THE NEW AMERICAN BIBLE

THE
NEW TESTAMENT

Newly Translated from the Original Greek
with Critical Use of the Ancient Sources
by Members of the
Catholic Biblical Association of America

SPONSORED BY THE BISHOPS' COMMITTEE

of the

CONFRATERNITY OF CHRISTIAN DOCTRINE

WITH SUPPLEMENTAL MAPS

Maps by permission of
Catholic Book Publishing Co., New York

ST. ANTHONY GUILD PRESS
PATERSON, NEW JERSEY

Nihil obstat:

STEPHEN J. HARTDEGEN, O.F.M., S.S.L.
CHRISTIAN P. CEROKE, O.CARM., S.T.D.

Imprimatur:

†PATRICK CARDINAL O'BOYLE, D.D.
Archbishop of Washington

July 27, 1970

Library of Congress Catalog Card No. 78-141767
SBN 0-87236-313-9

(The complete NEW AMERICAN BIBLE Library of Congress
Catalog Card Number is 71-141768
SBN 0-87236-310-4)

PRINTED IN THE UNITED STATES OF AMERICA

For the faithful in all English-speaking countries the publication of *The New American Bible* represents a notable achievement. Its pages contain a new Catholic version of the Bible in English, along with illustrations and explanations that facilitate the understanding of the text.

For more than a quarter of a century, members of the Catholic Biblical Association of America, sponsored by the Bishops' Committee of the Confraternity of Christian Doctrine, have labored to create this new translation of the Scriptures from the original languages or from the oldest extant form in which the texts exist.

In so doing, the translators have carried out the directive of our predecessor, Pius XII, in his famous Encyclical *Divino afflante Spiritu,* and the decree of the Second Vatican Council (*Dei Verbum*), which prescribed that "up-to-date and appropriate translations be made in the various languages, by preference from the original texts of the sacred books," and that "with the approval of Church authority, these translations may be produced in cooperation with our separated brethren" so that "all Christians may be able to use them."

The holy task of spreading God's word to the widest possible readership has a special urgency today. Despite all his material achievements, man still struggles with the age-old problems of how to order his life for the glory of God, for the welfare of his fellows and the salvation of his soul. Therefore we are gratified to find in this new translation of the Scriptures a new opportunity for men to give themselves to frequent reading of, and meditation on, the living Word of God. In its pages we recognize His voice, we hear a message of deep significance for every one of us. Through the spiritual dynamism and prophetic force of the Bible, the Holy Spirit spreads his light and his warmth over all men, in whatever historical or sociological situation they find themselves.

On all who have contributed to this translation, and all who seek in its pages the sacred teaching and the promise of salvation of Jesus Christ our Lord, we gladly bestow our paternal Apostolic Blessing.

From the Vatican, September 18, 1970

Paulus PP. VI

THE NEW TESTAMENT

On September 30, 1943, His Holiness Pope Pius XII issued his now famous encyclical on Scripture studies, *Divino afflante Spiritu.* He wrote: "We ought to explain the original text which was written by the inspired author himself and has more authority and greater weight than any, even the very best, translation whether ancient or modern. This can be done all the more easily and fruitfully if to the knowledge of languages be joined a real skill in literary criticism of the same text."

Early in 1944, in conformity with the spirit of the encyclical, and with the encouragement of Archbishop Cicognani, Apostolic Delegate to the United States, the Bishops' Committee of the Confraternity of Christian Doctrine requested members of the Catholic Biblical Association of America to translate the Sacred Scriptures from the original languages or from the oldest extant form of the text, and to present the sense of the biblical text in as correct a form as possible.

THE NEW AMERICAN BIBLE has accomplished this in response to the need of the church in America today. It is the achievement of some fifty biblical scholars, the greater number of whom, though not all, are Catholics. In particular, the editors-in-chief have devoted twenty-five years to this work. The collaboration of scholars who are not Catholic fulfills the directive of the Second Vatican Council, not only that "correct translations be made into different languages especially from the original texts of the sacred books," but that, "with the approval of the church authority, these translations be produced in cooperation with separated brothers" so that "all Christians may be able to use them."

The text of the books contained in THE NEW AMERICAN BIBLE is a completely new translation. From the original or the oldest extant texts of the sacred books, it aims to convey as directly as possible the thought and individual style of the inspired writers. The better understanding of Hebrew and Greek, and the steady development of the science of textual criticism, the fruit of patient study since the time of St. Jerome, have allowed the translators and editors in their use of all available materials to approach more closely than ever before the sense of what the sacred authors actually wrote.

This New Testament translation has been approached with essentially the same fidelity to the thought and individual style of the biblical writers as was applied in the Old Testament. In some cases, however, the problem of marked literary peculiarities must be met. What by any Western standard are the limited vocabularies and stylistic infelicities of the evangelists cannot be retained in the exact form in which they appear in the originals without displeasing the modern ear. A compromise is here attempted whereby some measure of the poverty of the evangelists' expression is kept and placed at the service of their message in its richness. Similarly, the syntactical shortcomings of Paul, his frequent lapses into anacoluthon, and the like, are rendered as they occur in his epistles rather than "smoothed out." Only thus, the translators suppose, will contemporary readers have some adequate idea of the kind of writing they have before them. When the prose of the original flows more smoothly, as in Luke, Acts, and Hebrews, it is reflected in the translation.

The Gospel according to John comprises a special case. Absolute fidelity to his technique of reiterated phrasing would result in an assault on the English ear, yet the softening of the vocal effect by substitution of other words and phrases would destroy the effectiveness of his poetry. Again, resort is had to compromise. This is not an easy matter when the very repetitiousness which the author deliberately employed is at the same time regarded by those who read and speak English to be a serious stylistic defect. Only those familiar with the Greek originals can know what a relentless tattoo Johannine poetry can produce. A similar observation could be made regarding other New Testament books as well. Matthew and Mark are given to identical phrasing twice and three times in the same sentence. As for the rhetorical overgrowth and mixed figures of speech in the letters of Peter, James, and Jude, the translator must resist a powerful compulsion to tidy them up if only to enable him to render these epistles intelligibly.

Without seeking refuge in complaints against the inspired authors, however, the translators of THE NEW AMERICAN BIBLE here state that what they have attempted is a translation rather than a paraphrase. To be sure, all translation can be called paraphrase by definition. Any striving for complete fidelity will shortly end in infidelity. Nonetheless, it must be pointed out that the temptation to improve overladen sentences by the consolidation or elimination of multiplied adjectives, or the simplification of clumsy hendiadys, has been resisted here. For the most part, rhetorically ineffective words and phrases are retained in this translation in some form, even when it is clear that a Western contemporary writer would never have employed them.

The spelling of proper names in THE NEW AMERICAN BIBLE follows the customary forms found in most English Bibles since the Authorized Version.

Despite the arbitrary character of the divisions into numbered verses (a scheme which in its present form is only four centuries old), the translators have made a constant effort to keep within an English verse the whole verbal content of the Greek verse. At times the effort has not seemed worth the result since it often does violence to the original author's flow of expression, which preceded it by so many centuries. If this translation had been prepared for purposes of public reading only, the editors would have forgone the effort at an early stage. But since they never departed from the threefold objective of preparing a translation suitable for liturgical use, private reading, and the purposes of students, the last-named consideration prevailed. Those familiar with Greek should be able to discover how the translators of the New Testament have rendered any given original verse of Scripture, if their exegetical or theological tasks require them to know this. At the same time, the fact should be set down here that the editors did not commit themselves in the synoptic gospels to rendering repeated words or phrases identically.

This leads to a final remark regarding the Greek text used for the New Testament. Here, punctuation and verse division are at least as important as variant readings. In general, Nestle-Aland's *Novum Testamentum Graece* (25th edition, 1963) was followed. Some help was derived from *The Greek New Testament* (Aland, Black, Metzger, Wikgren), produced for the use of translators by the United Bible Societies in 1966. However, the editors did not confine themselves strictly to these texts; at times, they inclined toward readings otherwise attested. The omission of alternative translations does not mean that the translators think them without merit, but only that in every case they had to make a choice.

Poorly attested readings do not occur in this translation. Doubtful readings of some merit appear within brackets; public readers may include such words or phrases, or omit them entirely without any damage to sense. Parentheses are used, as ordinarily in English, as a punctuation device. Material they enclose is in no sense textually doubtful. It is simply thought to be parenthetical in the intention of the biblical author, even though there is no such punctuation mark in Greek. The difficulty in dealing with quotation marks is well known. Since they do not appear in any form in the original text, wherever they occur here they constitute an editorial decision.

The work of translating the Bible has been characterized as "the sacred and apostolic work of interpreting the word of God and of presenting it to the laity in translations as clear as the difficulty of the matter and the limitations of human knowledge permit" (A. G. Cicognani, Apostolic Delegate, in *The Catholic Biblical Quarterly,* 6 [1944], 389f). In the appraisal of the present work, it is hoped that the words of the encyclical *Divino afflante Spiritu* will serve as a guide: "Let all the sons of the church bear in mind that the efforts of these resolute laborers in the vineyard of the Lord should be judged not only with equity and justice but also with the greatest charity; all moreover should abhor that intemperate zeal which imagines that whatever is new should for that very season be opposed or suspected."

Conscious of their personal limitations for the task thus defined, those who have prepared this text cannot expect that it will be considered perfect; but they can hope that it may deepen in its readers "the right understanding of the divinely given Scriptures," and awaken in them "that piety by which it behooves us to be grateful to the God of all providence, who from the throne of his majesty has sent these books as so many personal letters to his own children" (*Divino afflante Spiritu*).

THE BOOKS OF THE NEW TESTAMENT

THE BOOKS OF THE OLD AND NEW TESTAMENTS
AND THEIR ABBREVIATIONS

Genesis . . . . Gn	Proverbs . . . . Prv
Exodus . . . . Ex	Ecclesiastes . . . . Eccl
Leviticus Lv	Song of Songs . . . . Sg
Numbers . . . . Nm	Wisdom . . . . Wis
Deuteronomy . . . . Dt	Sirach . . . . Sir
Joshua . . . . Jos	Isaiah . . . . Is
Judges . . . . Jgs	Jeremiah . . . . Jer
Ruth . . . . Ru	Lamentations . . . . Lam
1 Samuel . . . . 1 Sm	Baruch . . . . Bar
2 Samuel . . . . 2 Sm	Ezekiel . . . . Ez
1 Kings . . . . 1 Kgs	Daniel . . . . Dn
2 Kings . . . . 2 Kgs	Hosea . . . . Hos
1 Chronicles . . . . 1 Chr	Joel . . . . Jl
2 Chronicles . . . . 2 Chr	Amos . . . . Am
Ezra . . . . Ezr	Obadiah . . . . Ob
Nehemiah . . . . Neh	Jonah . . . . Jon
Tobit . . . . Tb	Micah . . . . Mi
Judith . . . . Jdt	Nahum . . . . Na
Esther . . . . Est	Habakkuk . . . . Hb
1 Maccabees . . . . 1 Mc	Zephaniah . . . . Zep
2 Maccabees . . . . 2 Mc	Haggai . . . . Hg
Job . . . . Jb	Zechariah . . . . Zec
Psalms . . . . Ps(s)	Malachi . . . . Mal
Matthew . . . . Mt	1 Timothy . . . . 1 Tm
Mark . . . . Mk	2 Timothy . . . . 2 Tm
Luke . . . . Lk	Titus . . . . Ti
John . . . . Jn	Philemon . . . . Phlm
Acts of the Apostles . . . Acts	Hebrews . . . . Heb
Romans . . . . Rom	James . . . . Jas
1 Corinthians . . . . 1 Cor	1 Peter . . . . 1 Pt
2 Corinthians . . . . 2 Cor	2 Peter . . . . 2 Pt
Galatians . . . . Gal	1 John . . . . 1 Jn
Ephesians . . . . Eph	2 John . . . . 2 Jn
Philippians . . . . Phil	3 John . . . . 3 Jn
Colossians . . . . Col	Jude . . . . Jude
1 Thessalonians . . . . . . 1 Thes	Revelation . . . . Rv
2 Thessalonians . . . . . . 2 Thes	

In the Scriptural text which follows:

[ ] indicates a gloss.

THE GOSPEL ACCORDING TO MATTHEW

INTRODUCTION

Matthew's gospel in its present form was written in a Jewish milieu, probably after the destruction of Jerusalem in 70 A.D. There are evidences of the fulfillment of the Mosaic law (1, 19; 5, 18), and also references to violence (21, 38-41), to the burning of a city (22, 7), and to punishment in the wake of Jesus' death (27, 25).

There is also the anti-Pharisee and anti-scribe polemic in Matthew which indicates a fairly complete rift between Christians and official Judaism. By the year 85 A.D. Christians were unwelcome in Jewish synagogues—called *their synagogues* by Matthew to distinguish Jewish from Christian worship (4, 23; 9, 35; 12, 9; 13, 54).

There is thus an ambivalence between Matthew's earlier Jewishness, reflected in the elements of the gospel as they were in the process of formation, and his alienation from Jewish tradition even before these elements were incorporated into the finished gospel.

Ignatius, bishop of Antioch (†110), in his letters to certain churches of Asia Minor, uses several sayings of Jesus found only in this gospel (12, 35; 15, 13; 19, 12). Papias, bishop of Hierapolis in Phrygia, wrote (c 135) that Matthew had compiled a collection of sayings of the Lord "in the Hebrew tongue" (most likely Aramaic), "and each person translated them as he was able." This seems to indicate that various Greek versions of the early collection attributed to Matthew were in existence; one of them may have been the apocryphal gospel of the Hebrews.

Besides the sayings of the Lord, it is certain that the author of Matthew had access to the present Gospel of Mark because of the Marcan verses he uses in chapters 3, 8f, 12-17, 19-22, 24, 26ff. Matthew is obviously an expanded version of Mark, considered the first gospel form to be written. Very few scholars hold that Mark is a condensed version of Matthew.

Both Matthew and Luke, neither of whom can be proved to have copied from the other, seem to have had, besides the Gospel of Mark, another source of some 240 verses which Mark does not include. This source, not found but deduced, is designated simply as Q from Quelle, the German term for "source."

Beginning with a series of reflections relating Jesus and his parentage to the messianism of the Old Testament (1, 1-25), the gospel places his birth in the hostile political environment of the time (2, 1-23). Like the other gospels, Matthew introduces the public ministry of Jesus with a summary of the mission of John the Baptizer (3, 1-17). After the account of the temptation of Jesus (4, 1-11), the gospel reports his teaching and miracles, locating all these in Galilee and its vicinity, exclusive of Jerusalem (4, 12—20, 34). It concludes with the final events and teaching of Jesus, locating them in Jerusalem, and centering them around his passion, death and resurrection (21, 1—28, 20). For this general outline of a gospel, see Acts 1, 21f; 10, 37-41.

The Gospel of Matthew is distinctive for its practice of citing the Old Testament in connection with Jesus' activity and teaching, and for a structured presentation of his doctrine in the form of sermons or discourses (5, 1-7, 29; 10, 5-42; 13, 1-52; 18, 1-35; 24, 1—25, 46). The discourses are followed by collections of miracle-accounts and incidents which reflect Jesus' doctrinal teaching. They are presented by the evangelist in such a way as to be meaningful to the Christian communities of his time.

The gospel as a whole revolves around the concept, no doubt originally developed in Judaeo-Christian circles, that Jesus is the expected Messiah-king of Israel, mysteriously unacceptable to his own people, but no less mysteriously acceptable to many Gentiles.

The universal importance of Christ in this gospel does not derive from the notion of messianic kingship alone, but more especially from his divinity (1, 23; 16, 16; 28, 18). This makes possible his presence in Christian communities in word and sacrament (18, 19; 26, 29) and constitutes him the divine teacher of all nations (28, 19). The bond in Matthew between christology and ecclesiology portrays the mediating mission of the Christian community, that of giving witness to Christ in the world. In the judgment of modern scholars this mission is a theological development within the gospel tradition that requires a date for the Gospel of Matthew later than that of Mark and Luke. Current and more common opinion dates the composition of the Gospel of Matthew between 80-100 A.D., or roughly, 85 A.D. There is also the compelling evidence for the dependence of Matthew on Mark: namely, the 600 of Mark's 661 verses found in Matthew, as well as the relationship of language and order in these two gospels.

The principal divisions of the Gospel of Matthew are as follows:

THE GOSPEL ACCORDING TO MATTHEW

I: PROLOGUE: THE COMING OF THE SAVIOR

1

Genealogy of Jesus

¹ A family record of Jesus Christ, son of David, son of Abraham. ² Abraham was the father of Isaac, Isaac the father of Jacob, Jacob the father of Judah and his brothers. ³ Judah was the father of Perez and Zerah, whose mother was Tamar. Perez was the father of Hezron, Hezron the father of Ram. ⁴ Ram was the father of Amminadab, Amminadab the father of Nahshon, Nahshon the father of Salmon. ⁵ Salmon was the father of Boaz, whose mother was Rahab, Boaz was the father of Obed, whose mother was Ruth. Obed was the father of Jesse, ⁶ Jesse the father of King David. David was the father of Solomon, whose mother had been the wife of Uriah. ⁷ Solomon was the father of Rehoboam, Rehoboam the father of Abijah, Abijah the father of Asa. ⁸ Asa was the father of Jehoshaphat, Jehoshaphat the father of Joram, Joram the father of Uzziah. ⁹ Uzziah was the father of Jotham, Jotham the father of Ahaz, Ahaz the father of Hezekiah. ¹⁰ Hezekiah was the father of Manasseh, Manasseh the father of Amos, Amos the father of Josiah. ¹¹ Josiah became the father of Jechoniah and his brothers at the

---

1, 1-17: Lk 3, 23-38.
  1: 9, 27; Gal 3, 16.
  2: Gn 21, 3; 25, 26; 29, 35; Heb 7, 14.
  3: Gn 38, 29f; Ru 4, 18; 1 Chr 2, 4f.
  4: Nm 7, 12; Ru 4, 20.
  5: Ru 4, 21.
  6: 2 Sm 12, 24.
  7: 1 Kgs 11, 43; 14, 31; 15, 8.
  8: 2 Kgs 8, 16.
  9: 2 Chr 26, 23; 27, 9; 28, 27.
  10: 2 Chr 32, 33; 33, 20.25.
  11: 2 Chr 36, 9ff.20f.

1, 1: *A family record of Jesus Christ:* the Greek may also be taken to mean "book of the history of the origin of Jesus Christ." In this sense the opening verse is a title for the whole gospel, which then begins with the genealogy of Christ; cf Gn 2, 4. *Jesus:* the Greek and Latin form of the late Hebrew and Aramaic name *Jeshua,* meaning "The Lord is salvation." *Christ:* in v 17 and elsewhere, a title from the Greek *Christos,* which translates the Hebrew *Mashiah,* "Anointed One," applied to the expected representative of God on earth. Matthew in v 1 uses "Jesus Christ" as a proper name, as was customary in later Christian circles; cf Jn 1, 17; Phil 2, 11.

1, 2-17: The genealogy points out Jesus' Davidic lineage through Joseph who, however, is called "the husband of Mary." (1, 16), not the father of Jesus. In 1, 18-25, the evangelist explains the reason for the foster paternity of Joseph. The genealogy recalls the messianic hope of Israel by alluding to the divine promises to the patriarchs (2) and to David (6); cf 2 Sm 7, 12-16. It places this hope in the context of Israel's sinfulness by allusion to David's murder of Uriah (6), and also to the Babylonian captivity (11). The constant repetition of the term "was the father of," literally "begot," implies the continuous presence of God in Israel sustaining the faith and hope of the people. For the implication of the divine presence in the Greek term, cf 1 Cor 4, 15; Gal 4, 24.

time of the Babylonian exile. [12] After the Babylonian exile Jechoniah was the father of Shealtiel, Shealtiel the father of Zerubbabel. [13] Zerubbabel was the father of Abiud, Abiud the father of Eliakim, Eliakim the father of Azor. [14] Azor was the father of Zadok, Zadok the father of Achim, Achim the father of Eliud. [15] Eliud was the father of Eleazar, Eleazar the father of Matthan, Matthan the father of Jacob. [16] Jacob was the father of Joseph the husband of Mary. It was of her that Jesus who is called the Messiah was born. [17] Thus the total number of generations is: from Abraham to David, fourteen generations; from David to the Babylonian captivity, fourteen generations; from the Babylonian captivity to the Messiah, fourteen generations.

The Birth of Jesus

[18] Now this is how the birth of Jesus Christ came about. When his mother Mary was engaged to Joseph, but before they lived together, she was found with child through the power of the Holy Spirit. [19] Joseph her husband, an upright man unwilling to expose her to the law, decided to divorce her quietly. [20] Such was his intention when suddenly the angel of the Lord appeared in a dream and said to him: "Joseph, son of David, have no fear about taking Mary as your wife. It is by the Holy Spirit that she has conceived this child. [21] She is to have a son and you are to name him Jesus because he will save his people from

20: 2, 13.19; Lk 1, 31.35.

1, 17: The genealogy is artificially constructed out of three groups of fourteen names each, taken principally from Genesis, Ruth, 1 Chronicles and 2 Kings. The list of names beginning with Abiud in 1, 13 is unknown to the Old Testament. The number 14 is undoubtedly a mnemonic device, perhaps chosen because the numerical value of the three letters of David's name (DVD) yields in Hebrew the sum of 14.

1, 18-25: The evangelist shows that Jesus was introduced into the Davidic line through the divine choice of Joseph as his legal father. Throughout the public ministry of Jesus it was understandably the common opinion that Joseph was the natural father of Jesus; cf Mt 13, 55; Jn 6, 42.

1, 18: *Mary was engaged to Joseph:* they were living in a state of espousal which usually lasted one year in Galilee.

1, 19: A common opinion from the time of the Church Fathers ascribes to Joseph the fear that Mary's child was a consequence of adultery. The evangelist depicts Joseph in a dilemma: he feels it would not be honorable for him to assume the paternity of the child in view of the requirements of "justice" under Mosaic law; but at the same time he realizes that even a private divorce in the presence of only a few witnesses would eventually expose Mary to the popular suspicion of adultery.

1, 20f: To what extent the angelic visitation of Joseph through a dream is reality or popular description surrounding the divine message to him is subject to discussion. In either case the evangelist makes it abundantly clear to his readers that Joseph accepted Mary as his wife, together with the child, because he saw the will of God expressed in the circumstances. *He will save his people from their sins:* the child will not be a warrior-king overcoming the enemies of Israel, but will free the people from sin.

their sins." [22] All this happened to fulfill what the Lord had said through the prophet:

> [23] "The virgin shall be with child
> and give birth to a son,
> and they shall call him Emmanuel,"

a name which means "God is with us." [24] When Joseph awoke he did as the angel of the Lord had directed him and received her into his home as his wife. [25] He had no relations with her at any time before she bore a son, whom he named Jesus.

2

The Astrologers

[1] After Jesus' birth in Bethlehem of Judea during the reign of King Herod, astrologers from the east arrived one day in Jerusalem [2] inquiring, "Where is the newborn king of the Jews? We observed his star at its rising and have come to pay him homage." [3] At this news King Herod became greatly disturbed, and with him all Jerusalem. [4] Summoning all of the chief priests and scribes of the people, he inquired of them where the Mes-

---

23: Is 7, 14.   2, 2: Nm 24, 17.
25: Lk 2, 7.

1, 22f: This is a prophetic reinterpretation of Is 7, 14, in the light of the facts Matthew has outlined: the virginal conception of Jesus, his Davidic messianic role in a spiritual sense, Joseph's legal paternity, and the unique presence of God in Jesus, which the church of the evangelist's time had to come to understand as his divinity. All these things about Jesus that were faintly traced in Is 7, 14 are now seen by Matthew to be fully brought to light as God's plan.

1, 25: *He had no relations with her at any time before:* the evangelist emphasizes the virginity of the mother of Jesus from the moment of his conception to his birth. He does not concern himself here with the period that followed the birth of Jesus, but merely wishes to show that Joseph fully respected the legal character of the paternity imposed on him by the divine will. Moreover the New Testament makes no mention anywhere of children of Joseph and Mary.

2, 1-25: The episodes which follow the explanation of Jesus' Davidic origin through the legal paternity of Joseph raise the question: Do we have here a historical composition with theological overtones or a theological composition resting on a broad historical basis? The latter supposition finds support in the typology of the second chapter of Matthew, which parallels Jesus with Israel and Moses in a way that suggests an influence of extra-biblical Jewish religious traditions.

2, 1: *King Herod:* called "the Great" because of his political astuteness and his achievements in building, which included the temple in Jerusalem. In 40 B. C. the Roman senate appointed him king of Judea. From then on Herod succeeded in extending his rule to other parts of Palestine. Since Herod is known to have died in 4 B. C., scholars assign 7 or 6 B. C. as the actual date of the birth of Jesus; cf Mt 2, 16. *Astrologers from the east:* the various personages designated by the Greek term *magoi* did not include kings. Many think that the allusion is to learned men from Babylon who had contact with Jewish messianism; cf Dn 2, 2.

siah was to be born. ⁵ "In Bethlehem of Judea," they informed him. "Here is what the prophet has written:

⁶ 'And you, Bethlehem, land of Judah,
  are by no means least among the princes of Judah,
  since from you shall come a ruler
  who is to shepherd my people Israel.' "

⁷ Herod called the astrologers aside and found out from them the exact time of the star's appearance. ⁸ Then he sent them to Bethlehem, after having instructed them: "Go and get detailed information about the child. When you have found him, report it to me so that I may go and offer him homage too."

⁹ After their audience with the king, they set out. The star which they had observed at its rising went ahead of them until it came to a standstill over the place where the child was. ¹⁰ They were overjoyed at seeing the star, ¹¹ and on entering the house, found the child with Mary his mother. They prostrated themselves and did him homage. Then they opened their coffers and presented him with gifts of gold, frankincense, and myrrh.

¹² They received a message in a dream not to return to Herod, so they went back to their own country by another route.

The Flight into Egypt

¹³ After they had left, the angel of the Lord suddenly appeared in a dream to Joseph with the command: "Get up, take the child and his mother, and flee to Egypt. Stay there until I tell you otherwise. Herod is searching for the child to destroy him." ¹⁴ Joseph got up and took the child and his mother and left that night for Egypt. ¹⁵ He stayed there until the death of

---

5: Jn 7, 42.   11: Ps 72, 10f; Is 60, 5f.
6: Mi 5, 1.   15: Hos 11, 1.

2, 5f: The citation combines Mi 5, 1 and 2 Sm 5, 2. It emphasizes the fulfillment of Old Testament prophecy concerning Bethlehem, the birthplace of Jesus. For the expression of a current opinion that the Messiah was to come from Bethlehem, cf Jn 7, 42.
2, 9f: The action of the star implies that in the evangelist's thought it is a supernatural phenomenon. It is a symbol of faith leading the Gentiles to the discovery of Jesus as their king and savior; cf 2 Pt 1, 19.
2, 11: *The house:* Matthew's tradition of the astrologers' visit to a *house* is unrelated to the place of Jesus' birth as reported in Luke 2, 12. *Gold, frankincense and myrrh:* such gifts were customary in the Orient as signs of homage. The association of 2, 11 with Ps 72, 10f occasioned the mistaken supposition that the astrologers were kings. For the Old Testament oracles concerning the Gentiles' homage to Yahweh, cf Nm 24, 17; Is 49, 23; 60, 5f.
2, 13: *Flee to Egypt:* from the time of the Maccabees, Egypt had been a customary place of refuge. An earlier example is Jeroboam's flight to Egypt (1 Kgs 11, 40).
2, 15: The citation of Hos 11, 1, relates Jesus to Israel. Just as God called Israel out of Egypt to create a people peculiarly his own, so he

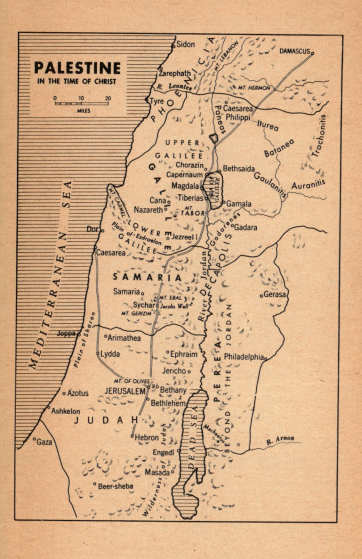

Herod, to fulfill what the Lord had said through the prophet:

"Out of Egypt I have called my son."

The Innocents

[16] Once Herod realized that he had been deceived by the astrologers, he became furious. He ordered the massacre of all the boys two years old and under in Bethlehem and its environs, making his calculations on the basis of the date he had learned from the astrologers. [17] What was said through Jeremiah the prophet was then fulfilled:

> [18] "A cry was heard at Ramah,
> sobbing and loud lamentation:
> Rachel bewailing her children;
> no comfort for her, since they are no more."

The Return to Nazareth

[19] But after Herod's death, the angel of the Lord appeared in a dream to Joseph in Egypt [20] with the command: "Get up, take the child and his mother, and set out for the land of Israel. Those who had designs on the life of the child are dead." [21] He got up, took the child and his mother, and returned to the land of Israel. [22] He heard, however, that Archelaus had succeeded his father Herod as king of Judea, and he was afraid to go back there. Instead, because of a warning received in a dream, Joseph went to the region of Galilee. [23] There he settled in a town called Nazareth. In this way what was said through the prophets was fulfilled:

"He shall be called a Nazorean."

18: Jer 31, 15.   4, 34; Jn 19, 19.
20: Ex 4, 19.   **3**, 1-12: Mk 1, 2-8; Lk 3, 2-17.
23: 13, 54; Lk 2, 39;

---

called Jesus out of Egypt into the land of Israel to accomplish his purpose of creating the new Israel or people of God. The story of the flight into Egypt illustrates the divine concealment of the child so that he might fulfill his role as head of the new Israel.

2,17f: The plaint over the massacre is not ascribed to the people of Bethlehem but figuratively to Rachel bewailing Israel's exile (Jer 31, 15f). She is comforted by a promise of restoration. A note of consolation seems implied in Matthew's citation, which views the massacre of infants as a guarantee of God's action to create the new people of God through Jesus; cf Rv 6, 9ff.

2, 22: *Archelaus:* i. e., "leader of the people," a son of Herod the Great and brother of Herod Antipas; see note on Acts 4, 27. He ruled as ethnarch of Judea, Samaria and Idumea from 4 B. C. to 6 A. D., when he was deposed by the Emperor Augustus.

2, 23: *He shall be called a Nazorean:* unidentifiable in any Old Testament passage. Jesus' residence in Galilee amid a mixed population of Jews and Gentiles is viewed as a providential indication of his messianic mission to the Gentiles; cf Is 66, 18f; Am 9, 11f.

II: PROMULGATION OF THE REIGN OF GOD

3

John the Baptizer

¹ When John the Baptizer made his appearance as a preacher in the desert of Judea, this was his theme: ² "Reform your lives! The reign of God is at hand." ³ It was of him that the prophet Isaiah had spoken when he said:

> "A herald's voice in the desert:
> 'Prepare the way of the Lord,
> make straight his paths.' "

⁴ John was clothed in a garment of camel's hair, and wore a leather belt around his waist. Grasshoppers and wild honey were his food. ⁵ At that time Jerusalem, all Judea, and the whole region around the Jordan were going out to him. ⁶ They were being baptized by him in the Jordan River as they confessed their sins.

⁷ When he saw that many of the Pharisees and Sadducees were stepping forward for this bath, he said to them: "You brood of vipers! Who told you to flee from the wrath to come? ⁸ Give some evidence that you mean to reform. ⁹ Do not pride yourselves on the claim, 'Abraham is our father.' I tell you, God can raise up children to Abraham from these very stones. ¹⁰ Even now the ax is laid to the root of the tree. Every tree that is not fruitful will be cut down and thrown into the fire. ¹¹ I baptize you in water for the sake of reform, but the one who

---

2: 4, 17; 10, 7; Acts 2, 38.
3: Is 40, 3.
4: 11, 7f; Zec 13, 4.
6: 21, 25.

7: 12, 34; 23, 33; Is 59, 5.
9: Jn 8, 33.39; Rom 9, 7f;
   Gal 4, 21-31.
11: Jn 1, 15.24-27.33; Acts 1, 5.

3, 1-17: This narrative is concerned with the prophetic message and person of John (1-5), his baptism (6), his critique of the Pharisees and Sadducees (7-10), his message concerning Jesus (11f), and his baptism of Jesus, with its theological significance (13-17).

3, 2: *Reform your lives!:* on the notion of repentance, see note on Acts 2, 38. *The reign of God is at hand:* literally, "the kingdom of heaven." "Heaven" is a conventional expression which avoids using the divine name. The term invokes God's sovereign authority over the human race. It announces that a new intervention of God is beginning in history which invites Israel to accept the prophetic manifestation of his will through the Baptizer.

3, 4: The Baptizer's garb recalls that of Elijah in 2 Kgs 1, 8: Jesus speaks of the Baptizer as Elijah who *has already come* (Mt 17, 10ff; Mk 9, 10ff); cf Mal 3, 24.

3, 7-10: John's criticism of the Pharisees and Sadducees implies that they have come to receive baptism for the purpose of gaining popular favor rather than to exercise their religious leadership in a national program of true reform. Matthew sees the Christian community to be the true *children* of *Abraham* who fulfill the Baptizer's prophetic words (v 10).

3, 11f: The baptism of John prepares for the purifying action *in the Holy*

will follow me is more powerful than I. I am not even fit to carry his sandals. He it is who will baptize you in the Holy Spirit and fire. [12] His winnowing-fan is in his hand. He will clear the threshing floor and gather his grain into the barn, but the chaff he will burn in unquenchable fire."

The Baptism of Jesus

[13] Later Jesus, coming from Galilee, appeared before John at the Jordan to be baptized by him. [14] John tried to refuse him with the protest, "I should be baptized by you, yet you come to me!" [15] Jesus answered: "Give in for now. We must do this if we would fulfill all of God's demands." So John gave in. [16] After Jesus was baptized, he came directly out of the water. Suddenly the sky opened and he saw the Spirit of God descend like a dove and hover over him. [17] With that, a voice from the heavens said, "This is my beloved Son. My favor rests on him."

4

The Temptation

[1] Then Jesus was led into the desert by the Spirit to be tempted by the devil. [2] He fasted forty days and forty nights, and afterward was hungry. [3] The tempter approached and said to him, "If you are the Son of God, command these stones to turn into bread." [4] Jesus replied, "Scripture has it:

> 'Not on bread alone is man to live
> but on every utterance that comes from the
> mouth of God.' "

12: 13, 42.50; Is 41, 16;
    Jer 15, 7.
13-17: Mk 1, 9-11; Lk 3, 21f;
    Jn 1, 31-34.
16: Is 11, 2.
17: 12, 18; 17, 5: Is 42, 1;

49, 3.
4, 1-11: Mk 1, 12f; Lk 4, 1-13.
  1: Heb 2, 18.
  2: Ex 24, 18; 34, 28.
  4: Dt 8, 3.

Spirit and fire which Jesus will effect; cf Is 1, 25; Zec 13, 9; Mal 3, 2. Refusal of this baptism of Jesus leads to a final judgment of condemnation *in unquenchable fire;* cf Is 34, 8ff; Jer 7, 20.

3, 13-17: For the theological significance of this account of Jesus' baptism, see note on Mk 1, 9ff.

4, 1-11: An introduction to the gospel proper; see note on Mk 1, 12f. Some regard the account as a Christian reflection on Jesus' messianic role: he refuses to use his miraculous power simply to relieve human need (3f), or to satisfy requests of unbelievers (5ff); he disdains a messianic role (8ff) that would be purely political in its implications. The central theme is the obedience of Jesus to God as he is known through the Old Testament.

4, 3: *If you are the Son of God:* in the sense of the messianic king of Ps 2.

4, 4: A citation of Dt 8, 3, signifying that the miracles of the Exodus were signs of God's religious, rather than physical, care of Israel.

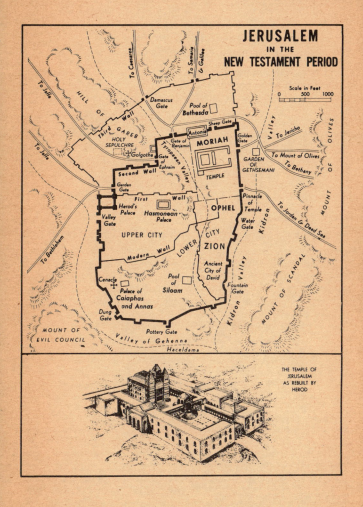

JERUSALEM
IN THE
NEW TESTAMENT PERIOD

Scale in Feet
0   500   1000

To Caesarea
To Samaria & Galilee
To Joppa
HILL OF GAREB
Third Wall
Damascus Gate
Pool of Bethesda
HOLY SEPULCHRE
Golgotha
Second Wall
Gate of Ephraim
Tyropoeon Valley
Gate of Benjamin
Antonia
Sheep Gate
MORIAH
Golden Gate
Valley
To Jericho
To Mount of Olives
To Bethany
GARDEN OF GETHSEMANI
TEMPLE
MOUNT OF OLIVES
Garden Gate
First Wall
Herod's Palace
Valley Gate
Hasmonean Palace
OPHEL
Pinnacle of Temple
Water Gate
To Jordan & Dead Sea
Kidron
UPPER CITY
Modern Wall
LOWER CITY
ZION
Ancient City of David
To Bethlehem
Cenacle
Palace of Caiaphas and Annas
Pool of Siloam
Fountain Gate
Kidron Valley
MOUNT OF SCANDAL
Dung Gate
Pottery Gate
Valley of Gehenna
Haceldama
MOUNT OF EVIL COUNCIL

THE TEMPLE OF JERUSALEM AS REBUILT BY HEROD

⁵ Next the devil took him to the holy city, set him on the parapet of the temple, ⁶ and said, "If you are the Son of God, throw yourself down. Scripture has it:

> 'He will bid his angels take care of you;
> with their hands they will support you
> that you may never stumble on a stone.' "

⁷ Jesus answered him, "Scripture also has it:

> 'You shall not put the Lord your God to the test.' "

⁸ The devil then took him up a very high mountain and displayed before him all the kingdoms of the world in their magnificence, promising, ⁹ "All these will I bestow on you if you prostrate yourself in homage before me." ¹⁰ At this, Jesus said to him, "Away with you, Satan! Scripture has it:

> 'You shall do homage to the Lord your God;
> him alone shall you adore.' "

¹¹ At that the devil left him, and angels came and waited on him.

¹² When Jesus heard that John had been arrested, he withdrew to Galilee. ¹³ He left Nazareth and went down to live in Capernaum by the sea near the territory of Zebulun and Naphtali, ¹⁴ to fulfill what had been said through Isaiah the prophet:

> ¹⁵ "Land of Zebulun, Land of Naphtali
> along the sea beyond the Jordan,
> heathen Galilee:
> ¹⁶ a people living in darkness
> has seen a great light.

6: Ps 91, 11f.
7: Dt 6, 16.
9: 16, 23.
10: Dt 6, 13.

12f: Mk 1, 14f; Lk 4, 14.31.
13: Jn 2, 12.
15f: Is 9, 1f.
16: Jn 8, 12.

4, 6f: The tempter here applies to the Messiah verse 11 of Psalm 91 dealing with God's protection of the just. Jesus' reply (Dt 6, 16) teaches that miracles are not to be demanded of God as evidence of his care of man.

4, 10: The citation expresses the basic attitude of worship which every man should have toward God.

4, 12-17: The gospel proper begins here with a summary introduction to the Galilean ministry: the Baptizer is arrested by Herod Antipas (12); Jesus makes Capernaum the center of his activity (13) and preaching (17). The citation from Is 9, 1f identifies the ministry of Jesus as fulfilling the prophecy of the restoration of the northern kingdom, destroyed by the Assyrians in 721 B. C.

On those who inhabit a land overshadowed by death,
light has arisen."

¹⁷ From that time on Jesus began to proclaim this theme: "Reform your lives! The kingdom of heaven is at hand."

The First Disciples Called

¹⁸ As he was walking along the Sea of Galilee he watched two brothers, Simon now known as Peter, and his brother Andrew casting a net into the sea. They were fishermen. ¹⁹ He said to them, "Come after me and I will make you fishers of men." ²⁰ They immediately abandoned their nets and became his followers. ²¹ He walked along farther and caught sight of two other brothers, James, Zebedee's son, and his brother John. They too were in their boat, getting their nets in order with their father, Zebedee. ²² He called them, and immediately they abandoned boat and father to follow him.

The Mission of Preaching

²³ Jesus toured all of Galilee. He taught in their synagogues, proclaimed the good news of the kingdom, and cured the people of every disease and illness. ²⁴ As a consequence of this, his reputation traveled the length of Syria. They carried to him all those afflicted with various diseases and racked with pain: the possessed, the lunatics, the paralyzed. He cured them all. ²⁵ The great crowds that followed him came from Galilee, the Ten Cities, Jerusalem and Judea, and from across the Jordan.

5

¹ When he saw the crowds he went up on the mountainside. After he had sat down his disciples gathered around him, ² and he began to teach them:

The Beatitudes

³ "How blest are the poor in spirit: the reign of God is theirs.

17: 3, 2; Lk 17, 20.
18-22: Mk 1, 16-20;
  Lk 5, 1-11.
23: 9, 35; Mk 1, 39;

Lk 4, 15.44.
25: Mk 3, 7; Lk 6, 17-19.
5, 3-12: Lk 6, 20-23.
3: 19, 21.29; 2 Cor 8, 9.

4, 17: See note on 3, 2.
4, 19: To be *fishers of men* requires abandonment of former means of livelihood in order to preach the kingdom of God and testify to its arrival in the name of Jesus; cf 10, 1f. It may be assumed that this complete dedication was accomplished only gradually.
5, 3-12: The beatitudes announce religious happiness for the *anawim*, i. e.,

⁴ Blest too are the sorrowing; they shall be consoled. ⁵ [Blest are the lowly; they shall inherit the land.] ⁶ Blest are they who hunger and thirst for holiness; they shall have their fill. ⁷ Blest are they who show mercy; mercy shall be theirs. ⁸ Blest are the single-hearted for they shall see God. ⁹ Blest too the peace-makers; they shall be called sons of God. ¹⁰ P'₂st are those persecuted for holiness' sake; the reign of God i₅ theirs. ¹¹ Blest are you when they insult you and persecute you and utter every kind of slander against you because of me. ¹² Be glad and re-joice, for your reward is great in heaven; they persecuted the prophets before you in the very same way.

The Disciples

¹³ "You are the salt of the earth. But what if salt goes flat? How can you restore its flavor? Then it is good for nothing but to be thrown out and trampled underfoot.

¹⁴ "You are the light of the world. A city set on a hill cannot be hidden. ¹⁵ Men do not light a lamp and then put it under a bushel basket. They set it on a stand where it gives light to all in the house. ¹⁶ In the same way, your light must shine before

---

4: Ps 126, 5; Is 61, 2f;
   Rv 21, 4.
5: Gn 13, 15; Ps 37, 11;
   Prv 2, 21.
6: Prv 21, 21.
8: Pss 24, 4f; 73, 1;
   Prv 22, 11.
10: 1 Pt 2, 20; 3, 14; 4, 14.

11: Acts 5, 41.
12: Phil 1, 29; Col 1, 24;
   Jas 1, 2.
13: Mk 9, 49; Lk 14, 34f.
14: Jn 8, 12.
15: Mk 4, 21; Lk 8, 16;
   11, 33.
16: Jn 3, 21.

---

those who lack material goods and stand in need of the spiritual blessings promised by God: cf Dt 24, 14; Ps 37, 14; 40, 18; Is 61, 1. This happiness is to reach its fulfillment through Christ. Recognition of the *anawim* contrasts with the religious thought of the time which regarded human affliction and sorrow as the punishment of personal sin. For the Christian attitude toward the poor and afflicted, cf Mt 25, 34-46; Jas 2, 15f; 1 Jn 4, 20.

5, 7: Matthew fashions the Sermon on the Mount from the sayings of Jesus concerning Moses and the law. Luke's corresponding Sermon on the Plain (6, 17-49) is differently arranged. A key factor is that Jesus came not to abolish but to fulfill the law and the prophets. Jesus makes greater demands on men than did the law of Moses; but he bestows the justice needed for meeting these demands (Rom 8, 1-11), and his disciples are bound to respond to the divine gift (5, 20; 7, 21.24-27). Though concerned with the relationship between God and the individual, the social implications of the Sermon on the Mount are evident.

5, 8: *The single-hearted:* those who serve God loyally for his own sake and not primarily out of self-interest.

5, 9: *The peacemakers:* those whose lives promote harmony within the human community (1 Thes 5, 14) as contrasted with those who foster strife through violence for personal advantage.

5, 10: *For holiness' sake:* fidelity to the divine precepts through which holiness is attained is deepened by the test of persecution.

5, 13-16: The disciples of Jesus, despite reproach and persecution (11f), make the human community valuable in God's eyes (*salt of the earth*) and enlighten the world with *the light* of God's prophetic word, which they preach by word and example (16).

men so that they may see goodness in your acts and give praise to your heavenly Father.

The Old Law and the New

[17] "Do not think that I have come to abolish the law and the prophets. I have come, not to abolish them, but to fulfill them. [18] Of this much I assure you: until heaven and earth pass away, not the smallest letter of the law, not the smallest part of a letter, shall be done away with until it all comes true. [19] That is why whoever breaks the least significant of these commands and teaches others to do so shall be called least in the kingdom of God. Whoever fulfills and teaches these commands shall be great in the kingdom of God. [20] I tell you, unless your holiness surpasses that of the scribes and Pharisees you shall not enter the kingdom of God.

Against Anger

[21] "You have heard the commandment imposed on your fore-fathers, 'You shall not commit murder; every murderer shall be liable to judgment.' [22] What I say to you is: everyone who grows angry with his brother shall be liable to judgment; any man who uses abusive language toward his brother shall be answerable to the Sanhedrin, and if he holds him in contempt he risks the fires of Gehenna. [23] If you bring your gift to the altar and there recall that your brother has anything against you, [24] leave your gift at the altar, go first to be reconciled with your brother, and then come and offer your gift. [25] Lose no time; settle with your opponent while on your way to court with him. Otherwise your opponent may hand you over to the judge, who will hand you over to the guard, who will throw you into prison. [26] I warn you, you will not be released until you have paid the last penny.

Occasions of Impurity

[27] "You have heard the commandment, 'You shall not commit

17: Rom 3, 31.
18: Lk 16, 17.
19: Jas 2, 10.
20: Rom 10, 3.
21: Ex 20, 13; Dt 5, 17.

22: Jas 1, 19f; 3, 6.
23: Sir 28, 2; Mk 11, 25.
25: Prv 17, 14; Lk 12, 58f.
27: Ex 20, 14; Dt 5, 18.

5, 17-20: Jesus' teaching does not reject the old law and the prophets; instead, it illumines the meaning God intended the Old Testament ultimately to have (17). Disregard of even the slightest detail of the law means failure to secure that fullness of the kingdom of God (19) which those achieve who both teach and fulfill the law. In contrast, the false justice of the Pharisees, their lack of true interior holiness, will exclude them from the kingdom (20).

5, 27-32: Women are to be accorded the respect due to their persons as

adultery.' [28] What I say to you is: anyone who looks lustfully at a woman has already committed adultery with her in his thoughts. [29] If your right eye is your trouble, gouge it out and throw it away! Better to lose part of your body than to have it all cast into Gehenna. [30] Again, if your right hand is your trouble, cut it off and throw it away! Better to lose part of your body than to have it all cast into Gehenna.

Divorce

[31] "It was also said, 'Whenever a man divorces his wife, he must give her a decree of divorce.' [32] What I say to you is: everyone who divorces his wife—lewd conduct is a separate case—forces her to commit adultery. The man who marries a divorced woman likewise commits adultery.

On Oaths

[33] "You have heard the commandment imposed on your forefathers, 'Do not take a false oath; rather, make good to the Lord all your pledges.' [34] What I tell you is: do not swear at all. Do not swear by heaven (it is God's throne), [35] nor by the earth (it is his footstool), nor by Jerusalem (it is the city of the great King); [36] do not swear by your head (you cannot make a single hair white or black). [37] Say, 'Yes' when you mean 'Yes' and 'No' when you mean 'No.' Anything beyond that is from the evil one.

New Law of Retaliation

[38] "You have heard the commandment, 'An eye for an eye, a tooth for a tooth.' [39] But what I say to you is: offer no resistance to injury. When a person strikes you on the right cheek, turn and offer him the other. [40] If anyone wants to go to law over your shirt, hand him your coat as well. [41] Should anyone

---

28: Sir 9, 5.
29: 18, 8f; Mk 9, 42.46.
31: 19, 3-9; Dt 24, 1;
    Mal 2, 14ff.
32: Lk 16, 18; 1 Cor 7, 10.
33: Lv 19, 12; Nm 30, 3.

34: Ps 11, 4; Sir 23, 9.
35: Is 66, 1.
37: Jas 5, 12.
38: Ex 21, 24; Lv 24, 19f.
39-48: Lk 6, 27-36.
41: Lam 3, 30; Rom 12, 19ff.

---

children of the same God as men. The deeper implications of the divine law are seen to prohibit, not merely indecent actions against the religious dignity of the human person, but impure thoughts and desires as well. Jesus here repudiates the norm contained in Dt 24, 1 which allows a husband to dismiss his wife with a written decree of divorce for the purpose of remarriage. See note on Mt 19, 3-8.
5, 33-37: In the ordinary conduct of human affairs, personal trustworthiness should be such that the invocation of the divine name as evidence of truth is altogether unnecessary.

press you into service for one mile, go with him two miles.
⁴² Give to the man who begs from you. Do not turn your back
on the borrower.

Love of Enemies

⁴³ "You have heard the commandment, 'You shall love your
countryman but hate your enemy.' ⁴⁴ My command to you is:
love your enemies, pray for your persecutors. ⁴⁵ This will prove
that you are sons of your heavenly Father, for his sun rises on
the bad and the good, he rains on the just and the unjust. ⁴⁶ If
you love those who love you, what merit is there in that? Do
not tax collectors do as much? ⁴⁷ And if you greet your brothers
only, what is so praiseworthy about that? Do not pagans do as
much? ⁴⁸ In a word, you must be made perfect as your heavenly
Father is perfect.

6

Purity of Intention

¹ "Be on guard against performing religious acts for people to
see. Otherwise expect no recompense from your heavenly Father.
² When you give alms, for example, do not blow a horn before
you in synagogues and streets like hypocrites looking for ap-
plause. You can be sure of this much, they are already repaid.
³ In giving alms you are not to let your left hand know what
your right hand is doing. ⁴ Keep your deeds of mercy secret,
and your Father who sees in secret will repay you.

Prayer

⁵ "When you are praying, do not behave like the hypocrites
who love to stand and pray in synagogues or on street corners
in order to be noticed. I give you my word, they are already repaid. ⁶ Whenever you pray, go to your room, close your door,

42: Dt 15, 7f.
43: Lv 19, 18.
46: Lk 6, 32.
48: Lv 11, 44; 19, 2;
    Jas 1, 4; 1 Pt 1, 16;

1 Jn 3, 3.
6, 1: 23, 5; Lk 16, 15.
2: Jn 12, 43.
6: Tb 3, 10f; Dn 6, 11.

5, 43-48: As God invites the unjust to respond to him through the evidence of his love, so the disciples of Jesus must be the bearers of the same
love toward their enemies.
5, 48: The perfection of the Father is revealed in his redemptive love of
mankind, cf Jn 3, 16; 1 Jn 4, 9ff. For an application of the principle, cf 1
Cor 8, 7-11.
6, 1-6.16ff: To be of value in the eyes of God, religious duties, public and
private, must be performed for the single-hearted purpose of serving God,
and not for human esteem.

and pray to your Father in private. Then your Father, who sees what no man sees, will repay you. [7] In your prayer do not rattle on like the pagans. They think they will win a hearing by the sheer multiplication of words. [8] Do not imitate them. Your Father knows what you need before you ask him. [9] This is how you are to pray:

> 'Our Father in heaven,
> hallowed be your name,
> [10] your kingdom come,
> your will be done
> on earth as it is in heaven.
> [11] Give us today our daily bread,
> [12] and forgive us the wrong we have done
> as we forgive those who wrong us.
> [13] Subject us not to the trial
> but deliver us from the evil one.'

[14] "If you forgive the faults of others, your heavenly Father will forgive you yours. [15] If you do not forgive others, neither will your Father forgive you.

Fasting

[16] "When you fast, you are not to look glum as the hypocrites do. They change the appearance of their faces so that others may see they are fasting. I assure you, they are already repaid. [17] When you fast, see to it that you groom your hair and wash your face. [18] In that way no one can see you are fasting but your Father who is hidden; and your Father who sees what is hidden will repay you.

True Riches

[19] "Do not lay up for yourselves an earthly treasure. Moths and rust corrode; thieves break in and steal. [20] Make it your practice instead to store up heavenly treasure, which neither moths nor rust corrode nor thieves break in and steal. [21] Re-

9: Lk 11, 2ff; Jn 17, 26.	2 Thes 3, 3.
10: Mt 26, 42.	14: 18, 35; Sir 28, 1-5;
11: Prv 30, 8f;	Mk 11, 25.
Jn 6, 32.35.	15: Jas 2, 13.
12: 18, 21f; Sir 28, 2.	19: Lk 12, 33.
13: Jn 17, 15;	20: Jas 5, 2f.

6, 19ff: A concluding parable to confirm Jesus' teaching on the true service of God; recompense for good works is to be expected from him alone.

6, 22f: A person with proper vision can easily direct the movements of his body. In a similar way, one who makes use of the prophetic vision of Christ can direct his way to God.

member, where your treasure is, there your heart is also. ²² The eye is the body's lamp. If your eyes are good, your body will be filled with light; ²³ if your eyes are bad, your body will be in darkness. And if your light is darkness, how deep will the darkness be! ²⁴ No man can serve two masters. He will either hate one and love the other or be attentive to one and despise the other. You cannot give yourself to God and money. ²⁵ I warn you then: do not worry about your livelihood, what you are to eat or drink or use for clothing. Is not life more than food? Is not the body more valuable than clothes?

²⁶ "Look at the birds in the sky. They do not sow or reap, they gather nothing into barns; yet your heavenly Father feeds them. Are not you more important than they? ²⁷ Which of you by worrying can add a moment to his life-span? ²⁸ As for clothes, why be concerned? Learn a lesson from the way the wild flowers grow. They do not work; they do not spin. ²⁹ Yet I assure you, not even Solomon in all his splendor was arrayed like one of these. ³⁰ If God can clothe in such splendor the grass of the field, which blooms today and is thrown on the fire tomorrow, will he not provide much more for you, O weak in faith! ³¹ Stop worrying, then, over questions like, 'What are we to eat, or what are we to drink, or what are we to wear?' ³² The unbelievers are always running after these things. Your heavenly Father knows all that you need. ³³ Seek first his kingship over you, his way of holiness, and all these things will be given you besides. ³⁴ Enough, then, of worrying about tomorrow. Let tomorrow take care of itself. Today has troubles enough of its own.

7

Avoiding Judgment

¹ "If you want to avoid judgment, stop passing judgment. ² Your verdict on others will be the verdict passed on you. The measure with which you measure will be used to measure you. ³ Why look at the speck in your brother's eye when you miss the plank in your own? ⁴ How can you say to your brother, 'Let me take that speck out of your eye,' while all the time the plank remains in your own? ⁵ You hypocrite! Remove the plank from

---

22f: Lk 11, 34ff.
24: Lk 16, 13.
25-33: Lk 12, 22-31.
26: Pss 145, 15f; 147, 9.

33: Wis 1, 1.
7, 1: Rom 2, 1f; 1 Cor 4, 5.
2: Wis 12, 22; Mk 4, 24.
4: Jn 8, 7.

7, 1-5: Judgments of condemnation upon one's neighbor and refusal to pardon him entail loss of God's pardon for one's own sins.

your own eye first; then you will see clearly to take the speck from your brother's eyes.

[6] "Do not give what is holy to dogs or toss your pearls before swine. They will trample them under foot, at best, and perhaps even tear you to shreds.

The Power of Prayer

[7] "Ask, and you will receive. Seek, and you will find. Knock, and it will be opened to you. [8] For the one who asks, receives. The one who seeks, finds. The one who knocks, enters. [9] Would one of you hand his son a stone when he asks for a loaf, [10] or a poisonous snake when he asks for a fish? [11] If you, with all your sins, know how to give your children what is good, how much more will your heavenly Father give good things to anyone who asks him!

The Golden Rule

[12] "Treat others the way you would have them treat you: this sums up the law and the prophets.

[13] "Enter through the narrow gate. The gate that leads to damnation is wide, the road is clear, and many choose to travel it. [14] But how narrow is the gate that leads to life, how rough the road, and how few there are who find it!

[15] "Be on your guard against false prophets, who come to you in sheep's clothing but underneath are wolves on the prowl. [16] You will know them by their deeds. Do you ever pick grapes from thornbushes, or figs from prickly plants? Never! [17] Any sound tree bears good fruit, while a decayed tree bears bad fruit. [18] A sound tree cannot bear bad fruit any more than a decayed tree can bear good fruit. [19] Every tree that does not bear good fruit is cut down and thrown into the fire. [20] You can tell a tree by its fruit. [21] None of those who cry out, 'Lord,

---

6: Prv 23, 9.
7-11: Mk 11, 24; Lk 11, 9-13.
7: 18, 19.
8: Lk 18, 1-8; Jn 14, 13.
11: 1 Jn 5, 14f.
12: Lk 6, 31; Rom 13, 8.

13: Sir 21, 10; Lk 13, 24.
15: 2 Pt 2, 1.
16f: 12, 33; Sir 27, 6; Lk 6, 43f.
18: Jn 15, 6.
19: 3, 10.

7, 6: The teaching of the gospel will be rejected by some precisely because it is holy, and those who teach it will themselves be subjected to attack.

7, 7-11: The persevering prayer of sinful humanity receives a divine response because of the generosity of God.

7, 12: An isolated saying introduced to show that the moral teaching concerning neighbor in the reign of God is the golden rule of true fraternal charity.

7, 13-27: A series of parables warning that only through the good works outlined in the Sermon does man find the way of life that leads to the happiness God has in store for him.

Lord,' will enter the kingdom of God but only the one who does the will of my Father in heaven. 22 When that day comes, many will plead with me, 'Lord, Lord, have we not prophesied in your name? Have we not exorcised demons by its power? Did we, not do many miracles in your name as well?' 23 Then I will declare to them solemnly, 'I never knew you. Out of my sight, you evildoers!'

Conclusion of the Sermon

24 "Anyone who hears my words and puts them into practice is like the wise man who built his house on rock. 25 When the rainy season set in, the torrents came and the winds blew and buffeted his house. It did not collapse; it had been solidly set on rock. 26 Anyone who hears my words but does not put them into practice is like the foolish man who built his house on sandy ground. 27 The rains fell, the torrents came, the winds blew and lashed against his house. It collapsed under all this and was completely ruined."

28 Jesus finished this discourse and left the crowds spellbound at his teaching. 29 The reason was that he taught with authority and not like their scribes.

III: PREACHING THE REIGN OF GOD

8

The Leper

1 When he came down from the mountain, great crowds followed him. 2 Suddenly a leper came forward and did him homage, saying to him, "Sir, if you will to do so, you can cure me." 3 Jesus stretched out his hand and touched him and said, "I do will it. Be cured." Immediately the man's leprosy disap-

---

21: Is 29, 13.
22: 25, 11f; Jas 2, 14-17.
23: Ps 5, 5.
24-27: 'Lk 6, 47ff.
25: Prv 10, 25.

29: Mk 1, 22; Lk 4, 32; Jn 7, 15ff.
8, 1-4: Mk 1, 40-44; Lk 5, 12ff.

7, 28: A general formula used in Matthew at the conclusion of the five collections of the sayings of Jesus (11, 1; 13, 53; 19, 1; 26, 1).
7, 29—9, 38: By means of miracle narratives and other events, Matthew portrays Jesus' unique power in word and action. Jesus uses the twofold charism of miracles and prophecy in behalf of the people to invite them to accept the new sovereign rule of God which he proclaims (8, 16-22; 9, 13.36). The miracle accounts appear in groups of three (8, 1-15; 8, 23—9, 8; 9, 18-34). Other incidents and comments are interspersed between these groupings.

peared. ⁴ Then Jesus said to him: "See to it that you tell no one. Go and show yourself to the priest and offer the gift Moses prescribed. That should be the proof they need."

The Centurion's Servant

⁵ As Jesus entered Capernaum, a centurion approached him with this request: ⁶ "Sir, my serving boy is at home in bed paralyzed, suffering painfully." ⁷ He said to him, "I will come and cure him." ⁸ "Sir," the centurion said in reply, "I am not worthy to have you under my roof. Just give an order and my boy will get better. ⁹ I am a man under authority myself and I have troops assigned to me. If I give one man the order, 'Dismissed,' off he goes. If I say to another, 'Come here,' he comes. If I tell my slave, 'Do this,' he does it." ¹⁰ Jesus showed amazement on hearing this and remarked to his followers, "I assure you, I have never found this much faith in Israel. ¹¹ Mark what I say! Many will come from the east and the west and will find a place at the banquet in the kingdom of God with Abraham, Isaac, and Jacob, ¹² while the natural heirs of the kingdom will be driven out into the dark. Wailing will be heard there, and the grinding of teeth." ¹³ To the centurion Jesus said, "Go home. It shall be done because you trusted." That very moment the boy got better.

Peter's Mother-in-law

¹⁴ Jesus entered Peter's house and found Peter's mother-in-law in bed with a fever. ¹⁵ He took her by the hand and the fever left her. She got up at once and began to wait on him.

Other Miracles

¹⁶ As evening drew on, they brought him many who were possessed. He expelled the spirits by a simple command and cured all who were afflicted, ¹⁷ thereby fulfilling what had been said through Isaiah the prophet:

4: Lv 14, 2f; Lk 17, 14.
5-13: Lk 7, 1-10.
11f: 22, 13; 24, 51; 25, 30; Lk 13, 28f.

14ff: Mk 1, 29-34; Lk 4, 38-41.
15: 9, 25.
17: Is 53, 4.

8, 4: See note on Mk 1, 40-45.
8, 10ff: The great trust of the centurion consisted in his honest acceptance of the religious authority of Jesus, displayed in curing the sick. Jesus' comment invites his contemporaries to match the centurion's trust.
8, 17: Matthew sees in Jesus the true servant of Yahweh (Is 53, 4), whose miraculous healings are the external sign of the redemption which Jesus was now accomplishing as *he bore*, i. e., "took upon himself," *our infirmities*, i. e., "our sins," to free us from them.

"It was our infirmities he bore,
our sufferings he endured."

Conditions for Following Jesus

[18] Seeing the people crowd around him, Jesus gave orders to cross to the other shore. [19] A scribe approached him and said, "Teacher, wherever you go I will come after you." [20] Jesus said to him, "The foxes have lairs, the birds in the sky have nests, but the Son of Man has nowhere to lay his head." [21] Another, a disciple, said to him, "Lord, let me go and bury my father first." [22] But Jesus told him, "Follow me, and let the dead bury their dead."

Storm on the Lake

[23] He got into the boat and his disciples followed him. [24] Without warning a violent storm came up on the lake, and the boat began to be swamped by the waves. [25] Jesus was sleeping soundly, so they made their way toward him and woke him: "Lord, save us! We are lost!" [26] He said to them: "Where is your courage? How little faith you have!" Then he stood up and took the winds and the sea to task. Complete calm ensued; [27] the men were dumbfounded. "What sort of man is this," they said, "that even the winds and the sea obey him?"

19-22: Lk 9, 57-60.
23-27: Mk 4, 35-40;

Lk 8, 22-25.
26: Ps 107, 29.

8, 20: *Son of Man:* an enigmatic title of Christ used in the gospels and in Acts 7, 56. Jesus is reported as using it frequently of himself; it was well adapted to his purpose of both veiling and revealing his person and mission. On the one hand, it simply meant "man" (Ez 2, 1) and emphasized the lowliness of the human condition (Mt 8, 20; 11, 19; 20, 28), especially in Christ's humiliation and death (17, 22). On the other hand, it expressed the triumph of Jesus' resurrection (17, 9), his return to glory (24, 30; Dn 7, 13), and his second coming as judge of the world (25, 31).

At his trial before the Sanhedrin, Jesus is described as using the title *Son of Man* in a well-defined religious sense (26, 64). Though he stood before his accusers an innocent victim, charged with blasphemy and condemned to die, he prophesied his vindication and future glory, *seated at the right hand of the Power*, i. e., God, not merely as man but as Lord (Dn 7, 13; Mk 14, 62).

Jewish apocalyptic literature (1 Enoch, 2 Ezra, 2 Baruch) employed the title to describe a unique religious personage endowed with extraordinary spiritual power, who would receive the kingdom from God at the end of time. Early Christian communities held this title in reverence because it reminded them of Jesus' awareness of his double destiny, of humiliation and of glory, in which the Christian community also shares (Mt 24, 30f).

8, 22: Jesus has subordinated family ties to the needs of his mission of salvation (8, 20). He requires the same sacrifice of those called to share this mission with him, when other members of the family can perform the deeds of filial piety. These latter are *dead* only in the sense that they have not received the divine call to separate themselves from family responsibility in order to preach the gospel of the kingdom. They can, however, be Jesus' disciples in another sense.

Expulsion of the Demons in Gadara

[28] As he approached the Gadarene boundary, he encountered two men coming out of the tombs. They were possessed by demons and were so savage that no one could travel along that road. [29] With a sudden shriek they cried: "Why meddle with us, Son of God? Have you come to torture us before the appointed time?" [30] Some distance away a large herd of swine was feeding. [31] The demons kept appealing to him, "If you expel us, send us into the herd of swine." [32] He answered, "Out with you!" At that they came forth and entered the swine. The whole herd went rushing down the bluff into the sea and were drowned.

[33] The swineherds took to their heels, and upon their arrival in the town related everything that had happened, including the story about the two possessed men. [34] The upshot was that the entire town came out to meet Jesus. When they caught sight of him, they begged him to leave their neighborhood.

9

A Paralytic at Capernaum

[1] Then he reentered the boat, made the crossing, and came back to his own town. [2] There the people at once brought to him a paralyzed man lying on a mat. When Jesus saw their faith he said to the paralytic, "Have courage, son, your sins are forgiven." [3] At that some of the scribes said to themselves, "The man blasphemes." [4] Jesus was aware of what they were thinking and said: "Why do you harbor evil thoughts? [5] Which is less trouble to say, 'Your sins are forgiven' or 'Stand up and walk'? [6] To help you realize that the Son of Man has authority on earth to forgive sins"—he then said to the paralyzed man—"Stand up! Roll up your mat, and go home." [7] The man stood up and went toward his home. [8] At the sight, a feeling of awe came over the crowd, and they praised God for giving such authority to men.

28-34: Mk 5, 1-17;
     Lk 8, 26-37.
  31: Lk 4, 34ff;
     Acts 10, 38.
9, 1-8: Mk 2, 3-12;

Lk 5, 18-26.
  2: Lk 7, 48.
  6: Jn 5, 27.
  7: Jn 5, 8f.

8, 29: *Son of God:* see note on Mk 3, 12. *Before the appointed time:* a phrase peculiar to Matthew in this account. Even in pagan territory the demons already feel the threat of Jesus before the destruction of Satan's power at the end of the world (1 Cor 15, 24f).

9, 8: *Such authority to men:* the principal issue of Jesus' authority here is the power to forgive sins. Matthew's use of the plural *men* suggests the power of the Christian community to forgive sins in Jesus' name; cf Acts 2, 38; Jas 5, 16.

Call of Matthew

⁹ As he moved on, Jesus saw a man named Matthew at his post where taxes were collected. He said to him, "Follow me." Matthew got up and followed him. ¹⁰ Now it happened that, while Jesus was at table in Matthew's home, many tax collectors and those known as sinners came to join Jesus and his disciples at dinner. ¹¹ The Pharisees saw this and complained to his disciples, "What reason can the Teacher have for eating with tax collectors and those who disregard the law?" ¹² Overhearing the remark, he said: "People who are in good health do not need a doctor; sick people do. ¹³ Go and learn the meaning of the words, 'It is mercy I desire and not sacrifice.' I have come to call, not the self-righteous, but sinners."

The Question of Fasting

¹⁴ Later on, John's disciples came to him with the objection, "Why is it that while we and the Pharisees fast, your disciples do not?" Jesus said to them: ¹⁵ "How can wedding guests go in mourning so long as the groom is with them? When the day comes that the groom is taken away, then they will fast. ¹⁶ Nobody sews a piece of unshrunken cloth on an old cloak; the very thing he has used to cover the hole will pull, and the rip only get worse. ¹⁷ People do not pour new wine into old wineskins. If they do, the skins burst, the wine spills out, and the skins are ruined. No, they pour new wine into new wineskins, and in that way both are preserved."

A Dead Girl; a Woman with a Hemorrhage

¹⁸ Before Jesus had finished speaking to them, a synagogue leader came up, did him reverence, and said: "My daughter has just died. Please come and lay your hand on her and she will come back to life." ¹⁹ Jesus stood up and followed him, and his

---

9-13: Mk 2, 14-17;
    Lk 5, 27-32.
10: 19, 1-10.
13: 12, 7; Hos 6, 6.
14-17: Mk 2, 18-22;

    Lk 5, 33-39.
16: Rom 7, 6; 2 Cor 5, 17.
18-26: Mk 5, 22-43;
    Lk 8, 41-56.

9, 13: Jesus' association with tax collectors and violators of the law is conformable to his teaching about the need of repentance (4, 17). He cites Hos 6, 6 to show that love of neighbor gives value to sacrifices offered as evidence of love of God.

9, 14-17: Jesus' presence among men during his public ministry is comparable to that of a bridegroom during the marriage feast. The time of fasting is temporarily set aside until after Jesus' death to bring about those changes in the human person required for assimilating the new doctrinal ideas.

9, 18-26: See note on Mk 5, 21-43.

disciples did the same. [20] As they were going, a woman who had suffered from hemorrhages for twelve years came up behind him and touched the tassel on his cloak. [21] "If only I can touch his cloak," she thought, "I shall get well." [22] Jesus turned around and saw her and said, "Courage, daughter! Your faith has restored you to health." That very moment the woman got well.

[23] When Jesus arrived at the synagogue leader's house and saw the flute players and the crowd who were making a din, he said, [24] "Leave, all of you! The little girl is not dead. She is asleep." At this they began to ridicule him. [25] When the crowd had been put out he entered and took her by the hand, and the little girl got up. [26] News of this circulated throughout the district.

Two Blind Men

[27] As Jesus moved on from there, two blind men came after him crying out, "Son of David, have pity on us!" [28] When he got to the house, the blind men caught up with him. Jesus said to them, "Are you confident I can do this?" "Yes, Lord," they told him. [29] At that he touched their eyes and said, "Because of your faith it shall be done to you"; [30] and they recovered their sight. Then Jesus warned them sternly, "See to it that no one knows of this." [31] But they went off and spread word of him through the whole area.

A Possessed Mute

[32] As they were leaving, suddenly some people brought him a mute who was possessed by a demon. [33] Once the demon was expelled the mute began to speak, to the great surprise of the crowds. "Nothing like this has ever been seen in Israel!" they exclaimed. [34] But the Pharisees were saying, "He casts out demons through the prince of demons."

Mission of the Twelve

[35] Jesus continued his tour of all the towns and villages. He taught in their synagogues, he proclaimed the good news of God's reign, and he cured every sickness and disease. [36] At the

---

21: 14, 36; Nm 15, 37;
    Acts 19, 12.
27: 15, 22.
32ff: 12, 22ff; Lk 11, 14f.

33: Mk 7, 37.
34: 10, 25.
35: Lk 8, 1.

9, 27-31: See note on Mk 10, 46-52.
9, 35—10, 1: Having preached and ministered widely in Galilee, Jesus sees the people's need for prophetic leadership; cf Nm 27, 17. He therefore expands his missionary activity by conferring his own powers on certain of his disciples.

sight of the crowds, his heart was moved with pity. They were lying prostrate from exhaustion, like sheep without a shepherd. [37] He said to his disciples: "The harvest is good but laborers are scarce. Beg the harvest master [38] to send out laborers to gather his harvest."

10

[1] Then he summoned his twelve disciples and gave them authority to expel unclean spirits and to cure sickness and disease of every kind.

[2] The names of the twelve apostles are these: first Simon, now known as Peter, and his brother Andrew; James, Zebedee's son, and his brother John; [3] Philip and Bartholomew, Thomas and Matthew the tax collector; James, son of Alphaeus, and Thaddaeus; [4] Simon the Zealot Party member, and Judas Iscariot, who betrayed him. [5] Jesus sent these men on mission as the Twelve, after giving them the following instructions:

"Do not visit pagan territory and do not enter a Samaritan town. [6] Go instead after the lost sheep of the house of Israel. [7] As you go, make this announcement: 'The reign of God is at hand!' [8] Cure the sick, raise the dead, heal the leprous, expel demons. The gift you have received, give as a gift. [9] Provide yourselves with neither gold nor silver nor copper in your belts; [10] no traveling bag, no change of shirt, no sandals, no walking staff. The workman, after all, is worth his keep.

[11] "Look for a worthy person in every town or village you come to and stay with him until you leave. [12] As you enter his home bless it. [13] If the home is deserving, your blessing will descend on it. If it is not, your blessing will return to you. [14] If anyone does not receive you or listen to what you have to say, leave that house or town, and once outside it shake its dust from your feet. [15] I assure you, it will go easier for the region of

36: Jer 50, 6; Ez 34, 5;
    Mk 6, 34.
37f: Lk 10, 2; Jn 4, 35.
10, 2-5: Mk 3, 16-19;
    Lk 6, 13-16; Acts 1, 13.
6: 15, 24.
7: 3, 2; 4, 17.

9: Mk 6, 8f; Lk 9, 3; 10, 4.
10: Lk 10, 7; 1 Cor 9, 14;
    3 Jn 8.
11-15: Mk 6, 10f; Lk 9, 4f;
    10, 5-12.
14: Acts 13, 51; 18, 6.
15: 11, 24; Jude 7.

10, 2-33: These verses, which conserve Jesus' instructions to his disciples for their missionary activity, constitute a norm for all Christian missioners. Certain of his prophecies are incorporated into the discourse because they reflected the church's experience (10, 17-21); cf 2 Cor 11, 23ff; Acts 5, 40; 24, 1-23.

10, 12f: The blessing referred to is a wish of peace. The blessing, once invoked, is considered to continue to exist. An undeserving household will not receive it; therefore it returns and benefits the one who uttered it.

Sodom and Gomorrah on the day of judgment than it will for that town.

[16] "What I am doing is sending you out like sheep among wolves. You must be clever as snakes and innocent as doves. Be on your guard with respect to others. [17] They will hale you into court, they will flog you in their synagogues. [18] You will be brought to trial before rulers and kings, to give witness before them and before the Gentiles on my account. [19] When they hand you over, do not worry about what you will say or how you will say it. When the hour comes, you will be given what you are to say. [20] You yourselves will not be the speakers; the Spirit of your Father will be speaking in you.

[21] "Brother will hand over brother to death, and the father his child; children will turn against parents and have them put to death. [22] You will be hated by all on account of me. But whoever holds out till the end will escape death. [23] When they persecute you in one town, flee to the next. I solemnly assure you, you will not have covered the towns of Israel before the Son of Man comes.

[24] "No pupil outranks his teacher, no slave his master. [25] The pupil should be glad to become like his teacher, the slave like his master. If they call the head of the house Beelzebul, how much more the members of his household! [26] Do not let them intimidate you. Nothing is concealed that will not be revealed, and nothing hidden that will not become known. [27] What I tell you in darkness, speak in the light. What you hear in private, proclaim from the housetops.

[28] "Do not fear those who deprive the body of life but cannot destroy the soul. Rather, fear him who can destroy both body and soul in Gehenna. [29] Are not two sparrows sold for next to nothing? Yet not a single sparrow falls to the ground without your Father's consent. [30] As for you, every hair of your head has been counted; [31] so do not be afraid of anything. You

---

16: Lk 10, 3; 1 Cor 14, 20.
17-22: Mk 13, 9-13;
     Lk 21, 12-19;
     Jn 16, 1-4.
17: Acts 5, 40.
18: Jn 15, 27.
19: Ex 4, 11f; Jer 1, 6-10;
     Lk 12, 11f.

21f: 24, 9.13.
24f: Lk 6, 40; Jn 13, 16;
     15, 20.
26-33: Lk 12, 2-9.
26: Mk 4, 22; Lk 8, 17;
     1 Tm 5, 25.
28: 1 Pt 3, 14; Rv 2, 10.

10, 23: The missionaries are not to risk their lives unnecessarily. *You will not have covered . . . the Son of Man comes:* Jesus implies, not that he expects the parousia (see note on 1 Thes 4, 13-18) and God's final judgment before the termination of his disciples' mission, but rather that the divine plan of Israel's salvation will not be completed before the parousia because of hostility.

are worth more than an entire flock of sparrows. [32] Whoever acknowledges me before men I will acknowledge before my Father in heaven. [33] Whoever disowns me before men I will disown before my Father in heaven.

[34] "Do not suppose that my mission on earth is to spread peace. My mission is to spread, not peace, but division. [35] I have come to set a man at odds with his father, a daughter with her mother, a daughter-in-law with her mother-in-law: [36] in short, to make a man's enemies those of his own household. [37] Whoever loves father or mother, son or daughter, more than me is not worthy of me. [38] He who will not take up his cross and come after me is not worthy of me. [39] He who seeks only himself brings himself to ruin, whereas he who brings himself to nought for me discovers who he is.

[40] "He who welcomes you welcomes me, and he who welcomes me welcomes him who sent me. [41] He who welcomes a prophet because he bears the name of prophet receives a prophet's reward; he who welcomes a holy man because he is known to be holy receives a holy man's reward. [42] And I promise you that whoever gives a cup of cold water to one of these lowly ones because he is a disciple will not want for his reward."

11

[1] When Jesus had finished instructing his twelve disciples, he left that locality to teach and preach in their towns.

IV: MYSTERY OF THE REIGN OF GOD

The Baptizer's Deputation

[2] Now John in prison heard about the works Christ was performing, and sent a message by his disciples to ask him, [3] "Are you 'He who is to come' or do we look for another?" [4] In reply, Jesus said to them: "Go back and report to John what you hear and see: [5] the blind recover their sight, cripples walk, lepers are

32: Lk 12, 8f.
33: Mk 8, 38; Lk 9, 26;
     2 Tm 2, 12; Rv, 3, 5.
34f: Lk 2, 34; 12, 51ff.
37ff: 16, 24f; Lk 14, 26f.
39: Mk 8, 35; Lk 9, 24;
     Jn 12, 25.

40: Lk 10, 16; Jn 12, 44;
     13, 20.
42: 25, 40; Mk 9, 41.
11, 2-11: Lk 7, 18-28.
5: 8, 3f; Is 26, 19; 29, 18f;
     35, 5f.

11, 2—12, 50: Jesus' messianic role is questioned and rejected. John sends a query to Jesus about his role (11, 2-6). Jesus himself comments on the resistance to his message in certain key cities of Galilee (11, 20-24). The scribes and Pharisees, and even Jesus' relatives, are hostile to him (12, 1-50).

11, 3: John is puzzled because Jesus continues to appeal for repentance rather than inflict final divine punishment on the unrepentant; cf Mt 3, 12.

cured, the deaf hear, dead men are raised to life, and the poor have the good news preached to them. ⁶ Blest is the man who finds no stumbling block in me."

Christ's Witness to John

⁷ As the messengers set off, Jesus began to speak to the crowds about John: "What did you go out to the wasteland to see—a reed swaying in the wind? ⁸ Tell me, what did you go out to see—someone luxuriously dressed? Remember, those who dress luxuriously are to be found in royal palaces. ⁹ Why then did you go out—to see a prophet? A prophet indeed, and something more! ¹⁰ It is about this man that Scripture says,

'I send my messenger ahead of you
to prepare your way before you.'

¹¹ "I solemnly assure you, history has not known a man born of woman greater than John the Baptizer. Yet the least born into the kingdom of God is greater than he. ¹² From John the Baptizer's time until now the kingdom of God has suffered violence, and the violent take it by force. ¹³ All the prophets as well as the law spoke prophetically until John. ¹⁴ If you are prepared to accept it, he is Elijah, the one who was certain to come. ¹⁵ Heed carefully what you hear!

The Wayward Children

¹⁶ "What comparison can I use to describe this breed? They are like children squatting in the town squares, calling to their playmates:

¹⁷ 'We piped you a tune but you did not dance!
We sang you a dirge but you did not wail!'

¹⁸ In other words, John appeared neither eating nor drinking, and people say, 'He is mad!' ¹⁹ The Son of Man appeared eating

---

7: 3, 3f.
10: Mal 3, 1; Mk 1, 2;
Lk 1, 76f.
12: Lk 16, 16.

14: 16, 14; 17, 10-13;
Mal 3, 23; Lk 1, 17.
16-19: Lk 7, 31-35.
18: Lk 1, 15.

11, 7-15: In this collection of sayings Jesus eulogizes the strength of John the Baptizer's religious convictions, the austerity of his life (7f), and his unique prophetic role as the messianic precursor (9-15).

11, 11: *Greater than he:* the disciples benefit from Jesus' prophetic light, which surpasses that of John.

11, 12: A highly enigmatic saying—probably so because of isolation from its original historical context. It contrasts Jesus' message of renewal through repentance and the faith that leads to admission into God's kingdom, with the false messianism of the "holy war" advocated, e. g., by the Zealots and the sectaries of Qumran.

and drinking, and they say, 'This one is a glutton and drunkard, a lover of tax collectors and those outside the law!' Yet time will prove where wisdom lies."

The Impenitent Towns

²⁰ He began to reproach the towns where most of his miracles had been worked, with their failure to reform: ²¹ "It will go ill with you, Chorazin! And just as ill with you, Bethsaida! If the miracles worked in you had taken place in Tyre and Sidon, they would have reformed in sackcloth and ashes long ago. ²² I assure you, it will go easier for Tyre and Sidon than for you on the day of judgment. ²³ As for you, Capernaum,

'Are you to be exalted to the skies?
You shall go down to the realm of death!'

If the miracles worked in you had taken place in Sodom, it would be standing today. ²⁴ I assure you, it will go easier for Sodom than for you on the day of judgment."

Jesus and His Father

²⁵ On one occasion Jesus spoke thus: "Father, Lord of heaven and earth, to you I offer praise; for what you have hidden from the learned and the clever you have revealed to the merest children. ²⁶ Father, it is true. You have graciously willed it so. ²⁷ Everything has been given over to me by my Father. No one knows the Son but the Father, and no one knows the Father but the Son—and anyone to whom the Son wishes to reveal him.

²⁸ "Come to me, all you who are weary and find life burdensome, and I will refresh you. ²⁹ Take my yoke upon your

---

19: 9, 10f.
20-24: Lk 10, 12-15.
23: Is 14, 13ff.
24: 10, 15.

25ff: Lk 10, 21f;
1 Cor 1, 26-29.
27: Jn 3, 35; 6, 46; 7, 28.
28: Sir 24, 18.

11, 19: *Time will prove where wisdom lies:* neither the austere preaching and penance of John the Baptizer nor the gentle persuasion of Jesus elicits the good will of unbelievers. God's wisdom triumphs over them in the end.
11, 20-24: Sayings of Jesus, uttered perhaps during his preaching in these cities, and summarized here. They are directed against those who fail to recognize the presence of God in Jesus so as to avoid repentance.
11, 27: This verse has a Johannine ring in thought and style (Jn 3, 16f; 5, 19-23) and uses as introduction a saying of the risen Christ (Mt 28, 18). Only God the Father fully comprehends Jesus' mission, and only Jesus fully understands God's saving plan which he gradually unveils to men. This saying may have originated in the instruction of the risen Lord; cf Acts 1, 3.
11, 28: *Who are weary . . . burdensome:* a probable allusion to the moral and legal prescriptions of rabbinic Judaism, which needed to be balanced by prophetic vision in order to give joy and peaceful expectancy to the Mosaic tradition.
11, 29: *Your souls will find rest:* through acceptance of the gospel teach-

shoulders and learn from me, for I am gentle and humble of heart. Your souls will find rest, ³⁰ for my yoke is easy and my burden light."

12

The Disciples and the Sabbath

¹ Once on a sabbath Jesus walked through the standing grain. His disciples felt hungry, so they began to pull off the heads of grain and eat them. ² When the Pharisees spied this, they protested: "See here! Your disciples are doing what is not permitted on the sabbath." ³ He replied: "Have you not read what David did when he and his men were hungry, ⁴ how he entered God's house and ate the holy bread, a thing forbidden to him and his men or anyone other than priests? ⁵ Have you not read in the law how the priests on temple duty can break the sabbath rest without incurring guilt? ⁶ I assure you, there is something greater than the temple here. ⁷ If you understood the meaning of the text, 'It is mercy I desire and not sacrifice,' you would not have condemned these innocent men. ⁸ The Son of Man is indeed Lord of the sabbath."

A Man with a Shriveled Hand

⁹ He left that place and went into their synagogue. ¹⁰ A man with a shriveled hand happened to be there, and they put this question to Jesus, hoping to bring an accusation against him:

12, 1-8: Ex 20, 8; Mk 2, 23-28;
     Lk 6, 1-5.
   3: 1 Sm 21, 6.
   4: Lv 24, 5-9.

   7: 1 Sm 15, 22; Hos 6, 6.
   8: Jn 5, 16f.
 9-15: Mk 3, 1-7.
  10: Lk 20, 20.

---

ing which satisfies the longings of those who are wearied by the burdens of life.

12, 3-6: Jesus responds to the objection of the Pharisees: if they hold so rigidly to their interpretation of the law, they should be critical of David's action (1 Sm 21, 1-6), and also that of the priests who on the sabbath prepare the offerings of the lambs (Nm 28, 9f). If these violations of the law in the temple, God's dwelling, are above criticism, neither should Jesus be criticized, for God is present in him as is manifested through his miracles; cf Jn 10, 38.

12, 8: See note on Mk 2, 28.

12, 10: *Is it lawful to work a cure on the sabbath?:* curing on the sabbath was a frequent issue against Jesus in the gospels and one of considerable tension between him and the religious authorities (Jn 7, 23f). The basis of this altercation is not entirely clear. The sabbath healings did not accord with the teaching of the rabbis on the limited degree of aid to be given the sick or injured on that day. It seems, however, from the complete gospel that the issue was more complex than one of mere legalism. The healings produced clamorous crowds and processions of other sick persons (Lk 13, 14), which greatly disturbed the sabbath rest. At times Jesus overrode the sabbath restrictions (Jn 5, 18), challenged the authority of the scribes and Pharisees, and thoroughly involved them in his message. They had no choice but to take a stand, whether favorable or hostile, to Jesus.

"Is it lawful to work a cure on the sabbath?" [11] He said in response: "Suppose one of you has a sheep and it falls into a pit on the sabbath. Will he not take hold of it and pull it out? [12] Well, think how much more precious a human being is than a sheep. Clearly, good deeds may be performed on the sabbath."

[13] To the man he said, "Stretch out your hand." He did so, and it was perfectly restored; it became as sound as the other. [14] When the Pharisees were outside they began to plot against him to find a way to destroy him. [15] Jesus was aware of this, and so he withdrew from that place.

The Mercy of Jesus

Many people followed him and he cured them all, [16] though he sternly ordered them not to make public what he had done. [17] This was to fulfill what had been said through Isaiah the prophet:

> [18] "Here is my servant whom I have chosen,
> my loved one in whom I delight.
> I will endow him with my spirit
> and he will proclaim justice to the Gentiles.
> [19] He will not contend or cry out,
> nor will his voice be heard in the streets.
> [20] The bruised reed he will not crush;
> the smoldering wick he will not quench
> until judgment is made victorious.
> [21] In his name, the Gentiles will find hope."

Blasphemy of the Pharisees

[22] A possessed man who was brought to him was blind and mute. He cured the man so that he could speak and see. [23] All in the crowd were astonished. "Might this not be David's son?" they asked. [24] When the Pharisees heard this, they charged, "This man can expel demons only with the help of Beelze-

---

11: Dt 22, 4.
14: Jn 5, 18; 11, 53.
18-21: Is 42, 1-4.

22ff: Lk 9, 32ff; 11, 14f.
23: 9, 27.
24: 10.25; Mk 3, 22.

12, 15-21: Jesus shows no inclination to counteract the hostility of the Pharisees by any action on his part, such as enlisting popular support against them. Instead he withdraws *from that place*, even orders those cured *not to make public what he had done*. The free citation of Is 42, 1-4 is a reflection of the meekness of Jesus, the harbinger of the divine mercy to Jews and Gentiles.

12, 24-29: To the Pharisees' charge that Jesus performs exorcisms by a pact with Satan, he replies by showing that the objection lacks common sense (25f), overlooks the tradition of exorcistic power in Israel (27), and refuses to acknowledge, in the person and teaching of Christ, the new reign of God, capable of destroying Satan's power (28f).

bul, the prince of demons." [25] Knowing their thoughts, he said to them: "A kingdom torn by strife is headed for its downfall. A town or household split into factions cannot last for long. [26] If Satan is expelling Satan, he must be torn by dissension. How, then, can his dominion last? [27] If I expel demons with Beelzebul's help, by whose help do your people expel them? Let them be the ones to judge you. [28] But if it is by the Spirit of God that I expel demons, then the reign of God has overtaken you.

[29] "How can anyone enter a strong man's house and make off with his property unless he first ties him securely? Only then can he rob his house. [30] He who is not with me is against me, and he who does not gather with me scatters.

[31] "That, I assure you, is why every sin, every blasphemy, will be forgiven men, but blasphemy against the Spirit will not be forgiven. [32] Whoever says anything against the Son of Man will be forgiven, but whoever says anything against the Holy Spirit will not be forgiven, either in this age or in the age to come. [33] Declare a tree good and its fruit good or declare a tree rotten and its fruit rotten, one or the other, for you can tell a tree by its fruit. [34] How can you utter anything good, you brood of vipers, when you are so evil? The mouth speaks whatever fills the mind. [35] A good man produces good from his store of goodness; an evil man produces evil from his evil store. [36] I assure you, on judgment day people will be held accountable for every unguarded word they speak. [37] By your words you will be acquitted, and by your words you will be condemned."

The Sign of Jonah

[38] Some of the scribes and Pharisees then spoke up, saying,

---

25-29: Mk 3, 23-27;
　　　Lk 11, 17-22.
28: Lk 8, 29.
30: Mk 9, 40; Lk 11, 23.

31f: Mk 3, 28ff; Lk 12, 10.
33: Lk 6, 43ff.
34: 3, 7; 23, 33; 15, 11f.
36f: Jas 3, 1f.

12, 31f: The Pharisees are said to attribute Jesus' exorcisms to satanic power and thus to deny the unique presence of God in Jesus. They thereby assign his entire work and teaching to an evil principle, making it anti-God. This is the *blasphemy against the Spirit* that *will not be forgiven*, because it negates the evidence of God's saving action in history. However, misunderstanding of Jesus' teaching and misconceptions of his Person due to human error or prejudice will be forgiven (Acts 9, 4f; 1 Tm 1, 13).

12, 33-37: Those who charge that Jesus is in league with Satan reflect a basic evil in themselves that can be cured only by a radical renewal of faith and love.

12, 38ff: A current opinion in Judaism (Jn 7, 31) was that the Messiah would perform a unique kind of miracle. This view was not supported by the Old Testament but was apparently adhered to in circles of apocalyptic thought. The only additional sign to be given the faithless is that of Jesus' death and resurrection, typified by the story of Jonah in the belly of the fish.

"Teacher, we want to see you work some signs." [39] He answered: "An evil and unfaithful age is eager for a sign! No sign will be given it but that of the prophet Jonah. [40] Just as Jonah spent three days and three nights in the belly of the whale, so will the Son of Man spend three days and three nights in the bowels of the earth. [41] At the judgment, the citizens of Nineveh will rise with the present generation and be the ones to condemn it. At the preaching of Jonah they reformed their lives; but you have a greater than Jonah here. [42] At the judgment, the queen of the South will rise with the present generation and be the one to condemn it. She came from the farthest corner of the earth to listen to the wisdom of Solomon; but you have a greater than Solomon here.

[43] "When the unclean spirit departs from a man, it roams through arid wastes searching for a place of rest and finding none. [44] Then it says, 'I will go back where I came from,' and returns to find the dwelling unoccupied, though swept and tidied now. [45] Off it goes again to bring back with it this time seven spirits more evil than itself. They move in and settle there. Thus the last state of that man becomes worse than the first. And that is how it will be with this evil generation."

Jesus and His Family

[46] He was still addressing the crowds when his mother and his brothers appeared outside to speak with him. [47] Someone said to him, "Your mother and your brothers are standing out there and they wish to speak to you." [48] He said to the one who had told him, "Who is my mother? Who are my brothers?" [49] Then, extending his hand toward his disciples, he said, [50] "There are my mother and my brothers. Whoever does the will of my heavenly Father is brother and sister and mother to me."

13

[1] That same day, on leaving the house, Jesus sat down by the

---

39-42: 16, 4; Jon 2, 1; 3, 5;
Lk 11, 29-32.
42: 1 Kgs 10, 1-6.

43ff: Lk 11, 24ff.
46-50: Mk 3, 31-35; Lk 8, 19ff.
13, 1-14: Mk 4, 1-12; Lk 8, 4-10.

The allusion to Jesus' resurrection could not have been grasped by his audience at the time.
12, 41f: The sayings insist that Jesus' message of repentance has been more forcefully presented than in the preaching of Jonah and that his teaching shows greater divine wisdom than the perceptions of Solomon.
12, 43ff: The religious history of man is a repetitious interchange of good and evil. The sayings warn that the option for evil can reach the point of taking full possession of a man.
12, 46-50: See note on Mk 3, 20-35.
13, 1-53: The main theme of this collection of parables is the mystery of

lakeshore. ² Such great crowds gathered around him that he went and took his seat in a boat while the crowd stood along the shore. ³ He addressed them at length in parables, speaking in this fashion:

Parable of the Seed

⁴ "One day a farmer went out sowing. Part of what he sowed landed on a footpath, where birds came and ate it up. ⁵ Part of it fell on rocky ground, where it had little soil. It sprouted at once since the soil had no depth, ⁶ but when the sun rose and scorched it, it began to wither for lack of roots. ⁷ Again, part of the seed fell among thorns, which grew up and choked it. ⁸ Part of it, finally, landed on good soil and yielded grain a hundred- or sixty- or thirtyfold. ⁹ Let everyone heed what he hears!"

¹⁰ When the disciples got near him, they asked him, "Why do you speak to them in parables?" ¹¹ He answered: "To you has been given a knowledge of the mysteries of the reign of God, but it has not been given to the others. ¹² To the man who has, more will be given until he grows rich; the man who has not, will lose what little he has.

¹³ "I use parables when I speak to them because they look but do not see, they listen but do not hear or understand. ¹⁴ Isaiah's prophecy is fulfilled in them which says:

'Listen as you will, you shall not understand,
look intently as you will, you shall not see.
¹⁵ Sluggish indeed is this people's heart.
They have scarcely heard with their ears,
they have firmly closed their eyes;
otherwise they might see with their eyes,
and hear with their ears,
and understand with their hearts,
and turn back to me,
and I should heal them.'

12: 25, 29; Mk 4, 25;
    Lk 8, 18; 19, 26.
13: Jn 9, 39.

14f: Is 6, 9f; Jn 12, 40;
    Acts 28, 26; Rom 11, 8.

---

the reign or kingship of God, a plan hidden in God and only incompletely manifested to men (10-17.34f); cf Eph 3, 4ff. The teaching of Jesus reveals that it is God who introduces his reign into history (3-9), intangibly brings it to fruition among men through his power (31ff), and will perfect it in his own good time (24-30). A secondary theme encourages adherence to Jesus' teaching despite hardships (18-23), and acceptance of God's toleration of evil (36-43.47-50). It places the reign proclaimed by Jesus above all the things in human existence which men hold dear (44ff).

13, 10-15: Precisely because the prophetic message is understandable, it can be, and frequently is, rejected (cf Is 6, 9f).

¹⁶ "But blest are your eyes because they see and blest are your ears because they hear. ¹⁷ I assure you, many a prophet and many a saint longed to see what you see but did not see it, to hear what you hear but did not hear it.

¹⁸ "Mark well, then, the parable of the sower. ¹⁹ The seed along the path is the man who hears the message about God's reign without understanding it. The evil one approaches him to steal away what was sown in his mind. ²⁰ The seed that fell on patches of rock is the man who hears the message and at first receives it with joy. ²¹ But he has no roots, so he lasts only for a time. When some setback or persecution involving the message occurs, he soon falters. ²² What was sown among briers is the man who hears the message, but then worldly anxiety and the lure of money choke it off. Such a one produces no yield. ²³ But what was sown on good soil is the man who hears the message and takes it in. He it is who bears a yield of a hundred- or sixty- or thirtyfold."

The Weeds

²⁴ He proposed to them another parable: "The reign of God may be likened to a man who sowed good seed in his field. ²⁵ While everyone was asleep, his enemy came and sowed weeds through his wheat, and then made off. ²⁶ When the crop began to mature and yield grain, the weeds made their appearance as well. ²⁷ The owner's slaves came to him and said, 'Sir, did you not sow good seed in your field? Where are the weeds coming from?' ²⁸ He answered, 'I see an enemy's hand in this.' His slaves said to him, 'Do you want us to go out and pull them up?' ²⁹ 'No,' he replied, 'pull up the weeds and you might take the wheat along with them. ³⁰ Let them grow together until harvest; then at harvest time I will order the harvesters, First collect the weeds and bundle them up to burn, then gather the wheat into my barn.' "

The Mustard Seed and the Leaven

³¹ He proposed still another parable: "The reign of God is like a mustard seed which someone took and sowed in his field. ³² It is the smallest seed of all, yet when full-grown it is the largest of plants. It becomes so big a shrub that the birds of the sky come and build their nests in its branches."

16f: Lk 10, 23f; Acts 22, 15.
18-23: Mk 4, 13-20; Lk 8, 11-15.
23: Jn 15, 8.16.
24: Mk 4, 26.
30: 3, 12; Jn 15, 6.
31f: Mk 4, 30ff; Lk 13, 18f.

33 He offered them still another image: "The reign of God is like yeast which a woman took and kneaded into three measures of flour. Eventually the whole mass of dough began to rise." 34 All these lessons Jesus taught the crowds in the form of parables. He spoke to them in parables only, 35 to fulfill what had been said through the prophet:

"I will open my mouth in parables,
I will announce what has lain hidden since the creation
of the world."

36 Then, dismissing the crowds, he went home. His disciples came to him with the request, "Explain to us the parable of the weeds in the field." 37 He said in answer: "The farmer sowing good seed is the Son of Man; 38 the field is the world, the good seed the citizens of the kingdom. The weeds are the followers of the evil one 39 and the enemy who sowed them is the devil. The harvest is the end of the world, while the harvesters are the angels. 40 Just as weeds are collected and burned, so will it be at the end of the world. 41 The Son of Man will dispatch his angels to collect from his kingdom all who draw others to apostasy, and all evildoers. 42 The angels will hurl them into the fiery furnace where they will wail and grind their teeth. 43 Then the saints will shine like the sun in their Father's kingdom. Let everyone heed what he hears!

The Treasure and the Pearl

44 "The reign of God is like a buried treasure which a man found in a field. He hid it again, and rejoicing at his find went and sold all he had and bought that field. 45 Or again, the kingdom of heaven is like a merchant's search for fine pearls. 46 When he found one really valuable pearl, he went back and put up for sale all that he had and bought it.

Parable of the Net

47 "The reign of God is also like a dragnet thrown into the lake, which collected all sorts of things. 48 When it was full they hauled it ashore and sat down to put what was worthwhile into containers. What was useless they threw away. 49 That is how it will be at the end of the world. Angels will go out and separate the wicked from the just 50 and hurl the wicked into the fiery furnace, where they will wail and grind their teeth.

33: Lk 13, 20f.
34: Jn 16, 25.
35: Ps 78, 2.
39: Rv 14, 15.

41: Zep 1, 3.
42: 8, 12; Rv 21, 8.
43: Wis 3, 7; Dn 12, 3.
44: 19, 21; Prv 4, 7.

⁵¹ "Have you understood all this?" "Yes," they answered; ⁵² to which he replied, "Every scribe who is learned in the reign of God is like the head of a household who can bring from his storeroom both the new and the old."

⁵³ When Jesus had finished these parables, he moved on from that district.

V: THE REIGN BECOME CHURCH

Jesus at Nazareth

⁵⁴ Jesus next went to his native place and spent his time teaching them in their synagogue. They were filled with amazement, and said to one another, "Where did this man get such wisdom and miraculous powers? ⁵⁵ Isn't this the carpenter's son? Isn't Mary known to be his mother and James, Joseph, Simon, and Judas his brothers? ⁵⁶ Aren't his sisters our neighbors? Where did he get all this?" ⁵⁷ They found him altogether too much for them. Jesus said to them, "No prophet is without honor except in his native place, indeed in his own house." ⁵⁸ And he did not work many miracles there because of their lack of faith.

14

Death of the Baptizer

¹ On one occasion Herod the tetrarch, having heard of Jesus'

54-58: Mk 6, 1-6.
   54: 2, 23; Jn 1, 46.
   55: 12, 46; 27, 56; Jn 6, 42.

57: Jn 4, 44.
14, 1-12: Mk 6, 14-29; Lk 9, 7ff.
   1: Lk 3, 1.

13, 51f: Jesus' teaching on the mystery of the kingdom of God is a prophetic development of the doctrine of the Old Testament requiring spiritual discernment for its acceptance; cf 1 Cor 2, 10-16.

13, 53—19, 1: The main purpose in this section of the gospel is to place the Person of Jesus at the very center of the mystery of the reign of God. Beginning with the rejection of Jesus at Nazareth and the execution of John (13, 53—14, 12), the evangelist alludes to the eucharistic mystery in the accounts of the multiplication of the loaves (14, 19; 15, 36), and of the walking on the water (14, 22-33); reports the doctrinal conflict between Jesus and the religious authorities (15, 1-20); raises again the question of the sign of Jonah (16, 1-4; see note on 12, 38ff), later explained to mean the passion, death and resurrection of Jesus (16, 21ff) which must occur before the reign of God reaches a new stage (16, 28). This is the message of the transfiguration (17, 5). A second purpose of the evangelist is to pattern the life of the Christian community after the model-life of Jesus (18, 1-35). This discourse takes its cue from Jesus' role as Servant of Yahweh (Is 42, 1) alluded to in 17, 5. Under the imagery of children, Jesus' disciples are identified with the *anawim*, who are so profoundly changed that they place the service of God entirely above personal gain; cf 2 Cor 11, 7. These members of the Christian community enjoy the divine favor, which will pursue them should they fall as a result of the entrapments set out for them by others (18, 5-14). This is to be borne in mind if the discipline of the gospel is to be enforced on those members who have deviated from it (18, 15f). If completely recalcitrant, they are to be cut off from the community; if repentant, they may be reinstated because of the limitless forgiveness within the community (18, 17-34).

13, 55: See note on Mk 6, 1-6.

reputation, ² exclaimed to his courtiers, "This man is John the Baptizer—it is he in person, raised from the dead; that is why such miraculous powers are at work in him!" ³ Recall that Herod had had John arrested, put in chains, and imprisoned on account of Herodias, the wife of his brother Philip. ⁴ That was because John had told him, "It is not right for you to live with her." ⁵ Herod wanted to kill John but was afraid of the people, who regarded him as a prophet. ⁶ Then on Herod's birthday Herodias' daughter performed a dance before the court which delighted Herod so much ⁷ that he swore he would grant her anything she asked for. ⁸ Prompted by her mother she said, "Bring me the head of John the Baptizer on a platter." ⁹ The king immediately had his misgivings, but because of his oath and the guests who were present he gave orders that the request be granted. ¹⁰ He sent the order to have John beheaded in prison. ¹¹ John's head was brought in on a platter and given to the girl, who took it to her mother. ¹² Later his disciples presented themselves to carry his body away and bury it. Afterward, they came and informed Jesus.

Jesus Feeds Five Thousand

¹³ When Jesus heard this, he withdrew by boat from there to a deserted place by himself. The crowds heard of it and followed him on foot from the towns. ¹⁴ When he disembarked and saw the vast throng, his heart was moved with pity, and he cured their sick. ¹⁵ As evening drew on, his disciples came to him with the suggestion: "This is a deserted place and it is already late. Dismiss the crowds so that they may go to the villages and buy some food for themselves." ¹⁶ Jesus said to them: "There is no need for them to disperse. Give them something to eat yourselves." ¹⁷ "We have nothing here," they replied, "but five loaves and a couple of fish." ¹⁸ "Bring them here," he said. ¹⁹ Then he ordered the crowds to sit down on the grass. He took the five loaves and two fish, looked up to heaven, blessed and broke them and gave the loaves to the disciples, who in turn gave them to the people. ²⁰ All those present ate their fill. The fragments remaining, when gathered up, filled twelve baskets. ²¹ Those who ate were about five thousand, not counting women and children.

3f: Mk 6, 17f; Lk 3, 19f.   13-21: 15, 32-38; Mk 6, 32-44;
4: Lv 18, 16; 20, 21.   Lk 9, 10-17; Jn 6, 1-13.
5: 21, 26.

14, 19: The rite of blessing and distribution anticipates the Last Supper.

Jesus Walks on the Water

²² Immediately afterward, while dismissing the crowds, Jesus insisted that his disciples get into the boat and precede him to the other side. ²³ When he had sent them away, he went up on the mountain by himself to pray, ²⁴ remaining there alone as evening drew on. Meanwhile the boat, already several hundred yards out from shore, was being tossed about in the waves raised by strong head winds. ²⁵ At about three in the morning, he came walking toward them on the lake. ²⁶ When the disciples saw him walking on the water, they were terrified. "It is a ghost!" they said, and in their fear they began to cry out. ²⁷ Jesus hastened to reassure them: "Get hold of yourselves! It is I. Do not be afraid!" ²⁸ Peter spoke up and said, "Lord, if it is really you, tell me to come to you across the water." ²⁹ "Come!" he said. So Peter got out of the boat and began to walk on the water, moving toward Jesus. ³⁰ But when he perceived how strong the wind was, becoming frightened, he began to sink and cried out, "Lord, save me!" ³¹ Jesus at once stretched out his hand and caught him. "How little faith you have!" he exclaimed. "Why did you falter?" ³² Once they had climbed into the boat, the wind died down. ³³ Those who were in the boat showed him reverence, declaring, "Beyond doubt you are the Son of God!"

Other Miracles

³⁴ After making the crossing they reached the shore at Gennesaret; ³⁵ and when the men of that place recognized him they spread the word throughout the region. People brought him all the afflicted, ³⁶ with the plea that he let them do no more than touch the tassel of his cloak. As many as touched it were fully restored to health.

22-32: Mk 6, 45-51;
　　　 Jn 6, 16-21.
　23: Mk 1, 35.
　31: 8, 25f.

33-36: Mk 6, 53-56.
　33: 16, 16.
　36: 9, 20ff.

14, 22-33: See note on Mk 6, 45-52.
14, 28-31: These verses are proper to Matthew. Peter, who exercised the leading role among the Twelve through the decision of Christ (16, 18; Acts 1, 15), had also to find his salvation in Jesus.
14, 33: *Beyond doubt you are the Son of God:* during the mortal life of Jesus, his divine nature was concealed. The confession therefore cannot be taken as evidence that the disciples comprehended Jesus' divine status at this time (Phil 2, 5-8). In the Old Testament the term "son" of God is applied to those who enjoy God's favor (Ex 4, 23; Ps 2, 7). However, the confession may be the evangelist's retrojection of the post-Easter faith into the time of Jesus' ministry; cf Mt 16, 16.

15

Jesus and the Pharisees

[1] Pharisees and scribes from Jerusalem approached Jesus with the question: [2] "Why do your disciples act contrary to the tradition of our ancestors? They do not wash their hands, for example, before eating a meal." [3] In reply he said to them: "Why do you for your part act contrary to the commandment of God for the sake of your 'tradition'? [4] For instance, God has said, 'Honor your father and your mother,' and, 'Whoever curses father or mother shall be put to death.' [5] Yet you declare, 'Whoever says to his father or his mother, Any support you might have had from me is dedicated to God, [6] need not honor his father or his mother.' This means that for the sake of your tradition you have nullified God's word.

[7] "You hypocrites! How accurately did Isaiah prophesy about you when he said:

[8] 'This people pays me lip service
but their heart is far from me.
[9] They do me empty reverence,
making dogmas out of human precepts.'"

[10] He summoned the crowd and said to them: "Give ear and try to understand. [11] It is not what goes into a man's mouth that makes him impure; it is what comes out of his mouth." [12] His disciples approached him and said, "Do you realize the Pharisees were scandalized when they heard your pronouncement?" [13] "Every planting not put down by my heavenly Father will be uprooted," he replied. [14] "Let them go their way; they are blind leaders of the blind. If one blind man leads another, both will end in a pit." [15] Then Peter spoke up to say, "Explain the parable to us." [16] "Are you, too, still incapable of understanding?" he asked. [17] "Do you not see that everything that

---

15, 1-20: Mk 7, 1-23.
  2: Lk 11, 38.
  4: Ex 20, 12; 21, 17;
    Lv 20, 9; Dt 5, 16;
    Prv 20, 20;
    Sir 3, 12; Eph 6, 2.

8: Ps 78, 36f;
  Is 29, 13.
9: Col 2, 23.
10: Mk 7, 14.
14: 23, 16.19; Lk 6, 39;
  Jn 9, 40.

15, 5f: Property dedicated by vow was considered sacred, and therefore not to be claimed by parents for their support. But since ownership of the property was still retained, the vow and its effect became a mere figment of law and a means of escape from the duty of filial piety. However, rabbinic evidence suggests that such was not the ordinary teaching of the rabbis.
15, 10f: Before God, human guilt or innocence stems from deliberate human decision, not from any (presumed) evil in material creation. How difficult it was to change this mentality of Jesus' contemporaries is evident from Acts 10, 9-16.

enters the mouth passes into the stomach and is discharged into the latrine, [18] but what comes out of the mouth originates in the mind? It is things like these that make a man impure. [19] From the mind stem evil designs—murder, adulterous conduct, fornication, stealing, false witness, blasphemy. [20] These are the things that make a man impure. As for eating with unwashed hands—that makes no man impure."

The Canaanite Woman

[21] Then Jesus left that place and withdrew to the district of Tyre and Sidon. [22] It happened that a Canaanite woman living in that locality presented herself, crying out to him, "Lord, Son of David, have pity on me! My daughter is terribly troubled by a demon." [23] He gave her no word of response. His disciples came up and began to entreat him, "Get rid of her. She keeps shouting after us." [24] "My mission is only to the lost sheep of the house of Israel," Jesus replied. [25] She came forward then and did him homage with the plea, "Help me, Lord!" [26] But he answered, "It is not right to take the food of sons and daughters and throw it to the dogs." [27] "Please, Lord," she insisted, "even the dogs eat the leavings that fall from their masters' tables." [28] Jesus then said in reply, "Woman, you have great faith! Your wish will come to pass." That very moment her daughter got better.

Jesus Heals the Suffering

[29] Jesus left that place and passed along the Sea of Galilee. He went up onto the mountainside and sat down there. [30] Large crowds of people came to him bringing with them cripples, the deformed, the blind, the mute, and many others besides. They laid them at his feet and he cured them. [31] The result was great astonishment in the crowds as they beheld the mute speaking, the deformed made sound, cripples walking about, and the blind seeing. They glorified the God of Israel.

Jesus Feeds Four Thousand

[32] Jesus called his disciples to him and said: "My heart is moved with pity for the crowd. By now they have been with me

18: 12, 34; Ti 1, 15.
21-28: Mk 7, 24-30.
  25: 10, 6; Rom 15, 8.
  28: 8, 10.

30: Is 35, 5f.
31: 8, 3.
32-39: Mk 8, 1-10.

15, 21-28: See note on Mk 7, 24-30.
15, 32-38: See note on Mk 8, 1-9.

three days, and have nothing to eat. I do not wish to send them away hungry, for fear they may collapse on the way." [33] His disciples said to him, "How could we ever get enough bread in this deserted spot to satisfy such a crowd?" [34] But Jesus asked them, "How many loaves of bread do you have?" "Seven," they replied, "and a few small fish." [35] Then he directed the crowd to seat themselves on the ground. [36] He took the seven loaves and the fish, and after giving thanks he broke them and gave them to the disciples, who in turn gave them to the crowds. [37] All ate until they were full. When they gathered up the fragments left over, these filled seven hampers. [38] The people who were fed numbered four thousand, apart from women and children.

[39] Then, after he had dismissed the crowds, he got into the boat and went to the district of Magadan.

16

The Pharisees and Sadducees

[1] The Pharisees and Sadducees came along, and as a test asked him to show them some sign in the sky. [2] He gave them this reply: ["In the evening you say, 'Red sky at night, the day will be bright'; [3] but in the morning, 'Sky red and gloomy, the day will be stormy.' If you know how to interpret the look of the sky, can you not read the signs of the times?] [4] An evil, faithless age is eager for a sign, but no sign will be given it except that of Jonah." With that he left them abruptly.

The Leaven of the Pharisees

[5] The disciples discovered when they arrived at the other side that they had forgotten to bring any bread along. [6] When Jesus said to them, "Be on the lookout against the yeast of the Pharisees and Sadducees," [7] they could think only, "This is because we have brought no bread." [8] Jesus knew their thoughts and said, "Why do you suppose it is because you have no bread? How weak your faith is! [9] Do you still not understand? Do you not remember the five loaves among five thousand and how many baskets-full you picked up? [10] Or the seven loaves among four thousand and how many hampers-full you retrieved? [11] Why is it you do not see that I was not speaking about bread at all but warning you against the yeast of the Pharisees?" [12] They finally

37: 16, 10.
16, 1-10: Mk 8, 11-21.
3: Lk 12, 54.
4: 12, 39; Jon 2, 1.
5: Mk 8, 14.
6: Lk 12, 1.
9: 14, 17.21; Jn 6, 9.
10: 15, 34.38.

realized he was not issuing a warning against yeast [used for bread] but against the Pharisees' and Sadducees' teaching.

Peter the Rock

[13] When Jesus came to the neighborhood of Caesarea Philippi, he asked his disciples this question: "Who do people say that the Son of Man is?" [14] They replied, "Some say John the Baptizer, others Elijah, still others Jeremiah or one of the prophets." [15] "And you," he said to them, "who do you say that I am?" [16] "You are the Messiah," Simon Peter answered, "the Son of the living God!" [17] Jesus replied, "Blest are you, Simon son of John! No mere man has revealed this to you, but my heavenly Father. [18] I for my part declare to you, you are 'Rock,' and on this rock I will build my church, and the jaws of death shall not prevail against it. [19] I will entrust to you the keys of the kingdom of heaven. Whatever you declare bound on earth shall be bound in heaven; whatever you declare loosed on earth shall be loosed in heaven." [20] Then he strictly ordered his disciples not to tell anyone that he was the Messiah.

13-16: Mk 8, 27ff; Lk 9, 18ff.
14: 14, 2.
16: Jn 6, 69f.
18: Jn 1, 42.
19: Is 22, 22; Rv 3, 7.

16, 16-20: To the tradition of Peter's confession at Caesarea Philippi (Mk 8, 27-30), Matthew adds the doctrine of the divinity of Christ, together with Jesus' prophecy that he will successfully build a new Israel, i. e., the church, upon Peter. Considering the unresolved dispute among the Twelve as to who was the greatest (Mt 20, 20-24), it is probable that this prophecy as a whole was made by the risen Christ (Jn 21, 15ff). The importance of the prophecy is seen from the fact that Matthew conserves it three decades after Peter's martyrdom, when his leadership of the Jerusalem community is already a thing of the past. In Matthew, the building of the new Israel on Peter pertains to Jesus' own role in the mystery of the reign of God that has appeared in history; see notes on 13, 1-53; 13, 53—19, 1. Jesus cannot begin to build his church upon Peter until after his death and resurrection (16, 21ff). For Matthew, Jesus' building of the new people of God upon Peter is a continuing reality for the Christian community of his time.

16, 17: Jesus' messianic identity and divinity cannot be truly known from human reason, but only from God's revelation (1 Cor 12, 3).

16, 18: *You are "Rock":* the Greek *petros* and its Aramaic equivalent *kepha,* "rock" is here conferred on Simon as a personal name to indicate his role as the firm foundation on which Jesus builds his church. *The jaws of death:* literally, "the gates of Sheol" (Nm 16, 33), i. e., death's realm, here used to signify the power or force of evil responsible first for physical then for spiritual death. The new people of God will overcome both forms of death to achieve the glorious entrance into the final kingdom (Rv 20, 4ff).

16, 19: *I will entrust . . . kingdom of heaven:* i. e., spiritual power to be exercised over the life of God's people, in contrast to the previously mentioned "gates," i. e., the evil power of death that would not prevail against the church. Simon Peter is the keeper of the keys, the one who has power to open and to close, to "bind" and to "loose," to allow and to forbid; cf Is 22, 22. The exercise of this responsibility is here compared to the disciplinary and doctrinal authority of the rabbis who in Jesus' time interpreted the Old Testament for the faith and life of the people. The exact nature of the extraordinary power here conferred became clear through the historical development of the Christian community in terms of the primacy of Peter, i. e., his supreme authority in teaching, governing and sanctifying the people of God.

First Prophecy of Passion and Resurrection

²¹ From then on Jesus [the Messiah] started to indicate to his disciples that he must go to Jerusalem and suffer greatly there at the hands of the elders, the chief priests, and the scribes, and to be put to death, and raised up on the third day. ²² At this, Peter took him aside and began to remonstrate wiʰ him. "May you be spared, Master! God forbid that any sᵤch thing ever happen to you!" ²³ Jesus turned on Peter and said, "Get out of my sight, you satan! You are trying to make me trip and fall. You are not judging by God's standards but by man's."

Doctrine of the Cross

²⁴ Jesus then said to his disciples: "If a man wishes to come after me, he must deny his very self, take up his cross, and begin to follow in my footsteps. ²⁵ Whoever would save his life will lose it, but whoever loses his life for my sake will find it. ²⁶ What profit would a man show if he were to gain the whole world and destroy himself in the process? What can a man offer in exchange for his very self? ²⁷ The Son of Man will come with his Father's glory accompanied by his angels. When he does, he will repay each man according to his conduct. ²⁸ I assure you, among those standing here there are some who will not experience death before they see the Son of Man come in his kingship."

17

Jesus Transfigured

¹ Six days later Jesus took Peter, James, and his brother John and led them up on a high mountain by themselves. ² He was transfigured before their eyes. His face became as dazzling as the sun, his clothes as radiant as light. ³ Suddenly Moses and Elijah appeared to them conversing with him. ⁴ Then Peter said

---

21-28: Mk 8, 31—9, 1;
      Lk 9, 22-27.
  21: 17, 22f; 20, 17ff; 13, 33;
      Acts 10, 40.
  24: Lk 14, 27.
  25: Lk 17, 33; Jn 12, 25.

27: 25, 31f; Jb 34, 11;
     Ps 62, 13; Jer 17, 10;
     2 Thes 1, 7f.
  28: 24, 30; 26, 64.
17, 1-8: Mk 9, 1-7; Lk 9, 28-36.
  3: 28, 2.

16, 24ff: See note on Mk 8, 34—9, 1.
16, 27f: These two sayings seem to refer to distinct phases of the kingdom of God: the reign of Christ in and through the new Christian community, with its orientation through faith to the second coming of Christ (27); and the eschatological kingdom of the Father, to be inaugurated when the Son of Man comes in glory at the end of time (28). See note on Mk 9, 1; Acts 1, 11.
17, 1-8: See note on Mk 9, 2-8.

to Jesus, "Lord, how good that we are here! With your permission I will erect three booths here, one for you, one for Moses, and one for Elijah." [5] He was still speaking when suddenly a bright cloud overshadowed them. Out of the cloud came a voice which said, "This is my beloved Son on whom my favor rests. Listen to him." [6] When they heard this the disciples fell forward on the ground, overcome with fear. [7] Jesus came toward them and laying his hand on them, said, "Get up! Do not be afraid." [8] When they looked up they did not see anyone but Jesus.

The Coming of Elijah

[9] As they were coming down the mountainside Jesus commanded them, "Do not tell anyone of the vision until the Son of Man rises from the dead." [10] The disciples put this question to him: "Why do the scribes claim that Elijah must come first?" [11] In reply he said: "Elijah is indeed coming, and he will restore everything. [12] I assure you, though, that Elijah has already come, but they did not recognize him and they did as they pleased with him. The Son of Man will suffer at their hands in the same way." [13] The disciples then realized that he had been speaking to them about John the Baptizer.

The Possessed Boy

[14] As they approached the crowd, a man came up to him and knelt before him. [15] "Lord," he said, "take pity on my son, who is demented and in a serious condition. For example, he often falls into the fire and frequently into the water. [16] I have brought him to your disciples but they could not cure him." [17] In reply Jesus said: "What an unbelieving and perverse lot you are! How long must I remain with you? How long can I endure you? Bring him here to me!" [18] Then Jesus reprimanded him, and the demon came out of him. That very moment the boy was cured.

[19] The disciples approached Jesus at that point and asked him privately, "Why could we not expel it?" [20] "Because you have so little trust," he told them. "I assure you, if you had faith the size of a mustard seed, you would be able to say to this moun-

5: 3, 17; 2 Pt 1, 17.
9-13: Mk 9, 9f.
10: Mal 3, 23f.
11: Lk 1, 17.
12: 11, 14; 16, 21; 17, 22f.

14-21: Mk 9, 14-29; Lk 9, 37-43.
18: 8, 29.
19: 21, 21; Lk 17, 6.
20: 1 Cor 13, 2.

17, 9: Misunderstanding the necessity of the passion, they are not to reveal the vision until after Jesus' resurrection.
17, 14-20: See note on Mk 9, 14-29.

tain, 'Move from here to there,' and it would move. Nothing would be impossible for you. [21] [This kind does not leave but by prayer and fasting.]"

Second Prophecy of the Passion

[22] When they met again in Galilee, Jesus said to them, "The Son of Man is going to be delivered into the hands of men [23] who will put him to death, and he will be raised up on the third day." At these words they were overwhelmed with grief.

Paying the Temple Tax

[24] When they entered Capernaum, the collectors of the temple tax approached Peter and said, "Does your master not pay the temple tax?" [25] "Of course he does," Peter replied. Then Jesus on entering the house asked, without giving him time to speak: "What is your opinion, Simon? Do the kings of the world take tax or toll from their sons, or from foreigners?" [26] When he replied, "From foreigners," Jesus observed: "Then their sons are exempt. [27] But for fear of disedifying them go to the lake, throw in a line, and take out the first fish you catch. Open its mouth and you will discover there a coin worth twice the temple tax. Take it and give it to them for you and me."

18

Against Ambition

[1] Just then the disciples came up to Jesus with the question, "Who is of greatest importance in the kingdom of God?" [2] He called a little child over and stood him in their midst [3] and said: "I assure you, unless you change and become like little children, you will not enter the kingdom of God. [4] Whoever makes himself lowly, becoming like this child, is of greatest importance in that heavenly reign.

Avoiding Scandal

[5] "Whoever welcomes one such child for my sake welcomes me. [6] On the other hand, it would be better for anyone who leads astray one of these little ones who believe in me, to be drowned by a millstone around his neck, in the depths of the sea. [7] What terrible things will come on the world through scandal! It is inevitable that scandal should occur. Nonetheless, woe

---

22f: 16, 21.
24: Ex 30, 15.
18, 1-5: Mk 9, 36f; Lk 9, 46ff.
3: 19, 14; 1 Cor 14, 20.

4: 23, 12; Mk 10, 15;
Lk 18, 17.
6: Mk 9, 42; Lk 17, 1f.
8f: 5, 30; Mk 9, 43-47.

to that man through whom scandal comes! [8] If your hand or foot is your undoing, cut it off and throw it from you! Better to enter life maimed or crippled than be thrown with two hands or two feet into endless fire. [9] If your eye is your downfall, gouge it out and cast it from you! Better to enter life with one eye than be thrown with both into fiery Gehenna.

The Straying Sheep

[10] "See that you never despise one of these little ones. I assure you, their angels in heaven constantly behold my heavenly Father's face. [12] What is your thought on this: A man owns a hundred sheep and one of them wanders away; will he not leave the ninety-nine out on the hills and go in search of the stray? [13] If he succeeds in finding it, believe me he is happier about this one than about the ninety-nine that did not wander away. [14] Just so, it is no part of your heavenly Father's plan that a single one of these little ones shall ever come to grief.

Fraternal Correction

[15] "If your brother should commit some wrong against you, go and point out his fault, but keep it between the two of you. If he listens to you, you have won your brother over. [16] If he does not listen, summon another, so that every case may stand on the word of two or three witnesses. [17] If he ignores them, refer it to the church. If he ignores even the church, then treat him as you would a Gentile or a tax collector. [18] I assure you, whatever you declare bound on earth shall be held bound in heaven, and whatever you declare loosed on earth shall be held loosed in heaven.

The Power of United Prayer

[19] "Again I tell you, if two of you join your voices on earth to pray for anything whatever, it shall be granted you by my Father in heaven. [20] Where two or three are gathered in my name, there am I in their midst."

11: Lk 19, 10.	1 Tm 5, 19f.
12ff: Ez 34, 1ff.16; Lk 15, 3-7.	17: 1 Cor 5, 9-13.
15: Lv 19, 17; Sir 19, 13;	18: Jn 20, 23.
Gal 6, 1.	19: 7, 7f; Jn 15, 7.
16: Dt 19, 15; Jn 8, 17;	20: 1 Cor 5, 4.

18, 11: Omitted here with many MSS.
18, 15-18: Note the transition from fraternal correction to the further action (17) of delivering the obstinate sinner to the authority of the church. Exclusion and readmission of such a one is a function of the power of binding and loosing which belongs to the Christian community. There is no concrete evidence as to how the communities of New Testament times exercised this power.

The Merciless Official

²¹ Then Peter came up and asked him, "Lord, when my brother wrongs me, how often must I forgive him? Seven times?" ²² "No," Jesus replied, "not seven times; I say, seventy times seven times. ²³ That is why the reign of God may be said to be like a king who decided to settle accounts with his officials. ²⁴ When he began his auditing, one was brought in who owed him a huge amount. ²⁵ As he had no way of paying it, his master ordered him to be sold, along with his wife, his children, and all his property, in payment of the debt. ²⁶ At that the official prostrated himself in homage and said, 'My lord, be patient with me and I will pay you back in full.' ²⁷ Moved with pity, the master let the official go and wrote off the debt. ²⁸ But when that same official went out he met a fellow servant who owed him a mere fraction of what he himself owed. He seized him and throttled him. 'Pay back what you owe,' he demanded. ²⁹ His fellow servant dropped to his knees and began to plead with him, 'Just give me time and I will pay you back in full.' ³⁰ But he would hear none of it. Instead, he had him put in jail until he paid back what he owed. ³¹ When his fellow servants saw what had happened they were badly shaken, and went to their master to report the whole incident. ³² His master sent for him and said, 'You worthless wretch! I canceled your entire debt when you pleaded with me. ³³ Should you not have dealt mercifully with your fellow servant, as I dealt with you?' ³⁴ Then in anger the master handed him over to the torturers until he paid back all that he owed. ³⁵ My heavenly Father will treat you in exactly the same way unless each of you forgives his brother from his heart."

19

¹ When Jesus had finished this discourse, he left Galilee and came to the district of Judea across the Jordan. ² Great crowds followed him and he cured them there.

VI: FIRST STEPS IN ESTABLISHING GOD'S REIGN

The Question of Divorce

³ Some Pharisees came up to him and said, to test him, "May

21: 6, 12; Lk 17, 4.   35: 6, 12; Jas 2, 13.
23: 25, 19; Sir 28, 4.   **19**, 1-9: Mk 10, 1-12.
33: 1 Jn 4, 11.

19, 3-8: The Pharisees wish to force Jesus to take sides on the question of divorce for the purpose of remarriage. (The stringent position at the time was that of the school of Shammai, while leniency was advocated by the

a man divorce his wife for any reason whatever?" [4] He replied, "Have you not read that at the beginning the Creator made male and female [5] and declared, 'For this reason a man shall leave his father and mother and cling to his wife, and the two shall become as one'? [6] Thus they are no longer two but one flesh. Therefore, let no man separate what God has joined." [7] They said to him, "Then why did Moses command divorce and the promulgation of a divorce decree?" [8] "Because of your stubbornness Moses let you divorce your wives," he replied; "but at the beginning it was not that way. [9] I now say to you, whoever divorces his wife (lewd conduct is a separate case) and marries another commits adultery, and the man who marries a divorced woman commits adultery."

[10] His disciples said to him, "If that is the case between man and wife, it is better not to marry." [11] He said, "Not everyone can accept this teaching, only those to whom it is given to do so. [12] Some men are incapable of sexual activity from birth; some have been deliberately made so; and some there are who have freely renounced sex for the sake of God's reign. Let him accept this teaching who can."

Jesus Blesses the Children

[13] At one point, children were brought to him so that he

4: Gn 1, 27.	7, 10; Eph 5, 31.	Lk 16, 18;
5: Gn 2, 24;	7: Dt 24, 1-4.	1 Cor 7, 11.
1 Cor 6, 16;	9: 5, 32;	13ff: Mk 10, 13-16.

---

school of Hillel.) In reply, Jesus proclaims the indissolubility of marriage, citing Gn 1, 27 and 2, 24. He declares this scriptural doctrine to be God's ultimate intent for marriage in human society, explaining that the divorce granted in the Old Testament was due to the stubbornness of the Jews, i. e., to their cultural *mores,* which God in his wisdom chose to leave unenlightened. *Let no man separate what God has joined:* not by mere legislation, for neither civil law, nor social custom, nor mutual consent forges the unbreakable bond, but rather the divine involvement in the union of marriage. The citation of Gn 2, 24 indicates that in the divine "joining together," God ratifies the mutual love of persons; their sexual union serves as a pledge of exclusive fidelity to each other; cf Mk 10, 2-12; Lk 16, 18; 1 Cor 7, 10f. For reflection on the theological implications of the Lord's new teaching, cf Eph 5, 21-33.

19, 9: *Lewd conduct is a separate case:* literally "except for porneia," i. e., immorality, fornication, even incest. A growing number of scholars consider this to refer to Christians who, prior to their conversion, had married within the prohibited degree of blood relationship as stated in Lv 18, 6-18. The same position seems to be taken in Acts 15, 20. As it stands, however, this Matthean clause of exception and that of 5, 32 cannot easily be reconciled with the absolute prohibition of divorce repeated in Mk 10, 11f and Lk 16, 18. Whatever may have been the situation prevailing among the Christians for whom Matthew wrote, the more stringent understanding of Jesus' words prevailed throughout the church.

19, 12: This verse is proper to Matthew. While there is no consensus on its meaning, some exegetes understand it to refer to voluntary and perpetual celibacy for members of the Christian community who wish to dedicate themselves completely to the kingdom of God; cf Mt 13, 44ff; 19, 29.

19, 13ff: Children were the symbol Jesus used for the *anawim,* the poor

[51]

could place his hands on them in prayer. The disciples began to scold them, [14] but Jesus said, "Let the children come to me. Do not hinder them. The kingdom of God belongs to such as these." [15] And he laid his hands on their heads before he left that place.

The Danger of Riches

[16] Another time a man came up to him and said, "Teacher, what good must I do to possess everlasting life?" [17] He answered, "Why do you question me about what is good? There is One who is good. If you wish to enter into life, keep the commandments." [18] "Which ones?" he asked. Jesus replied, " 'You shall not kill'; 'You shall not commit adultery'; 'You shall not steal'; 'You shall not bear false witness'; [19] 'Honor your father and your mother'; and 'Love your neighbor as yourself.' " [20] The young man said to him, "I have kept all these; what do I need to do further?" [21] Jesus told him, "If you seek perfection, go, sell your possessions, and give to the poor. You will then have treasure in heaven. Afterward come back and follow me." [22] Hearing these words, the young man went away sad, for his possessions were many.

[23] Jesus said to his disciples: "I assure you, only with difficulty will a rich man enter into the kingdom of God. [24] I repeat what I said: it is easier for a camel to pass through a needle's eye than for a rich man to enter the kingdom of God." [25] When the disciples heard this they were completely overwhelmed, and exclaimed, "Then who can be saved?" [26] Jesus looked at them and said, "For man it is impossible; but for God all things are possible." [27] Then it was Peter's turn to say to him: "Here we have put everything aside to follow you. What can we expect

---

14: 18, 3.
16-29: Mk 10, 17-30;
    Lk 18, 18-30.
17-20: Lk 10, 25-28.
18: Ex 20, 12-16;
    Dt 5, 16-20.
19: Jn 13, 34.

21: 6, 20; 13, 44ff.
23-26: Mk 10, 23-27.
24: 7, 14.
27-30: Mk 10, 28-31;
    Lk 18, 28ff.
27: 4, 20.22.

---

in spirit or the lowly, within the Christian community; see note on 5, 3-12. Like the apostles, these have surrendered personal possessions (16-30) for total dedication to his ministry.

19, 16: See note on Mk 10, 17f.

19, 21: The young man is invited to join the *anawim*.

19, 23-26: Jesus' contemporaries consider wealth a sign of divine favor. When he denies this and shows that wealth can even obstruct the spiritual perception of his message, the disciples conclude that virtually no one can be saved. Jesus replies that the rich as well as the poor are dependent on God for their salvation.

19, 27-30: Voluntary renunciation of home, property and relatives for the sake of Christ will evoke the divine generosity in this life and in the next.

from it?" ²⁸ Jesus said to them: "I give you my solemn word, in the new age when the Son of Man takes his seat upon a throne befitting his glory, you who have followed me shall likewise take your places on twelve thrones to judge the twelve tribes of Israel. ²⁹ Moreover, everyone who has given up home, brothers or sisters, father or mother, wife or children or property for my sake will receive many times as much and inherit everlasting life. ³⁰ Many who are first shall come last, and the last shall come first.

20

The Laborers in the Vineyard

¹ "The reign of God is like the case of the owner of an estate who went out at dawn to hire workmen for his vineyard. ² After reaching an agreement with them for the usual daily wage, he sent them out to his vineyard. ³ He came out about midmorning and saw other men standing around the marketplace without work, ⁴ so he said to them, 'You too go along to my vineyard and I will pay you whatever is fair.' ⁵ At that they went away. He came out again around noon and midafternoon and did the same. ⁶ Finally, going out in late afternoon he found still others standing around. To these he said, 'Why have you been standing here idle all day?' ⁷ 'No one has hired us,' they told him. He said, 'You go to the vineyard too.' ⁸ When evening came the owner of the vineyard said to his foreman, 'Call the workmen and give them their pay, but begin with the last group and end with the first.' ⁹ When those hired late in the afternoon came up they received a full day's pay, ¹⁰ and when the first group appeared they supposed they would get more; ¹¹ yet they received the same daily wage. Thereupon they complained to the owner, ¹² 'This last group did only an hour's work, but you have put them on the same basis as us who have worked a full day in the scorching heat.' ¹³ 'My friend,' he said to one in reply, 'I do you no injustice. You agreed on the usual wage, did you not? ¹⁴ Take your pay and go home. I intend to give this man who was hired last the same

---

28: Dn 7, 22; Rv 3, 21;
    20, 4.

30: 19, 30; 20, 16;
    Mk 10, 31; Lk 13, 30.

20, 1-34: A development of the thought of 19, 30: God requires service of his followers while reserving to himself the modes and occasions of his generosity (1-16). He makes the same requirement of Jesus himself (17ff) and of his apostles (20-28), without indicating what will be the nature of God's generous return. The cure of the blind men (29-34) shows that Jesus is still the servant of men as he proceeds to his death in Jerusalem.

pay as you. [15] I am free to do as I please with my money, am I not? Or are you envious because I am generous?' [16] Thus the last shall be first and the first shall be last."

Third Prophecy: Passion and Resurrection

[17] As Jesus was starting to go up to Jerusalem, he took the Twelve aside on the road and said to them: [18] "We are going up to Jerusalem now. There the Son of Man will be handed over to the chief priests and scribes, who will condemn him to death. [19] They will turn him over to the Gentiles, to be made sport of and flogged and crucified. But on the third day he will be raised up."

The Mother of James and John

[20] The mother of Zebedee's sons came up to him accompanied by her sons, to do him homage and ask of him a favor. [21] "What is it you want?" he said. She answered, "Promise me that these sons of mine will sit, one at your right hand and the other at your left, in your kingdom." [22] In reply Jesus said, "You do not know what you are asking. Can you drink of the cup I am to drink of?" "We can," they said. [23] He told them: "From the cup I drink of, you shall drink. But sitting at my right hand or my left is not mine to give. That is for those to whom it has been reserved by my Father." [24] The other ten, on hearing this, became indignant at the two brothers. [25] Jesus then called them together and said: "You know how those who exercise authority among the Gentiles lord it over them; their great ones make their importance felt. [26] It cannot be like that with you. Anyone among you who aspires to greatness must serve the rest, [27] and whoever wants to rank first among you must serve the needs of all. [28] Such is the case with the Son of Man who has come, not to be served by others, but to serve, to give his own life as a ransom for the many."

The Two Blind Men at Jericho

[29] As they were leaving Jericho a large crowd followed him, [30] and suddenly two blind men sitting by the roadside, who heard that Jesus was passing by, began to shout, "Lord, Son of

20, 16: 19, 30.   27: Mk 9, 35; Jn 13, 14.
  17ff: 16, 21; 17, 22f;   28: 26, 28; Rom 5, 6;
         Mk 10, 32ff;   1 Tm 2, 6.
         Lk 18, 31ff.   29-34: Mk 10, 46-52;
    19: Acts 10, 40.   Lk 18, 35-43.
 20-28: Mk 10, 35-45.   30: 9, 27.
 24-27: Lk 22, 25ff.

David, have pity on us!" [31] The crowd began to scold them in an effort to reduce them to silence, but they only shouted the louder, "Lord, Son of David, have pity on us!" [32] Jesus then stopped and called out to them, "What do you want me to do for you?" [33] "Lord," they told him, "open our eyes!" [34] Moved with compassion, Jesus touched their eyes, and immediately they could see; and they became his followers.

21

Triumphal Entry into Jerusalem

[1] As they drew near Jerusalem, entering Bethphage on the Mount of Olives, Jesus sent off two disciples [2] with the instructions: "Go into the village straight ahead of you and you will immediately find an ass tethered and her colt with her. Untie them and lead them back to me. [3] If anyone says a word to you, say, 'The Master needs them.' Then he will let them go at once." [4] This came about to fulfill what was said through the prophet:

[5] "Tell the daughter of Zion,
> Your king comes to you without display
> astride an ass, astride a colt,
> the foal of a beast of burden."

[6] So the disciples went off and did what Jesus had ordered; [7] they brought the ass and the colt and laid their cloaks on them, and he mounted. [8] The huge crowd spread their cloaks on the road, while some began to cut branches from the trees and lay them along his path. [9] The groups preceding him as well as those following kept crying out:

"Hosanna to the Son of David!
Blessed is he who comes in the name of the Lord!
Hosanna in the highest!"

[10] As he entered Jerusalem the whole city was stirred to its

---

21, 1-9: Mk 11, 1-9;
Lk 19, 28-38;
Jn 12, 12-15.

5: Is 62, 11; Zec 9, 9.
8: 2 Kgs 9, 13.
9: Ps 118, 25f.

21, 1-11: See note on Mk 11, 1-11.
21, 5: A free citation of Is 62, 11 and Zec 9, 9 indicating that Jesus entered Jerusalem as king of peace, riding, not the horse, symbol of the conqueror (Jer 22, 4), but the ass, the work beast of the poor.
21, 9: A citation of Ps 118, 25f used for the purpose of acknowledging Jesus to be the Messiah and son of David. See note on Mk 11, 1-11. *God save* (the Hebrew *Hōšî'ah-nnā*, literally "Do save!"): meant here as an acclamation or shout of praise honoring Jesus as the Savior.

depths, demanding, "Who is this?" [11] And the crowd kept answering, "This is the prophet Jesus from Nazareth in Galilee."

Cleaning out the Temple

[12] Jesus entered the temple precincts and drove out all those engaged there in buying and selling. He overturned the money changers' tables and the stalls of the dove-sellers, [13] saying to them: "Scripture has it,

> 'My house shall be called a house of prayer,'

but you are turning it into a den of thieves." [14] The blind and the lame came to him inside the temple area and he cured them. [15] The chief priests and the scribes became indignant when they observed the wonders he worked, and how the children were shouting out in the temple precincts, "Hosanna to the Son of David!" [16] "Do you hear what they are saying?" they asked him. Jesus said to them, "Of course I do! Did you never read this:

> 'From the speech of infants and children
> you have framed a hymn of praise'?"

[17] With that he left them and went out of the city to Bethany, where he spent the night.

Jesus Curses a Fig Tree

[18] At dawn, as Jesus was returning to the city, he felt hungry. [19] Seeing a fig tree by the roadside he went over to it, but found nothing there except leaves. He said to it, "Never again shall you produce fruit!"; and it withered up instantly. [20] The disciples were dumbfounded when they saw this. They asked, "Why did the fig tree wither up so quickly?" [21] Jesus said: "Believe me, if you trust and do not falter, not only will you do what I did to the fig tree, but if you say to this mountain, "Be lifted up and thrown into the sea,' even that will happen. [22] You will receive all that you pray for, provided you have faith."

The Authority of Jesus

[23] After Jesus had entered the temple precincts, and while he

---

12-16: Mk 11, 15-18;
    Lk 19, 45ff; Jn 2, 14ff.
12: Neh 13, 8.
13: Is 56, 7; Jer 7, 11.
16: Ps 8, 2; Wis 10, 21.

18-22: Mk 11, 12ff.20-24.
19: Jer 8, 13; Lk 13, 6-9.
20: Hos 9, 16.
21: 17, 20; Lk 17, 6.
22: 7, 7; 1 Jn 3, 22.

21, 12-22: See notes on Mk 11, 15-19 and on 11, 12ff, in that order.

was teaching, the chief priests and elders of the people came up to him and said: "On what authority are you doing these things? Who has given you this power?" 24 Jesus answered: "I too will ask a question. If you answer it for me, then I will tell you on what authority I do the things I do. 25 What was the origin of John's baptism? Was it divine or merely human?" They thought to themselves, "If we say 'divine,' he will ask us, 'Then why did you not put faith in it?'; 26 while if we say, 'merely human,' we shall have reason to fear the people, who all regard John as a prophet." 27 So their answer to Jesus was, "We do not know." He said in turn, "Then neither will I tell you on what authority I do the things I do.

Parable of the Two Sons

28 "What do you think of this case? There was a man who had two sons. He approached the elder and said, 'Son, go out and work in the vineyard today.' 29 The son replied, 'I am on my way, sir'; but he never went. 30 Then the man came to his second son and said the same thing. This son said in reply, 'No, I will not'; but afterward he regretted it and went. 31 Which of the two did what the father wanted?" They said, "The second." Jesus said to them, "Let me make it clear that tax collectors and prostitutes are entering the kingdom of God before you. 32 When John came preaching a way of holiness, you put no faith in him; but the tax collectors and the prostitutes did believe in him. Yet even when you saw that, you did not repent and believe in him.

Parable of the Tenants

33 "Listen to another parable. There was a property owner who planted a vineyard, put a hedge around it, dug out a vat, and erected a tower. Then he leased it out to tenant farmers and went on a journey. 34 When vintage time arrived he dispatched his slaves to the tenants to obtain his share of the grapes. 35 The tenants responded by seizing the slaves. They beat one, killed another, and stoned a third. 36 A second time he dispatched even more slaves than before, but they treated them the same way. 37 Finally he sent his son to them, thinking, 'They will respect my son.' 38 When they saw the son, the tenants said to

23-27: Mk 11, 27-33;
    Lk 20, 1-8.
23: 28, 18; Jn 2, 18.
25: Jn 3, 27.
26: 14, 5; 21, 32.

31: Lk 7, 29f.
33-46: Is 5, 1-7; Mk 12, 1-12;
    Lk 20, 9-19.
38: 26, 4; 27, 1; Jn 3, 16;
    11, 53.

one another. 'Here is the one who will inherit everything. Let us kill him and then we shall have his inheritance!' [39] With that they seized him, dragged him outside the vineyard, and killed him. [40] What do you suppose the owner of the vineyard will do to those tenants when he comes?" [41] They replied, "He will bring that wicked crowd to a bad end and lease his vineyard out to others who will see to it that he has grapes at vintage time." [42] Jesus said to them, "Did you never read in the Scriptures,

> 'The stone which the builders rejected
> has become the keystone of the structure.
> It was the Lord who did this
> and we find it marvelous to behold'?

[43] For this reason, I tell you, the kingdom of God will be taken away from you and given to a nation that will yield a rich harvest. [44] [The man who falls upon that stone will be smashed to bits; and he on whom it falls will be crushed.]"

[45] When the chief priests and the Pharisees heard these parables, they realized he was speaking about them. Although they sought to arrest him, they had reason to fear the crowds who regarded him as a prophet.

22

The Wedding Banquet

[1] Jesus began to address them, once more using parables. [2] "The reign of God may be likened to a king who gave a wedding banquet for his son. [3] He dispatched his servants to summon the invited guests to the wedding, but they refused to come. [4] A second time he sent other servants, saying: 'Tell those who were invited, See, I have my dinner prepared! My bullocks and corn-fed cattle are killed; everything is ready. Come to the feast.' [5] Some ignored the invitation and went their way, one to his farm, another to his business. [6] The rest laid hold of his servants, insulted them, and killed them. [7] At this the king grew furious and sent his army to destroy those murderers and burn their city. [8] Then he said to his servants: 'The banquet is ready, but those who were invited were unfit to come. [9] That is why you must go out into the byroads and invite to the wedding

---

39: Heb 13, 12.
42: Dn 2, 45; Ps 118, 22; Is 28, 16; Acts 4, 11; Rom 9, 33; 1 Pt 2, 4-7.

43: Rom 11, 11.
22, 2: Prv 9, 1-6; Rv 19, 9.
2-9: Lk 14, 16-24.
6: 21, 35.

anyone you come upon.' [10] The servants then went out into the byroads and rounded up everyone they met, bad as well as good. This filled the wedding hall with banqueters.

[11] "When the king came in to meet the guests, however, he caught sight of a man not properly dressed for a wedding feast. [12] 'My friend,' he said, 'how is it you came in here not properly dressed?' The man had nothing to say. [13] The king then said to the attendants, 'Bind him hand and foot and throw him out into the night to wail and grind his teeth.' [14] The invited are many, the elect are few."

Paying Tax to the Emperor

[15] Then the Pharisees went off and began to plot how they might trap Jesus in speech. [16] They sent their disciples to him, accompanied by Herodian sympathizers, who said: "Teacher, we know you are a truthful man and teach God's way sincerely. You court no one's favor and do not act out of human respect. [17] Give us your opinion, then, in this case. Is it lawful to pay tax to the emperor or not?" [18] Jesus recognized their bad faith and said to them, "Why are you trying to trip me up, you hypocrites? [19] Show me the coin used for the tax." When they handed him a small Roman coin he asked them, [20] "Whose head is this, and whose inscription?" [21] "Caesar's," they replied. At that he said to them, "Then give to Caesar what is Caesar's, but give to God what is God's." [22] Taken aback by this reply, they went off and left him.

The Sadducees and the Resurrection

[23] That same day some Sadducees, who hold there is no resurrection, came to him with a question: [24] "Teacher, Moses declared, 'If a man dies without children, his brother must take the wife and produce offspring for his brother.' [25] Once there were seven brothers. The eldest died after marrying, and since he had no children, left his wife to his brother. [26] The same thing happened to the second, the third, and so on, down to the seventh. [27] Last of all the woman died too. [28] At the resur-

---

13: 8, 12; 25, 30.
15-22: Mk 12, 13-17;
Lk 20, 20-26.
15: Lk 11, 54.
21: Rom 13, 7.

23-33: Mk 12, 18-27;
Lk 20, 27-38;
Acts 23, 8.
23: Jn 11, 25.
24: Gn 38, 8; Dt 25, 5.

22, 14: The failure of Israel to accept Jesus' prophetic message deserved the punishment of deprivation—a warning of divine judgment against Christians who fail to live according to their faith.

rection, whose wife will she be, since all seven of them married her?" [29] Jesus replied: "You are badly misled because you fail to understand the Scriptures and the power of God. [30] When people rise from the dead, they neither marry nor are given in marriage but live like angels in heaven. [31] As to the fact that the dead are raised, have you not read what God said to you,

> [32] 'I am the God of Abraham, the God of Isaac,
> the God of Jacob'?

He is the God of the living, not of the dead." [33] The crowds who listened were spellbound by his teaching.

The Great Commandment

[34] When the Pharisees heard that he had silenced the Sadducees, they assembled in a body; [35] and one of them, a lawyer, in an attempt to trip him up, asked him, [36] "Teacher, which commandment of the law is the greatest?" [37] Jesus said to him:

> " 'You shall love the Lord your God
> with your whole heart,
> with your whole soul,
> and with all your mind.'

[38] This is the greatest and first commandment. [39] The second is like it:

> 'You shall love your neighbor as yourself.'

[40] On these two commandments the whole law is based, and the prophets as well."

The Son of David

[41] In turn Jesus put a question to the assembled Pharisees, [42] "What is your opinion about the Messiah? Whose son is he?" "David's," they answered. [43] He said to them, "Then how is it that David under the Spirit's influence calls him 'lord,' as he does:

> [44] 'The Lord said to my lord, Sit at my right hand,
> until I humble your enemies beneath your feet'?

32: Ex 3, 6.
34-40: Mk 12, 28-34;
    Lk 10, 25-28.
34: Jn 13, 34f.
36: 1 Jn 4, 21.
37: Dt 6, 5.

39: Lv 19, 18; Jas 2, 8.
40: Rom 13, 8ff; Gal 5, 14.
41-46: Mk 12, 35ff.
42: 9, 27.
44: Ps 110, 1; Acts 2, 35;
    Heb 1, 13.

[45] If David calls him 'lord,' how can he be his son?" [46] No one could give him an answer; therefore no one dared, from that day on, to ask him any questions.

23

Hypocrisy of the Scribes and Pharisees

[1] Then Jesus told the crowds and his disciples: [2] "The scribes and the Pharisees have succeeded Moses as teachers; [3] therefore, do everything and observe everything they tell you. But do not follow their example. [4] Their words are bold but their deeds are few. They bind up heavy loads, hard to carry, to lay on other men's shoulders, while they themselves will not lift a finger to budge them. [5] All their works are performed to be seen. They widen the phylacteries and wear huge tassels. [6] They are fond of places of honor at banquets and the front seats in synagogues, [7] of marks of respect in public and of being called 'Rabbi.' [8] As to you, avoid the title 'Rabbi.' One among you is your teacher, the rest are learners. [9] Do not call anyone on earth your father. Only one is your father, the One in heaven. [10] Avoid being called teachers. Only one is your teacher, the Messiah. [11] The greatest among you will be the one who serves the rest. [12] Whoever exalts himself shall be humbled, but whoever humbles himself shall be exalted.

[13] "Woe to you scribes and Pharisees, you frauds! You shut the doors of the kingdom of God in men's faces, neither entering yourselves nor admitting those who are trying to enter. [15] Woe to you scribes and Pharisees, you frauds! You travel over sea and land to make a single convert, but once he is converted you make a devil of him twice as wicked as yourselves. [16] It is an evil day for you, blind guides! You declare,

---

46: Lk 20, 40.
23, 1: Rom 2, 22f.
3: Rom 2, 23f.
4: Lk 11, 46.
5: 6, 1-6; Ex 13, 9;
Nm 15, 38; Dt 6, 8.

6: Mk 12, 38f; Lk 11, 43.
7: Lk 20, 46.
11: 20, 26.
12: 18, 4; Lk 1, 52f; 14, 11; 18, 14.
13: Jer 8, 8.
16: 15, 14; Jn 9, 38-41.

23, 1-36: These strong criticisms of the scribes and Pharisees are found also in Mk 12, 38ff. The collection of them in Matthew is probably explained by a hostility that had developed between Judaism and Christianity. See note on Acts 8, 3. It may also be that some members of the Judaeo-Christian communities still adhered to certain ideas and practices of the Pharisees which are here reprobated.
23, 8ff: Typical hyperbolic speech of the time. It does not reject authority in principle, but authoritarianism; not the use of titles, but the failure to acknowledge that authority exists to serve God, his anointed One, and one's neighbor.
23, 14: Omitted here with many MSS.

'If a man swears by the temple it means nothing, but if he swears by the gold of the temple he is obligated.' [17] Blind fools! Which is more important, the gold or the temple which makes it sacred? [18] Again you declare, 'If a man swears by the altar he is obligated.' [19] How blind you are! Which is more important, the offering or the altar which makes the offering sacred? [20] The man who swears by the altar is swearing by it and by everything on it. [21] The man who swears by the temple is swearing by it and by him who dwells there. [22] The man who swears by heaven is swearing by God's throne and by him who is seated on that throne. [23] Woe to you scribes and Pharisees, you frauds! You pay tithes on mint and herbs and seeds while neglecting the weightier matters of the law, justice and mercy and good faith. It is these you should have practiced, without neglecting the others.

[24] "Blind guides! You strain out the gnat and swallow the camel! [25] Woe to you scribes and Pharisees, you frauds! You cleanse the outside of cup and dish, and leave the inside filled with loot and lust! [26] Blind Pharisee! First cleanse the inside of the cup so that its outside may be clean. [27] Woe to you scribes and Pharisees, you frauds! You are like white-washed tombs, beautiful to look at on the outside but inside full of filth and dead men's bones. [28] Thus you present to view a holy exterior while hypocrisy and evil fill you within. [29] Woe to you scribes and Pharisees, you frauds! You erect tombs for the prophets and decorate the monuments of the saints. [30] You say, 'Had we lived in our forefathers' time we would not have joined them in shedding the prophets' blood.' [31] Thus you show that you are the sons of the prophets' murderers. [32] Now it is your turn: fill up the vessel measured out by your forefathers. [33] Vipers' nest! Brood of serpents! How can you escape condemnation to Gehenna? [34] For this reason I shall send you prophets and wise men and scribes. Some you will kill and crucify, others you will flog in your synagogues and hunt down from city to city; [35] until retribution overtakes you for all the blood of the just ones shed on earth, from the blood of holy Abel to the blood of Zechariah son of Barachiah, whom you

19: 15, 14.
20: 5, 33-37; Sir 23, 9.
23: Dt 14, 22; Lk 11, 42.
25: Mk 7, 4f; Lk 11, 39f; Ti 1, 15.
27: Acts 23, 3.
28: Lk 16, 15; 18, 9.

30: Lk 11, 47.
31: Acts 7, 52.
33: 3, 7; 12, 34.
34f: 5, 12; 2 Chr 24, 21f; 36, 16; Lk 11, 49ff; Rv 18, 24.

murdered between the temple building and the altar. [36] All this, I assure you, will be the fate of the present generation. [37] O Jerusalem, Jerusalem, murderess of prophets and stoner of those who were sent to you! How often have I yearned to gather your children, as a mother bird gathers her young under her wings, but you refused me. [38] Recall the saying, 'You will find your temple deserted.' [39] I tell you, you will not see me from this time on until you declare, 'Blessed is he who comes in the name of the Lord!' "

24

Beginning of Calamities

[1] Jesus left the temple precincts then, and his disciples came up and pointed out to him the buildings of the temple area. [2] His comment was: "Do you see all these buildings? I assure you, not one stone will be left on another—it will all be torn down." [3] While he was seated on the Mount of Olives, his disciples came up to him privately and said: "Tell us, when will all this occur? What will be the sign of your coming and the end of the world?" [4] In reply Jesus said to them: "Be on guard! Let no one mislead you. [5] Many will come attempting to impersonate me. 'I am the Messiah!' they will claim, and they will deceive many. [6] You will hear of wars and rumors of wars. Do not be alarmed. Such things are bound to happen, but that is not yet the end. [7] Nation will rise against nation, one kingdom against another. There will be famine and pestilence and earthquakes in many places. [8] These are the early stages of the birth pangs. [9] They will hand you over to torture and kill you. [10] Indeed, you will be hated by all nations on my account. Many will falter then, betraying and hating one another. [11] False prophets will rise in great numbers to mislead many. [12] Because of the increase of evil, the love of most will grow cold. [13] The man who holds out to the end, however, is the one who will see salvation. [14] This good news of the kingdom will be proclaimed throughout the world as a witness to all the nations. Only after that will the end come.

37ff: Lk 13, 34f; 19, 41-44.
37: 21, 35; 22, 6.
38: 26, 5f.
24, 1-51: Mk 13, 1-37;
    Lk 21, 5-36.
2: Lk 19, 44.

4f: Lk 21, 8.
6: Jer 51, 46.
9: 10, 17.
10: 10, 21.
13: 10, 22.
14: Rom 10, 18.

24, 1-51: See note on Mk 13, 1-37.

The Final Test

[15] "When you see the abominable and destructive thing which the prophet Daniel foretold standing on holy ground (let the reader take note!), [16] those in Judea must flee to the mountains. [17] If a man is on the roof terrace, he must not come down to get anything out of his house. [18] If a man is in the field, he must not turn back to pick up his cloak. [19] It will be hard on pregnant or nursing mothers in those days. [20] Keep praying that you will not have to flee in winter or on a sabbath, [21] for those days will be more filled with anguish than any from the beginning of the world until now or in all ages to come. [22] Indeed, if the period had not been shortened, not a human being would be saved. For the sake of the chosen, however, the days will be shortened. [23] If anyone tells you at that time, 'Look, the Messiah is here,' or 'He is there,' do not believe it. [24] False messiahs and false prophets will appear, performing signs and wonders so great as to mislead even the chosen if that were possible. [25] Remember, I have told you all about it beforehand; [26] so if they tell you, 'Look, he is in the desert,' do not go out there; or 'He is in the innermost rooms,' do not believe it. [27] As the lightning from the east flashes to the west, so will the coming of the Son of Man be. [28] Where the carcass lies, there the vultures gather.

Coming of the Son of Man

[29] "Immediately after the stress of that period, 'the sun will be darkened, the moon will not shed her light, the stars will fall from the sky, and the hosts of heaven will be shaken loose.' [30] Then the sign of the Son of Man will appear in the sky, and 'all the clans of earth will strike their breasts' as they see 'the Son of Man coming on the clouds of heaven' with power and great glory. [31] He will dispatch his angels 'with a mighty trumpet blast, and they will assemble his chosen from the four winds, from one end of the heavens to the other.' [32] From the fig tree learn a lesson. When its branch grows tender and sprouts leaves, you realize that summer is near. [33] Likewise, when you see all these things happening, you will know that he is near, standing at your door. [34] I assure you, the present generation

15: Dn 11, 31; 12, 11;
    Mk 13, 14.
16: Lk 21, 20.
17: Lk 17, 31.
21: Dn 12, 1.
23: Lk 17, 23; 2 Thes 2, 3ff.
24: 2 Pt 2, 1ff; 1 Jn 4, 1.

28: Lk 17, 37.
29: Is 13, 10; Ez 32, 7;
    Am 8, 9; Lk 21, 25.
30: Dn 7, 13; 1 Thes 4, 16;
    Rv 1, 7.
31: 1 Cor 15, 52.
32: Mk 13, 28; Lk 21, 29.

will not pass away until all this takes place. [35] The heavens and the earth will pass away but my words will not pass.

The Need for Watchfulness

[36] "As for the exact day or hour, no one knows it, neither the angels in heaven nor the Son, but the Father only. [37] The coming of the Son of Man will repeat what happened in Noah's time. [38] In the days before the flood people were eating and drinking, marrying and being married, right up to the day Noah entered the ark. [39] They were totally unconcerned until the flood came and destroyed them. [40] So will it be at the coming of the Son of Man. Two men will be out in the field; one will be taken and one will be left. [41] Two women will be grinding meal; one will be taken and one will be left. [42] Stay awake, therefore! You cannot know the day your Lord is coming.

[43] "Be sure of this: if the owner of the house knew when the thief was coming he would keep a watchful eye and not allow his house to be broken into. [44] You must be prepared in the same way. The Son of Man is coming at the time you least expect. [45] Who is the faithful, farsighted servant whom the master has put in charge of his household to dispense food at need? [46] Happy that servant whom his master discovers at work on his return! [47] I assure you, he will put him in charge of all his property. [48] But if the servant is worthless and tells himself, 'My master is a long time in coming,' [49] and begins to beat his fellow servants, to eat and drink with drunkards, [50] that man's master will return when he is not ready and least expects him. [51] He will punish him severely and settle with him as is done with hypocrites. There will be wailing then and grinding of teeth.

25

Parable of the Ten Virgins

[1] "The reign of God can be likened to ten bridesmaids who took their torches and went out to welcome the groom. [2] Five of them were foolish, while the other five were sensible. [3] The foolish ones, in taking their torches, brought no oil along, [4] But

---

35: Is 40, 8; 51, 6;
    Heb 12, 27.
36: Acts 1, 7.
39: Gn 7, 11-23; 2 Pt 3, 6.

42: 25, 13; Rv 3, 3.
43-51: Lk 12, 39-46.
    43: 1 Thes 5, 6.
    51: 13, 42; 25, 30.

25, 1-46. The parables teach that the Christian community is to be ever ready to meet the Lord at his second coming (1-13); to function with a sense of personal responsibility for divine gifts received (14-30); and to be constantly aware of the primacy of love of neighbor (31-46).

the sensible ones took flasks of oil as well as their torches. [5] The groom delayed his coming, so they all began to nod, then to fall asleep. [6] At midnight someone shouted, 'The groom is here! Come out and greet him!' [7] At the outcry all the virgins woke up and got their torches ready. [8] The foolish ones said to the sensible, 'Give us some of your oil. Our torches are going out.' [9] But the sensible ones replied, 'No, there may not be enough for you and us. You had better go to the dealers and buy yourselves some.' [10] While they went off to buy it the groom arrived, and the ones who were ready went in to the wedding with him. Then the door was barred. [11] Later the other bridesmaids came back. 'Master, master!' they cried. 'Open the door for us.' [12] But he answered, 'I tell you, I do not know you.' [13] The moral is: keep your eyes open, for you know not the day or the hour.

Parable of the Silver Pieces

[14] "The case of a man who was going on a journey is similar. He called in his servants and handed his funds over to them according to each man's abilities. [15] To one he disbursed five thousand silver pieces, to a second two thousand, and to a third a thousand. Then he went away. [16] Immediately the man who received the five thousand went to invest it and made another five. [17] In the same way, the man who received the two thousand doubled his figure. [18] The man who received the thousand went off instead and dug a hole in the ground, where he buried his master's money. [19] After a long absence, the master of those servants came home and settled accounts with them, [20] The man who had received the five thousand came forward bringing the additional five. 'My lord,' he said, 'you let me have five thousand. See, I have made five thousand more.' [21] His master said to him, 'Well done! You are an industrious and reliable servant. Since you were dependable in a small matter I will put you in charge of larger affairs. Come, share your master's joy!' [22] The man who had received the two thousand then stepped forward. 'My lord,' he said, 'you entrusted me with two thousand and I have made two thousand more.' [23] His master said to him, 'Cleverly done! You too are an industrious and reliable servant. Since you were dependable in a small matter I will put you in charge of larger affairs. Come, share your master's joy!"

25, 11: Lk 13, 25.   14-30: Lk 19, 12-27.
       13: 24, 42; Mk 13, 33.   21: Lk 16, 10.

²⁴ "Finally the man who had received the thousand stepped forward. 'My lord,' he said, 'I knew you were a hard man. You reap where you did not sow and gather where you did not scatter, ²⁵ so out of fear I went off and buried your thousand silver pieces in the ground. Here is your money back.' ²⁶ His master exclaimed: 'You worthless, lazy lout! You know I reap where I did not sow and gather where I did not scatter. ²⁷ All the more reason to deposit my money with the bankers, so that on my return I could have had it back with interest. ²⁸ You, there! Take the thousand away from him and give it to the man with the ten thousand. ²⁹ Those who have, will get more until they grow rich, while those who have not, will lose even the little they have. ³⁰ Throw this worthless servant into the darkness outside. where he can wail and grind his teeth.

The Last Judgment

³¹ "When the Son of Man comes in his glory, escorted by all the angels of heaven, he will sit upon his royal throne, ³² and all the nations will be assembled before him. Then he will separate them into two groups, as a shepherd separates sheep from goats. ³³ The sheep he will place on his right hand, the goats on his left. ³⁴ The king will say to those on his right: 'Come. You have my Father's blessing! Inherit the kingdom prepared for you from the creation of the world. ³⁵ For I was hungry and you gave me food, I was thirsty and you gave me drink. I was a stranger and you welcomed me, ³⁶ naked and you clothed me. I was ill and you comforted me, in prison and you came to visit me.' ³⁷ Then the just will ask him: 'Lord, when did we see you hungry and feed you or see you thirsty and give you drink? ³⁸ When did we welcome you away from home or clothe you in your nakedness? ³⁹ When did we visit you when you were ill or in prison?' ⁴⁰ The king will answer them: 'I assure you, as often as you did it for one of my least brothers, you did it for me.'

⁴¹ "Then he will say to those on his left: 'Out of my sight, you condemned, into that everlasting fire prepared for the devil and his angels! ⁴² I was hungry and you gave me no food, I was thirsty and you gave me no drink. ⁴³ I was away from home and you gave me no welcome, naked and you gave me no

29: 13, 12; Mk 4, 25;
    Lk 8, 18; 19, 26.
31: 16, 27.
32: 2 Cor 5, 10.
35: Is 58, 7.

36: Ez 18, 7ff; Heb 13, 3.
40: 10, 40.
41: 7, 23; Lk 13, 27.
42: Jb 22, 7; Jas 2, 14-17.

clothing. I was ill and in prison and you did not come to comfort me.' [44] Then they in turn will ask: 'Lord, when did we see you hungry or thirsty or away from home or naked or ill or in prison and not attend you in your needs?' [45] He will answer them: 'I assure you, as often as you neglected to do it to one of these least ones, you neglected to do it to me.' [46] These will go off to eternal punishment and the just to eternal life."

26

Epilogue

[1] Now when Jesus had finished all these discourses, he declared to his disciples, [2] "You know that in two days' time it will be Passover, and that the Son of Man is to be handed over to be crucified."

VII: THE PASSION AND RESURRECTION

The Conspiracy

[3] At that time the chief priests and elders of the people were assembled in the palace of the high priest, whose name was Caiaphas. [4] They plotted to arrest Jesus by some trick and kill him; [5] but they said, "Not during the festival, for fear of a riot among the people."

The Anointing at Bethany

[6] While Jesus was in Bethany at the house of Simon the leper, [7] a woman carrying a jar of costly perfume came up to him at table and began to pour it on his head. [8] When the disciples saw this they grew indignant, protesting: "What is the point of such extravagance? [9] This could have been sold for a good price and the money given to the poor." [10] Jesus became aware of this and said to them: "Why do you criticize the woman? It is a good deed she has done for me. [11] The poor you will always have with you but you will not always have me. [12] By pouring this perfume on my body, she has contributed toward my burial preparation. [13] I assure you, wherever the good news is proclaimed throughout the world, what she did will be spoken of as her memorial."

[14] Then one of the Twelve whose name was Judas Iscariot

46: Dn 12, 2.
26, 2-5: Mk 14, 1f; Lk 22, 1f.
4: Jn 11, 47-53.

6-13: Mk 14, 3-9; Jn 12, 1-8.
11: Dt 15, 11.
14ff: Mk 14, 10f; Lk 22, 3-6.

26, 1-75: See note on Mk 14, 1—15, 57.

went off to the chief priests [15] and said, "What are you willing to give me if I hand him over to you?" They paid him thirty pieces of silver, [16] and from that time on he kept looking for an opportunity to hand him over.

Passover Preparation

[17] On the first day of the feast of Unleavened Bread, the disciples came up to Jesus and said, "Where do you wish us to prepare the Passover supper for you?" [18] He said, "Go to this man in the city and tell him, 'The Teacher says, My appointed time draws near. I am to celebrate the Passover with my disciples in your house.' "
[19] The disciples then did as Jesus had ordered, and prepared the Passover supper.

The Betrayer

[20] When it grew dark he reclined at table with the Twelve. [21] In the course of the meal he said, "I assure you, one of you is about to betray me." [22] Distressed at this, they began to say to him one after another, "Surely it is not I, Lord?" [23] He replied: "The man who has dipped his hand into the dish with me is the one who will hand me over. [24] The Son of Man is departing, as Scripture says of him, but woe to that man by whom the Son of Man is betrayed. Better for him if he had never been born."
[25] Then Judas, his betrayer, spoke: "Surely it is not I, Rabbi?" Jesus answered, "It is you who have said it."

The Holy Eucharist

[26] During the meal Jesus took bread, blessed it, broke it, and gave it to his disciples. "Take this and eat it," he said, "this is my body." [27] Then he took a cup, gave thanks, and gave it to them. "All of you must drink from it," he said, [28] "for this is my blood, the blood of the covenant, to be poured out in behalf of many for the forgiveness of sins. [29] I tell you, I will not drink this fruit of the vine from now until the day when I drink it new with you in my Father's reign." [30] Then, after singing songs of praise, they walked out to the Mount of Olives.

15: 27, 3f; Gn 37, 28.
17-24: Mk 14, 21;
      Lk 22, 7-14.21ff.
20f: Jn 13, 21-26.
23: Jn 13, 18.
24: Jn 17, 12.
26-29: Mk 14, 22-25;

Lk 22, 18ff;
      1 Cor 11, 23ff.
26: Jn 6, 51-58.
27: 1 Cor 10, 16.
28: Is 53, 12.
30-35: Mk 14, 26-31.

Peter's Denial Foretold

³¹ Jesus then said to them, "Tonight your faith in me will be shaken, for Scripture has it:

'I will strike the shepherd
and the sheep of the flock will be dispersed.'

³² But after I am raised up, I will go to Galilee ahead of you." ³³ Peter responded, "Though all may have their faith in you shaken, mine will never be shaken!" ³⁴ Jesus said to him, "I give you my word, before the cock crows tonight you will deny me three times." ³⁵ Peter replied, "Even though I have to die with you, I will never disown you." And all the other disciples said the same.

The Agony in the Garden

³⁶ Then Jesus went with them to a place called Gethsemani. He said to his disciples, "Stay here while I go over there and pray." ³⁷ He took along Peter and Zebedee's two sons, and began to experience sorrow and distress. Then he said to them, ³⁸ "My heart is nearly broken with sorrow. Remain here and stay awake with me." ³⁹ He advanced a little and fell prostrate in prayer. "My Father, if it is possible, let this cup pass me by. Still, let it be as you would have it, not as I." ⁴⁰ When he returned to his disciples, he found them asleep. He said to Peter, "So you could not stay awake with me for even an hour? ⁴¹ Be on guard, and pray that you may not undergo the test. The spirit is willing but nature is weak." ⁴² Withdrawing a second time, he began to pray: "My Father, if this cannot pass me by without my drinking it, your will be done!" ⁴³ Once more, on his return, he found them asleep; they could not keep their eyes open. ⁴⁴ He left them again, withdrew somewhat, and began to pray a third time, saying the same words as before. ⁴⁵ Finally he returned to his disciples and said to them: "Sleep on now. Enjoy your rest! The hour is on us when the Son of Man is to be handed over to the power of evil men. ⁴⁶ Get up! Let us be on our way! See, my betrayer is here."

Jesus Arrested

⁴⁷ While he was still speaking, Judas, one of the Twelve, ar-

31: Zec 13, 7; Jn 16, 32.
32: Mk 16, 7.
34: Lk 22, 33f; Jn 13, 37f.
35: 26, 69-75.
36-46: Mk 14, 32-42;
  Lk 22, 40-46.

36: Jn 18, 1; Heb 5, 7ff.
39: 6, 10.
40: Jn 4, 34; 6, 38;
  Phil 2, 8.
42: Heb 10, 9.
46: Jn 14, 31.

rived accompanied by a great crowd with swords and clubs. They had been sent by the chief priests and elders of the people. [48] His betrayer had arranged to give them a signal, saying, "The man I shall embrace is the one; take hold of him." [49] He immediately went over to Jesus, said to him, "Peace, Rabbi," and embraced him. [50] Jesus answered, "Friend, do what you are here for!" At that moment they stepped forward to lay hands on Jesus, and arrested him. [51] Suddenly one of those who accompanied Jesus put his hand to his sword, drew it, and slashed at the high priest's servant, cutting off his ear. [52] Jesus said to him: "Put back your sword where it belongs. Those who use the sword are sooner or later destroyed by it. [53] Do you not suppose I can call on my Father to provide at a moment's notice more than twelve legions of angels? [54] But then how would the Scriptures be fulfilled which say it must happen this way?"

[55] At that very time Jesus said to the crowd: "Am I a brigand, that you have come armed with swords and clubs to arrest me? From day to day I sat teaching in the temple precincts, yet you never arrested me. [56] Nonetheless, all this has happened in fulfillment of the writings of the prophets." Then all the disciples deserted him and fled.

Jesus before the Sanhedrin

[57] Those who had apprehended Jesus led him off to Caiaphas the high priest, where the scribes and elders were convened. [58] Peter kept following him at a distance as far as the high priest's residence. Going inside, he sat down with the guards to see the outcome. [59] The chief priests, with the whole Sanhedrin, were busy trying to obtain false testimony against Jesus so that they might put him to death. [60] They discovered none, despite the many false witnesses who took the stand. Finally two came forward [61] who stated: "This man has declared, 'I can destroy God's sanctuary and rebuild it in three days.'" [62] The high priest rose to his feet and addressed him: "Have you no answer to the testimony leveled against you?" [63] But Jesus remained silent. The high priest then said to him: "I order you to tell us under oath before the living God whether you are the Messiah, the Son of God." [64] Jesus answered: "It is you who say it. But I tell you this: Soon you will see the Son of

47-56: Mk 14, 43-49;
　　　Lk 22, 47-53;
　　　Jn 18, 3-11.
　49: Prv 27, 6.
57-68: Mk 14, 53-65;

　　　Lk 22, 54; Jn 18, 12-24.
　61: Jn 2, 19.
63-66: Lk 22, 67-71.
　63: Is 53, 7.
　64: 16, 27; Dn 7, 13.

Man seated at the right hand of the Power and coming on the clouds of heaven." [65] At this the high priest tore his robes: "He has blasphemed! What further need have we of witnesses? [66] Remember, you heard the blasphemy. What is your verdict?" They answered, "He deserves death!" [67] Then they began to spit in his face and hit him. Others slapped him, saying: [68] "Play the prophet for us, Messiah! Who struck you?"

Peter's Denial

[69] Peter was sitting in the courtyard when one of the serving girls came over to him and said, "You too were with Jesus the Galilean." [70] He denied it in front of everyone: "I do not know what you are talking about!" [71] When he went out to the gate another girl saw him and said to those nearby, "This man was with Jesus the Nazorean." [72] Again he denied it with an oath: "I do not know the man!" [73] A little while later some bystanders came over to Peter and said, "You are certainly one of them! Even your accent gives you away!" [74] At that he began cursing, and swore, "I do not even know the man!" Just then a cock began to crow [75] and Peter remembered the prediction Jesus had made: "Before the cock crows, you will deny me three times." He went out and began to weep bitterly.

27

[1] At daybreak all the chief priests and the elders of the people took formal action against Jesus to put him to death. [2] They bound him and led him away to be handed over to the procurator Pilate.

The End of Judas

[3] Then Judas, who had handed him over, seeing that Jesus had been condemned, began to regret his action deeply. He took the thirty pieces of silver back to the chief priests and elders and said, [4] "I did wrong to deliver up an innocent man!" They

---

67: Wis 2, 19; Is 50, 6;
　　52, 14; Mk 14, 65;
　　Lk 22, 63f.
69-75: Mk 14, 66-72;
　　Lk 22, 55-62;

Jn 18, 17f.
75: 26, 34.
27, 1f: Mk 15, 1; Lk 22, 66;
　　23, 1; Jn 18, 28.
3: 26, 15.

27, 3-10: The tragic death of Judas is elsewhere related only in Acts 1, 18; see note. Despite differences in the accounts, there is agreement in essentials: a plot of land near Jerusalem, popularly called the "Field of Blood," was purchased with the money Judas received for betraying Jesus, and the traitor died an infamous death. Matthew's free citation of Jer 18, 2f; 19, 1f; 32, 6-15 and Zec 11, 13 shows that he regards Judas' death as a divine judgment.

retorted, "What is that to us? It is your affair!" [5] So Judas flung the money into the temple and left. He went off and hanged himself. [6] The chief priests picked up the silver, observing, "It is not right to deposit this in the temple treasury since it is blood money." [7] After consultation, they used it to buy the potter's field as a cemetery for foreigners. [8] That is why that field, even today, is called Blood Field. [9] On that occasion, what was said through Jeremiah the prophet was fulfilled:

"They took the thirty pieces of silver, the value of a man with a price on his head, a price set by the Israelites, [10] and they paid it out for the potter's field just as the Lord had commanded me."

Jesus before Pilate

[11] Jesus was arraigned before the procurator, who questioned him: "Are you the king of the Jews?" Jesus responded, "As you say." [12] Yet when he was accused by the chief priests and elders, he had made no reply. [13] Then Pilate said to him, "Surely you hear how many charges they bring against you?" [14] He did not answer him on a single count, much to the procurator's surprise.

[15] Now on the occasion of a festival the procurator was accustomed to release one prisoner, whom the crowd would designate. [16] They had at the time a notorious prisoner named Barabbas. [17] Since they were already assembled, Pilate said to them, "Which one do you wish me to release for you, Barabbas or Jesus the so-called Messiah?" [18] He knew, of course, that it was out of jealousy that they had handed him over.

[19] While he was still presiding on the bench, his wife sent him a message: "Do not interfere in the case of that holy man. I had a dream about him today which has greatly upset me."

[20] Meanwhile, the chief priests and elders convinced the crowds that they should ask for Barabbas and have Jesus put to death. [21] So when the procurator asked them, "Which one do you wish me to release for you?" they said, "Barabbas." [22] Pilate said to them, "Then what am I to do with Jesus, the

---

11-14: Mk 15, 2-5; Lk 23, 2f;
          Jn 18, 29-38.
      12: Wis 2, 19.
15-26: Mk 15, 6-15;

Lk 23, 17-25;
Jn 18, 39f.
      20: Acts 3, 14.

27, 19f: This passage is proper to Matthew. The episode concerning Pilate's wife accords with evidence that women sometimes intervened in the political affairs of the Roman world. Her concern is for the welfare of her husband rather than of Jesus; for this reason she does not wish Pilate to become involved in the religious affairs of the Jews.

so-called Messiah?" "Crucify him!" they all cried. [23] He said, "Why, what crime has he committed?" But they only shouted the louder, "Crucify him!" [24] Pilate finally realized that he was making no impression and that a riot was breaking out instead. He called for water and washed his hands in front of the crowd, declaring as he did so, "I am innocent of the blood of this just man. The responsibility is yours." [25] The whole people said in reply, "Let his blood be on us and on our children." [26] At that, he released Barabbas to them. Jesus, however, he first had scourged; then he handed him over to be crucified.

The Crowning with Thorns

[27] The procurator's soldiers took Jesus inside the praetorium and collected the whole cohort around him. [28] They stripped off his clothes and wrapped him in a scarlet military cloak. [29] Weaving a crown out of thorns they fixed it on his head, and stuck a reed in his right hand. Then they began to mock him by dropping to their knees before him, saying, "All hail, king of the Jews!" [30] They also spat at him. Afterward they took hold of the reed and kept striking him on the head. [31] Finally, when they had finished making a fool of him, they stripped him of the cloak, dressed him in his own clothes, and led him off to crucifixion.

The Way of the Cross

[32] On their way out they met a Cyrenian named Simon. This man they pressed into service to carry the cross. [33] Upon arriving at a site called Golgotha (a name which means Skull Place), [34] they gave him a drink of wine flavored with gall, which he tasted but refused to drink.

The Crucifixion

[35] When they had crucified him, they divided his clothes among them by casting lots; [36] then they sat down there and kept watch over him. [37] Above his head they had put the charge against him in writing: "THIS IS JESUS, KING OF THE JEWS." [38] Two insurgents were crucified along with him, one at his

25: Acts 18, 6.
27-31: Mk 15, 16-20; Jn 19, 2f.
29: 27, 11.
30: Is 50, 6.
32: Mk 15, 21; Lk 23, 36.

33-50: Mk 15, 22-34;
Lk 23, 32-38; 44ff;
Jn 19, 17ff.23f.28ff.
35: Ps 22, 19.
38: Lk 22, 37.

27, 25: *Let his blood be on us and on our children:* probably the evangelist's commentary on the responsibility for Jesus' death; cf Jer 51, 35.

right and one at his left. [39] People going by kept insulting him, tossing their heads [40] and saying: "So you are the one who was going to destroy the temple and rebuild it in three days! Save yourself, why don't you? Come down off that cross if you are God's Son!" [41] The chief priests, the scribes, and the elders also joined in the jeering: [42] "He saved others but he cannot save himself! So he is the king of Israel! Let's see him come down from that cross and then we will believe in him. [43] He relied on God; let God rescue him now if he wants to. After all, he claimed, 'I am God's Son.'" [44] The insurgents who had been crucified with him kept taunting him in the same way.

The Death of Jesus

[45] From noon onward, there was darkness over the whole land until midafternoon. [46] Then toward midafternoon Jesus cried out in a loud tone, *"Eli, Eli, lema sabachthani?"*, that is, "My God, my God, why have you forsaken me?" [47] This made some of the bystanders who heard it remark, "He is invoking Elijah!" [48] Immediately one of them ran off and got a sponge. He soaked it in cheap wine, and sticking it on a reed, tried to make him drink. [49] Meanwhile the rest said, "Leave him alone. Let's see whether Elijah comes to his rescue." [50] Once again Jesus cried out in a loud voice, and then gave up his spirit.

[51] Suddenly the curtain of his sanctuary was torn in two from top to bottom. [52] The earth quaked, boulders split, tombs opened. [53] Many bodies of saints who had fallen asleep were raised. After Jesus' resurrection they came forth from their tombs and entered the holy city and appeared to many. [54] The centurion and his men who were keeping watch over Jesus were terror-stricken at seeing the earthquake and all that was happening, and said, "Clearly this was the Son of God!"

[55] Many women were present looking on from a distance. They had followed Jesus from Galilee to attend to his needs. [56] Among them were Mary Magdalene, and Mary the mother of James and Joseph, and the mother of Zebedee's sons.

39: Ps 22, 8.
40: Jn 2, 19.
43: Ps 22, 9.
46: Ps 22, 2.
48: Lk 23, 36; Jn 19, 29.
49: Ps 69, 21.

51: Heb 6, 19.
52: 1 Pt 3, 18.
54ff: Mk 15, 39ff;
Lk 23, 47ff.
55: Jn 19, 25.
56: 13, 55.

27, 51ff: The tearing of the sanctuary veil between the holy place and the holy of holies symbolizes a break with the past; the other phenomena portend the resurrection of all men, the final cosmic event of human history; cf Is 13, 9f; 34, 4; Dn 12, 2; Jl 2, 10.

The Burial

[57] When evening fell, a wealthy man from Arimathea arrived, Joseph by name. He was another of Jesus' disciples, [58] and had gone to request the body of Jesus. Thereupon Pilate issued an order for its release. [59] Taking the body, Joseph wrapped it in fresh linen [60] and laid it in his own new tomb which had been hewn from a formation of rock. Then he rolled a huge stone across the entrance of the tomb and went away. [61] But Mary Magdalene and the other Mary remained sitting there, facing the tomb.

Precautions of the Chief Priests

[62] The next day, the one following the Day of Preparation, the chief priests and the Pharisees called at Pilate's residence. [63] "Sir," they said, "we have recalled that that impostor while he was still alive made the claim, 'After three days I will rise.' [64] You should issue an order having the tomb kept under surveilance until the third day. Otherwise his disciples may go and steal him and tell the people, 'He has been raised from the dead!' This final imposture would be worse than the first." [65] Pilate told them, "You have a guard. Go and secure the tomb as best you can." [66] So they went and kept it under surveillance of the guard, after fixing a seal to the stone.

28

The Women at the Tomb

[1] After the sabbath, as the first day of the week was dawning, Mary Magdalene came with the other Mary to inspect the tomb. [2] Suddenly there was a mighty earthquake, as the angel of the Lord descended from heaven. He came to the stone, rolled it back, and sat on it. [3] In appearance he resembled a flash of lightning while his garments were as dazzling as snow. [4] The guards grew paralyzed with fear of him and fell down like dead men. [5] Then the angel spoke, addressing the women: "Do not be

---

57-61: Mk 15, 42-47;
   Lk 23, 50ff;
   Jn 19, 38-42.
60: Is 53, 9.

64: Acts 10, 40.
28, 1-8: Mk 16, 1-8;
   Lk 24, 1-10.
3: 17, 2.

27, 62-66: This account is proper to Matthew. It is thought to have originated among Judaeo-Christians in response to a Jewish allegation that Jesus' disciples had stolen the body. Matthew wishes to emphasize the supernatural character of Jesus' departure from the tomb, to which there was no human witness; cf 28, 2ff.

28, 1-20: See note on Lk 24, 1-53.

frightened. I know you are looking for Jesus the crucified, [6] but he is not here. He has been raised, exactly as he promised. Come and see the place where he was laid. [7] Then go quickly and tell his disciples: 'He has been raised from the dead and now goes ahead of you to Galilee, where you will see him.' That is the message I have for you."

[8] They hurried away from the tomb half-overjoyed, half-fearful, and ran to carry the good news to his disciples. [9] Suddenly, without warning, Jesus stood before them and said, "Peace!" The women came up and embraced his feet and did him homage. [10] At this Jesus said to them, "Do not be afraid! Go and carry the news to my brothers that they are to go to Galilee, where they will see me."

Tale of the Guards and Chief Priests

[11] As the women were returning, some of the guard went into the city and reported to the chief priests all that had happened. [12] They, in turn, convened with the elders and worked out their strategy, giving the soldiers a large bribe [13] with the instructions: "You are to say, 'His disciples came during the night and stole him while we were asleep.' [14] If any word of this gets to the procurator, we will straighten it out with him and keep you out of trouble." [15] The soldiers pocketed the money and did as they had been instructed. This is the story that circulates among the Jews to this very day.

Commission of the Apostles

[16] The eleven disciples made their way to Galilee, to the mountain to which Jesus had summoned them. [17] At the sight of him, those who had entertained doubts fell down in homage. [18] Jesus came forward and addressed them in these words:

> "Full authority has been given to me
> both in heaven and on earth;
> [19] go, therefore, and make disciples of all the nations.

7: 26, 32.
10: Acts 1, 3.

19: Mk 16, 15f; Lk 24, 47.

28, 11-15: The chief priests and elders are not concerned with the resurrection itself, which they simply deem impossible, but with the repercussions on the people of the apostolic preaching concerning the resurrection.

28, 16: The tradition of Jesus' appearance to his disciples in Galilee is also reflected in Jn 21, 1-23.

28, 17: *Those who had entertained doubts:* literally, "but some doubted"; probably a summary allusion to the initial doubts of the disciples over the reality of the resurrection; cf Lk 24, 22ff.38; Jn 20, 27. The resurrection narratives are characterized by a condensed description of events.

28, 19: *Go, therefore, and make . . . the nations:* some regard these words

Baptize them in the name
'of the Father,
and of the Son,
and of the Holy Spirit.'
20Teach them to carry out
everything I have commanded you.
And know that I am with you alwayc
until the end of the world!"

20: Jn 14, 18-21.

---

as an interpretation of Jesus' final instructions in the light of the church's early change from a mission to the Jews to one in behalf of the Gentiles; see Introduction to Acts. *Baptize them . . . Holy Spirit:* The baptismal formula reflects the church's gradual understanding of God as three Persons (Acts 2, 38; 2 Cor 13, 13).

28, 20: The apostles are to teach the world not merely the doctrine of the resurrection but the historical teaching of Jesus. This the evangelist Matthew obviously considers to be contained in the gospel he has written. *I am with you always:* The power of the risen Christ (18) will ever sustain those whom he has commissioned to preach the "good news" of salvation to the world.

THE GOSPEL ACCORDING TO MARK
INTRODUCTION

The gospel of Mark is invaluable for grasping the essential characteristics of Jesus' public ministry. The gospels of Matthew and Luke are better understood in the light of the data provided by Mark because of their direct dependence on him. Like the other evangelists, Mark, in addressing himself to Christian readers, places his gospel within the framework of Christian tradition on the identity of Jesus which developed during the course of the apostolic teaching. In Mark's day, the title "Christ" had already become part of Jesus' proper name; for the Gentile Christian it had the religious implication of "savior" or "redeemer" rather than "Messiah," which would be meaningless to all but Jews; cf Rom 9, 5. The title "Son of God" had become the most characteristic name of Jesus, designating him as the God-man; cf Rom 1, 1-4.

The gospel of Mark revolves around the two titles "Christ" and "Son of God." The evangelist shows how the Christian community's faith in Jesus as Savior harmonized with his own knowledge of his divine destiny to suffer, die, and rise again. The miraculous powers of Jesus which so mystified his contemporaries find their satisfactory explanation in the doctrine of Jesus' divinity, which the Christian community grasped only after his resurrection. Although the gospel of Mark is developed in connection with Christian faith in Jesus as redeemer and Son of God, its contents indicate the historical reality of the person and ministry of Jesus in a manner less refined by theological reflection than the accounts of the other evangelists. In Mark, the person of Jesus is depicted with an unaffected naturalness. He reacts to events with authentic human emotion: apprehension (1, 44), anger (3, 5), triumph (4, 40), sympathy (5, 36; 6, 34), surprise (5, 30; 6, 6), admiration (7, 29), sadness (14, 33f), indignation (14, 48f). His disciples take positions toward him that are critical (4, 38; 5, 31; 6, 37; 8, 4.32) or inattentive (7, 16f). He acknowledges that there are things he does not know, e.g., the appointed time for the end of the world, known only to the Father (13, 32); cf also 5, 30; 6, 38.

From a literary standpoint this gospel is divided into clearly distinguishable parts: the title (1, 1), the prologue (1, 2-13), the ministry of Jesus (1, 14—13, 37), his passion, death, and burial (14, 1—15, 47), his resurrection, the commission of the apostles, and his ascension (16, 1-20).

The account of the ministry is doctrinal rather than chronological or geographical. The reader's attention is fixed on the mystery of Jesus' person. The average man recognizes in the teaching of Jesus something authentically new (1, 22), and he is thoroughly impressed by Jesus' curative powers (1, 37f; 3, 8-11). The religious leaders are disconcerted when Jesus challenges them on their own ground (2, 16—3, 6). The relatives of Jesus fear for his safety (3, 20f), and his disciples discover that their understanding of him is deficient (4, 36-40; 6, 47-52). Jesus accepts the title of prophet, but he lays no explicit claim to the role of Messiah; he even imposes silence concerning his miracles (1, 44; 5, 43; 7, 36; 8, 26).

At Caesarea Philippi Jesus departs from this reticence and elicits two admissions from his disciples: one is that popular opinion concedes him the role of prophet; the other is that the disciples themselves consider him to be the Messiah (8, 27-30). At this point Mark's gospel reaches its first climax concerning the identity of Jesus, to which it has been building up. Jesus proceeds beyond the messianic confession of his disciples to state clearly his own prophetic understanding of his role: it is the divine will that he should suffer and die at the hands of the Sanhedrin. The mystery of the crucified Messiah, which is a stumbling block to the Jews (1 Cor 1, 23), is traced by Mark to Jesus' self-awareness throughout his ministry. Though the remainder of the gospel incorporates an occasional miracle story (9, 17-27; 10, 46-52; 11, 12ff.20f), and much of Jesus' teaching, it is dominated by his self-revelation as the chosen instrument who is to suffer, die, and rise again (9, 9f.31f; 10, 32ff; 12, 1-12; 14, 1—16, 8). Within the passion narrative, the second and chief climax of Jesus' self-revelation occurs when, in the inquest before the high priest, he is shown by Mark to express the church's faith that he is both Messiah and Son of God (14, 62).

Mark's geographical framework places the ministry of Jesus not only in the Galilean area (1, 14—6, 13), but outside it as well (6, 30—10, 31). The journey to Jerusalem begins in 10, 32 and ends in 11, 1 near that city, where the final days of the ministry are to be spent (11, 1—15, 37).

According to Papias (†135 A.D.), the author of the second gospel was Mark who served as Peter's "interpreter" (editor of Petrine material?). Irenaeus (c 202), Clement of Alexandria (c 215), Tertullian (c 220), and Origen (c 254) attest a similar relationship. There is no need to reject the identification of the author with that John Mark whom the New Testament associates with St. Paul (Acts 12, 25; 15, 37.39; Col 4, 10; 2 Tm 4, 11; Phlm 24), and with St. Peter (Acts 12, 12; 1 Pt 5, 13).

The Petrine influence on Mark should not be exaggerated. Modern scholarship has shown quite clearly that Mark's sources cannot be explained solely in terms of Peter's preaching. On the basis of manuscript and stylistic evidence, Mk 16, 9-20 derives from a hand other than Mark's. The gospel originally ended at 16, 8. The so-called longer ending (vv 9-20), which the Council of Trent declared to be inspired and canonical, was known to Justin Martyr (c 165), Tatian (c 170), and Irenaeus (c 202).

Data in the gospel clearly indicate that it was intended for Gentile Christian readers (7, 3f.11), or at least readers unfamiliar with Jewish customs; nonetheless, the place of composition is uncertain. Following the suggestion of Clement of Alexandria and Origen, the majority of modern scholars consider the gospel to have been written in Rome. The date of composition is c 70 A.D.

The gospel of Mark has contributed much to the other gospels for the Christian understanding of Jesus and his ministry.

The principal division of the gospel of Mark are as follows:

THE GOSPEL ACCORDING TO MARK

I: PROLOGUE: PREPARATION FOR
THE MINISTRY OF JESUS

1

John the Baptizer

¹ Here begins the gospel of Jesus Christ, the Son of God. ² In Isaiah the prophet it is written:

> "I send my messenger before you
>   to prepare your way:
> ³ a herald's voice in the desert, crying,
> 'Make ready the way of the Lord,
>   clear him a straight path.'"

⁴ Thus it was that John the Baptizer appeared in the desert, proclaiming a baptism of repentance which led to the forgiveness of sins. ⁵ All the Judean countryside and the people of Jerusalem went out to him in great numbers. They were being baptized by him in the Jordan River as they confessed their sins. ⁶ John was clothed in camel's hair, and wore a leather belt around his waist. His food was grasshoppers and wild honey. ⁷ The theme of his preaching was: "One more powerful than I is to come after me. I am not fit to stoop and untie his sandal straps. ⁸ I have baptized you in water; he will baptize you in the Holy Spirit."

The Baptism of Jesus

⁹ During that time, Jesus came from Nazareth in Galilee and

1, 2-8: Mt 3, 1-11; Lk 3, 2-16.
2: Mal 3, 1.
3: Is 40, 3; Jn 1, 23.
8: Jn 1, 27; Acts 1, 5;

11, 16.
9ff: Mt 3, 13-17; Lk 3, 21f;
Jn 1, 32f.

1, 1: This verse is probably the title of the entire gospel, which Mark regards as the account of Jesus' ministry of redemption. Several important early manuscripts lack the phrase *Son of God;* its authenticity, however, is accepted by most modern scholars.
1, 2f: Portions of Exodus (23, 20), Malachi (3, 1) and Isaiah (40, 3) are combined here; cf Mt 11, 10; Lk 7, 26. Mark mentions only Isaiah.
1, 3f: The historical concept of God's fulfillment of prophecy is the same as in Matthew. See note on Mt 3, 1. On repentance, see note on Acts 2, 38.
1, 5: See note on Mt 3, 11f. *They confessed their sins:* whether the confessions was explicit and individual or general and collective is not determinable from the text.
1, 6: *Clothed in camel's hair . . . waist:* see note on Mt 3, 4.
1, 7f: Here the figure of Jesus is kept foremost in the Baptizer's preaching. He is the *One more powerful* who *is to come.* Matthew (3, 7-10) and Luke (3, 7-14) add elements of warning against those who hear the invitation to repentance and fail to heed it.
1, 9ff: The synoptic gospels concentrate on the baptism of Jesus, while

was baptized in the Jordan by John. ¹⁰ Immediately on coming up out of the water he saw the sky rent in two and the Spirit descending on him like a dove. ¹¹ Then a voice came from the heavens: "You are my beloved Son. On you my favor rests."

The Temptation

¹² At that point the Spirit sent him out toward the desert. ¹³ He stayed in the wasteland forty days, put to the test there by Satan. He was with the wild beasts, and angels waited on him.

II: THE MYSTERY OF JESUS

Call of the First Disciples

¹⁴ After John's arrest, Jesus appeared in Galilee proclaiming the good news of God: ¹⁵ "This is the time of fulfillment. The reign of God is at hand! Reform your lives and believe in the gospel!"

¹⁶ As he made his way along the Sea of Galilee, he observed Simon and his brother Andrew casting their nets into the sea; they were fishermen. ¹⁷ Jesus said to them, "Come after me; I will make you fishers of men." ¹⁸ They immediately abandoned

---

11: Ps 2, 7.
12: Mt 4, 1-11; Lk 4, 1-13.
14: Mt 4, 12-17.

15: Mt 3, 2.
16-20: Mt 4, 18-22; Lk 5, 2-11.

---

the fourth gospel (Jn 1, 24-37) is concerned with the role of the Baptizer in identifying Jesus as the One who is to come. The synoptics ascribe directly to God the Father the identification of Jesus as "Servant of Yahweh." The dove is the symbol of the Holy Spirit (Mk 1, 10), derived perhaps from the image of the creative spirit of God hovering over the waters (Gn 1, 2). The intimation is that Jesus, possessor of the Spirit, is the creator of the new people of God. The occasion of Jesus' baptism is the response to the prayer in Is 64, 1 for the heavens to open and rain down messianic salvation (1, 10). The designation of Jesus as God's Son reflects the early Christian usage of Ps 2, 7, which sees the sonship there spoken of as prophetically fulfilled in Jesus' resurrection.

1, 12f: Jesus, possessor of the Spirit, is directed irresistibly to a confrontation with Satan over the course of forty days. Both angels and wild beasts are present. Though the sense of the imagery is uncertain, some evidence in New Testament times shows demons symbolized by wild beasts. Following the extra-biblical Jewish literary tradition of holy men subjected to temptation, Mark depicts Jesus as the faithful servant of Yahweh, loyal to God in his time of trial (Heb 2, 14-18). The temptation narrative expresses, in terms of a drama, Jesus' ministry, passion and death as a conflict with satanic power.

1, 14f: Jesus appeared . . . the good news of God: a summary statement concerning Jesus' preaching, to introduce his public ministry. This is the time of fulfillment: the period in human history appointed by God for making good his messianic promises. The reign of God is at hand: see note on Mt 3, 1. Though some scholars maintain that Jesus proclaimed the kingdom as imminent but not yet arrived, it is more probable that he announced it as actually arrived yet awaiting future development. Reform your lives: see note on Acts 2, 38.

1, 16-20: See note on Mt 4, 19.

their nets and became his followers. [19] Proceeding a little farther along, he caught sight of James, Zebedee's son, and his brother John. They too were in their boat putting their nets in order. He summoned them on the spot. [20] They abandoned their father Zebedee, who was in the boat with the hired men, and went off in his company. [21] Shortly afterward they came to Capernaum, and on the sabbath he entered the synagogue and began to teach. [22] The people were spellbound by his teaching because he taught with authority, and not like the scribes.

Cure of a Demoniac

[23] There appeared in their synagogue a man with an unclean spirit that shrieked: [24] "What do you want of us, Jesus of Nazareth? Have you come to destroy us? I know who you are—the holy One of God!" [25] Jesus rebuked him sharply: "Be quiet! Come out of the man!" [26] At that the unclean spirit convulsed the man violently and with a loud shriek came out of him. [27] All who looked on were amazed. They began to ask one another: "What does this mean? A completely new teaching in a spirit of authority! He gives orders to unclean spirits and they obey!" [28] From that point on his reputation spread throughout the surrounding region of Galilee.

Peter's Mother-in-law

[29] Immediately upon leaving the synagogue, he entered the house of Simon and Andrew with James and John. [30] Simon's mother-in-law lay ill with a fever, and the first thing they did was to tell him about her. [31] He went over to her and grasped her hand and helped her up, and the fever left her. She immediately began to wait on them.

Other Miracles

[32] After sunset, as evening drew on, they brought him all who

---

21-28: Lk 4, 31-37.   29-34: Mt 8, 14ff; Lk 4, 38-41.
22: Mt 7, 28f.

1, 21f: The people realize that Jesus presents himself as a prophet who does not depend on rabbinic tradition for his teaching.

1, 23-28: This account of exorcism is the first of four such narratives in Mark (5, 1-20; 7, 24-30; 9, 14-27). The gospel also contains several allusions to Jesus' numerous exorcisms (1, 34.39; 3, 11f), and records a debate between Jesus and the scribes over their meaning (3, 22-30). Matthew and Luke present some of the same traditional accounts as Mark but add no new ones. Note that Jesus neither declares diabolical "possession" to be a phenomenon in Israel nor contests any affirmation of the presence of diabolic beings. When the scribes accuse Jesus of performing exorcisms by the power of Satan, they imply that there are diabolic manifestations among the sick brought to Jesus. Apart from the case of the Syro-Phoenician woman's daughter (see note on 7, 24-30), nowhere is Jesus asked precisely to perform an exorcism.

were ill, and those possessed by demons. ³³ Before long the whole town was gathered outside the door. ³⁴ Those whom he cured, who were variously afflicted, were many, and so were the demons he expelled. But he would not permit the demons to speak, because they knew him. ³⁵ Rising early the next morning, he went off to a lonely place in the desert; there he was absorbed in prayer. ³⁶ Simon and his companions managed to track him down, and ³⁷ when they found him, they told him, "Everybody is looking for you!" ³⁸ He said to them: "Let us move on to the neighboring villages so that I may proclaim the good news there also. That is what I have come to do." ³⁹ So he went into their synagogues preaching the good news and expelling demons throughout the whole of Galilee.

A Leper

⁴⁰ A leper approached him with a request, kneeling down as he addressed him: "If you will to do so, you can cure me." ⁴¹ Moved with pity, Jesus stretched out his hand, touched him, and said: "I do will it. Be cured." ⁴² The leprosy left him then and there, and he was cured. ⁴³ Jesus gave him a stern warning and sent him on his way. ⁴⁴ "Not a word to anyone, now," he said. "Go off and present yourself to the priest and offer for your cure what Moses prescribed. That should be a proof for them." ⁴⁵ The man went off and began to proclaim the whole matter freely, making the story public. As a result of this, it was no longer possible for Jesus to enter a town openly. He stayed in desert places; yet people kept coming to him from all sides.

2

A Paralytic at Capernaum

¹ He came back to Capernaum after a lapse of several days and word got around that he was at home. ² At that they began

---

35-39: Lk 4, 42ff.   42: Lk 17, 14.
40-44: Mt 8, 2ff; Lk 5, 12ff.   44: Lv 14, 2-32.
   41: 5, 30.   2, 1-12: Mt 9, 2-8; Lk 5, 18-26.

1, 34: *Because they knew him:* probably the knowledge which the demons had about Jesus is to be understood in the broad sense, i.e., they are reported as having recognized Jesus as their enemy without having specific knowledge of his actual identity.
1, 40-45: For the various forms of skin disease, cf Lv 13, 1-50 and the note on Lv 13, 2ff. Jesus shows concern for the proper interpretation of his miracles. He assumes that the priests will perceive the messianic significance of the miracle. On the "messianic secret" involved in this narrative, see note on 8, 27-30.
2, 1-12: Besides his power over demonic spirits and physical illness, Jesus manifests his power to forgive sins. This miracle story constitutes a

to gather in great numbers. There was no longer any room for them, even around the door. [3] While he was delivering God's word to them, some people arrived bringing a paralyzed man to him. The four who carried him [4] were unable to bring him to Jesus because of the crowd, so they began to open up the roof over the spot where Jesus was. When they had made a hole, they let down the mat on which the paralytic was lying. [5] When Jesus saw their faith, he said to the paralyzed man, "My son, your sins are forgiven." [6] Now some of the scribes were sitting there asking themselves: [7] "Why does the man talk in that way? He commits blasphemy! Who can forgive sins except God alone?" [8] Jesus was immediately aware of their reasoning, though they kept it to themselves, and he said to them: "Why do you harbor these thoughts? [9] Which is easier, to say to the paralytic, 'Your sins are forgiven,' or to say, 'Stand up, pick up your mat, and walk again'? [10] That you may know that the Son of Man has authority on earth to forgive sins" (he said to the paralyzed man), [11] "I command you: Stand up! Pick up your mat and go home." [12] The man stood and picked up his mat and went outside in the sight of everyone. They were awestruck; all gave praise to God, saying, "We have never seen anything like this!"

The Call of Levi

[13] Another time, while he went walking along the lakeshore, people kept coming to him in crowds and he taught them. [14] As he moved on he saw Levi the son of Alphaeus at his tax collector's post, and said to him, "Follow me." Levi got up and became his follower. [15] While Jesus was reclining to eat in Levi's house, many tax collectors and those known as sinners joined him and his disciples at dinner. The number of those who followed him was large. [16] When the scribes who belonged to the Pharisee party saw that he was eating with tax collectors and offenders against the law, they complained to his disciples, "Why does he eat with such as these?" [17] Overhearing the remark, Jesus said to them, "People who are healthy do not need a doctor; sick people do. I have come to call sinners, not the self-righteous."

7: Is 43, 25.   14-17: Mt 9, 9-13; Lk 5, 27-32.
13: 4, 1.

transition to the conflict narratives which follow. Once Christians believed in the divinity of Jesus after his resurrection, they realized that he forgave sins through the power he had conferred on the community; cf Mt 9, 8.
2, 15ff: See note on Mt 9, 13.

The Question of Fasting

¹⁸ Now John's disciples and the Pharisees were accustomed to fast. People came to Jesus with the objection, "Why do John's disciples and those of the Pharisees fast while yours do not?" ¹⁹ Jesus replied: "How can the guests at a wedding fast as long as the groom is still among them? So long as the groom stays with them, they cannot fast. ²⁰ The day will come, however, when the groom will be taken away from them; on that day they will fast. ²¹ No one sews a patch of unshrunken cloth on an old cloak. If he should do so, the very thing he has used to cover the hole would pull away—the new from the old—and the tear would get worse. ²² Similarly, no man pours new wine into old wineskins. If he does so, the wine will burst the skins and both wine and skins will be lost. No, new wine is poured into new skins."

The Disciples and the Sabbath

²³ It happened that he was walking through standing grain on the sabbath, and his disciples began to pull off heads of grain as they went along. ²⁴ At this the Pharisees protested: "Look! Why do they do a thing not permitted on the sabbath?" ²⁵ He said to them: "Have you never read what David did when he was in need and he and his men were hungry? ²⁶ How he entered God's house in the days of Abiathar the high priest and ate the holy bread which only the priests were permitted to eat? He even gave it to his men." ²⁷ Then he said to them: "The sabbath was made for man, not man for the sabbath. ²⁸ That is why the Son of Man is lord even of the sabbath."

3

A Man with a Withered Hand

¹ He returned to the synagogue where there was a man whose hand was shriveled up. ² They kept an eye on Jesus to see whether he would heal him on the sabbath, hoping to be able

---

23-28: Mt 12, 1-8; Lk 6, 1-5.
24: Dt 23, 25.
26: 1 Sm 21, 2-7; Lv 24, 5-9.

27: 2 Mc 5, 19.
3, 1-6: Mt 12, 9-14; Lk 6, 6-11.

2, 18-22: See note on Mt 9, 14-17.
2, 23-27: See note on Mt 12, 3-6.
2, 28: This statement seems to be an editorial addition to teach that the early Christian community's freedom from Jewish sabbath regulations relies on the authority of Jesus, now fully vindicated by his resurrection and ascension. On the title *Son of Man*, see note on 8, 31ff.
3, 1-6: See note on Mt 12, 10.

to bring an accusation against him. ³ He addressed the man with the shriveled hand: "Stand up here in front!" ⁴ Then he said to them: "Is it permitted to do a good deed on the sabbath— or an evil one? To preserve life—or to destroy it?" At this they remained silent. ⁵ He looked around at them with anger, for he was deeply grieved that they had closed their minds against him. Then he said to the man, "Stretch out your hand." The man did so and his hand was perfectly restored. ⁶ When the Pharisees went outside, they immediately began to plot with the Herodians how they might destroy him.

The Mercy of Jesus

⁷ Jesus withdrew toward the lake with his disciples. A great crowd followed him from Galilee, ⁸ and an equally great multitude came to him from Judea, Jerusalem, Idumea, Transjordan, and the neighborhood of Tyre and Sidon, because they had heard what he had done. ⁹ In view of their numbers, he told his disciples to have a fishing boat ready for him so that he could avoid the press of the crowd against him. ¹⁰ Because he had cured many, all who had afflictions kept pushing toward him to touch him. ¹¹ Unclean spirits would catch sight of him, fling themselves down at his feet, and shout, "You are the Son of God!", ¹² while he kept ordering them sternly not to reveal who he was.

Choice of the Twelve

¹³ He then went up the mountain and summoned the men he himself had decided on, who came and joined him. ¹⁴ He named twelve as his companions whom he would send to preach the good news; ¹⁵ they were likewise to have authority to expel demons. ¹⁶ He appointed the Twelve as follows: ¹⁷ Simon to whom he gave the name Peter; James, son of Zebedee; and John, the brother of James (he gave these two the name

5: Lk 14, 4.
7-12: Mt 4, 23ff; Lk 6, 17ff.
10: 5, 30.
11: 1, 34; Lk 4, 41.

13-19: Mt 10, 1-4; Lk 6, 12-16.
14: 6, 7.
17: Mt 16, 18; Jn 1, 42.

3, 12: Jesus refuses to receive witness concerning his identity from evil spirits. Since this identity can be known only from divine revelation, Mark does not ascribe true knowledge of Jesus to evil spirits. See note on Mt 16, 17.

3, 13-19: Within the circle of Jesus' disciples, the Twelve were given a privileged position. They alone were present with Jesus at the Last Supper (14, 17). Later they exercised leadership over the primitive community in Jerusalem (Acts 1, 26; 2, 14; 5, 20f), and were responsible for the information about Jesus that developed into the gospel tradition (Acts 6, 2.4).

Boanerges, or "sons of thunder"); [18] Andrew, Philip, Bartholomew, Matthew, Thomas, James son of Alphaeus; Thaddaeus, Simon of the Zealot party, [19] and Judas Iscariot, who betrayed him.

Blasphemy of the Scribes

[20] He returned to the house with them and again the crowd assembled, making it impossible for them to get any food whatever. [21] When his family heard of this they came to take charge of him, saying, "He is out of his mind"; [22] while the scribes who arrived from Jerusalem asserted, "He is possessed by Beelzebul," and "He expels demons with the help of the prince of demons." [23] Summoning them, he then began to speak to them by way of examples: "How can Satan expel Satan? [24] If a kingdom is torn by civil strife, that kingdom cannot last. [25] If a household is divided according to loyalties, that household will not survive. [26] Similarly, if Satan has suffered mutiny in his ranks and is torn by dissension, he cannot endure; he is finished. [27] No one can enter a strong man's house and despoil his property unless he has first put him under restraint. Only than can he plunder his house.

[28] "I give you my word, every sin will be forgiven mankind and all the blasphemies men utter, [29] but whoever blasphemes against the Holy Spirit will never be forgiven. He carries the guilt of his sin without end." [30] He spoke thus because they had said, "He is possessed by an unclean spirit."

Jesus and His Family

[31] His mother and his brothers arrived, and as they stood outside they sent word to him to come out. [32] The crowd seated around him told him, "Your mother and your brothers and sisters are outside asking for you." [33] He said in reply, "Who are my mother and my brothers?" [34] And gazing around him at those seated in the circle he continued, "These are my mother and my brothers. [35] Whoever does the will of God is brother and sister and mother to me."

20: 2, 2.
21: Jn 10, 20.
22-30: Mt 12, 24-32;

Lk 11, 15-22.
28: Lk 12, 10.
31-35: Mt 12, 46-50; Lk 8, 19ff.

3, 20-35: Reactions to the person and teaching of Jesus are varied: the crowds are favorable to him (1, 27.37.45; 2, 15; 3, 8); the scribes and Pharisees are increasingly hostile (2, 13—3, 6); his relatives are unbelieving (3, 20f). Faith in Jesus' prophetic word creates a relationship superior to that between himself and his relatives.

4

Parable of the Seed

¹ On another occasion he began to teach beside the lake. Such a huge crowd gathered around him that he went and sat in a boat on the water, while the crowd remained on the shore nearby. ² He began to instruct them at great length, by the use of parables, and in the course of his teaching said: ³ "Listen carefully to this. A farmer went out sowing. ⁴ Some of what he sowed landed on the footpath, where the birds came along and ate it. ⁵ Some of the seed landed on rocky ground where it had little soil; it sprouted immediately because the soil had no depth. ⁶ Then, when the sun rose and scorched it, it began to wither for lack of roots. ⁷ Again, some landed among thorns, which grew up and choked it off, and there was no yield of grain. ⁸ Some seed, finally, landed on good soil and yielded grain that sprang up to produce at a rate of thirty- and sixty- and a hundredfold." ⁹ Having spoken this parable, he added: "Let him who has ears to hear me, hear!"

¹⁰ Now when he was away from the crowd, those present with the Twelve questioned him about the parables. ¹¹ He told them: "To you the mystery of the reign of God has been confided. To the others outside it is all presented in parables, ¹² so that they will look intently and not see, listen carefully and not understand, lest perhaps they repent and be forgiven."

¹³ He said to them: "You do not understand this parable? How then are you going to understand other figures like it? ¹⁴ What the sower is sowing is the word. ¹⁵ Those on the path are the ones to whom, as soon as they hear the word, Satan comes to carry off what was sown in them. ¹⁶ Similarly, those sown on rocky ground are people who on listening to the word accept it joyfully at the outset. ¹⁷ Being rootless, they last only

---

4, 1-12: Mt 13, 18-23; Lk 8, 4-10. Acts 28, 26; Rom 11, 8.
  1: 2, 13; Lk 5, 1. 13-20: Mt 13, 18-23;
  12: Is 6, 9; Jn 12, 40; Lk 8, 11-15.

4, 1-34: See note on Mt 13, 1-53 for the sense of the parables of the sower, the mustard seed, and the leaven.

4, 10ff: In Mt 13, 10, attention centers on the method of teaching in parables. Jesus gives the same response here as he gave there. The light shed by the parables on the reign of God, though real, is far from complete. For the disciples, well-disposed to accept the teaching, questions are answered; not so for the crowds, ill-prepared at this time to abandon their false preconceptions. Thus Mark indicates a gradual unveiling of the mystery, beginning with the parables and continuing as a slow realization on the part of hearers that the traditional conceptions about God's reign were false and contrary to his plan; cf Mt 13, 33. Divine wisdom is described as justified in this procedure in terms of Is 6, 9f.

a while. When some pressure or persecution overtakes them because of the word, they falter. [18] Those sown among thorns are another class. They have listened to the word, [19] but anxieties over life's demands, and the desire for wealth, and cravings of other sorts come to choke it off; it bears no yield. [20] But those sown on good soil are the ones who listen to the word, take it to heart, and yield at thirty- and sixty- and a hundredfold."

Purpose of This Teaching

[21] He said to them: "Is a lamp acquired to be put under a bushel basket or hidden under a bed? Is it not meant to be put on a stand? [22] Things are hidden only to be revealed at a later time; they are covered so as to be brought out into the open. [23] Let him who has ears to hear me, hear!" [24] He said to them another time: "Listen carefully to what you hear. In the measure you give you shall receive, and more besides. [25] To those who have, more will be given; from those who have not, what little they have will be taken away."

Seed Grows of Itself

[26] He also said: "This is how it is with the reign of God. A man scatters seed on the ground. [27] He goes to bed and gets up day after day. Through it all the seed sprouts and grows without his knowing how it happens. [28] The soil produces of itself first the blade, then the ear, finally the ripe wheat in the ear. [29] When the crop is ready he 'wields the sickle, for the time is ripe for harvest.' "

The Mustard Seed

[30] He went on to say: "What comparison shall we use for the reign of God? What image will help to present it? [31] It is like mustard seed which, when planted in the soil, is the smallest of all the earth's seeds, [32] yet once it is sown, springs up to be-

---

21-25: Lk 8, 16ff.
  21: Mt 5, 15; Lk 11, 33.
  22: Mt 10, 26; Lk 12, 2.
  24: Mt 7, 2; Lk 6, 38.

  25: Mt 13, 12; Lk 19, 26.
26-29: Jas 5, 7.
30-32: Mt 13, 31f; Lk 13, 18f.

4, 21-25: These sayings, found in other contexts as well (Mt 5, 15; 7, 2; 10, 26; 13, 12), are here presented as commentary on the revelation of the reign of God. Jesus' teaching in parables begins this revelation (21); time and events will make it more clear (22). Acceptance of the original light gives promise of more in the future (24). Conversely, rejection of that light results in greater obscurity and misunderstanding (25).
4, 26-29: This parable is found only in Mark. Through the ministry of Jesus, God's sovereign rule over men is made manifest. It comes without warning; it is destined to spread throughout the world and to continue for the length of time set by God.

come the largest of shrubs, with branches big enough for the birds of the sky to build nests in its shade." [33] By means of many such parables he taught them the message in a way they could understand. [34] To them he spoke only by way of parable, while he kept explaining things privately to his disciples.

The Storm on the Sea

[35] That day as evening drew on he said to them, "Let us cross over to the farther shore." [36] Leaving the crowd, they took him away in the boat in which he was sitting, while the other boats accompanied him. [37] It happened that a bad squall blew up. The waves were breaking over the boat and it began to ship water badly. [38] Jesus was in the stern through it all, sound asleep on a cushion. They finally woke him and said to him, "Teacher, does it not matter to you that we are going to drown?" [39] He awoke and rebuked the wind and said to the sea: "Quiet! Be still!" The wind fell off and everything grew calm. [40] Then he said to them, "Why are you so terrified? Why are you lacking in faith?" [41] A great awe overcame them at this. They kept saying to one another, "Who can this be that the wind and the sea obey him?"

5

Expulsion of the Devils in Gerasa

[1] They came to Gerasene territory on the other side of the lake. [2] As he got out of the boat, he was immediately met by a man from the tombs who had an unclean spirit. [3] The man had taken refuge among the tombs; he could no longer be restrained even with a chain. [4] In fact, he had frequently been secured with handcuffs and chains, but had pulled the chains apart and smashed the fetters. No one had proved strong enough to tame him. [5] Uninterruptedly night and day, amid the tombs and on the hillsides, he screamed and gashed himself with stones. [6] Catching sight of Jesus at a distance, he ran up and did him homage, [7] shrieking in a loud voice, "Why meddle with me, Jesus, Son of God Most High? I implore you in God's name,

---

35-40: Mt 8, 18.23-27;
　　　Lk 8, 22-25.
41: 1, 27.

5, 1-17: Mt 8, 28-34;
　　　　Lk 8, 26-37.

4, 33f: See note on 4, 10ff.
4, 35-41: The sequence of action in this event is rearranged in Mt 8, 23-27 to teach the Christian community what great trust in Jesus it must have in time of peril. In Mark, the disciples' panic is reflected in their reproachful question to Jesus. He in return interprets the event for them as showing the need for absolute confidence in him.

do not torture me!" [8] (Jesus had been saying to him, "Unclean spirit, come out of the man!") [9] "What is your name?" Jesus asked him. "Legion is my name," he answered. "There are hundreds of us." [10] He pleaded hard with Jesus not to drive them away from that neighborhood.

[11] It happened that a large herd of swine was feeding there on the slope of the mountain. [12] "Send us into the swine," they begged him. "Let us enter them." [13] He gave the word, and with it the unclean spirits came out and entered the swine. The herd of about two thousand went rushing down the bluff into the lake, where they began to drown. [14] The swineherds ran off and brought the news to field and village, and the people came to see what had happened. [15] As they approached Jesus, they caught sight of the man who had been possessed by Legion sitting fully clothed and perfectly sane, and they were seized with fear. [16] The spectators explained what had happened to the possessed man, and told them about the swine. [17] Before long they were begging him to go away from their district. [18] As Jesus was getting into the boat, the man who had been possessed was pressing to accompany him. [19] Jesus did not grant his request, but told him instead: "Go home to your family and make it clear to them how much the Lord in his mercy has done for you." [20] At that the man went off and began to proclaim throughout the Ten Cities what Jesus had done for him. They were all amazed at what they heard.

The Daughter of Jairus; the Woman with a Hemorrhage

[21] Now when Jesus had crossed back to the other side again in the boat, a large crowd gathered around him and he stayed close to the lake. [22] One of the officials of the synagogue, a man named Jairus, came near. [23] Seeing Jesus, he fell at his feet and made this earnest appeal: "My little daughter is critically ill. Please come and lay your hands on her so that she may get well and live." [24] The two went off together and a large crowd followed, pushing against Jesus.

9: Mt 12, 45; Lk 8, 2; 11, 26.
21: 2, 13.

22-43: Mt 9, 18-26; Lk 8, 41-56.

5, 21-43: This narrative is significant for Christology. Jesus knows that a cure has occurred in favor of someone who touched him; he does not know the person's identity (30). Informed of the death of Jairus' daughter, he decides his course of action from the development of events; he recognizes in them the divine will to raise the girl to life (35f). His assertion, *The child is not dead. She is asleep*, leaves the girl's condition unclear (38), so that he can more easily prohibit the witnesses from speaking of the event as an unmistakable manifestation of his power to raise the dead (43).

²⁵ There was a woman in the area who had been afflicted with a hemorrhage for a dozen years. ²⁶ She had received treatment at the hands of doctors of every sort and exhausted her savings in the process, yet she got no relief; on the contrary, she only grew worse. ²⁷ She had heard about Jesus and came up behind him in the crowd and put her hand to his cloak. ²⁸ "If I just touch his clothing," she thought, "I shall get well." ²⁹ Immediately her flow of blood dried up and the feeling that she was cured of her affliction ran through her whole body. ³⁰ Jesus was conscious at once that healing power had gone out from him. Wheeling about in the crowd, he began to ask, "Who touched my clothing?" ³¹ His disciples said to him, "You can see how this crowd hems you in, yet you ask, 'Who touched me?' ³² Despite this, he kept looking around to see the woman who had done it. ³³ Fearful and beginning to tremble now as she realized what had happened, the woman came and fell in front of him and told him the whole truth. ³⁴ He said to her, "Daughter, it is your faith that has cured you. Go in peace and be free of this illness."

³⁵ He had not finished speaking when people from the official's house arrived saying, "Your daughter is dead. Why bother the Teacher further?" ³⁶ Jesus disregarded the report that had been brought and said to the official: "Fear is useless. What is needed is trust." ³⁷ He would not permit anyone to follow him except Peter, James, and James's brother John. ³⁸ As they approached the house of the synagogue leader, Jesus was struck by the noise of people wailing and crying loudly on all sides. ³⁹ He entered and said to them: "Why do you make this din with your wailing? The child is not dead. She is asleep." ⁴⁰ At this they began to ridicule him. Then he put them all out.

Jesus took the child's father and mother and his own companions and entered the room where the child lay. ⁴¹ Taking her hand he said to her, *"Talitha, koum,"* which means, "Little girl, get up." ⁴² The girl, a child of twelve, stood up immediately and began to walk around. At this the family's astonishment knew no bounds. ⁴³ He enjoined them strictly not to let anyone know about it, and told them to give her something to eat.

6

Jesus at Nazareth

¹ He departed from there and returned to his own part of

34: Lk 7, 50.
39f: Acts 9, 40.

6, 1-6: Mt 13, 54-58;
Lk 4, 16-30.

the country followed by his disciples. ² When the sabbath came he began to teach in the synagogue in a way that kept his large audience amazed. They said: "Where did he get all this? What kind of wisdom is he endowed with? How is it that such miraculous deeds are accomplished by his hands? ³ Is this not the carpenter, the son of Mary, a brother of James and Joses and Judas and Simon? Are not his sisters our neighbors here?" They found him too much for them. ⁴ Jesus' response to all this was: "No prophet is without honor except in his native place, among his own kindred, and in his own house." ⁵ He could work no miracle there, apart from curing a few who were sick by laying hands on them, ⁶ so much did their lack of faith distress him. He made the rounds of the neighboring villages instead, and spent his time teaching.

Mission of the Twelve

⁷ Jesus summoned the Twelve and began to send them out two by two, giving them authority over unclean spirits. ⁸ He instructed them to take nothing on the journey but a walking stick—no food, no traveling bag, not a coin in the purses in their belts. ⁹ They were, however, to wear sandals. "Do not bring a second tunic," he said, ¹⁰ and added: "Whatever house you find yourself in, stay there until you leave the locality. ¹¹ If any place will not receive you or hear you, shake its dust from your feet in testimony against them as you leave." ¹² With that they went off, preaching the need of repentance. ¹³ They expelled many demons, anointed the sick with oil, and worked many cures.

Death of the Baptizer

¹⁴ King Herod came to hear of Jesus, for his reputation had become widespread and people were saying, "John the Baptizer has been raised from the dead; that is why such miraculous

---

3: 15, 40; Mt 12, 46; Jn 6, 42.
4: Jn 4, 44.
7-11: Mt 10, 1.9-14; Lk 9, 1; 10, 4-11.
13: Jas 5, 14.
14f: Lk 9, 7f.
14-29: Mt 14, 1-12.

6, 1-6: The townsmen of Jesus were not disposed to believe in him because he had not first exercised his power of miracles in their midst (2f). *"Is this not the carpenter . . . our neighbors here?":* some manuscripts have. "Is this not the carpenter's son?" The question about the brothers of Jesus and *his sisters* (V3) cannot easily be decided on linguistic grounds. Greek-speaking Semites used the terms *adelphos* and *adelphē,* not only in the ordinary sense of blood brother and sister, but also for nephew, niece, half-brother, half-sister, and cousin. The question of meaning here would not have arisen but for the faith of the church in Mary's perpetual virginity.

powers are at work in him." [15] Others were saying, "He is Elijah"; still others, "He is a prophet equal to any of the prophets." [16] On hearing of Jesus, Herod exclaimed, "John, whose head I had cut off, has been raised up!" [17] Herod was the one who had ordered John arrested, chained, and imprisoned on account of Herodias, the wife of his brother Philip, whom he had married. [18] That was because John had told Herod, "It is not right for you to live with your brother's wife." [19] Herodias harbored a grudge against him for this and wanted to kill him but was unable to do so. [20] Herod feared John, knowing him to be an upright and holy man, and kept him in custody. When he heard him speak he was very much disturbed; yet he felt the attraction of his words. [21] Herodias had her chance one day when Herod held a birthday dinner for his court circle, military officers, and the leading men of Galilee. [22] Herodias' own daughter came in at one point and performed a dance which delighted Herod and his guests. The king told the girl, "Ask for anything you want and I will give it to you." [23] He went so far as to swear to her: "I will grant you whatever you ask, even to half my kingdom!" [24] She went out and said to her mother, "What shall I ask for?" The mother answered, "The head of John the Baptizer." [25] At that the girl hurried back to the king's presence and made her request: "I want you to give me, at once, the head of John the Baptizer on a platter." [26] The king bitterly regretted the request; yet because of his oath and the presence of the guests, he did not want to refuse her. [27] He promptly dispatched an executioner, ordering him to bring back the Baptizer's head. [28] The man went and beheaded John in the prison. He brought in the head on a platter and gave it to the girl, and the girl gave it to her mother. [29] Later, when his disciples heard about this, they came and carried his body away and laid it in a tomb.

Return of the Disciples

[30] The apostles returned to Jesus and reported to him all that they had done and what they had taught. [31] He said to them, "Come by yourselves to an out-of-the-way place and rest a little." People were coming and going in great numbers, making it impossible for them to so much as eat. [32] So Jesus and the

15: Mt 16, 14.
17: Lk 3, 19f.
18: Lv 18, 16.
23: Est 5, 3.
27f: Lk 9, 9.

31: 3, 20; Mt 14, 13; Lk 9, 10.
32-44: Mt 14, 13-21; Lk 9, 10-17; Jn 6, 1-13.

apostles went off in the boat by themselves to a deserted place. [33] People saw them leaving, and many got to know about it. People from all the towns hastened on foot to the place, arriving ahead of them.

Jesus Feeds Five Thousand

[34] Upon disembarking Jesus saw a vast crowd. He pitied them, for they were like sheep without a shepherd; and he began to teach them at great length. [35] It was now getting late and his disciples came to him with a suggestion: "This is a deserted place and it is already late. [36] Why do you not dismiss them so that they can go to the crossroads and villages around here and buy themselves something to eat?" [37] "You give them something to eat," Jesus replied. At that they said, "Are we to go and spend two hundred days' wages for bread to feed them?" [38] "How many loaves have you?" Jesus asked. "Go and see." When they learned the number they answered, "Five, and two fish." [39] He told them to make the people sit down on the green grass in groups or parties. [40] The people took their places in hundreds and fifties, neatly arranged like flower beds. [41] Then, taking the five loaves and the two fish, Jesus raised his eyes to heaven, pronounced a blessing, broke the loaves, and gave them to the disciples to distribute. He divided the two fish among all of them [42] and they ate until they had their fill. [43] They gathered up enough leftovers to fill twelve baskets, besides what remained of the fish. [44] Those who had eaten the loaves numbered five thousand men.

Jesus Walks on the Water

[45] Immediately afterward he insisted that his disciples get into the boat and precede him to the other side toward Bethsaida, while he dismissed the crowd. [46] When he had taken leave of them, he went off to the mountain to pray. [47] As evening drew on, the boat was far out on the lake while he was alone on the land. [48] Then, seeing them tossed about as they tried to row with the wind against them, he came walking toward them on the water; the time was between three and six in the morning. He meant to pass them by. [49] When they saw him walking

---

45-51: Mt 14, 22-32; Jn 6, 15-21.

6, 45-52: Mt 14, 22-33 and Jn 6, 15-21, as well as Mark, place the event of Jesus' walking on the sea after the miracle of the loaves and fish. The disciples would not have been so astonished at it had they understood the meaning of the multiplication of the loaves (51f). But contrast Matthew's conclusion in 14, 33.

on the lake, they thought it was a ghost and they began to cry out. [50] They had all seen him and were terrified. He hastened to reassure them: "Get hold of yourselves! It is I. Do not be afraid!" [51] He got into the boat with them and the wind died down. They were taken aback by these happenings, [52] for they had not understood about the loaves. On the contrary, their minds were completely closed to the meaning of the events.

Other Miracles

[53] After making the crossing they came ashore at Gennesaret, and tied up there. [54] As they were leaving the boat people immediately recognized him. [55] The crowds scurried about the adjacent area and began to bring in the sick on bedrolls to the place where they heard he was. [56] Wherever he put in an appearance, in villages, in towns, or at crossroads, they laid the sick in the market places and begged him to let them touch just the tassel of his cloak. All who touched him got well.

7

Jesus and the Pharisees

[1] The Pharisees and some of the experts in the law who had come from Jerusalem gathered around him. [2] They had observed a few of his disciples eating meals without having purified— that is to say, washed—their hands. [3] The Pharisees, and in fact all Jews, cling to the custom of their ancestors and never eat without scrupulously washing their hands. [4] Moreover, they never eat anything from the market without first sprinkling it. There are many other traditions they observe—for example, the washing of cups and jugs and kettles. [5] So the Pharisees and the scribes questioned him: "Why do your disciples not follow the tradition of our ancestors, but instead take food without purifying their hands?" [6] He said to them: "How accurately Isaiah prophesied about you hypocrites when he wrote,

---

52: 4, 13.
56: 5, 27f; Acts 5, 15.

7, 1-30: Mt 15, 1-28.
6: Is 29, 13.

6, 53-56: This summary statement conveys the popular faith in Jesus. *Came ashore at Gennesaret:* in Jn 6, 24 the name of the place is Capernaum, an apparent indication of two traditions underlying the account.

7, 1-23: The reference to ceremonial washings (2ff) reflects, no doubt, the opposition of the early Christian communities to them. Jesus is described as criticizing the overconcern of the scribes and Pharisees for their traditions to the neglect of the commandments enunciated in the Scriptures (6ff); see note on Mt 15, 5f. Even among Gentile Christians scruples existed concerning the moral implications supposedly inherent in the eating of certain foods (Rom 14, 2f.6), a fact that accounts for the editorial observation in Mk 7, 19.

'This people pays me lip service
but their heart is far from me.
[7] Empty is the reverence they do me
because they teach as dogmas
mere human precepts.'

[8] You disregard God's commandment and cling to what is human tradition."

[9] He went on to say: "You have made a fine art of setting aside God's commandment in the interests of keeping your traditions! [10] For example, Moses said, 'Honor your father and your mother'; and in another place, 'Whoever curses father or mother shall be put to death.' [11] Yet you declare, 'If a person says to his father or mother, Any support you might have had from me is *korban*' (that is, dedicated to God), [12] you allow him to do nothing more for his father or mother. [13] That is the way you nullify God's word in favor of the traditions you have handed on. And you have many other such practices besides." [14] He summoned the crowd again and said to them: "Hear me, all of you, and try to understand. [15] Nothing that enters a man from outside can make him impure; that which comes out of him, and only that, constitutes impurity. [16] Let everyone heed what he hears!"

[17] When he got home, away from the crowd, his disciples questioned him about the proverb. [18] "Are you, too, incapable of understanding?" he asked them. "Do you not see that nothing that enters a man from outside can make him impure? [19] It does not penetrate his being, but enters his stomach only and passes into the latrine." Thus did he render all foods clean. [20] He went on: "What emerges from within a man, that and nothing else is what makes him impure. [21] Wicked designs come from the deep recesses of the heart: acts of fornication, theft, murder, [22] adulterous conduct, greed, maliciousness, deceit, sensuality, envy, blasphemy, arrogance, an obtuse spirit. [23] All these evils come from within and render a man impure."

A Canaanite Woman

[24] From that place he went off to the territory of Tyre and

---

10: Ex 21, 17; Lv 20, 9;
Dt 5, 16; Eph 6, 2.
14-23: Mt 15, 10-20.
17: 4, 10.13.

19: Acts 10, 15.
21: Jer 17, 9.
24-30: Mt 15, 21-28.

7, 24-30: The Syro-Phoenician woman ascribes her daughter's illness to an evil spirit. The mind of the time was inclined to attribute the more

Sidon. He retired to a certain house and wanted no one to recognize him; however, he could not escape notice. 25 Soon a woman, whose small daughter had an unclean spirit, heard about him. She approached him and crouched at his feet. 26 The woman who was Greek—a Syro-Phoenician by birth—began to beg him to expel the demon from her daughter. 27 He told her: "Let the sons of the household satisfy themselves at table first. It is not right to take the food of the children and throw it to the dogs." 28 "Please, Lord," she replied, "even the dogs under the table eat the family's leavings." 29 Then he said to her, "For such a reply, be off now! The demon has already left your daughter." 30 When she got home, she found the child lying in bed and the demon gone.

Healing of a Deaf-mute

31 He then left Tyrian territory and returned by way of Sidon to the Sea of Galilee, into the district of the Ten Cities. 32 Some people brought him a deaf man who had a speech impediment and begged him to lay his hand on him. 33 Jesus took him off by himself away from the crowd. He put his fingers into the man's ears and, spitting, touched his tongue; 34 then he looked up to heaven and emitted a groan. He said to him, *"Ephphata!"* (that is, "Be opened!") 35 At once the man's ears were opened; he was freed from the impediment, and began to speak plainly. 36 Then he enjoined them strictly not to tell anyone; but the more he ordered them not to, the more they proclaimed it. 37 Their amazement went beyond all bounds: "He has done everything well! He makes the deaf hear and the mute speak!"

8

Jesus Feeds Four Thousand

1 At about that time another large crowd assembled, and they

26: Mt 8, 29.
31-37: Mt 15, 29ff.

37: Mt 15, 31.
8, 1-10: Mt 15, 32-39; 6, 34-44.

---

baffling sicknesses to satanic power. Without contesting the woman's assertion, Jesus pronounces the curing word in the same terms: *The demon has already left your daughter.*
Jewish authors sometimes used the term "dogs" of Gentiles to express their scorn of paganism. Because the woman's subtle response acknowledges her dependence on the God of Israel, whom Jesus represents, he cures her daughter.
7, 31-37: The actions attributed to Jesus (33f) were used by healers of the time, who considered them effective in themselves. With Jesus, however, they have a sacramental purpose inasmuch as they are effective by his power through his relation to the Father: cf Jn 11, 41; 17, 1.
8, 1-9: Many scholars regard this as a second version of the one multiplication of loaves, set in a Gentile context because of the eucharistic sig-

were without anything to eat. He called the disciples over to him and said: [2] "My heart is moved with pity for the crowd. By now they have been with me three days and have nothing to eat. [3] If I send them home hungry, they will collapse on the way. Some of them have come a great distance." [4] His disciples replied, "How can anyone give these people sufficient bread in this deserted spot?" [5] Still he asked them, "How many loaves do you have?" "Seven," they replied. [6] Then he directed the crowd to take their places on the ground. Taking the seven loaves he gave thanks, broke them, and gave them to his disciples to distribute, and they handed them out to the crowd. [7] They also had a few small fish; asking a blessing on the fish, he told them to distribute these also. [8] The people in the crowd ate until they had their fill; then they gathered up seven wicker baskets of leftovers. [9] Those who had eaten numbered about four thousand.

[10] He dismissed them and got into the boat with his disciples to go to the neighborhood of Dalmanutha.

The Pharisees Ask a Sign

[11] The Pharisees came forward and began to argue with him. They were looking for some heavenly sign from him as a test. [12] With a sigh from the depths of his spirit he said, "Why does this age seek a sign? I assure you, no such sign will be given it!" [13] Then he left them, got into the boat again, and went off to the other shore.

The Leaven of the Pharisees

[14] They had forgotten to bring any bread along; except for one loaf they had none with them in the boat. [15] So when he instructed them, "Keep your eyes open! Be on your guard against the yeast of the Pharisees and the yeast of Herod," [16] they concluded among themselves that it was because they had no

---

11ff: Mt 12, 38f; 16, 1-4.
11: Lk 11, 16.

14f: Mt 16, 5f; Lk 12, 1.

---

nificance which the early Christian communities saw in it. Note that in this account Jesus' initiative in feeding the crowd is emphasized; the disciples appear helpless except in dependence on him (2ff).

8, 11f: The Pharisees object that the miracles wrought by Jesus are unsatisfactory as proof of the arrival of God's reign. This is comparable to the complaint in Jn 6, 30f. Jesus replies that a request for a sign which originates in human distrust will not be provided.

8, 15: *Be on your guard against the yeast . . . of Herod:* Mt 16, 12 explains the leaven as the teaching of the religious authorities; Lk 12, 1 takes it to symbolize their hypocrisy. In the light of Mk 8, 11f, the reference here is to their deep-seated hostility toward Jesus, which for different reasons Herod also shares.

bread. [17] Aware of this he said to them, "Why do you suppose that it is because you have no bread? Do you still not see or comprehend? Are your minds completely blinded? [18] Have you eyes but no sight? Ears but no hearing? [19] Do you remember when I broke the five loaves for the five thousand, how many baskets of fragments did you collect?" They answered, "Twelve." [20] When I broke the seven loaves for the four thousand, how many full hampers of fragments did you collect?" They answered, "Seven." [21] He said to them again, "Do you still not understand?"

A Blind Man at Bethsaida

[22] When they arrived at Bethsaida, some people brought him a blind man and begged him to touch him. [23] Jesus took the blind man's hand and led him outside the village. Putting spittle on his eyes he laid his hands on him and asked, "Can you see anything?" [24] The man opened his eyes and said, "I can see people but they look like walking trees!" [25] Then a second time Jesus laid hands on his eyes, and he saw perfectly; his sight was restored and he could see everything clearly. [26] Jesus sent him home with the admonition, "Do not even go into the village."

III: THE MYSTERY BEGINS TO BE REVEALED

The Messiah

[27] Then Jesus and his disciples set out for the villages around Caesarea Philippi. On the way he asked his disciples this question: "Who do people say that I am?" [28] They replied, "Some, John the Baptizer, others, Elijah, still others, one of the prophets." [29] "And you," he went on to ask, "who do you say that I am?" Peter answered him, "You are the Messiah!" [30] Then he gave them strict orders not to tell anyone about him.

17: 4, 13.
18: Jer 5, 21; Ez 12, 2.

23: 7, 33; Jn 9, 6.
27ff: Mt 16, 13-16; Lk 9, 18ff.

8, 22-26: Jesus' actions and the gradual cure of the blind man probably have the same purpose as in the case of the deaf man; see note on 7, 31-37. Some authors regard the cure as an intended symbol of the gradual enlightenment of the disciples concerning the difference between Jesus' teaching and the views of the authorities.

8, 27-30: This episode marks a turning point in Mark's portrait of Jesus in his public ministry. Varieties of popular opinion concerning him concur in regarding him as a prophet. The disciples, by contrast, believe him to be the Messiah. He is described as acknowledging this identification, but prohibits them from making his messianic office known.

First Teaching of the Paschal Event

³¹ He began to teach them that the Son of Man had to suffer much, be rejected by the elders, the chief priests, and the scribes, be put to death, and rise three days later. ³² He said these things quite openly. Peter then took him aside and began to remonstrate with him. ³³ At this he turned around and, eyeing the disciples, reprimanded Peter: "Get out of my sight, you satan! You are not judging by God's standards but by man's!"

The Doctrine of the Cross

³⁴ He summoned the crowd with his disciples and said to them: "If a man wishes to come after me, he must deny his very self, take up his cross, and follow in my steps. ³⁵ Whoever would preserve his life will lose it, but whoever loses his life for my sake and the gospel's will preserve it. ³⁶ What profit does a man show who gains the whole world and destroys himself in the process? ³⁷ What can a man offer in exchange for his life? ³⁸ If anyone in this faithless and corrupt age is ashamed of me and my doctrine, the Son of Man will be ashamed of him when he comes with the holy angels in his Father's glory."

9

¹ He also said to them: "I assure you, among those standing here there are some who will not taste death until they see the reign of God established in power."

Jesus Transfigured

² Six days later, Jesus took Peter, James, and John off by

31-38: Mt 16, 21-27;
          Lk 9, 22-26.
    34: Mt 10, 38f; 16, 24-27;
          Lk 14, 26f.

35: Jn 12, 25.
38: Mt 10, 33; Lk 12, 8.
9, 2-13: Mt 17, 1-13;
          Lk 9, 28-36.

8, 31ff: *Son of Man:* an enigmatic title. Jewish apocryphal tradition (1 Enoch, 4 Ezra, 2 Baruch) uses it to describe a unique religious personage, a messiah with extraordinary spiritual endowments. Jesus' use of it seems to derive from Ez 2, where it is a title of humility, and Dn 7, 13f, where it indicates a clearly messianic figure. It expresses for him his twofold destiny, of suffering (8, 31; 9, 11.31; 10, 33; 12, 31; 14, 21) and of glory (8, 38; 12, 36; 14, 62). Peter, along with the other disciples, fails (despite his confession) to grasp the association of suffering and death with the office of Messiah.

8, 34—9, 1: Mt 16, 24-28 and Lk 9, 23-27 place these sayings in the same context as Mark, namely, Peter's messianic confession and Jesus' rebuke to Peter and the disciples in the prophecy of the passion. Mark and Luke apply the doctrine of the cross to Christians in general. The disciples are instructed to sacrifice even life itself to follow Jesus (34). To strengthen their waning confidence, Jesus foretells that some of them will live to see the arrival of the reign of God in power (9, 1).

9, 2-8: The synoptic gospels place the transfiguration of Jesus six days

themselves with him and led them up a high mountain. He was transfigured before their eyes [3] and his clothes became dazzlingly white—whiter than the work of any bleacher could make them. [4] Elijah appeared to them along with Moses; the two were in conversation with Jesus. [5] Then Peter spoke to Jesus: "Rabbi, how good it is for us to be here! Let us erect three booths on this site, one for you, one for Moses, and one for Elijah." [6] He hardly knew what to say, for they were all overcome with awe. [7] A cloud came, overshadowing them, and out of the cloud a voice: "This is my Son, my beloved. Listen to him." [8] Suddenly looking around they no longer saw anyone with them—only Jesus.

On the Coming of Elijah

[9] As they were coming down the mountain, he strictly enjoined them not to tell anyone what they had seen, before the Son of Man had risen from the dead. [10] They kept this word of his to themselves, though they continued to discuss what "to rise from the dead" meant. [11] Finally they put to him this question: "Why do the scribes claim that Elijah must come first?" [12] He told them: "Elijah will indeed come first and restore everything. Yet why does Scripture say of the Son of Man that he must suffer much and be despised? [13] Let me assure you, Elijah has already come. They did entirely as they pleased with him, as the Scriptures say of him."

A Possessed Boy

[14] As they approached the disciples, they saw a large crowd standing around, and scribes in lively discussion with them. [15] Immediately on catching sight of Jesus, the whole crowd was

---

9: 8, 31.
11f: Is 53, 3; Mal 3, 23.
13: 1 Kgs 19, 2-10.

14-29: Mt 17, 14-21;
Lk 9, 37-44.

---

after the first prediction of his passion and death and his instruction to the disciples on the doctrine of the cross (Mt 17, 1-8; Lk 9, 28-36). Thus it counterbalances the prediction of the passion by affording certain of the disciples' insight into the divine glory which he possessed. His glory will overcome his death and that of his disciples; cf 2 Pt 1, 16ff; 2 Cor 3, 18. The heavenly voice (6) prepares the disciples to understand that in the divine plan Jesus must die ignominiously before his messianic glory is made manifest; cf Lk 24, 25ff. The appearance of Moses and Elijah indicates that the purpose of both the law and the prophets was to prepare for Christ.

9, 14-29: The disciples' failure to effect a cure seems to reflect unfavorably on Jesus (14-18). In response, he exposes their lack of trust in God (19) and scores their neglect of prayer, i.e., of the conscious reliance on God's power when acting in Jesus' name. Mark and Matthew (17, 14-18) concur on this point; Luke (9, 37-43) centers attention on Jesus' sovereign power.

overcome with awe. They ran up to greet him. [16] He asked them, "What are you discussing among yourselves?" [17] "Teacher," a man in the crowd replied, "I have brought my son to you because he is possessed by a mute spirit. [18] Whenever it seizes him it throws him down; he foams at the mouth and grinds his teeth and becomes rigid. Just now I asked your disciples to expel him, but they were unable to do so." [19] He replied by saying to the crowd, "What an unbelieving lot you are! How long must I remain with you? How long can I endure you? Bring him to me." [20] When they did so the spirit caught sight of Jesus and immediately threw the boy into convulsions. As he fell to the ground he began to roll around and foam at the mouth. [21] Then Jesus questioned the father: "How long has this been happening to him?" "From childhood," the father replied. [22] "Often it throws him into fire and into water. You would think it would kill him. If out of the kindness of your heart you can do anything to help us, please do!" [23] Jesus said, "'If you can'? Everything is possible to a man who trusts." [24] The boy's father immediately exclaimed, "I do believe! Help my lack of trust!" [25] Jesus, on seeing a crowd rapidly gathering, reprimanded the unclean spirit by saying to him, "Mute and deaf spirit, I command you: Get out of him and never enter him again!" [26] Shouting, and throwing the boy into convulsions, it came out of him; the boy became like a corpse, which caused many to say, "He is dead." [27] But Jesus took him by the hand and helped him to his feet. [28] When Jesus arrived at the house his disciples began to ask him privately, "Why is it that we could not expel it?" [29] He told them, "This kind you can drive out only by prayer."

Second Teaching: Passion and Resurrection

[30] They left that district and began a journey through Galilee, but he did not want anyone to know about it. [31] He was teaching the disciples in this vein: "The Son of Man is going to be delivered into the hands of men who will put him to death; three days after his death he will rise." [32] Though they failed to understand his words, they were afraid to question him.

30: Jn 7, 1.   Lk 9, 44.
31: 8, 31; Mt 17, 22;   32: Lk 9, 45.

9, 30ff: Although the disciples heard Jesus' new prediction concerning his passion, they failed to accept its truth because they did not understand his messianic role.

IV: THE FULL REVELATION OF THE MYSTERY

Against Ambition and Envy

³³ They returned to Capernaum and Jesus, once inside the house, began to ask them, "What were you discussing on the way home?" ³⁴ At this they fell silent, for on the way they had been arguing about who was the most important. ³⁵ So he sat down and called the Twelve around him and said, "If anyone wishes to rank first, he must remain the last one of all and the servant of all." ³⁶ Then he took a little child, stood him in their midst, and putting his arms around him, said to them, ³⁷ "Whoever welcomes a child such as this for my sake welcomes me. And whoever welcomes me welcomes, not me, but him who sent me."

³⁸ John said to him, "Teacher, we saw a man using your name to expel demons and we tried to stop him because he is not of our company." ³⁹ Jesus said in reply: "Do not try to stop him. No man who performs a miracle using my name can at the same time speak ill of me. ⁴⁰ Anyone who is not against us is with us. ⁴¹ Any man who gives you a drink of water because you belong to Christ will not, I assure you, go without his reward. ⁴² But it would be better if anyone who leads astray one of these simple believers were to be plunged in the sea with a great millstone fastened around his neck.

⁴³ "If your hand is your difficulty, cut it off! Better for you to enter life maimed than to keep both hands and enter Gehenna with its unquenchable fire. ⁴⁵ If your foot is your undoing, cut it off! Better for you to enter life crippled than to be thrown into Gehenna with both feet. ⁴⁷ If your eye is your downfall,

---

33-37: Mt 18, 1-5; Lk 9, 46ff.	Lk 9, 49f.
35: Mt 20, 27.	40: Mt 12, 30.
37: Mt 9, 40; 18, 5;	41: Mt 10, 42; 1 Cor 3, 23.
Jn 13, 20.	42-47: Mt 5, 29f; 18, 6-9.
38-41: Nm 11, 28; 1 Cor 12, 3;	42: Lk 17, 2.

9, 33-37: The evangelist probably intends this incident and the sayings that follow as a commentary on the disciples' lack of undersanding (9, 32). Their role in Jesus' work is one of service, especially to the poor and lowly. For this concept of the child, see note on Mt 19, 13ff.
9, 38-41: Jesus warns against jealousy and intolerance toward good works, such as exorcism, performed in his name by those whose faith is imperfect. The saying in 9, 40 is a broad principle of the divine tolerance: God repays men for the smallest courtesies they show to those who teach in Jesus' name.
9, 42-50: A collection of Jesus' sayings, rather loosely connected. Vv 44 and 46 are omitted here as additions to the text taken from v 48 and a modified citation of Is 66, 24. The concluding sayings in vv 49f probably allude to the sacrifices required for loyal adherence to the teaching of Jesus. For the imagery of salt, cf Lv 2, 13 and note.
9,44.46: Not found in many manuscripts.

tear it out! Better for you to enter the kingdom of God with one eye than to be thrown with both eyes into Gehenna, [48] where 'the worm dies not and the fire is never extinguished.' [49] Everyone will be salted with fire. [50] Salt is excellent in its place; but if salt becomes tasteless, how can you season it? Keep salt in your hearts and you will be at peace with one another."

10

[1] From there he moved on to the districts of Judea and across the Jordan. Once more crowds gathered around him, and as usual he began to teach them.

The Question of Divorce

[2] Then some Pharisees came up and as a test began to ask him whether it was permissible for a husband to divorce his wife. [3] In reply he said, "What command did Moses give you?" [4] They answered, "Moses permitted divorce and the writing of a decree of divorce." [5] But Jesus told them: "He wrote that commandment for you because of your stubbornness. [6] At the beginning of creation God made them male and female; [7] for this reason a man shall leave his father and mother [8] and the two shall become as one. They are no longer two but one flesh. [9] Therefore let no man separate what God has joined." [10] Back in the house again, the disciples began to question him about this. [11] He told them, "Whoever divorces his wife and marries another commits adultery against her; [12] and the woman who divorces her husband and marries another commits adultery."

Jesus Blesses the Children

[13] People were bringing their little children to him to have him touch them, but the disciples were scolding them for this. [14] Jesus became indignant when he noticed it and said to them: "Let the children come to me and do not hinder them. It is to just such as these that the kingdom of God belongs. [15] I assure you that whoever does not accept the reign of God like a little

48: Is 66, 24.
50: Lv 2, 13; Mt 5, 13;
    Lk 14, 34f; Col 4, 6.
10, 2-12: Mt 19, 3-9.
    4: Dt 24, 1-4.
    6: Gn 1, 27.
    7f: Gn 2, 24; 1 Cor 6, 16;

Eph 5, 31.
11f: Mt 5, 32; Lk 16, 18;
    1 Cor 7, 10f.
13-16: Mt 19, 13ff;
    Lk 18, 15ff.
13: Lk 9, 47.
15: Mt 18, 3.

10, 1-12: See notes on Mt 19, 3-8 and 19, 9.
10, 13-16: See note on Mt 19, 13ff.

child shall not take part in it." ¹⁶ Then he embraced them and blessed them, placing his hands on them.

The Danger of Riches

¹⁷ As he was setting out on a journey a man came running up, knelt down before him and asked, "Good Teacher, what must I do to share in everlasting life?" ¹⁸ Jesus answered, "Why do you call me good? No one is good but God alone. ¹⁹ You know the commandments:

> 'You shall not kill;
> You shall not commit adultery;
> You shall not steal;
> You shall not bear false witness;
> You shall not defraud;
> Honor your father and your mother.' "

²⁰ He replied, "Teacher, I have kept all these since my childhood." ²¹ Then Jesus looked at him with love and told him, "There is one thing more you must do. Go and sell what you have and give to the poor; you will then have treasure in heaven. ²² After that, come and follow me." ²² At these words the man's face fell. He went away sad, for he had many possessions. ²³ Jesus looked around and said to his disciples, "How hard it is for the rich to enter the kingdom of God!" ²⁴ The disciples could only marvel at his words. So Jesus repeated what he had said: "My sons, how hard it is to enter the kingdom of God! ²⁵ It is easier for a camel to pass through a needle's eye than for a rich man to enter the kingdom of God."

²⁶ They were completely overwhelmed at this, and exclaimed to one another, "Then who can be saved?" ²⁷ Jesus fixed his gaze on them and said, "For man it is impossible but not for God. With God all things are possible."

²⁸ Peter was moved to say to him: "We have put aside everything to follow you!" ²⁹ Jesus answered: "I give you my word, there is no one who has given up home, brothers or sisters, mother or father, children or property, for me, and for the

---

17-31: Mt 19, 16-30;
      Lk 18, 18-30.
19: Ex 20, 12-16;

Dt 5, 16-21.
23: Prv 11, 28.

10, 17f: Jesus' repudiation of the term "good" is probably in response to the man's implication that Jesus will reveal to him the secret of eternal life. What Jesus requires of the man is not necessarily congenial to his ideas. The remainder of the story in vv 19-22 bears out the point.
10, 23-27: See note on Mt 19, 23-26.
10, 28-31: See note on Mt 19, 27-30.

gospel [30] who will not receive in this present age a hundred times as many homes, brothers and sisters, mothers, children and property—and persecution besides—and in the age to come, everlasting life. [31] Many who are first shall come last, and the last shall come first."

Third Teaching: Passion and Resurrection

[32] The disciples were on the road going up to Jerusalem, with Jesus walking in the lead. Their mood was one of wonderment, while that of those who followed was fear. Taking the Twelve aside once more, he began to tell them what was going to happen to him. [33] "We are on our way up to Jerusalem, where the Son of Man will be handed over to the chief priests and the scribes. [34] They will condemn him to death and hand him over to the Gentiles, who will mock him and spit at him, flog him, and finally kill him. But three days later he will rise."

Ambition of James and John

[35] Zebedee's sons, James and John, approached him. "Teacher," they said, "we want you to grant our request." [36] "What is it?" he asked. [37] They replied, "See to it that we sit, one at your right and the other at your left, when you come into your glory." [38] Jesus told them, "You do not know what you are asking. Can you drink the cup I shall drink or be baptized in the same bath of pain as I?" [39] "We can," they told him. Jesus said in response, "From the cup I drink of you shall drink; the bath I am immersed in you shall share. [40] But as for sitting at my right or my left, that is not mine to give; it is for those to whom it has been reserved." [41] The other ten, on hearing this,

31: Mt 19, 30; Lk 13, 30.
32ff: 8, 31; Mt 20, 17ff;
  Lk 18, 31ff.

35-45: Mt 20, 20-28.
38: Lk 12, 50.

10, 32ff: The disciples are apprehensive because Jesus, after prophesying his execution in Jerusalem, now proceeds deliberately to confront it (Lk 9, 51; Jn 11, 16). No doubt the prophecies in the synoptic tradition about the passion of Christ have been schematized through the influence of the event of the crucifixion. There seems to be no question, however, that frequent repetition of a passion prophecy by Jesus was part of the original tradition.
10, 35-45: If Mark has placed this narrative in its actual historical context (cf Mt 20, 20), the petition of James and John becomes dramatic: they declare themselves ready to risk death with Jesus provided he will guarantee to them the highest positions in the kingdom. While accepting their pledge to suffer with him, Jesus observes that it lies beyond his personal authority to make such concessions (35-40). If not in its actual historical context, the petition of James and John has been placed here by the evangelist to align the sacrifices required of disciples with the personal sacrifice made by Jesus. Whatever authority the disciples exercise is to be viewed, like the authority of Jesus (v 45), in terms of service to others rather than as a sign of personal eminence (42ff).

became indignant at James and John. ⁴² Jesus called them together and said to them: "You know how among the Gentiles those who seem to exercise authority lord it over them; their great ones make their importance felt. ⁴³ It cannot be like that with you. Anyone among you who aspires to greatness must serve the rest; ⁴⁴ whoever wants to rank first among you must serve the needs of all. ⁴⁵ The Son of Man has r ₊ come to be served but to serve—to give his life in ransom for the many."

The Blind Bartimaeus

⁴⁶ They came to Jericho next, and as he was leaving that place with his disciples and a sizable crowd, there was a blind beggar Bartimaeus ("son of Timaeus") sitting by the roadside. ⁴⁷ On hearing that it was Jesus of Nazareth, he began to call out, "Jesus, Son of David, have pity on me!" ⁴⁸ Many people were scolding him to make him keep quiet, but he shouted all the louder, "Son of David, have pity on me!" ⁴⁹ Then Jesus stopped and said, "Call him over." So they called the blind man over, telling him as they did so, "You have nothing to fear from him! Get up! He is calling you!" ⁵⁰ He threw aside his cloak, jumped up and came to Jesus. ⁵¹ Jesus asked him, "What do you want me to do for you?" "Rabboni," the blind man said, "I want to see." ⁵² Jesus said in reply, "Be on your way. Your faith has healed you." Immediately he received his sight and started to follow him up the road.

11

Triumphal Entry into Jerusalem

¹ Then, as they neared Bethphage and Bethany on the Mount of Olives, close to Jerusalem, he sent off two of his disciples

---

42-45: Lk 22, 25ff.
46-52: Mt 20, 29-34; Lk 18, 35-43.

11, 1-10: Mt 21, 1-9; Lk 19, 29-38; Jn 12, 12-15.

10, 46-52: The synoptic gospels locate this event at Jericho on Jesus' last journey to Jerusalem (Mt 20, 29-34; Lk 18, 35-43). The blind man, unaffected by what he heard of Jesus' lowly condition, accords him the messianic title, "Son of David." He requests a cure in order that he may see Jesus. On this basis his sight is restored.

11, 1-11: The nature of Jesus' entry into Jerusalem is not entirely clear in the synoptic tradition. In Jn 12, 12f the popular excitement upon his arrival in the city is associated with his raising of Lazarus to life (Jn 12, 18). This explains the acclaim Jesus receives on entering the city. In Mk 11, 9f the greeting Jesus receives stops short of proclaiming him Messiah. He is greeted rather as the prophet of the coming messianic kingdom; cf Mt 21, 11. Matthew introduces the notion of fulfillment of Old Testament prophecy (Zec 9, 9).

² with the instruction: "Go to the village straight ahead of you, and as soon as you enter it you will find tethered there a colt on which no one has ridden. Untie it and bring it back. ³ If anyone says to you, 'Why are you doing that?' say, 'The Master needs it but he will send it back here at once.'" ⁴ So they went off, and finding a colt tethered out on the street near a gate, they untied it. ⁵ Some of the bystanders said to them, "What do you mean by untying that colt?" ⁶ They answered as Jesus had told them to, and the men let them take it. ⁷ They brought the colt to Jesus and threw their cloaks across its back, and he sat on it. ⁸ Many people spread their cloaks on the road, while others spread reeds which they had cut in the fields. ⁹ Those preceding him as well as those who followed cried out:

"Hosanna!
Blessed is he who comes in the name of the Lord!
¹⁰ Blessed is the reign of our father David to come!
Hosanna in the highest!"

¹¹ He entered Jerusalem and went into the temple precincts. He inspected everything there, but since it was already late in the afternoon, he went out to Bethany accompanied by the Twelve.

Jesus Curses a Fig Tree

¹² The next day when they were leaving Bethany he felt hungry. ¹³ Observing a fig tree some distance off, covered with foliage, he went over to see if he could find anything on it. When he reached it he found nothing but leaves; it was not the time for figs. ¹⁴ Then addressing it he said, "Never again shall anyone eat of your fruit!" His disciples heard all this.

Cleansing of the Temple

¹⁵ When they reached Jerusalem he entered the temple precincts and began to drive out those who were engaged in buying and selling. He overturned the money-changers' tables and

---

9f: 2 Sm 7, 16; Ps 118, 26.   15-18: Mt 21, 12f; Lk 19, 45f;
11: Mt 21, 10.17.   Jn 2, 14ff.
12ff: Mt 21, 18ff; Lk 13, 6-9.

11, 12ff: Jesus' search for fruit on the fig tree recalls the prophets' earlier use of this image to designate Israel; cf Jer 8, 13; Ez 17, 24; Jl 1, 7; Hos 9, 10. Cursing the fig tree is a parable in action representing Christ's judgment on barren Israel for failing to receive his teaching.
11, 15-19: The expulsion of the buyers and sellers from the temple does not seem to be properly understood if regarded simply as an objection to the practice within the temple precincts, for it was fairly well controlled by the religious authorities. The key to an understanding of the incident is the citation of Is 56, 7 and Jer 7, 11. Both prophets objected that the wor-

the stalls of the men selling doves; [16] moreover, he would not permit anyone to carry things through the temple area.

[17] Then he began to teach them: "Does not Scripture have it,

'My house shall be called a house of prayer
for my peoples'—?

but you have turned it into a den of thieves." [18] The chief priests and the scribes heard of this and began to look for a way to destroy him. They were at the same time afraid of him because the whole crowd was under the spell of his teaching. [19] When evening drew on, Jesus and his disciples went out of the city. [20] Early next morning, as they were walking along, they saw the fig tree withered to its roots. [21] Peter remembered and said to him, "Rabbi, look! The fig tree you cursed has withered up." [22] In reply Jesus told them: "Put your trust in God. [23] I solemnly assure you, whoever says to this mountain, 'Be lifted up and thrown into the sea,' and has no inner doubts but believes that what he says will happen, shall have it done for him. [24] I give you my word, if you are ready to believe that you will receive whatever you ask for in prayer, it shall be done for you. [25] When you stand to pray, forgive anyone against whom you have a grievance so that your heavenly Father may in turn forgive you your faults."

The Authority of Jesus

[27] They returned once more to Jerusalem. As he was walking in the temple precincts the chief priests, the scribes, and the elders approached him [28] and said to him, "On what authority are you doing these things? Who has given you the power to do them?" [29] Jesus said to them, "I will ask you a question. If you give me an answer, I will tell you on what authority I do the things I do. [30] Tell me, was John's baptism of divine origin

---

17: Is 56, 7; Jer 7, 11.
19: Lk 21, 37.
20-24: Mt 21, 20ff.
23: Mt 17, 20f; Lk 17, 6.

24: Mt 7, 7; Jn 11, 22;
    14, 13.
25: Mt 6, 14; 18, 35.
27-33: Mt 21, 23-27; Lk 20, 1-8.

---

ship in the temple was not consistent with true conversion. Jesus' action is a symbol of God's judgment against the abuses of his temple, due to the priests' failure to instruct the people in the meaning of temple worship.
11, 26: Omitted with many MSS.
11, 27—12, 27: For a similar series of conflicts see Mk 2, 1—3, 6. The parable of the vineyard tenants (Mt 21, 33-46; Lk 20, 1-12) indicates Jesus' self-awareness of his unique divine sonship (12, 1-12). His superior wisdom sees no conflict between Roman taxation and Israel's worship of God (12, 13-17). His prophetic insight exposes the specious arguments against resurrection of the dead adduced by the Sadducees, who fail to understand that the messianic promises benefit here and hereafter all who have hoped in God (12, 18-27).

or merely from men?" [31] They thought to themselves, "If we say 'divine,' he will ask, 'Then why did you not put faith in it?' [32] But can we say, 'merely human'?" (They had reason to fear the people, who all regarded John as a true prophet.) [33] So their answer to Jesus was, "We do not know." In turn, Jesus said to them, "Then neither will I tell you on what authority I do the things I do."

12

Parable of the Tenants

[1] He began to address them once more in parables: "A man planted a vineyard, put a hedge around it, dug out a vat, and erected a tower. Then he leased it to tenant farmers and went on a journey. [2] In due time he dispatched a man in his service to the tenants to obtain from them his share of produce from the vineyard. [3] But they seized him, beat him, and sent him off empty-handed. [4] The second time he sent them another servant; him too they beat over the head and treated shamefully. [5] He sent yet another and they killed him. So too with many others: some they beat; some they killed. [6] He still had one to send—the son whom he loved. He sent him to them as a last resort, thinking, 'They will have to respect my son.' [7] But those tenants said to one another, 'Here is the one who will inherit everything. Come, let us kill him, and the inheritance will be ours.' [8] Then they seized and killed him and dragged him outside the vineyard. [9] What do you suppose the owner of the vineyard will do? He will come and destroy those tenants and turn his vineyard over to others. [10] Are you not familiar with this passage of Scripture:

'The stone rejected by the builders
　　has become the keystone of the structure.
[11] It was the Lord who did it
　　and we find it marvelous to behold'?"

[12] They wanted to arrest him at this, yet they had reason to fear the crowd. (They knew well enough that he meant the parable for them.) Finally they left him and went off.

Tribute to the Emperor

[13] They next sent some Pharisees and Herodians after him to

12, 1-12: Mt 21, 33-46;
　　Lk 20, 9-19.
　1: Is 5, 1-7; Jer 2, 21.
　10f: Ps 118, 22f; Is 28, 16.

13-27: Mt 22, 15-33;
　　Lk 20, 20-39.
　13: Mk 3, 6.

catch him in his speech. [14] The two groups came and said to him: "Teacher, we know you are a truthful man, unconcerned about anyone's opinion. It is evident you do not act out of human respect but teach God's way of life sincerely. Is it lawful to pay the tax to the emperor or not? Are we to pay or not to pay?" [15] Knowing their hypocrisy he said to them, "Why are you trying to trip me up? Bring me a coin and let me see it." [16] When they brought one, he said to them, "Whose head is this and whose inscription is it?" "Caesar's," they told him. [17] At that Jesus said to them, "Give to Caesar what is Caesar's, but give to God what is God's." Their amazement at him knew no bounds.

The Sadducees and the Resurrection

[18] Then some Sadducees who hold there is no resurrection came to him with a question: [19] "Teacher, we were left this in writing by Moses: 'If anyone's brother dies leaving a wife but no child, his brother must take the wife and produce offspring for his brother.' [20] There were these seven brothers. The eldest took a wife and died, leaving no children. [21] The second took the woman, and he too died childless. The same thing happened to the third; [22] in fact none of the seven left any children behind. Last of all, the woman also died. [23] At the resurrection, when they all come back to life, whose wife will she be? All seven married her." [24] Jesus said: "You are badly misled, because you fail to understand the Scriptures or the power of God. [25] When people rise from the dead, they neither marry nor are given in marriage but live like angels in heaven. [26] As to the raising of the dead, have you not read in the book of Moses, in the passage about the burning bush, how God told him,

'I am the God of Abraham, the God of Isaac,
the God of Jacob'?

[27] He is the God of the living, not of the dead. You are very much mistaken."

The Great Commandment

[28] One of the scribes came up, and when he heard them arguing he realized how skillfully Jesus answered them. He de-

17: Rom 13, 7. 26: Ex 3, 6.
19: Dt 25, 5. 28-34: Mt 22, 34-40.

cided to ask him, "Which is the first of all the commandments?" [29] Jesus replied: "This is the first:

'Hear, O Israel! The Lord our God is Lord alone!
[30] Therefore you shall love the Lord your God
with all your heart,
with all your soul,
with all your mind,
and with all your strength.'

[31] This is the second,

'You shall love your neighbor as yourself.'

There is no other commandment greater than these." [32] The
scribe said to him: "Excellent, Teacher! You are right in saying, 'He is the One, there is no other than he.' [33] Yes, 'to love
him with all our heart, with all our thoughts and with all our
strength, and to love our neighbor as ourselves' is worth more
than any burnt offering or sacrifice." [34] Jesus approved the insight of this answer and told him, "You are not far from the
reign of God." And no one had the courage to ask him any
more questions.

The Son of David

[35] As Jesus was teaching in the temple precincts he went on
to say: "How can the scribes claim, 'The Messiah is David's
son'? [36] David himself, inspired by the Holy Spirit, said,

'The Lord said to my Lord: Sit at my right hand
until I make your enemies your footstool.'

[37] If David himself addresses him as 'Lord,' in what sense can
he be his son?" The majority of the crowd heard this with
delight.

Hypocrisy of the Opponents of Jesus

[38] In the course of his teaching he said: "Be on guard against
the scribes, who like to parade around in their robes and ac-

30: Dt 6, 4f.
31: Lv 19, 18; Rom 13, 9;
   Gal 5, 14; Jas 2, 8.
33: Dt 6, 4; Ps 40, 7ff.
34: Mt 22, 46; Lk 20, 40.

35ff: Mt 22, 41-45;
   Lk 20, 41-44.
36: Ps 110, 1.
38ff: Mt 23, 1-7; Lk 11, 43;
   20, 45ff.

12, 35-44: Jesus questions the claim of the scribes about the Davidic
descent of the Messiah, not to deny it (Mt 1, 1; Acts 2, 20.34; Rom 1, 3; 2
Tm 2, 8), but to imply that he is more than this. His superiority derives
from his transcedent origin (35ff), to which David himself attested when

cept marks of respect in public, [39] front seats in the synagogues, and places of honor at banquets. [40] These men devour the savings of widows and recite long prayers for appearance' sake; it is they who will receive the severest sentence."

The Widow's Mite

[41] Taking a seat opposite the treasury, he observed the crowd putting money into the collections box. Many of the wealthy put in sizable amounts; [42] but one poor widow came and put in two small copper coins worth a few cents. [43] He called his disciples over and told them: "I want you to observe that this poor widow contributed more than all the others who donated to the treasury. [44] They gave from their surplus wealth, but she gave from her want, all that she had to live on."

13

Questions about the Temple

[1] As he was making his way out of the temple area, one of his disciples said to him, "Teacher, look at the huge blocks of stone and the enormous buildings!" [2] Jesus said to him, "You see these great buildings? Not one stone will be left upon another—all will be torn down." [3] While he was seated on the Mount of Olives facing the temple, Peter, James, John, and Andrew began to question him privately. [4] "Tell us, when will this occur? What will be the sign that all this is coming to an end?"

Beginning of Calamities

[5] Jesus began his discourse: "Be on your guard. Let no one mislead you. [6] Any number will come attempting to impersonate me. 'I am he,' they will claim, and will lead many astray. [7] When you hear about wars and threats of war, do not yield to panic. Such things are bound to happen, but this is not yet the end. [8] Nation will rise against nation, one kingdom

---

41-44: Lk 21, 1-4.
13, 1-37: Mt 24, 1-51;

Lk 21, 5-36.
5: Eph 5, 6; 2 Thes 2, 3.

---

he addressed the Messiah with the name reserved for Yahweh (Ps 110, 1).
Jesus was pained by the scribes' abuse of religious position (38ff). At the same time he was deeply sympathetic toward the religious generosity of the poor (41-44).
13, 1-37: This chapter and its parallels (Mt 24, 1-44; Lk 21, 5-36) express the principal New Testament thought on the second coming of Christ; cf 1 Thes 4, 13-18 and note. Each of the three evangelists in his own way relates the second coming to Jesus' prophecy of the destruction of Jerusalem. The *abominable and destructive presence* (Dn 9, 27), i.e., the profanation

against another. There will be earthquakes in various places and there will be famine. This is but the onset of the pains of labor. [9] Be constantly on your guard. They will hand you over to the courts. You will be beaten in synagogues. You will be arraigned before governors and kings on my account and have to testify to your faith before them. [10] But the good news must first be proclaimed to all the Gentiles. [11] When men take you off into custody, do not worry beforehand about what to say. In that hour, say what you are inspired to say. It will not be yourselves speaking but the Holy Spirit. [12] Brother will hand over brother for execution and likewise the father his child; children will turn against their parents and have them put to death. [13] Because of my name, you will be hated by everyone. Nonetheless, the man who holds out till the end is the one who will come through safe.

The Supreme Tribulation

[14] "When you see the abominable and destructive presence standing where it should not be—let the reader take note!—those in Judea must flee to the mountains. [15] If a man is on the roof terrace, he must not come down or enter his house to get anything out of it. [16] If a man is in the field, he must not turn back to pick up his cloak. [17] It will go badly with pregnant and nursing women in those days. [18] Keep praying that none of this happens in winter. [19] Those times will be more distressful than any between God's work of creation and now, and for all time to come. [20] Indeed, had the Lord not shortened the period, not a person would be saved. But for the sake of those he has chosen, he has shortened the days. [21] If anyone tells you at that time, 'Look, the Messiah is here!' 'Look, he is there!'—do not believe it. [22] False messiahs and false prophets will appear performing signs and wonders to mislead, if it were possible, even the chosen. [23] So be constantly on guard! I have told you about it beforehand.

11ff: Mt 10, 19-22;   15: Lk 17, 31.
      Lk 12, 11f.   19: Dn 12, 1.
14: Dn 9, 27; Mt 24, 15.

---

of the temple by the Roman power, will be the sign of imminent destruction. Jesus urges flight from Jerusalem rather than defense of the city through misguided messianic hope (14-23). Intervention will only occur after the destruction (24-27), which itself is to occur before the end of the first Christian generation (28-31). No one but the Father knows the precise time, nor that of Jesus' second coming (32), hence the necessity of constant vigilance (33-37). The chronological proximity of the second coming and the destruction of the temple is not determined (2-27). Luke sets the second coming at a later date, in *the times of the Gentiles* (Lk 21, 24).

Last Act of the Drama

[24] "During that period after trials of every sort the sun will be darkened, the moon will not shed its light, [25] stars will fall out of the skies, and the heavenly hosts will be shaken. [26] Then men will see the Son of Man coming in the clouds with great power and glory. [27] He will dispatch his angels and assemble his chosen from the four winds, from the farthest bounds of earth and sky. [28] Learn a lesson from the fig tree. Once the sap of its branches runs high and it begins to sprout leaves, you know that summer is near. [29] In the same way, when you see these things happening, you will know that he is near, even at the door. [30] I assure you, this generation will not pass away until all these things take place. [31] The heavens and the earth will pass away but my words will not pass.

Need for Watchfulness

[32] "As to the exact day or hour, no one knows it, neither the angels in heaven nor even the Son, but only the Father. [33] Be constantly on the watch! Stay awake! You do not know when the appointed time will come. [34] It is like a man traveling abroad. He leaves home and places his servants in charge, each with his own task; and he orders the man at the gate to watch with a sharp eye. [35] Look around you! You do not know when the master of the house is coming, whether at dusk, at midnight, when the cock crows, or at early dawn. [36] Do not let him come suddenly and catch you asleep. [37] What I say to you, I say to all. Be on guard!"

14

The Official Decision

[1] The feasts of Passover and Unleavened Bread were to be observed in two days' time, and therefore the chief priests and scribes began to look for a way to arrest him by some trick and kill him. [2] Yet they pointed out, "Not during the festival, or the people may riot."

24-27: Mt 24, 29ff;
    Lk 21, 25ff.
  24: Is 13, 10; Ez 32, 7;
    Jl 2, 10.
  26: 14, 62; Dn 7, 13f.
28-32: Mt 24, 32-36;

Lk 21, 29-33.
33-37: Mt 24, 42; 25, 13ff.
  34: Mt 25, 14-30;
    Lk 19, 12-27.
14, 1f: Mt 26, 2-5;
    Lk 22, 1f.

14, 1—15, 47: In this solemn narrative the principal facts on the sufferings and death of Jesus are interwoven with implication; of their religious significance. The facts include: a plan to arrest Jesus secretly and thus prevent

The Anointing at Bethany

³ When Jesus was in Bethany reclining at table in the house of Simon the leper, a woman entered carrying an alabaster jar of perfume made from expensive aromatic nard. Breaking the jar, she began to pour the perfume on his head. ⁴ Some were saying to themselves indignantly: "What is the point of this extravagant waste of perfume? ⁵ It could have been sold for over three hundred silver pieces and the money given to the poor." They were infuriated at her. ⁶ But Jesus said: "Let her alone. Why do you criticize her? She has done me a kindness. ⁷ The poor you will always have with you and you can be generous to them whenever you wish, but you will not always have me. ⁸ She has done what she could. By perfuming my body she is anticipating its preparation for burial. ⁹ I assure you, wherever the good news is proclaimed throughout the world, what she has done will be told in her memory."

The Betrayal

¹⁰ Then Judas Iscariot, one of the Twelve, went off to the chief priests to hand Jesus over to them. ¹¹ Hearing what he had to say, they were jubilant and promised to give him money. He for his part kept looking for an opportune way to hand him over.

Passover Preparation

¹² On the first day of Unleavened Bread, when it was cus-

3-9: Mt 26, 6-13; Jn 12, 1-8.   12-16: Mt 26, 17ff; Lk 22, 7-11.
10f: Mt 26, 14ff.

---

tumult (1ff); facilitation of the plan through Judas' betrayal (10f); the arrest of Jesus (43-47); inquest before the Sanhedrin and indictment for blasphemy (35-49); transfer to Pilate's court and the insinuation of political sedition (15, 1-5); official and popular demand for Jesus' condemnation and crucifixion; Pilate's consent under pressure (15, 6-15); the mockery, scourging and crucifixion (15, 15-27); death on the cross (15, 29-39); and burial by Joseph of Arimathea (15, 42-47).

Jesus is described as interpreting the events of his passion as follows: the anointing at Bethany as a preparation for his death (14, 3-9); his celebration of the Passover (12-16) as the inauguration of a new and lasting covenant in which his body and blood are to be shared in the form of bread and wine, symbols of his passion and death (22ff). He prophesies Peter's denial and the apostles' desertion and subsequent reunion (26ff). Jesus declares his acceptance of the passion to be in conformity with his Father's will (32-42), and confesses his awareness of what was foretold by the Scriptures concerning him (48f). He refuses to throw himself on the mercy of Pilate (15, 2-5) and rejects the drug that would cloud his mind to the reality of the crucifixion (36). He prays Psalm 22 from the cross (34). The Roman centurion's tribute to Jesus' courage (39) is actually a concluding Marcan confession of faith, put on Gentile lips.

The religious cast of the Marcan passion narrative derives from the consistent theme of fulfillment of prophecy, even concerning the conduct of Jesus' disciples. Though complete in itself, this narrative is closely joined to the account of Jesus' ministry. One single item remains to be fulfilled: the prophecy of his future vindication (14, 62).

tomary to sacrifice the paschal lamb, his disciples said to him, "Where do you wish us to go to prepare the Passover supper for you?" [13] He sent two of his disciples with these instructions: "Go into the city and you will come upon a man carrying a water jar. Follow him. [14] Whatever house he enters, say to the owner, 'The Teacher asks, Where is my guest room where I may eat the Passover with my disciples?' [15] Then he will show you an upstairs room, spacious, furnished, and all in order. That is the place you are to get ready for us." [16] The disciples went off. When they reached the city they found it just as he had told them, and they prepared the Passover supper.

The Betrayer

[17] As it grew dark he arrived with the Twelve. [18] They reclined at table, and in the course of the meal Jesus said, "I give you my word, one of you is about to betray me, yes, one who is eating with me." [19] They began to say to him sorrowfully, one by one, "Surely not I!" [20] He said, "It is one of the Twelve—a man who dips into the dish with me. [21] The Son of Man is going the way the Scripture tells of him. Still, accursed be that man by whom the Son of Man is betrayed. It were better for him had he never been born."

The Holy Eucharist

[22] During the meal he took bread, blessed and broke it, and gave it to them. "Take this," he said, "this is my body." [23] He likewise took a cup, gave thanks and passed it to them, and they all drank from it. [24] He said to them: "This is my blood, the blood of the covenant, to be poured out on behalf of many. [25] I solemnly assure you, I will never again drink of the fruit of the vine until the day when I drink it new in the reign of God."

[26] After singing songs of praise, they walked out to the Mount of Olives.

Peter's Denial Foretold

[27] Jesus then said to them: "Your faith in me shall be shaken, for Scripture has it,

'I will strike the shepherd
and the sheep will be dispersed.'

17-21: Mt 26, 20-24;
    Lk 22, 21ff; Jn 13, 21-26.
22-25: Mt 26, 26-30;
    Lk 22, 19f;

1 Cor 11, 23ff.
27-31: Mt 26, 31-35;
    Lk 22, 31-34; Jn 13, 36ff.
27: Zec 13, 7; Jn 16, 32.

²⁸ But after I am raised up, I will go to Galilee ahead of you."
²⁹ Peter said to him, "Even though all are shaken in faith, it will not be that way with me." ³⁰ Jesus answered, "I give you my assurance, this very night before the cock crows twice, you will deny me three times." ³¹ But Peter kept reasserting vehemently, "Even if I have to die with you, I will not deny you." They all said the same.

The Agony in the Garden

³² They went then to a place named Gethsemani. "Sit down here while I pray," he said to his disciples; ³³ at the same time he took along with him Peter, James, and John. ³⁴ Then he began to be filled with fear and distress. He said to them, "My heard is filled with sorrow to the point of death. Remain here and stay awake." ³⁵ He advanced a little and fell to the ground, praying that if it were possible this hour might pass him by. ³⁶ He kept saying, *"Abba* (O Father), you have the power to do all things. Take this cup away from me. But let it be as you would have it, not as I." ³⁷ When he returned he found them asleep. He said to Peter, "Asleep, Simon? You could not stay awake for even an hour? ³⁸ Be on guard and pray that you may not be put to the test. The spirit is willing but nature is weak." ³⁹ Going back again he began to pray in the same words. ⁴⁰ Once again he found them asleep on his return. They could not keep their eyes open, nor did they know what to say to him. ⁴¹ He returned a third time and said to them, "Still sleeping? Still taking your ease? It will have to do. The hour is on us. You will see that the Son of Man is to be handed over to the clutches of evil men. ⁴² Rouse yourselves and come along. See! My betrayer is near."

Jesus Arrested

⁴³ Even while he was still speaking, Judas, one of the Twelve, made his appearance accompanied by a crowd with swords and clubs; these people had been sent by the chief priests, the scribes, and the elders. ⁴⁴ The betrayer had arranged a signal for them, saying, "The man I shall embrace is the one; arrest him and lead him away, taking every precaution." ⁴⁵ He then went directly over to him and said, "Rabbi!" and embraced him. ⁴⁶ At this, they laid hands on him and arrested him. ⁴⁷ One of

32-42: Mt 26, 36-46;
     Lk 22, 40-46.
32: Jn 18, 1.
38: Rom 7, 5.

43-50: Mt 26, 47-56;
Lk 22, 47-53;
Jn 18, 3-11.

the bystanders drew his sword and struck the high priest's slave, cutting off his ear. [48] Addressing himself to them, Jesus said: "You have come out to arrest me armed with swords and clubs as if against a brigand. [49] I was within your reach daily, teaching in the temple precincts, yet you never arrested me. But now, so that the Scriptures may be fulfilled . . ." [50] With that, all deserted him and fled. [51] There was a young man following him who was covered by nothing but a linen cloth. As they seized him [52] He left the cloth behind and ran off naked.

Jesus before the Sanhedrin

[53] Then they led Jesus off to the high priest, and all the chief priests, the elders and the scribes came together. [54] Peter followed him at a distance right into the high priest's courtyard, where he found a seat with the temple guard and began to warm himself at the fire. [55] The chief priests with the whole Sanhedrin were busy soliciting testimony against Jesus that would lead to his death, but they could not find any. [56] Many spoke against him falsely under oath but their testimony did not agree. [57] Some, for instance, on taking the stand, testified falsely by alleging, [58] "We heard him declare, 'I will destroy this temple made by human hands,' and 'In three days I will construct another not made by human hands.'" [59] Even so, their testimony did not agree.

[60] The high priest rose to his feet before the court and began to interrogate Jesus: "Have you no answer to what these men testify against you?" [61] But Jesus remained silent; he made no reply. Once again the high priests interrogated him: "Are you the Messiah, the Son of the Blessed One?" [62] Then Jesus answered: "I am; and you will see the Son of Man seated at the right hand of the Power and coming with the clouds of heaven." [63] At that the high priest tore his robes and said: "What further need do we have of witnesses? [64] You have heard the blasphemy. What is your verdict?" They all concurred in the verdict "guilty," with its sentence of death. [65] Some of them then began to spit on him. They blindfolded him and hit him, saying, "Play the prophet!" while the officers manhandled him.

Peter's Denial

[66] While Peter was down in the courtyard, one of the servant

---

53-65: Mt 26, 57-68;
    Lk 22, 54.63ff; Jn 18, 12f.
58: 15, 29; 2 Cor 5, 1.
62: 13, 26; Ps 110, 1;
·Dn 7, 13; Mt 24, 30.
65: Lk 22, 63ff.
66-72: Mt 26, 69-75;
    Lk 22, 55-62;

girls of the high priest came along. [67] When she noticed Peter warming himself, she looked at him more closely and said, "You too were with Jesus of Nazareth." [68] But he denied it: "I do not know what you are talking about! What are you getting at?' Then he went out into the gateway. [At that moment a cock crowed.] [69] The servant girl, keeping an eye on him, started again to tell the bystanders, "This man is one of them." [70] Once again he denied it. A little later 'the bystanders said to Peter once more, "You are certainly one of them! You are a Galilean, are you not?" [71] He began to curse, and to swear, "I do not even know the man you are talking about!" [72] Just then a second cockcrow was heard and Peter recalled the prediction Jesus had made to him, "Before the cock crows twice you will deny me three times." He broke down and began to cry.

15

Jesus before Pilate

[1] As soon as it was daybreak the chief priests, with the elders and scribes (that is, the whole Sanhedrin), reached a decision. They bound Jesus, led him away, and handed him over to Pilate. [2] Pilate interrogated him: "Are you the king of the Jews?" "You are the one who is saying it," Jesus replied. [3] The chief priests, meanwhile, brought many accusations against him. [4] Pilate interrogated him again: "Surely you have some answer? See how many accusations they are leveling against you. [5] But greatly to Pilate's surprise, Jesus made no further response.

[6] Now on the occasion of a festival he would release for them one prisoner—any man they asked for. [7] There was a prisoner named Barabbas jailed along with the rebels who had committed murder in the uprising. [8] When the crowd came up to press their demand that he honor the custom, [9] Pilate rejoined, "Do you want me to release the king of the Jews for you?" [10] He was aware, of course, that it was out of jealousy that the chief priests had handed him over. [11] Meanwhile, the chief priests incited the crowd to have him release Barabbas instead. [12] Pilate again asked them, "What am I to do with the man you call the king of the Jews?" [13] They shouted back, "Crucify him!" [14] Pilate protested, "Why? What crime has he committed?" They only shouted the louder, "Crucify him!" [15] So Pilate, who wished to satisfy the crowd, released Barabbas to

Jn 18, 16ff.25ff.
72: Jn 13, 38.
15, 1-5: Mt 27, 11-14;
Lk 23, 1ff.

1: Jn 18, 28.
6-15: Mt 27, 15-26;
Lk 23, 17-25;
Jn 18, 39f.

them; and after he had had Jesus scourged, he handed him over to be crucified.

The Crowning with Thorns

16 The soldiers now led Jesus away into the hall known as the praetorium; at the same time they assembled the whole cohort. 17 They dressed him in royal purple, then wove a crown of thorns and put it on him, 18 and began to salute him, "All hail! King of the Jews!" 19 Continually striking Jesus on the head with a reed and spitting at him, they reguflected before him and pretended to pay him homage. 20 When they had finished mocking him, they stripped him of the purple, dressed him in his own clothes, and led him out to crucify him.

The Way of the Cross: the Crucifixion

21 A man named Simon of Cyrene, the father of Alexander and Rufus, was coming in from the fields, and they pressed him into service to carry the cross. 22 When they brought Jesus to the site of Golgotha (which means "Skull Place"), 23 they tried to give him wine drugged with myrrh, but he would not take it. 24 Then they crucified him and divided up his garments by rolling dice for them to see what each should take. 25 It was about nine in the morning when they crucified him. 26 The inscription proclaiming his offense read, "THE KING OF THE JEWS."

27 With him they crucified two insurgents, one at his right and one at his left. 29 People going by kept insulting him, tossing their heads and saying, "Ha, ha! So you were going to destroy the temple and rebuild it in three days! 30 Save yourself now by coming down from that cross!" 31 The chief priests and the scribes also joined in and jeered: "He saved others but he cannot save himself! 32 Let the 'Messiah,' the 'King of Israel,' come down from that cross here and now so that we can see it and believe in him!" The men who had been crucified with him likewise kept taunting him.

Death of Jesus

33 When noon came, darkness fell on the whole countryside and lasted until midafternoon. 34 At that time Jesus cried in a

---

16-20: Mt 27, 27-31;
     Jn 19, 2f.
  21: Mt 27, 32; Lk 23, 26.
22-38: Mt 27, 33-51; Lk 23,
     32-46; Jn 19, 17ff.

24: Ps 22, 18.
27: Lk 23, 33.
29: Jn 2, 19.
32: Lk 23, 39.
34: Ps 22, 2.

15, 28: Omitted with many MSS.

loud voice, *"Eloi, Eloi, lama sabachthani?"* which means, "My God, my God, why have you forsaken me?" [35] A few of the bystanders who heard it remarked, "Listen! He is calling on Elijah!" [36] Someone ran off, and soaking a sponge in sour wine, stuck it on a reed to try to make him drink. The man said, "Now let's see whether Elijah comes to take him down."

[37] Then Jesus, uttering a loud cry, breathed his last. [38] At that moment the curtain in the sanctuary was torn in two from top to bottom. [39] The centurion who stood guard over him, on seeing the manner of his death, declared, "Clearly this man was the Son of God!" [40] There were also women present looking on from a distance. Among them were Mary Magdalene, Mary the mother of James the younger and Joses, and Salome. [41] These women had followed Jesus when he was in Galilee and attended to his needs. There were also many others who had come up with him to Jerusalem.

The Burial

[42] As it grew dark (it was Preparation Day, that is, the eve of the sabbath), [43] Joseph from Arimathea arrived—a distinguished member of the Sanhedrin. He was another who looked forward to the reign of God. He was bold enough to seek an audience with Pilate and urgently requested the body of Jesus. [44] Pilate was surprised that Jesus should have died so soon. He summoned the centurion and inquired whether Jesus was already dead. [45] Learning from him that he was dead, Pilate released the corpse to Joseph. [46] Then, having bought a linen shroud, Joseph took him down, wrapped him in the linen, and laid him in a tomb which had been cut out of rock. Finally he rolled a stone across the entrance of the tomb. [47] Meanwhile, Mary Magdalene and Mary the mother of Joses observed where he had been laid.

16

The Women at the Tomb

[1] When the sabbath was over, Mary Magdalene, Mary the

39ff: Mt 27, 54ff;
Lk 23, 47ff.
40: 6, 3; Lk 8, 2f.
42-47: Mt 27, 57-61;
Lk 23, 50-56;

Jn 19, 38-42.
16, 1-8: Mt 28, 1-8; Lk 24, 1-10;
Jn 20, 1-10.
1f: Mt 28, 1; Lk 23, 56.

16, 1-8: The purpose of this narrative is to show, in the mystery of Jesus' resurrecton, the fulfillment of Jesus' prophecy before the Sanhedrin. The women find the tomb empty and an angel stationed there announces to them what has happened: *He has been raised up; he is not here.* They are

mother of James, and Salome bought perfumed oils with which they intended to go and anoint Jesus. [2] Very early, just after sunrise, on the first day of the week they came to the tomb. [3] They were saying to one another, "Who will roll back the stone for us from the entrance to the tomb?" [4] When they looked, they found that the stone had been rolled back. (It was a huge one.) [5] On entering the tomb they saw a young man sitting at the right, dressed in a white robe. [6] This frightened them thoroughly, but he reassured them: "You need not be amazed! You are looking for Jesus of Nazareth, the one who was crucified. He has been raised up; he is not here. See the place where they laid him. [7] Go now and tell his disciples and Peter, 'He is going ahead of you to Galilee, where you will see him just as he told you.' " [8] They made their way out and fled from the tomb bewildered and trembling; and because of their great fear, they said nothing to anyone.

The Longer Ending: 16, 9-20

[9] Jesus rose from the dead early on the first day of the week. He first appeared to Mary Magdalene, out of whom he had cast seven demons. [10] She went to announce the good news to his followers, who were now grieving and weeping. [11] But when they heard that he was alive and had been seen by her, they refused to believe it. [12] Later on, as two of them were walking along on their way to the country, he was revealed to them completely changed in appearance. [13] These men retraced their steps and announced the good news to the others; but the others put no more faith in them than in Mary Magdalene. [14] Finally, as they were at table, Jesus was revealed to the Eleven. He took them to task for their disbelief and their stubbornness,

---

5: Jn 20, 12.
7: 14, 28.
9-20: Mt 28, 1-10;
     Jn 20, 11-18.

10f: Lk 24, 10f; Jn 20, 18.
12ff: Lk 24, 13-35.
14: Lk 24, 36-49;
     1 Cor 15, 5.

---

told to proclaim the news to Peter and the disciples in order to prepare them for a reunion with him. Mark's composition of the gospel ends at 16, 8 with the women silenced by the mystery. This abrupt termination causes many to believe that the original ending of this gospel may have been lost. See note on vv 9-20.

16, 9-20: This passage, termed "the longer ending" to the Marcan gospel by comparison with a much briefer conclusion found in some less important manuscripts, has traditionally been accepted as an inspired part of the gospel. Early citations of it by the Fathers indicate that it was composed in the first century, although vocabulary and style argue strongly that it was written by someone other than Mark. It is a general résumé of the material concerning the appearances of the risen Jesus, reflecting, in particular, traditions found in Luke (24) and John (20).

since they had put no faith in those who had seen him after he had been raised.

[15] Then he told them: "Go into the whole world and proclaim the good news to all creation. [16] The man who believes in it and accepts baptism will be saved; the man who refuses to believe in it will be condemned. [17] Signs like these will accompany those who have professed their faith: they will use my name to expel demons, they will speak entirely new languages, [18] they will be able to handle serpents, they will be able to drink deadly poison without harm, and the sick upon whom they lay their hands will recover." [19] Then, after speaking to them, the Lord Jesus was taken up into heaven and took his seat at God's right hand. [20] The Eleven went forth and preached everywhere. The Lord continued to work with them throughout and confirm the message through the signs which accompanied them.

The Shorter Ending*

They promptly reported to Peter and his companions all that had been announced to them. Later on it was through them that Jesus himself sent out from east to west the sacred and immortal proclamation of eternal salvation.

The Freer Logion**

They offered this excuse: "This lawless and faithless age is under Satan, who does not allow what is unclean and dominated by spirits to grasp the true power of God. Therefore," they said to Christ, "reveal your just authority now." Christ replied: "The measure of the years of Satan's power has been fulfilled, but other terrible things are imminent. Yet it was for the sake of sinners that I was handed over to death, that they might return to the truth and sin no more, and inherit the spiritual and immortal glory of justification in heaven."

15f: 13, 10; Mt 28, 18ff;
    Lk 24, 47; Jn 20, 21.
18: Mt 10, 1; Lk 10, 19;

Acts 28, 3-6.
19: Lk 24, 50-53.
20: 1 Tm 3, 16.

*Found after Mark 16, 8 before the Longer Ending, in some late Greek manuscripts as well as some ancient versions.
**Found after Mark 16, 14 in a fourth-fifth century manuscript preserved in the Freer Gallery of Art, Washington, D. C. This ending was known to St. Jerome.

THE GOSPEL ACCORDING TO LUKE
INTRODUCTION

In accordance with the custom of Greek writers of the time, Luke introduces his gospel narrative with a brief preface (1, 1-4) probably intended to cover the Acts of the Apostles as well. Luke here alludes to his predecessors and stresses the care with which he has collected and judged his material. He regards those who wrote the gospel message before him as comprising two groups: "eye-witnesses and ministers of the word," i.e., the Twelve, who were the fundamental source of the gospel tradition (1, 2; Acts 1, 21f; 10, 39); and the "many," who attempted to arrange the preaching and teaching of the Twelve in narrative form (1, 1). Luke places himself in the latter group (1, 3)—not eyewitnesses like the Twelve, but catechists and writers who had familiarized themselves with the traditions about Jesus (the gospel) and the experiences of the Christian communities (Acts of the Apostles).

Luke dedicates his two books to a certain Theophilus (1, 3; Acts 1, 1) —a common name in the Greek world meaning "God's friend." This personage, whether a literary figure signifying Gentiles as such, or a historical individual with some degree of political importance, has received information on Christian teaching. Luke sees him either as a person of influence favorable disposed toward Christian teaching and worthy of more information, or as a Christian seeking more knowledge concerning the practical implications of his faith (1, 4). Perhaps this ambiguity concerning the religious status of Theophilus is deliberate; compare Lk 1, 4 with Acts 18, 25; 21, 21.24.

Many scholars discern in the Lucan gospel and Acts an apologetic strain presumably directed against unfounded criticisms of Christian teaching. Written after the persecution of Nero that began in 64 A.D. and caused hostility toward Christians throughout the empire, Luke-Acts reveal that Jesus himself was accounted innocent by the Roman governor Pontius Pilate (Lk 23, 4.15.22), and that St. Paul, founder of many Christian communities in the empire, was often acquitted by the Roman magistrates of charges against him (Acts 16, 36; 18, 12-17; 25, 26; 26, 32).

The evangelist portrays Christianity, not as a political movement, nor as a sect organized for an initiated few, but as a religious faith open to all men. His portrait of Jesus, drawn from the gospel tradition, manifests the Savior's concern for humanity (10, 25-37; 13, 10-16; 14, 12ff; 15, 11-32), and his identification with the poor (9, 57f; 12, 13-21), the outcast (15, 1f; 17, 11-19), and the criminal (19, 1-10; 23, 39-43). Although the apologetic thought in Luke's writings must be acknowledged, it was nevertheless not his chief purpose to produce an apology for Christianity.

Unlike the other evangelists, Luke presents no main thesis. He is content to let the material of the gospel narrative speak for itself without any argumentative intrusion of his own. The correct understanding of the importance of the Christian gospel is delicately introduced into the traditional material. By aligning Jesus' birth (2, 1ff) and the preaching of John the Baptizer (3, 1f) with the facts of secular history, the evangelist indicates that the gospel tradition did not originate in a myth about gods, but was lived out by Jesus of Nazareth in the real world wherein all men are born, struggle over the meaning of their existence, and die. He depicts Jesus as resolutely facing the reality which that world had in store for him (9, 51). Luke also, in harmony with the growing realization of the Christian communities of his time, removes the concept of the proximate parousia so prominent in Mark 13. But neither these concepts nor any particular aspects of Jesus' teaching that Luke chosses to emphasize are presented in any but a serene fashion. His reverence extends, not only to Jesus as God's Son (1, 35), and to the invisible persons of the Father (11, 2) and the Holy Spirit (11, 13), but also to humanity itself as the fruitful recipient of God's word.

No other evangelist has placed such emphasis on the prophetic word of Jesus; no other is so optimistic over the favorable response it is destined to receive. Nothing that the divine word enacts in history can fail (1, 37). The word of Jesus on love of enemies (6, 27-42) is seen as the only weapon which the small Christian communities of Luke's time possess to combat the forces of persecution. The word of God is the teaching of Jesus, to be planted in the hearts of men (8, 11). And it is the function of the Christian community (24, 27) to confront humanity with this word, which undergoes vicissitudes but inevitably finds out those who will hear, believe, and act (8, 15.21; 11, 28).

Most scholars agree that Luke made use of Mark's gospel as one of his sources; some even consider it to be Luke's principal source, to which he added other material (Lk 1-2; 6, 20—8, 3; 9, 51—18, 14) including an independently derived passion-narrative (22, 1—24, 53). In the view of others, Luke used Mark only as a supplementary source for rounding out the material he took from other traditions. Certainly, Luke's aim was not to improve upon Mark's account of the public ministry of Jesus, but rather to provide material for those like Theophilus, God's friends, desirous of living out the message of Jesus in the world.

Early Christian tradition ascribes the companion volumes of the Lucan gospel and Acts of the Apostles to approximately 75 A.D., and identifies the author with Luke the physician, friend of St. Paul, mentioned in Col 4, 14; Phlm 24; and 2 Tm 4, 11.

The Gospel of Luke is divided as follows:
Preface (1, 1-4)
  I: The Infancy Narrative (1, 5—2, 52)
 II: Preparation for the Public Ministry (3, 1—4, 13)
III: The Ministry in Galilee (4, 14—9, 50)
 IV: The Journey Through Perea (9, 51—19, 27)
  V: The Jerusalem Ministry (19, 28—29, 38)
 VI: The Passion of Jesus (22, 1—23, 56)
VII: Appearances after the Resurrection (24, 1-53)

THE GOSPEL ACCORDING TO LUKE
PREFACE

1

¹ Many have undertaken to compile a narrative of the events which have been fulfilled in our midst, ² precisely as those events were transmitted to us by the original eyewitnesses and ministers of the word. ³ I too have carefully traced the whole sequence of events from the beginning, and have decided to set it in writing for you, Theophilus, ⁴ so that Your Excellency may see how reliable the instruction was that you received.

I: THE INFANCY NARRATIVE

Announcement of the Birth of John

⁵ In the days of Herod, king of Judea, there was a priest named Zechariah of the priestly class of Abijah; his wife was a descendant of Aaron named Elizabeth. ⁶ Both were just in the eyes of God, blamelessly following all the commandments and ordinances of the Lord. ⁷ They were childless, for Elizabeth was sterile; moreover, both were advanced in years.

⁸ Once, when it was the turn of Zechariah's class and he was fulfilling his functions as a priest before God, ⁹ it fell to him by lot according to priestly usage to enter the sanctuary of the Lord and offer incense. ¹⁰ While the full assembly of people was praying outside at the incense hour, ¹¹ an angel of the Lord appeared to him, standing at the right of the altar of incense. ¹² Zechariah was deeply disturbed upon seeing him, and overcome by fear.

¹³ The angel said to him: "Do not be frightened, Zechariah; your prayer has been heard. Your wife Elizabeth shall bear a

---

1, 1-4: Acts 1, 1; 1 Cor 15, 3.
  5: 1 Chr 24, 10.
  7: Gn 18, 11; Jgs 13, 2-5;

1 Sm 1, 5f.
  9: Ex 30, 7.
  13: 1, 57.60.63; Mt 1, 20.

1, 5—2, 52: Beneath the simple beauty of Luke's infancy narrative there lies a remarkable depth of theological reflection. It centers about the similarity and the contrast between the religious mission of John the Baptizer and that of Jesus. By presenting the parallel announcements of their conception and birth (1, 5-25; 1, 26-38; 1, 57f; 2, 1-20) and the parallel narratives of their circumcision (1, 59-63; 2, 21), to which are added prophecies concerning the unique religious importance of Jesus (2, 22-40), the evangelist brings into sharp focus the transcendence of Jesus' person and mission over John's.

This parallelism in literary structure, along with the pervading use of Old Testament passages and ideas, conveys the basically theological character of the infancy gospel.

Mary is presented as the virgin divinely chosen in Israel to be the mother of Jesus and to experience the mystery and the spiritual benefits of his redemptive mission (1, 34-38.42.45-55; 2, 19.35.51). She is the prefiguration of the life and destiny of the Christian community.

son whom you shall name John. [14] Joy and gladness will be yours, and many will rejoice at his birth; [15] for he will be great in the eyes of the Lord. He will never drink wine or strong drink, and he will be filled with the Holy Spirit from his mother's womb. [16] Many of the sons of Israel will he bring back to the Lord their God. [17] God himself will go before him, in the spirit and power of Elijah, to turn the hearts of fathers to their children and the rebellious to the wisdom of the just, and to prepare for the Lord a people well-disposed."

[18] Zechariah said to the angel: "How am I to know this? I am an old man; my wife too is advanced in age." [19] The angel replied: "I am Gabriel, who stand in attendance before God. I was sent to speak to you and bring you this good news. [20] But now you will be mute—unable to speak—until the day these things take place, because you have not trusted my words. They will all come true in due season." [21] Meanwhile, the people were waiting for Zechariah, wondering at his delay in the temple. [22] When he finally came out he was unable to speak to them, and they realized that he had seen a vision inside. He kept making signs to them, for he remained speechless.

[23] Then, when his time of priestly service was over, he went home.

[24] Afterward, his wife Elizabeth conceived. She went into seclusion for five months, saying: [25] "In these days the Lord is acting on my behalf; he has seen fit to remove my reproach among men."

Announcement of the Birth of Jesus

[26] In the sixth month, the angel Gabriel was sent from God to a town of Galilee named Nazareth, [27] to a virgin betrothed to a man named Joseph, of the house of David. The virgin's name was Mary. [28] Upon arriving, the angel said to her: "Rejoice, O highly favored daughter! The Lord is with you. Blessed are you among women." [29] She was deeply troubled by his words, and wondered what his greeting meant. [30] The angel went on

---

15: Nm 6, 2f.
16: 1, 76.
17: Sir 48, 10; Mal 3, 23f;

Mt 17, 10-13.
27: Mt 1, 18.
28: Ru 2, 4; Jdt 13, 18.

1, 20: Though Zechariah's punishment is usually thought to have been due to unbelief in the angelic message concerning the child's conception, the sign he was asking for (1, 18) may have been some proof within his own lifetime of the child's future prophetic role.

1, 28: *Highly favored daughter:* Mary is to be the recipient of the divine favor, i.e., of the sanctifying power of God, in view of her office of mother of the Messiah, which the angel announces to her.

1, 30-34: The angel's message to Mary (30f) shows a certain similarity

to say to her: "Do not fear, Mary. You have found favor with God. [31] You shall conceive and bear a son and give him the name Jesus. [32] Great will be his dignity and he will be called Son of the Most High. The Lord God will give him the throne of David his father. He will rule over the house of Jacob forever [33] and his reign will be without end."

[34] Mary said to the angel, "How can this be since I do not know man?" [35] The angel answered her: "The Holy Spirit will come upon you and the power of the Most High will overshadow you; hence, the holy offspring to be born will be called Son of God. [36] Know that Elizabeth your kinswoman has conceived a son in her old age; she who was thought to be sterile is now in her sixth month, [37] for nothing is impossible with God."

[38] Mary said: "I am the servant of the Lord. Let it be done to me as you say." With that the angel left her.

The Visit

[39] Thereupon Mary set out, proceeding in haste into the hill country to a town of Judah, [40] where she entered Zechariah's house and greeted Elizabeth. [41] When Elizabeth heard Mary's greeting, the baby leapt in her womb. Elizabeth was filled with the Holy Spirit [42] and cried out in a loud voice: "Blest are you among women and blest is the fruit of your womb. [43] But who am I that the mother of my Lord should come to me? [44] The moment your greeting sounded in my ears, the baby leapt in my womb for joy. [45] Blest is she who trusted that the Lord's words to her would be fulfilled."

32: Is 9, 6; Mi 4, 7.
33: Dn 2, 44; 7, 14.
35: Mt 1, 20.

37: Gn 18, 14; Jer 32, 27;
Mt 19, 26.
42: Jgs 5, 24; Jdt 13, 18.

---

to the announcements made to some sterile women of the Old Testament who by God's intervention became the mothers of personages illustrious in salvation history: Sarah, mother of Isaac (Gn 17, 16.19); Samson's mother (Jgs 13, 2f); Hannah, mother of Samuel (1 Sm 1, 9-20). Mary, however, who is betrothed but not yet married (27), cannot be called sterile. Her question, then, directs itself precisely to the issue of divine favor in her case (30-33). How is she to know that the child she is now to conceive will be the Son of the Most High?

1, 34: *I do not know man:* i.e., as husband. Scholars generally explain this verse as a literary form emphasizing the faith of the first-century church in the virginal conception and birth of the Messiah.

1, 35ff: The overshadowing of Mary recalls the cloud that covered with glory the Meeting Tent (Ex 40, 34f) and the temple of the Lord (1 Kgs 8, 10; Hg 2, 7). The descent of the Holy Spirit upon her, the designation of her child as Son of God, are further signs of God's favor. As a divine pledge of this, she is informed of the approaching maternity of her aged and hitherto sterile cousin Elizabeth.

Mary's Canticle

⁴⁶ Then Mary said:

"My being proclaims the greatness of the Lord,
⁴⁷ my spirit finds in God my savior,
⁴⁸ For he has looked upon his servant in her lowliness;
all ages to come shall call me blessed.
⁴⁹ God who is mighty has done great things for me,
holy is his name;
⁵⁰ His mercy is from age to age
on those who fear him.

⁵¹ "He has shown might with his arm;
he has confused the proud in their inmost thoughts.
⁵² He has deposed the mighty from their thrones
and raised the lowly to high places.
⁵³ The hungry he has given every good thing,
while the rich he has sent empty away.
⁵⁴ He has upheld Israel his servant,
ever mindful of his mercy;
⁵⁵ Even as he promised our fathers,
promised Abraham and his descendants forever."

⁵⁶ Mary remained with Elizabeth about three months and then returned home.

⁵⁷ When Elizabeth's time for delivery arrived, she gave birth to a son. ⁵⁸ Her neighbors and relatives, upon hearing that the Lord had extended his mercy to her, rejoiced with her. ⁵⁹ When they assembled for the circumcision of the child on the eighth day, they intended to name him after his father Zechariah. ⁶⁰ At this his mother intervened, saying, "No, he is to be called John." ⁶¹ They pointed out to her, "None of your relatives has this name." ⁶² Then, using signs, they asked the father what he wished him to be called.

⁶³ He signaled for a writing tablet and wrote the words, "His name is John." This astonished them all. ⁶⁴ At that moment his mouth was opened and his tongue loosed, and he began to speak in praise of God.

⁶⁵ Fear descended on all in the Neighborhood; throughout

46: Is 61, 10.
48: 11, 27; Ps 113, 7.
50: Ps 103, 17.
51: Ps 138, 6; Jb 5, 12.
52: Ps 75, 8.
53: Ps 107, 9.
54: Ps 98, 3; Is 41, 9.
55: Gn 13, 15; 22, 18.
59: Gn 17, 10; Lv 12, 3.
63: 1, 13.
64: 1, 20.

the hill country of Judea these happenings began to be re-counted to the last detail. [66] All who heard stored these things up in their hearts, saying, "What will this child be?" and, "Was not the hand of the Lord upon him?"

Zechariah's Canticle

[67] Then Zechariah his father, filled with the Holy Spirit, uttered this prophecy:

[68] "Blessed be the Lord the God of Israel
    because he has visited and ransomed his people.
  [69] He has raised a horn of saving strength for us
    in the house of David his servant,
  [70] As he promised through the mouths of his holy ones,
    the prophets of ancient times:
  [71] Salvation from our enemies
    and from the hands of all our foes.
  [72] He has dealt mercifully with our fathers
    and remembered the holy covenant he made,
  [73] The oath he swore to Abraham our father he would grant
    us;
    [74] that, rid of fear and delivered from the enemy,
  [75] We should serve him devoutly and through all our days
    be holy in his sight.
  [76] And you, O child, shall be called
    prophet of the Most High;
    For you shall go before the Lord
    to prepare straight paths for him,
  [77] Giving his people a knowledge of salvation
    in freedom from their sins.
  [78] All this is the work of the kindness of our God;
    he, the Dayspring, shall visit us in his mercy
  [79] To shine on those who sit in darkness and in the shadow
    of death,
    to guide our feet into the way of peace."

[80] The child grew up and matured in spirit. He lived in the desert until the day when he made his public appearance in Israel.

68: Pss 74, 12; 111, 9.
70: Jer 30, 10.
71: Ps 106, 10.
72f: Lv 26, 42; Mi 7, 20.

76f: 1, 16; Is 40, 3;
    Mal 3, 1; Mt 11, 10.
78f: Is 42, 7; Jn 8, 12;
    2 Pt 1, 19.

2

Birth of Jesus

¹ In those days Caesar Augustus published a decree ordering a census of the whole world. ² This first census took place while Quirinius was governor of Syria. ³ Everyone went to register, each to his own town. ⁴ And so Joseph went from the town of Nazareth in Galilee to Judea, to David's town of Bethlehem—because he was of the house and lineage of David—⁵ to register with Mary, his espoused wife, who was with child.

⁶ While they were there the days of her confinement were completed. ⁷ She gave birth to her first-born son and wrapped him in swaddling clothes and laid him in a manger, because there was no room for them in the place where travelers lodged.

The Shepherds

⁸ There were shepherds in that locality, living in the fields and keeping night watch by turns over their flocks. ⁹ The angel of the Lord appeared to them as the glory of the Lord shone around them, and they were very much afraid. ¹⁰ The angel said to them: "You have nothing to fear! I come to proclaim good news to you—tidings of great joy to be shared by the whole people. ¹¹ This day in David's city a savior has been born to you, the Messiah and Lord. ¹² Let this be a sign to you: in a manger you will find an infant wrapped in swaddling clothes." ¹³ Suddenly, there was with the angel a multitude of the heavenly host, praising God and saying,

¹⁴ "Glory to God in high heaven,
      peace on earth to those on whom his favor rests."

2, 4: Mi 5, 2; Mt 2, 6.
5: Mt 1, 18.
11: Mt 1, 21.

12: Is 9, 5f.
14: 19, 38.

2, 1-5: Luke introduces the census to explain the time of Jesus' birth at Bethlehem. Scholars interpret inscriptions found near Tivoli in 1764, and at Antioch in Pisidia in 1912, to point to Cyrinus as governor of Syria between the years 10 and 8 B. C. The census may well have been inaugurated by him and hence named after him, even if continued and completed under Saturinus, his successor (8-6 B. C.).

2, 7: *Her first-born son:* a reference to the preferential status of the eldest son rather than an implication of subsequent offspring. In Israel the rights of primogeniture—authority, responsibility, succession—accrued to the first-born. He was considered holy; he belonged to God (Ex 13, 1f.14f; 22, 28; 34, 19f) and had to be redeemed, i. e., ransomed by an offering of five shekels made to the sanctuary (Nm 3, 47f; 18, 5f).

2, 14: *Those on whom his favor rests:* an allusion to the mystery of divine election that bestows the gift of faith upon people of divine choice. To these, the messianic mission of Jesus also brings a special gift of peace, the restored friendship between God and man.

¹⁵ When the angels had returned to heaven, the shepherds said to one another: "Let us go over to Bethlehem and see this event which the Lord has made known to us." ¹⁶ They went in haste and found Mary and Joseph, and the baby lying in the manger; ¹⁷ once they saw, they understood what had been told them concerning this child. ¹⁸ All who heard of it were astonished at the report given them by the shepherds.

¹⁹ Mary treasured all these things and reflected on them in her heart. ²⁰ The shepherds returned, glorifying and praising God for all they had heard and seen, in accord with what had been told them.

Circumcision of Jesus

²¹ When the eighth day arrived for his circumcision, the name Jesus was given the child, the name the angel had given him before he was conceived.

Presentation in the Temple

²² When the day came to purify them according to the law of Moses, the couple brought him up to Jerusalem so that he could be presented to the Lord, ²³ for it is written in the law of the Lord, "Every first-born male shall be consecrated to the Lord." ²⁴ They came to offer in sacrifice "a pair of turtledoves or two young pigeons," in accord with the dictate in the law of the Lord.

²⁵ There lived in Jerusalem at the time a certain man named Simeon. He was just and pious, and awaited the consolation of Israel, and the Holy Spirit was upon him. ²⁶ It was revealed to him by the Holy Spirit that he would not experience death until he had seen the Anointed of the Lord. ²⁷ He came to the temple now, inspired by the Spirit; and when the parents brought in the child Jesus to perform for him the customary ritual of the law, ²⁸ he took him in his arms and blessed God in these words:

²⁹ "Now, Master, you can dismiss your servant in peace;
     you have fulfilled your word.
³⁰ For my eyes have witnessed your saving deed
     ³¹ displayed for all the peoples to see:
³² A revealing light to the Gentiles,
     the glory of your people Israel."

20: 5, 26; 7, 16.
21: 1, 31; Gn 17, 12;
    Mt 1, 21.
22: Lv 12, 2-6.

23f: Ex 13, 2; Lv 12, 8.
30ff: Is 46, 13; 49, 6; 52, 10;
     Jn 8, 12.

[33] The child's father and mother were marveling at what was being said about him. [34] Simeon blessed them and said to Mary his mother: "This child is destined to be the downfall and the rise of many in Israel, a sign that will be opposed— [35] and you yourself shall be pierced with a sword—so that the thoughts of many hearts may be laid bare."

The Prophetess

[36] There was also a certain prophetess, Anna by name, daughter of Phanuel of the tribe of Asher. She had seen many days, having lived seven years with her husband after her marriage [37] and then as a widow until she was eighty-four. She was constantly in the temple, worshipping day and night in fasting and prayer. [38] Coming on the scene at this moment, she gave thanks to God and talked about the child to all who looked forward to the deliverance of Jerusalem.

[39] When the pair had fulfilled all the prescriptions of the law of the Lord, they returned to Galilee and their own town of Nazareth. [40] The child grew in size and strength, filled with wisdom, and the grace of God was upon him.

The Finding in the Temple

[41] His parents used to go every year to Jerusalem for the feast of the Passover, [42] and when he was twelve they went up for the celebration as was their custom. [43] As they were returning at the end of the feast, the child Jesus remained behind unknown to his parents. [44] Thinking he was in the party, they continued their journey for a day, looking for him among their relatives and acquaintances.

[45] Not finding him, they returned to Jerusalem in search of him. [46] On the third day they came upon him in the temple sitting in the midst of the teachers, listening to them and asking them questions. [47] All who heard him were amazed at his intelligence and his answers.

[48] When his parents saw him they were astonished, and his mother said to him: "Son, why have you done this to us? You see that your father and I have been searching for you in sorrow." [49] He said to them: "Why did you search for me? Did you not know I had to be in my Father's house?" [50] But they did not grasp what he said to them.

34: 12, 51ff.
35: Jn 9, 39; 19, 25ff; Rom 9, 33; 1 Pt 2, 7.

39: Mt 2, 23.
41: Ex 23, 15.
47: 4, 22.

---

⁵¹ He went down with them then, and came to Nazareth, and was obedient to them. His mother meanwhile kept all these things in memory. ⁵² Jesus, for his part, progressed steadily in wisdom and age and grace before God and men.

II: PREPARATION FOR THE PUBLIC MINISTRY

3

John the Baptizer

¹ In the fifteenth year of the rule of Tiberius Caesar, when Pontius Pilate was procurator of Judea, Herod tetrarch of Galilee, Philip his brother tetrarch of the region of Ituraea and Trachonitis, and Lysanias tetrarch of Abilene, ² during the high-priesthood of Annas and Caiaphas, the word of God was spoken to John son of Zechariah in the desert. ³ He went about the entire region of the Jordan proclaiming a baptism of repentance which led to the forgiveness of sins, ⁴ as is written in the book of the words of Isaiah the prophet:

"A herald's voice in the desert, crying,
　'Make ready the way of the Lord,
　　Clear him a straight path.
⁵ Every valley shall be filled
　　And every mountain and hill shall be leveled.
The windings shall be made straight
　　And the rough ways smooth,
⁶ And all mankind shall see the salvation of God.' "

⁷ He would say to the crowds that came out to be baptized by him: "You brood of vipers! Who told you to flee from the wrath to come? ⁸ Give some evidence that you mean to reform. Do not begin by saying to yourselves, 'Abraham is our father.' I tell you, God can raise up children to Abraham from these stones. ⁹ Even now the ax is laid to the root of the tree. Every tree that is not fruitful will be cut down and thrown into the fire."

¹⁰ The crowds asked him, "What ought we to do?" ¹¹ In reply

52: 2, 19.
3, 3-10: Mt 3, 1-10; Mk 1, 2-6.
　4: Is 40, 3ff; Jn 1, 23.

10f: Acts 2, 37; Jas 2, 15;
1 Jn 3, 17.

3, 1: *In the fifteenth year . . . Caesar:* this chronological datum enables scholars to calculate that John the Baptizer began his mission sometime between 27 and 29 A. D.
3, 2-18: See notes on the verses in Mt 3, 1-17. The Lucan account of the Baptizer's mission gives examples which clarify the meaning of repentance (3, 10-14).

he said, "Let the man with two coats give to him who has none. The man who has food should do the same."

¹² Tax collectors also came to be baptized, and they said to him, "Teacher, what are we to do?" ¹³ He answered them, "Exact nothing over and above your fixed amount."

¹⁴ Soldiers likewise asked him, "What about us?" He told them, "Don't bully anyone. Denounce no one falsely. Be content with your pay."

¹⁵ The people were full of anticipation, wondering in their hearts whether John might be the Messiah. ¹⁶ John answered them all by saying: "I am baptizing you in water, but there is one to come who is mightier than I. I am not fit to loosen his sandal strap. He will baptize you in the Holy Spirit and in fire. ¹⁷ His winnowing-fan is in his hand to clear his threshing floor and gather the wheat into his granary; but the chaff he will burn in unquenchable fire." ¹⁸ Using exhortations of this sort, he preached the good news to the people.

¹⁹ Herod the tetrarch was censured by John on the subject of Herodias, his brother's wife, and for all his other crimes. ²⁰ He added to his guilt by shutting John up in prison.

Baptism of Jesus

²¹ When all the people were baptized, and Jesus was at prayer after likewise being baptized, the skies opened ²² and the Holy Spirit descended on him in visible form like a dove. A voice from heaven was heard to say: "You are my beloved Son. On you my favor rests."

Genealogy of Jesus

²³ When Jesus began his work he was about thirty years of age, being—so it was supposed—the son of Joseph, son of Heli, ²⁴ son of Matthat, son of Levi, son of Melchi, son of Jannai, son of Joseph, ²⁵ son of Mattathias, son of Amos, son of Nahum, son of Esli, son of Naggai, ²⁶ son of Maath, son of Mattathias,

15-18: Mt 3, 11f; Mk 1, 7f; Acts 13, 25.
16: Jn 1, 27; Acts 1, 5; 11, 16.
17: Mt 3, 12.
19f: Mt 14, 3; Mk 6, 17f.
21f: Mt 3, 13-17; Jn 1, 32ff.
22: 2 Pt 1, 17.
23-38: Mt 1, 1-17.
23: Mt 13, 55.

3, 15: This popular conception concerning John the Baptizer closely resembles that in John 1, 20.25.
3, 21f: See note on Mk 1, 9ff.
3, 23-38: Luke traces the genealogy of Jesus to Adam in order to identify Jesus with all humanity; Matthew (1, 1-16) traces it to Abraham to identify Jesus with Israel.

son of Semein, son of Josech, son of Joda, [27] son of Joanan, son of Rhesa, son of Zerubbabel, son of Shealtiel, son of Neri, [28] son of Melchi, son of Addi, son of Cosam, son of Elmadam, son of Er, [29] son of Joshua, son of Eliezer, son of Jorim, son of Matthat, son of Levi, [30] son of Simeon, son of Judah, son of Joseph, son of Jonam, son of Eliakim, [31] son of Melea, son of Menna, son of Mattatha, son of Nathan, son of David, [32] son of Jesse, son of Obed, son of Boaz, son of Sala, son of Nahshon, [33] son of Amminadab, son of Admin, son of Arni, son of Hezron, son of Perez, son of Judah, [34] son of Jacob, son of Isaac, son of Abraham, son of Terah, son of Nahor, [35] son of Serug, son of Reu, son of Peleg, son of Eber, son of Shelah, [36] son of Cainan, son of Arphaxad, son of Shem, son of Noah, son of Lamech, [37] son of Methusaleh, son of Enoch, son of Jared, son of Mahalaleel, son of Cainan, [38] son of Enos, son of Seth, son of Adam, son of God.

4

Temptation in the Desert

[1] Jesus, full of the Holy Spirit, then returned from the Jordan and was conducted by the Spirit into the desert [2] for forty days, where he was tempted by the devil. During that time he ate nothing, and at the end of it he was hungry. [3] The devil said to him, "If you are the Son of God, command this stone to turn into bread." [4] Jesus answered him, "Scripture has it, 'Not on bread alone shall man live.'"

[5] Then the devil took him up higher and showed him all the kingdoms of the world in a single instant. [6] He said to him, "I will give you all this power and the glory of these kingdoms; the power has been given to me and I give it to whomever I wish. [7] Prostrate yourself in homage before me, and it shall all be yours." [8] In reply, Jesus said to him, "Scripture has it,

'You shall do homage to the Lord your God;
    him alone shall you adore.'"

[9] Then the devil led him to Jerusalem, set him on the parapet of the temple, and said to him, "If you are the Son of God, throw yourself down from here, [10] for Scripture has it,

---

27: 1 Chr 3, 17.
33: Gn 38, 29; Ru 4, 18.
4, 1-13: Mt 4, 1-11; Mk 1, 12f.

4: Dt 8, 3.
6: Jer 27, 5; Rv 13, 2ff.
8: Dt 6, 13.

4, 1-13: See note on Mt 4, 1-11.

'He will bid his angels watch over you';

¹¹ and again,

'With their hands they will support you,
that you may never stumble on a stone.' "

¹² Jesus said to him in reply, "It also says, 'You shall not put the Lord your God to the test.' "

¹³ When the devil had finished all the tempting he left him, to await another opportunity.

III: THE MINISTRY IN GALILEE

Beginning of Preaching

¹⁴ Jesus returned in the power of the Spirit to Galilee, and his reputation spread throughout the region. ¹⁵ He was teaching in their synagogues, and all were loud in his praise.

¹⁶ He came to Nazareth where he had been reared, and entering the synagogue on the sabbath as he was in the habit of doing, he stood up to do the reading. ¹⁷ When the book of the prophet Isaiah was handed him, he unrolled the scroll and found the passage where it was written:

¹⁸ "The spirit of the Lord is upon me;
therefore he has anointed me.
He has sent me to bring glad tidings to the poor,
to proclaim liberty to captives,
Recovery of sight to the blind
and release to prisoners,
¹⁹ To announce a year of favor from the Lord."

²⁰ Rolling up the scroll he gave it back to the assistant and sat down. All in the synagogue had their eyes fixed on him. ²¹ Then he began by saying to them, "Today this Scripture passage is fulfilled in your hearing." ²² All who were present spoke favorably of him; they marveled at the appealing discourse

---

10: Ps 91, 11f.
12: Dt 6, 16.
13: Jn 13, 2.27.
14: 5, 15; Mt 3, 16.

16-30: Mt 13, 53-58;
Mk 6, 1-6.
18: Is 61, 1f; Mt 3, 16.

4, 14-30: After noting Jesus' initial popularity throughout Galilee, Luke combines, into a single scene laid at Nazareth, the favorable reception given to him which Jesus senses in the attitude of his townsmen (23-27; see note on Mk 6, 1-6), and their personal attack on him for refusing to work many miracles for them because of their lack of faith (28ff). Luke intends the entire scene to be prophetic of the ultimate rejection of Jesus by his contemporaries.

which came from his lips. They also asked, "Is not this Joseph's son?"

²³ He said to them, "You will doubtless quote me the proverb, 'Physician, heal yourself,' and say, 'Do here in your own country the things we have heard you have done in Capernaum.' ²⁴ But in fact," he went on, "no prophet gains acceptance in his native place. ²⁵ Indeed, let me remind you, th .e were many widows in Israel in the days of Elijah when the heavens remained closed for three and a half years and a great famine spread over the land. ²⁶ It was to none of these that Elijah was sent, but to a widow of Zarephath near Sidon. ²⁷ Recall, too, the many lepers in Israel in the time of Elisha the prophet; yet not one was cured except Naaman the Syrian."

²⁸ At these words the whole audience in the synagogue was filled with indignation. ²⁹ They rose up and expelled him from the town, leading him to the brow of the hill on which it was built ³⁰ and intending to hurl him over the edge. But he went straight through their midst and walked away.

Jesus Teaches in Capernaum

³¹ He then went down to Capernaum, a town of Galilee, where he began instructing them on the sabbath day. ³² They were spellbound by his teaching, for his words had authority.

Cure of a Demoniac

³³ In the synagogue there was a man with an unclean spirit, who shrieked in a loud voice: ³⁴ "Leave us alone! What do you want of us, Jesus of Nazareth? Have you come to destroy us? I know who you are: the Holy One of God." ³⁵ Jesus said to him sharply, "Be quiet! Come out of him." At that, the demon threw him to the ground before everyone's eyes and came out of him without doing him any harm. ³⁶ All were struck with astonishment, and they began saying to one another: "What is there about his speech? He commands the unclean spirits with authority and power, and they leave." ³⁷ His renown kept spreading through the surrounding country.

³⁸ Leaving the synagogue, he entered the house of Simon. Simon's mother-in-law was in the grip of a severe fever, and they interceded with him for her. ³⁹ He stood over her and ad-

---

27: 2 Kgs 5, 14.   31-37: Mt 4, 13; Mk 1, 21-28.
29: Jn 7, 30.   32: Mt 7, 28f.
30: Jn 8, 59.   38f: Mt 8, 14ff; Mk 1, 29ff.

4, 33-37: See note on Mk 1, 23-28.

dressed himself to the fever, and it left her. She got up immediately and waited on them.

⁴⁰ At sunset, all who had people sick with a variety of diseases took them to him, and he laid hands on each of them and cured them. ⁴¹ Demons departed from many, crying out as they did so, "You are the son of God!" He rebuked them and did not allow them to speak because they knew that he was the Messiah.

⁴² The next morning he left the town and set out into the open country. The crowds went in search of him, and when they found him they tried to keep him from leaving them. But he said to them, ⁴³ "To other towns I must announce the good news of the reign of God, because that is why I was sent." ⁴⁴ And he continued to preach in the synagogues of Judea.

5

Call of the First Disciples

¹ As he stood by the Lake of Gennesaret, and the crowd pressed in on him to hear the word of God, ² he saw two boats moored by the side of the lake; the fishermen had disembarked and were washing their nets. ³ He got into one of the boats, the one belonging to Simon, and asked him to pull out a short distance from the shore; then, remaining seated, he continued to teach the crowds from the boat. ⁴ When he had finished speaking he said to Simon, "Put out into deep water and lower your nets for a catch." ⁵ Simon answered, "Master, we have been hard at it all night long and have caught nothing; but if you say so, I will lower the nets." ⁶ Upon doing this they caught such a great number of fish that their nets were at the breaking point. ⁷ They signaled to their mates in the other boat to come and help them. These came, and together they filled the two boats until they nearly sank.

⁸ At the sight of this, Simon Peter fell at the knees of Jesus saying, "Leave me, Lord. I am a sinful man." ⁹ For indeed, amazement at the catch they had made seized him and all his

---

40f: Mt 8, 16; Mk 1, 32ff.   5, 1-11: Mt 4, 18-22; Mk 1, 16-20.
42f: Mk 1, 35-38.   4: Jn 21, 6.

5, 1-11: This scene of the miraculous catch of fish parallels the call of the disciples in Mt 4, 18-22; Mk 1, 16-20. Probably it is related to the miraculous catch after the resurrection, mentioned in Jn 21, 1-8, to which it bears a certain affinity. The final mandate which the risen Christ gave Simon Peter and the other disciples is here anticipated by Luke in an account which portrays Simon's leadership of the disciples and their role of continuing the spiritual mission of Jesus.

shipmates, [10] as well as James and John, Zebedee's sons, who were partners with Simon. Jesus said to Simon, "Do not be afraid. From now on you will be catching men." [11] With that they brought their boats to land, left everything, and became his followers.

Cure of a Leper

[12] On one occasion in a certain town, a man full of leprosy came to him. Seeing Jesus, he bowed down to the ground and said to him, "Lord, if you will to do so, you can cure me." [13] Jesus stretched out his hand to touch him and said, "I do will it. Be cured." Immediately the leprosy left him. [14] Jesus then instructed the man: "Tell no one, but go and show yourself to the priest. Offer for your healing what Moses prescribed; that should be a proof for them." [15] His reputation spread more and more, and great crowds gathered to hear him and to be cured of their maladies. [16] He often retired to deserted places and prayed.

A Paralyzed Man Cured

[17] One day Jesus was teaching, and the power of the Lord made him heal. Sitting close by were Pharisees and teachers of the law who had come from every village of Galilee and from Judea and Jerusalem. [18] Some men came along carrying a paralytic on a mat. They were trying to bring him in and lay him before Jesus; [19] but they found no way of getting him through because of the crowd, so they went up on the roof. There they let him down with his mat through the tiles into the middle of the crowd before Jesus. [20] Seeing their faith, Jesus said, "My friend, your sins are forgiven you."

[21] The scribes and the Pharisees began a discussion, saying: "Who is this man who utters blasphemies? Who can forgive sins but God alone?" [22] Jesus, however, knew their reasoning and answered them by saying: "Why do you harbor these thoughts? [23] Which is easier: to say, 'Your sins are forgiven you,' or to say, 'Get up and walk'? [24] In any case, to make it clear to you that the Son of Man has authority on earth to forgive sins"—he then addressed the paralyzed man: "I say to you, get up! Take your mat with you, and return to your house."

12ff: Mt 8, 2ff;   17-26: Mt 9, 1-8;
    Mk 1, 40-44.   Mk 2, 1-12.
14: Lv 14, 2-32.

5, 12ff: See note on Mk 1, 40-45.
5, 17-26: See note on Mk 2, 1-12.

²⁵ At once the man stood erect before them. He picked up the mat he had been lying on and went home praising God. ²⁶ At this they were all seized with astonishment. Full of awe, they gave praise to God, saying, "We have seen incredible things today!"

The Call of Levi

²⁷ Afterward he went out and saw a tax collector named Levi sitting at his customs post. He said to him, "Follow me." ²⁸ Leaving everything behind, Levi stood up and became his follower. ²⁹ After that Levi gave a great reception for Jesus in his house, in which he was joined by a large crowd of tax collectors and others at dinner. ³⁰ The Pharisees and the scribes of their party said to his disciples, "Why do you eat and drink with tax collectors and non-observers of the law?" ³¹ Jesus said to them, "The healthy do not need a doctor; sick people do. ³² I have not come to invite the self-righteous to a change of heart, but sinners."

The Question of Fasting

³³ They said to him: "John's disciples fast frequently and offer prayers; the disciples of the Pharisees do the same. Yours, on the contrary, eat and drink freely." ³⁴ Jesus replied: "Can you make guests of the groom fast while the groom is still with them? ³⁵ But when the days come that the groom is removed from their midst, they will surely fast in those days."

³⁶ He then proposed to them this figure: "No one tears a piece from a new coat to patch an old one. If he does, he will only tear the new coat, and the piece taken from it will not match the old. ³⁷ Moreover, no one pours new wine into old wine-skins. Should he do so, the new wine will burst the old skins, the wine will spill out, and the skins will be lost. ³⁸ New wine should be poured into fresh skins. ³⁹ No one, after drinking old wine, wants new. He says, 'I find the old wine better.' "

6

The Disciples and the Sabbath

¹ Once on a sabbath Jesus was walking through the standing

27-38: Mt 9, 9-17;
   Mk 2, 14-22.
29-32: Mt 9, 10-13;
   Mk 2, 15ff.

33-39: Mt 9, 14-17;
   Mk 2, 18-22.
6, 1-5: Mt 12, 1-8;
   Mk 2, 23-28.

5, 33-39: See note on Mt 9, 14-17.
6, 1-5: See note on Mt 12, 3-6.

grain. His disciples were pulling off grain-heads, shelling them with their hands, and eating them. [2] Some of the Pharisees asked, "Why are you doing what is prohibited on the sabbath?" [3] Jesus said to them: "Have you not read what David did when he and his men were hungry—[4] how he entered God's house and took and ate the holy bread and gave it to his men, even though only priests are allowed to eat it?" [5] Then he said to them, "The Son of Man is Lord even of the sabbath."

[6] On another sabbath he came to teach in a synagogue where there was a man whose right hand was withered. [7] The scribes and Pharisees were on the watch to see if he would perform a cure on the sabbath so that they could find a charge against him. [8] He knew their thoughts, however, and said to the man whose hand was withered, "Get up and stand here in front." The man rose and remained standing. [9] Jesus said to them, "I ask you, is it lawful to do good on the sabbath—or evil? To preserve life—or destroy it?" [10] He looked around at them all and said to the man, "Stretch out your hand." The man did so and his hand was perfectly restored.

[11] At this they became frenzied and began asking one another what could be done to Jesus.

Choice of the Twelve

[12] Then he went out to the mountain to pray, spending the night in communion with God. [13] At daybreak he called his disciples and selected twelve of them to be his apostles: [14] Simon, to whom he gave the name Peter, and Andrew his brother, James and John, Philip and Bartholomew, [15] Matthew and Thomas, James son of Alphaeus, and Simon called the Zealot, [16] Judas son of James, and Judas Iscariot, who turned traitor.

The Great Discourse

[17] Coming down the mountain with them, he stopped at a level stretch where there were many of his disciples; a large crowd of people was with them from all Judea and Jerusalem and the coast of Tyre and Sidon, [18] people who came to hear him and be healed of their diseases. Those who were troubled with unclean spirits were cured; [19] indeed, the whole crowd was trying to touch him because power went out from him

---

4: 1 Sm 21, 7.
6-11: 14, 1-6; Mt 12, 9-14; Mk 3, 1-6.

12-16: Mt 10, 1-4; Mk 3, 13-19.
17ff: Mt 4, 24f; Mk 3, 7-12.

6, 6-11: See note on Mt 12, 10.
6, 12-16: See note on Mk 3, 13-19.

which cured all. [20] Then, raising his eyes to his disciples, he said:

"Blest are you poor; the reign of God is yours.
  Blest are you who hunger; [21] you shall be filled.
  Blest are you who are weeping; you shall laugh.

[22] "Blest shall you be when men hate you, when they ostracize you and insult you and proscribe your name as evil because of the Son of Man. [23] On the day they do so, rejoice and exult, for your reward shall be great in heaven. Thus it was that their fathers treated the prophets.

[24] "But woe to you rich, for your consolation is now.
  [25] Woe to you who are full; you shall go hungry.
  Woe to you who laugh now; you shall weep in your grief.

[26] "Woe to you when all speak well of you. Their fathers treated the false prophets in just this way.

Love of One's Enemy

[27] "To you who hear me, I say: Love your enemies, do good to those who hate you; [28] bless those who curse you and pray for those who maltreat you. [29] When someone slaps you on one cheek, turn and give him the other; when someone takes your coat, let him have your shirt as well. [30] Give to all who beg from you. When a man takes what is yours, do not demand it back. [31] Do to others what you would have them do to you. [32] If you love those who love you, what credit is that to you? Even sinners love those who love them. [33] If you do good to those who do good to you, how can you claim any credit? Sinners do as much. [34] If you lend to those from whom you

20-23: Mt 5, 1-12.
24: Is 5, 8-12; Am 6, 1.
25: Prv 14, 13; Is 65, 13f;
  Jas 5, 1.
27: Mt 5, 44.

28: 1 Pt 3, 9.
29f: Mt 5, 39-42.
31: Mt 7, 12.
32: Mt 5, 46.
34: Dt 15, 8; Mt 5, 42.

6, 20-49: The Lucan Sermon on the Plain characterizes the Christian as distinctive for his poverty (20-23), cautious against the dangers of wealth (24f), loving toward his enemy (27-38), critical of himself (39-45), and obedient to the teaching of Jesus (46-49). It is reasonable to assume that this Lucan arrangement of Jesus' teaching was addressed to the economically deprived and politically threatened Christian communities of Asia Minor and Greece. It thus possesses a special poignancy, born of Luke's faith in the inevitable victory of the Christian message in a hostile environment, provided Christians accept their poverty in the spirit of Christ and endeavor to conquer their persecutors by the love they show them. The sermon seems to intimate a relevance between the actual situation of the Christian communities it addresses and the teaching of Jesus.

expect repayment, what merit is there in it for you? Even sinners lend to sinners, expecting to be repaid in full.

³⁵ "Love your enemy and do good; lend without expecting repayment. Then will your recompense be great. You will rightly be called sons of the Most High, since he himself is good to the ungrateful and the wicked.

³⁶ "Be compassionate, as your Father is compassionate. ³⁷ Do not judge, and you will not be judged. Do not condemn, and you will not be condemned. Pardon, and you shall be pardoned. ³⁸ Give, and it shall be given to you. Good measure pressed down, shaken together, running over, will they pour into the fold of your garment. For the measure you measure with will be measured back to you."

³⁹ He also used images in speaking to them: "Can a blind man act as guide to a blind man? Will they not both fall into a ditch? ⁴⁰ A student is not above his teacher; but every student when he has finished his studies will be on a par with his teacher.

⁴¹ "Why look at the speck in your brother's eyes when you miss the plank in your own? ⁴² How can you say to your brother, 'Brother, let me remove the speck from your eye,' yet fail yourself to see the plank lodged in your own? Hypocrite, remove the plank from your own eye first; then you will see clearly enough to remove the speck from your brother's eye.

⁴³ "A good tree does not produce decayed fruit any more than a decayed tree produces good fruit. ⁴⁴ Each tree is known by its yield. Figs are not taken from thornbushes, nor grapes picked from brambles. ⁴⁵ A good man produces goodness from the good in his heart; an evil man produces evil out of his store of evil. Each man speaks from his heart's abundance. ⁴⁶ Why do you call me 'Lord, Lord,' and not put into practice what I teach you? ⁴⁷ Any man who desires to come to me will hear my words and put them into practice. I will show you with whom he is to be compared. ⁴⁸ He may be likened to the man who, in building a house, dug deeply and laid the foundation on a rock. When the floods came the torrent rushed in on that house, but failed to shake it because of its solid foundation. ⁴⁹ On the other hand, anyone who has heard my words but not put them into practice is like the man who built his

---

37: Mt 7, 1; Jas 2, 13.
38: Mk 4, 24.
39: Mt 15, 14.
40: Mt 10, 24; Jn 13, 16.
41f: Mt 7, 3ff.

43ff: Mt 7, 16ff; 12, 33ff.
46: Mt 7, 21; Rom 2, 13; Jas 1, 22.
47ff: Mt 7, 24-27.

house on the ground without any foundation. When the torrent rushed upon it, it immediately fell in and was completely destroyed."

7

Cure of the Centurion's Servant

[1] When he had finished this discourse in the hearing of the people, he entered Capernaum. [2] A centurion had a servant he held in high regard, who was at that moment sick to the point of death. [3] When he heard about Jesus he sent some Jewish elders to him, asking him to come and save the life of his servant. [4] Upon approaching Jesus they petitioned him earnestly. [5] "He deserves this favor from you," they said, "because he loves our people, and even built our synagogue for us." [6] Jesus set out with them. When he was only a short distance from the house, the centurion sent friends to tell him: "Sir, do not trouble yourself, for I am not worthy to have you enter my house. [7] That is why I did not presume to come to you myself. Just give the order and my servant will be cured. [8] I too am a man who knows the meaning of an order, having soldiers under my command. I say to one, 'On your way,' and off he goes; to another, 'Come here,' and he comes; to my slave, 'Do this,' and he does it." [9] Jesus showed amazement on hearing this, and turned to the crowd which was following him to say, "I tell you, I have never found so much faith among the Israelites." [10] When the deputation returned to the house, they found the servant in perfect health.

The Widow's Son

[11] Soon afterward he went to a town called Naim, and his disciples and a large crowd accompanied him. [12] As he approached the gate of the town a dead man was being carried out, the only son of a widowed mother. A considerable crowd of townsfolk were with her. [13] The Lord was moved with pity upon seeing her and said to her, "Do not cry." [14] Then he

---

7, 1-10: Mt 8, 5-13.   9: Mt 8, 10.

7, 1-10: The placement of this event after the Sermon on the Plain (6, 46-49) serves as an example of that practical acknowledgment of Jesus' authority which is recommended at the conclusion of the sermon.
7, 11-17: This account of the raising to life of the widow's son prepares for Jesus' response about his ministry, made to the inquiring disciples of John the Baptizer (20.22). The observation in 7, 15, *Jesus gave him back to his mother* relates the mission of Jesus to that of Elijah (1 Kgs 17, 23).

stepped forward and touched the litter; at this, the bearers halted. He said, "Young man, I bid you get up." [15] The dead man sat up and began to speak. Then Jesus gave him back to his mother. [16] Fear seized them all and they began to praise God. "A great prophet has risen among us," they said; and, "God has visited his people." [17] This was the report that spread about him throughout Judea and the surrounding country.

Jesus' Testimony

[18] The disciples of John brought their teacher word of all these happenings. Summoning two of them, [19] John sent them to ask the Lord, "Are you 'He who is to come' or are we to expect someone else?" [20] When the men came to him they said, "John the Baptizer sends us to you with this question: 'Are you "He who is to come" or do we look for someone else?' " [21] (At that time he was curing many of their diseases, afflictions, and evil spirits; he also restored sight to many who were blind.) [22] Jesus gave this response: "Go and report to John what you have seen and heard. The blind recover their sight, cripples walk, lepers are cured, the deaf hear, dead men are raised to life, and the poor have the good news preached to them. [23] Blest is that man who finds no stumbling block in me."

[24] When the messengers of John had set off, Jesus began to speak about him to the crowds. "What did you go out to see in the desert—a reed swayed by the wind? [25] What, really, did you go out to see—someone dressed luxuriously? Remember, those who dress in luxury and eat in splendor are to be found in royal palaces. [26] Then what did you go out to see—a prophet? He is that, I assure you, and something more. [27] This is the man of whom Scripture says,

> 'I send my messenger ahead of you
> to prepare your way before you.'

[28] I assure you, there is no man born of woman greater than John. Yet the least born into the kingdom of God is greater than he."

John's Baptism

[29] The entire populace that had heard Jesus, even the tax

16: 1 Kgs 17, 23;
    Mt 16, 14; Jn 4, 19.
17: 4, 14.
18-27: Mt 11, 2-11.

22: Is 35, 5f.
27: Is 40, 3; Mal 3, 1.
29: Mt 21, 32.

7, 18-23: See note on Mt 11, 3.
7, 24-35: See notes on Mt 11, 7-15; 11, 11; 11, 19.

collectors, gave praise to God, for they had received from John the baptismal bath he administered. ³⁰ The Pharisees and the lawyers, on the other hand, by failing to receive his baptism defeated God's plan in their regard.

Christ's Verdict

³¹ "What comparison can I use for the men of today? What are they like? ³² They are like children squatting in the city squares and calling to their playmates,

> 'We piped you a tune but you did not dance,
> We sang you a dirge but you did not wail.'

³³ I mean that John the Baptizer came neither eating bread nor drinking wine, and you say, 'He is mad!' ³⁴ The Son of Man came and he both ate and drank, and you say, 'Here is a glutton and a drunkard, a friend of tax collectors and sinners!' ³⁵ God's wisdom is vindicated by all who accept it."

The Penitent Woman

³⁶ There was a certain Pharisee who invited Jesus to dine with him. Jesus went to the Pharisee's home and reclined to eat. ³⁷ A woman known in the town to be a sinner learned that he was dining in the Pharisee's home. She brought in a vase of perfumed oil ³⁸ and stood behind him at his feet, weeping so that her tears fell upon his feet. Then she wiped them with her hair, kissing them and perfuming them with the oil. ³⁹ When his host, the Pharisee, saw this, he said to himself, "If this man were a prophet, he would know who and what sort of woman this is that touches him—that she is a sinner." ⁴⁰ In answer to his thoughts, Jesus said to him, "Simon, I have something to propose to you." "Teacher," he said, "speak."

⁴¹ "Two men owed money to a certain money-lender; one owed a total of five hundred coins, the other fifty. ⁴² Since neither was able to repay, he wrote off both debts. Which of them was more grateful to him?" ⁴³ Simon answered, "He, I presume, to whom he remitted the larger sum." Jesus said to him, "You are right."

31-35: Mt 11, 16-19.   Mk 14, 3-9; Jn 12, 1-8.
36: 11, 37; 14, 1.   37: Mt 21, 32.
37ff: Mt 26, 6-13;

7, 36-50: Jesus admits both the gravity of the woman's sins and the relative justice of Simon. But he points out her superiority to the Pharisee, for she expresses the love that stems from repentance, whereas Simon's pride prevents him from acknowledging his real, though lesser, sinfulness.

⁴⁴ Turning then to the woman, he said to Simon: "You see this woman? I came to your home and you provided me with no water for my feet. She has washed my feet with her tears and wiped them with her hair. ⁴⁵ You gave me no kiss, but she has not ceased kissing my feet since I entered. ⁴⁶ You did not anoint my head with oil, but she has anointed my feet with perfume. ⁴⁷ I tell you, that is why her many sins are forgiven— because of her great love. Little is forgiven the one whose love is small."

⁴⁸ He said to her then, "Your sins are forgiven"; ⁴⁹ at which his fellow guests began to ask among themselves, "Who is this that he even forgives sins?" ⁵⁰ Meanwhile he said to the woman, "Your faith has been your salvation. Now go in peace."

8

The Women Who Served

¹ After this he journeyed through towns and villages preaching and proclaiming the good news of the kingdom of God. The Twelve accompanied him, ² and also some women who had been cured of evil spirits and maladies: Mary called the Magdalene, from whom seven devils had gone out, ³ Joanna, the wife of Herod's steward Chuza, Susanna, and many others who were assisting them out of their means.

Parable of the Sower

⁴ A large crowd was gathering, with people resorting to him from one town after another. He spoke to them in a parable: ⁵ "A farmer went out to sow some seed. In the sowing, some fell on the footpath where it was walked on and the birds of the air ate it up. ⁶ Some fell on rocky ground, sprouted up, then withered through lack of moisture. ⁷ Some fell among briers, and the thorns growing up with it stifled it. ⁸ But some fell on good soil, grew up, and yielded again a hundredfold."

As he said this he exclaimed: "Let everyone who has ears attend to what he has heard." ⁹ His disciples began asking him

48: Mt 9, 2. Jn 19, 25.
8, 1: 4, 43; Mk 1, 39. 9-15: Mt 13, 10-23;
   2: 24, 10; Mt 27, 55f; Mk 4, 10-20.
   Mk 15, 40f; 16, 9;

8, 1ff: Luke notes Jesus' acceptance of the aid of women during his ministry. The evangelist probably also has in mind their contributions to the early Christian communities.

8, 4-15: On the meaning of the parable of the sower and its explanation, see the note on Mt 13, 1-53.

what the meaning of this parable might be. [10] He replied, "To you the mysteries of the reign of God have been confided, but to the rest in parables that,

> 'Seeing they may not perceive,
> and hearing they may not understand.'

[11] This is the meaning of the parable. The seed is the word of God. [12] Those on the footpath are people who hear, but the devil comes and takes the word out of their hearts lest they believe and be saved. [13] Those on the rocky ground are the ones who, when they hear the word, receive it with joy. They have no root; they believe for a while, but fall away in time of temptation. [14] The seed fallen among briers are those who hear, but their progress is stifled by the cares and riches and pleasures of life and they do not mature. [15] The seed on good ground are those who hear the word in a spirit of openness, retain it, and bear fruit through perseverance.

Parable of the Lamp

[16] "No one lights a lamp and puts it under a bushel basket or under a bed; he puts it on a lampstand so that whoever comes in can see it. [17] There is nothing hidden that will not be exposed, nothing concealed that will not be known and brought to light. [18] Take heed, therefore, how you hear: to the man who has, more will be given; and he who has not, will lose even the little he thinks he has."

True Kindred of Jesus

[19] His mother and brothers came to be with him, but they could not reach him because of the crowd. [20] He was told, "Your mother and your brothers are standing outside and they wish to see you." [21] He told them in reply, "My mother and my brothers are those who hear the word of God and act upon it."

10: Is 6, 9; Jn 12, 40;
  Acts 28, 26.
16ff: Mk 4, 21-25.
  16: 11, 33; Mt 5, 15.
  17: 12, 2; Mt 10, 26.

18: 19, 26; Mt 13, 12;
  25, 29.
19ff: Mt 12, 46-50;
  Mk 3, 31-35.
  21: 11, 27f.

8, 19ff: This passage is to be understood in the light of Luke's theological conception of the mother of Jesus as the figure or type of the Christian community. She acquiesces fully, as the Christian should, to the mystery of God's word; cf 1, 38.

Calming of the Tempest

²² One day he got into a boat with his disciples and said to them, "Let us cross over to the far side of the lake." So they set out, ²³ and as they sailed he slept. A windstorm descended on the lake, and they began to ship water and to be in danger. ²⁴ They came to awaken him, saying, "Master, master, we are lost!" He awoke and rebuked the wind and the tumultuous waves. The waves subsided and it grew calm. ²⁵ Then he asked them, "Where is your faith?" Filled with fear and admiration, they said to one another, "What sort of man can this be who commands even the winds and the sea and they obey him?"

The Gerasene Demoniac

²⁶ They sailed to the country of the Gerasenes, which is opposite Galilee. ²⁷ When he came to land, he was met by a man from the town who was possessed by demons. For a long time he had not worn any clothes; he did not live in a house, but among the tombstones. ²⁸ On seeing Jesus he began to shriek; then he fell at his feet and exclaimed at the top of his voice, "Jesus, Son of God Most High, why do you meddle with me? Do not torment me, I beg you." ²⁹ By now Jesus was ordering the unclean spirit to come out of the man. This spirit had taken hold of him many a time. The man used to be tied with chains and fetters, but he would break his bonds and the demon would drive him into places of solitude. ³⁰ "What is your name?" Jesus demanded. "Legion," he answered, because the demons who had entered him were many. ³¹ They pleaded with him not to order them back to the abyss. ³² It happened that a large herd of swine was feeding nearby on the hillside, and the demons asked him to permit them to enter the swine. This he granted. ³³ The demons then came out of the man and entered the swine, and the herd charged down the bluff into the lake, where they drowned.

³⁴ When the swineherds saw what had happened, they took to their heels and brought the news to the town and country roundabout. ³⁵ The people went out to see for themselves what had happened. Coming on Jesus, they found the man from

---

22-25: Mt 8, 23-27;   Mk 5, 1-20.
        Mk 4, 35-41.   28: 4, 34; Mt 4, 3.
26-39: Mt 8, 28-34;

8, 22-25: See note on Mk 4, 35-41.
8, 26-39: See note on Mk 1, 23-28 concerning the exorcisms performed by Jesus.

whom the devils had departed sitting at his feet dressed and in his full senses; this sight terrified them. [36] They were told by witnesses how the possessed man had been cured. [37] Shortly afterward, the entire population of the Gerasene territory asked Jesus to leave their neighborhood, for a great fear had seized them; so he got into the boat and went back across the lake.

[38] The man from whom the devils had departed asked to come with him, [39] but he sent him away with the words, "Go back home and recount all that God has done for you." The man went all through the town making public what Jesus had done for him.

Jairus' Child; a Hemorrhage Victim

[40] On his return, Jesus was welcomed by the crowd; indeed, they were all waiting for him. [41] A man named Jairus, who was chief of the synagogue, came up and fell at Jesus' feet, begging that he come to his home [42] because his only daughter, a girl of about twelve, was dying. As Jesus went, the crowds almost crushed him. [43] A woman with a hemorrhage of twelve years' duration, incurable at any doctor's hands, [44] came up behind him and touched the tassel on his cloak. Immediately her bleeding stopped. [45] Jesus asked, "Who touched me?" Everyone disclaimed doing it, while Peter said, "Lord, the crowds are milling and pressing around you!" [46] Jesus insisted, "Someone touched me; I know that power has gone forth from me." [47] When the woman saw that her act had not gone unnoticed, she came forward trembling. Falling at his feet, she related before the whole assemblage why she had touched him and how she had been instantly cured. [48] Jesus said to her, "Daughter, it is your faith that has cured you. Now go in peace."

[49] He was still speaking when a man came from the ruler's house with the announcement, "Your daughter is dead; do not bother the Teacher further." [50] Jesus heard this, and his response was: "Fear is useless; what is needed is trust and her life will be spared." [51] Once he had arrived at the house, he permitted no one to enter with him except Peter, John, James, and the child's parents. [52] While everyone wept and lamented her, he said, "Stop crying for she is not dead but asleep." [53] They laughed at him, being certain she was dead. [54] He took her by the hand and spoke these words: "Get up, child." [55] The

40-56: Mt 9, 18-26;   46: 6, 19.
        Mk 5, 21-43.

8, 40-56: See note on Mk 5, 21-43.

breath of life returned to her and she got up immediately; whereupon he told them to give her something to eat. [56] Her parents were astounded, but he ordered them not to tell anyone what had happened.

9

Mission of the Twelve

[1] Jesus now called the Twelve together and gave them power and authority to overcome all demons and to cure diseases. [2] He sent them forth to proclaim the reign of God and heal the afflicted. [3] Jesus advised them: "Take nothing for the journey, neither walking staff nor traveling bag; no bread, no money. No one is to have two coats. [4] Stay at whatever house you enter and proceed from there. [5] When people will not receive you, leave that town and shake its dust from your feet as a testimony against them." [6] So they set out and went from village to village, spreading the good news everywhere and curing diseases.

Herod Learns of Jesus

[7] Herod the tetrarch heard of all that was happening and was perplexed, for some were saying, "John has been raised from the dead"; [8] others, "Elijah has appeared"; and still others, "One of the prophets of old has risen." [9] But Herod said, "John I beheaded. Who is this man about whom I hear all these reports?" He was very curious to see him.

Multiplication of the Loaves

[10] The apostles on their return related to Jesus all they had accomplished. Taking them with him, he retired to a town called Bethsaida, [11] but the crowds found this out and followed him. He received them and spoke to them of the reign of God, and he healed all who were in need of healing.

[12] As sunset approached the Twelve came and said to him, "Dismiss the crowd so that they can go into the villages and farms in the neighborhood and find themselves lodging and food, for this is certainly an out-of-the-way place." [13] He answered them, "Why do you not give them something to eat yourselves?" They replied, "We have nothing but five loaves

9, 1-6: Mt 10, 1.8-14;
     Mk 3, 13-16; 6, 7-13.
   4: 10, 7.
   5: Acts 13, 51.

7ff: Mt 14, 1f; Mk 6, 14ff.
10-17: Mt 14, 13-21;
      Mk 6, 30-44; Jn 6, 1-13.

and two fish. Or shall we ourselves go and buy food for all these people?" [14] (There were about five thousand men.) Jesus said to his disciples, "Have them sit down in groups of fifty or so." [15] They followed his instructions and got them all seated. [16] Then, taking the five loaves and the two fish, Jesus raised his eyes to heaven, pronounced a blessing over them, broke them, and gave them to his disciples for distribution to the crowd. [17] They all ate until they had enough. What they had left, over and above, filled twelve baskets.

Peter's Profession of Faith

[18] One day when Jesus was praying in seclusion and his disciples were with him, he put the question to them, "Who do the crowds say that I am?" [19] "John the Baptizer," they replied, "and some say Elijah, while others claim that one of the prophets of old has returned from the dead." [20] "But you— who do you say that I am?" he asked them. Peter said in reply, "The Messiah of God." [21] He strictly forbade them to tell this to anyone. [22] "The Son of Man," he said, "must first endure many sufferings, be rejected by the elders, the high priests and the scribes, and be put to death, and then be raised up on the third day."

Conditions of Discipleship

[23] Jesus said to all: "Whoever wishes to be my follower must deny his very self, take up his cross each day, and follow in my steps. [24] Whoever would save his life will lose it, and whoever loses his life for my sake will save it. [25] What profit does he show who gains the whole world and destroys himself in the process? [26] If a man is ashamed of me and my doctrine, the Son of Man will be ashamed of him when he comes in his glory and that of his Father and his holy angels. [27] I assure you, there are some standing here who will not taste death until they see the reign of God."

18-21: Mt 16, 13-20;
    Mk 8, 27-30.
  22: 24, 7.26; Mt 16, 21;
    Mk 8, 31.
23-26: Mt 16, 24-28;
    Mk 8, 34-38; 9, 1.

23: 14, 27; Mt 10, 38.
24: 17, 33; Mt 10, 39;
    Jn 12, 25f.
26: 12, 9; Mt 10, 33.
27: Mt 16, 28; Mk 9, 1.

9, 18-22: Luke omits reference to Caesarea Philippi (Mt 16, 13; Mk 8, 27) as the locale of Peter's confession. This is because his chief interest in the event centers upon Jesus' awareness of his messianic identity in his onward movement toward Jerusalem (not away from it) to achieve the climax of his mission through the passion and resurrection.
9, 23-27: See note on Mk 8, 34—9, 1.

Jesus Transfigured

²⁸ About eight days after saying this he took Peter, John and James, and went up onto a mountain to pray. ²⁹ While he was praying, his face changed in appearance and his clothes became dazzlingly white. ³⁰ Suddenly two men were talking with him— Moses and Elijah. ³¹ They appeared in glory and spoke of his passage, which he was about to fulfill in Jerusalem. ³² Peter and those with him had fallen into a deep sleep; but awakening, they saw his glory and likewise saw the two men who were standing with him. ³³ When these were leaving, Peter said to Jesus: "Master, how good it is for us to be here. Let us set up three booths, one for you, one for Moses, and one for Elijah." (He did not really know what he was saying.) ³⁴ While he was speaking, a cloud came and overshadowed them, and the disciples grew fearful as the others entered it. ³⁵ Then from the cloud came a voice which said, "This is my Son, my Chosen One. Listen to him." ³⁶ When the voice fell silent, Jesus was there alone. The disciples kept quiet, telling nothing of what they had seen at that time to anyone.

A Possessed Boy

³⁷ The following day they came down from the mountain and a large crowd met them. ³⁸ Suddenly a man from the crowd exclaimed: "Teacher, I beg you to look at my son; he is my only child. ³⁹ A spirit takes possession of him and with a sudden cry throws him into a convulsion and makes him foam at the mouth, then abandons him in his shattered condition. ⁴⁰ I asked your disciples to cast out the spirit but they could not." ⁴¹ Jesus said in reply: "What an unbelieving and perverse lot you are! How long must I remain with you? How long can I endure you? Bring your son here to me." ⁴² As he was being brought, the spirit threw him into convulsions on the ground. Jesus then rebuked the unclean spirit, cured the boy, and restored him to his father. ⁴³ And all who saw it marveled at the greatness of God.

Second Prediction of the Passion

In the midst of their amazement at all that he was doing,

28-36: Mt 17, 1-9; Mk 9, 2-10.   37-43: Mt 17, 14-18;
35: 2 Pt 1, 17.   Mk 9, 14-27.

9, 28-36: See note on Mk 9, 2-8. Lk 9, 31 explicitly associates the transfiguration with Jesus' passion and resurrection.
9, 37-43: See note on Mk 9, 14-29.

Jesus said to his disciples: [44] "Pay close attention to what I tell you: the Son of Man must be delivered into the hands of men." [45] They failed, however, to understand this warning; its meaning was so concealed from them they did not grasp it at all, and they were afraid to question him about the matter.

Against Ambition

[46] A discussion arose among them as to which of them was the greatest. [47] Jesus, who knew their thoughts, took a little child and placed it beside him, [48] after which he said to them, "Whoever welcomes this little child on my account welcomes me, and whoever welcomes me welcomes him who sent me; for the least one among you is the greatest."

[49] It was John who said, "Master, we saw a man using your name to expel demons, and we tried to stop him because he is not of our company." [50] Jesus told him in reply, "Do not stop him, for any man who is not against you is on your side."

IV: THE JOURNEY THROUGH PEREA

Samaritan Inhospitality

[51] As the time approached when he was to be taken from this world, he firmly resolved to proceed toward Jerusalem, and sent messengers on ahead of him. [52] These entered a Samaritan town to prepare for his passing through, [53] but the Samaritans would not welcome him because he was on his way to Jerusalem. [54] When his disciples James and John saw this, they said, "Lord,

---

44f: Mt 17, 22f; Mk 9, 30ff.
46ff: Mt 18, 1-5;
        Mk 9, 33-37.
46: 22, 24.

48: Mt 10, 40; 18, 5; Jn 13, 20.
51: 13, 22; 17, 11; 18, 31;
     19, 28; 24, 51.

9, 44f: See note on Mk 9, 30ff.
9, 46ff: See note on Mk 9, 33-37.
9, 49f: See note on Mk 9, 38-41.
9, 51—18, 14: This section, composed mainly of sayings, parables, and incidents found only in Luke, is derived from special sources at Luke's disposal and has come to be called "the great insertion." The evangelist presents these things within the framework of a geographical theme of Jesus' last journey to Jerusalem (9, 53.57; 10, 1; 13, 22.33; 17, 11). The several incidents recounted show the superior wisdom of Jesus, e. g., his response to the lawyer concerning the way to eternal life (10, 25-28), and his defense of healing on the sabbath (13, 10-17; 14, 1-6).

The principal themes of Jesus' teaching in this section concern the sacrifices required for discipleship (9, 57-62); God's action in history directing the gospel message to the simple ones (10, 21); reliance on persevering prayer (11, 1-13; 18, 1-8); the supreme value of man's response to God's word (10, 38-42; 11, 27f); the gravity of the refusal to repent (11, 29-32; 13, 1-5); the sinfulness of hypocrisy (11, 37—12, 3); the threat to salvation presented by material wealth (12, 13-34; 16, 1-15.19-31); constant readiness for divine judgment (12, 35-48.54-59; 13, 6-9.22-30; 14, 16-24; 17, 20-37); and the bestowal of the divine mercy upon sinners (15, 3-32).

would you not have us call down fire from heaven to destroy them?" ⁵⁵ He turned toward them only to reprimand them. ⁵⁶ Then they set off for another town.

The Apostles' Requirements

⁵⁷ As they were making their way along, someone said to him, "I will be your follower wherever you go." ⁵⁸ Jesus said to him, "The foxes have lairs, the birds of the sky have nests, but the Son of Man has nowhere to lay his head." ⁵⁹ To another he said, "Come after me." The man replied, "Let me bury my father first." ⁶⁰ Jesus said to him, "Let the dead bury their dead; come away and proclaim the kingdom of God." ⁶¹ Yet another said to him, "I will be your follower, Lord, but first let me take leave of my people at home." ⁶² Jesus answered him, "Whoever puts his hand to the plow but keeps looking back is unfit for the reign of God."

10

Mission of the Seventy-two

¹ After this, the Lord appointed a further seventy-two and sent them in pairs before him to every town and place he intended to visit. ² He said to them: "The harvest is rich but the workers are few; therefore ask the harvest-master to send workers to his harvest. ³ Be on your way, and remember: I am sending you as lambs in the midst of wolves. ⁴ Do not carry a walking staff or traveling bag; wear no sandals and greet no one along the way. ⁵ On entering any house, first say, 'Peace to this house.' ⁶ If there is a peaceable man there, your peace will rest on him; if not, it will come back to you. ⁷ Stay in the one house eating and drinking what they have, for the laborer is worth his wage. Do not move from house to house.

⁸ "Into whatever city you go, after they welcome you, eat what they set before you, ⁹ and cure the sick there. Say to them, 'The reign of God is at hand.' ¹⁰ If the people of any town you enter do not welcome you, go into its streets and say, ¹¹ 'We shake the dust of this town from our feet as testimony against you. But know that the reign of God is near.' ¹² I assure you, on that day the fate of Sodom will be less severe than

57-60: Mt 8, 19-22.   7: Mt 10, 10; 1 Tm 5, 18.
   61: 1 Kgs 19, 19ff.   9: Mt 3, 2; 4, 17.
10, 2: Mt 9, 37; Jn 4, 35.   10: Mt 10, 7.
   3: Mt 10, 16.   11: Acts 13, 51.
   4-7: 9, 3ff.   13: Mt 11, 21-24.

that of such a town. [13] It will go ill with you, Chorazin! And just as ill with you, Bethsaida! If the miracles worked in your midst had occurred in Tyre and Sidon, they would long ago have reformed in sackcloth and ashes. [14] It will go easier on the day of judgment for Tyre and Sidon than for you. [15] And as for you, Capernaum, 'Are you to be exalted to the skies? You shall be hurled down to the realm of death!'

[16] "He who hears you, hears me. He who rejects you, rejects me. And he who rejects me, rejects him who sent me."

[17] The seventy-two returned in jubilation saying, "Master, even the demons are subject to us in your name." [18] He said in reply: "I watched Satan fall from the sky like lightning. [19] See what I have done; I have given you power to tread on snakes and scorpions and all the forces of the enemy, and nothing shall ever injure you. [20] Nevertheless, do not rejoice so much in the fact that the devils are subject to you as that your names are inscribed in heaven."

Hymn of Praise

[21] At that moment Jesus rejoiced in the Holy Spirit and said: "I offer you praise, O Father, Lord of heaven and earth, because what you have hidden from the learned and the clever you have revealed to the merest children.

[22] "Yes, Father, you have graciously willed it so. Everything has been given over to me by my Father. No one knows the Son except the Father and no one knows the Father except the Son—and anyone to whom the Son wishes to reveal him."

Privilege of the Disciples

[23] Turning to his disciples he said to them privately: "Blest are the eyes that see what you see. I [24] tell you, many prophets and kings wished to see what you see but did not see it, and to hear what you hear but did not hear it."

The Good Samaritan

[25] On one occasion a lawyer stood up to pose him this problem: "Teacher, what must I do to inherit everlasting life?"

15: Is 14, 13ff.
16: Mt 10, 40; Jn 13, 20.
18: Is 14, 12.
19: Ps 91, 13; Rv 12, 9.
20: Rv 20, 12.

21f: Mt 11, 25ff.
23f: Mt 13, 16f.
25-28: Mt 22, 34-39;
Mk 12, 28-31.
25: Mt 19, 16.

26 Jesus answered him: "What is written in the law? How do you read it?" 27 He replied:

> "You shall love the Lord your God
> with all your heart,
> with all your soul,
> with all your strength,
> and with all your mind;
> and your neighbor as yourself."

28 Jesus said, "You have answered correctly. Do this and you shall live." 29 But because he wished to justify himself he said to Jesus, "And who is my neighbor?" 30 Jesus replied: "There was a man going down from Jerusalem to Jericho who fell prey to robbers. They stripped him, beat him, and then went off leaving him half-dead. A 31 priest happened to be going down the same road; he saw him but continued on. 32 Likewise there was a Levite who came the same way; he saw him and went on. 33 But a Samaritan who was journeying along came on him and was moved to pity at the sight. 34 He approached him and dressed his wounds, pouring in oil and wine. He then hoisted him on his own beast and brought him to an inn, where he cared for him. 35 The next day he took out two silver pieces and gave them to the innkeeper with the request: 'Look after him, and if there is any further expense I will repay you on my way back.'

36 "Which of these three, in your opinion, was neighbor to the man who fell in with the robbers?" 37 The answer came, "The one who treated him with compassion." Jesus said to him, "Then go and do the same."

Martha and Mary

38 On their journey Jesus entered a village where a woman named Martha welcomed him to her home. 39 She had a sister named Mary, who seated herself at the Lord's feet and listened to his words. 40 Martha, who was busy with all the details of hospitality, came to him and said, "Lord, are you not concerned that my sister has left me to do the household tasks all alone? Tell her to help me."

41 The Lord in reply said to her: "Martha, Martha, you are anxious and upset about many things; 42 one thing only is required. Mary has chosen the better portion and she shall not be deprived of it."

27: Lv 19, 18; Dt 6, 5.   28: Lv 18, 5; Prv 19, 16.   38: Jn 11, 1f.

11

The Our Father

¹ One day he was praying in a certain place. When he had finished, one of his disciples asked him, "Lord, teach us to pray, as John taught his disciples." ² He said to them, "When you pray, say:

> "Father,
> hallowed be your name,
> your kingdom come.
> ³ Give us each day our daily bread.
> ⁴ Forgive us our sins
> for we too forgive all who do us wrong;
> and subject us not to the trial."

Two Parables on Prayer

⁵ Jesus said to them: "If one of you knows someone who comes to him in the middle of the night and says to him, 'Friend, lend me three loaves, ⁶ for a friend of mine has come in from a journey and I have nothing to offer him'; ⁷ and he from inside should reply, 'Leave me alone. The door is shut now and my children and I are in bed. I cannot get up to look after your needs'—I ⁸ tell you, even though he does not get up and take care of the man because of friendship, he will do so because of his persistence, and give him as much as he needs.

⁹ "So I say to you, 'Ask and you shall receive; seek and you shall find; knock and it shall be opened to you.'

¹⁰ 'For whoever asks, receives; whoever seeks, finds; whoever knocks, is admitted. ¹¹ What father among you will give his son a snake if he asks for a fish, ¹² or hand him a scorpion if he asks for an egg? ¹³ If you, with all your sins, know how to give your children good things, how much more will the heavenly Father give the Holy Spirit to those who ask him."

Jesus and Beelzebul

¹⁴ Jesus was casting out a devil which was mute, and when the devil was cast out the dumb man spoke. The crowds were amazed at this. ¹⁵ Some of them said, "It is by Beelzebul, the prince of devils, that he casts out devils." ¹⁶ Others, to test him, were demanding of him a sign from heaven.

11, 2ff: Mt 6, 9-13.
9-13: Mt 7, 7-11.
9: Mk 11, 24.

14-22: Mt 12, 22-29; Mk 3, 22-27.
16: Mt 16, 1; Mk 8, 11.

¹⁷ Because he knew their thoughts, he said to them: "Every kingdom divided against itself is laid waste. Any house torn by dissension falls. ¹⁸ If Satan is divided against himself, how can his kingdom last?—since you say it is by Beelzebul that I cast out devils. ¹⁹ If I cast out devils by Beelzebul, by whom do your people cast them out? In such case, let them act as your judges. ²⁰ But if it is by the finger of God that I cast out devils, then the reign of God is upon you.

²¹ "When a strong man fully armed guards his courtyard, his possessions go undisturbed. ²² But when someone stronger than he comes and overpowers him, such a one carries off the arms on which he was relying and divides the spoils. ²³ He who is not with me is against me, and he who does not gather with me scatters.

²⁴ "When an unclean spirit has gone out of a man, it wanders through arid wastes searching for a resting-place; failing to find one, it says, 'I will go back to where I came from.' ²⁵ It then returns, to find the house swept and tidied. ²⁶ Next it goes out and returns with seven other spirits far worse than itself, who enter in and dwell there. The result is that the last state of the man is worse than the first."

True Happiness

²⁷ While he was saying this a woman from the crowd called out, "Blest is the womb that bore you and the breasts that nursed you!" ²⁸ "Rather," he replied, "blest are they who hear the word of God and keep it."

The Sign of Jonah

²⁹ While the crowds pressed around him he began to speak to them in these words: "This is an evil age. It seeks a sign. But no sign will be given it except the sign of Jonah. ³⁰ Just as Jonah was a sign for the Ninevites, so will the Son of Man be a sign for the present age. ³¹ The queen of the South will rise at the judgment along with the men of this generation, and she will condemn them. She came from the farthest corner of the world to listen to the wisdom of Solomon, but you have a greater than Solomon here. ³² At the judgment, the citizens of Nineveh will rise along with the present generation, and they

20: Mt 12, 28.
23: Mt 12, 30.
24ff: Mt 12, 43ff.
28: Rv 1, 3.
29-32: Mt 12, 38-42.

29: Mt 16, 1; Mk 9, 11f;
    Jn 6, 30f.
31: 1 Kgs 10, 1-10.
32: Jon 3, 5.

will condemn it. For at the preaching of Jonah they reformed, but you have a greater than Jonah here.

Parable of the Lamp

[33] "One who lights a lamp does not put it in the cellar or under a bushel basket, but rather on a lampstand, so that they who come in may see the light. [34] The eye is the lamp of your body. When your eyesight is sound, your whole body is lighted up, but when your eyesight is bad, your body is in darkness. [35] Take care, then, that your light is not darkness. [36] If your whole body is lighted up and not partly in darkness, it will be as fully illumined as when a lamp shines brightly for you."

Hypocrisy of Pharisees and Lawyers

[37] As he was speaking, a Pharisee invited him to dine at his house. He entered and reclined at table. [38] Seeing this, the Pharisee was surprised that he had not first performed the ablutions prescribed before eating. [39] The Lord said to him: "You Pharisees! You cleanse the outside of cup and dish, but within you are filled with rapaciousness and evil. [40] Fools! Did not he who made the outside make the inside too? [41] But if you give what you have as alms, all will be wiped clean for you. [42] Woe to you Pharisees! You pay tithes on mint and rue and all the garden plants, while neglecting justice and the love of God. These are the things you should practice, without omitting the others. [43] Woe to you Pharisees! You love the front seats in synagogues and marks of respect in public. [44] Woe to you! You are like hidden tombs over which men walk unawares."

[45] In reply one of the lawyers said to him, "Teacher, in speaking this way you insult us too." [46] Jesus answered: "Woe to you lawyers also! You lay impossible burdens on men but will not lift a finger to lighten them. [47] Woe to you! You build the tombs of the prophets, but it was your fathers who murdered them. [48] You show that you stand behind the deeds of your fathers: they committed the murders and you erect the tombs. [49] That is why the wisdom of God has said, 'I will send them prophets and apostles, and some of these they will persecute and kill'; [50] so that this generation will have to account

33: 8, 16; Mt 5, 15;
    Mk 4, 21.
37: 7, 36; 14, 1.
38: Mt 15, 2; Mk 7, 2.5.
39: Mt 23, 25f.
42: Mt 23, 23.

43: 20, 46; Mt 23, 6f;
    Mk 12, 38f.
44: Mt 23, 27.
46: Mt 23, 4.
47f: Mt 23, 29ff.
49ff: Mt 23, 34ff.

for the blood of all the prophets shed since the foundation of the world. [51] Their guilt stretches from the blood of Abel to the blood of Zechariah, who met his death between the altar and the sanctuary! Yes, I tell you, this generation will have to account for it. [52] Woe to you lawyers! You have taken away the key of knowledge. You yourselves have not gained access, yet you have stopped those who wished to enter!"

[53] After he had left this gathering, the scribes and Pharisees began to manifest fierce hostility to him and to make him speak on a multitude of questions, [54] setting traps to catch him in his speech.

12

Courage under Persecution

[1] Meanwhile a crowd of thousands had gathered, so dense that they were treading on one another. He began to speak first to his disciples: "Be on guard against the yeast of the Pharisees, which is hypocrisy. [2] There is nothing concealed that will not be revealed, nothing hidden that will not be made known. [3] Everything you have said in the dark will be heard in the daylight; what you have whispered in locked rooms will be proclaimed from the rooftops.

[4] "I say to you who are my friends: Do not be afraid of those who kill the body and can do no more. [5] I will show you whom you ought to fear. Fear him who has power to cast into Gehenna after he has killed. Yes, I tell you, fear him. [6] Are not five sparrows sold for a few pennies? Yet not one of them is neglected by God. [7] In very truth, even the hairs of your head are counted! Fear nothing, then. You are worth more than a flock of sparrows.

[8] "I tell you, whoever acknowledges me before men—the Son of Man will acknowledge him before the angels of God. [9] But the man who has disowned me in the presence of men will be disowned in the presence of the angels of God. [10] Anyone who speaks against the Son of Man will be forgiven, but whoever blasphemes the Holy Spirit will never be forgiven. [11] When they bring you before synagogues, rulers and authorities, do not worry about how to defend yourselves or what to say. [12] The

51: Gn 4, 8; 2 Chr 24, 20ff.
52: Mt 23, 13.
53: 6, 11; Mt 22, 15f.
12, 1: Mt 16, 6.12; Mk 8, 15.
2: 8, 17.
2-9: Mt 10, 26-33.

3: Mk 4, 22.
9: 9, 26; Mk 8, 38;
   2 Tm 2, 12.
10: Mt 12, 31f; Mk 3, 28f.
11f: 21, 12-15; Mt 10, 17-20;
    Mk 13, 11.

Holy Spirit will teach you at that moment all that should be said."

Trust in God, Not in Possessions

13 Someone in the crowd said to him, "Teacher, tell my brother to give me my share of our inheritance." 14 He replied, "Friend, who has set me up as your judge or arbiter?" 15 Then he said to the crowd, "Avoid greed in all its forms. A man may be wealthy, but his possessions do not guarantee him life."

16 He told them a parable in these words: "There was a rich man who had a good harvest. 17 'What shall I do?' he asked himself. 'I have no place to store my harvest. 18 I know!' he said. 'I will pull down my grain bins and build larger ones. All my grain and my goods will go there. 19 Then I will say to myself: You have blessings in reserve for years to come. Relax! Eat heartily, drink well. Enjoy yourself.' 20 But God said to him, 'You fool! This very night your life shall be required of you. To whom will all this piled-up wealth of yours go?' 21 That is the way it works with the man who grows rich for himself instead of growing rich in the sight of God."

Dependence on Providence

22 He said to his disciples: "That is why I warn you, Do not be concerned for your life, what you are to eat, or for your body, what you are to wear. 23 Life is more important than food and the body more than clothing. 24 Consider the ravens: they do not sow, they do not reap, they have neither cellar nor barn—yet God feeds them. How much more important you are than the birds! 25 Which of you by worrying can add a moment to his lifespan? 26 If the smallest things are beyond your power, why be anxious about the rest?

27 "Or take the lilies: they do not spin, they do not weave; but I tell you, Solomon in all his splendor was not arrayed like any one of them. 28 If God clothes in such splendor the grass of the field, which grows today and is thrown on the fire tomorrow, how much more will he provide for you, O weak in faith! 29 It is not for you to be in search of what you are to eat or drink. Stop worrying. 30 The unbelievers of this world are always running after these things. Your Father knows that you need such things. 31 Seek out instead his kingship over you, and the rest will follow in turn.

19: Prv 27, 1; Sir 11, 24;
    1 Tm 6, 17.
21: Mt 6, 19ff.

22-31: Mt 6, 25-33.
22: Ps 55, 23; 1 Pt 5, 7.

The Heart's Treasure

[32] "Do not live in fear, little flock. It has pleased your Father to give you the kingdom. [33] Sell what you have and give alms. Get purses for yourselves that do not wear out, a never-failing treasure with the Lord which no thief comes near nor any moth destroys. [34] Wherever your treasure lies, there your heart will be.

Preparedness for the Master's Return

[35] "Let your belts be fastened around your waists and your lamps be burning ready. [36] Be like men awaiting their master's return from a wedding, so that when he arrives and knocks, you will open for him without delay. [37] It will go well with those servants whom the master finds wide-awake on his return. I tell you, he will put on an apron, seat them at table, and proceed to wait on them. [38] Should he happen to come at midnight or before sunrise and find them prepared, it will go well with them. [39] You know as well as I that if the head of the house knew when the thief was coming he would not let him break into his house. [40] Be on guard, therefore. The Son of Man will come when you least expect him."

[41] Peter said, "Do you intend this parable for us, Lord, or do you mean it for everyone?" [42] The Lord said, "Who in your opinion is that faithful, farsighted steward whom the master will set over his servants to dispense their ration of grain in season? [43] That servant is fortunate whom his master finds busy when he returns. [44] Assuredly, his master will put him in charge of all his property. [45] But if the servant says to himself, 'My master is taking his time about coming,' and begins to abuse the housemen and servant girls, to eat and drink and get drunk, [46] that servant's master will come back on a day when he does not expect him, at a time he does not know. He will punish him severely and rank him among those undeserving of trust. [47] The slave who knew his master's wishes but did not prepare to fulfill them will get a severe beating, [48] whereas the one who did not know them and who nonetheless deserved to be flogged will get off with fewer stripes. When much has been given a man, much will be required of him. More will be asked of a man to whom more has been entrusted.

[49] "I have come to light a fire on the earth. How I wish the blaze were ignited! [50] I have a baptism to receive. What anguish

33: Mt 6, 20f; 19, 21.   39f: Mt 24, 43f.
36: Mt 25, 1-13.   42-46: Mt 24, 45-51.
36ff: Mk 13, 34f.   50: 9, 22.

I feel till it is over! [51] Do you think I have come to establish peace on the earth? I assure you, the contrary is true; I have come for division. [52] From now on, a household of five will be divided three against two and two against three; [53] father will be split against son and son against father, mother against daughter and daughter against mother, mother-in-law against daughter-in-law, daughter-in-law against mother-in-law."

Signs of the Times

[54] He said to the crowds: "When you see a cloud rising in the west, you say immediately that rain is coming—and so it does. [55] When the wind blows from the south, you say it is going to be hot—and so it is. [56] You hypocrites! If you can interpret the portents of earth and sky, why can you not interpret the present time? [57] Tell me, why do you not judge for yourselves what is just? [58] When you are going with your opponent to appear before a magistrate, try to settle with him on the way lest he turn you over to the judge, and the judge deliver you up to the jailer, and the jailer throw you into prison. [59] I warn you, you will not be released from there until you have paid the last penny."

13

Providential Calls to Penance

[1] At that time, some were present who told him about the Galileans whose blood Pilate had mixed with their sacrifices. [2] He said in reply: "Do you think that these Galileans were the greatest sinners in Galilee just because they suffered this? [3] By no means! But I tell you, you will all come to the same end unless you reform. [4] Or take those eighteen who were killed by a falling tower in Siloam. Do you think they were more guilty than anyone else who lived in Jerusalem? [5] Certainly not! But I tell you, you will all come to the same end unless you reform."

The Barren Fig Tree

[6] Jesus spoke this parable: "A man had a fig tree growing in his vineyard, and he came out looking for fruit on it but did not find any. [7] He said to the vinedresser, 'Look here! For three years now I have come in search of fruit on this fig tree and

---

51ff: Mt 10, 34ff.   54: Mt 16, 2f.
  51: 2, 34.   58: Mt 5, 25.
  53: Mi 7, 6.   **13,** 5: Jn 8, 24.

found none. Cut it down. Why should it clutter up the ground?' [8] In answer, the man said, 'Sir, leave it another year, while I hoe around it and manure it; [9] then perhaps it will bear fruit. If not, it shall be cut down.' "

A Sabbath Cure

[10] On a sabbath day he was teaching in one of the synagogues. [11] There was a woman there who for eighteen years had been possessed by a spirit which drained her strength. She was badly stooped—quite incapable of standing erect. [12] When Jesus saw her, he called her to him and said, "Woman, you are free of your infirmity." [13] He laid his hand on her, and immediately she stood up straight and began thanking God.

[14] The chief of the synagogue, indignant that Jesus should have healed on the sabbath, said to the congregation, "There are six days for working. Come on those days to be cured, not on the sabbath." [15] The Lord said in reply, "O you hypocrites! Which of you does not let his ox or ass out of the stall on the sabbath to water it? [16] Should not this daughter of Abraham here who has been in the bondage of Satan for eighteen years have been released from her shackles on the sabbath?" [17] At these words, his opponents were covered with confusion; meanwhile, everyone else rejoiced at the marvels Jesus was accomplishing.

Parable of the Mustard Seed

[18] Then he said: "What does the reign of God resemble? To what shall I liken it? [19] It is like mustard seed which a man took and planted in his garden. It grew and became a large shrub and the birds of the air nested in its branches."

Parable of the Yeast

[20] He went on: "To what shall I compare the reign of God? [21] It is like yeast which a woman took to knead into three measures of flour until the whole mass of dough began to rise."

The Narrow Door

[22] He went through cities and towns teaching—all the while making his way toward Jerusalem. [23] Someone asked him, "Lord, are they few in number who are to be saved?" [24] He replied:

10-17: 14, 1-6.   18f: Mt 13, 31f; Mk 4, 30ff.
  14: Ex 20, 8f.   20f: Mt 13, 33.
  15: 14, 5; Mt 12, 11.   24: Mt 7, 13f.

"Try to come in through the narrow door. Many, I tell you, will try to enter and be unable. ²⁵ When once the master of the house has risen to lock the door and you stand outside knocking and saying, 'Sir, open for us,' he will say in reply, 'I do not know where you come from.' ²⁶ Then you will begin to say, 'We ate and drank in your company. You taught in our streets.' ²⁷ But he will answer, 'I tell you, I do not know where you come from. Away from me, you evildoers!'

²⁸ "There will be wailing and grinding of teeth when you see Abraham, Isaac, Jacob, and all the prophets safe in the kingdom of God, and you yourselves rejected. ²⁹ People will come from the east and the west, from the north and the south, and will take their place at the feast in the kingdom of God. ³⁰ Some who are last will be first and some who are first will be last."

Herod the Fox

³¹ It was then that certain Pharisees came to him. "Go on your way!" they said. "Leave this place! Herod is trying to kill you." ³² His answer was: "Go tell that fox, 'Today and tomorrow I cast out devils and perform cures, and on the third day my purpose is accomplished. ³³ For all that, I must proceed on course today, tomorrow, and the day after, since no prophet can be allowed to die anywhere except in Jerusalem.'

Apostrophe to Jerusalem

³⁴ "O Jerusalem, Jerusalem, you slay the prophets and stone those who are sent to you! How often have I wanted to gather your children together as a mother bird collects her young under her wings, and you refused me! ³⁵ Your temple will be abandoned. I say to you, you shall not see me until the time comes when you say, 'Blessed is he who comes in the name of the Lord.'"

14

Cure and a Lesson in Humility

¹ When Jesus came on a sabbath to eat a meal in the house of one of the leading Pharisees, they observed him closely. ² Directly in front of him was a man who suffered from dropsy. ³ Jesus asked the lawyers and the Pharisees, "Is it lawful to cure

25: Mt 25, 10ff.
27: Mt 7, 23; 25, 41.
28: Mt 8, 11f.
30: Mt 19, 30; 20, 16; Mk 10, 31.

34f: 19, 41-44; Mt 23, 37ff.
35: Ps 118, 26.
14, 1-6: 6, 6-11; 13, 10-17.
3: Mk 3, 4.

on the sabbath or not?" ⁴ At this they kept silent. He took the man, healed him, and sent him on his way. ⁵ Then he addressed himself to them: "If one of you has a son or an ox and he falls into a pit, will he not immediately rescue him on the sabbath day?" ⁶ This they could not answer.

⁷ He went on to address a parable to the guests, noticing how they were trying to get the places of honor at the table: ⁸ "When you are invited by someone to a wedding party, do not sit in the place of honor in case some greater dignitary has been invited. ⁹ Then the host might come and say to you, 'Make room for this man,' and you would have to proceed shamefacedly to the lowest place. ¹⁰ What you should do when you have been invited is go and sit in the lowest place, so that when your host approaches you he will say, 'My friend, come up higher.' This will win you the esteem of your fellow guests. ¹¹ For everyone who exalts himself shall be humbled and he who humbles himself shall be exalted."

The Poor

¹² He said to the one who had invited him: "Whenever you give a lunch or dinner, do not invite your friends or brothers or relatives or wealthy neighbors. They might invite you in return and thus repay you. ¹³ No, when you have a reception, invite beggars and the crippled, the lame and the blind. ¹⁴ You should be pleased that they cannot repay you, for you will be repaid in the resurrection of the just." ¹⁵ At these words one in the party said to him, "Happy is he who eats bread in the kingdom of God." ¹⁶ Jesus responded: "A man was giving a large dinner and he invited many. ¹⁷ At dinner time he sent his servant to say to those invited, 'Come along, everything is ready now.' ¹⁸ But they began to excuse themselves, one and all. The first one said to the servant, 'I have bought some land and must go out and inspect it. Please excuse me.' ¹⁹ Another said, 'I have bought five yoke of oxen and I am going out to test them. Please excuse me.' ²⁰ A third said, 'I am newly married and so I cannot come.' ²¹ The servant returning reported all this to his master. The master of the house grew angry at the account. He said to his servant, 'Go out quickly into the streets and alleys of the town and bring in the poor and the crippled, the blind and the lame.' ²² The servant reported, after some time, 'Your

---

5: Mt 12, 11.
8f: Prv 25, 6f.
11: 18, 14; Mt 23, 12.

12: 6, 32-35.
16-23: Mt 22, 2-10.

orders have been carried out, my lord, and there is still room.' ²³ The master then said to the servant, 'Go out into the highways and along the hedgerows and force them to come in. I want my house to be full, ²⁴ but I tell you that not one of those invited shall taste a morsel of my dinner.' "

²⁵ On one occasion when a great crowd was with him, he turned to them and said, ²⁶ "If anyone comes to me without turning his back on his father and mother, his wife and his children, his brothers and sisters, indeed his very self, he cannot be my follower. ²⁷ Anyone who does not take up his cross and follow me cannot be my disciple. ²⁸ If one of you decides to build a tower, will he not first sit down and calculate the outlay to see if he enough money to complete the project? ²⁹ He will do that for fear of laying the foundation and then not being able to complete the work; for all who saw it would jeer at him, ³⁰ saying, 'That man began to build what he could not finish.'

³¹ "Or if a king is about to march on another king to do battle with him, will he not sit down first and consider whether, with ten thousand men, he can withstand an enemy coming against him with twenty thousand? ³² If he cannot, he will send a delegation while the enemy is still at a distance, asking for terms of peace. ³³ In the same way, none of you can be my disciple if he does not renounce all his possessions. ³⁴ Salt is good, but if salt loses its flavor what good is it for seasoning? ³⁵ It is fit for neither the soil nor the manure heap; it has to be thrown away. Let him who hears this, heed it."

15

Parable of Divine Mercy

¹ The tax collectors and sinners were all gathering around to hear him, ² at which the Pharisees and the scribes murmured, "This man welcomes sinners and eats with them." ³ Then he addressed this parable to them: ⁴ "Who among you, if he has a hundred sheep and loses one of them, does not leave the ninety-nine in the wasteland and follow the lost one until he finds it? ⁵ And when he finds it, he puts it on his shoulders in jubilation. ⁶ Once arrived home, he invites friends and neighbors in and says to them, 'Rejoice with me because I have found my lost

26: Mt 10, 37.
27: 9, 23; Mt 10, 38;
  16, 24; Mk 8, 34.
34: Mt 5, 13; Mk 9, 50.

15, 2-7: Mt 9, 10-13.
  2: 19, 7.
  4f: Mt 18, 12ff.
  6: 19, 10.

sheep.' ⁷ I tell you, there will likewise be more joy in heaven over one repentant sinner than over ninety-nine righteous people who have no need to repent.

⁸ "What woman, if she has ten silver pieces and loses one, does not light a lamp and sweep the house in a diligent search until she has retrieved what she lost? ⁹ And when she finds it, she calls in her friends and neighbors to say, 'Rejoice with me! I have found the silver piece I lost.' ¹⁰ I tell you, there will be the same kind of joy before the angels of God over one repentant sinner."

The Prodigal Son

¹¹ Jesus said to them: "A man had two sons. ¹² The younger of them said to his father, 'Father, give me the share of the estate that is coming to me.' So the father divided up the property. ¹³ Some days later this younger son collected all his belongings and went off to a distant land, where he squandered his money on dissolute living. ¹⁴ After he had spent everything, a great famine broke out in that country and he was in dire need. ¹⁵ So he attached himself to one of the propertied class of the place, who sent him to his farm to take care of the pigs. ¹⁶ He longed to fill his belly with the husks that were fodder for the pigs, but no one made a move to give him anything. ¹⁷ Coming to his senses at last, he said: 'How many hired hands at my father's place have more than enough to eat, while here I am starving! ¹⁸ I will break away and return to my father, and say to him, Father, I have sinned against God and against you; I no longer deserve to be called your son. ¹⁹ Treat me like one of your hired hands.' ²⁰ With that he set off for his father's house. While he was still a long way off, his father caught sight of him and was deeply moved. He ran out to meet him, threw his arms around his neck, and kissed him. ²¹ The son said to him, 'Father, I have sinned against God and against you; I no longer deserve to be called your son.' ²² The father said to his servants: 'Quick! bring out the finest robe and put it on him; put a ring on his finger and shoes on his feet. ²³ Take the fatted calf and kill it. Let us eat and celebrate ²⁴ because this son of mine was dead and has come back to life. He was lost and is found.' Then the celebration began.

²⁵ "Meanwhile the elder son was out on the land. As he neared the house on his way home, he heard the sound of music and dancing. ²⁶ He called one of the servants and asked

---

7: Ez 18, 23; 33, 11.

him the reason for the dancing and the music. [27] The servant answered, 'Your brother is home, and your father has killed the fatted calf because he has him back in good health.' [28] The son grew angry at this and would not go in; but his father came out and began to plead with him.

[29] "He said to his father in reply: 'For years now I have slaved for you. I never disobeyed one of your orders, yet you never gave me so much as a kid goat to celebrate with my friends. [30] Then, when this son of yours returns after having gone through your property with loose women, you kill the fatted calf for him.'

[31] "'My son,' replied the father, 'you are with me always, and everything I have is yours. [32] But we had to celebrate and rejoice! This brother of yours was dead, and has come back to life. He was lost, and is found.'"

16

The Wily Manager

[1] Another time he said to his disciples: "A rich man had a manager who was reported to him for dissipating his property. [2] He summoned him and said, 'What is this I hear about you? Give me an account of your service, for it is about to come to any end.' [3] The manager thought to himself, 'What shall I do next? My employer is sure to dismiss me. I cannot dig ditches. I am ashamed to go begging. [4] I have it! Here is a way to make sure that people will take me into their homes when I am let go.'

[5] "So he called in each of his master's debtors, and said to the first, 'How much do you owe my master?' [6] The man replied, 'A hundred jars of oil.' The manager said, 'Take your invoice, sit down quickly, and make it fifty.' [7] Then he said to a second, 'How much do you owe?' The answer came, 'A hundred measures of wheat,' and the manager said, 'Take your invoice and make it eighty.'

[8] "The owner then gave his devious employee credit for being enterprising! Why? Because the worldly take more initiative than the other-worldly when it comes to dealing with their own kind.

Right Use of Money

[9] "What I say to you is this: Make friends for yourselves

16, 9: 12, 33; Sir 29, 12.

through your use of this world's goods, so that when they fail you, a lasting reception will be yours. [10] If you can trust a man in little things, you can also trust him in greater; while anyone unjust in a slight matter is also unjust in greater. [11] If you cannot be trusted with elusive wealth, who will trust you with lasting? [12] And if you have not been trustworthy with someone else's money, who will give you what is your own?

[13] "No servant can serve two masters. Either he will hate the one and love the other or be attentive to the one and despise the other. You cannot give yourself to God and money." [14] The Pharisees, who were avaricious men, heard all this and began to deride him. [15] He said to them: "You justify yourselves in the eyes of men, but God reads your hearts. What man thinks important, God holds in contempt.

The Law

[16] "The law and the prophets were in force until John. From his time on, the good news of God's kingdom has been proclaimed, and people of every sort are forcing their way in. [17] It is easier for the heavens and the earth to pass away than for a single stroke of a letter of the law to pass. [18] Everyone who divorces his wife and marries another commits adultery. The man who marries a woman divorced from her husband likewise commits adultery.

The Rich Man and Lazarus

[19] "Once there was a rich man who dressed in purple and linen and feasted splendidly every day. [20] At his gate lay a beggar named Lazarus who was covered with sores. [21] Lazarus longed to eat the scraps that fell from the rich man's table. The dogs even came and licked his sores. [22] Eventually the beggar died. He was carried by angels to the bosom of Abraham. The rich man likewise died and was buried. [23] From the abode of the dead where he was in torment, he raised his eyes and saw Abraham afar off, and Lazarus resting in his bosom.

[24] "He called out, 'Father Abraham, have pity on me. Send Lazarus to dip the tip of his finger in water to refresh my tongue, for I am tortured in these flames.' [25] 'My child,' replied Abraham, 'remember that you were well off in your lifetime, while Lazarus was in misery. Now he has found consolation

10: 19, 17; Mt 25, 21.
15: 18, 9-14.
16: Mt 11, 12.
17: Mt 5, 18.

18: Mt 5, 32; 19, 9;
    Mk 10, 11f;
    1 Cor 7, 10f.
25: 6, 24f.

here, but you have found torment. 26 And that is not all. Between you and us there is fixed a great abyss, so that those who might wish to cross from here to you cannot do so, nor can anyone cross from your side to us.'

27 " 'Father, I ask you, then,' the rich man said, 'send him to my father's house 28 where I have five brothers. Let him be a warning to them so that they may not end in this place of torment.' 29 Abraham answered, 'They have Moses and the prophets. Let them hear them.' 30 'No, Father Abraham,' replied the rich man. 'But if someone would only go to them from the dead, then they would repent.' 31 Abraham said to him, 'If they do not listen to Moses and the prophets, they will not be convinced even if one should rise from the dead.' "

17

Four Sayings of Jesus

1 He said to his disciples: "Scandals will inevitably arise, but woe to him through whom they come. 2 He would be better off thrown into the sea with a millstone around his neck than giving scandal to one of these little ones.

3 "Be on your guard. If your brother does wrong, correct him; if he repents, forgive him. 4 If he sins against you seven times a day, and seven times a day turns back to you saying, 'I am sorry,' forgive him."

5 The apostles said to the Lord, "Increase our faith," 6 and he answered: "If you had faith the size of a mustard seed, you could say to this sycamore, 'Be uprooted and transplanted into the sea,' and it would obey you.

7 "If one of you had a servant plowing or herding sheep and he came in from the fields, would you say to him, 'Come and sit down at table'? 8 Would you not rather say, 'Prepare my supper. Put on your apron and wait on me while I eat and drink. You can eat and drink afterward'? 9 Would he be grateful to the servant who was only carrying out his orders? 10 It is quite the same with you who hear me. When you have done all you have been commanded to do, say, 'We are useless servants. We have done no more than our duty.' "

Ten Lepers

11 On his journey to Jerusalem he passed along the borders of Samaria and Galilee. 12 As he was entering a village, ten

---

31: Jn 5, 46f.
17, 1f: Mt 18, 6f.

4: Mt 18, 21f.
6: Mt 21, 21; Mk 11, 23.

lepers met him. Keeping their distance, [13] they raised their voices and said, "Jesus, Master, have pity on us!" [14] When he saw them, he responded, "Go and show yourselves to the priests." On their way there they were cured. [15] One of them, realizing that he had been cured, came back praising God in a loud voice. [16] He threw himself on his face at the feet of Jesus and spoke his praises. This man was a Samaritan.

[17] Jesus took the occasion to say, "Were not all ten made whole? Where are the other nine? [18] Was there no one to return and give thanks to God except this foreigner?" [19] He said to the man, "Stand up and go your way; your faith has been your salvation."

Coming of the Reign of God

[20] Once, on being asked by the Pharisees when the reign of God would come, he replied: "You cannot tell by careful watching when the reign of God will come. [21] Neither is it a matter of reporting that it is 'here' or 'there.' The reign of God is already in your midst."

Day of the Son of Man

[22] He said to the disciples: "A time will come when you will long to see one day of the Son of Man but will not see it. [23] They will tell you he is to be found in this place or that. Do not go running about excitedly. [24] The Son of Man in his day will be like the lightning that flashes from one end of the sky to the other. [25] First, however, he must suffer much and be rejected by the present age. [26] As it was in the days of Noah, so will it be in the days of the Son of Man. [27] They ate and drank, they took husbands and wives, right up to the day Noah entered the ark—and when the flood came, it destroyed them all. [28] It was much the same in the days of Lot: they ate and drank, they bought and sold, they built and planted. [29] But on the day Lot left Sodom, fire and brimstone rained down from heaven and destroyed them all.

[30] "It will be like that on the day the Son of Man is revealed. [31] On that day, if a man is on the rooftop and his belongings are in the house, he should not go down to get them; neither should the man in the field return home. [32] Remember Lot's

---

14: 5, 14; Lv 13, 9-34;
     Mt 8, 4; Mk 1, 44.
23f: Mt 24, 23.26f;
     Mk 13, 21.

26f: Gn 6—8; Mt 24, 37ff.
28f: Gn 19, 1-29.
31: 21, 21; Mt 24, 17f; Mk 13, 15f.
32: Gn 19, 26.

wife. [33] Whoever tries to preserve his life will lose it; whoever loses it will keep it. [34] I tell you, on that night there will be two men in one bed; one will be taken and the other left. [35] Two women will be grinding grain together; one will be taken and the other left." [37] "Where, Lord?" they asked him, and he answered, "Wherever the carcass is, there will the vultures gather."

18

The Corrupt Judge

[1] He told them a parable on the necessity of praying always and not losing heart: [2] "Once there was a judge in a certain city who respected neither God nor man. [3] A widow in that city kept coming to him saying, 'Give me my rights against my opponent.' [4] For a time he refused, but finally he thought, 'I care little for God or man, [5] but this widow is wearing me out. I am going to settle in her favor or she will end by doing me violence.'" [6] The Lord said, "Listen to what the corrupt judge has to say. [7] Will not God then do justice to his chosen who call out to him day and night? Will he delay long over them, do you suppose? [8] I tell you, he will give them swift justice. But when the Son of Man comes, will he find any faith on the earth?"

The Pharisee and the Tax Collector

[9] He then spoke this parable addressed to those who believed in their own self-righteousness while holding everyone else in contempt: [10] "Two men went up to the temple to pray; one was a Pharisee, the other a tax collector. [11] The Pharisee with head unbowed prayed in this fashion: 'I give you thanks, O God, that I am not like the rest of men—grasping, crooked, adulterous—or even like this tax collector. [12] I fast twice a week. I pay tithes on all I possess.' [13] The other man, however, kept his distance, not even daring to raise his eyes to heaven. All he did was beat his breast and say, 'O God, be merciful to me, a sinner.' [14] Believe me, this man went home from the temple justified but the other did not. For everyone who exalts himself shall be humbled while he who humbles himself shall be exalted."

33: 9, 24; Mt 10, 39;
    Mk 8, 35; Jn 12, 25.
35: Mt 24, 40f.

37: Mt 24, 28.
18, 9: 16, 15; Mt 23, 28.
14: 14, 11; Mt 23, 12.

17, 36: Omitted here with many MSS.

Jesus and the Children; a Rich Man

¹⁵ They even brought babies to be touched by him. When the disciples saw this, they scolded them roundly; ¹⁶ but Jesus called for the children, saying: "Let the little children come to me. Do not shut them off. The reign of God belongs to such as these. ¹⁷ Trust me when I tell you that whoever does not accept the kingdom of God as a child will not enter into it."

¹⁸ One of the ruling class asked him then, "Good teacher, what must I do to share in everlasting life?" ¹⁹ Jesus said to him, "Why call me 'good'? None is good but God alone. ²⁰ You know the commandments:

> "You shall not commit adultery.
> You shall not kill.
> You shall not steal.
> You shall not bear dishonest witness.
> Honor your father and your mother."

²¹ He replied, "I have kept all these since I was a boy." ²² When Jesus heard this he said to him: "There is one thing further you must do. Sell all you have and give to the poor. You will have treasure in heaven. Then come and follow me." ²³ On hearing this he grew melancholy, for he was a very rich man. ²⁴ When Jesus observed this he said: "How hard it will be for the rich to go into the kingdom of God! ²⁵ Indeed, it is easier for a camel to go through a needle's eye than for a rich man to enter the kingdom of heaven."

²⁶ His listeners asked him, "Who, then, can be saved?" ²⁷ to which he replied, "Things that are impossible for men are possible for God." ²⁸ Peter said, "We have left all we own to become your followers." ²⁹ His answer was, "I solemnly assure you, there is no one who has left home or wife or brothers, parents or children, for the sake of the kingdom of God ³⁰ who will will not receive a plentiful return in this age and life everlasting in the age to come."

15ff: Mt 19, 13ff.
18-30: Mt 19, 16-29;
      Mk 10, 17-30.
20: Ex 20, 12-16;

Dt 5, 16-20.
22: 12, 33.
29: 14, 26.

18, 15ff: See note on Mt 19, 13ff.
18, 18-21: See note on Mk 10, 17f.
18, 24-27: See note on Mt 19, 23-26.
18, 28ff: See note on Mt 19, 27-30.

³¹ Taking the Twelve aside, he said to them: "We must now go up to Jerusalem so that all that was written by the prophets concerning the Son of Man may be accomplished. ³² He will be delivered up to the Gentiles. He will be mocked and outraged and spat upon. ³³ They will scourge him and put him to death, and on the third day he will rise again."

³⁴ They understood nothing of this. His utterance remained obscure to them, and they did not grasp his meaning.

³⁵ As he drew near Jericho a blind man sat at the side of the road begging. ³⁶ Hearing a crowd go by the man asked, "What is that?" ³⁷ The answer came that Jesus of Nazareth was passing by. ³⁸ He shouted out, "Jesus, Son of David, have pity on me!" ³⁹ Those in the lead sternly ordered him to be quiet, but he cried out all the more, "Son of David, have pity on me!" ⁴⁰ Jesus halted and ordered that he be brought to him. When he had come close, Jesus asked him, ⁴¹ "What do you want me to do for you?" "Lord," he answered, "I want to see." ⁴² Jesus said to him, "Receive your sight. Your faith has healed you." ⁴³ At that very moment he was given his sight and began to follow him, giving God the glory. All the people witnessed it and they too gave praise to God.

19

Zacchaeus the Tax Collector

¹ Entering Jericho, he passed through the city. ² There was a man there named Zacchaeus, the chief tax collector and a wealthy man. ³ He was trying to see what Jesus was like, but being small of stature, was unable to do so because of the crowd. ⁴ He first ran on in front, then climbed a sycamore tree which was along Jesus' route, in order to see him. ⁵ When Jesus came to the spot he looked up and said, "Zacchaeus, hurry down. I mean to stay at your house today." ⁶ He quickly descended, and welcomed him with delight. ⁷ When this was observed, everyone began to murmur, "He has gone to a sinner's house as a guest." ⁸ Zacchaeus stood his ground and said to the Lord: "I give half my belongings, Lord, to the poor. If I have defrauded anyone in the least, I pay him back fourfold." ⁹ Jesus said to him: "Today salvation has come to this house,

31ff: 9, 22; Mt 20, 17ff;   Mk 10, 46-52.
     Mk 10, 32ff.   39: Mt 9, 27.
33: Acts 3, 18.   19, 9: Mt 21, 31.
35-43: Mt 20, 29-34;

18, 31-34: See note on Mk 10, 32ff.
18, 35-43: See note on Mk 10, 46-52.

for this is what it means to be a son of Abraham. ¹⁰ The Son of Man has come to search out and save what was lost."

Parable of the Sums of Money

¹¹ While they were listening to these things he went on to tell a parable, because he was near Jerusalem where they thought that the reign of God was about to appear. ¹² He said: "A man of noble birth went to a faraway country to become its king, and then return. ¹³ He summoned ten of his servants and gave them sums of ten units each, saying to them, 'Invest this until I get back.' ¹⁴ But his fellow citizens despised him, and they immediately sent a deputation after him with instructions to say, 'We will not have this man rule over us.' ¹⁵ He returned, however, crowned as king. Then he sent for the servants to whom he had given the money, to learn what profit each had made. ¹⁶ The first presented himself and said, 'Lord, the sum you gave me has earned you another ten.' ¹⁷ 'Good man!' he replied. 'You showed yourself capable in a small matter. For that you can take over ten villages.' ¹⁸ The second came and said, 'Your investment, my lord, has netted you five.' ¹⁹ His word to him was, 'Take over five villages.' ²⁰ The third came in and said: 'Here is your money, my lord, which I hid for safekeeping. ²¹ You see, I was afraid of you because you are a hard man. You withdraw what you never deposited. You reap what you never sowed.' ²² To him the king said: 'You worthless lout! I intend to judge you on your own evidence. You knew I was a hard man, withdrawing what I never deposited, reaping what I never sowed! ²³ Why, then, did you not put my money out on loan, so that on my return I could get it back with interest?' ²⁴ He said to those standing around, 'Take from him what he has, and give it to the man with the ten.' ²⁵ 'Yes, but he already has ten,' they said. ²⁶ He responded with, 'The moral is: whoever has will be given more, but the one who has not will lose the little he has. ²⁷ Now about those enemies of mine who do not want me to be king, bring them in and slay them in my presence.' "

10: 15, 6.9; Mt 18, 11.
11-27: Mt 25, 14-30.
17: 16, 10.

26: 8, 18; Mt 13, 12; Mk 4, 25.

19, 11-27: The parable of the sums of money presents two principal ideas: 1) Jesus is the Messiah-king; he understands this office to be a religious one despite the opposition of his contemporaries (19, 12-15). The reign of God is actually present in his person and teaching. 2) In exercising his messianic kingship Jesus demands the response of men to the gifts of God. The kingdom will appear in its permanent form when Christ renders the final judgment on humanity's response to him (19, 15-27).

V: THE JERUSALEM MINISTRY

Messianic Entry into Jerusalem

²⁸ Having spoken thus he went ahead with his ascent to Jerusalem. ²⁹ As he approached Bethphage and Bethany on the mount called Olivet, he sent two of the disciples ³⁰ with these instructions: "Go into the village straight ahead of you. Upon entering it you will find an ass tied there which no one has yet ridden. Untie it and lead it back. ³¹ If anyone should ask you, 'Why are you untying the beast?' say, 'The Master has need of it.' "

³² They departed on their errand and found things just as he had said. ³³ As they untied the ass, its owners said to them, "Why are your doing that?" ³⁴ They explained that the Master needed it. ³⁵ Then they led the animal to Jesus, and laying their cloaks on it, helped him mount. ³⁶ They spread their cloaks on the roadway as he moved along; ³⁷ and on his approach to the descent from Mount Olivet, the entire crowd of disciples began to rejoice and praise God loudly for the display of power they had seen, ³⁸ saying:

> "Blessed be he who comes a king
>   in the name of the Lord!
> Peace in heaven
>   and glory in the highest!"

³⁹ Some of the Pharisees in the crowd said to him, "Teacher, rebuke your disciples." ⁴⁰ He replied, "If they were to keep silence, I tell you the very stones would cry out."

Lamentation for Jerusalem

⁴¹ Coming within sight of the city, he wept over it and said: ⁴² "If only you had known the path to peace this day; but you have completely lost it from view! ⁴³ Days will come upon you

---

28-38: Mt 21, 1-9; Mk 11, 1-10;
      Jn 12, 12-15.
38: Ps 118, 26.

39f: Mt 21, 15f.
41-44: 13, 34f.

19, 28-38: See note on Mk 11, 1-11.
19, 41-44: This lamentation over Jerusalem implies that Jesus has previously visited the city in his public ministry, a fact that is brought out only in John (2, 13; 5, 1; 7, 10.14; 10, 22; 12, 12).
Here the thought of the impending destruction of Jerusalem because of its refusal to accept the Messiah is contrasted with the city's potentiality as the principal center of the Christian message. Jerusalem became that center for only a short time, as the Acts attest (9, 31; 12, 1-5); the city was destroyed in 70 A.D. The allusions here are drawn from Jeremiah: v 42 (Jer 6, 8.10.14); v 43 (Jer 6, 6); v 44 (Jer 6, 2.11.17.21).

when your enemies encircle you with a rampart, hem you in, and press you hard from every side. ⁴⁴ They will wipe you out, you and your children within your walls, and leave not a stone on a stone within you, because you failed to recognize the time of your visitation."

The Traders Expelled

⁴⁵ Then he entered the temple and began ejecting the traders ⁴⁶ saying: "Scripture has it,

> 'My house is meant for a house of prayer'

but you have made it a den of thieves.' "

⁴⁷ He was teaching in the temple area from day to day. The chief priests and scribes meanwhile were looking for a way to destroy him, as were the leaders of the people, ⁴⁸ but they had no idea how to achieve it, for indeed the entire populace was listening to him and hanging on his words.

20

The authority of Jesus

¹ One day when he was teaching the people in the temple and proclaiming the good news, the high priests and Pharisees, accompanied by the elders, approached him ² with the question, "Tell us, by what authority do you do these things? In other words, who has authorized you?" ³ He replied, "Let me put a question for you to answer: ⁴ Did the baptism of John come from God or from men?" ⁵ They held a brief conference during which someone said, "If we answer, 'From God,' he will say, 'Then why do you not believe in it?'; ⁶ whereas if we say, 'From men,' the people will stone us, so convinced are they that John was a prophet." ⁷ They ended by replying they did not know where it came from. ⁸ Jesus said to them, "In that case, neither will I tell you by whose authority I act."

Parable of the Tenants

⁹ He then began to tell the people the following parable: "A

43: Is 29, 3.
44: 21, 6; Mt 24, 2;
    Mk 13, 2.
45f: Mt 21, 12f; Mk 11, 15ff;
    Jn 2, 14ff.
46: Is 56, 7; Jer 7, 11.

20, 1-8: Mt 21, 23-27;
    Mk 11, 27-33.
     2: Acts 4, 7.
9-19: Mt 21, 33-46;
    Mk 12, 1-12.

19, 45f: See note on Mk 11, 15-19.
20, 1-40: See note on Mk 11, 27—12, 27.

man planted a vineyard, leased it to tenant farmers, and went away for a long time. [10] At vintage time he sent a servant to the tenant farmers to receive his share of the crop from them; but they beat him and sent him away empty-handed. [11] He sent a second servant whom they also beat. Him too they sent away empty-handed, after treating him shamefully. [12] He sent still a third, whom they likewise maltreated before driving him away. [13] The owner of the vineyard asked himself, 'What am I do do now? Perhaps if I send the son I love, they will respect him.'

[14] "But when the tenant farmers saw the son, they reflected, 'This is the heir. Let us kill him so that the inheritance will be ours.' [15] With that, they dragged him outside the vineyard and killed him. What fate do you suppose the owner of the vineyard has in store for them? [16] I will tell you. He will make an end to those tenant farmers and give the vineyard to others."

When they heard this they said, "God forbid!" [17] He looked directly at them and said, "What do the Scriptures mean when they say,

'The stone which the builders rejected
Has become the keystone of the structure'?

[18] The man who falls on that stone will be smashed to pieces. It will make dust of anyone on whom it falls." [19] At these words the scribes and high priests tried to get their hands on him, but they were afraid of the people. They were well aware that he had told the parable with them in mind.

Tribute to the Emperor

[20] Waiting their chance, they sent spies to him in the guise of honest men to trap him in speech, so that they might then hand him over to the office and authority of the procurator. [21] They put to him this problem: "Teacher, we know that your words and your doctrine are completely forthright, that you are no respecter of persons but teach the way of God in truth. [22] May we pay tax to the emperor or not?" [23] Realizing their duplicity he said, [24] "Show me a coin. Whose head is this? Whose inscription do you read?" "Caesar's," they replied, [25] to which he said, "Then give to Caesar what is Caesar's, but give to God what is God's." [26] They were unable to trap him pub-

---

17: Ps 118, 22; Is 28, 16.
20-26: Mt 22, 15-22;

Mk 12, 13-17.
25: Rom 13, 7.

licly in speech. His answer completely disconcerted them and reduced them to silence.

Resurrection of the Dead

27 Some Sadducees came forward (the ones who claim there is no resurrection) 28 to pose this problem to him: "Master, Moses prescribed that if a man's brother dies leaving a wife and no child, the brother should marry the widow and raise posterity to his brother. 29 Now there were seven brothers. 30 The first one married and died childless. 31 Next, the second brother married the widow, then the third, and so on. All seven died without leaving her any children. 32 Finally the widow herself died. 33 At the resurrection, whose wife will she be? Remember, seven married her."

34 Jesus said to them: "The children of this age marry and are given in marriage, 35 but those judged worthy of a place in the age to come and of resurrection from the dead do not. 36 They become like angels and are no longer liable to death. Sons of the resurrection, they are sons of God. 37 Moses in the passage about the bush showed that the dead rise again when he called the Lord the God of Abraham, and the God of Isaac, and the God of Jacob. 38 God is not the God of the dead but of the living. All are alive for him."

39 Some of the scribes responded, "Well said, Teacher." 40 They did not dare ask him anything else.

Jesus, Son and Lord of David

41 Jesus then said to them: "How can they say that the Messiah is the son of David? 42 Does not David himself say in the psalms,

'The Lord said to my lord: Sit at my right hand
43 while I make your enemies your footstool'?

44 Now if David accords him the title 'lord,' how can he be his son?"

The Scribes Condemned

45 In the hearing of all the people, Jesus said to his disciples:

27-38: Mt 22, 23-33;
Mk 12, 18-27.
28: Dt 25, 5.
37: Ex 3, 6.15f.

41-44: Mt 22, 41-45;
Mk 12, 35ff.
42: Ps 110, 1.

20, 41—21, 4: See note on Mk 12, 35-44.

⁴⁶ "Beware of the scribes, who like to parade around in their robes, and love marks of respect in public, front seats in synagogues, and places of honor at banquets. ⁴⁷ These men are going through the savings of widows while they recite long prayers to keep up appearances. The heavier sentence will be theirs."

21

The Widow's Mite

¹ He glanced up and saw the rich putting their offerings into the treasury, ² and also a poor widow putting in two copper coins. At that he said: ³ "I assure you, this poor widow has put in more than all the rest. ⁴ They make contributions out of their surplus, but she from her want has given what she could not afford—every penny she had to live on."

The Cataclysm To Come

⁵ Some were speaking of how the temple was adorned with precious stones and votive offerings. ⁶ He said, "These things you are contemplating—the day will come when not one stone will be left on another, but it will all be torn down." ⁷ They asked him, "When will this be, Teacher? And what will be the sign that it is going to happen?" ⁸ He said, "Take care not to be misled. Many will come in my name saying, 'I am he' and 'The time is at hand.' Do not follow them. ⁹ Neither must you be perturbed when you hear of wars and insurrections. These things are bound to happen first, but the end does not follow immediately."

¹⁰ He said to them further: "Nation will rise against nation and kingdom against kingdom. ¹¹ There will be great earthquakes, plagues and famines in various places—and in the sky fearful omens and great signs. ¹² But before any of this, they will manhandle and persecute you, summoning you to synagogues and prisons, bringing you to trial before kings and governors, all because of my name. ¹³ You will be brought to give witness on account of it. ¹⁴ I bid you resolve not to worry about your defense beforehand, ¹⁵ for I will give you words and a wisdom which none of your adversaries can take exception to

46: 11, 43; Mt 23, 6f;
    Mk 12, 38ff.
21, 1-4: Mk 12, 41-44.
5-19: Mt 24, 1-14;

Mk 13, 1-13.
12-15: 12, 11f; Mt 10, 17-20.
15: Acts 6, 10.

21, 5-36: See note on Mk 13, 1-37.

or contradict. ¹⁶ You will be delivered up even by your parents, brothers, relatives and friends, and some of you will be put to death. ¹⁷ All will hate you because of me, ¹⁸ yet not a hair of your head will be harmed. ¹⁹ By patient endurance you will save your lives.

Siege and Fall of Jerusalem

²⁰ "When you see Jerusalem encircled by soldiers, know that its devastation is near. ²¹ Those in Judea at the time must flee to the mountains; those in the heart of the city must escape it; those in the country must not return. ²² These indeed will be days of retribution, when all that is written must be fulfilled.

²³ "The women who are pregnant or nursing at the breast will fare badly in those days! The distress in the land and the wrath against this people will be great. ²⁴ The people will fall before the sword; they will be led captive in the midst of the Gentiles. Jerusalem will be trampled by the Gentiles, until the times of the Gentiles are fulfilled.

Coming of the Son of Man

²⁵ "There will be signs in the sun, the moon and the stars. On the earth, nations will be in anguish, distraught at the roaring of the sea and the waves. ²⁶ Men will die of fright in anticipation of what is coming upon the earth. ²⁷ The powers in the heavens will be shaken. After that, men will see the Son of Man coming on a cloud with great power and glory. ²⁸ When these things begin to happen, stand erect and hold your heads high, for your deliverance is near at hand."

Parable of the Fig Tree

²⁹ Then he told them a parable: "Notice the fig tree, or any other tree. ³⁰ You observe them when they are budding, and know for yourselves that summer is near. ³¹ Likewise when you see all the things happening of which I speak, know that the reign of God is near. ³² Let me tell you this: the present generation will not pass away until all this takes place. ³³ The heavens and the earth will pass away, but my words will not pass.

³⁴ "Be on guard lest your spirits become bloated with in-

20-23: Mt 24, 15-20;
    Mk 13, 14-18.
21: 17, 31.
25ff: Mt 24, 29f;
    Mk 13, 24ff.
25: Is 13, 10; Ez 32, 7;

Jl 4, 15.
27: Dn 7, 13.
29-33: Mt 24, 32-35;
    Mk 13, 28-31.
32: 9, 27; Mt 16, 28.
34: 1 Thes 5, 3.

dulgence and drunkenness and worldly cares. The great day will suddenly close in on you like a trap. [35] The day I speak of will come upon all who dwell on the face of the earth. [36] So be on the watch. Pray constantly for the strength to escape whatever is in prospect, and to stand secure before the Son of Man."

Last Days of Jesus

[37] He would teach in the temple by day, and leave the city to spend the night on the Mount of Olives. [38] At daybreak all the people came to hear him in the temple.

VI: THE PASSION OF JESUS

1. The Paschal Meal

22

The Council and the Betrayal

[1] The feast of unleavened bread known as the Passover was drawing near, [2] and the high priests and scribes began to look for some way to dispose of him; but they were afraid of the people. [3] Then Satan took possession of Judas, the one called Iscariot, a member of the twelve. [4] He went off to confer with the chief priests and officers about a way to hand him over to them. [5] They were delighted, and agreed to give him money. [6] He accepted, then kept looking for an opportunity to hand him over without creating a disturbance.

The Passover Preparation

[7] The day of Unleavened Bread arrived on which it was appointed to sacrifice the paschal lamb. [8] Accordingly, Jesus sent

---

22, 1f: Mt 26, 2.5; Mk 14, 1f.
3: Jn 13, 2.27.
4f: Mt 26, 14ff;

7-13: Mt 26, 17ff;
Mk 14, 10f.
Mk 14, 12-16.

22, 1—23, 56: Certain features of this narrative of the passion of Jesus are distinctive of Luke. There are omissions: the flight of the disciples at the arrest of Jesus (Mk 14, 50ff), the false witnesses (Mk 14, 55-59), which many consider a Marcan insertion into traditional materials, the mistreatment at the hands of the Roman soldiery (Mk 15, 16-20), the offering of a narcotic to Jesus before the crucifixion (Mk 15, 23), and the praying of Psalm 22 from the cross (Mk 15, 34ff).

Additions found in Luke include: the elements of Jesus' farewell address at the Last Supper (22, 15.25-30.35-38); reference to the angel at the agony, which heightens the religious solemnity of the scene (22, 43); Jesus' look at Peter after his denial (22, 61); the appearance of Jesus before Herod (23, 6-11); his conversation with the women of Jerusalem (23, 27-31); and his words from the cross (23, 34.43.46).

Luke depicts Jesus throughout his passion as the innocent victim (23, 4.14.22.47) of satanic activity (22, 3), who forgives his enemies (22, 51; 23, 34) and accepts his suffering and death as the will of his Father (23, 46).

Peter and John off with the instruction, "Go and prepare your Passover supper for us." [9] They asked him, "Where do you want us to get it ready?" [10] He explained to them: "Just as you enter the city, you will come upon a man carrying a water jar. Follow him into the house he enters, and say to the owner, [11] 'The Teacher asks you: Do you have a guest room where I may eat the Passover with my disciples?' [12] That man will show you an upstairs room, spacious and furnished. It is there you are to prepare." [13] They went off and found everything just as he had said; and accordingly they prepared the Passover supper.

The Holy Eucharist

[14] When the hour arrived, he took his place at table, and the apostles with him. [15] He said to them: "I have greatly desired to eat this Passover with you before I suffer. [16] I tell you, I will not eat again until it is fulfilled in the kingdom of God." [17] Then taking a cup he offered a blessing in thanks and said: "Take this and divide it among you; [18] I tell you, from now on I will not drink of the fruit of the vine until the coming of the reign of God."

[19] Then, taking bread and giving thanks, he broke it and gave it to them, saying: "This is my body to be given for you. Do this as a remembrance of me." [20] He did the same with the cup after eating, saying as he did so: "This cup is the new covenant in my blood, which will be shed for you.

The Betrayer

[21] "And yet the hand of my betrayer is with me at this table. [22] The Son of Man is following out his appointed course, but woe to that man by whom he is betrayed?? [23] Then they began to dispute among themselves as to which of them would do such a deed.

Who Is Greatest?

[24] A dispute arose among them about who should be regarded as the greatest. [25] He said: "Earthly kings lord it over their people. Those who exercise authority over them are called their benefactors. [26] Yet it cannot be that way with you. Let the

18: Mt 26, 29; Mk 14, 25.
19f: Mt 26, 26ff;
     Mk 14, 22ff;
     1 Cor 11, 23ff.
21ff: Mt 26, 20-25;

Mk 14, 17-21;
     Jn 13, 21-30.
25ff: Mt 20, 25-28;
      Mk 10, 42ff.

greater among you be as the junior, the leader as the servant.
²⁷ Who, in fact, is the greater—he who reclines at table or he who serves the meal? Is it not the one who reclines at table? Yet I am in your midst as the one who serves you. ²⁸ You are the ones who have stood loyally by me in my temptations. ²⁹ I for my part assign to you the dominion my Father has assigned to me. ³⁰ In my kingdom you will eat and drink at my table, and you will sit on thrones judging the twelve tribes of Israel.

Peter's Denials Foretold

³¹ "Simon, Simon! Remember that Satan has asked for you, to sift you all like wheat. ³² But I have prayed for you that your faith may never fail. You in turn must strengthen your brothers." ³³ "Lord," he said to him, "at your side I am prepared to face imprisonment and death itself." ³⁴ Jesus replied, "I tell you, Peter, the cock will not crow today until you have three times denied that you know me."

³⁵ He asked them, "When I sent you on mission without purse or traveling bag or sandals, were you in need of anything?" "Not a thing," they replied. ³⁶ He said to them: "Now, however, the man who has a purse must carry it; the same with the traveling bag. And the man without a sword must sell his coat and buy one. ³⁷ It is written in Scripture,

'He was counted among the wicked,'

and this, I tell you, must come to be fulfilled in me. All that has to do with me approaches its climax." ³⁸ They said, "Lord, here are two swords!" He answered, "Enough."

2. The Passion, Death and Burial

The Agony in the Garden

³⁹ Then he went out and made his way, as was his custom, to the Mount of Olives; his disciples accompanied him. ⁴⁰ On reaching the place he said to them, "Pray that you may not be put to the test." ⁴¹ He withdrew from them about a stone's throw, then went down on his knees and prayed in these words:

27: Jn 13, 4-15.
30: Mt 19, 28.
34: 22, 61; Mt 26, 33ff; Mk 14, 29ff; Jn 13, 36ff.

35: 10, 4; Mt 10, 9.
37: 23, 32; Is 53, 12.
39-46: Mt 26, 30.36-46; Mk 14, 26.32-42.

22, 28: *My temptations:* both from Satan (4, 13) and from the enemies of Jesus who served the purposes of Satan.

[42] "Father, if it is your will, take this cup from me; yet not my will but yours be done." [43] An angel then appeared to him from heaven to strengthen him. [44] In his anguish he prayed with all the greater intensity, and his sweat became like drops of blood falling to the ground. [45] Then he rose from prayer and came to his disciples, only to find them asleep, exhausted with grief. [46] He said to them, "Why are you sleeping? Wake up, and pray that you may not be subjected to the trial."

Jesus Arrested

[47] While he was still speaking a crowd came, led by the man named Judas, one of the Twelve. He approached Jesus to embrace him. [48] Jesus said to him, "Judas, would you betray the Son of Man with a kiss?" [49] When the companions of Jesus saw what was going to happen, they said, "Lord, shall we use the sword?" [50] One of them went so far as to strike the high priest's servant and cut off his right ear. [51] Jesus said in answer to their question, "Enough!" Then he touched the ear and healed the man. [52] But to those who had come out against him —the chief priests, the chiefs of the temple guard, and the ancients—Jesus said, "Am I a criminal that you come out after me armed with swords and clubs? [53] When I was with you day after day in the temple you never raised a hand against me. But this is your hour—the triumph of darkness!"

Peter's Denial

[54] They led him away under arrest and brought him to the house of the high priest, while Peter followed at a distance. [55] Later they lighted a fire in the middle of the courtyard and were sitting beside it, and Peter sat among them. [56] A servant girl saw him sitting in the light of the fire. She gazed at him intently, then said, [57] "This man was with him." He denied the fact, saying, "Woman, I do not know him." [58] A little while later someone else saw him and said, "You are one of them too." But Peter said, "No, sir, not I!" [59] About an hour after that another spoke more insistently: "This man was certainly with him, for he is a Galilean." [60] Peter responded, "My friend, I do not know what you are talking about." At the very moment he was saying this, a cock crowed. [61] The Lord turned around

---

47-53: Mt 26, 47-56;
    Mk 14, 43-50;
    Jn 18, 3-11.
54-62: Mt 26, 58.69-75;
    Mk 14, 54.66-72;

Jn 18, 15-18.25ff.
61: 22, 34;
    Mt 26, 34;
    Mk 14, 30;
    Jn 13. 38.

and looked at Peter, and Peter remembered the word that the Lord had spoken to him, "Before the cock crows today you will deny me three times." [62] He went out and wept bitterly.

Jesus before the Sanhedrin

[63] Meanwhile the men guarding Jesus amused themselves at his expense. [64] They blindfolded him first, slapped him, and then taunted him: "Play the prophet; which one struck you?" [65] And they directed many other insulting words at him.

[66] At daybreak, the elders of the people, the chief priests, and the scribes assembled again. Once they had brought him before their council, they said, "Tell us, are you the Messiah?" [67] He replied, "If I tell you, you will not believe me, [68] and if I question you, you will not answer. [69] This much only will I say: 'From now on, the Son of Man will have his seat at the right hand of the Power of God.'" [70] "So you are the Son of God?" they asked in chorus. He answered, "It is you who say I am." [71] They said, "What need have we of witnesses? We have heard it from his own mouth."

23

Jesus before Pilate

[1] Then the entire assembly rose up and led him before Pilate. [2] They started his prosecution by saying, "We found this man subverting our nation, opposing the payment of taxes to Caesar, and calling himself the Messiah, a king." [3] Pilate asked him, "Are you the king of the Jews?" He answered, "That is your term." [4] Pilate reported to the chief priests and the crowds, "I do not find a case against this man." [5] But they insisted, "He stirs up the people by his teaching throughout the whole of Judea, from Galilee, where he began, to this very place." [6] On hearing this Pilate asked if the man was a Galilean; [7] and when he learned that he was under Herod's jurisdiction, he sent him to Herod, who also happened to be in Jerusalem at the time.

[8] Herod was extremely pleased to see Jesus. From the reports about him he had wanted for a long time to see him, and he was hoping to see him work some miracle. [9] He questioned

63f: Mt 26, 67ff; Mk 14, 65.
66-71: Mt 26, 59-66;
Mk 14, 55-64.
66: Mt 27, 1; Mk 15, 1.
70: Wis 2, 13; Jn 10, 30.
23, 1: Mt 27, 1f; Jn 18, 28.
2-6: Mt 27, 11-14;

Mk 15, 2-5;
Jn 18, 29-38.
2: 20, 22-25; Acts 17, 7;
24, 5.
3: Mt 27, 11; Mk 15, 2;
Jn 18, 33.

Jesus at considerable length, but Jesus made no answer. [10] The chief priests and scribes were at hand to accuse him vehemently. [11] Herod and his guards then treated him with contempt and insult, after which they put a magnificent robe on him and sent him back to Pilate. [12] Herod and Pilate, who had previously been set against each other, became friends from that day.

Jesus Again before Pilate

[13] Pilate then called together the chief priests, the ruling class, and the people, [14] and said to them: "You have brought this man before me as one who subverts the people. I have examined him in your presence and have no charge against him arising from your allegations. [15] Neither has Herod, who therefore has sent him back to us; obviously this man has done nothing that calls for death. [16] Therefore I mean to release him, once I have taught him a lesson." [18] The whole crowd cried out, "Away with this man; release Barabbas for us!" [19] This Barabbas had been thrown in prison for causing an uprising in the city, and for murder. [20] Pilate addressed them again, for he wanted Jesus to be the one he released.

[21] But they shouted back, "Crucify him, crucify him!" [22] He said to them for the third time, "What wrong is this man guilty of? I have not discovered anything about him that calls for the death penalty. I will therefore chastise him and release him." [23] But they demanded with loud cries that he be crucified, and their shouts increased in violence. [24] Pilate then decreed that what they demanded should be done. [25] He released the one they asked for, who had been thrown in prison for insurrection and murder, and delivered Jesus up to their wishes.

The Way of the Cross

[26] As they led him away, they laid hold of one Simon the Cyrenean who was coming in from the fields. They put a crossbeam on Simon's shoulder for him to carry along behind Jesus. [27] A great crowd of people followed him, including women who beat their breasts and lamented over him. [28] Jesus turned to them and said: "Daughters of Jerusalem, do not weep for me. Weep for yourselves and for your children. [29] The days are

---

14: Jn 19, 4.
18-25: Mt 27, 15-26;
Mk 15, 7-15;

Jn 18, 39—19, 16.
24f: Acts 3, 14f.
26: Mt 27, 31f; Mk 15, 20f.

23, 17: Omit with some MSS. Others read: "At the festival time he had to release a prisoner to them."

coming when they will say, 'Happy are the sterile, the wombs that never bore and the breasts that never nursed.' [30] Then they will begin saying to the mountains, 'Fall on us,' and to the hills, 'Cover us.' [31] If they do these things in the green wood, what will happen in the dry?"

The Crucifixion

[32] Two others who were criminals were led along with him to be crucified. [33] When they came to Skull Place, as it was called, they crucified him there and the criminals as well, one on his right and the other on his left. [34] [Jesus said, "Father, forgive them; they do not know what they are doing."] They divided his garments, rolling dice for them.

[35] The people stood there watching, and the leaders kept jeering at him, saying, "He saved others; let him save himself if he is the Messiah of God, the chosen one." [36] The soldiers also made fun of him, coming forward to offer him their sour wine [37] and saying, "If you are the king of the Jews, save yourself." [38] There was an inscription over his head:

"THIS IS THE KING OF THE JEWS."

[39] One of the criminals hanging in crucifixion blasphemed him: "Aren't you the Messiah? Then save yourself and us." [40] But the other one rebuked him: "Have you no fear of God, seeing you are under the same sentence? [41] We deserve it, after all. We are only paying the price for what we've done, but this man has done nothing wrong." [42] He then said, "Jesus, remember me when you enter upon your reign." [43] And Jesus replied, "I assure you: this day you will be with me in paradise."

Jesus Dies on the Cross

[44] It was now around midday, and darkness came over the whole land until midafternoon with an eclipse of the sun. [45] The curtain in the sanctuary was torn in two. [46] Jesus uttered a loud cry and said,

"Father, into your hands I commend my spirit."

After he said this, he expired. [47] The centurion, upon seeing

30: Hos 10, 8; Rv 6, 16.
32: 22, 37; Is 53, 12.
33f: Mt 27, 33; Mk 15, 22ff;
   Jn 19, 17.
34: Ps 22, 19; Acts 7, 60.
35-38: Mt 27, 39-43;
   Mk 15, 29-32.
36: Mt 27, 48.
38: Jn 19, 19.
39: Mt 27, 44; Mk 15, 32.
44ff: Mt 27, 45-50;
   Mk 15, 33-37.
46: Ps 31, 6; Jn 19, 30;
   Acts 7, 60.
47: Mt 27, 54; Mk 15, 39.

what had happened, gave glory to God by saying, "Surely this was an innocent man." ⁴⁸ When the crowd which had assembled for this spectacle saw what had happened, they went home beating their breasts. ⁴⁹ All his friends and the women who had accompanied him from Galilee were standing at a distance watching everything.

The Burial

⁵⁰ There was a man named Joseph, an upright and holy member of the Sanhedrin, ⁵¹ who had not been associated with their plan or their action. He was from Arimathea, a Jewish town, and he looked expectantly for the reign of God. ⁵² This man approached Pilate with a request for Jesus' body. ⁵³ He took it down, wrapped it in fine linen, and laid it in a tomb hewn out of the rock, in which no one had yet been buried.

⁵⁴ That was the Day of Preparation, and the sabbath was about to begin. ⁵⁵ The women who had come with him from Galilee followed along behind. They saw the tomb and how his body was buried. ⁵⁶ Then they went home to prepare spices and perfumes. They observed the sabbath as a day of rest, in accordance with the law.

VII: APPEARANCES AFTER THE RESURRECTION

24

The Women at the Tomb

¹ On the first day of the week, at dawn, the women came to the tomb bringing the spices they had prepared. ² They

---

49: 24, 10.
50-55: Mt 27, 57-61;
  Mk 15, 42-47;
  Jn 19, 38-41.

56: Mk 16, 1.
24, 1-8: Mt 28, 1-8; Mk 16, 1-8.
  1ff: Jn 20, 1ff.

24, 1-53: The resurrection narratives in the gospels do not derive directly from the primitive stage when the apostolic testimony was as yet unchallenged by the unbeliever. They reflect a somewhat later period, when the average Christian was aware of the unbeliever's principal counter-arguments against the doctrine of the resurrection; namely, that Jesus' disciples had removed his body from the tomb, or that they were victims of visionary or other objectively unreal experiences. The gospels and the tradition that preceded them carefully interwove the data of the resurrection with the replies to these arguments, so that Christians might remain in peaceful possession of their faith.

The narratives, then, begin with the account of the women's visit to the tomb—no doubt to make clear that up to this point the male disciples of Jesus had not come near the tomb (1-8). The reaction of the disciples to the women's report reveals that they did not anticipate Jesus' immediate resurrection (10f), much less think of creating a resurrection myth by removal of the body. The stress on the incredulity of the disciples (11.25.41;

found the stone rolled back from the tomb; ³ but when they
entered the tomb, they did not find the body of the Lord Jesus.
⁴ While they were still at a loss over what to think of this, two
men in dazzling garments stood beside them. ⁵ Terrified, the
women bowed to the ground. The men said to them: "Why do
you search for the Living One among the dead? ⁶ He is not
here; he has been raised up. Remember what he said to you
while he was still in Galilee—⁷ that the Son of Man must be
delivered into the hands of sinful men, and be crucified, and
on the third day rise again." ⁸ With this reminder, his words
came back to them.

⁹ On their return from the tomb, they told all these things
to the Eleven and the others. ¹⁰ The women were Mary of
Magdala, Joanna, and Mary the mother of James. The other
women with them also told the apostles, ¹¹ but the story seemed
like nonsense and they refused to believe them. ¹² Peter, however, got up and ran to the tomb. He stooped down but could
see nothing but the wrappings. So he went away full of amazement at what had occurred.

Emmaus

¹³ Two of them that same day were making their way to a
village named Emmaus seven miles distant from Jerusalem,
¹⁴ discussing as they went all that had happened. ¹⁵ In the
course of their lively exchange, Jesus approached and began to
walk along with them. ¹⁶ However, they were restrained from
recognizing him. ¹⁷ He said to them, "What are you discussing
as you go your way?" ¹⁸ They halted, in distress, and one of
them, Cleopas by name, asked him, "Are you the only resident

7: 9, 22; Mt 16, 21;   12: Jn 20, 3-7.
    17, 22f; Mk 9, 31.   13: Mk 16, 12f.
9ff: Mk 16, 10f.   16: Jn 20, 14; 21, 4.
10: 8, 2f.

cf Mt 28, 17; Jn 20, 24-29) depicts them as men not easily convinced
of the resurrection event: *They thought they were seeing a ghost* (37). But
their experience of his presence for the duration of meals (42f; cf Jn 20,
9-13), and their conversation with him in which they recognized that his
earlier teaching actually culminated in these new circumstances (44; cf Jn
20, 21; 21, 15ff), required the acceptance of the one before them as
Jesus of Nazareth, who had returned to life after undergoing the reality of
death.

The greater problem of the disciples in accepting the fact of the resurrection was, no doubt, its messianic implications. These new and unan-
ticipated concepts presented an extraordinary challenge to the faith of Israel,
a point that Luke's resurrection narrative is careful to make (25ff.44-47).
In addition to the apologetic response to the denials of the resurrection,
Luke (44-49), like Matthew (28, 19f) and John (20, 21ff), incorporates into
his gospel the instructions of the risen Jesus concerning the mission of
the disciples and of the Christian community.

of Jerusalem who does not know the things that went on there these past few days?" [19] He said to them, "What things?" They said: "All those that had to do with Jesus of Nazareth, a prophet powerful in word and deed in the eyes of God and all the people; [20] how our chief priests and leaders delivered him up to be condemned to death, and crucified him. [21] We were hoping that he was the one who would set Israel free. Besides all this, today, the third day since these things happened, [22] some women of our group have just brought us some astonishing news. They were at the tomb before dawn [23] and failed to find his body, but returned with the tale that they had seen a vision of angels who declared he was alive. [24] Some of our number went to the tomb and found it to be just as the women said; but him they did not see."

[25] Then he said to them, "What little sense you have! How slow you are to believe all that the prophets have announced! [26] Did not the Messiah have to undergo all this so as to enter into his glory?" [27] Beginning, then, with Moses and all the prophets, he interpreted for them every passage of Scripture which referred to him. [28] By now they were near the village to which they were going, and he acted as if he were going farther. [29] But they pressed him: "Stay with us. It is nearly evening—the day is practically over." So he went in to stay with them.

[30] When he had seated himself with them to eat, he took bread, pronounced the blessing, then broke the bread and began to distribute it to them. [31] With that their eyes were opened and they recognized him; whereupon he vanished from their sight. [32] They said to one another, "Were not our hearts burning inside us as he talked to us on the road and explained the Scriptures to us?" [33] They got up immediately and returned to Jerusalem, where they found the Eleven and the rest of the company assembled. They were greeted with, [34] "The Lord has been raised! It is true! He has appeared to Simon." [35] Then they recounted what had happened on the road and how they had come to know him in the breaking of bread.

Jesus Appears to the Eleven

[36] While they were still speaking about all this, he himself stood in their midst [and said to them, "Peace to you."]. [37] In

---

19: Mt 2, 23; Acts 2, 22. 27: 1 Pt 1, 10f.
21: 1, 54; 2, 38. 36: Jn 20, 19f.
25f: 18, 31; Acts 3, 24.

their panic and fright they thought they were seeing a ghost.
[38] He said to them, "Why are you disturbed? Why do such
ideas cross your mind? [39] Look at my hands and my feet; it is
really I. Touch me, and see that a ghost does not have flesh and
bones as I do." [40] As he said this he showed them his hands
and feet. [41] They were still incredulous for sheer joy and wonder,
so he said to them, "Have you anything here to eat?" [42] They
gave him a piece of cooked fish, [43] which he took and ate in
their presence. [44] Then he said to them, "Recall those words I
spoke to you when I was still with you: everything written
about me in the law of Moses and the prophets and psalms
had to be fulfilled." [45] Then he opened their minds to the understanding of the Scriptures.

[46] He said to them: "Thus it is written that the Messiah must
suffer and rise from the dead on the third day. [47] In his name,
penance for the remission of sins is to be preached to all the
nations, beginning at Jerusalem. [48] You are witnesses of this.
See, [49] I send down upon you the promise of my Father. Remain here in the city until you are clothed with power from on
high."

The Ascension

[50] Then he led them out near Bethany, and with hands up-
raised, blessed them. [51] As he blessed, he left them, and was
taken up to heaven. [52] They fell down to do him reverence,
then returned to Jerusalem filled with joy. [53] There they were
to be found in the temple constantly, speaking the praises of
God.

40f: Jn 21, 9f.13.   Mk 16, 15f; Acts 10, 41.
46: 9, 22.   49: Jn 14, 26; Acts 1, 4; 2, 3f.
47: Mt 3, 2; 28, 19f;   50f: Mk 16, 19; Acts 1, 9ff.

THE GOSPEL ACCORDING TO JOHN
INTRODUCTION

The reputed author of the fourth gospel was John, son of Zebedee, who published it at Ephesus in the last years of his life. Within the Christian community, this is the only important tradition that has come down from antiquity concerning this gospel. In its essentials the tradition is found in Irenaeus ("Adversus Haereses," 3:1, 1) toward the close of the second century. He claims to have had it from Polycarp of Smyrna, who knew John. Thus "the beloved disciple" himself becomes identified as the source of the tradition (19, 35; 21, 24); cf 19, 26f.

While the attestation of this tradition is impressive, it should be remembered that for the ancients authorship was a much broader concept than it is today. In their time a man could be called the "author" of a work if he was the authority behind it, even though he did not write it. Modern critical analysis makes it difficult to accept the idea that the gospel as it now stands was written by one man. Chapter 21 seems to have been added after the gospel was completed (20, 30f); it exhibits a Greek style somewhat different from the rest of the work. The Prologue (1, 1-18) was apparently an independent hymn, subsequently adapted to serve as a preface to the gospel. Within the gospel itself there are signs of some disorder; e.g., there are two endings to Jesus' discourse at the Last Supper (14, 31; 18, 1).

To solve these problems, scholars have proposed various rearrangements that would produce a smoother order. However, more and more students of this gospel are coming to believe that the inconsistencies were probably produced by subsequent editing in which homogeneous materials were added to a shorter original. Other difficulties for the theory of eyewitness authorship are presented by the gospel's highly developed theology, and by certain elements of its literary style. For instance, some of the miracles of Jesus have been worked into highly effective dramatic scenes (ch 9); there has been a careful attempt to have the miracles followed by discourses which explain them (chs 5 and 6); the sayings of Jesus have been woven into long discourses of a quasi-poetic form resembling the speeches of personified Wisdom in the Old Testament.

How can the ancient tradition about the authorship of the fourth gospel be reconciled with modern biblical scholarship? Many scholars, Protestant and Catholic, are coming to accept a theory which tries to do justice to both. This proposes that behind the fourth gospel there was an ancient tradition of the words and deeds of Jesus, a tradition of real historical value, similar in general to, but independent of, the traditions that underlie the synoptic gospels. Thus, just as the name "Peter" has been associated with one of the traditions behind the synoptic gospels, so the name "John, son of Zebedee," may well be attached to the tradition behind the fourth gospel. John, as one of the three privileged disciples who were closest to Jesus, may have preserved and preached this basic tradition about Jesus.

The theory further proposes that it was one of John's disciples who actually developed the tradition into the pattern of the gospel as we know it. Perhaps, under John's guidance, this disciple was the real evangelist: an artistic and theological genius, who gave to the tradition the distinctive literary features which we call "Johannine," and who used the gospel message to respond to the pressing theological needs of his time. All of this would have required the selection and reworking of details from the tradition, and would probably have been based on a long history of Johannine preaching.

Later, the theory continues, still another disciple of John was responsible for the editing of the evangelist's original gospel. He is often called the disciple-redactor, or editor, to distinguish him from the disciple-evangelist. This man added other material which had come down from the wide circle of Johannine disciples (the Prologue and chapter 21), and seems to have included a large body of material from the disciple-evangelist which had not been incorporated into the original edition of the gospel. For instance, if the Last Discourse of Jesus in the original edition came to an end at 14, 31, the redactor added three more chapters of Last Discourse material (15—17), quite like the material in chapter 14 and even duplicating it. But since he did not wish to tamper with the original gospel, he let the original conclusion of 14, 31 stand.

Such a theory respects the ancient tradition that John the Apostle was the authority behind the gospel. It also explains, on the basis of critical analysis, that a disciple of John, here called the disciple-evangelist, was not an eyewitness, and that more than one hand was involved in the writing of the gospel. Moreover it teaches us how to evaluate what we find therein. This gospel contains many valid historical details about Jesus not found in the synoptic gospels: e.g., that after his baptism by John, Jesus was engaged in a baptizing ministry before he changed exclusively to preaching (3, 22); that Jesus' public ministry lasted for several years (see note on 2, 13); that he traveled to Jerusalem on various feasts and met serious opposition long before his death (2, 14ff; chs 5 and 7-10); that he was put to death on the day before Passover (18, 28). These events are not always in order, however, because of the development and editing that ensued.

The fourth gospel is not simply history; the narrative has been organized and adapted to serve the evangelist's theological purposes as well. Among them are: opposition to the synagogue and to such of John the Baptizer's sectarians as tried to exalt their master at Jesus' expense; desire to show that Jesus was the Messiah; desire to convince Christians that their religious belief and practice must be rooted in Jesus. Such theological purposes have caused the evangelist to bring to the fore motifs which, as can be seen by comparison with the synoptic gospels, were not so clear in the synoptic account of Jesus' ministry, e.g., the explicit emphasis on his divinity.

The polemic between the synagogue and the church influenced Johannine language toward harshness especially by reason of the hostility toward Jesus manifested by the authorities—Pharisees and Sadducees—who are referred to frequently as "the Jews" (see note on Jn 1, 19). Such opponents are even described in Jn 8, 44 as springing from their father the devil, whose conduct they imitate in opposing God by rejecting the One whom God has sent. Today, there is a very real effort by Christians and Jews to understand and respect one another and thus to eliminate all embittered criticism.

The final editing of the gospel and arrangement in its present form probably dates between A.D. 90 and 100. Ephesus is still favored by most scholars as the place of composition, though some have proposed the Syrian city of Antioch.

The chief divisions of the Gospel of John are as follows:

   I: Prologue 1, 1-18
  II: The Book of Signs (1, 19—12, 50)
 III: The Book of Glory (13, 1—20, 31)
 IV: Appendix: The Resurrection Appearance in Galilee (21, 1-25)

THE GOSPEL ACCORDING TO JOHN
I: PROLOGUE

1

¹ In the beginning was the Word;
the Word was in God's presence,
and the Word was God.
² He was present to God in the beginning.
³ Through him all things came into being,
and apart from him nothing came to be.
⁴ Whatever came to be in him, found life,
life for the light of men.
⁵ The light shines on in darkness,
a darkness that did not overcome it.

⁶ There was a man named John sent by God, ⁷ who came as a witness to testify to the light, so that through him all men might believe—⁸ but only to testify to the light, for he himself was not the light. ⁹ The real light which gives light to every man was coming into the world.

¹⁰ He was in the world,
and through him the world was made,

1, 1: 10, 30; Gn 1, 1-5.
Prv 8, 22-25; 1 Jn 1, 1f;
Rv 19, 14.
3: Ps 33, 9; 1 Cor 8, 6;
Col 1, 15; Heb 1, 2.
4: 5, 26.

5: 3, 19; 8, 12; 1 Jn 2, 8.
6: Mt 3, 1; Mk 1, 4;
Lk 3, 2f.
7: 1, 19-34.
9: 8, 12; 12, 46.

1, 1-18: The Prologue is a hymn, formally poetic in style—perhaps originally an independent composition and only later adapted and edited to serve as an overture to the gospel. Its closest parallel is found in the christological hymns in Col 1, 15-20; Phil 2, 6-11; 1 Tm 3, 16. The Roman writer Pliny (A. D. 111) mentions the Christians of Asia Minor as singing hymns to Christ as a god. Commentators are divided on whether the initial reference to the earthly ministry of Jesus Christ is in 1, 9 or 1, 14.
1, 1: *In the beginning:* these, the first words of Gn 1, 1, serve as the Hebrew title of that book. Here, however, they introduce the two verses describing the situation before creation. *Was:* three times in the first verse this verb is used of the Word. First, it indicates timeless existence; next, relationship to the Father; finally, identity with God.
1, 3f: In the Clementine Vulgate, the words *whatever came to be* are put at the end of v 3: *"Apart from him,* nothing came into being which came to be. In him was life, etc."* The best evidence favors the division given above. *Found life:* literally "was life."
1, 3: The creation was through the Word and in the Word; cf Col 1, 16.
1, 5: *Overcome:* if this translation is accepted, hostility between darkness and light is indicated, perhaps a reference to the sin of Gn 3. Other possible translations—"grasp," "comprehend," "receive"—are preferred by those who regard the verse as referring to the ministry of Jesus.
1, 6ff: These are more prosaic than the other verses of the Prologue, and their content is intrusive, separating 5 from 9 or 10. Vv 6ff, perhaps including 9, are to be regarded as a parenthetical addition by the Johannine editor of the hymn. For him, the reference to the ministry of Jesus came after 6ff.
1, 9: The earlier versions make *every man* (instead of *the light*) the subject of *coming into the world.*

yet the world did not know who he was.
[11] To his own he came,
yet his own did not accept him.
[12] Any who did accept him
he empowered to become children of God.

These are they who believe in his name—[13] who were begotten
not by blood, nor by carnal desire, nor by man's willing it, but
by God.

[14] The Word became flesh
and made his dwelling among us,
and we have seen his glory:
the glory of an only Son coming from the Father,
filled with enduring love.

[15] John testified to him by proclaiming: "This is he of whom I
said, 'The one who comes after me ranks ahead of me, for he
was before me.'"

[16] Of his fullness
we have all had a share—
love following upon love.

12: Gal 3, 26; 4, 6f;   14: 1 Jn 1, 2.
   1 Jn 3, 2.   15: 1, 30; 3, 27-30.
13: 3, 5f.

1, 11: *His own:* in 11a, a neuter expression, probably meaning his own
country, the Holy Land; in 11b, *his own* is masculine, and refers to Israel
or to the Jews.

1, 12f: *Empowered:* or "gave authority." *These are they who believe in
his name,* etc.: many regard these verses as part of the final edition rather
than of the original hymn.

1, 13: *Who were begotten:* some minor textual witnesses and some early
Fathers read "he who was begotten"—a reference to Jesus. This is probably
a free adaptation of the text to illustrate the virgin birth. *Not by blood . . .
desire:* no human agency, male or female, begets God's children. That is
done through baptism and the Holy Spirit; cf 3, 5.

1, 14: *Made his dwelling:* literally, "set up his tent, or tabernacle." In the
Exodus the tabernacle or tent of meeting was the site of God's dwelling
among men (Ex 25, 8f); now that site is the Word-made-flesh. *Glory:* the
glory of God (the visible manifestation of his majesty in power), which once
filled the tabernacle (Ex 40, 34) and the temple (1 Kgs 8, 10f.27), is now
centered in Jesus. *Filled with enduring love:* It is not clear whether *filled*
modifies *glory* or *Word* or *only Son.* The two words *love* and *enduring*
(often translated "grace and truth") represent two Old Testament terms used
to describe the dealings of the God of the covenant with Israel (Ex 34, 6):
love signifying God's love in choosing Israel and his steadfast expression of
that love in the covenant; *enduring* signifying his faithfulness to his covenant
promises. Jesus is a new manifestation of God's covenant, *enduring love,* replacing the old; cf v 16.

1, 15: This verse, of the same nature as 6ff, seems to be drawn from v
30; it interrupts vv 14 and 16, which belong together.

1, 16: *Love following upon love:* the endless accumulation of God's goodness in Jesus. Other possible translations are: "love in place of love"—the
love manifested in Jesus replacing the love manifested in Moses (cf 1, 17)—
and "love for love"—our love corresponding to Jesus' love.

[17] For while the law was given through Moses, this enduring love came through Jesus Christ. [18] No one has ever seen God. It is God the only Son, ever at the Father's side, who has revealed him.

II: THE BOOK OF SIGNS

Testimony of John to the Envoys

[19] The testimony John gave when the Jews sent priests and Levites from Jerusalem to ask, "Who are you?" [20] was the direct statement, "I am not the Messiah." [21] They questioned him further, "Who, then? Elijah?" "I am not Elijah," he answered. "Are you the Prophet?" "No," he replied.

[22] Finally they said to him: "Tell us who you are, so that we can give some answer to those who sent us. What do you have to say for yourself?" [23] He said, quoting the prophet Isaiah, "I am

> 'a voice in the desert, crying out:
> Make straight the way of the Lord!' "

[24] Those whom the Pharisees had sent [25] proceeded to question him further: "If you are not the Messiah, nor Elijah, nor the Prophet, why do you baptize?" [26] John answered them: "I baptize with water. There is one among you whom you do not recognize—[27] the one who is to come after me—the strap of whose sandal I am not worthy to unfasten.'

17: Dt 33, 4.
18: 6, 46; Ex 33, 20;
    1 Jn 4, 12.
20: 3, 28; Acts 13, 25.

23: Is 40, 3; Mt 3, 3;
    Mk 1, 2; Lk 3, 4.
26: Mt 3, 11; Mk 1, 8;
    Lk 3, 16.

1, 17f: Many commentators regard these verses as explanation rather than part of the pre-Prologue hymn. *God the only Son:* other MSS read "the Son, the only one" or "the only Son." *Ever at the Father's side:* literally, "in [to] the bosom of the Father."

1, 19: *The Jews:* Throughout most of the gospel, with the notable exception of chapters 11 and 12, the "Jews" are not the Jewish people as such. They are the hostile authorities, the Pharisees and Sadducees, particularly those in Jerusalem, who refuse to believe in Jesus. The use of the term reflects the atmosphere at the end of the first century, when polemics expressed the hostility between the synagogue and the church.

1, 21: *"Elijah?" "I am not":* the Baptizer himself did not claim to be Elijah returned to earth; with greater insight, Jesus (Mt 11, 14) explained the Baptizer's career as fulfilling the role Malachi (4, 5) attributed to Elijah. *The Prophet:* probably the prophet like Moses of Dt 18, 15; cf Acts 3, 22.

1, 24: *Those whom the Pharisees had sent:* it would be very unusual for the priestly and levitical envoys of v 19 to have been of the Pharisees' party rather than that of the Sadducees. Some would translate: "There were some Pharisees sent," or "Some of the Pharisees' party were sent." If the latter translation is correct, the evangelist has simplified party distinctions, since the Sadducees were no longer important in the late first century.

²⁸ This happened in Bethany, across the Jordan, where John was baptizing.

His Testimony to Jesus

²⁹ The next day, when John caught sight of Jesus coming toward him, he exclaimed:

> "Look! There is the Lamb of God
> who takes away the sin of the world!

³⁰ It is he of whom I said:

> 'After me is to come a man
> who ranks ahead of me,
> because he was before me.'

³¹ I confess I did not recognize him, though the very reason I came baptizing with water was that he might be revealed to Israel."

³² John gave this testimony also:

> "I saw the Spirit descend
> like a dove from the sky,
> and it came to rest on him.

³³ But I did not recognize him. The one who sent me to baptize with water told me, 'When you see the Spirit descend and rest on someone, it is he who is to baptize with the Holy Spirit.' ³⁴ Now I have seen for myself and have testified, 'This is God's chosen One.' "

30: 1, 15; Mt 3, 11;
Mk 1, 7; Lk 3, 16.
32: Is 11, 2; Mt 3, 16;
Mk 1, 10; Lk 3, 21f.

33: Mt 3, 11; Mk 1, 8;
Lk 3, 16.
34: Is 42, 1; Mt 3, 17;
Mk 1, 11; Lk 9, 35.

1, 28: *Bethany, across the Jordan:* this is not the Bethany near Jerusalem (11, 18); the actual site is unknown. "Bethabara" ("place of crossing over") is read by the Old Syriac, and Origen accepted it as the correct reading.

1, 29: *The Lamb of God:* perhaps, for the Baptizer this meant the great apocalyptic lamb who would destroy evil in the world (Rv 17, 14). The evangelist may see a reference to the paschal lamb, and/or to the suffering servant led like a lamb to the slaughter as an offering for sin (Is 53, 7.10).

1, 30: *He was before me:* preexistence is a Johannine theme (1, 1; 8, 58; 17, 5).

1, 32: John the Evangelist does not actually describe the baptism of Jesus, but the occasion of the vision narrated here is almost certainly to be understood as the baptism.

1, 34: *God's chosen One:* the better Greek MSS have "God's Son." The heavenly voice in the synoptic gospels proclaims: "This is my beloved Son" (Mt 3, 17; Mk 1, 11; Lk 3, 22). It is difficult to see why scribes would change "God's Son" to "God's chosen One," and easy to see why for harmonizing and theological purposes a change in the opposite direction would be made. *Chosen One* is probably a reference to the Servant of Yahweh (Is 42, 1).

The First Disciples

[35] The next day John was there again with two of his disciples. [36] As he watched Jesus walk by he said, "Look! There is the Lamb of God!" [37] The two disciples heard what he said, and followed Jesus. [38] When Jesus turned around and noticed them following him, he asked them, "What are you looking for?" They said to him, "Rabbi (which means Teacher), where do you stay?" [39] "Come and see," he answered. So they went to see where he was lodged, and stayed with him that day. (It was about four in the afternoon.)

[40] One of the two who had followed him after hearing John was Simon Peter's brother Andrew. [41] The first thing he did was seek out his brother Simon and tell him, "We have found the Messiah!" (This term means the Anointed.) [42] He brought him to Jesus, who looked at him and said, "You are Simon, son of John; your name shall be Cephas (which is rendered Peter)."

[43] The next day he wanted to set out for Galilee, but first he came upon Philip. "Follow me," Jesus said to him. [44] Now Philip was from Bethsaida, the same town as Andrew and Peter. [45] Philip sought out Nathanael and told him, "We have found the one Moses spoke of in the law—the prophets too—Jesus, son of Joseph, from Nazareth." [46] Nathanael's response to that was, "Can anything good come from Nazareth?" and Philip replied, "Come, see for yourself." [47] When Jesus saw Nathanael coming toward him, he remarked: "This man is a true Israelite. There is no guile in him." "How do you know me?" [48] Nathanael asked him. "Before Philip called you," Jesus answered, "I saw you under the fig tree." [49] "Rabbi," said Nathanael, "you are the Son of God; you are the king of Israel." [50] Jesus responded:

41: 4, 25.
42: Mt 16, 18; Mk 3, 16.

49: 12, 13.

1, 37: *Two disciples:* one is Andrew (v 40); the other, unnamed here, is traditionally identified as John, son of Zebedee. See note on 13, 23.
1, 39: *Four in the afternoon:* literally, the tenth hour. The evangelists seem to use the Roman method of reckoning time; the hours from sunrise (6 A. M.) are counted as the daylight hours. Some suggest that it was a Friday afternoon; the next day, beginning at sunset, would be the sabbath, which was why they *stayed with him.*
1, 41: The reading of *first* is uncertain: our interpretation follows the best MSS, including the early papyri. *The Messiah:* the actual Aramaic word *meshiha*—"anointed one"—appears in the Greek as the transliterated *messias* here and in 4, 25. Elsewhere the Greek translation *christos* is used.
1, 43: The subject of the first two verbs is not clear; grammatically it could be Peter, but logically it is probably Jesus.
1, 47: *A true Israelite:* Jacob was the first to bear the name "Israel" (Gn 22, 28ff), but Jacob was a man of guile (Gn 27, 35).
1, 50f: *You will see . . . :* these verses may be a play on the name "Israel," which was popularly interpreted as "a man who sees God." There may be a reference in v 51 to Jacob's ladder (Gn 28, 12). *I solemnly as-*

"Do you believe just because I told you I saw you under the fig tree? You will see much greater things than that."

[51] He went on to tell them, "I solemnly assure you, you shall see the sky opened and the angels of God ascending and descending on the Son of Man."

2

The Wedding at Cana

[1] On the third day there was a wedding at Cana in Galilee, and the mother of Jesus was there. [2] Jesus and his disciples had likewise been invited to the celebration. [3] At a certain point the wine ran out, and Jesus' mother told him, "They have no more wine." [4] Jesus replied, "Woman, how does this concern of yours involve me? My hour has not yet come." [5] His mother instructed those waiting on table, "Do whatever he tells you." [6] As prescribed for Jewish ceremonial washings, there were at hand six stone water jars, each one holding fifteen to twenty-five gallons. [7] "Fill those jars with water," Jesus ordered, at which they filled them to the brim. [8] "Now," he said, "draw some out and take it to the waiter in charge." They did as he instructed them. [9] The waiter in charge tasted the water made wine, without knowing where it had come from; only the waiters knew, since they had drawn the water. Then the waiter in charge called the groom over [10] and remarked to him: "People usually serve the choice wine first; then when the guests have been drinking awhile, a lesser vintage. What you have done is keep the choice wine until now." [11] Jesus performed this first

---

2, 1: 4, 46.　　　　　　　　　　13, 1.
4: 7, 30; 8, 20; 12, 23;　　　　　11: 4, 54.

---

sure you: literally, "Amen, amen." The double "amen" is characteristic of John.

2, 4: *Woman:* this form of address, normally given by Jesus to the women he encountered during his ministry (Mt 15, 28; Lk 13, 12) is entirely courteous. However, there is no attestation of a son's use of "woman," without any qualification, to address his mother; and so some commentators suggest a symbolic meaning. Mary is again called "woman" in 19, 26, and the mother of the Messiah in Rv 12, 1-5 is described as "a woman clothed with the sun." Is there symbolic reference to Eve, "the woman" of Genesis? *How does this concern of yours involve me?:* literally, "What is this to me and to you?"— a Hebrew expression; e. g., 2 Kgs 3, 13, where it denies the speaker's involvement in a project proposed by another. *My hour has not yet come:* the translation of this as a question ("Has not my hour now come?") is quite unlikely from a comparison with 7, 6.30. The *hour* is the hour of Jesus' passion, death, resurrection and ascension (13, 1).

2, 6: *Fifteen to twenty-five gallons:* literally, "two or three measures"; the measure in question was of eight or nine gallons.

2, 8: *Waiter in charge:* it is not clear if the official is a major domo, or a friend of the family who acted as master of ceremonies; see Sir 32, 1.

of his signs at Cana in Galilee. Thus did he reveal his glory, and his disciples believed in him.

¹² After this he went down to Capernaum, along with his mother and brothers [and his disciples] but they stayed there only a few days.

Cleansing of the Temple

¹³ As the Jewish Passover was near, Jesus went up to Jerusalem. ¹⁴ In the temple precincts he came upon people engaged in selling oxen, sheep and doves, and others seated changing coins. ¹⁵ He made a [kind of] whip of cords and drove sheep and oxen alike out of the temple area, and knocked over the money-changers' tables, spilling their coins. ¹⁶ He told those who were selling doves: "Get them out of here! Stop turning my Father's house into a marketplace!" ¹⁷ His disciples recalled the words of Scripture: "Zeal for your house consumes me."

¹⁸ At this the Jews responded, "What sign can you show us authorizing you to do these things?" ¹⁹ "Destroy this temple," was Jesus' answer, "and in three days I will raise it up." ²⁰ They retorted, "This temple took forty-six years to build, and you are going to 'raise it up in three days'!" ²¹ Actually he was talking about the temple of his body. ²² Only after Jesus had been raised from the dead did his disciples recall that he had said this, and come to believe the Scripture and the word he had spoken.

²³ While he was in Jerusalem during the Passover festival, many believed in his name, for they could see the signs he was performing. ²⁴ For his part, Jesus would not trust himself to them because he knew them all. ²⁵ He needed no one to give

---

13-22: Mt 21, 12f; Mk 11, 15ff;
     Lk 19, 45f.
  17: Ps 69, 10.
  18: 6, 30.

19: Mt 26, 61.
22: 5, 39.
23: 4, 45.

2, 12: This transitional verse may be a harmonization with the synoptic tradition in Lk 4, 31 and Mt 4, 13. There are many textual variants.

2, 13: *Passover:* this is the first Passover mentioned in John; a second is mentioned in 6, 4, a third in 13, 1. If these chronological indications are to be taken literally, they point to a ministry of at least two years.

2, 14ff: This is almost certainly the same cleansing the other gospels place in the last days of Jesus' life (Mt, on the day Jesus entered Jerusalem; Mk, on the next day). The order of events in the gospel narratives is often determined by theological motives rather than by chronological data.

2, 15: *Sheep and oxen:* in John the cleansing is a more violent attack on the temple, because the animals necessary for sacrifice are expelled.

2, 19: This saying is reported by the false witnesses in the synoptic account of Jesus' trial before Caiaphas (Mk 14, 58; Mt 26, 61); see also Mk 15, 29; Acts 6, 14. According to John, Jesus says that it is the Jewish authorities themselves who will destroy the temple; the false witnesses say that Jesus threatened to destroy it.

him testimony about human nature. He was well aware of what was in man's heart.

3

Nicodemus

[1] A certain Pharisee named Nicodemus, a member of the Jewish Sanhedrin, [2] came to him at night. "Rabbi," he said, "we know you are a teacher come from God, for no man can perform signs and wonders such as you perform unless God is with him." [3] Jesus gave him this answer:

> "I solemnly assure you,
> no one can see the reign of God
> unless he is begotten from above."

[4] "How can a man be born again once he is old?" retorted Nicodemus. "Can he return to his mother's womb and be born over again?" [5] Jesus replied:

> "I solemnly assure you,
> no one can enter into God's kingdom
> without being begotten of water and Spirit.
> [6] Flesh begets flesh,
> Spirit begets spirit.
> [7] Do not be surprised that I tell you
> you must all be begotten from above.
> [8] The wind blows where it will.
> You hear the sound it makes
> but you do not know where it comes from,
>   or where it goes.
> So it is with everyone begotten of the Spirit."

[9] "How can such a thing happen?" asked Nicodemus. [10] Jesus

---

3, 1: 7, 50f; 19, 39.
2: 9, 16.33; 10, 21.
4: 1, 13.

6: 6, 63; 1 Cor 15, 44-50.
8: Acts 2, 2ff.

3, 3: *Begotten:* the Greek verb can mean "born" from a female principle, or "begotten" by a male principle. As in 1, 13, John primarily means it as "begotten," though many early versions translate it as "born" or even, with heightened baptismal symbolism, "reborn." *From above:* the Greek term *anothen* means both "again" and "from above." V 31 below shows that Jesus means it as "from above," but Nicodemus misunderstands. (A misunderstanding that brings out Jesus' teaching is a common literary device in John.)
3, 5: The Council of Trent declared that *water* here is not a metaphor but means real water. This passage has had an important role in baptismal theology.
3, 8: *Wind:* the Greek word *pneuma* means both "wind" and "spirit." We can see from the context that John is playing on the double meaning, with wind as the primary comparison.

responded: "You hold the office of teacher of Israel and still you do not understand these matters?

¹¹ "I solemnly assure you,
we are talking about what we know,
we are testifying to what we have seen,
but you do not accept our testimony.
¹² If you do not believe
when I tell you about earthly things,
how are you to believe
when I tell you about those of heaven?
¹³ No one has gone up to heaven
except the One who came down from there—
the Son of Man [who is in heaven].
¹⁴ Just as Moses lifted up the serpent in the desert,
so must the Son of Man be lifted up,
¹⁵ that all who believe
may have eternal life in him,
¹⁶ Yes, God so loved the world
that he gave his only Son,
that whoever believes in him may not die
but may have eternal life.
¹⁷ God did not send the Son into the world
to condemn the world,
but that the world might be saved through him.
¹⁸ Whoever believes in him avoids condemnation,
but whoever does not believe is already condemned
for not believing in the name of God's only Son.
¹⁹ The judgment of condemnation is this:

11: 3, 32.34; 8, 14;   14: Nm 21, 9; Wis 16, 5ff.
Mt 11, 27.   16: 1 Jn 4, 9.
12: 6, 62ff; Wis 9, 16f.   17: 12, 47.
13: 1, 18.   19: 8, 12.

3, 13: *Has gone up to heaven:* the seeming reference to the ascension in the past tense is difficult, but tenses in John seem to be somewhat timeless; see 8, 58. *Who is in heaven:* if this is a true reading, it may be compared to 1, 18.

3, 14: *Lifted up:* the first of three references (8, 28; 12, 32) to the "lifting up" of Jesus the Son of Man: i. e., in crucifixion, resurrection, and ascension. These are comparable to the three references to the passion and resurrection in the synoptics (Mk 8, 31; 9, 30; 10, 31).

3, 15: This might be translated "that everyone who believes in him may have eternal life." *Eternal life,* used here for the first time in John, stresses the quality of the life rather than its duration.

3, 16: *Gave:* a reference to both the incarnation and the death of Jesus; cf Rom 8, 32.

3, 16: *Condemn . . . judgment:* the same Greek root is involved, and it has both shades of meaning. Jesus' coming provokes judgment; his purpose is to save, but some condemn themselves by turning from the light.

3, 19: John stresses that judgment is not only a matter of the future but is partially realized here and now.

> the light came into the world,
> but men loved darkness rather than light
> because their deeds were wicked.
> [20] Everyone who practices evil
> hates the light;
> he does not come near it
> for fear his deeds will be exposed.
> [21] But he who acts in truth
> comes into the light,
> to make clear
> that his deeds are done in God."

Final Witness of the Baptizer

[22] Later on, Jesus and his disciples came into Judean territory, and he spent some time with them there baptizing. [23] John too was baptizing at Aenon near Salim where water was plentiful, and people kept coming to be baptized. [24] (John, of course, had not yet been thrown into prison.) [25] A controversy about purification arose between John's disciples and a certain Jew. [26] So they came to John, saying, "Rabbi, the man who was with you across the Jordan—the one about whom you have been testifying—is baptizing now, and everyone is flocking to him." [27] John answered:

> "No one can lay hold on anything
> unless it is given him from on high.

[28] "You yourselves are witnesses to the fact that I said: 'I am not the Messiah; I am sent before him.'

> [29] "It is the groom who has the bride.
> The groom's best man
> waits there listening for him
> and is overjoyed to hear his voice.

20: Jb 24, 13-17.
21: Mt 5, 14ff.
22f: 4, 1f.
27: 19, 11; 2 Cor 3, 5;

Heb 5, 4.
28: Lk 3, 15.
29: Mt 9, 15.

3, 22: *Baptizing:* that after his baptism Jesus conducted a baptizing ministry is not mentioned by the synoptics; cf 4, 2.
3, 23: *Aenon near Salim:* uncertain site, either in the upper Jordan valley or in Samaria.
3, 25: *Controversy:* perhaps this dispute concerned the relative value of the two baptisms or the value of baptism vs. Jewish purifications (2, 6).
3, 27: *No one:* it is more likely that this refers to Jesus than to the Baptizer.
3, 29: *Groom's best man:* the one who arranged the wedding and acted as go-between for groom and bride.

That is my joy, and it is complete.
[30] He must increase,
while I must decrease.

Discourse Concluded

[31] "The One who comes from above is above all;
the one who is of the earth is earthly,
and he speaks on an earthly plane.
The One who comes from heaven [who is above all]
[32] testifies to what he has seen and heard,
but no one accepts his testimony.
[33] Whoever does accept this testimony
certifies that God is truthful,
[34] For the One whom God has sent
speaks the words of God;
he does not ration his gift of the Spirit.
[35] The Father loves the Son
and has given everything over to him.
[36] "Whoever believes in the Son
has life eternal.
Whoever disobeys the Son
will not see life,
but must endure the wrath of God."

4

[1] Now when Jesus learned that the Pharisees had heard that
he was winning over and baptizing more disciples than John
[2] (in fact, however, it was not Jesus himself who baptized, but
his disciples), [3] he left Judea and started back for Galilee again.

The Samaritan Woman

[4] He had to pass through Samaria, [5] and his journey brought
him to a Samaritan town named Shechem near the plot of

32: 3, 11;
33f: 8. 26; 1 Jn 5, 10.

35: Mt 28, 18.
4, 5: Gn 33, 18f.

3, 31-36: It is uncertain whether these words are spoken by the Baptizer,
by Jesus, or by the evangelist. Perhaps an originally independent discourse of
Jesus has been brought here by way of comment on the two preceding
scenes of ch 3. *His gift:* it is uncertain to whom the "his" refers: to God
or to Jesus.
4, 2: An editorial refinement on 3, 22, perhaps against followers of the
Baptizer in the late first century who exalted the Baptizer above Jesus.
4, 5f: *Shechem:* most MSS have Sychar which St. Jerome identifies with
Shechem. He may be correct in saying that copyists mistakenly put "Sychar"
for "Shechem." *Jacob's well* (unmentioned in the Old Testament) is the
well of Shechem. The town is situated in the valley between Mounts Gerizim
and Ebal; cf Dt 27; Jos 3, 30.

land which Jacob had given to his son Joseph. [6] This was the site of Jacob's well. Jesus, tired from his journey, sat down at the well.

The hour was about noon. [7] When a Samaritan woman came to draw water, Jesus said to her, "Give me a drink." [8] (His disciples had gone off to the town to buy provisions.) [9] The Samaritan woman said to him, "You are a Jew. How can you ask me, a Samaritan and a woman, for a drink?" (Recall that Jews have nothing to do with Samaritans.)
[10] Jesus replied:

> "If only you recognized God's gift,
>   and who it is that is asking you for a drink,
>   you would have asked him instead,
>   and he would have given you living water."

[11] "Sir," she challenged him, "You do not have a bucket and this well is deep. Where do you expect to get this flowing water? [12] Surely you do not pretend to be greater than our ancestor Jacob, who gave us this well and drank from it with his sons and his flocks?" [13] Jesus replied:

> "Everyone who drinks this water
>   will be thirsty again.
>   [14] But whoever drinks the water I give him
>   will never be thirsty;
>   no, the water I give
>   shall become a fountain within him,
>   leaping up to provide eternal life."

[15] The woman said to him, "Give me this water, sir, so that I shall not grow thirsty and have to keep coming here to draw water."

[16] He said to her, "Go, call your husband, and then come back here." [17] "I have no husband," replied the woman. "You are right in saying you have no husband!" Jesus exclaimed. [18] "The fact is, you have had five, and the man you are living with now is not your husband. What you said is true."

9: Sir 50, 25f; Mt 10, 5.   14: 6, 35; 7, 37ff; Jl 4, 18.

4, 9: Samaritan women were regarded as ritually impure, and therefore Jews were forbidden to drink from any vessel they had handled.

4, 10f: *Living water:* Jesus is speaking of the water of life; the woman thinks of *flowing water,* so much more desirable than stale cistern water. This is a typical example of Johannine use of a hearer's misunderstanding; cf note on 3, 3.

¹⁹ "Sir," answered the woman, "I can see you are a prophet.
²⁰ Our ancestors worshiped on this mountain, but you people
claim that Jerusalem is the place where men ought to worship
God." ²¹ Jesus told her:

"Believe me, woman,
   an hour is coming
   when you will worship the Father
   neither on this mountain
   nor in Jerusalem.
²² You people worship what you do not understand,
while we understand what we worship;
after all, salvation is from the Jews.
²³ Yet an hour is coming, and is already here,
when authentic worshipers
will worship the Father in Spirit and truth.
Indeed, it is just such worshipers
the Father seeks.
²⁴ God is Spirit,
and those who worship him
must worship in Spirit and truth."

²⁵ The woman said to him: "I know there is a Messiah coming."
(This term means Anointed.) "When he comes, he will tell us
everything." ²⁶ Jesus replied, "I who speak to you am he."

²⁷ His disciples, returning at this point, were surprised that
Jesus was speaking with a woman. No one put a question,
however, such as "What do you want of him?" or "Why are
you talking with her?" ²⁸ The woman then left her water
jar and went off into the town. She said to the people: ²⁹ "Come
and see someone who told me everything I ever did! Could
this not be the Messiah?" ³⁰ At that they set out from the town
to meet him.

22: 2 Kgs 17, 27.   26: 9, 37.

4, 19: *Sir:* the original word (used also in v 11) means either "Sir" or
"Lord"; here the latter term may be more appropriate if the woman is
moving toward faith.
4, 20: The Samaritans included among the ten commandments the obligation to worship on Mount Gerizim. It was an ancient holy place. "Ebal" is
probbaly an anti-Samaritan Jewish emendation of "Gerizim"; cf Dt 27, 4.
4, 23: *In Spirit and truth:* this is not a reference to an interior worship
within man's spirit. The Spirit is the Spirit of truth (14, 16f), the Spirit given
by God which reveals truth and raises up man to worship God on the appropriate level. This idea presupposes the "begetting by Spirit" in 3, 5.
4, 25: The expectations of the Samaritans are expressed here in more
familiar Jewish terminology. They did not expect a messianic king of the
house of David but a prophet like Moses (Dt 18, 15).

³¹ Meanwhile the disciples were urging him, "Rabbi, eat something." ³² But he told them:

"I have food to eat
of which you do not know."

³³ At this the disciples said to one another, "Do you suppose that someone has brought him something to eat?" ³⁴ Jesus explained to them:

"Doing the will of him who sent me
and bringing his work to completion is my food.
³⁵ Do you not have a saying:
'Four months more
and it will be harvest!'?
Listen to what I say:
Open your eyes and see!
The fields are shining for harvest!
³⁶ The reaper already collects his wages
and gathers a yield for eternal life,
that sower and reaper may rejoice together.
³⁷ Here we have the saying verified:
'One man sows; another reaps.'
³⁸ I sent you to reap
what you had not worked for.
Others have done the labor,
and you have come into their gain."

³⁹ Many Samaritans from that town believed in him on the strength of the woman's word of testimony: "He told me everything I ever did." ⁴⁰ The result was that, when these Samaritans came to him, they begged him to stay with them awhile. So he stayed there two days, ⁴¹ and through his own spoken word many more came to faith. ⁴² As they told the woman: "No longer does our faith depend on your story. We have heard for ourselves, and we know that this really is the Savior of the world."

Return to Galilee

⁴³ When the two days were over, he left for Galilee. ⁴⁴ (Jesus himself had testified that no one esteems a prophet in his own

---

34: 6, 38; 17, 4.   36: Ps 126, 5f.
35: Mt 9, 37f; Lk 10, 2.

4, 35: This is probably a proverb rather than a real time indication; cf Mt 9, 37f.
4, 36: *Already:* it is possible that this word belongs at the end of v 35.

country.) ⁴⁵ When he arrived in Galilee, the people there welcomed him. They themselves had been at the feast and had seen all that he had done in Jerusalem on that occasion.

Second Sign at Cana

⁴⁶ He went to Cana in Galilee once more, where he had made the water wine. At Capernaum there happened to be a royal official whose son was ill. ⁴⁷ When he heard that Jesus had come back from Judea to Galilee, he went to him and begged him to come down and restore health to his son, who was near death. ⁴⁸ Jesus replied, "Unless you people see signs and wonders, you do not believe." ⁴⁹ "Sir," the royal official pleaded with him, "come down before my child dies." ⁵⁰ Jesus told him, "Return home. Your son will live." The man put his trust in the word Jesus spoke to him, and started for home.

⁵¹ He was on his way there when his servants met him with the news that his boy was going to live. ⁵² When he asked them at what time the boy had shown improvement, they told him, "The fever left him yesterday afternoon about one." ⁵³ It was at that very hour, the father realized, that Jesus had told him, "Your son is going to live." He and his whole household thereupon became believers. ⁵⁴ This was the second sign that Jesus performed on returning from Judea to Galilee.

5

Cure on a Sabbath Feast

¹ Later, on the occasion of a Jewish feast, Jesus went up to Jerusalem. ² Now in Jerusalem by the Sheep Pool there is a

---

44: Mt 13, 57.   54: 2, 11.
48: Mt 12, 38.   5, 1: 6, 4.

4, 44: The parenthetical verse is probably the reminiscence of a tradition similar to that in Mk 6, 4.

4, 46-52: The story of the royal official's son is probably a third version of the story of the centurion's boy (Mt 8, 5-13) or servant (Lk 7, 1-10) found in slightly different forms in the synoptic tradition. The variants are inconsequential details, of the sort that could arise in oral tradition.

4, 50f.53: *Live:* this theme of life will be commented on by Jesus in 5, 21ff.

4, 53: The author ends a section by referring back to its beginning (2, 11).

5, 1: This was probably not a winter feast or the people would not have been in open porticoes. The reference later in the discourse to Moses (5, 45f) leads some scholars to think that the feast was Pentecost (fifty days after Passover; the feast of the giving of the law to Moses on Sinai). Another suggestion is Passover. All that John emphasizes is that it was a sabbath.

5, 2: Another possible translation is "Now in Jerusalem, by the Sheep [Gate], there is a pool with the Hebrew name Bethesda." The name of the region was given to the pool as well. Variants of *Bethesda* are "Bethsaida" and "Be(t)zatha." This pool with its five porticoes has been excavated in recent years in the area northeast of the temple.

place with the Hebrew name Bethesda. Its five porticoes [3] were crowded with sick people lying there blind, lame or disabled [waiting for the movement of the water] . . . [4]. [5] There was one man who had been sick for thirty-eight years. [6] Jesus, who knew he had been sick a long time, said when he saw him lying there, "Do you want to be healed?" [7] "Sir," the sick man answered, "I do not have anyone to plunge me into the pool once the water has been stirred up. By the time I get there, someone else has gone in ahead of me." [8] Jesus said to him, "Stand up! Pick up your mat and walk!" [9] The man was immediately cured; he picked up his mat and began to walk.

The day was a sabbath. [10] Consequently, some of the Jews began telling the man who had been cured, "It is the sabbath, and you are not allowed to carry that mat around." [11] He explained: "It was the man who cured me who told me, 'Pick up your mat and walk.' " [12] "This person who told you to pick it up and walk," they asked, "who is he?" [13] The man who had been restored to health had no idea who it was. The crowd in that place was so great that Jesus had been able to slip away.

[14] Later on, Jesus found him in the temple precincts and said to him: "Remember, now, you have been cured. Give up your sins so that something worse may not overtake you." [15] The man went off and informed the Jews that Jesus was the one who had cured him.

Discourse on His Sabbath Work

[16] It was because Jesus did things such as this on the sabbath that they began to persecute him. [17] But he had an answer for them:

10: Ex 20, 8; Jer 17, 21-27.   16: 7, 23; Mt 12, 8.

5, 3: Some good Western MSS, including St. Jerome's Vulgate, have the additional phrase [waiting for the movement of the water]. We may conclude from v 7 that there was an intermittent spring in the pool that bubbled up occasionally. People attributed a curative value to the turbulence produced by the spring.

5, 4: Toward the end of the second century in the West, and among the fourth-century Greek Fathers, there is knowledge of an additional verse: "For [from time to time] an angel of the Lord used to come down into the pool; and the water was stirred up, so the first one to get in [after the bubbling of the water] was healed of whatever sickness he had had." The appearance of the angel is probably a popular explanation of the turbulence and the healing powers attributed to it. This verse is missing in our best early Greek witnesses, and the earliest versions; it is not to be found in St. Jerome's original Vulgate. The vocabulary of the verse is markedly non-Johannine.

5, 10: Carrying a sleeping mat on the sabbath was specifically forbidden in rabbinic law.

5, 14: *Give up your sins:* Jesus never draws a one-to-one connection between sin and sickness or misfortune; cf Jn 9, 3; Lk 12, 1-5. Nevertheless he regards sickness as part of the evil introduced into the world by sin, and his mission is to destroy the kingdom of evil in all its forms (Mk 2, 8-11).

"My Father is at work until now,
and I am at work as well."

¹⁸ The reason why the Jews were even more determined to kill
him was that he not only was breaking the sabbath but, worse
still, was speaking of God as his own father, thereby making
himself God's equal.

The Work of the Son

¹⁹ This was Jesus' answer:

"I solemnly assure you,
the Son cannot do anything by himself—
he can do only what he sees the Father doing.
For whatever the Father does,
the Son does likewise.
²⁰ For the Father loves the Son
and everything the Father does he shows him.
Yes, to your great wonderment,
he will show him even greater works than these.
²¹ Indeed, just as the Father raises the dead and grants life,
so the Son grants life to those to whom he wishes.
²² The Father himself judges no one,
but has assigned all judgment to the Son,
²³ so that all men may honor the Son
just as they honor the Father.
He who refuses to honor the Son
refuses to honor the Father who sent him.
²⁴ I solemnly assure you,
the man who hears my word
and has faith in him who sent me
possesses eternal life.
He does not come under condemnation,
but has passed from death to life.
²⁵ I solemnly assure you,
an hour is coming, has indeed come,
when the dead shall hear the voice of the Son of God,
and those who have heeded it shall live.

20: 3, 35.   22: Acts 10, 42.
21: Dt 32, 29; 2 Kgs 5, 7;   24: 3, 18.
    Wis 16, 13.   25: 8, 51; 11, 25f.

5, 17: The sabbath observance was based on God's resting after the six
days of creation, but the Jewish theologians were perfectly aware that divine
providence remained active on the sabbath, keeping all things in existence.
It was obvious that on the sabbath God gave life in birth and took
it away in death. Jesus is claiming the same right to work as the Father,
and, in the discourse that follows, the same power over life and death.

²⁶ Indeed, just as the Father possesses life in himself,
so has he granted it to the Son to have life in himself.
²⁷ The Father has given over to him power to pass judgment
because he is Son of Man;
²⁸ no need for you to be surprised at this,
for an hour is coming
in which all those in their tombs
shall hear his voice and come forth.
²⁹ Those who have done right shall rise to live;
the evildoers shall rise to be damned.
³⁰ I cannot do anything of myself.
I judge as I hear,
and my judgment is honest
because I am not seeking my own will
but the will of him who sent me.

Witnesses to Jesus

³¹ "If I witness on my own behalf,
    you cannot verify my testimony;
     ³² but there is another who is testifying on my behalf,
and the testimony he renders me
I know can be verified.
     ³³ You have sent to John,
who has testified to the truth.
     ³⁴ (Not that I myself accept such human testimony—
I refer to these things only for your salvation.)
     ³⁵ He was the lamp, set aflame and burning bright,
and for a while you exulted willingly in his light.
     ³⁶ Yet I have testimony greater than John's,
namely, the works the Father has given me to accomplish.
These very works which I perform
testify on my behalf
that the Father has sent me.
     ³⁷ Moreover, the Father who sent me
has himself given testimony on my behalf.
His voice you have never heard,

26: 3, 35; 1 Jn 5, 11.
27: 5, 22; Dn 7, 13.
28: 11, 43.
29: Mt 16, 27; Acts 24, 15;
    2 Cor 5, 10.
30: 6, 38.

31f: 8, 13f.18.
33: 1, 19-27; Mt 11, 10f.
35: 1, 8; Sir 48, 1.
36: 10, 25.
37: 8, 18; Dt 4, 12.15;
    1 Jn 5, 9.

5, 32: *Another:* this is generally understood to be the Father who in four
different ways gives testimony to Jesus, as indicated in the verse groupings
33f; 36; 37f; 39f.
5, 35: *Lamp:* this may reflect the description of Elijah in Sir 48, 1.

his form you have never seen,
³⁸ neither do you have his word abiding in your hearts
because you do not believe
the One he has sent.
³⁹ Search the Scriptures
in which you think you have eternal life—
they also testify on my behalf.
⁴⁰ Yet you are unwilling to come to me
to possess that life.

Unbelief of Jesus' Hearers

⁴¹ "It is not that I accept human praise—
⁴² it is simply that I know you,
and you do not have the love of God in your hearts.
⁴³ I have come in my Father's name,
yet you do not accept me.
But let someone come in his own name
and him you will accept.
⁴⁴ How can people like you belive,
when you accept praise from one another
yet do not seek the glory that comes from the One [God]?
⁴⁵ Do not imagine that I will be your accuser before the
    Father;
the one to accuse you is Moses
on whom you have set your hopes.
⁴⁶ If you believed Moses
you would then believe me,
for it was about me that he wrote.
⁴⁷ But if you do not believe what he wrote,
how can you believe what I say?"

6

Multiplication of the Loaves at Passover

¹ Later on, Jesus crossed the Sea of Galilee [to the shore]

39: 12, 16; 19, 28; 20, 9.
42: 1 Jn 2, 15.
43: Mt 24, 24.
44: 12, 43.
46: 5, 39; Dt 18, 15;

6, 1-13: Mt 14, 13-21;
Lk 16, 31, 24, 44.
Mk 6, 32-44;
Lk 9, 10-17.

5, 39: *Search:* this may be a statement: "You search the Scriptures because you think [them] to have eternal life."
5, 41: *Praise:* the same Greek word means "praise" (from men) and
"glory" (from God). There will be a play on this in v 44.
6, 1: *Of Tiberias:* if the bracketed clause is omitted, "Tiberias" stands in
awkward apposition as another name of the lake. It was only considerably
later than Jesus' time that this name was given to the lake, since the city of
Tiberias was completed only just before Jesus' ministry. If the clause is left
in, then the multiplication took place near Tiberias.

of Tiberias; [2] a vast crowd kept following him because they saw the signs he was performing for the sick. [3] Jesus then went up the mountain and sat down there with his disciples. [4] The Jewish feast of Passover was near; [5] when Jesus looked up and caught sight of a vast crowd coming toward him, he said to Philip, "Where shall we buy bread for these people to eat?" [6] He knew well what he intended to do but he asked this to test Philip's response.) [7] Philip replied, "Not even with two hundred days' wages could we buy loaves enough to give each of them a mouthful!"

[8] One of Jesus' disciples, Andrew, Simon Peter's brother, remarked to him, [9] "There is a lad here who has five barley loaves and a couple of dried fish, but what good is that for so many?" [10] Jesus said, "Get the people to recline." Even though the men numbered about five thousand, there was plenty of grass for them to find a place on the ground. [11] Jesus then took the loaves of bread, gave thanks, and passed them around to those reclining there; he did the same with the dried fish, as much as they wanted. [12] When they had had enough, he told his disciples, "Gather up the crusts that are left over so that nothing will go to waste." [13] At this, they gathered twelve baskets full of pieces left over by those who had been fed with the five barley loaves.

[14] When the people saw the sign he had performed they began to say, "This is undoubtedly the Prophet who is to come into the world." [15] At that, Jesus realized that they would come and carry him off to make him king, so he fled back to the mountain alone.

Walking on the Sea

[16] As evening drew on, his disciples came down to the lake. [17] They embarked, intending to cross the lake toward Capernaum. By this time it was dark, and Jesus had still not joined them; [18] moreover, with a strong wind blowing, the sea was becoming rough. [19] Finally, when they had rowed three or four

---

4: 2, 13; 11, 55.   15: 18, 36.
11: 21, 13.   16-21: Mt 14, 22-33;
13: 2 Kgs 4, 42ff.   Mk 6, 45-52.

6, 5ff: The Gospels of John and Luke have only one account of a multiplication of loaves and fish; Mark and Matthew have two accounts.

6, 14: *The Prophet:* probably the prophet like Moses (see note on 1, 21). Jesus, like Moses, had fed the people miraculously.

6, 19: *Walking on the water:* the Greek would permit a translation "on the seashore" or "by the sea." This would eliminate the miraculous from the story and leave it pointless. In Mt 14, 24-25, it is quite clear that Jesus walked upon the sea.

miles, they sighted Jesus approaching the boat, walking on the water. They were frightened, [20] but he told them, "It is I; do not be afraid." [21] They wanted to take him into the boat, but suddenly it came aground on the shore they had been approaching.

[22] The crowd remained on the other side of the lake. The next day they realized that there had been only one boat there and that Jesus had not left in it with his disciples; rather, they had set out by themselves. [23] Then some boats came out from Tiberias near the place where they had eaten the bread after the Lord had given thanks. [24] Once the crowd saw that neither Jesus nor his disciples were there, they too embarked in the boats and went to Capernaum looking for Jesus.

Discourse on the Bread of Life

[25] When they found him on the other side of the lake, they said to him, "Rabbi, when did you come here?" [26] Jesus answered them:

"I assure you,
> you are not looking for me because you have seen signs
> but because you have eaten your fill of the loaves.
> [27] You should not be working for perishable food
> but for food that remains unto life eternal,
> food which the Son of Man will give you;
> it is on him that God the Father has set his seal."

[28] At this they said to him, "What must we do to perform the works of God?" [29] Jesus replied:

"This is the work of God:
> have faith in the One whom he sent."

[30] "So that we can put faith in you," they asked him, "what sign are you going to perform for us to see? What is the 'work' you do? [31] Our ancestors had manna to eat in the desert; ac-

---

30: Mt 16, 1-4; Lk 11, 29f.   31: Ex 16, 4f; Ps 78, 24.

6, 20: *It is I:* literally, "I am"—perhaps the expression intended to connote divinity; see note on 8, 24.

6, 21: It is not clear whether Jesus got into the boat, or whether the sudden arrival at the shore is presented as miraculous. Possibly both are intended.

6, 22ff: These verses have many variants in the manuscripts and are awkward and somewhat illogical. Were all five thousand transported? There may be several forms of the account combined in our present readings.

6, 23: *From Tiberias near the place:* it is not clear whether Tiberias is near the place or the boats came near to the place; cf v 1 and the note there.

6, 31: There is evidence that the Jews believed the miracle of the manna would be repeated in the last days; hence their challenge to discover whether these were the last days.

cording to Scripture, 'He gave them bread from the heavens to eat.' " [32] Jesus said to them:

"I solemnly assure you,
it was not Moses who gave you bread from the heavens;
it is my Father who gives you the real heavenly bread.
[33] God's bread comes down from heaven
and gives life to the world."

[34] "Sir, give us this bread always," they besought him.
[35] Jesus explained to them:

"I myself am the bread of life.
No one who comes to me shall ever be hungry,
no one who believes in me shall ever thirst.
[36] But as I told you—
though you have seen me, you still do not believe.
[37] All that the Father gives me shall come to me;
no one who comes will I ever reject,
[38] because it is not to do my own will
that I have come down from heaven,
but to do the will of him who sent me.
[39] It is the will of him who sent me
that I should lose nothing of what he has given me;
rather, that I should raise it up on the last day.
[40] Indeed, this is the will of my Father,
that everyone who looks upon the Son
and believes in him
shall have eternal life.
Him I will raise up on the last day."

[41] At this the Jews started to murmur in protest because he claimed, "I am the bread that came down from heaven." [42] They kept saying: "Is this not Jesus, the son of Joseph? Do

---

32: Mt 6, 11.
35: Is 55, 1ff.
38: 4, 34; Mt 26, 39;
    Heb 10, 9.

39: 10, 28f; 17, 12; 18, 9.
40: 1 Jn 2, 25.
42: Mt 13, 54-57; Mk 6, 1-4.

6, 33: *God's bread comes down:* the Greek is ambiguous for it literally reads, "God's bread is that which [or he who] comes down," etc.

6, 35: What does Jesus mean by "the bread of life"? Because of the emphasis on believing and teaching in vv 35-50, most scholars today think of the bread in these verses as primarily a figurative reference to Jesus' revelation or teaching. There may well be a secondary reference to the Eucharist. In vv 51-58, however, the eucharistic theme comes to the fore. Many, then, place a break in the discourse between vv 50 and 51.

6, 37.39: *All that . . . nothing:* for a reason not totally clear, the evangelist uses the neuter in these verses. Some think it is a grammatical peculiarity with no special significance; others see it as a reading indicative of universality.

we not know his father and mother? How can he claim to have come down from heaven?"

⁴³ "Stop your murmuring," Jesus told them;

⁴⁴ "No one can come to me
unless the Father who sent me draws him;
I will raise him up on the last day.
⁴⁵ It is written in the prophets:
'They shall all be taught by God.'
Everyone who has heard the Father
and learned from him
comes to me.
⁴⁶ Not that anyone has seen the Father—
only the one who is from God
has seen the Father.
⁴⁷ Let me firmly assure you,
he who believes has eternal life.
⁴⁸ I am the bread of life.
⁴⁹ Your ancestors ate manna in the desert, but they died.
⁵⁰ This is the bread that comes down from heaven
for a man to eat and never die.

⁵¹ I myself am the living bread
come down from heaven.
If anyone eats this bread
he shall live forever;
the bread I will give
is my flesh, for the life of the world."

⁵² At this the Jews quarreled among themselves, saying, "How can he give us his flesh to eat?" ⁵³ Thereupon Jesus said to them:

"Let me solemnly assure you,
if you do not eat the flesh of the Son of Man
and drink his blood,
you have no life in you.
⁵⁴ He who feeds on my flesh
and drinks my blood

45: Is 54, 13.   51: Mt 26, 26f; Lk 22, 19.
46: 7, 29; Ex 33, 20.

6, 51: The last two lines of 51 may be compared to the Lucan eucharistic formula (22, 19): "This [bread] is my body which is given for you."
6, 54-58: *Feeds:* the verb that John uses in these verses is not the regular verb "to eat," but a very realistic verb with a rather crude connotation of "munch, gnaw." This may be part of John's emphasis on the reality of the flesh and blood of Jesus; cf v 55.

has life eternal,
and I will raise him up on the last day.
⁵⁵ For my flesh is real food
and my blood real drink.
⁵⁶ The man who feeds on my flesh
and drinks my blood
remains in me, and I in him.
⁵⁷ Just as the Father who has life sent me
and I have life because of the Father,
so the man who feeds on me
will have life because of me.
⁵⁸ This is the bread that came down from heaven.
Unlike your ancestors who ate and died nonetheless,
the man who feeds on this bread shall live forever."

⁵⁹ He said this in a synagogue instruction at Capernaum.

Effect of the Discourse

⁶⁰ After hearing his words, many of his disciples remarked, "This sort of talk is hard to endure! How can anyone take it seriously?" ⁶¹ Jesus was fully aware that his disciples were murmuring in protest at what he had said. "Does it shake your faith?" he asked them.

⁶² "What, then, if you were to see the Son of Man
ascend to where he was before . . . ?
⁶³ It is the spirit that gives life;
the flesh is useless.
The words I spoke to you
are spirit and life.
⁶⁴ Yet among you there are some who do not believe."

(Jesus knew from the start, of course, the ones who refused to believe, and the one who would hand him over.) ⁶⁵ He went on to say:

57: 5, 26.

6, 57: *Because of me:* this can mean either "from me" (as the source) or "for my sake" (as the reason).
6, 60ff: These verses seem to refer more to the themes of vv 35-50, than to those of vv 51-58.
6, 62: This unfinished conditional sentence is obscure. Probably there is a reference to vv 49-51. Jesus claims to be *the bread that comes down from heaven;* this claim provokes incredulity (v 60); and so Jesus asks what will be said when he goes up to heaven.
6, 63: *Spirit . . . flesh:* probably not a reference to the eucharistic flesh of Jesus but to the supernatural and the natural, as in 3, 6.
6, 65: *I have told:* presumably, this is a reference to v 44 combined with v 37.

"This is why I have told you
that no one can come to me
unless it is granted him by the Father."

66 From this time on, many of his disciples broke away and would not remain in his company any longer. 67 Jesus then said to the Twelve, "Do you want to leave me too?" 68 Simon Peter answered him, "Lord, to whom shall we go? You have the words of eternal life. 69 We have come to believe; we are convinced that you are God's holy one."

70 Jesus replied, "Did I not choose the Twelve of you myself? Yet one of you is a devil." 71 (He was talking about Judas, son of Simon the Iscariot, who, though one of the Twelve, was going to hand Jesus over.)

7

Feast of Booths

1 After this, Jesus moved about within Galilee. He had decided not to travel in Judea because some of the Jews were looking for a chance to kill him. 2 However, as the Jewish feast of Booths drew near, 3 his brothers had this to say: "You ought to leave here and go to Judea so that your disciples there may see the works you are performing. 4 No one who wishes to be known publicly keeps his actions hidden. If you are going to do things like these, you may as well display yourself to the world at large." 5 (As a matter of fact, not even his brothers had much confidence in him.) 6 Jesus answered them:

"It is not yet the right time for me,
whereas the time is always right for you.
7 The world is incapable of hating you,
but it does hate me

69: 11, 27; Mt 16, 16.
71: 13, 2.27.

7, 2: Lv 23, 34; Nm 29, 12;
Zec 14, 16-19.

6, 71: Here and in 13, 2.26, it is not entirely clear whether Iscariot (man from Kerioth?) modifies *Judas* or *Simon*.

7, 2: *Booths:* the autumn harvest feast lasting eight days, during which the people lived in huts. This was looked on as a reminiscence of their ancestors' life in tents in the desert after the Exodus. The Hebrew name for this festival and its booths is Sukkoth.

7, 3: *Brothers:* these relatives are never portrayed as disciples until after the resurrection (Acts 1, 14). Mt 13, 55 and Mk 6, 3 give the names of four of them.

7, 6: *Time:* a synonym for "hour" (see 2, 4), the period of Jesus' death and resurrection. The Christian reader of the gospel understands the theological play on words: this feast does not yet mark the time of Jesus' glorification; he will not die at this time.

because of the evidence I bring against it
that what it does is evil.

8 Go up yourselves to the festival. I am not going up to this festival because the time is not yet ripe for me." 9 Having said this, he stayed on in Galilee. 10 However, once his brothers had gone up to the festival he too went up, but as if in secret and not for all to see.

11 During the festival, naturally, the Jews were looking for him, asking, "Where is that troublemaker?" 12 Among the crowds there was much guarded debate about him. Some maintained, "He is a good man," while others kept saying, "Not at all—he is only misleading the crowd!" 13 No one dared talk openly about him, however, for fear of the Jews.

First Episode

14 The feast was half over by the time Jesus went into the temple area and began to teach. 15 The Jews were filled with amazement and said, "How did this man get his education when he had no teacher?" 16 This was Jesus' answer:

"My doctrine is not my own;
it comes from him who sent me.
17 Any man who chooses to do his will
will know about this doctrine—
namely, whether it comes from God
or is simply spoken on my own.
18 Whoever speaks on his own
is bent on self-glorification.
The man who seeks glory for him who sent him
is truthful;
there is no dishonesty in his heart.
19 Moses has given you the law, has he not?
Yet not one of you keeps it.
Why do you look for a chance to kill me?"

20 "You are mad!" the crowd retorted. "Who wants to kill you?" 21 Jesus answered:

13: 9, 22; 12, 42.   15: Lk 2, 47.   20: 10, 20.

7, 8: *I am not going up:* another play on words. "Go up" refers to his elevation in crucifixion, resurrection, and ascension; cf 20, 17.
7, 15: *Education:* literally, "How does he know letters . . . ?" Children were taught to read and write by means of the Scriptures. But here more than Jesus' literacy is being discussed; the people are wondering how he can teach like a rabbi. Rabbis were trained by other rabbis and loved to quote their teachers.

"I have performed a single work
and you profess astonishment over it.
22 Moses gave you circumcision
(though it did not originate with Moses but with
    the patriarchs).
And so, even on a sabbath you circumcise a man.
23 If a man can be circumcised on the sabbath
to prevent a violation of Mosaic law,
how is it you are angry with me
for curing a whole man on the sabbath?
24 Stop judging by appearances
and make an honest judgment."

25 This led some of the people of Jerusalem to remark: "Is this not the one they want to kill? 26 Here he is speaking in public and they don't say a word to him! Perhaps even the authorities have decided that this is the Messiah. 27 Still, we know where this man is from. When the Messiah comes, no one is supposed to know his origins."

28 At this, Jesus, who was teaching in the temple area, cried out:

"So you know me,
and you know my origins?
The truth is, I have not come of myself.
I was sent by One who has the right to send,
and him you do not know.
29 I know him
because it is from him I come:
he sent me."

30 At this they tried to seize him, but no one laid a finger on him because his hour had not yet come. 31 Many in the crowd came to believe in him. They kept saying, "When the Messiah comes, can he be expected to perform more signs than this man?" 32 The Pharisees overheard this debate about him among the crowd, and the chief priests and Pharisees together sent

22: Gn 17, 10.
23: 5, 2-9.16; Mt 12, 11f;
    Lk 14, 5.
27: Heb 7, 3.

28: 8, 19.
29: 6, 46; 8, 55.
30: 7, 44; 8, 20; Lk 4, 29f.
31: 2, 11; 10, 42; 11, 45.

7, 20: *Mad:* literally, "You have a demon." The insane were thought to possess or be possessed by a demonical spirit. One has to determine from the context whether the charge in our terms is one of insanity or of possession.

7, 26: *Authorities:* the Sanhedrin members; the same term is used to describe Nicodemus (3, 1).

temple guard to arrest him.

³³ Jesus then said to them:

> "Only a little while longer am I to be with you,
> then I am going away to him who sent me.
> ³⁴ You will look for me, but you will not find me;
> where I am you cannot come."

³⁵ This caused the Jews to exclaim among themselves: "Where does he intend to go that we will not find him? Surely he is not going off to the Diaspora among the Greeks, to teach them? ³⁶ What does he mean by saying, 'You will look for me, but you will not find me,' and, 'Where I am you cannot come'?"

Second Episode

³⁷ On the last and greatest day of the festival, Jesus stood up and cried out:

> "If anyone thirsts, let him come to me;
> let him drink ³⁸ who believes in me.
> Scripture has it:
> 'From within him rivers of living water shall flow.'"

³⁹ (Here he was referring to the Spirit, whom those that came to believe in him were to receive. There was, of course, no Spirit as yet, since Jesus had not yet been glorified.) ⁴⁰ Some in the crowd who heard these words began to say, "This must be the Prophet." ⁴¹ Others were claiming, "He is the Messiah." But an objection was raised: "Surely the Messiah is not to come from Galilee? ⁴² Does not Scripture say that the Messiah, being of David's family, is to come from Bethlehem, the village where David lived?" ⁴³ In this fashion the crowd

---

33: 13, 33; 16, 16.
34: 8, 21; Prv 1, 28.
38: 4, 10.14; 19, 34;
   Is 12, 3.

39: 16, 7.
42: 2 Sm 7, 12; Ps 89, 4f;
   Mi 5, 1; Mt 2, 5f.

7, 35: *Diaspora:* the Jews living outside Palestine. *Greeks:* probably refers to the Gentiles in the Mediterranean area; cf 12, 20.

7, 37f: *Last and greatest day:* probably the seventh day, since the eighth was a day of rest after the feast. There is some MS evidence for the omission of *greatest* as a copyist's clarification.

The translation given makes Christ the source of the living water. Another reading is possible which makes the believer himself the source; in that case a period is placed after *drink* and what remains becomes an independent sentence, "He who believes in me," etc. *Scripture has it* is not an exact citation of any passage. Perhaps the reference is to the rock that Moses tapped during the Exodus. *From within him:* literally, "from his belly."

7, 39: *No Spirit as yet:* in relation to the Christian, the sending of the Spirit was not to take place until Jesus' death, resurrection, and ascension; cf 20, 22.

was sharply divided over him. [44] Some of them even wanted to apprehend him. However, no one laid hands on him.

[45] When the temple guards came back, the chief priests and Pharisees asked them, "Why did you not bring him in?" [46] "No man ever spoke like that before," the guards replied. [47] "Do not tell us you too have been taken in!" the Pharisees retorted. [48] "You do not see any of the Sanhedrin believing in him, do you? Or the Pharisees? [49] Only this lot, that knows nothing about the law—and they are lost anyway!" [50] One of their own number, Nicodemus (the man who had come to him), spoke up to say, [51] "Since when does our law condemn any man without first hearing him and knowing the facts?" [52] "Do not tell us you are a Galilean too," they taunted him. "Look it up. You will not find the Prophet coming from Galilee."

8

The Adulteress

[7, 53] [Then each went off to his own house, [8, 1] while Jesus went out to the Mount of Olives. [2] At daybreak he reappeared in the temple area; and when the people started coming to him, he sat down and began to teach them. [3] The scribes and the Pharisees led a woman forward who had been caught in adultery. They made her stand there in front of everyone. [4] "Teacher," they said to him, "this woman has been caught in the act of adultery. [5] In the law, Moses ordered such women to be stoned. What do you have to say about the case?" [6] (They were posing this question to trap him, so that they could have something to accuse him of.) Jesus bent down and started tracing on the ground with his finger. [7] When they persisted in their questioning, he straightened up and said to them, "Let the man among you who has no sin be the first to cast a stone at her." [8] A second time he bent down and wrote on the ground. [9] Then the audience drifted away one by one, beginning with the elders.

50: 3, 1; 19, 39.
51: Dt 1, 16f.
8, 1f: Lk 2, 37f.

5: Lv 20, 10; Dt 22, 22ff.
7: Mt 7, 1-5.

7, 53ff: The story of the adulteress is missing from the best early Greek MSS. Where it does appear, it is found in different places in different MSS: here; or after 7, 36; or at the end of this gospel; or after Lk 21, 38. It seems to have been preserved largely in Western and Latin circles. There are many non-Johannine features in the language, and there are also many doubtful readings. It appears in Jerome's Vulgate. However, it is certainly out of place here; it fits better with the general situation in Lk 21, 38. The Catholic Church accepts it as inspired Scripture.

8, 6: *Tracing:* or "writing" or "recording"; whether Jesus was writing something meaningful is not clear.

This left him alone with the woman, who continued to stand there before him. [10] Jesus finally straightened up and said to her, "Woman, where did they all disappear to? Has no one condemned you?" [11] "No one, sir," she answered. Jesus said, "Nor do I condemn you. You may go. But from now on, avoid this sin."]

Third Episode

[12] Jesus spoke to them once again:

"I am the light of the world.
No follower of mine shall every walk in darkness;
no, he shall possess the light of life."

[13] This caused the Pharisees to break in with: "You are your own witness. Such testimony cannot be valid." [14] Jesus answered:

"What if I am my own witness?
My testimony is valid nonetheless,
because I know where I came from
and where I am going;
you know neither the one nor the other.
[15] You pass judgment according to appearances
but I pass judgment on no man.
[16] Even if I do judge,
that judgment of mine is valid
because I am not alone:
I have at my side the One who sent me [the Father].
[17] It is laid down in your law
that evidence given by two persons is valid.
[18] I am one of those testifying in my behalf,
the Father who sent me is the other."

[19] They pressed him: "And where is this 'Father' of yours?" Jesus replied:

"You know neither me nor my Father.
If you knew me, you would know my Father too."

10: Ez 33, 11.
11: 5, 14.
12: 1, 5.9; 12, 46;
    Ex 13, 22; Is 42, 6.
14: 5, 31.
15: 12, 47.

16: 5, 30.
17: Dt 17, 6: 19, 15;
    Nm 35, 30.
18: 5, 23.37.
19: 7, 28; 14, 7; 15, 21.

8, 15: *Appearances:* literally, "according to the flesh."
8, 16: The last line is literally, "but I and the One who sent me [the Father]."

²⁰ He spoke these words while teaching at the temple treasury. Still, he went unapprehended, because his hour had not yet come.

Warning to Unbelievers

²¹ Again he said to them:

> "I am going away. You will look for me
> but you will die in your sins.
> Where I am going you cannot come."

²² At this some of the Jews began to ask, "Does he mean he will kill himself when he claims, 'Where I am going you cannot come'? ²³ He went on:

> "You belong to what is below;
> I belong to what is above.
> You belong to this world—
> a world which cannot hold me.
> ²⁴ That is why I said you would die in your sins.
> You will surely die in your sins
> unless you come to believe that I AM."

²⁵ "Who are you, then?" they asked him. Jesus answered:

> "What I have been telling you from the beginning.
> ²⁶ I could say much about you in condemnation,
> but no, I only tell the world
> what I have heard from him,
> the truthful One who sent me."

²⁷ They did not grasp that he was speaking to them of the Father. ²⁸ Jesus continued:

> "When you lift up the Son of Man,
> you will come to realize that I AM
> and that I do nothing by myself.
> I say only what the Father has taught me.
> ²⁹ The One who sent me is with me.

20: 7, 30.
21: 7, 34; 13, 33.
23: 3, 31; 17, 14; 18, 36.

25: 10, 24.
26: 12, 50.
28: 3, 14; 12, 34.

8, 24.28: *I AM,* an expression which late Jewish tradition understands as a name for God; cf 8, 58.

8, 25: *What I have been telling you from the beginning:* this is a very unclear verse and several other translations are possible: (I am) "what I say to you"; "How is it that I speak to you at all?" The earliest attested reading (Bodmer Papyrus P⁶⁶) has, "I told you at the beginning what I am also telling you (now)."

He has not deserted me
since I always do what pleases him."

30 Because he spoke this way, many came to believe in him.

Jesus and Abraham

31 Jesus then went on to say to those Jews who believed in him:

"If you live according to my teaching,
you are truly my disciples;
32 then you will know the truth,
and the truth will set you free."

33 "We are descendants of Abraham," was their answer. "Never have we been slaves to anyone. What do you mean by saying, 'You will be free'?" 34 Jesus answered them:

"I give you my assurance,
everyone who lives in sin
is the slave of sin.
35 (No slave has a permanent place in the family,
but the son has a place there forever.)
36 That is why, if the son frees you,
you will really be free.
37 I realize you are of Abraham's stock.
Nonetheless, you are trying to kill me
because my word finds no hearing among you.
38 I tell what I have seen in the Father's presence;
you do what you have heard from your father."

39 They retorted, "Our father is Abraham." Jesus told them:

"If you were Abraham's children,
you would be following Abraham's example.
40 The fact is, you are trying to kill me,
a man who has told you the truth

32: Is 42, 7; Gal 4, 31.   35: Gn 21, 10; Gal 4, 30.
33: Mt 3, 9.

8, 37: *Finds no hearing:* or "finds no place in you"; "does not continue in you"; "takes no hold in you."
8, 38: The translation given in the text understands the second part of the verse to be a sarcastic reference to the descent of the Jews from their father, the devil. There are good grounds, however, for another translation in which (as in the first part of the verse) *father* means God. "You should do what you have heard from the Father."
8, 40: Nowhere else in the New Testament is Jesus described as *a man* in this broad sense. Probably the phrase is a Semitic expression for "someone."

which I have heard from God.
Abraham did nothing like that.
⁴¹ Indeed you are doing your father's works!"

They cried, "We are no illegitimate breed! We have but one
father and that is God himself." ⁴² Jesus answered:

"Were God your father
you would love me,
for I come forth from God, and am here.
I did not come of my own will;
it was he who sent me.
⁴³ Why do you not understand what I say?
It is because you cannot bear to hear my word.
⁴⁴ The father you spring from is the devil,
and willingly you carry out his wishes.
He brought death to man from the beginning,
and has never based himself on truth;
the truth is not in him.
Lying speech
is his native tongue;
he is a liar and the father of lies.
⁴⁵ But because I deal in the truth,
you give me no credence.
⁴⁶ Can any one of you convict me of sin?
If I am telling the truth,
why do you not believe me?
⁴⁷ Whoever is of God
hears every word God speaks.
The reason you do not hear
is that you are not of God."

⁴⁸ The Jews answered, "Are we not right, after all, in saying
you are a Samaritan, and possessed besides?" ⁴⁹ Jesus replied:

"I am not possessed.
However, I revere my Father,

42: 1 Jn 5, 1.
44: 3, 1f; Wis 1, 13; 2, 24;
    Acts 13, 10; 1 Jn 3, 8-15.

46: Heb 4, 15; 1 Pt 2, 22.
47: 10, 26; 1 Jn 4, 6.

8, 41: *Illegitimate:* literally, "of fornication"; in the Old Testament, fornication signifies the worship of false gods.
8, 44: *The father of lies:* literally, "of him [i. e., the liar]" or "of it
[i. e., the lie]."
8, 48: *Samaritan:* the Samaritans were noted for an interest in magical
powers; see Simon Magus in Acts 7, 14-24.

while you fail to respect me.
⁵⁰ I seek no glory for myself;
there is one who seeks it, and it is he who judges.
⁵¹ I solemnly assure you,
if a man is true to my word
he shall never see death."

⁵² "Now we are sure you are possessed," the Jews retorted. "Abraham is dead. The prophets are dead. Yet you claim, 'A man shall never know death if he keeps my word.' ⁵³ Surely you do not pretend to be greater than our father Abraham, who died! Or the prophets, who died! Whom do you make yourself out to be?" ⁵⁴ Jesus answered:

"If I glorify myself,
that glory comes to nothing.
He who gives me glory is the Father,
the very one you claim for your God,
⁵⁵ even though you do not know him.
But I know him.
Were I to say I do not know him,
I would be no better than you—a liar!
Yes, I know him well,
and I keep his word.
⁵⁶ Your father Abraham rejoiced
that he might see my day.
He saw it and was glad."

⁵⁷ At this the Jews objected: "You are not yet fifty! How can you have seen Abraham?" ⁵⁸ Jesus answered them:

"I solemnly declare it:
before Abraham came to be, I AM."

⁵⁹ At that they picked up rocks to throw at Jesus, but he hid himself and slipped out of the temple precincts.

50: 7, 18.
51: 5, 24-29; 6, 40.47;
11, 25f.
53: 4, 12.
55: 7, 28f.

56: Mt 13, 17; Lk 17, 22.
58: 1, 30; 17, 5.
59: 10, 31.39; 11, 8;
Lk 4, 29f.

8, 56: *He saw it:* presumably this is a reference to the birth of Jacob (Israel), which was the beginning of the fulfillment of the promises concerning Abraham's seed; see Gn 17, 7 and 21, 6. But there may also be a reference to a popular Jewish tradition that Abraham saw all of his descendants.
8, 57: There is equally good evidence for reading: "How can Abraham have seen you?"

9

The Man Born Blind

¹ As he walked along, he saw a man who had been blind from birth. ² His disciples asked him, "Rabbi, was it his sin or that of his parents that caused him to be born blind?" ³ "Neither," answered Jesus:

"It was no sin, either of this man
or of his parents.
Rather, it was to let God's works show forth in him.
⁴ We must do the deeds of him who sent me
while it is day.
The night comes on
when no one can work.
⁵ While I am in the world
I am the light of the world."

⁶ With that Jesus spat on the ground, made mud with his saliva, and smeared the man's eyes with the mud. ⁷ Then he told him, "Go, wash in the pool of Siloam." (This name means "One who has been sent.") So the man went off and washed, and came back able to see.

⁸ His neighbors and the people who had been accustomed to see him begging began to ask, "Isn't this the fellow who used to sit and beg?" ⁹ Some were claiming it was he; others maintained it was not but someone who looked like him. The man himself said, "I am the one." ¹⁰ They said to him then, "How were your eyes opened?" ¹¹ He answered: "That man they call Jesus made mud and smeared it on my eyes, telling me to go to Siloam and wash. When I did go and wash, I was able to see." ¹² "Where is he?" they asked. He replied, "I have no idea."

¹³ Next, they took the man who had been born blind to the Pharisees. ¹⁴ (Note that it was on a sabbath that Jesus had made the mud paste and opened his eyes.) ¹⁵ The Pharisees, in

---

9, 1f: Is 42, 7.
  3: 11, 4.
  4: 11, 9f; 12, 35f.

5: 8, 12.
6: 5, 11; Mk 7, 33; 8, 23.

9, 1: It is difficult to be certain where or when this scene took place. The similarity of 9, 5 and 8, 12 may indicate that the scene is also part of the "Booths" setting. The next time indication is in 10, 22, three months after the feast of Booths. The evangelist may have given to this story a secondary baptismal symbolism by stressing that the man was born blind and was healed by the waters of the pool (v 7).

9, 7: *One who has been sent:* a reference to Jesus, sent by the Father.

9, 14: In using spittle, and in kneading mud, Jesus had broken the sabbath rules laid down by the scribes.

turn, began to inquire how he had recovered his sight. He told them, "He put mud on my eyes. I washed it off, and now I can see." [16] This prompted some of the Pharisees to assert, "This man cannot be from God because he does not keep the sabbath." Others objected, "If a man is a sinner, how can he perform signs like these?" They were sharply divided over him. [17] Then they addressed the blind man again: "Since it was your eyes he opened, what do you have to say about him?" "He is a prophet," he replied.

[18] The Jews refused to believe that he had really been born blind and had begun to see, until they summoned the parents of this man who now could see. [19] "Is this your son?" they asked, "and if so, do you attest that he was blind at birth? How do you account for the fact that now he can see?" [20] The parents answered: "We know this is our son, and we know he was blind at birth. [21] But how he can see now, or who opened his eyes, we have no idea. Ask him. He is old enough to speak for himself." [22] (His parents answered in this fashion because they were afraid of the Jews, who had already agreed among themselves that anyone who acknowledged Jesus as the Messiah would be put out of the synagogue. [23] That was why his parents said, "He is of age—ask him.")

[24] A second time they summoned the man who had been born blind and said to him, "Give glory to God! First of all, we know this man is a sinner." [25] "I do not know whether he is a sinner or not," he answered. "I know this much: I was blind before; now I can see." [26] They persisted: "Just what did he do to you? How did he open your eyes?" [27] "I have told you once, but you would not listen to me," he answered them. "Why do you want to hear it all over again? Do not tell me you want to become his disciples too?" [28] They retorted scornfully: "You are the one who is that man's disciple. We are disciples of Moses. [29] We know that God spoke to Moses, but we have no idea where this man comes from." [30] He came back at them: "Well, this is news! You do not know where he comes from, yet he

---

16: 3, 2; Mt 12, 10f;
    Lk 13, 10f; 14, 1-4.
22: 7, 13.

23: 12, 42.
31: 10, 21.

9, 22f: This parenthetical explanation seems to envisage a situation during the writer's lifetime after Jesus' ministry. Rejection from the synagogue of those Jews who confessed Jesus as the Messiah seems to have begun in the late eighties, when the curse against the *minim* or heretics was introduced.

9, 24: *Give glory to God:* this oath formula before taking testimony is attested in Jos 7, 19.

opened my eyes. [31] We know that God does not hear sinners, but that if someone is devout and obeys his will, he listens to him. [32] It is unheard of that anyone ever gave sight to a person blind from birth. [33] If this man were not from God, he could never have done such a thing." [34] "What!" they exclaimed, "You are steeped in sin from your birth, and you are giving us lectures?" With that they threw him out bodily.

[35] When Jesus heard of his expulsion, he sought him out and asked him, "Do you believe in the Son of Man?" [36] He answered, "Who is he, sir, that I may believe in him?" [37] "You have seen him," Jesus replied. "He is speaking to you now." [38] ["I do believe, Lord," he said, and bowed down to worship him. [39] Then Jesus said:]

> "I came into this world to divide it,
>   to make the sightless see
>   and the seeing blind."

[40] Some of the Pharisees around him picked this up, saying, "You are not calling us blind, are you?" [41] To which Jesus replied:

> "If you were blind
>   there would be no sin in that.
> 'But we see,' you say,
>   and your sin remains."

The Good Shepherd

10

> [1] "Truly I assure you:
>   Whoever does not enter the sheepfold through the gate
>   but climbs in some other way
>   is a thief and a marauder.
>   [2] The one who enters through the gate
>   is shepherd of the sheep;
>   [3] the keeper opens the gate for him.

37: 4, 26.　　　　　　　　　　　Rom 2, 19.
39: Mt 13, 13ff.　　　　　　**10**, 1-5: Jer 23, 1ff; Ez 34, 1-31.
40: Mt 15, 14; 23, 26;

9, 38: This verse, omitted in important MSS, may be an addition from a baptismal liturgy.
10, 1: The exact time when these parables were spoken is difficult to determine—whether at the feast of Booths, as in chapters 7—9, or at the feast of the Dedication, as in 10, 22; but they continue the theme of attack on the Pharisees that ends chapter 9.

The sheep hear his voice
as he calls his own by name
and leads them out.
⁴ When he has brought out [all] those that are his,
he walks in front of them,
and the sheep follow him
because they recognize his voice.
⁵ They will not follow a stranger;
such a one they will flee,
because they do not recognize a stranger's voice."

⁶ Even though Jesus used this figure with them, they did not grasp what he was trying to tell them. ⁷ He therefore said [to them again]:

"My solemn word is this:
I am the sheepgate.
⁸ All who came before me
were thieves and marauders
whom the sheep did not heed.
⁹ "I am the gate.
Whoever enters through me
will be safe.
He will go in and out,
and find pasture.
¹⁰ The thief comes
only to steal and slaughter and destroy.
I came that they might have life
and have it to the full.
¹¹ I am the good shepherd;
the good shepherd lays down his life for the sheep.
¹² The hired hand—who is no shepherd
nor owner of the sheep—
catches sight of the wolf coming
and runs away, leaving the sheep
to be snatched and scattered by the wolf.

4: Mi 2, 12f.   11: Heb 13, 20.
9: Ps 23, 1ff; Is 49, 9f.   12: Zec 11, 17.

10, 6: *Figure:* John uses a different word for illustrative speech than the "parable" of the synoptics, but the idea is the same.

10, 7-10: In 7f, the figure is of a gate for the shepherd to come to the sheep; in 9f, of a gate for the sheep to *go in and out.*

10, 11.14: The normal Greek word for *good* does not occur here. Were not the expression *good shepherd* traditional, it might be preferable to translate "model" or "noble" shepherd.

¹³ That is because he works for pay;
he has no concern for the sheep.

¹⁴ "I am the good shepherd.
I know my sheep
and my sheep know me
¹⁵ in the same way that the Father knows me
and I know the Father;
for these sheep I will give my life.
¹⁶ I have other sheep
that do not belong to this fold.
I must lead them, too,
and they shall hear my voice.
There shall be one flock then, one shepherd.
¹⁷ The Father loves me for this:
that I lay down my life
to take it up again.
¹⁸ No one takes it from me;
I lay it down freely.
I have power to lay it down,
and I have power to take it up again.
This command I received from my Father."

¹⁹ Because of these words, the Jews were sharply divided once more. ²⁰ Many were claiming: "He is possessed by a devil—out of his mind! Why pay any attention to him?" ²¹ Others maintained: "These are not the words of a madman. Surely a devil cannot open the eyes of the blind!"

Feast of the Dedication

²² It was winter, and the time came for the feast of the Dedication in Jerusalem. ²³ Jesus was walking in the temple area, in

---

16: Jer 23, 3; Eph 2, 14f.
17: Heb 10, 10.
18: 19, 11.

20: 7, 20; 8, 48.
21: 3, 2.
22: 1 Mc 4, 54.59.

10, 16: *Other sheep:* the Gentiles, God's dispersed children destined to be gathered into one (11, 52). *One flock:* St. Jerome in the Vulgate translates "one fold," but there is no evidence in Greek or Latin to support this reading. Translating the Greek word as "sheep-herd" would bring out the word-play involved as the Greek terms for "flock" and "shepherd" are as much alike as "sheep-herd" and "shepherd."

10, 22: *Feast of the Dedication:* held in December, three months after the feast of Booths (7, 2), to celebrate the Maccabees' rededication of the altar and reconsecration of the temple in 164 B.C., after their desecration by the Syrians (1 Mc 4, 36.59). Under its Hebrew name, Hanukkah, this feast is still a regular part of Jewish religious observance.

10, 23: *Solomon's Portico* was on the east side of the temple area and would offer protection from the cold winds sweeping in from the desert.

Solomon's Portico, [24] when the Jews gathered around him and said, "How long are you going to keep us in suspense? If you really are the Messiah, tell us so in plain words." [25] Jesus answered:

"I did tell you, but you do not believe.
The works I do in my Father's name
give witness in my favor,
[26] but you refuse to believe
because you are not my sheep.
[27] My sheep hear my voice.
I know them,
and they follow me.
[28] I give them eternal life,
and they shall never perish.
No one shall snatch them out of my hand.
[29] My Father is greater than all, in what he has given me,
and there is no snatching out of his hand.
[30] The Father and I are one."

[31] When some of the Jews again reached for rocks to stone him, [32] Jesus protested to them, "Many good deeds have I shown you from the Father. For which of these do you stone me?" [33] "It is not for any 'good deed' that we are stoning you," the Jews retorted, "but for blaspheming. You who are only a man are making yourself God." [34] Jesus answered:

"Is it not written in your law,
'I have said, You are gods'?
[35] If it calls those men gods
to whom God's word was addressed—
and Scripture cannot lose its force—
[36] do you claim that I blasphemed
when, as he whom the Father consecrated

24: Lk 22, 67.
25: 5, 36.
26: 8, 47.
28: Dt 32, 39.
29: Wis 3, 1; Is 43, 13.

30: 1, 1; 12, 45; 14, 9.
31: 8, 59.
33: 5, 18; 19, 7.
34: Ps 82, 6.
36: 5, 18.

10, 24: *Keep us in suspense:* The literal translation of the words is "How long will you take away our life?" Cf 11, 48ff.

10, 29: The textual evidence for the first clause is very divided; it may also be translated: "As for the Father, what he has given me is greater than all."

10, 34: This is a reference to the judges who, since they exercised the divine prerogative to judge (Dt 1, 17), were called "gods"; cf Ex 21, 6, besides Ps 82, 6 from which the quotation comes.

10, 36: *Consecrated:* may be a reference to the theme of the Hanukkah feast; see note on 10, 22. In place of the rededicated temple altar, Jesus is consecrated by the Father.

and sent into the world,
I said, 'I am God's Son'?
[37] If I do not perform my Father's works,
put no faith in me.
[38] But if I do perform them,
even though you put no faith in me,
put faith in these works,
so as to realize what it means
that the Father is in me
and I in him."

[39] At these words they again tried to arrest him, but he eluded their grasp.

Return to the Jordan

[40] Then he went back across the Jordan to the place where John had been baptizing earlier, and while he stayed there [41] many people came to him. "John may never have performed a sign," they commented, "but whatever John said about this man was true." [42] In that place, many came to believe in him.

11

The Raising of Lazarus

[1] There was a certain man named Lazarus who was sick. He was from Bethany, the village of Mary and her sister Martha. [2] (This Mary whose brother Lazarus was sick was the one who anointed the Lord with perfume and dried his feet with her hair.) [3] The sisters sent word to Jesus to inform him, "Lord, the one you love is sick." [4] Upon hearing this, Jesus said:

"This sickness is not to end in death;
rather it is for God's glory,
that through it the Son of God may be glorified."

[5] Jesus loved Martha and her sister and Lazarus very much. [6] Yet, after hearing that Lazarus was sick, he stayed on where he was for two days more. [7] Finally he said to his disciples, "Let us go back to Judea." [8] "Rabbi," protested the disciples, "with the Jews only recently trying to stone you, you are going back up there again?" [9] Jesus answered:

38: 14, 10f.20.   **11,** 1f: 12, 1-8; Lk 10, 38f.
40: 1, 28.   8: 8, 59; 10, 31.

11, 1: *Bethany:* a town near Jerusalem (v 18), distinct from Bethany in the Transjordan (1, 28). Among the synoptics, only Luke (10, 38) writes of Mary and Martha, but he locates the scene involving them in the journey from Galilee toward Jerusalem.

"Are there not twelve hours of daylight?
If a man goes walking by day he does not stumble
because he sees the world bathed in light.
¹⁰ But if he goes walking at night he will stumble
since there is no light in him."

¹¹ After uttering these words, he added, "Our beloved Lazarus has fallen asleep, but I am going there to wake him." ¹² At this the disciples objected, "Lord, if he is asleep his life will be saved." ¹³ Jesus had been speaking about his death, but they thought he meant sleep in the sense of slumber. ¹⁴ Finally Jesus said plainly: "Lazarus is dead. ¹⁵ For your sakes I am glad I was not there, that you may come to believe. In any event, let us go to him." ¹⁶ Then Thomas (the name means "Twin") said to his fellow disciples, "Let us go along, to die with him."

¹⁷ When Jesus arrived at Bethany, he found that Lazarus had already been in the tomb four days. ¹⁸ The village was not far from Jerusalem—just under two miles—¹⁹ and many Jewish people had come out to console Martha and Mary over their brother. ²⁰ When Martha heard that Jesus was coming she went to meet him, while Mary sat at home. ²¹ Martha said to Jesus, "Lord, if you had been here, my brother would never have died. ²² Even now, I am sure that God will give you whatever you ask of him." ²³ "Your brother will rise again," Jesus assured her. ²⁴ "I know he will rise again," Martha replied, "in the resurrection on the last day." ²⁵ Jesus told her:

"I am the resurrection and the life:
²⁶ whoever believes in me,
though he should die, will come to life;
and whoever is alive and believes in me
will never die.

Do you believe this?" ²⁷ "Yes, Lord," she replied. "I have come to believe that you are the Messiah, the Son of God: he who is come into the world."
²⁸ When she had said this she went back and called her sister

---

9: 8, 12; 9, 4.
9f: 12, 35; 1 Jn 2, 10.
13: Mt 9, 24.
19: 12, 9.17f.

21: 11, 32.
24: 5, 29.
25: 5, 24; 8, 51.
27: 1, 9; 6, 69.

11, 10: *No light in him:* the ancient Palestinians apparently did not grasp clearly the entry of light *through* the eye, but seem to have thought of it as being *in* the eye; cf Lk 11, 34; Mt 6, 23.
11, 16: *The name means "Twin":* or "Thomas, the one called Didymus." "Thomas" is derived from the Hebrew word for twin; "Didymus," a Greek personal name of the time, from the Greek word for twin.

Mary. "The Teacher is here, asking for you," she whispered. [29] As soon as Mary heard this, she got up and started out in his direction. [30] (Actually Jesus had not yet come into the village but was still at the spot where Martha had met him.) [31] The Jews who were in the house with Mary consoling her saw her get up quickly and go out, so they followed her, thinking she was going to the tomb to weep there. [32] When Mary came to the place where Jesus was, seeing him, she fell at his feet and said to him, "Lord, if you had been here my brother would never have died." [33] When Jesus saw her weeping, and the Jews who had accompanied her also weeping, he was troubled in spirit, moved by the deepest emotions. [34] "Where have you laid him?" he asked. "Lord, come and see," they said. [35] Jesus began to weep, [36] which caused the Jews to remark, "See how much he loved him!" [37] But some said, "He opened the eyes of that blind man. Why could he not have done something to stop this man from dying?" [38] Once again troubled in spirit, Jesus approached the tomb.

It was a cave with a stone laid across it. [39] "Take away the stone," Jesus directed. Martha, the dead man's sister, said to him, "Lord, it has been four days now; surely there will be a stench!" [40] Jesus replied, "Did I not assure you that if you believed you would see the glory of God displayed?" [41] They then took away the stone and Jesus looked upward and said:

"Father, I thank you for having heard me.
[42] I know that you always hear me
but I have said this for the sake of the crowd,
that they may believe that you sent me."

[43] Having said this, he called loudly, "Lazarus, come out!" [44] The dead man came out, bound hand and foot with linen strips, his face wrapped in a cloth. "Untie him," Jesus told them, "and let him go free."

Session of the Sanhedrin

[45] This caused many of the Jews who had come to visit Mary, and had seen what Jesus did, to put their faith in him. [46] Some others, however, went to the Pharisees and reported what Jesus had done. [47] The result was that the chief priests and the Phari-

---

35: Lk 19, 41.   42: 12, 30.   47: 12, 19; Mt 26, 3ff;

11, 33: *He was troubled in spirit . . . deepest emotions:* probably signifies that Jesus was angry, perhaps at the lack of faith or at the presence of evil (death).

11, 47: *What are we to do?:* could be the rhetorical "Why are we doing nothing?"

sees called a meeting of the Sanhedrin. "What are we to do," they said, "with this man performing all sorts of signs? ⁴⁸ If we let him go on like this, the whole world will believe in him. Then the Romans will come in and sweep away our sanctuary and our nation." ⁴⁹ One of their number named Caiaphas, who was high priest that year, addressed them at this point: "You have no understanding whatever! ⁵⁰ Can you not see that it is better for you to have one man die [for the people] than to have the whole nation destroyed?" ⁵¹ (He did not say this on his own. It was rather as high priest for that year that he prophesied that Jesus would die for the nation—⁵² and not for this nation only, but to gather into one all the dispersed children of God.)

⁵³ From that day onward there was a plan afoot to kill him. ⁵⁴ In consequence, Jesus no longer moved about freely in Jewish circles. He withdrew instead to a town called Ephraim in the region near the desert, where he stayed with his disciples.

The Last Passover

⁵⁵ The Jewish Passover was near, which meant that many people from the country went up to Jerusalem for Passover purification. ⁵⁶ They were on the lookout for Jesus, various people in the temple vicinity saying to each other, "What do you think? Is he likely to come for the feast?" ⁵⁷ (The chief priests and the Pharisees had given orders that anyone who knew where he was should report it, so that they could apprehend him.)

12

Anointing at Bethany

¹ Six days before Passover Jesus came to Bethany, the village of Lazarus whom Jesus had raised from the dead. ² There they

---

              Lk 22, 2; Acts 4, 16.   **12,** 1-11: Mt 26, 6-13; Mk 14, 3-9.
49f: 18, 13f.   1f: 11, 1.
  53: 5, 18; 7, 1; Mt 12, 14.   2: Lk 10, 38ff.
  55: 2, 13; 5, 1; 6, 4; 18, 28.

11, 49: *That year:* emphasizes the conjunction of the office and the year. The Jews attributed a gift of prophecy, sometimes unconscious, to the high priest.

11, 50: *For the people:* this phrase is omitted in some impressive patristic witnesses, and may be a gloss. If it is original, Caiaphas meant "in place of the people"; but in v 51, John takes it to mean "on behalf of."

11, 54: Ephraim is usually located about twelve miles northeast of Jerusalem, as the mountains descend into the Jordan valley.

12, 1ff: This is probably the same scene of anointing that we find in Mk 14, 3-9. The anointing reported in Lk 7, 36-38 is part of a different scene. Details from these various episodes may have become interchanged.

gave him a banquet, at which Martha served. Lazarus was one of those at table with him. [3] Mary brought a pound of costly perfume made from genuine aromatic nard, with which she anointed Jesus' feet. Then she dried his feet with her hair, and the house was filled with the ointment's fragrance. [4] Judas Iscariot, one of his disciples (the one about to hand him over), protested; [5] "Why was not this perfume sold? It could have brought three hundred silver pieces, and the money have been given to the poor." [6] (He did not say this out of concern for the poor, but because he was a thief. He held the purse, and used to help himself to what was deposited there.) [7] To this Jesus replied: "Leave her alone. Let her keep it against the day they prepare me for burial. [8] The poor you always have with you, but me you will not always have."

[9] The great crowd of Jews discovered he was there and came out, not only because of Jesus but also to see Lazarus, whom he had raised from the dead. [10] The fact was, the chief priests planned to kill Lazarus too, [11] because many Jews were going over to Jesus and believing in him on account of Lazarus.

Entry into Jerusalem

[12] The next day the great crowd that had come for the feast heard that Jesus was to enter Jerusalem, [13] so they got palm branches and came out to meet him. They kept shouting:

> "Hosanna!
> Blessed is he who comes in the name of the Lord!
> Blessed is the King of Israel!"

[14] Jesus found a donkey and mounted it, in accord with Scripture:

3: 11, 2.
6: 13, 29.
9: 11, 19.
11: 11, 45.
12-19: Mt 21, 1-16;

Mk 11, 1-10;
Lk 19, 28-40.
13: 1, 49; Ps 118, 26;
Rv 7, 9.

12, 3: *Perfume made from genuine aromatic nard:* this phrase, found also in Mk 14, 3, is of uncertain meaning.

12, 5: *Silver pieces:* literally, "denarii." A denarius is a day's wage in Mt 20, 2.

12, 7: An obscure verse. It could be taken to mean that Mary was to keep the perfume for Jesus' future burial, though Mk 14, 8 and Jn 19, 39 seem to rule out a future reference. The present scene probably represents Jesus' embalming in a figurative sense.

12, 9: The expression *the great crowd,* here and in v 12, is even more awkward in Greek than in English; many textual witnesses have smoothed it out by omitting the article. It seems to have the function of uniting the crowd of the entry scene with the witnesses of the Lazarus miracle.

12, 13: See Psalm 118, 25f, and the note there on *Hosanna.*

¹⁵ "Fear not, O daughter of Zion!
  Your king approaches you
  on a donkey's colt."

¹⁶ (At first, the disciples did not understand all this, but after Jesus was glorified they recalled that the people had done to him precisely what had been written about him.) ¹⁷ The crowd that was present when he called Lazarus out of the tomb and raised him from the dead kept testifying to it. ¹⁸ The crowd came out to meet him because they heard he had performed this sign. ¹⁹ The Pharisees remarked to one another, "See, there is nothing you can do! The whole world has run after him."

The Coming of Jesus' Hour

²⁰ Among those who had come up to worship at the feast were some Greeks. ²¹ They approached Philip, who was from Bethsaida in Galilee, and put this request to him: "Sir, we should like to see Jesus." ²² Philip went to tell Andrew; Philip and Andrew in turn came to inform Jesus. ²³ Jesus answered them:

  "The hour has come
    for the Son of Man to be glorified.
    ²⁴ I solemnly assure you,
    unless the grain of wheat falls to the earth and dies,
    it remains just a grain of wheat.
    But if it dies,
    it produces much fruit.
    ²⁵ The man who loves his life
    loses it,

15: Zec 9, 9.
16: 2, 22.
19: 11, 47f; Mt 21, 16.
21: 1, 43.
22: 1, 40.

23: 2, 4.
24: Is 53, 10ff;
    1 Cor 15, 36.
25: Mt 16, 25; Mk 8, 35;
    Lk 9, 24.

12, 17f: There seem to be two different crowds in these verses. There are good witnesses to the text which have another reading for v 17: "Then the crowd that was with him began to testify that he had called Lazarus out of the tomb and raised him from the dead."

12, 19: *The whole world:* the sense is that everyone is following Jesus, but John has an ironic play on *world;* he alludes to the universality of salvation (3, 17; 4, 42).

12, 20: *Greeks:* Not used here in a nationalistic sense. These are Gentile proselytes to Judaism; cf 7, 35.

12, 24: *It remains just a grain of wheat:* literally, "it remains alone."

12, 25: *His life:* the Greek word *psyche* refers to a man's natural life. It does not mean "soul," for Hebrew anthropology did not postulate body/soul dualism in the way that is familiar to us.

while the man who hates his life in this world
preserves it to life eternal.
²⁶ If anyone would serve me,
let him follow me;
where I am,
there will my servant be.
If anyone serves me,
him the Father will honor.
²⁷ My soul is troubled now,
yet what should I say—
Father, save me from this hour?
But it was for this that I came to this hour.
²⁸ Father, glorify your name!"

Then a voice came from the sky:

"I have glorified it,
and will glorify it again."

²⁹ When the crowd of bystanders heard the voice, they said it
was thunder. Others maintained, "An angel was speaking to
him." ³⁰ Jesus answered, "That voice did not come for my sake,
but for yours.

³¹ "Now has judgment come upon this world,
now will this world's prince be driven out,
³² and I—once I am lifted up from earth—
will draw all men to myself."

³³ (This statement indicated the sort of death he had to die.)
³⁴ The crowd objected to his words: "We have heard it said in
the law that the Messiah is to remain forever. How can you
claim that the Son of Man must be lifted up? Just who is this
'Son of Man'?" ³⁵ Jesus answered:

"The light is among you only a little longer.
Walk while you still have it
or darkness will come over you.
The man who walks in the dark
does not know where he is going.

26: 14, 3; 17, 24; Mt 16, 24.
27: 6, 38; 18, 11; Lk 22, 42;
  Heb 5, 7f.
28: 2, 11; 17, 5.
30: 11, 42; 16, 11.

31: Lk 10, 18; Rv 12, 9.
32: 3, 14; 8, 28.
34: Ps 89, 5; Is 9, 6;
  Dn 7, 14.
35: 9, 4; Jb 5, 14.

12, 34: There is no passage in the Old Testament that states precisely that
the Messiah is to remain forever. Perhaps the closest is Ps 89, 37.

³⁶ While you have the light,
keep faith in the light;
thus you will become sons of light."

After this utterance, Jesus left them and went into hiding.

Evaluation of the Ministry

³⁷ Despite his many signs performed in their presence, they refused to believe in him. ³⁸ This was to fulfill the word of the prophet Isaiah:

"Lord, who has believed what has reached our ears?
To whom has the night of the Lord been revealed?"

³⁹ The reason they could not believe was that, as Isaiah says elsewhere:

⁴⁰ "He has blinded their eyes,
and numbed their hearts,
lest they see
or comprehend,
or have a change of heart—
and I should heal them."

⁴¹ Isaiah uttered these words because he had seen Jesus' glory, and it was of him he spoke.
⁴² There were many, even among the Sanhedrin, who believed in him; but they refused to admit it because of the Pharisees, for fear they might be ejected from the synagogue.
⁴³ They preferred the praise of men to the glory of God.

Summary Proclamation

⁴⁴ Jesus proclaimed aloud:

"Whoever puts faith in me
believes not so much in me
as in him who sent me;
⁴⁵ and whoever looks on me
is seeing him who sent me.

38: Is 53, 1; Rom 10, 16.
40: Mt 13, 13f; Is 6, 9f.
41: 5, 39; Is 6, 1.4.
42: 9, 22.

43: 5, 44.
44: 13, 20; 14, 1.
45: 14, 7ff.

12, 38ff: John gives a historical explanation of Jewish disbelief, not a psychological one. The Old Testament had to be fulfilled in the New; the disbelief that met Isaiah's message was a foreshadowing of the disbelief that Jesus encountered. In 12, 42 and also in 3, 20, we see that there is no negation of freedom.

⁴⁶ I have come to the world as its light,
to keep anyone who believes in me
from remaining in the dark.
⁴⁷ If anyone hears my words and does not keep them,
I am not the one to condemn him,
for I did not come to condemn the world
but to save it.
⁴⁸ Whoever rejects me and does not accept my words
already has his judge,
namely, the word I have spoken—
it is that which will condemn him on the last day.
⁴⁹ For I have not spoken on my own;
no, the Father who sent me
has commanded me
what to say and how to speak.
⁵⁰ Since I know that his commandment means
    eternal life,
whatever I say
is spoken just as he instructed me."

III: THE BOOK OF GLORY

13

The Washing of the Feet

¹ Before the feast of Passover, Jesus realized that the hour had come for him to pass from this world to the Father. He had loved his own in this world, and would show his love for them to the end. ² The devil had already induced Judas, son of Simon Iscariot, to hand him over; and so, during the supper, ³ Jesus—fully aware that he had come from God and was going to God, the Father who had handed everything over to him— ⁴ rose from the meal and took off his cloak. He picked up a towel and tied it around himself. ⁵ Then he poured water into a basin and began to wash his disciples' feet and dry them with the towel he had around him. ⁶ Thus he came to Simon Peter, who said to him, "Lord, are you going to wash my feet?" ⁷ Jesus

---

46: 1, 9; 8, 12.
47: 3, 17.
48: Lk 10, 16.
49: 14, 10.31; Dt 18, 18f.
13, 1: 2, 4; 7, 30; 8, 20;

Mt 26, 17.
2: 6, 71; 17, 12;
Mt 26, 20; Lk 22, 3.
3: 3, 35.

13, 2: *Induced:* literally, "The devil put into the heart that Judas should hand him over." It is uncertain into whose heart, Judas' or the devil's.
13, 5: *Basin:* the exact vessel is not certain, but it was used for washing, perhaps by pouring, in which case the translation should be "pitcher."

answered, "You may not realize now what I am doing, but later you will understand." [8] Peter replied, "You shall never wash my feet!" "If I do not wash you," Jesus answered, "you will have no share in my heritage." [9] "Lord," Simon Peter said to him, "then not only my feet, but my hands and head as well." [10] Jesus told him, "The man who has bathed has no need to wash [except for his feet]; he is entirely cleansed, just as you are; though not all." [11] (The reason he said, "Not all are washed clean," was that he knew his betrayer.)

[12] After he had washed their feet, he put his cloak back on and reclined at table once more. He said to them:

> "Do you understand what I just did for you?
> [13] You address me as 'Teacher' and 'Lord,'
> and fittingly enough,
> for that is what I am.
> [14] But if I washed your feet—
> I who am Teacher and Lord—
> then you must wash each other's feet.
> [15] What I just did was to give you an example:
> as I have done, so you must do.
> [16] I solemnly assure you,
> no slave is greater than his master;
> no messenger outranks the one who sent him.
> [17] Once you know all these things,
> blest will you be if you put them into practice.

Role of Judas

> [18] "What I say is not said of all,
> for I know the kind of men I chose.
> My purpose here is the fulfillment of Scripture:
> 'He who partook of bread with me
> has raised his heel against me.'
> [19] I tell you this now, before it takes place,
> so that when it takes place you may believe
> that I AM.

10: 15, 3.
11: 6, 70.
15: Lk 22, 27.

16: 15, 20; Mt 10, 24;
     Lk 6, 40.
18: Ps 41, 10.

13, 10: *Bathed:* many have suggested that this passage is a symbolic reference to baptism. The Greek root involved is used in baptismal contexts in 1 Cor 6, 11; Eph 5, 26; Ti 3, 5; Heb 10, 22. The washing of the feet was connected with baptism in early Christian liturgy.

13, 16: *Messenger:* the Greek has *apostolos,* the only occurrence of the term in John. It is not used in the technical sense here.

^{20} I solemnly assure you,
he who accepts anyone I send
accepts me,
and in accepting me
accepts him who sent me."

^{21} After saying this, Jesus grew deeply troubled. He went on to give this testimony:

"I tell you solemnly,
one of you will betray me."

^{22} The disciples looked at one another, puzzled as to whom he could mean. ^{23} One of them, the disciple whom Jesus loved, reclined close to him as they ate. ^{24} Simon Peter signaled him to ask Jesus whom he meant. ^{25} He leaned back against Jesus' chest and said to him, "Lord, who is he?" ^{26} Jesus answered, "The one to whom I give the bit of food I dip in the dish." He dipped the morsel, then took it and gave it to Judas, son of Simon Iscariot. ^{27} Immediately after, Satan entered his heart. Jesus addressed himself to him: "Be quick about what you are to do." ^{28} (Naturally, none of those reclining at table understood why Jesus said this to him. ^{29} A few had the idea that, since Judas held the common purse, Jesus was telling him to buy what was needed for the feast, or to give something to the poor.) ^{30} No sooner had Judas eaten the morsel than he went out. It was night.
^{31} Once Judas had left, Jesus said:

"Now is the Son of Man glorified
and God is glorified in him.
^{32} [If God has been glorified in him,]
God will, in turn, glorify him in himself,
and will glorify him soon.

20: Mt 10, 40; Mk 9, 37;
    Lk 9, 48.
21-30: Mt 26, 21-25;
    Mk 14, 18-21;
    Lk 22, 21ff.

23: 19, 26; 20, 2; 21, 7.20.
27: 13, 2; Lk 22, 3.
29: 12, 5f.
32: 17, 1-5.

13, 23: *The disciple whom Jesus loved* is mentioned in 19, 26; 20, 2; 21, 7. A disciple, called *another disciple* or *the other disciple,* is mentioned in 18, 15 and 20, 2; and in the latter reference he is identified with the disciple whom Jesus loved. There is also an unnamed dsciple in 1, 35-40. It has been traditional to identify the disciple thus variously referred to as St. John.
13, 31-38: These verses form an introduction to the last discourse of Jesus, which runs through chapters 14—17. In it John has collected Jesus' words to *his own* (cf 13, 1). There are indications that several speeches have been fused together, e. g., in 14, 31 and 17, 1.
13, 32: *God will . . . glorify him in himself:* the concluding word probably refers to the Father rather than to Jesus; cf 17, 5.21.

³³ My children, I am not to be with you much longer.
You will look for me,
but I say to you now
what I once said to the Jews:
'Where I am going, you cannot come.'
³⁴ I give you a new commandment:
Love one another.
Such as my love has been for you,
so must your love be for each other.
³⁵ This is how all will know you for my disciples:
your love for one another."

Peter's Denial Predicted

³⁶ "Lord," Simon Peter said to him, "Where do you mean to go?" Jesus answered:

"I am going where you cannot follow me now;
later on you shall come after me."

³⁷ "Lord," Peter said to him, "why can I not follow you now? I will lay down my life for you!" ³⁸ "You will lay down your life for me, will you?" Jesus answered. "I tell you truly, the cock will not crow before you have three times disowned me!

Last Discourse

14

¹ "Do not let your hearts be troubled.
Have faith in God
and faith in me.
² In my Father's house there are many dwelling places;
otherwise, how could I have told you
that I was going to prepare a place for you?
³ I am indeed going to prepare a place for you,
and then I shall come back to take you with me,
that where I am you also may be.
⁴ You know the way that leads where I go."

⁵ "Lord," said Thomas, "we do not know where you are going. How can we know the way?" ⁶ Jesus told him:

33: 7, 33; 8, 21.
34: 15, 12f.17; Lv 19, 18.
36: Mk 14, 27; Lk 22, 33.

38: 18, 27; Mt 26, 33ff;
  Mk 14, 29ff; Lk 22, 33f.
14, 3: 12, 26; 17, 24.

14, 2: A number of MSS omit *that* in this sentence, thus giving different inflections of meaning to the verse, with three distinct statements in it.

"I am the way, and the truth, and the life;
no one comes to the Father but through me.
[7] If you really knew me, you would know my Father also.
From this point on you know him; you have seen him."

[8] "Lord," Philip said to him, "show us the Father and that
will be enough for us." [9] "Philip," Jesus replied, "after I have
been with you all this time, you still do not know me?

"Whoever has seen me has seen the Father.
How can you say, 'Show us the Father'?
[10] Do you not believe that I am in the Father
and the Father is in me?
The words I speak are not spoken of myself;
it is the Father who lives in me accomplishing
  his works.
[11] Believe me and I am in the Father
and the Father is in me,
or else, believe because of the works I do.
[12] I solemnly assure you,
the man who has faith in me
will do the works I do,
and greater far than these.
Why? Because I go to the Father,
[13] and whatever you ask in my name
I will do,
so as to glorify the Father in the Son.
[14] Anything you ask me in my name
I will do.
[15] If you love me
and obey the commands I give you,
[16] I will ask the Father

7: 8, 19; 12, 45.
9: 1, 18; 10, 30; 12, 45.
10: 1, 1; 12, 49.
11: 10, 38.
13: 15, 7.16; 16, 23f;

Mt 7, 7-11.
15: 15, 10; Wis 6, 18;
    1 Jn 2, 3.
16: 15, 26.

14, 7: An alternative reading is: "If you know me, then you know my
Father also." The form in the text above is a rebuke akin to 8, 19.
14, 15: There is attestation for several other readings of this verse: "If
you love me, keep my commandments" or "If you love me, you will keep my
commandments."
14, 16: *Another Paraclete:* evidently Jesus is the first Paraclete; see 1 Jn 2,
2, where Jesus is a Paraclete in the sense of heavenly intercessor. However,
this verse could be translated: "another, a Paraclete." The Johannine term
paraclete derived from Greek legal terminology is used secularly for a defense attorney, a spokesman, an intercessor, although none of these terms
fits precisely in John. The Paraclete in John is a teacher, a witness to
Jesus, and a prosecutor of the world. He represents the continued presence
on earth of the Jesus who has returned to the Father.

and he will give you another Paraclete—
to be with you always:
[17] the Spirit of truth,
whom the world cannot accept,
since it neither sees him nor recognizes him;
but you can recognize him
because he remains with you
and will be within you.
[18] I will not leave you orphaned;
I will come back to you.
[19] A little while now and the world will see me
  no more;
but you see me
as one who has life, and you will have life.
[20] On that day you will know
that I am in my Father,
and you in me, and I in you.
[21] He who obeys the commandments he has from me
is the man who loves me;
and he who loves me will be loved by my Father.
I too will love him
and reveal myself to him."

[22] Judas (not Judas Iscariot) said to him, "Lord, why is it that you will reveal yourself to us and not to the world?" [23] Jesus answered:

"Anyone who loves me
will be true to my word,
and my Father will love him;
we will come to him
and make our dwelling place with him.
[24] He who does not love me does not keep my words.
Yet the word you hear is not mine;
it comes from the Father who sent me.

17: 16, 13; Mt 28, 20;
  2 Jn 1f.
19: 16, 16.

21: Jn 16, 27; 1 Jn 2, 5;
  3, 24.
23: Rv 3, 20.

14, 17: The Greek word for "Spirit" is neuter, and while we use personal pronouns in English ("he," "his," "him"), most Greek MSS employ "it."
14, 19: The last part can be made a separate sentence: "Because I have life, you also will have life."
14, 22: *Not Judas Iscariot:* other readings are "Judas the Cananean" and "Judas Thomas." Perhaps the original had simply "Judas." There is a *Judas son of James* in the Lucan lists of the Twelve (Lk 6, 16; Acts 1, 13), but there is no corresponding name in the Matthean or Marcan lists.

²⁵ This much have I told you while I was still
with you;
²⁶ the Paraclete, the Holy Spirit
whom the Father will send in my name,
will instruct you in everything,
and remind you of all that I told you.
²⁷ 'Peace' is my farewell to you,
my peace is my gift to you;
I do not give it to you as the world gives peace.
Do not be distressed or fearful.
²⁸ You have heard me say,
'I go away for a while, and I come back to you.'
If you truly loved me
you would rejoice to have me go to the Father,
for the Father is greater than I.
²⁹ I tell you this now, before it takes place,
so that when it takes place you may believe.
³⁰ I shall not go on speaking to you longer;
the Prince of this world is at hand.
He has no hold on me,
³¹ but the world must know that I love the Father
and do as the Father has commanded me.
Come, then! Let us be on our way.

15

The Vine and the Branches

¹ "I am the true vine
and my Father is the vinegrower.
² He prunes away
every barren branch,

26: 15, 26; 16, 13f.
27: Eph 2, 14-18.
29: 13, 19; 16, 4.

31: 6, 38.
15, 1: Is 5, 1.

14, 27: *Peace:* Jesus gives to his disciples the traditional Hebrew salutation "Shalom"; but his *shalom* is a gift of salvation and not a conventional
word of farewell, as it is among other men.
15, 1: In the Bible Israel is spoken of as a vineyard (Is 5, 1-7; Mt 21, 33-
46) and as a vine (Jer 2, 21). The identification of the vine as the son of
man in Ps 80, 16, and Wisdom's description of herself as a vine in Sir 24,
17, are important background for Jesus' use of this figure as a self-descrip-
tion. In the synoptic account of the institution of the Eucharist at the Last
Supper, we hear of "the fruit of the vine" (Mk 12, 25). The Didache refers
to the eucharistic cup as "the holy vine of David your servant revealed
through Jesus Christ." Consequently there may be secondary eucharistic symbolism here.
15, 2: *Prunes away . . . trims clean:* in Greek there is a play on two related verbs, *airein* and *kathairein.*

but the faithful ones
he trims clean
to increase their yield.
³ You are clean already,
thanks to the word I have spoken to you.
⁴ Live on in me, as I do in you.
No more than a branch can bear fruit of itself
apart from the vine,
can you bear fruit
apart from me.
⁵ I am the vine, you are the branches.
He who lives in me and I in him,
will produce abundantly,
for apart from me you can do nothing.
⁶ A man who does not live in me
is like a withered, rejected branch,
picked up to be thrown in the fire and burnt.
⁷ If you live in me,
and my words stay part of you,
you may ask what you will—
it will be done for you.
⁸ My Father has been glorified
in your bearing much fruit
and becoming my disciples.

A Disciple's Love

⁹ "As the Father has loved me,
so I have loved you.
Live on in my love.
¹⁰ You will live in my love
if you keep my commandments,
even as I have kept my Father's commandments,
and live in his love.
¹¹ All this I tell you
that my joy may be yours
and your joy may be complete.
¹² This is my commandment:

3: 13, 10.	8: Mt 5, 16.
5: Ps 127, 1.	9: 17, 23.
6: Ez 15, 6f; 19, 10ff;	10: 8, 29; 14, 15.
3, 10.	11: 16, 22; 17, 13.
7: 14, 13; 1 Jn 5, 14.	12: 13, 34.

15, 4-7: *Live on in . . . live in . . . stay part of:* these all represent the same Greek expression for "remain in."

love one another
as I have loved you.
¹³ There is no greater love than this:
to lay down one's life for one's friends.
¹⁴ You are my friends
if you do what I command you.
¹⁵ I no longer speak of you as slaves,
for a slave does not know what his master is about.
Instead, I call you friends,
since I have made known to you all that I heard
  from my Father.
¹⁶ It was not you who chose me,
it was I who chose you
to go forth and bear fruit.
Your fruit must endure,
so that all you ask the Father in my name
he will give you.
¹⁷ The command I give you is this,
that you love one another.

The World's Hate

¹⁸ "If you find that the world hates you,
know that it has hated me before you.
¹⁹ If you belonged to the world,
it would love you as its own;
the reason it hates you
is that you do not belong to the world.
But I chose you out of the world.
²⁰ Remember what I told you:
no slave is greater than his master.
They will harry you
as they harried me.
They will respect your words
as much as they respected mine.

13: Rom 5, 6ff; 1 Jn 3, 16.
15: Rom 8, 15; Gal 4, 7.
16: 14, 13; Dt 7, 6.
17: 13, 34; 1 Jn 3, 23;
4, 21.
18: 7, 7; 1 Jn 3, 13.
19: 17, 14ff; 1 Jn 4, 5.
20: 13, 16; Mt 10, 24.

15, 13: *For one's friends:* in 9-13a, the words for love are related to the Greek *agapan.* In 13b-15, the words for love are related to the Greek *philein.* For John, the two roots are synonymous and mean "to love." The word *philos* in vv 13ff, is here translated "friend."
15, 18: The section 15, 18—16, 4 has numerous parallels with predictions of persecution made by Jesus in the synoptic gospels—especially with Mt 10, 17-25.
15, 20: *What I told you:* a reference to 13, 16.

²¹ And this they will do to you because of my name,
for they know nothing of him who sent me.
²² If I had not come to them and spoken to them,
they would not be guilty of sin;
now, however, their sin cannot be excused.
²³ To hate me is to hate my Father.
²⁴ Had I not performed such works among them
as no one has ever done before,
they would not be guilty of sin;
but as it is, they have seen,
and they go on hating me and my Father.
²⁵ However, this only fulfills the text in their law:
'They hated me without cause.'
²⁶ When the Paraclete comes,
the Spirit of truth who comes from the Father—
and whom I myself will send from the Father—
he will bear witness on my behalf.
²⁷ You must bear witness as well,
for you have been with me from the beginning.

16

¹ "I have told you all this
to keep your faith from being shaken.
² Not only will they expel you from synagogues;
a time will come
when anyone who puts you to death
will claim to be serving God!

21: 8, 19; 16, 3.
22: 8, 21.24.
23: 5, 23; 1 Jn 2, 23.
24: 3, 2; 9, 32.

26: 14, 26.
27: Lk 1, 2; Acts 1, 8.
16, 2: 9, 22; 12, 42; Mt 10, 17;
Lk 21, 12; Acts 26, 11.

15, 21: *Because of my name:* the idea of persecution because of Jesus'
name is frequent in the New Testament (Mt 10, 22; 24, 9; Acts 9, 14). For
John, association with Jesus' name implies union with Jesus.
15, 22.24: Jesus' words (*spoken*) and deeds (*works performed*) are the
great motives of credibility. *They have seen, . . . go on hating:* probably
means they have seen his works and still have hated; but the Greek can be
read: "have seen both me and my Father and still have hated both me and
my Father."
15, 25: *Law:* a larger concept than the Pentateuch, for the reference is to
Ps 35, 19 or 69, 5. See notes on 10, 34; 12, 34.
15, 26: *Comes from the Father:* refers to the mission of the Spirit to men,
not to the eternal procession of the Spirit. Compare 14, 26, where the Father,
not Jesus, is said to send the Spirit.
15, 27: *You . . . as well:* this witness of the disciples is not different or
distinct from that of the Paraclete; rather, it exteriorizes the Paraclete's internal witness.
16, 2: *Time* is literally "hour"—not "the hour" of Jesus but the period
of persecution.

³ All this they will do [to you]
because they knew neither the Father nor me.
⁴ But I have told you these things
that when their hour comes
you may remember my telling you of them.

Jesus' Departure; Coming to the Paraclete

"I did not speak of this with you from the beginning
because I was with you.
⁵ Now that I go back to him who sent me,
not one of you asks me, 'Where are you going?'
⁶ Because I have had all this to say to you,
you are overcome with grief.
⁷ Yet I tell you the sober truth:
It is much better for you that I go.
If I fail to go,
the Paraclete will never come to you,
whereas if I go,
I will send him to you.
⁸ When he comes,
he will prove the world wrong
about sin,
about justice,
about condemnation.
⁹ About sin—
in that they refuse to believe in me;
¹⁰ about justice—
from the fact that I go to the Father
and you can see me no more;
¹¹ about condemnation—
for the prince of this world has been condemned.
¹² I have much more to tell you,
but you cannot bear it now.

3: 15, 21.
4: 13, 19; 14, 29.
7: 14, 16.26.

9: 8, 21-24; 15, 22.
11: 12, 31.

16, 5: *Not one of you asks me:* the difficulty of reconciling this with Simon
Peter's question in 13, 36 and Thomas' words in 14, 5 strengthens the supposition that the last discourse has been made up of several collections of
Johannine material.
16, 8-11: These verses illustrate the forensic character of the Paraclete's
role: in the forum of the disciples' conscience he prosecutes the world. He
leads believers to see (a) that the basic sin of men was and is their refusal
to believe in Jesus; (b) that, although Jesus was found guilty and apparently died in disgrace, in reality justice has triumphed, for Jesus has returned to his Father; (c) finally, that it is the prince of this world, Satan,
who has been condemned through Jesus' death (12, 32).

¹³ When he comes, however,
being the Spirit of truth
he will guide you to all truth.
He will not speak on his own,
but will speak only what he hears,
and will announce to you the things to come.
¹⁴ In doing this he will give glory to me,
because he will have received from me
what he will announce to you.
¹⁵ All that the Father has belongs to me.
That is why I said that what he will announce to you
he will have from me.
¹⁶ Within a short time you will lose sight of me,
but soon after that you shall see me again."

The Return of Jesus

¹⁷ At this, some of his disciples asked one another: "What can he mean, 'Within a short time you will lose sight of me, but soon after that you will see me'? And did he not say that he is going back to the Father?" ¹⁸ They kept asking: "What does he mean by this 'short time'? We do not know what he is talking about." ¹⁹ Since Jesus was aware that they wanted to question him, he said: "You are asking one another about my saying, 'Within a short time you will lose sight of me, but soon after that you will see me.'

²⁰ "I tell you truly:
you will weep and mourn
while the world rejoices;
you will grieve for a time,
but your grief will be turned to joy.
²¹ When a woman is in labor
she is sad that her time has come.

13: 14, 26.   20: Ps 126, 6.
16: 7, 33; 14, 19.   21: Is 26, 17f; Jer 31, 13.

16, 13: *Announce to you the things to come:* this is not necessarily a reference to new future predictions; the Greek verb is used in Daniel for interpretation, in relation to the present and the future, of what has already happened. The Paraclete makes Jesus' message continually relevant for each generation.
16, 17: The disciples are puzzled by the contrast between their seeing Jesus soon again (v 16) and his return to the Father (v 10), presumably to stay.
16, 20: Jesus does not discuss the *short time* mentioned in v 18, but the contrast between sorrow and joy implicit in v 16. The *grief* of this verse and the *pain* of the next are the same Greek word as the *grief* of v 6. The promise of joy will be fulfilled in 20, 20.

When she has borne her child,
she no longer remembers her pain
for joy that a man has been born into the world.
²² In the same way, you are sad for a time,
but I shall see you again;
then your hearts will rejoice
with a joy no one can take from you.
²³ On that day you will have no questions to ask me.
I give you my assurance,
whatever you ask the Father,
he will give you in my name.
²⁴ Until now you have not asked for anything in
   my name.
Ask and you shall receive,
that your joy may be full.
²⁵ I have spoken these things to you in veiled language.
A time will come when I shall no longer do so,
but shall tell you about the Father in plain speech.
²⁶ On that day you will ask in my name
and I do not say that I will petition the Father
   for you.
²⁷ The Father already loves you,
because you have loved me
and have believed that I came from God.
²⁸ [I did indeed come from the Father;]
I came into the world.
Now I am leaving the world
to go to the Father."

²⁹ "At last you are speaking plainly," his disciples exclaimed,
"without talking in veiled language! ³⁰ We are convinced that
you know everything. There is no need for anyone to ask you
questions. We do indeed believe you came from God." ³¹ Jesus
answered them:

22: 14, 19; 15, 11; 20, 20.	26: 14, 13.
23: 14, 13.	28: 1, 1.
25: Mt 13, 34f.	

16, 23: Having no questions to ask is a matter of seeking or not seeking
understanding. "Ask and you shall receive" is a matter of petitioning.
16, 25: *In veiled language:* may be a reference to the parabolic comparisons of the vine and the branches (15, 1-16) and the woman in labor (16,
21).
16, 30: The reference is seemingly to the fact that Jesus could anticipate
their question in v 19. The disciples naively think they have the full understanding that is the climax of "the hour" of Jesus' death, resurrection and
ascension (v 25), but the only part of the hour that is at hand for them
is their share in the passion (v 32).

"Do you really believe?
³² An hour is coming—has indeed already come—
when you will be scattered and each will go his way,
leaving me quite alone.
(Yet I can never be alone;
the Father is with me.)
³³ I tell you all this
that in me you may find peace.
you will suffer in the world.
But take courage!
I have overcome the world."

17

Completion of Jesus' Work

¹ After he had spoken these words, Jesus looked up to heaven
and said:

"Father, the hour has come!
Give glory to your Son
that your Son may give glory to you,
² inasmuch as you have given him authority over
all mankind.
that he may bestow eternal life on those you gave him.
³ (Eternal life is this:
to know you, the only true God,
and him whom you have sent, Jesus Christ.)
⁴ I have given you glory on earth
by finishing the work you gave me to do.
⁵ Do you now, Father, give me glory at your side,
a glory I had with you before the world began.

32: 8, 29; Zec 13, 7;
   Mt 26, 31.
33: 14, 27.
17, 1: 13, 31.

2: 3, 35; Mt 28, 18.
3: Wis 14, 7; 1 Jn 5, 20.
5: 12, 28; Phil 2, 6.9ff.

17, 1-26: Since the sixteenth century this part of the last discourse has
been called the "high priestly prayer" of Jesus. Here his words are addressed
directly to the Father rather than to the disciples, who only overhear. Although still in the world (v 13), Jesus looks on his earthly ministry as a
thing of the past (vv 4.12). Whereas Jesus has hitherto stated that the disciples could not follow him (13, 33.36), now he wishes them to be with him
in union with the Father (vv 12ff). He is crossing the threshold of eternity.
17, 1: The action of looking up to heaven and the address *Father* are
typical of Jesus at prayer; cf 11, 41.
17, 2: Another possible interpretation is to treat the first line of the verse
as parenthetical and the second as an appositive to the clause that ends v
1: *that your Son may give glory to you (inasmuch . . . mankind), that he
may bestow eternal life. . . .*
17, 3: This verse was clearly added in the editing of the gospel, for Jesus
would hardly have referred to himself as Jesus Christ.

⁶ I have made your name known
to those you gave me out of the world.
These men you gave me were yours;
they have kept your word.
⁷ Now they realize
that all that you gave me comes from you.
⁸ I entrusted to them
the message you entrusted to me,
and they received it.
They have known that in truth I came from you,
they have believed it was you who sent me.

Prayer for the Disciples

⁹ "For these I pray—
not for the world
but for these you have given me,
for they are really yours.
¹⁰ (Just as all that belongs to me is yours,
so all that belongs to you is mine.)
It is in them that I have been glorified.
¹¹ I am in the world no more,
but these are in the world
as I come to you.
O Father most holy,
protect them with your name which you have given me
[that they may be one, even as we are one].
¹² As long as I was with them,
I guarded them with your name which you gave me.
I kept careful watch,
and not one of them was lost,
none but him who was destined to be lost—
in fulfillment of Scripture.
¹³ Now, however, I come to you;
I say all this while I am still in the world
that they may share my joy completely.
¹⁴ I gave them your word,

10: 16, 15; 2 Thes 1, 10.12.   13: 15, 11.
12: 13, 18; 18, 9; Ps 41, 10;   14: 15, 19.
    Mt 26, 24; Acts 1, 16.

17, 6: *I have made your name known:* perhaps the name is *I AM;* cf 8, 24.28.58; 13, 19.
17, 11: *Protect them with your name which you have given me:* here and in the next verse, some witnesses read: "Protect with your name those whom you have given to me."
17, 12: *Scripture:* Jn 13, 18 cites Ps 41, 10.

and the world has hated them for it;
they do not belong to the world
[any more than I belong to the world].
¹⁵ I do not ask you to take them out of the world,
but to guard them from the evil one.
¹⁶ They are not of the world,
any more than I belong to the world.
¹⁷ Consecrate them by means of truth—
'Your word is truth.'
¹⁸ As you have sent me into the world,
so I have sent them into the world;
¹⁹ I consecrate myself for their sakes now,
that they may be consecrated in truth.

Prayer for All Believers

²⁰ "I do not pray for them alone.
I pray also for those who will believe in me
   through their word,
²¹ that all may be one
as you, Father, are in me, and I in you;
I pray that they may be [one] in us,
that the world may believe that you sent me.
²² I have given them the glory you gave me
that they may be one, as we are one—
²³ I living in them, you living in me—
that their unity may be complete.
So shall the world know that you sent me,
and that you loved them as you loved me.
²⁴ Father,
all those you gave me
I would have in my company
where I am,
to see this glory of mine

15: Mt 6, 13; 1 Jn 5, 18.   21: 10, 30; 14, 10f.20.
17: 1 Pt 1, 22.   24: 14, 3; 1 Thes 4, 17.

17, 15: Note the resemblance to the petition of the Our Father, "deliver us from the evil one." Both probably refer to the devil rather than to abstract evil.

17, 17: *'Your word is truth':* seemingly a citation from the Greek form of Ps 119, 142, as found in Codex Sinaiticus.

17, 21: For other Johannine passages on unity, see 10, 16; 11, 52. The world (21.23) is once more to be challenged by the mission of the disciples and given the opportunity of self-judgment inasmuch as it will either accept or reject Jesus.

17, 24: *Where I am:* Jesus prays for the believers ultimately to join him in heaven. Then they will not see his glory as in a mirror but clearly (2 Cor 3, 18; 1 Jn 3, 2).

which is your gift to me,
because of the love you bore me before the world
    began.
25 Just Father,
the world has not known you,
but I have known you;
and these men have known that you sent me.
26 To them I have revealed your name,
and I will continue to reveal it
so that your love for me may live in them,
and I may live in them."

18

Jesus Arrested

1 After this discourse, Jesus went out with his disciples across
the Kidron Valley. There was a garden there, and he and his
disciples entered it. 2 The place was familiar to Judas as well
(the one who was to hand him over) because Jesus had often
met there with his disciples. 3 Judas took the cohort as well as
guards supplied by the chief priests and the Pharisees, and came
there with lanterns, torches and weapons. 4 Jesus, aware of all
that would happen to him, stepped forward and said to them,
"Who is it you want?" 5 "Jesus the Nazorean," they replied. "I
am he," he answered. (Now Judas, the one who was to hand
him over, was there with them.) 6 As Jesus said to them, "I
am he," they retreated slightly and fell to the ground. 7 Jesus
put the question to them again, "Who is it you want?" "Jesus
the Nazorean," they repeated. 8 "I have told you, I am he,"
Jesus said. "If I am the one you want, let these men go." 9 (This

---

25: 1, 10.
18, 1: Mt 26, 30.36;
     Mk 14, 26.32;
     Lk 22, 39.

3: Mt 26, 47-51;
     Mk 14, 43f; Lk 22, 47.
9: 6, 39; 17, 12.

17, 26: *Will continue to reveal:* through the Paraclete.
18, 1-13: John does not mention the agony in the garden and the kiss
of Judas, nor does he identify the place as Gethsemani or the Mount of
Olives.
18, 1: *Jesus went out:* see 14, 31, where it seems he is leaving the supper
room. *Kidron Valley:* literally, "the winter-flowing Kidron"; this wadi has
water only during the winter rains.
18, 3: *Cohort:* seems to refer to Roman troops, the full cohort of 600
soldiers or the maniple of 200 under their tribune (v 12). In this case John
is hinting at Roman collusion in the action against Jesus before he was
brought to Pilate.
18, 5: *Nazorean:* The form found in Matthew is here used in preference
to the *Nazarene* of Mark. *I am he:* this *Ego eimi* may be intended by the
evangelist as an expression of divinity; see note on 8, 24. John sets the confusion of the arresting party against the background of Jesus' divine majesty.
18, 9: The citation may refer to 17, 12; 6, 39; or 10, 28.

was to fulfill what he had said, "I have not lost one of those you gave me.")

¹⁰ Then Simon Peter, who had a sword, drew it and struck the slave of the high priest, severing his right ear. (The slave's name was Malchus.) ¹¹ At that Jesus said to Peter, "Put your sword back in its sheath. Am I not to drink the cup the Father has given me?"

¹² Then the soldiers of the cohort, their tribune, and the Jewish guards arrested Jesus and bound him. ¹³ They led him first to Annas, the father-in-law of Caiaphas who was high priest that year. ¹⁴ (It was Caiaphas who had proposed to the Jews the advantage of having one man die for the people.)

Peter's First Denial

¹⁵ Simon Peter, in company with another disciple, kept following Jesus closely. This disciple, who was known to the high priest, stayed with Jesus as far as the high priest's courtyard, ¹⁶ while Peter was left standing at the gate. The disciple known to the high priest came out and spoke to the woman at the gate, and then brought Peter in. ¹⁷ This servant girl who kept the gate said to Peter, "Are you not one of this man's followers?" "Not I," he replied.

¹⁸ Now the night was cold, and the servants and the guards who were standing around had made a charcoal fire to warm themselves by. Peter joined them and stood there warming himself.

14: 11, 49f.   Mk 14, 54.66f;
15ff: Mt 26, 58.69f;   Lk 22, 54.
13: Lk 3, 2.

18, 10: Only John gives the names of the two antagonists; both John and Luke mention the right ear.
18, 11: The theme of the cup is found in the synoptic account of the agony (Mk 14, 36) and parallels.
18, 13: *Annas:* only John mentions an inquiry before Annas, who is presumably the *high priest* of vv 16 and 19. Patriarch of a family of high priests, he had been deposed by the Romans in 15 A. D.; but since, according to Jewish law, the office was for life, Annas may still have been the legitimate high priest in the eyes of many. Luke (3, 2) and Acts (4, 6) mention him in terms of high priesthood. There have been many attempts by scribes and commentators to rearrange or interpret the verses of John so that Caiaphas does the interrogating. It may be said with reasonable certainty that this night time interrogation before Annas is not the same as the trial before Caiaphas placed by Matthew and Mark at night and by Luke in the morning.
18, 15: *Courtyard:* the Greek word can mean this or "palace."
18, 15f: *Another disciple:* many scholars identify him with *the other disciple* of 20, 2, who is the beloved disciple; see note on 13, 23. But how would a Galilean fisherman be *known to the high priest*? An early (but unlikely) tradition has it that John was himself a priest. See note on 19, 25 for John's possible relation to Mary, who had priestly relatives.

The Inquiry before Annas

[19] The high priest questioned Jesus, first about his disciples, then about his teaching. [20] Jesus answered by saying:

"I have spoken publicly to any who would listen.
I always taught in a synagogue or in the temple area
where all the Jews come together.
There was nothing secret about anything I said.

[21] Why do you question me? Question those who heard me when I spoke. It should be obvious that they will know what I said." [22] At this reply, one of the guards who was standing nearby gave Jesus a sharp blow on the face. "Is that the way to answer the high priest?" he said. [23] Jesus replied, "If I said anything wrong produce the evidence, but if I spoke the truth why hit me?" [24] Annas next sent him, bound, to the high priest Caiaphas.

The Further Denials

[25] All through this, Simon Peter had been standing there warming himself. They said to him, "Are you not a disciple of his?" He denied it and said, "I am not!" [26] "But did I not see you with him in the garden?" insisted one of the high priest's slaves—as it happened, a relative of the man whose ear Peter had severed. [27] Peter denied it again. At that moment a cock began to crow.

The Trial before Pilate

[28] At daybreak they brought Jesus from Caiaphas to the praetorium. They did not enter the praetorium themselves, for

---

20: 7, 26; Is 48, 16;
    Lk 19, 47; 22, 53.
22: Acts 23, 2.
24: Mt 26, 57.
25ff: Mt 26, 69-75;

Lk 22, 55-62;
    Mk 14, 66-72.
28-40: Mt 27, 11-25;
    Mk 15, 1-15;
    Lk 23, 1-4.13-25.

18, 20: *I always taught . . . in the temple area:* in the synoptics a similar statement appears in the garden scene (Mk 14, 49).
18, 24: *Caiaphas:* John may leave room here for the trial before Caiaphas not narrated by him but dealt with in the synoptic gospels. Details parelleling those of the synoptic trial are scattered throughout John.
18, 27: Cockcrow was the third Roman division of the night lasting from 12 to 3 A.M.
18, 28: *Daybreak:* literally, "the early hour," or fourth Roman division of the night, 3 to 6 A.M.; here presumably about 6 A.M. *Praetorium:* the residence of the Roman governor in Jerusalem was either the Herodian palace on the western hill or the fortress Antonia near the temple. *The Passover supper:* the synoptic gospels give the impression that the Thursday night supper was the Passover meal (Mk 14, 12); for John that meal is still to be eaten Friday night.

they had to avoid ritual impurity if they were to eat the Passover supper. [29] Pilate came out to them. "What accusation do you bring against this man?" he demanded. [30] "If he were not a criminal," they retorted, "we would certainly not have handed him over to you." [31] At this Pilate said, "Why do you not take him and pass judgment on him according to your law?" "We may not put anyone to death," the Jews answered. (This was to fulfill what Jesus had said indicating the sort of death he had to die.)

[33] Pilate went back into the praetorium and summoned Jesus. "Are you the King of the Jews?" he asked him. [34] Jesus answered, "Are you saying this on your own, or have others been telling you about me?" [35] "I am no Jew!" Pilate retorted. "It is your own people and the chief priests who have handed you over to me. What have you done?" [36] Jesus answered:

> "My kingdom does not belong to this world.
> If my kingdom were of this world,
> my subjects would be fighting
> to save me from being handed over to the Jews.
> As it is, my kingdom is not here."

[37] At this Pilate said to him, "So, then, you are a king?" Jesus replied:

> "It is you who say I am a king.
> The reason I was born,
> the reason why I came into the world,
> is to testify to the truth.
> Anyone committed to the truth hears my voice."

[38] "Truth!" said Pilate, "What does that mean?"

After this remark, Pilate went out again to the Jews and said to them: "Speaking for myself, I find no case against this man. [39] Recall your custom whereby I release someone to you

---

32: 3, 14; 8, 28; 12, 32f.   37: 8, 47.
36: 1, 10; 8, 23.   39f: Mt 27, 15; Lk 23, 20.

18, 31: *We may not put anyone to death:* only John gives this reason for their bringing Jesus to Pilate. Jewish sources are not clear on the competence of the Sanhedrin at this period to sentence and to execute for political crimes.

18, 32: The Jewish punishment for blasphemy was stoning (Lv 24, 16). In coming to the Romans to ensure that Jesus would be crucified, the Jewish authorities fulfilled his prophecy that he would be *lifted up;* cf 12, 32f.

18, 37: *It is you who say I am a king:* see Mt 26, 64 for a similar response to the high priest. It is a reluctant affirmative, equaling "Yes, but the terminology is yours."

18, 39: This privilege connected with *Passover* is not clearly attested outside the gospels.

at Passover time. Do you want me to release to you the king of the Jews?" ⁴⁰ They shouted back, "We want Barabbas, not this one!" (Barabbas was an insurrectionist.)

19

¹ Pilate's next move was to take Jesus and have him scourged. ² The soldiers then wove a crown of thorns and fixed it on his head, throwing around his shoulders a cloak of royal purple. ³ Repeatedly they came up to him and said, "All hail, king of the Jews!", slapping his face as they did so.

⁴ Pilate went out a second time and said to the crowd: "Observe what I do. I am going to bring him out to you to make you realize that I find no case [against him]." ⁵ When Jesus came out wearing the crown of thorns and the purple cloak, Pilate said to them, "Look at the man!" ⁶ As soon as the chief priests and the temple guards saw him they shouted, "Crucify him! Crucify him!" Pilate said, "Take him and crucify him yourselves; I find no case against him." ⁷ "We have our law," the Jews responded, "and according to that law he must die because he made himself God's Son." ⁸ When Pilate heard this kind of talk, he was more afraid than ever.

⁹ Going back into the praetorium, he said to Jesus, "Where do you come from?" Jesus would not give him any answer. ¹⁰ "Do you refuse to speak to me?" Pilate asked him. "Do you not know that I have the power to release you and the power to crucify you?" ¹¹ Jesus answered:

"You would have no power over me whatever
unless it were given you from above.
That is why he who handed me over to you
is guilty of the greater sin."

¹² After this, Pilate was eager to release him, but the Jews

19, 1-16: Mt 27, 27-31;
Mk 15, 16-21;
Lk 23, 13-25.
4: 18, 38.
5: Is 52, 14.

6: 18, 31; 19, 15.
7: 10, 33-36; Lv 24, 16.
9: 7, 28.
11: 3, 27; 10, 18.
12: Acts 17, 7.

18, 40: *Insurrectionist:* a guerrilla warrior fighting both for nationalistic aims and for gain, Barabbas had been arrested for murder in a recent insurrection (Mk 15, 7).

19, 1: Luke places the mockery of Jesus at the midpoint in the trial when Jesus was sent to Herod. Mark and Matthew place the scourging and mockery at the end of the trial after the sentence of death. Scourging was an integral part of the crucifixion penalty.

19, 7: *Made himself God's Son:* this question was not raised in John's account of the Jewish interrogations of Jesus as it was in the synoptic account. Nevertheless, see 5, 18; 8, 53; 10, 36.

19, 12: *'Friend of Caesar':* a technical Roman term of honor.

shouted, "If you free this man you are no 'Friend of Caesar.' Anyone who makes himself a king becomes Caesar's rival." [13] Pilate heard what they were saying, then brought Jesus outside and took a seat on a judge's bench at the place called the Stone Pavement—*Gabbatha* in Hebrew. [14] (It was the Preparation Day for Passover, and the hour was about noon.) He said to the Jews, "Look at your king!" [15] At this they shouted, "Away with him! Away with him! Crucify him!" "What!" Pilate exclaimed. "Shall I crucify your king?" The chief priests replied, "We have no king but Caesar." [16] In the end, Pilate handed Jesus over to be crucified.

Crucifixion and Death

[17] Jesus was led away, and carrying the cross by himself, went out to what is called the Place of the Skull (in Hebrew, *Golgotha*). [18] There they crucified him, and two others with him: one on either side, Jesus in the middle. [19] Pilate had an inscription placed on the cross which read,

JESUS THE NAZOREAN
THE KING OF THE JEWS

[20] This inscription, in Hebrew, Latin, and Greek, was read by many of the Jews, since the place where Jesus was crucified

---

17-22: Mt 27, 32-37;   Lk 23, 26.33.
        Mk 15, 21-26;

19, 13: *Took a seat:* many scholars think this should be translated transitively, "sat him down." In John's thought, Jesus is the real judge of men, and they suggest that John portrays him seated on the judgment bench. We find this tradition in the second century. *Stone Pavement:* under the fortress Antonia, one of the conjectured locations of the praetorium, a tremendous stone pavement has been uncovered. The Aramaic word *Gabbatha* probably means "ridge, elevation."

19, 14: *Preparation Day for Passover:* the synoptics describe this as Friday (Mk 15, 42). *Noon:* Mk 15, 25 has Jesus crucified "at the third hour," which means either 9 A. M. or the period from 9 to 12. Noon, the time when, according to John, Jesus was sentenced to death, was the hour at which the priests began to slaughter Passover lambs in the temple; see Jn 1, 29.

19, 16: *In the end, Pilate handed Jesus over to be crucified:* according to the sequence this would seem to mean "handed him over to the chief priests." Lk 23, 25 has a similar ambiguity. There is a polemic tendency in the later gospels to place the guilt of the crucifixion solely on the Jewish authorities and to excuse the Romans from blame. Actually, John later mentions the Roman soldiers, and it was to these soldiers that Pilate handed Jesus over.

19, 17: *Carrying the cross by himself:* this is a different picture from that of the synoptics, especially Lk 23, 26, where Simon of Cyrene is made to bear the cross, walking behind Jesus. In John's theology Jesus remained master of his destiny (10, 18). *Place of the Skull:* the Latin word for skull is *Calvaria;* hence "Calvary." *Golgotha* is actually an Aramaic rather than a Hebrew word.

19, 19: The inscription or "title," found here in its technical form appears with slightly different words in each of the four gospels. Only John mentions its polyglot character and Pilate's role in keeping the title unchanged.

was near the city. [21] The chief priests of the Jews tried to tell Pilate, "You should not have written, 'The King of the Jews.' Write instead, 'This man claimed to be King of the Jews.'" [22] Pilate answered, "What I have written, I have written."

[23] After the soldiers had crucified Jesus they took his garments and divided them four ways, one for each soldier. There was also his tunic, but this tunic was woven in one piece from top to bottom and had no seam. [24] They said to each other, "We should not tear it. Let us throw dice to see who gets it." (The purpose of this was to have the Scripture fulfilled:

"They divided my garments among them;
　　for my clothing they cast lots.")

And this was what the soldiers did.

[25] Near the cross of Jesus there stood his mother, his mother's sister, Mary the wife of Clopas, and Mary Magdalene. [26] Seeing his mother there with the disciple whom he loved, Jesus said to his mother, "Woman, there is your son." [27] In turn he said to the disciple, "There is your mother." From that hour onward, the disciple took her into his care.

[28] After that, Jesus, realizing that everything was now finished, said to fulfill the Scripture, "I am thirsty." [29] There was a jar there, full of common wine. They stuck a sponge soaked in

---

21: 18, 33; Lk 19, 14.
23f: Ps 22, 19; Mt 27, 35;
　　Mk 15, 24.
25: Mt 27, 55; Mk 15, 40f;

Lk 8, 2; 23, 49.
28ff: Mt 27, 48ff;
　　Mk 15, 36f.
28: Ps 22, 16; 69, 22.

19, 23: Perhaps this seamless tunic is meant to recall the tunic of the high priest which Josephus (*Antiquities* III, 8, 4) says was without seam. Rv 1, 13 shows Jesus in priestly robes. The synoptics do not have the details about Jesus' garments.

19, 25: It is not clear whether three or four women are meant (i. e., whether *Mary the wife of Clopas* is or is not in apposition with *his mother's sister*); the Syriac tradition has four women. Only John mentions the mother of Jesus. The synoptics have a group of women *at a distance* from the cross (Mk 15, 40). If *his mother's sister* is not *Mary the wife of Clopas*, is she to be identified with *Salome* of the synoptic account? Salome was the mother of James and John, the sons of Zebedee; and thus these two disciples would have been Jesus' cousins.

19, 26f: This scene is to be read in the light of the Cana story in chapter 2. The presence of the mother of Jesus, the use of *woman*, and the mention of the *hour*, are elements of both scenes. Now that the hour has come, Mary (a symbol of the church?) is given a role as the mother of Christians (personified by the beloved disciple).

19, 28: *The Scripture:* it is not certain whether the fulfillment is in the scene of 25-27, or in the *I am thirsty* of 28. If the latter, Pss 69, 22 and 22, 16 deserve consideration.

19, 29: *Common wine:* John does not mention the drugged wine, a narcotic which Jesus refused as the crucifixion began (Mk 15, 25), but only this final gesture of kindness at the end (Mk 15, 36). Hyssop, a small plant, is scarcely suitable for carrying a sponge (Mark mentions a reed) and may be a symbolic reference to the hyssop used to put the blood of the paschal lamb on the doorpost of the Hebrews (Ex 12, 22).

this wine on some hyssop and raised it to his lips. [30] When Jesus took the wine, he said, "Now it is finished." Then he bowed his head, and delivered over his spirit.

The Blood and Water

[31] Since it was the Preparation Day the Jews did not want to have the bodies left on the cross during the sabbath, for that sabbath was a solemn feast day. They asked Pilate that the legs be broken and the bodies be taken away. [32] Accordingly, the soldiers came and broke the legs of the men crucified with Jesus, first of the one, then of the other. [33] When they came to Jesus and saw that he was already dead, they did not break his legs. [34] One of the soldiers thrust a lance into his side, and immediately blood and water flowed out. [35] (This testimony has been given by an eyewitness, and his testimony is true. He tells what he knows is true, so that you may believe.) [36] These events took place for the fulfillment of Scripture:

"Break none of his bones."

[37] There is still another Scripture passage which says:

"They shall look on him whom they have pierced."

Burial

[38] Afterward, Joseph of Arimathea, a disciple of Jesus (although a secret one for fear of the Jews), asked Pilate's per-

---

30: 4, 34; 10, 18; 17, 4;
    Lk 23, 46.
31: Ex 12, 16; Dt 21, 23.
34: Nm 20, 11; 1 Jn 5, 6.
35: 7, 37ff; 21, 24.
36: Ex 12, 46; Nm 9, 12;

Ps 34, 21.
37: Nm 21, 9; Zec 12, 10;
    Rv 1, 7.
38-42: Mt 27, 57-60;
    Mk 15, 42-46;
    Lk 34, 50-54.

19, 30: *Delivered over his spirit:* it is awkward in English to preserve the possible double nuance of dying (giving up the last breath or spirit) and that of passing on the Holy Spirit; see 7, 39, which connects the giving of the Spirit with Jesus' glorious return to the Father.

19, 34f: John probably emphasizes these verses to show the reality of Jesus' death, against the Docetic heretics. In the blood and water there may also be a symbolic reference to the Eucharist and Baptism.

19, 35: *He tells:* it is not certain from the Greek that this *he* is the *eyewitness* of the first part of the sentence.

19, 36: The scriptural reference is probably to Ex 12, 46 (Nm 9, 12), which has directions for dealing with the Passover lamb. That Jesus is the Paschal Lamb is a Johannine theme, and thus at the end of the gospel we are called back to 1, 29. There may also be a reference to Ps 34, 21, describing God's safeguarding of an innocent man.

19, 37: John cites Zec 12, 10 (also cited in Rv 1, 7), but not exactly according to either the standard Hebrew reading or the Greek Old Testament. There was a Jewish tradition of uncertain date that this text referred to the Messiah.

19, 38-42: In the first three gospels there is no embalming on Friday. In Matthew and Luke the women come to the tomb on Sunday morning precisely to anoint Jesus.

mission to remove Jesus' body. Pilate granted it, so they came and took the body away. ³⁹ Nicodemus (the man who had first come to Jesus at night) likewise came, bringing a mixture of myrrh and aloes which weighed about a hundred pounds. ⁴⁰ They took Jesus' body, and in accordance with Jewish burial custom bound it up in wrappings of cloth with perfumed oils. ⁴¹ In the place where he had been crucified there was a garden, and in the garden a new tomb in which no one had ever been buried. ⁴² Because of the Jewish Preparation Day they buried Jesus there, for the tomb was close at hand.

20

Peter and the Disciple

¹ Early in the morning on the first day of the week, while it was still dark, Mary Magdalene came to the tomb. She saw that the stone had been moved away, ² so she ran off to Simon Peter and the other disciple (the one Jesus loved) and told them, "The Lord has been taken from the tomb! We don't know where they have put him!" ³ At that, Peter and the other disciple started out on their way toward the tomb. ⁴ They were running side by side, but then the other disciple outran Peter and reached the tomb first. ⁵ He did not enter but bent down to peer in, and saw the wrappings lying on the ground. ⁶ Presently, Simon Peter came along behind him and entered the tomb. He observed the wrappings on the ground ⁷ and saw the piece of cloth which had covered the head not lying with the wrappings, but rolled up in a place by itself. ⁸ Then the disciple who had arrived first at the tomb went in. He saw and believed. ⁹ (Remember, as yet they did not understand the Scripture that Jesus had to rise from the dead.) ¹⁰ With this, the disciples went back home.

39: 3, 1f; 7, 50.
20, 1-18: Mt 28, 1-10;
 Mk 16, 1-11;
 Lk 24, 1-11.

1: 19, 25.
6: Lk 24, 12.
7: 11, 44; 19, 40.
9: Acts 2, 26f; 1 Cor 15, 4.

20, 1: *Still dark:* according to Mark the sun had risen, and Matthew speaks of the first rays of light.
20, 3-10: The basic narrative is told of Peter alone in Lk 24, 12, a verse missing in important MSS and which may be borrowed from tradition similar to John. Lk 24, 24 also generally reflects this story.
20, 6-8: There was some special feature about the state of the burial wrappings that caused the beloved disciple to believe. Some suggest that Jesus had passed through them without their being unrolled.
20, 9: Probably a general reference to the Scriptures is intended, as in Lk 24, 26 and 1 Cor 15, 4. Some individual Old Testament passages suggested are Ps 16, 10; Hos 6, 2; Jon 1, 17; 2, 1.

Mary Magdalene

[11] Meanwhile, Mary stood weeping beside the tomb. Even as she wept, she stooped to peer inside, [12] and there she saw two angels in dazzling robes. One was seated at the head and the other at the foot of the place where Jesus' body had lain. [13] "Woman," they asked her, "why are you weeping?" She answered them, "Because the Lord has been taken away, and I do not know where they have put him." [14] She had no sooner said this than she turned around and caught sight of Jesus standing there. But she did not know him. [15] "Woman," he asked her, "why are you weeping? Who is it you are looking for?" She supposed he was the gardener, so she said, "Sir, if you are the one who carried him off, tell me where you have laid him and I will take him away." [16] Jesus said to her, "Mary!" She turned to him and said [in Hebrew], *"Rabbouni!"* (meaning "Teacher"). [17] Jesus then said: "Do not cling to me, for I have not yet ascended to the Father. Rather, go to my brothers and tell them, 'I am ascending to my Father and your Father, to my God and your God!' " [18] Mary Magdalene went to the disciples. "I have seen the Lord!" she announced. Then she reported what he had said to her.

Appearance to the Disciples

[19] On the evening of that first day of the week, even though the disciples had locked the doors of the place where they were for fear of the Jews, Jesus came and stood before them. "Peace be with you," he said. [20] When he had said this, he showed

---

14: 21, 4; Lk 24, 16.
15ff: Mt 28, 9f.
17: Acts 1, 9.
20: 14, 27.

20, 17: *Do not cling to me:* literally "Don't keep touching me." See Mt 28, 9, where the women take hold of his feet. *I have not yet ascended:* for John and many of the New Testament writers, the ascension in the theological sense of going to the Father to be glorified took place with the resurrection as one action. This scene in John dramatizes such an understanding, for by Easter night Jesus is glorified and can give the Spirit. Therefore his ascension takes place immediately after he has talked to Mary. In such a view, the ascension after forty days described in Acts 1, 1-11 would be simply the termination of earthly appearances. *My Father and your Father:* this echoes Ru 1, 16, *Your people shall be my people, and your God my God.* The Father of Jesus will now become the Father of the disciples because, once ascended, Jesus can give them the Spirit that comes from the Father and beget them as God's children (3, 5). That is why he calls them *my brothers.*

20, 19: *The disciples:* by implication from v 24, this means ten of the Twelve. Lk 24, 33 mentions a larger group; Mk 16, 14 refers to the Eleven. Presumably they are in Jerusalem; see Lk 24, 33. The "upper room" is first mentioned in Acts 1, 13, as the place to which the Eleven came forty days later, after Jesus' final departure. *Peace be with you:* although this could be an ordinary greeting, John intends here to echo 14, 27. The theme of rejoicing in v 20 echoes 16, 22.

20, 20: *Hands and . . . side:* Lk 24, 39f mentions "hands and feet"; cf Ps 22, 17.

them his hands and his side. At the sight of the Lord the disciples rejoiced. ²¹ "Peace be with you," he said again.

> "As the Father has sent me,
> so I send you."

²² Then he breathed on them and said:

> "Receive the Holy Spirit.
> ²³ If you forgive men's sins,
> they are forgiven them;
> if you hold them bound,
> they are held bound."

Thomas

²⁴ It happened that one of the Twelve, Thomas (the name means "Twin"), was absent when Jesus came. ²⁵ The other disciples kept telling him: "We have seen the Lord!" His answer was, "I will never believe it without probing the nail-prints in his hands, without putting my finger in the nailmarks and my hand into his side."

²⁶ A week later, the disciples were once more in the room, and this time Thomas was with them. Despite the locked doors, Jesus came and stood before them. "Peace be with you," he said; ²⁷ then, to Thomas: "Take your finger and examine my hands. Put your hand into my side. Do not persist in your unbelief, but believe!" ²⁸ Thomas said in response, "My Lord and my God!" ²⁹ Jesus then said to him:

21: 17, 18; Mt 28, 19;
    Mk 16, 15; Lk 24, 47f.
23: Mt 16, 19; 18, 18.

25: 1 Jn 1, 1.
26: 21, 14.
29: 4, 48; Lk 1, 45.

20, 21: By means of this sending, the Eleven were made *apostles,* that is, "those sent"; cf 17, 18. A solemn mission or "sending" is also the subject of the post-resurrection appearances to the Eleven in Mt 28, 19; Lk 24, 47; Mk 16, 15.

20, 22: According to the Second Council of Constantinople, the Spirit was truly given here and the breathing on the disciples was not merely symbolic. This action recalls Gn 2, 7, where God breathed on man and gave him the natural spirit or life-force; in John it is the life-source for supernatural life that is given. The apostles are recreated as new men, sons of God. The further giving of the Spirit in chapter 2 of Acts is a more public charism for the church.

20, 23: The Council of Trent defined that the power to forgive sins given here is the same power exercised in the Sacrament of Penance. See Mt 16, 19 and 18, 18. *If you hold them bound, they are held bound:* the reference of *they, them,* not wholly clear in the Greek, is more probably to *sins* than to *men.*

20, 28: The Second Council of Constantinople defined that this confession of Thomas referred to Christ and was not simply an expression of glory to God the Father. *Lord* and *God* are two Old Testament titles of God (Ps 35, 23).

"You became a believer because you saw me.
  Blest are they who have not seen and have believed."

Conclusion

[30] Jesus performed many other signs as well—signs not recorded here—in the presence of his disciples. [31] But these have been recorded to help you believe that Jesus is the Messiah, the Son of God, so that through this faith you may have life in his name.

IV: APPENDIX

THE RESURRECTION APPEARANCE IN GALILEE

21

The Fishermen

[1] Later, at the sea of Tiberias, Jesus showed himself to the disciples [once again]. This is how the appearance took place. [2] Assembled were Simon Peter, Thomas ("the Twin"), Nathanael (from Cana in Galilee), Zebedee's sons, and two other disciples. [3] Simon Peter said to them, "I am going out to fish." "We will join you," they replied, and went off to get into their boat. All through the night they caught nothing. [4] Just after daybreak Jesus was standing on the shore, though none of the disciples knew it was Jesus. [5] He said to them, "Children, have you caught anything to eat?" "Not a thing," they answered. [6] "Cast your net off to the starboard side," he suggested, "and you will find something." So they made a cast, and took so many fish they could not haul the net in. [7] Then the disciple Jesus loved cried out to Peter, "It is the Lord!" On hearing it was the

---

31: 1 Jn 5, 13.
21, 1: Mt 26, 32; 28, 7.

3: Mt 4, 18; Lk 5, 4-10.
5: Lk 24, 41.

20, 30f: These verses are clearly a conclusion to the gospel.
  20, 31: See 1 Jn 5, 13: *To help you believe:* it is difficult to determine whether the Greek should be read "that you may continue to believe" (i. e., the readers are Christians) or "that you may come to believe" (i. e., perhaps the readers are non-Christians).
  21, 1-23: There are many non-Johannine peculiarities in this chapter, some suggesting Lucan Greek style; yet there are many Johannine features as well. Perhaps the tradition was ultimately derived from John but preserved by some disciple other than the writer of the rest of the gospel. The appearances narrated seem to be independent of those in chapter 20. Even if a later addition, the chapter was added before publication of the gospel, for it appears in all MSS.
  21, 2: *Zebedee's sons:* the only mention by name of James and John in this gospel. Perhaps the phrase was inserted to identify the *two other disciples.* The anonymity of the latter phrase is more Johannine (1, 35).
  21, 3-6: This may be a variant of Luke's account of the catch of fish (5, 1-11), which he joined with the call of the first disciples.

Lord, Simon Peter threw on some clothes—he was stripped—and jumped into the water.

⁸ Meanwhile the other disciples came in the boat, towing the net full of fish. Actually they were not far from land—no more than a hundred yards.

⁹ When they landed, they saw a charcoal fire there with a fish laid on it and some bread. ¹⁰ "Bring some of the fish you just caught," Jesus told them. ¹¹ Simon Peter went aboard and hauled ashore the net loaded with sizable fish—one hundred fifty-three of them! In spite of the great number, the net was not torn.

¹² "Come and eat your meal," Jesus told them. Not one of the disciples presumed to inquire, "Who are you?" for they knew it was the Lord. ¹³ Jesus came over, took the bread and gave it to them, and did the same with the fish. ¹⁴ This marked the third time that Jesus appeared to the disciples after being raised from the dead.

Peter the Shepherd

¹⁵ When they had eaten their meal, Jesus said to Simon Peter, "Simon, son of John, do you love me more than these?" "Yes, Lord," he said, "you know that I love you." At which Jesus said, "Feed my lambs."

¹⁶ A second time he put his question, "Simon, son of John, do you love me?" "Yes, Lord," Peter said, "you know that I love you." Jesus replied, "Tend my sheep."

¹⁷ A third time Jesus asked him, "Simon, son of John, do you love me?" Peter was hurt because he had asked a third time, "Do you love me?" So he said to him: "Lord, you know

---

9: Lk 24, 41ff.
13: Lk 24, 42.
15: Lk 5, 10; Acts 20, 28.

17: 13, 37f; 18, 17.25ff;
Mt 16, 17ff; Lk 22, 31f.

21, 9.12f: It is strange that Jesus already has fish since none have yet been brought ashore. This meal may have had eucharistic significance for early Christians since v 13 recalls John 6, 11, which uses the vocabulary of Jesus' action at the Last Supper.

21, 11: The exact number, 153, is probably meant to have a symbolic meaning, perhaps in relation to the apostles' mission to catch men. The net which was not torn *may* represent the church.

21, 12: *Not one . . . presumed:* is Jesus' appearance strange to them? See Lk 24, 16; Mk 16, 12; Jn 20, 14.

21, 14: This verse connects chapters 20 and 21.

21, 15: *More than these:* probably "more than these disciples do" rather two different Greek verbs for *love;* two verbs for *feed/tend;* two or three nouns for *sheep;* two verbs for *know.* Apparently there is no difference of meaning. The First· Vatican Council cited this verse in defining that the risen Jesus gave Peter the jurisdiction of supreme shepherd and ruler over the whole flock.

21, 15: *More than these:* probably "more than these disciples do" rather than "more than you love these things [fishing, etc.]."

everything. You know well that I love you." Jesus said to him, "Feed my sheep.

> 18 "I tell you solemnly:
> as a young man
> you fastened your belt
> and went about as you pleased;
> but when you are older
> you will stretch out your hands,
> and another will tie you fast
> and carry you off against your will."

19 (What he said indicated the sort of death by which Peter was to glorify God.) When Jesus had finished speaking he said to him, "Follow me."

The Beloved Disciple

20 Peter turned around at that, and noticed that the disciple whom Jesus loved was following (the one who had leaned against Jesus' chest during the supper and said, "Lord, which one will hand you over?"). 21 Seeing him, Peter was prompted to ask Jesus, "But Lord, what about him?" 22 "Suppose I want him to stay until I come," Jesus replied, "how does that concern you? Your business is to follow me." 23 This is how the report spread among the brothers that this disciple was not going to die. Jesus never told him, as a matter of fact, that the disciple was not going to die; all he said was, "Suppose I want him to stay until I come [how does that concern you]?"

Conclusion

24 It is this same disciple who is the witness to these things; it is he who wrote them down and his testimony, we know, is true. 25 There are still many other things that Jesus did, yet if they were written about in detail, I doubt there would be room enough in the entire world to hold the books to record them.

18: 2 Pt 1, 14.   24: 15, 27; 19, 35.
19: 13, 36.   25: 20, 30.
20: 13, 25.

21, 18: A figurative reference to the crucifixion of Peter.
21, 23: This whole scene takes on more significance if the disciple is already dead. The death of the apostolic generation caused problems in the church because of a belief that Jesus was to have returned first. Loss of faith sometimes resulted; cf 2 Pt 3, 4.
21, 24: *Who wrote them down:* this does not necessarily mean he wrote them with his own hand. The same expression is used in 19, 9 of Pilate, who certainly did not write the inscription himself. *We know:* it is probably not the beloved disciple of v 7 who speaks here as *we.*

THE ACTS OF THE APOSTLES
INTRODUCTION

Luke is the only one of the evangelists who supplements his gospel with a second volume describing the origin and spread of the Christian communities in New Testament times. He attributes the establishment of these churches to the action of the Holy Spirit, specifically upon Peter (2, 14-18; 4, 8; 15, 8) and Paul (13, 2ff; 16, 6; 20, 22f). Peter was the leading member of the Twelve (1, 13.26) and the recognized authority over the Judaeo-Christian communities (12, 17; 15, 6-12). Paul eventually joined the church at Antioch (11, 25f), which subsequently commissioned him and Barnabas to undertake the spread of the gospel to Asia Minor. This missionary venture generally failed to win the Jews of the diaspora to the gospel, but enjoyed a measure of success among the Gentiles (13, 14—14, 27). Paul's refusal to impose the Mosaic law upon his Gentile converts provoked very strong objection among the Judaeo-Christians of Jerusalem (15, 1), but both Peter and James supported his position (15, 6-21). Paul's second and third missionary journeys (16, 36—21, 16) resulted in the same pattern: of failure among the Jews generally but of some success among the Gentiles.

In Acts, Luke has provided a broad survey of the church's development from the resurrection of Jesus to Paul's first Roman imprisonment, the point at which the book ends. Originally a Judaeo-Christian community in Jerusalem, the church was placed in circumstances impelling it to include within its membership people of other cultures: the Samaritans (8, 4-25), at first an occasional Gentile (8, 26-40; 10, 1-48), and finally the Gentiles on principle (11, 20f). Fear on the part of the Jewish people that Christian messianism, particularly as preached to the Gentiles, threatened their own cultural heritage caused them to be suspicious of Paul's gospel (15, 1-5; 13, 42-45; 28, 17-24). The inability of Christian missioners to allay this apprehension inevitably created a situation wherein the gospel was preached more and more to the Gentiles. Toward the end of Paul's career, the Christian communities, with the exception of those in Palestine itself (9, 31), were mainly of Gentile membership.

In the development of the church from a Judaeo-Christian origin in Jerusalem, with its roots in Jewish religious tradition, to a series of Christian communities among the Gentiles of the Roman Empire, Luke perceives the action of God in history laying open the hearts of all mankind to the divine message of salvation. His approach to the history of the church is predominantly theological. He conceives of the church as a mystery of God introduced into history through the apostolic preaching (1, 21f), which was forced to adapt itself to circumstances and so to carry forward the predestined spread of God's word among men, again in history. His preoccupation with the mystery of the church as the bearer of the word of salvation rules out of his book detailed histories of the various members of the Twelve as well as of the churches founded by Paul. Only the main lines of the roles of Peter and Paul serve Luke's interest. Nonetheless, the historical data he utilizes are of value for the understanding of the church's early life and development and as general background to the Pauline epistles. In the interpretation of Acts, care must be exercised to determine Luke's theological aims and interests and to evaluate his historical data without either exaggerating their literal accuracy or underestimating their factual worth. Concerning the date of Acts, see Introduction of the Gospel according to Luke.

The book of the Acts of the Apostles is divided as follows:

THE ACTS OF THE APOSTLES
I: PROLOGUE

1

Jesus' Final Instructions and Ascension

[1] In my first account, Theophilus, I dealt with all that Jesus did and taught [2] until the day he was taken up to heaven, having first instructed the apostles he had chosen through the Holy Spirit. [3] In the time after his suffering he showed them in many convincing ways that he was alive, appearing to them over the course of forty days and speaking to them about the reign of God. [4] On one occasion when he met with them, he told them not to leave Jerusalem: "Wait, rather, for the fulfillment of my Father's promise, of which you have heard me speak. [5] John baptized with water, but within a few days you will be baptized with the Holy Spirit."

[6] While they were with him they asked, "Lord, are you going to restore the rule to Israel now?" [7] His answer was: "The exact time it is not yours to know. The Father has reserved that to himself. [8] You will receive power when the Holy Spirit comes down on you; then you are to be my witnesses in Jerusalem,

1, 1: Lk 1, 1-4.
2: Mt 28, 19f; Lk 24, 51;
   1 Tm 3, 16.
4: Jn 14, 26.
5: 11, 16; Mt 3, 11;

Mk 1, 8; Lk 3, 16;
Jn 1, 26; Eph 1, 13.
7: Mt 24, 36; 1 Thes 5, 1f.
8: 2, 2; Is 43, 10;
Mt 28, 19.

1, 1-26: This introductory material connects Acts with Luke's gospel (1, 1f); shows that the apostles were instructed by the risen Jesus (1, 3ff); points out that the parousia or renewed presence of Jesus will occur as certainly as his resurrection occurred (1, 6-11); and lists the members of the Twelve, stressing their role as a body of divinely mandated witnesses to his life, teaching, and resurrection (1, 12-26).

1, 3: *In many convincing ways:* the meaning of the Greek is that the apostles received evidence of Jesus' resurrection decisive enough to eliminate doubt from their minds (Lk 24, 36-49). This divinely offered proof, however, entailed more than an appeal to human reason. It included prophetic illumination which rendered the apostles certain that the appearances of the risen Christ were actions of God manifesting himself to their human experience. *Appearing to them over the course of forty days:* Christian tradition considered especially sacred the interval in which the appearances and instructions of the risen Jesus occurred, and expressed it therefore in terms of the sacred number forty; cf Dt 8, 2.

According to John (20, 17), the ascension of Jesus to the kingdom of his Father took place on the day of his resurrection. Luke writes from a different perspective and speaks of a visible ascension of Jesus after forty days. For John, the ascension means primarily the risen Jesus' new existence with the Father, and the appearances are those of the risen and ascended One. For Luke, the ascension marks the end of the appearances of Jesus except for the extraordinary appearance to Paul.

1, 4: *My Father's promise:* the Holy Spirit, as is clear from 1, 5. This gift of the Spirit formed part of the instructions of the risen Jesus on the kingdom of God, of which Luke speaks in 1, 3. Probably this instruction is the source of the material on the Holy Spirit in Jn 15, 26f and 16, 7-15.

1, 7: This verse echoes the tradition that the precise time of the parousia is not revealed to men; cf Mk 13, 32; 1 Thes 5, 1ff.

throughout Judea and Samaria yes, even to the ends of the earth." [9] No sooner had he said this than he was lifted up before their eyes in a cloud which took him from their sight.

[10] They were still gazing up into the heavens when two men dressed in white stood beside them. [11] "Men of Galilee," they said, "why do you stand here looking up at the skies? This Jesus who has been taken from you will return, just as you saw him go up into the heavens."

[12] After that they returned to Jerusalem from the mount called Olivet near Jerusalem—a mere sabbath's journey away. [13] Entering the city, they went to the upstairs room where they were staying: Peter and John and James and Andrew; Philip and Thomas, Bartholomew and Matthew; James son of Alpheus; Simon, the Zealot party member, and Judas son of James. [14] Together they devoted themselves to constant prayer. There were some women in their company, and Mary the mother of Jesus, and his brothers.

II: THE COMMUNITY IN JERUSALEM FINDS MATURITY IN THE SPIRIT

Matthias Chosen

[15] At one point during those days, Peter stood up in the center of the brothers; there must have been a hundred and twenty gathered together. [16] "Brothers," he said, "the saying in Scripture uttered long ago by the Holy Spirit through the mouth of David was destined to be fulfilled in Judas, the one who guided those that arrested Jesus. [17] He was one of our number and he had been given a share in this ministry of ours.

[18] "That individual bought a piece of land with his unjust gains, and fell headlong upon it. His body burst wide open, all his entrails spilling out. [19] This event came to be known

---

9: 2 Kgs 2, 11; Mk 16, 19.   1 Pt 3, 22.
10: Jn 20, 17.   12ff: Lk 6, 14ff.
11: Lk 24, 51; Eph 4, 8ff;   16: Lk 22, 47.

1, 9: Comparison of this verse with Lk 24, 51 suggests that there were several visible ascensions of the risen Christ. Mt 28, 16-20 raises the possibility of a similar visible ascension of Christ in Galilee. The visible ascension accorded with the cosmological conception of the time that held the sky to be a solid vault above which was God's throne. On other occasions, Jesus simply vanished; cf Lk 24, 31. A visible ascension is not described in Jn 20, 17.

1, 18: Luke records a popular tradition on the death of Judas that seems to differ from that in Mt 27, 5, according to which Judas hanged himself. Here, though the text is not entirely clear, Judas is depicted as purchasing a piece of property with the betrayal money and being killed on it in a fall.

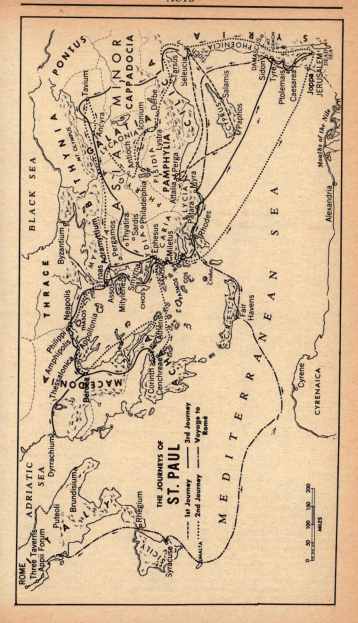

THE JOURNEYS OF
ST. PAUL

1st Journey ———
2nd Journey ·········
3rd Journey ———
Voyage to
Rome ·—·—·—·

0 50 100 150 200
MILES

by the inhabitants of Jerusalem, who named the property Field of Blood—'Akeldama' in their own language.

[20] "It is written in the Book of Psalms,

'Let his encampment be desolate.
  May no one dwell on it.'

And again,

'May another take his office.'

[21] It is entirely fitting, therefore, that one of those who was of our company while the Lord Jesus moved among us, [22] from the baptism of John until the day he was taken up from us, should be named as witness with us to his resurrection." [23] At that they nominated two, Joseph (called Barsabbas, also known as Justus) and Matthias. [24] Then they prayed: "O Lord, you read the hearts of men. Make known to us which of these two you choose [25] for this apostolic ministry, replacing Judas, who deserted the cause and went the way he was destined to go." [26] They then drew lots between the two men. The choice fell to Matthias, who was added to the eleven apostles.

2

Descent of the Holy Spirit

[1] When the day of Pentecost came it found them gathered in one place. [2] Suddenly from up in the sky there came a noise

---

20: Pss 69, 26; 109, 8;
    Jn 17, 12.
22: 1, 8; 10, 39.

2, 1: Ex 23, 14.
2f: Jn 3, 8.

1, 26: The need for replacing Judas so as to restore the apostolic college to the number of twelve was probably dictated by the symbolism of the number. It recalled the twelve tribes from which all Israelites were thought to be descended, and indicated that the messianic teaching about Jesus was to be directed first to the whole of Israel.

2, 2: *From up in the sky there came a noise like a strong, driving wind*: the wind and the Holy Spirit are associated in Jn 3, 8. The sound of a great rush of wind would aptly presage a new action of God in the history of salvation.

2, 1-41: Luke's pentecostal narrative consists of an introduction (2, 1-13), a speech ascribed to Peter declaring the resurrection of Jesus and its messianic significance (2, 14-36), and a favorable response from the audience (2, 39ff). It is likely that the narrative telescopes events that took place over a period of time and on a less dramatic scale. The Twelve were not originally in a position to proclaim publicly the messianic office of Jesus without incurring immediate reprisal from those religious authorities in Jerusalem who had encompassed Jesus' death precisely to stem the rising tide in his favor; cf Jn 11, 47f. Once the "new covenant" had acquired many adherents, public teaching could more easily be undertaken. In any case, these reflections point up Luke's emphasis on the Holy Spirit. He is at pains to show that Christianity cannot be accounted a mere religious sect within Judaism that developed its own brand of messianism. On the contrary, it declared itself from the beginning as originating in the inspiration and under the impulsion of God.

like a strong, driving wind which was heard all through the house where they were seated. [3] Tongues as of fire appeared, which parted and came to rest on each of them. [4] All were filled with the Holy Spirit. They began to express themselves in foreign tongues and make bold proclamation as the Spirit prompted them.

[5] Staying in Jerusalem at the time were devout Jews of every nation under heaven. [6] These heard the sound, and assembled in a large crowd. They were much confused because each one heard these men speaking his own language. [7] The whole occurrence astonished them. They asked in utter amazement, "Are not all of these men who are speaking Galileans? [8] How is it that each of us hears them in his native tongue? [9] We are Parthians, Medes, and Elamites. We live in Mesopotamia, Judea and Cappadocia, Pontus, the province of Asia, [10] Phrygia and Pamphylia, Egypt, and the regions of Libya around Cyrene. There are even visitors from Rome—[11] all Jews, or those who have come over to Judaism; Cretans and Arabs too. Yet each of us hears them speaking in his own tongue about the marvels God has accomplished." [12] They were dumbfounded, and could make nothing at all of what had happened.

"What does this mean?" they asked one another, while a few remarked with a sneer, [13] "They have had too much new wine!"

Peter's Discourse

[14] Peter stood up with the Eleven, raised his voice, and addressed them: "You who are Jews, indeed all of you staying in Jerusalem! Listen to what I have to say. [15] You must realize

---

4: 1, 5; 4, 31; 11, 16; 19, 6;
  Ps 104, 30; Jn 20, 33.
5: Wis 1, 7.

11: 10, 46.
13: 1 Cor 14, 23.

2, 3: *Tongues as of fire:* see Ex 19, 18, where fire symbolizes the presence of God to initiate the covenant on Sinai. Here the Holy Spirit acts upon the apostles, preparing them to proclaim the new covenant with its unique gift of the Spirit (2, 38).

2, 4: *To express themselves in foreign tongues:* ecstatic prayer in praise of God; cf 2, 11.

2, 6-13: The multitude receives the charism of interpretation of tongues (1 Cor 12, 10). The question of the meaning of this charism is raised. To some of the hearers, however, the language is unintelligible, and they conclude the apostles are drunk. Luke may have in mind here the varying reactions to the gift in the early Christian communities; cf 1 Cor 14, 22-25.

2, 14-36: The first of six discourses in Acts (see 3, 12-26; 4, 8-12; 5, 29-32; 10, 34-43; 13, 16-41) dealing with the substance of Christian messianism, the resurrection of Jesus and its messianic import. Five of these are attributed to Peter, the final one to Paul. In 1 Cor 15, 11 Paul refers to the apostolic teaching on the death and resurrection of Jesus as "the preaching" or "proclamation." Hence modern scholars term these discourses in Acts the "kerygma," the Greek word for proclamation.

In the present discourse, Peter appeals to the religious faith of the

that these men are not drunk, as you seem to think. It is only nine in the morning! [16] No it is what Joel the prophet spoke of:

[17] 'It shall come to pass in the last days, says God,
    that I will pour out a portion of my spirit on
      all mankind:
Your sons and daughters shall prophesy,
    your young men shall see visions
    and your old men shall dream dreams.
[18] Yes, even on my servants and handmaids
    I will pour out a portion of my spirit in those days,
    and they shall prophesy.
[19] I will work wonders in the heavens above
    and signs on the earth below:
    blood, fire, and a cloud of smoke.
[20] The sun shall be turned to darkness and the moon
      to blood
    before the coming of that great and glorious
      day of the Lord.
[21] Then shall everyone be saved who calls on the
      name of the Lord.'

[22] "Men of Israel, listen to me! Jesus the Nazorean was a man whom God sent to you with miracles, wonders, and signs as his credentials. These God worked through him in your midst, as you well know. [23] He was delivered up by the set purpose and plan of God; you even made use of pagans to crucify and kill him. [24] God freed him from death's bitter pangs, however, and raised him up again, for it was impossible that death should keep its hold on him. [25] David says of him:

17: Is 2, 2; 44, 3; Jl 3, 1-5.   23: 1 Thes 2, 15.
21: Rom 10, 13.   24: 13, 34.
22: 10, 38; Lk 24, 19.   25-28: Ps 16, 8-11.

---

audience and presents himself as one in possession of certain religious information given him by God together with the ability to interpret it. This is called a prophetic announcement. The following chief points are made: (1) The ecstatic prayer is due to the influence of the Spirit, which the prophet Joel foretold would be especially active in messianic times (16-21); (2) the crucifixion of Jesus of Nazareth, a man publicly known in Jerusalem because of his miracle-working, was an integral part of God's saving plan, as God has indicated by raising him from the dead (22ff); (3) the prophetic understanding of the Old Testament reveals that the resurrection and ascension of the Messiah was God's actual saving plan (25-35); (4) the true meaning of the death, resurrection and ascension of Jesus is that he is the divinely enthroned messianic King of Israel (36), bestowing the gift of the Spirit upon all who accept him as Savior (38).

The prophetic character of the kerygmatic discourses in Acts explains why they do not include accounts of the appearances of Jesus. Only to one who accepts the prophetic announcement of Jesus' resurrection will accounts of his subsequent appearances convey any meaning.

'I have set the Lord ever before me,
  with him at my right hand I shall not be disturbed.
26 My heart has been glad and my tongue has rejoiced,
  my body will live on in hope,
27 for you will not abandon my soul to the nether world,
  nor will you suffer your faithful one to undergo corruption.
28 You have shown me the paths of life;
  you will fill me with joy in your presence.'

29 "Brothers, I can speak confidently to you about our father David. He died and was buried, and his grave is in our midst to this day. 30 He was a prophet and knew that God had sworn to him that one of his descendants would sit upon his throne. 31 He said that he was not abandoned to the nether world, nor did his body undergo corruption, thus proclaiming beforehand the resurrection of the Messiah. 32 This is the Jesus God has raised up, and we are his witnesses. 33 Exalted at God's right hand, he first received the promised Holy Spirit from the Father, then poured this Spirit out on us. This is what you now see and hear. 34 David did not go up to heaven, yet David says,

'The Lord said to my Lord,
  Sit at my right hand
    35 until I make your enemies your footstool.'

36 Therefore let the whole house of Israel know beyond any doubt that God has made both Lord and Messiah this Jesus whom you crucified."

37 When they heard this, they were deeply shaken. They asked Peter and the other apostles, "What are we to do, brothers?" 38 Peter answered: "You must reform and be baptized, each one of you, in the name of Jesus Christ, that your sins may be forgiven; then you will receive the gift of the Holy Spirit. 39 It was to you and your children that the promise was made, and to all those still far off whom the Lord our God calls."

27: 13, 35.   34: Ps 110, 1.
30: 2 Sm 7, 12; Ps 132, 11.   36: 9, 22; Rom 10, 9;
31: 13, 35; Ps 16, 10.   Phil 2, 11.
33: 1, 4f.   38: 2, 33; 16, 31.

2, 38: *You must reform and be baptized:* repentance is a positive concept, a change of heart toward God reflected in the actual goodness of one's own life. It is in accord with the apostolic teaching derived from Jesus (2, 42) and ultimately recorded in the four gospels. Jesus made use of baptism at the beginning of his ministry (Jn 3, 22; 4, 2), but according to the synoptic evangelists abandoned the practice after the arrest of the Baptizer. Matthew tells us (28, 19) that the sacramental usage of baptism was an instruction given to the apostles by the risen Christ. Jesus spoke of this new baptism to Nicodemus (Jn 3, 5).

⁴⁰ In support of his testimony he used many other arguments, and kept urging, "Save yourselves from this generation which has gone astray." ⁴¹ Those who accepted his message were baptized; some three thousand were added that day.

Communal Life

⁴² They devoted themselves to the apostles' instruction and the communal life, to the breaking of bread and the prayers. ⁴³ A reverent fear overtook them all, for many wonders and signs were performed by the apostles. ⁴⁴ Those who believed shared all things in common; ⁴⁵ they would sell their property and goods, dividing everything on the basis of each one's need. ⁴⁶ They went to the temple area together every day, while in their homes they broke bread. With exultant and sincere hearts they took their meals in common, ⁴⁷ praising God and winning the approval of all the people. Day by day the Lord added to their number those who were being saved.

3

Cure of a Cripple

¹ Once, when Peter and John were going up to the temple

40: Lk 9, 41.	42: 1, 14; 6, 4.
41: 1, 5.	43: 5, 12-16.
42-47: 4, 32-35.	44: 4, 32.34f.

2, 42-47: The first of three summary passages (see 4, 32-37 and 5, 12-16) which outline, somewhat ideally, the chief characteristics of the Jerusalem community: adherence to the teachings of the Twelve concerning repentance; the centering of its religious life in the eucharistic liturgy (42); a system of distribution of goods that led wealthier Christians to sell their possessions when the needs of the community's poor required it (44 and note on 4, 32—5, 11); continued attendance at the Temple, since in this initial stage there was little or no thought of dividing lines between Judaism and Christianity.

2, 47: *Those who were being saved:* not that Christians are absolutely saved, but rather that to those who believe in Christ God directly reveals his saving action in their behalf. If Christians are not saved, it is because of their failure to respond to God's saving action; cf Rom 8, 1.

3, 1—4, 31: This section presents a series of related events: the dramatic cure of a lame beggar (3, 1-10) produces a large audience for the kerygmatic discourse of Peter (3, 11-26). The Sadducees, taking exception to the doctrine of resurrection, have Peter, John, and apparently the beggar as well arrested (4, 1-4) and brought to trial before the Sanhedrin. The issue concerns the authority on which Peter and John publicly teach religious doctrine in the temple (5ff). Peter replies with a brief summary of the kerygma, implying that his authority is prophetic (8-12). The court warns the apostles to abandon their practice of invoking prophetic authority in the name of Jesus (13-18). When Peter and John reply that the prophetic role cannot be abandoned to satisfy the objections of men, the court nevertheless releases them, afraid to do otherwise since the beggar, lame from birth and over forty years old, is a well-known figure in Jerusalem and the facts of his cure are common property (19-22). The narrative concludes with a prayer of the Christian community imploring divine aid against threats of persecution (23-31).

3, 1: *Prayer at the three o'clock hour:* when the evening sacrifice was offered in the temple; cf Ex 29, 38f.

for prayer at the three o'clock hour, ² a man crippled from birth was being carried in. They would bring him every day and put him at the temple gate called "the Beautiful" to beg from the people as they entered. ³ When he saw Peter and John on their way in, he begged them for an alms. ⁴ Peter fixed his gaze on the man; so did John. "Look at us!" Peter said. ⁵ The cripple gave them his whole attention, hoping to get something. ⁶ Then Peter said: "I have neither silver nor gold, but what I have I give you! In the name of Jesus Christ the Nazorean, walk!" ⁷ Then Peter took him by the right hand and pulled him up. Immediately the beggar's feet and ankles became strong; ⁸ he jumped up, stood for a moment, then began to walk around. He went into the temple with them—walking, jumping about, and praising God. ⁹ When the people saw him moving and giving praise to God, ¹⁰ they recognized him as that beggar who used to sit at the Beautiful Gate of the temple. They were struck with astonishment—utterly stupefied at what had happened to him.

Peter's Discourse

¹¹ As the man stood there clinging to Peter and John, the whole crowd rushed over to them excitedly in Solomon's Portico. ¹² When Peter saw this, he addressed the people as follows: "Fellow Israelites, why does this surprise you? Why do you stare at us as if we had made this man walk by some power or holiness of our own? ¹³ The God of Abraham, of Isaac, and of Jacob, the God of our fathers, has glorified his Servant Jesus, whom you handed over and disowned in Pilate's presence when Pilate was ready to release him. ¹⁴ You disowned the Holy and Just One and preferred instead to be granted the release of a murderer. ¹⁵ You put to death the Author of life.

3, 7: 4, 10.
  8: Is 35, 6; Lk 7, 22.
  12: 14, 15.

14: Mt 27, 20; Mk 15, 11;
  Lk 23, 18; Jn 18, 40.

3, 6-10: The miracle has a dramatic cast; it symbolizes the saving power of Christ and leads the beggar to enter the temple, where he hears Peter's proclamation of salvation through Jesus.
3, 13: *Servant:* the Greek word can be rendered "son" or even "child" here and also in 3, 26; 4, 25 (applied to David); 4, 27-30. Scholars are of the opinion, however, that the original concept reflected in the word identified Jesus in the early apostolic preaching with the suffering Servant of the Lord of Is 52, 13—53, 12. *Has glorified:* through the resurrection and ascension of Jesus, God reversed the judgment against him on the occasion of his trial.
3, 14: *Holy and Just One:* a characterization of Jesus as Messiah, emphasizing his sinlessness and extraordinary religious dignity, which are placed in sharp contrast with the guilt of those who rejected him in favor of Barabbas; Mt 27, 15-23.
3, 15: *The Author of life:* the source of the messianic benefits for Israel.

But God raised him from the dead, and we are his witnesses. [16] It is his name, and trust in this name, that has strengthened the limbs of this man whom you see and know well. Such faith has given him perfect health, as all of you can observe.

[17] "Yet I know, my brothers, that you acted out of ignorance, just as your leaders did. [18] God has brought to fulfillment by this means what he announced long ago through all the prophets: that his Messiah would suffer. [19] Therefore, reform your lives! Turn to God, that your sins may be wiped away! [20] Thus may a season of refreshment be granted you by the Lord when he sends you Jesus, already designated as your Messiah. [21] Jesus must remain in heaven until the time of universal restoration which God spoke of long ago through his holy prophets. [22] For Moses said:

"'The Lord God will raise up for you a prophet like me from among your own kinsmen: you shall listen to him in everything he says to you. [23] Anyone who does not listen to that prophet shall be ruthlessly cut off from the people.'

[24] "Moreover, all the prophets who have spoken, from Samuel onward, have announced the events of these days. [25] You are the children of those prophets, you are the heirs of the covenant God made with your fathers when he said to Abraham, 'In your offspring, all the families of the earth shall be blessed.' [26] When God raised up his servant, he sent him to you first to bless you by turning you from your evil ways."

4

[1] While Peter and John were still addressing the crowd, the

---

16: 4, 10.
17: 13, 27; 1 Cor 2, 8.
18: Lk 18, 31.
22: 7, 37; Dt 18, 15.18.

25: Gn 12, 3; 22, 18; Sir 44, 19ff.
26: Gal 3, 8f.

3, 17: *You acted out of ignorance, just as your leaders did:* even those actually responsible for the execution of Jesus were unaware of his messianic dignity.

3, 18: *Through all the prophets:* Christian prophetic insight into the Old Testament saw the crucifixion and death of Jesus as the main burden of messianic prophecy. The Jews themselves did not anticipate a suffering Messiah; they usually understood the Servant Song in Is 52, 13—53, 12 to signify their own suffering as a people (as most Jews still do to the present day).

3, 20: *Thus may a season of refreshment be granted you:* an allusion to the parousia or second coming of Christ, judged to be imminent in the apostolic age. This reference to its nearness is the only explicit one in Acts; see note on 5, 1-11.

3, 22: A loose citation of Dt 18, 15, which teaches that the Israelites are to learn the will of Yahweh from no one but their prophets. At the time of Jesus the Jews expected a unique prophet to come in fulfillment of this text (Jn 1, 21; 6, 14; 7, 40). Early Christianity understood this tradition and text as applying to Jesus, and used them especially in defense of the divergence of Christian teaching from traditional Judaism.

priests, the captain of the temple guard, and the Sadducees came up to them, ² angry because they were teaching the people and proclaiming the resurrection of the dead in the person of Jesus. ³ It was evening by now, so they arrested them and put them in jail for the night. ⁴ Despite this, many of those who had heard the speech believed; the number of the men came to about five thousand.

Before the Sanhedrin

⁵ When the leaders, the elders, and the scribes assembled the next day in Jerusalem, ⁶ Annas the high priest, Caiaphas, John, Alexander, and all who were of the high-priestly class were there. ⁷ They brought Peter and John before them and began the interrogation in this fashion: "By what power or in whose name have men of your stripe done this?"

⁸ Then Peter, filled with the Holy Spirit, spoke up: "Leaders of the people! Elders! ⁹ If we must answer today for a good deed done to a cripple and explain how he was restored to health, ¹⁰ Then you and all the people of Israel must realize that it was done in the name of Jesus Christ the Nazorean whom you crucified and whom God raised from the dead. In the power of that name this man stands before you perfectly sound. ¹¹ This Jesus is 'the stone rejected by you the builders which has become the cornerstone.' ¹² There is no salvation in anyone else, for there is no other name in the whole world given to men by which we are to be saved."

¹³ Observing the self-assurance of Peter and John, and realizing that the speakers were uneducated men of no standing, the questioners were amazed. Then they recognized these men as having been with Jesus. ¹⁴ When they saw the man who had been cured standing there with them, they could think of nothing to say, ¹⁵ so they ordered them out of the court while they held a consultation. "What shall we do with these men? ¹⁶ Everyone who lives in Jerusalem knows what a remarkable show of power took place through them. We cannot deny it. ¹⁷ To stop

---

4, 2: 23, 6ff; 24, 21.
    8: Mt 10, 20.
    11: Ps 118, 22; Is 28, 16;

Mt 21, 42; Mk 12, 10;
Lk 20, 17; Rom 9, 33;
1 Pt 2, 7.

4, 1: *The priests, the captain of the temple guard, and the Sadducees:* the priests performed the temple liturgy. The officer of the temple, a Levite, was in charge of the temple guard. The Sadducees, a party within Judaism at this time, rejected those doctrines (among them bodily resurrection) which they believed alien to the ancient Mosaic religion. The Sadducees were drawn from priestly families and the lay aristocracy.
4, 11: Early Christianity applied this citation from Ps 118, 22 to Jesus; cf Mk 12, 10; 1 Pt 2, 7.

this from spreading further among the people we must give them a stern warning never to mention that man's name to anyone again." [18] So they called them back and made it clear that under no circumstances were they to speak the name of Jesus or teach about him. [19] Peter and John answered, "Judge for yourselves whether it is right in God's sight for us to obey you rather than God. [20] Surely we cannot help speaking of what we have heard and seen." [21] At that point they were dismissed with further warnings. The court could find no way to punish them because of the people, all of whom were praising God for what had happened. [22] The fact was, the man thus miraculously cured was more than forty years of age.

Thanksgiving

[23] After being released, the two went back to their own people and told them what the priests and elders had said. [24] All raised their voices in prayer to God on hearing the story: "Sovereign Lord, who made heaven and earth and sea and all that is in them, [25] You have said by the Holy Spirit through the lips of our father David your servant:

'Why did the Gentiles rage,
    the peoples conspire in folly?
[26] The kings of the earth were aligned,
    the princes gathered together
        against the Lord and against his anointed.'

[27] Indeed, they gathered in this very city against your holy Servant, Jesus, whom you anointed—Herod and Pontius Pilate in league with the Gentiles and the peoples of Israel. [28] They have brought about the very things which in your powerful providence you planned long ago. [29] But now, O Lord, look at the threats they are leveling against us. Grant to your servants, even as they speak your words, complete assurance [30] by stretching forth your hand in cures and signs and wonders to be worked in the name of Jesus, your holy Servant."

25: Ps 2, 1f.   27: Lk 23, 12.

4, 24-30: An example of the type of prayer common in the early Christian community. After invoking God as Creator (4, 24) it cites the messianic Psalm 2, 1f, much favored in early Christianity, to recall men's impotence against God's designs (4, 25f), as exemplified by the resurrection of Jesus, which frustrated the actions of Herod and Pilate against him (4, 27f). It then appeals to the members of the community for courage to proclaim the Christian kerygma in a hostile world and pleads for divine aid through the bestowal of the charism to perform physical cures (4, 29f).

4, 27: *Herod:* Herod Antipas, ruler of Galilee and Perea from 4 B. C. to 39 A. D., who executed John the Baptizer, and before whom Jesus was arraigned; cf Lk 23, 6-12.

[31] The place where they were gathered shook as they prayed. They were filled with the Holy Spirit and continued to speak God's word with confidence.

Life of the Christians

[32] The community of believers were of one heart and one mind. None of them ever claimed anything as his own; rather, everything was held in common. [33] With power the apostles bore witness to the resurrection of the Lord Jesus, and great respect was paid to them all; [34] nor was there anyone needy among them, for all who owned property or houses sold them and donated the proceeds. [35] They used to lay them at the feet of the apostles to be distributed to everyone according to his need.

[36] There was a certain Levite from Cyprus named Joseph, to whom the apostles gave the name Barnabas (meaning "son of encouragement"). [37] He sold a farm that he owned and made a donation of the money, laying it at the apostles' feet.

5

Ananias and Sapphira

[1] Another man named Ananias and his wife Sapphira likewise sold a piece of property. [2] With the connivance of his wife he put aside a part of the proceeds for himself; the rest he took

---

36f: Gal 2, 1.

4, 31: *The place . . . shook:* the earthquake is used as a sign of the divine presence in Ex 19, 18; Is 6, 4. Here the shaking of the building symbolizes God's favorable response to prayer. Luke may have had as an additional reason for using the symbol in this sense the fact that it was familiar to the Hellenistic world. Ovid and Virgil also employ it.

4, 32-37: This is a second summary characterization of the Jerusalem community (see note on 2, 42-47). It highlights the system on the distribution of goods, and introduces Barnabas, who figures later in Acts as the friend and companion of Paul, and who, as noted here (v 37), endeared himself to the community by a donation of money through the sale of property. Careful examination of Luke's statements on *everything in common* indicates that: (1) members of the community were free to dispose of their property or to retain it as they saw fit; (2) donation of property or of money accruing from its sale was not a condition of membership in the community; and (3) the holding of property *in common* meant that the poor of the community were cared for through the substantial donations of the wealthier members.

5, 1-11: The peculiarities latent in this narrative afford the basis of its proper interpretation. The harsh treatment meted out to Ananias (3f) does not accord with Luke's portrait of the love operative within the community; cf 2, 44-47. This harshness becomes even more painfully evident when Sapphira is not informed of her husband's death, or of the fact that their deceit has been discovered (7f); neither of them is given that opportunity for repentance which lies at the heart of the teaching of the Christian community (2, 38).

Their sin did not consist in the withholding of part of the money, even deceitfully, but in their deception of the community. The true nature of this deceit is revealed in the light of the early Christian expectation of the parousia; cf Acts 3, 20; 1 Thes 4, 13-17. Their gift supposedly symbolized

and laid at the feet of the apostles. ³ Peter exclaimed: "Ananias, why have you let Satan fill your heart so as to make you lie to the Holy Spirit and keep for yourself some of the proceeds from that field? ⁴ Was it not yours so long as it remained unsold? Even when you sold it, was not the money still yours? How could you ever concoct such a scheme? You have lied not to men but to God!" ⁵ At the sound of these words, Ananias fell dead. Great fear came upon all who later heard of it. ⁶ Some of the young men came forward, wrapped up the body, and carried it out for burial. ⁷ Three hours later Ananias' wife came in, unaware of what had happened. ⁸ Peter said to her, "Tell me, did you sell that piece of property for such and such an amount?" She answered, "Yes, that was the sum." ⁹ Peter replied, "How could you two scheme to put the Spirit of the Lord to the test? The footsteps of the men who have just buried your husband can be heard at the door. They stand ready to carry you out too." ¹⁰ At that, she fell dead at his feet. The young men came in found her dead, and carried her out for burial beside her husband. ¹¹ Great fear came on the whole church and on all who heard of it.

Signs and Wonders

¹² Through the hands of the apostles, many signs and wonders occurred among the people. By mutual agreement they used to meet in Solomon's Portico. ¹³ No one else dared to join them, despite the fact that the people held them in great esteem. ¹⁴ Nevertheless more and more believers, men and women in great numbers, were continually added to the Lord. ¹⁵ The people carried the sick into the streets and laid them on cots and mattresses, so that when Peter passed by at least his shadow might fall on one or another of them. ¹⁶ Crowds from the towns around Jerusalem would gather, too, bringing their sick and those who were troubled by unclean spirits, all of whom were cured.

Second Trial before the Sanhedrin

¹⁷ The high priest and all his supporters (that is, the party of the Sadducees), filled with jealousy, ¹⁸ arrested the apostles and

their complete confidence in the proximity of Christ's final coming, which rendered earthly possessions unimportant. (For a similar line of thought, cf 1 Cor 7, 29ff.) Their deaths are ascribed to a lie to the Holy Spirit (3-9), i. e., they accepted the honor accorded them by the community for their apparent faith in the proximate parousia, but in reality they were not deserving of it.

5, 12-6: This, the third summary portrait of the Jerusalem community, underscores the Twelve as its bulwark, especially because of their charismatic power to heal the sick; cf 2, 42-47; 4, 32-37.

5, 17-42: A second action against the community is taken by the Sanhedrin

threw them into the public jail. ¹⁹ During the night, however, an angel of the Lord opened the gates of the jail, led them forth, and said, ²⁰ "Go out now and take your place in the temple precincts and preach to the people all about this new life." ²¹ Accordingly they went into the temple at dawn and resumed their teachings.

When the high priest and his supporters arrived they convoked the Sanhedrin, the full council of the elders of Israel. They sent word to the jail that the prisoners were to be brought in. ²² But when the temple guard got to the jail they could not find them, ²³ and hurried back with the report, "We found the jail securely locked and the guards at their posts outside the gates, but when we opened it we found no one inside."

²⁴ On hearing this report, the captain of the temple guard and the high priests did not know what to make of the affair. ²⁵ Someone then came up to them, pointing out, "Look, there! Those men you put in jail are standing over there in the temple, teaching the people." ²⁶ At that, the captain went off with the guard and brought them in, but without any show of force, for fear of being stoned by the crowd. ²⁷ When they had led them in and made them stand before the Sanhedrin, the high priest began the interrogation in this way: ²⁸ "We gave you strict orders not to teach about that name, yet you have filled Jerusalem with your teaching and are determined to make us responsible for that man's blood." ²⁹ To this, Peter and the apostles replied: "Better for us to obey God than men! ³⁰ The God of our fathers has raised up Jesus whom you put to death, hanging him on a tree. ³¹ He whom God has exalted at his right hand as ruler and savior is to bring repentence to Israel and forgiveness of sins. ³² We testify to this. So too does the Holy Spirit, whom God has given to those that obey him."

³³ When the Sanhedrin heard this, they were stung to fury

5, 19: 12, 7-10; 16, 25f.   28: Mt 27, 25.

---

in the arrest and trial of the Twelve; cf 4, 1ff. The motive is the jealousy of the religious authorities over the popularity of the apostles (17), who are now charged with defiance of the Sanhedrin's previous order to them to abandon their prophetic role (28; cf 4, 18). In this crisis the apostles are favored by a miraculous release from prison (18-24). (For similar incidents involving Peter and Paul, cf 12, 6-11; 16, 25-29.) The real significance of such an event, however, would be manifest only to men of faith, not to unbelievers; since the Sanhedrin had already judged the Twelve to be unauthentic prophets, it could disregard reports of their miracles. When the Twelve immediately resumed public teaching, the Sanhedrin determined to invoke upon them the penalty of death (5, 33) prescribed in Dt 13, 6-10. Gamaliel's advice against this course finally prevailed, but it did not save the Twelve from the punishment of scourging (5, 40f), in a last endeavor to shake their conviction of their prophetic mission.

and wanted to kill them. [34] Then a member of the Sanhedrin stood up, a Pharisee named Gamaliel, a teacher of the law highly regarded by all the people. He had the accused ordered out of court for a few minutes, [35] and then said to the assembly, "Fellow Israelites, think twice about what you are going to do with these men. [36] Not long ago a certain Theudas came on the scene and tried to pass himself off as someone of importance. About four hundred men joined him. However he was killed, and all those who had been so easily convinced by him were disbanded. In the end it came to nothing. [37] Next came Judas the Galilean at the time of the census. He too built up quite a following, but likewise died, and all his followers were dispersed. [38] The present case is similar. My advice is that you have nothing to do with these men. Let them alone. If their purpose or activity is human in its origins, it will destroy itself. [39] If, on the other hand, it comes from God, you will not be able to destroy them without fighting God himself."

This speech persuaded them. [40] In spite of it, however, the Sanhedrin called in the apostles and had them whipped. They ordered them not to speak again about the name of Jesus, and afterward dismissed them. [41] The apostles for their part left the Sanhedrin full of joy that they had been judged worthy of ill-treatment for the sake of the Name. [42] Day after day, both in the temple and at home, they never stopped teaching and proclaiming the good news of Jesus the Messiah.

III: SPREAD OF THE CHURCH THROUGH PERSECUTION IN JERUSALEM

6

The Need of Assistants

[1] In those days, as the number of disciples grew, the ones who spoke Greek complained that their widows were being neglected in the daily distribution of food, as compared with the widows of those who spoke Hebrew. [2] The Twelve assembled the community of the disciples and said, "It is not right for us to neglect

---

34: 22, 3.   41: Mt 5, 10f.
40: Mt 10, 17.

6, 1-11: An example of the solution of conflicts within the Christian community. It is probable that the seven men assigned to this duty from among the Hellenist Christians, i. e., Jews from the diaspora, already possessed standing in the community as catechists, a role later ascribed to Stephen (8ff) and Philip (8, 5).

6, 2.4: The essential function of the Twelve is the "service of the word," i. e., development of the kerygma by formulation of the teachings of Jesus. This became the material that went into the formation of the gospels.

the word of God in order to wait on tables. [3] Look around among your own number, brothers, for seven men acknowledged to be deeply spiritual and prudent, and we shall appoint them to this task. [4] This will permit us to concentrate on prayer and the ministry of the word." [5] The proposal was unanimously accepted by the community. Following this they selected Stephen, a man filled with faith and the Holy Spirit; Philip, Prochorus, Nicanor, Timon, Parmenas, and Nicolaus of Antioch, who had been a convert to Judaism. [6] They presented these men to the apostles, who first prayed over them and then imposed hands on them.

[7] The word of God continued to spread, while at the same time the number of the disciples in Jerusalem enormously increased. There were many priests among those who embraced the faith.

Stephen Accused

[8] The Stephen already spoken of was a man filled with grace and power, who worked great wonders and signs among the people. [9] Certain members of the so-called "Synagogue of Roman Freedmen" (that is, the Jews from Cyrene, Alexandria, Cilicia and Asia) would undertake to engage Stephen in debate, [10] but they proved no match for the wisdom and spirit with which he spoke. [11] They persuaded some men to make the charge that they had heard him speaking blasphemies against Moses and God, [12] and in this way they incited the people, the elders, and the scribes. All together they confronted him, seized him, and led him off to the Sanhedrin. [13] There they brought in false wit-

---

6, 11: 21, 21.   14: Mt 26, 59ff.

6, 6: *They . . . imposed hands on them:* the customary Jewish way of designating a person for a task and invoking upon him the divine blessing and power to perform it.

6, 8—8, 1: The summary statement (6, 7) on the progress of the Jerusalem community, illustrated by the conversion of the priests, is followed by a lengthy narrative regarding Stephen. Stephen's defense is not a response to the charges made against him, but takes the form of a discourse that reviews the fortunes of God's word to Israel and leads to a prophetic declaration: a plea for the hearing of that word as announced by Christ and now possessed by the Christian community.

The charges that Stephen depreciated the importance of the temple and the Mosaic law and elevated Jesus to a stature above Moses (6, 13f) were in fact true. Before a non-Christian audience such as the Sanhedrin, no defense against them was possible. With Stephen, who thus perceived the fuller implications of the teaching of Jesus, the differences between Judaism and Christianity began to appear. Luke's account of Stephen's martyrdom and its aftermath shows how the major impetus behind the Christian movement passed from Jerusalem, where temple and law prevailed, to Antioch in Syria, where these influences were less pressing.

6, 13: *False witnesses:* here and in his account of Stephen's execution (7, 54-60), Luke parallels the martyrdom of Stephen with the death of Jesus.

nesses, who said: "This man never stops making statements against the holy place and the law. [14] We have heard him claim that Jesus the Nazorean will destroy this place and change the customs which Moses handed down to us." [15] The members of the Sanhedrin who sat there stared at him intently. Throughout, Stephen's face seemed like that of an angel.

7

Stephen's Discourse ·

[1] The high priest asked whether the charges were true. [2] To this Stephen replied: "My brothers! Fathers! Listen to me. The God of glory appeared to our father Abraham when he was still in Mesopotamia and before he settled in Haran. [3] God said to him, Leave your country and your kinsfolk, and go to the land I will show you. [4] So he left the land of the Chaldeans and settled in Haran. After his father died, God made him move from there to this land where you now dwell. [5] God did not give him any of it as his heritage, not even a foot of land, but he promised to give it to him and his descendants after him as a possession—although he had no child. [6] These are the words God used: Abraham's posterity will be strangers in a foreign land, and they will be subject to slavery and oppressed four hundred years. [7] But I will judge that nation which they serve, God said, and after that they will worship me in this place.

[8] "God then made a covenant of circumcision with him, and Abraham, who had become the father of Isaac, circumcised him on the eighth day. Isaac did the same for Jacob, and Jacob for the twelve patriarchs. [9] Out of envy, the patriarchs sold Joseph into slavery in Egypt, [10] but God was with him and rescued him from all his tribulations. He granted him favor and wisdom in

---

7, 3: Gn 12, 1.
5: Gn 12, 7; 15, 2.
6f: Gn 15, 13f.

8: Gn 17, 10; 21, 2ff.
9: Gn 37, 28.
10: Gn 41, 37; Ps 105, 21.

6, 14: *Will destroy this place and change the customs:* a possible indication that Stephen and other members of the community had begun to reflect upon the religious significance of Christ's prophecy concerning the destruction of the temple (Mk 13, 1f) and upon his attitude toward the law; cf Mk 2, 18—3, 6.

7, 2: *God . . . appeared to . . . Abraham . . . in Mesopotamia:* the first of a number of minor discrepancies between the data of the Old Testament and the data of Stephen's discourse. According to Gn 12, 1 God first spoke to Abraham in Haran. The main discrepancies are these: In 7, 16 it is said that Jacob was buried in Shechem, whereas Gn 50, 13 says he was buried at Hebron; in the same verse it is said that the tomb was purchased by Abraham, but in Gn 33, 19 and Jos 24, 32 the purchase is attributed to Jacob himself. The exactitude of detail achievable by modern scholarship was not a concern of ancient writers—who in any case were dealing with a variety of biblical and extra-biblical traditions.

the court of the Pharaoh, king of Egypt, and made him the governor of Egypt and of the Pharaoh's entire household. [11] When famine and great trial came upon Egypt and Canaan, our fathers could find no sustenance. [12] Hearing that there was grain in Egypt, Jacob sent our fathers there on a first mission. [13] The second time, Joseph made himself known to his brothers, and his family ties became known to the Pharaoh. [14] Then Joseph sent for his father Jacob, inviting him and all his kinsfolk—seventy-five persons in all. [15] Jacob went down to Egypt and died there, as did our fathers. [16] Their remains were transferred to Shechem and placed in the tomb which Abraham had bought with silver from the sons of Hamor at Shechem.

[17] "When the time drew near for the fulfillment of the Promise made by God to Abraham, our people in Egypt grew more and more numerous, [18] Until a new king came to power in Egypt, who knew not Joseph. [19] This one dealt craftily with our people and oppressed them. He forced our fathers to abandon their infants to exposure so that the people would not survive.

[20] "It was at this time that Moses was born. He proved to be an exceedingly handsome child. For the first three months he was reared in his father's house, [21] but afterward he was abandoned, and Pharaoh's daughter adopted him and brought him up as her own son. [22] Moses was educated in all the lore of Egypt. He was a man powerful in word and deed. [23] When he was forty, he decided to visit his kinsmen, the Israelites. [24] Upon seeing one of them maltreated, he went to his aid and avenged the victim by slaying the Egyptian. [25] He assumed that his kinsmen would understand that God was using him to bring them deliverance; but they did not. [26] He appeared the next day while some of them were fighting, and tried to reconcile them by saying: 'Friends, you are blood brothers. Why are you trying to hurt each other?' [27] At that, the man who was wronging his neighbor pushed Moses aside. 'And who has appointed you ruler and judge over us?' he said. [28] 'Are you thinking of killing me as you killed the Egyptian yesterday?' [29] On hearing this, Moses fled. He took up his residence as an alien in the land of Midian, where he became the father of two sons.

[30] "Forty years later an angel appeared to him in the desert near Mount Sinai in the flame of a burning thornbush. [31] When

---

12: Gn 42, 2.
13: Gn 45, 3.
15: Gn 49, 32.
16: Gn 23, 15f; 50, 13;
    Jos 24, 32.

17: Ex 1, 7.
20: Ex 2, 2f; Heb 11, 23.
24: Ex 2, 12.
26: Ex 2, 13.
30-34: Ex 3, 2-10.

Moses saw it, he marveled at the sight. As he drew near to
observe it carefully, the voice of the Lord was heard: [32] 'I am
the God of your fathers, the God of Abraham, of Isaac, and of
Jacob.' Moses began to tremble and dared look no more. [33] The
Lord said to him: 'Remove the sandals from your feet, for the
place where you stand is holy ground. [34] I have witnessed the
affliction of my people in Egypt and have heard the . groaning,
and I have come down to rescue them. Come now, I will send
you into Egypt.'

[35] "This very Moses whom they had rejected with the words,
'Who has appointed you ruler and judge?', was the one whom
God, through the angel appearing to him in the thornbush, sent
to be their ruler and deliverer. [36] It was he who led them forth,
all the while performing wonders and signs in the land of
Egypt, in the Red Sea, and for forty years in the desert. [37] This
Moses is the one who said to the Israelites, 'God will raise up
for you from among your kinsmen a prophet like me.' [38] In that
assembly, it was he who was in conversation with the angel on
Mount Siani and with our fathers; he too received the oracles
of life to pass on to you. [39] He it was whom our fathers would
not obey; rather, they thrust him aside and longed to return
to Egypt. [40] 'Make us gods that will be our leaders,' they said
to Aaron. 'As for that Moses who brought us out of the land of
Egypt, we have no idea what has happened to him.' [41] It was
then that they fashioned the calf and offered sacrifice to the
idol, and had a festive celebration over the product of their
own hands. [42] But God turned away from them and abandoned
them to the worship of the galaxies in the heavens. So we find
it written in the Book of the Prophets:

> 'Did you bring me sacrifices and offerings
>   for forty years in the desert, O house of Israel?
> [43] Not at all! You took along the tent of Moloch
>   and the star of the god Rephan,
>   the images you had made for your cult.
> For that I will exile you beyond Babylon.'

[44] "Our fathers in the desert had the meeting tent as God
prescribed it when he spoke to Moses, ordering him to make it
according to the pattern he had seen. [45] The next generation of
our fathers inherited it. Under Joshua, they brought it into the

---

37: Dt 18, 15.
38: Ex 19, 3.
40: Ex 32, 1.

42: Am 5, 25.
44: Ex 25, 40.
45: Jos 3, 14.

land during the conquest of those peoples whom God drove out to make room for our fathers. So it was until the time of David, [46] who found favor with God and begged that he might find a dwelling place for the house of Jacob. [47] It was Solomon, however, who constructed the building for that house. [48] Yet the Most High does not dwell in buildings made by human hands, for as the prophet says:

> [49] 'The heavens are my throne,
>   the earth is my footstool;
>   What kind of house can you build me?
>   asks the Lord.
>   What is my resting-place to be like?
>   [50] Did not my hand make all these things?'

Conclusion

[51] "You stiff-necked people, uncircumcised in heart and ears, you are always opposing the Holy Spirit just as your fathers did before you. [52] Was there ever any prophet whom your fathers did not persecute? In their day, they put to death those who foretold the coming of the Just One; now you in your turn have become his betrayers and murderers. [53] You who received the law through the ministry of angels have not observed it."

Stephen's Martyrdom

[54] Those who listened to his words were stung to the heart; they ground their teeth in anger at him. [55] Stephen meanwhile, filled with the Holy Spirit, looked to the sky above and saw the glory of God, and Jesus standing at God's right hand. [56] "Look!" he exclaimed, "I see an opening in the sky, and the Son of Man standing at God's right hand." [57] The onlookers were shouting aloud, holding their hands over their ears as they did so. Then they rushed at him as one man, [58] dragged him out of the city, and began to stone him. The witnesses meanwhile were piling their cloaks at the feet of a young man named Saul. [59] As Stephen was being stoned he could be heard praying,

---

46: Ps 132, 5.
47: 1 Kgs 6, 1; 1 Chr 17, 12.

48: 17, 24.
49: Is 66, 1.

7, 55: *Stephen . . . saw . . . Jesus standing at God's right hand:* whether this statement is intended to introduce the description of a vision, or is a dramatized version of Stephen's expression of faith in Christ, is of less importance than the meaning Luke attaches to it for his Christian reader. Stephen affirms to the Sanhedrin that the prophecy Jesus made before them has been fulfilled (Mk 14, 62).

7, 57: *Holding their hands over their ears:* Stephen's declaration, like that of Jesus, is a scandal to the court, which regards it as blasphemy.

7, 59f: Compare Lk 23, 34.46.

"Lord Jesus, receive my spirit." [60] He fell to his knees and cried out in a loud voice, "Lord, do not hold this sin against them." And with that he died.

8

The Church Persecuted

[1] Saul, for his part, concurred in the act of killing. That day saw the beginning of a great persecution of the church in Jerusalem. All except the apostles scattered throughout the countryside of Judea and Samaria. [2] Devout men buried Stephen, bewailing him loudly as they did so. [3] After that, Saul began to harass the church. He entered house after house, dragged men and women out, and threw them into jail.

IV: THE COMMUNITY CARRIES THE MESSAGE TO SAMARIA, SYRIA AND CYPRUS

Philip in Samaria

[4] The members of the church who had been dispersed went about preaching the word. [5] Philip, for example, went down to the town of Samaria and there proclaimed the Messiah. [6] Without exception, the crowds that heard Philip and saw the miracles he performed attended closely to what he had to say. [7] There were many who had unclean spirits, which came out shrieking loudly. Many others were paralytics or cripples, and these were cured. [8] The rejoicing in that town rose to fever pitch.

Simon Magus

[9] A certain man named Simon had been practicing magic in

8, 3: 9, 1f.   4: 11, 19.   5: 6, 5; 21, 8.

8, 1-40: Some idea of the severity of the persecution that now breaks out against the Jerusalem community can be gathered from Acts 22, 4 and 26, 9ff. Luke, however, concentrates on the fortunes of the word of God among men, indicating how the dispersal of the Jerusalem community resulted in the conversion of the Samaritans (8, 4-17.25). His narrative is further expanded to include the account of Philip's acceptance of a Gentile from Ethiopia (8, 26-39).

8, 1: *All except the apostles scattered:* this observation leads some modern scholars to conclude that the persecution was limited to the Hellenist Christians, and that the Judaeo-Christians were not molested. Whatever the facts, it appears that the Twelve took no public stand regarding Stephen's position, choosing, instead, to await the development of events.

8, 3: *Saul began to harass the church:* like Stephen, Saul was able to perceive that the Christian movement contained the seeds of serious doctrinal divergence from Judaism. A pupil of Gamaliel (22, 3), and totally dedicated to the law as the way of salvation (Gal 1, 13f), Saul accepted the task of crushing the Christian movement, at least insofar as it detracted from the importance of the temple and the law. His vehement opposition to Christianity reveals how difficult it was for a Jew of his time to accept a messianism that differed so greatly from the general expectation.

the town and holding the Samaritans spellbound. He passed himself off as someone of great importance. [10] People from every rank of society were paying attention to him. "He is the power of the great God," they said. [11] Those who followed him had been under the spell of his magic over a long period; [12] but once they began to believe in the good news that Philip preached about the kingdom of God and the name of Jesus Christ, men and women alike accepted baptism. [13] Even Simon believed. He was baptized like the rest and became a devoted follower of Philip. He watched the signs and the great miracles as they occurred, and was quite carried away.

[14] When the apostles in Jerusalem heard that Samaria had accepted the word of God, they sent Peter and John to them. [15] The two went down to these people and prayed that they might receive the Holy Spirit. [16] It had not as yet come down upon any of them since they had only been baptized in the name of the Lord Jesus. [17] The pair upon arriving imposed hands on them and they received the Holy Spirit. [18] Simon observed that it was through the laying on of hands that the apostles conferred the Spirit, and he made them an offer of money [19] with the request, "Give me that power too, so that if I place my hands on anyone he will receive the Holy Spirit."

[20] Peter said in answer: "May you and your money rot—thinking that God's gift can be bought! [21] You can have no portion or lot in this affair. Your heart is not steadfastly set on God. [22] Reform your evil ways. Pray that the Lord may pardon you for thinking the way you have. [23] I see you poisoned with gall and caught in the grip of sin." [24] Simon responded, "I need the prayers of all of you to the Lord, so that what you have just said may never happen to me."

[25] After giving their testimony and proclaiming the word of the Lord, they went back to Jerusalem bringing the good news to many villages of Samaria on the way.

Philip and the Ethiopian

[26] An angel of the Lord then addressed himself to Philip:

20: 13, 10.

8, 9-13. 18-24: Sorcerers were well known in the ancient world. Probably the incident involving Simon and his altercation with Peter is introduced to show that the miraculous charisms possessed by members of the Christian community (8, 6f) were not to be confused with the magic of sorcerers.

8, 25: Stephen's insistence that the presence of God was not confined to the temple in Jerusalem (7, 48f) is now fully accepted by the apostles as a result of the success of Philip in Samaria.

8, 26-40: In the account of the conversion of the Ethiopian eunuch, Luke adduces additional evidence to show that the spread of Christianity

"Head south toward the road which goes from Jerusalem to Gaza, the desert route." Philip began the journey. [27] It happened that an Ethiopian eunuch, a court official in charge of the entire treasury of Candace (a name meaning queen) of the Ethiopians, had come on a pilgrimage to Jerusalem and was returning home. [28] He was sitting in his carriage reading the prophet Isaiah. [29] The Spirit said to Philip, "Go and catch up with that carriage." [30] Philip ran ahead and heard the man reading the prophet Isaiah. He said to him, "Do you really grasp what you are reading?" [31] "How can I," the man replied, "unless someone explains it to me?" With that, he invited Philip to get in and sit down beside him. [32] This was the passage of Scripture he was reading:

> "Like a sheep he was led to the slaughter,
>   like a lamb before its shearer he was silent
>   and opened not his mouth.
> [33] In his humiliation he was deprived of justice,
> Who will speak of his posterity
>   for he is deprived of his life on earth?"

[34] The eunuch said to Philip, "Tell me, if you will, of whom the prophet says this—himself or someone else?" [35] Philip launched out with this Scripture passage as his starting point, telling him the good news of Jesus. [36] As they moved along the road they came to some water, and the Eunuch said, [37] "Look, there is some water right there. What is to keep me from being baptized?" [38] He ordered the carriage stopped, and Philip went down into the water with the eunuch and baptized him. [39] When they came out of the water, the Spirit of the Lord snatched Philip away and the eunuch saw him no more. Nevertheless the man went on his way rejoicing. [40] Philip found himself at Azotus next, and he went about announcing the good news in all the towns until he reached Caesarea.

27: Is 56, 3ff.   36: 10, 47.
32f: Is 53, 7f.

---

outside the confines of Judaism itself was in accord with the plan of God. He does not make clear whether the Ethiopian was originally a convert to Judaism or, as is more probable, a "God-fearer" (10, 1), i. e., one who accepted Jewish monotheism and ethic and attended the synagogue but did not consider himself bound by other regulations. The story of his conversion to Christianity is given a strong supernatural cast by the introduction of an angel (8, 26), instruction from the Holy Spirit (8, 29), and the strange removal of Philip from the scene (8, 38).
8, 30-34: Philip is brought alongside the carriage at the very moment when the Ethiopian is pondering the meaning of Is 53, 7f, a passage which Christianity, from its earliest origins, has understood of Jesus; cf note on 3, 13.

9

The Vocation of Saul

¹ Saul, still breathing murderous threats against the Lord's disciples, went to the high priest ² and asked him for letters to the synagogues in Damascus which would empower him to arrest and bring to Jerusalem anyone he might find, man or woman, living according to the new way. ³ As he traveled along and was approaching Damascus, a light from the sky suddenly flashed about him. ⁴ He fell to the ground and at the same time heard a voice saying, "Saul, Saul, why do you persecute me?" ⁵ "Who are you, sir?" he asked. The voice answered, "I am Jesus, the one you are persecuting. ⁶ Get up and go into the city, where you will be told what to do." ⁷ The men who were traveling with him stood there speechless. They had heard the voice but could see no one. ⁸ Saul got up from the ground unable to see, even though his eyes were open. They had to take him by the hand and lead him into Damascus. ⁹ For three days he continued blind, during which time he neither ate nor drank.

Saul's Baptism

¹⁰ There was a disciple in Damascus named Ananias to whom the Lord had appeared in a vision. "Ananias!" he said. "Here I am, Lord," came the answer. ¹¹ The Lord said to him, "Go at once to Straight Street, and at the house of Judas ask for a certain Saul of Tarsus. ¹² He is there praying." (Saul saw in a vision a man named Ananias coming to him and placing his hands on him so that he might recover his sight.) ¹³ But Ananias protested: "Lord, I have heard from many sources about this man and all the harm he has done to your holy people in

---

9, 1: Gal 1, 13f.   5: Mt 25, 40.
   3: 22, 6; 1 Cor 15, 8.

9, 1-19: This is the first of three accounts of Paul's conversion (see 22, 3-16 and 26, 2-18), with some differences of detail. Paul's experience was not visionary but was precipitated by the actual appearance of Jesus, as he insists in 1 Cor 15, 8. The words of Jesus, *"Saul, Saul, why do you persecute me?",* related by Luke with no variation in all three accounts, exerted a profound and lasting influence on the thought of Paul. Under the impulsion of this experience he gradually developed his understanding of justification by faith (see Epistles to Galatians and Romans), and of the identification of the Christian community with Jesus Christ; cf Col 1, 18.
9, 2: *The new way:* an early name for Christian discipleship; cf 16, 17; 18, 26; 19, 9.23; 24, 14.22. The term, no doubt Christian in origin, expresses the idea that Christian discipleship is the culmination of God's revelation to men and of men's relationship to God.
9, 8: *Unable to see:* a temporary blindness (9, 18), miraculous in origin, symbolizing the religious blindness of Saul as persecutor.

Jerusalem. [14] He is here now with authorization from the chief priests to arrest any who invoke your name." [15] The Lord said to him: "You must go! This man is the instrument I have chosen to bring my name to the Gentiles and their kings and to the people of Israel. [16] I myself shall indicate to him how much he will have to suffer for my name." [17] With that Ananias left. When he entered the house he laid his hands on Saul and said, "Saul, my brother, I have been sent by the Lord Jesus who appeared to you on the way here, to help you recover your sight and be filled with the Holy Spirit." [18] Immediately something like scales fell from his eyes and he regained his sight. He got up and was baptized, [19] and his strength returned to him after he had taken food.

Saul Preaches in Damascus

Saul stayed some time with the disciples in Damascus, [20] and soon began to proclaim in the synagogues that Jesus was the Son of God. [21] Any who heard it were greatly taken aback. They kept saying: "Isn't this the man who worked such havoc in Jerusalem among those who invoke this name? Did he not come here purposely to apprehend such people and bring them before the chief priests?"

[22] Saul for his part grew steadily more powerful, and reduced the Jewish community of Damascus to silence with his proofs that this Jesus was the Messiah.

Saul Visits Jerusalem

[23] After quite some time had passed, certain Jews conspired to kill Saul, [24] but their plot came to his attention. They went so far as to keep close watch on the city gates day and night in an attempt to do away with him. [25] Some of his disciples, therefore, took him along the wall one night and lowered him to

---

18: Tb 11, 12ff.   24f: 2 Cor 11, 32f.

9, 15: *To bring my name to the Gentiles:* only gradually was the significance of this prophecy realized by Paul as the church was compelled to turn its attention more and more to the Gentiles.

9, 19-30: This is a brief résumé of Paul's initial experience as an apostolic preacher, though that aspect of his career did not begin immediately upon his conversion (Gal 1, 17). At first he found himself in the position of being both a turncoat to the Jews and an enigma to the Christian community of Jerusalem. His acceptance by the latter was finally brought about through his friendship with Barnabas.

9, 20: *The Son of God:* to be understood in the sense of "the Christ" in 9, 22; cf Acts 13, 33 citing Ps 2, 7 in this sense. Perhaps Luke chooses this expression here because, for Paul and Christians generally, the title "Son of God" soon became the one most expressive of Jesus' true dignity; cf 1 Thes 1, 10; Rom 1, 2ff.

the ground, using ropes and a hamper. ²⁶ When he arrived back in Jerusalem he tried to join the disciples there; but it turned out that they were all afraid of him. They even refused to believe that he was a disciple. ²⁷ Then Barnabas took him in charge and introduced him to the apostles. He explained to them how on his journey Saul had seen the Lord, who had conversed with him, and how Saul had been speaking out fearlessly in the name of Jesus at Damascus. ²⁸ Saul stayed on with them, moving freely about Jerusalem and expressing himself quite openly in the name of the Lord. ²⁹ He even addressed the Greek-speaking Jews and debated with them. They for their part responded by trying to kill him. ³⁰ When the brothers learned of this, some of them took him down to Caesarea and sent him off to Tarsus.

The Church at Peace

³¹ Meanwile throughout all Judea, Galilee, and Samaria the church was at peace. It was being built up and was making steady progress in the fear of the Lord; at the same time it enjoyed the increased consolation of the Holy Spirit.

Peter Visits Lydda and Joppa

³² Once when Peter was making numerous journeys, he went —among other places—to God's holy people living in Lydda. ³³ There he found a man named Aeneas, a paralytic who had been bedridden for eight years. ³⁴ Peter said to him, "Aeneas, Jesus Christ cures you! Get up and make your bed." The man got up at once. ³⁵ All the inhabitants of Lydda and Sharon, upon seeing him, were converted to the Lord.

³⁶ Now in Joppa there was a certain woman convert named Tabitha (in Greek Dorcas, meaning a gazelle). Her life was marked by constant good deeds and acts of charity. ³⁷ At about that time she fell ill and died. They washed her body and laid it out in an upstairs room. ³⁸ Since Lydda was near Joppa, the disciples who had heard that Peter was there sent two men to him with the urgent request, "Please come over to us without delay." ³⁹ Peter set out with them as they asked. Upon his ar-

9, 31-43: In the context of the period of peace enjoyed by the community through the cessation of Paul's activities against it, Luke introduces two traditions concerning the miraculous powers of Peter. The towns of Lydda, Sharon and Joppa were populated by both Jews and Gentiles, and their Christian communities may well have been mixed. No particular motive for the cure of Aeneas is assigned, though it is not said that he was a Christian prior to the cure. The actual motive for the raising of Tabitha may have been the expectation of the parousia; in view of her unique charity, the community apparently found it hard to understand her death before this event had occurred.

rival they took him upstairs to the room. All the widows came to him in tears and showed him the various garments Dorcas had made when she was still with them. ⁴⁰ Peter first made everyone go outside; then he knelt down and prayed. Turning to the dead body, he said, "Tabitha, stand up." She opened her eyes, then looked at Peter and sat up. ⁴¹ He gave her his hand and helped her to her feet. The next thing he did was to call in those who were believers and the widows to show them that she was alive. ⁴² This became known all over Joppa, and because of it, many came to believe in the Lord. ⁴³ Thus it happened that Peter stayed on in Joppa for a considerable time at the house of Simon, a tanner of leather.

10

The Vision of Cornelius

¹ Now in Caesarea there was a centurion named Cornelius, of the Roman cohort Italica, who was religious and God-fearing. The same was true of his whole household. ² He was in the habit of giving generously to the people and he constantly prayed to God. ³ One afternoon at about three he had a vision in which he clearly saw a messenger of God coming toward him and calling, "Cornelius!" ⁴ He stared at the sight and said in fear, "What is it, sir?" The answer came: "Your prayers and your generosity have risen in God's sight, and because of them he has remembered you. ⁵ Send some men to Joppa and summon a certain Simon, known as Peter. ⁶ He is a guest of Simon the leather-tanner whose house stands by the sea." ⁷ When the messenger who spoke these words had disappeared, he called two servants and a devout soldier from among those whom he could trust. ⁸ He explained everything to them and dispatched them to Joppa.

Peter's Vision

⁹ About noontime the next day, as the men were traveling

9, 43: The fact that Peter lodged with a tanner would have been significant to both Gentile and Judaeo-Christians, for Judaism considered the tanning occupation unclean.

10, 1-48: The narrative centers on the conversion of Cornelius, a Gentile and a "God-fearer" (see note on 8, 26-40). Luke considers the event of great importance, as is evident from his long treatment of it. The incident is again related in 11, 1-18 and alluded to in 15, 7ff. The narrative divides itself easily into a series of distinct episodes, concluding with Peter's presentation of the Christian kerygma (34-43), and a pentecostal experience undergone by Cornelius' household preceding their reception of baptism (44-48).

10, 7: *A devout soldier:* by using this adjective Luke probably intends to classify him as a "God-fearer." The point is that Cornelius is careful to select a soldier who will respect his account of the apparition.

along and approaching the city, Peter went up to the roof terrace to pray. [10] He became hungry and asked for some food, and while it was being prepared he fell into a trance. [11] He saw the sky open and an object come down that looked like a big canvas. It was lowered to the ground by its four corners. [12] Inside it were all the earth's four-legged creatures and reptiles and birds of the sky. [13] A voice said to him: "Get up, Peter! Slaughter, then eat." [14] He answered: "Sir, it is unthinkable! I have never eaten anything unclean or impure in my life." [15] The voice was heard a second time: "What God has purified you are not to call unclean." [16] This happened three times; then the object was snatched up into the sky. [17] While Peter was trying to make out the meaning of the vision he had had, the men sent by Cornelius arrived at the gate asking for the house of Simon. [18] They called out to inquire whether Simon Peter was a guest there. [19] Peter was still pondering the vision when the Spirit said to him: "There are two men in search of you. [20] Go downstairs and set out with them unhesitatingly, for it is I who sent them." [21] Peter went down to the men and said, "I am the man you are looking for. What brought you here?" [22] They answered: "The centurion Cornelius, who is an upright and God-fearing man, well thought of in the whole Jewish community, has been instructed by a holy messenger to summon you to his house. There he is to hear what you have to say." [23] With that, Peter invited them in and treated them as guests.

Peter in Caesarea

The next day he went off with them, accompanied by some of the brothers from Joppa. [24] The following day, he arrived in Caesarea. Cornelius, who was expecting them, had called in his relatives and close friends. [25] As Peter entered, Cornelius went to meet him, dropped to his knees before him and bowed low. [26] Peter said as he helped him to his feet, "Get up! I am only a man myself." [27] Peter then went in, talking with him all

---

10, 15: Lv 11, 1-42. 22: Lk 7, 4f.

10, 9-16: The vision is intended to prepare Peter to share the food of Cornelius' household without qualms of conscience (10, 48). The necessity of such instruction to Peter reveals that at first not even the apostles fully grasped the implications of Jesus' teaching on the law. The initial insight belongs to Stephen.
10, 17-23: The arrival of the Gentile emissaries with their account of the angelic apparition illuminates Peter's vision: he is to be prepared to admit Gentiles into the Christian community.
10, 24ff: So impressed is Cornelius with the apparition that he invites close personal friends to support him in his confrontation with Peter. But his understanding of the personage he is about to meet is not devoid of superstition. For a similar experience of Paul and Barnabas, see 14, 10-17.

the while. ²⁸ He found many people assembled there, and he began speaking to them thus: "You must know that it is not proper for a Jew to associate with a Gentile or to have dealings with him. But God has made it clear to me that no one should call any man unclean or impure. ²⁹ That is why I have come in response to your summons without raising any objection. I should, of course, like to know why you summoned me." ³⁰ Cornelius replied: "Just three days ago at this very hour, namely three o'clock, I was praying at home when a man in dazzling robes stood before me. ³¹ 'Cornelius,' he said, 'your prayer has been heard and your generosity remembered in God's presence. ³² Send someone to Joppa to invite Simon known as Peter to come here. He is a guest in the house of Simon the leather-tanner, by the sea.' ³³ I sent for you immediately, and you have been kind enough to come. All of us stand before God at this moment to hear whatever directives the Lord has given you."

Peter's Discourse

³⁴ Peter proceeded to address them in these words: "I begin to see how true it is that God shows no partiality. ³⁵ Rather, the man of any nation who fears God and acts uprightly is acceptable to him. ³⁶ This is the message he has sent to the sons of Israel, the good news of peace proclaimed through Jesus Christ who is Lord of all. ³⁷ I take it you know what has been reported all over Judea about Jesus of Nazareth, beginning in Galilee with the baptism John preached; ³⁸ of the way God anointed him with the Holy Spirit and power. He went about doing good works and healing all who were in the grip of the devil, and God was with him. ³⁹ We are witnesses to all that

---

28: Gal 2, 12.15f.
34: Dt 10, 17; 2 Chr 19, 7;
    Jb 34, 19; Wis 6, 8;

Rom 2, 11; Gal 2, 6;
Eph 6, 9; 1 Pt 1, 17.
37: Lk 4, 14.

10, 28: Peter now fully understands the meaning of his vision; see note on 10, 17-23.

10, 34f: *God shows no partiality:* the revelation of his choice of Israel to be the people of God did not mean he withheld the divine favor from other men.

10, 37: *You know what has been reported all over Judea about Jesus of Nazareth:* God's revelation of his plan for the destiny of mankind through Israel culminated in Jesus of Nazareth. Consequently, the ministry of Jesus is an integral part of God's revelation. This viewpoint explains why the early Christian communities were interested in conserving the historical substance of the ministry of Jesus, a tradition leading to the production of the four gospels.

10, 39: *We are witnesses:* the apostolic testimony was not restricted to the resurrection of Jesus but also included his historical ministry. This witness, however, was theological in character: the Twelve, divinely mandated as prophets, were empowered to interpret his sayings and deeds in

he did in the land of the Jews and in Jerusalem. [40] They killed him, finally, hanging him on a tree, only to have God raise him up on the third day and grant that he be seen, [41] not by all, but only by such witnesses as had been chosen beforehand by God—by us who ate and drank with him after he rose from the dead. [42] He commissioned us to preach to the people and to bear witness that he is the one set apart by God as judge of the living and the dead. [43] To him all the prophets testify, saying that everyone who believes in him has forgiveness of sins through his name."

Baptism of Cornelius

[44] Peter had not finished these words when the Holy Spirit descended upon all who were listening to Peter's message. [45] The circumcised believers who had accompanied Peter were surprised that the gift of the Holy Spirit should have been poured out on the Gentiles also, [46] whom they could hear speaking in tongues and glorifying God. Peter put the question at that point: [47] "What can stop these people who have received the Holy Spirit, even as we have, from being baptized with water?" [48] So he gave orders that they be baptized in the name of Jesus Christ. After this was done, they asked him to stay with them for a few days.

11

The Call of the Gentiles Explained

[1] All through Judea the apostles and the brothers heard that Gentiles, too, had accepted the word of God. [2] As a result, when Peter went up to Jerusalem some among the circumcised took issue with him, [3] saying, "You entered the house of uncircumcised men and ate with them." [4] Peter then explained the whole

---

41: Lk 24, 41ff.   44f: 15, 8.

---

the light of his redemptive death and resurrection. The meaning of these words and deeds was to be made clear to the developing Christian community as the bearer of the word of salvation; cf 1, 21-26.

10, 42: *As judge of the living and the dead:* the apostolic preaching to the Jews appealed to their messianic hope, while the appeal to the Gentiles stressed the coming divine judgment; cf 1 Thes 1, 10.

11, 1-18: Scholars differ regarding the historical realities behind this narrative and Luke's purpose in utilizing them. Simply understood, the narrative indicates the following:

(1) The Judaeo-Christians of Jerusalem were scandalized to learn of Peter's sojourn in the house of the Gentile Cornelius; (2) nonetheless they had to accept the divine directions given to both Peter and Cornelius; (3) they concluded that the setting aside of the legal barriers between Jew and Gentile was an exceptional ordinance of God in this one case to indicate that the apostolic kerygma was also to be directed to the Gentiles. As yet, the Jerusalem Christians were unwilling to accept mixed communities.

affair to them step by step from the beginning: [5] "I was at prayer in the city of Joppa when, in a trance, I saw a vision. An object like a big canvas came down; it was lowered down to me from the sky by its four corners. [6] As I stared at it I could make out four-legged creatures of the earth, wild beasts and reptiles, and birds of the sky. [7] I listened as a voice said to me, 'Get up, Peter! Slaughter, then eat.' [8] I replied: 'Not for a moment, sir! Nothing unclean or impure has ever entered my mouth!' [9] A second time the voice from the heavens spoke out: 'What God has purified you are not to call unclean.' [10] This happened three times; then the canvas with everything in it was drawn up again into the sky.

[11] "Immediately after that, the three men who had been sent to me from Caesarea came to the house where we were staying. [12] The Spirit instructed me to accompany them without hesitation. These six brothers came along with me, and we entered the man's house. [13] He informed us that he had seen an angel standing in his house and that the angel had said: 'Send someone to Joppa and fetch Simon, known also as Peter. [14] In the light of what he will tell you, you shall be saved, and all your household.' [15] As I began to address them the Holy Spirit came upon them, just as it had upon us at the beginning. [16] Then I remembered what the Lord had said: 'John baptized with water but you will be baptized with the Holy Spirit.' [17] If God was giving them the same gift he gave us when we first believed in the Lord Jesus Christ, who was I to interfere with him?" [18] When they heard this they stopped objecting, and instead began to glorify God in these words: "If this be so, then God has granted life-giving repentance even to the Gentiles."

The Church Established at Antioch

[19] Those in the community who had been dispersed by the persecution that arose because of Stephen went as far as Phoenicia, Cyprus and Antioch, making the message known to none but Jews. [20] However, some men of Cyprus and Cyrene

---

11, 16: 1, 5; 19, 4; Mt 3, 11. 17: 15, 8f.

11, 12: *These six brothers:* companions from the Christian community of Joppa; cf 10, 23.
11, 19-26: The Judaeo-Christian antipathy to the mixed community was reflected by the early missioners generally. The few among them who entertained a different view succeeded in introducing Gentiles into the community at Antioch (in Syria). When the disconcerted Jerusalem community sent Barnabas to investigate, he was so favorably impressed by what he observed that he persuaded his friend Saul to participate in the Antioch experiment. The venture was successful; within a year, members of the mixed community in Antioch had acquired the new name of "Christians."

among them who had come to Antioch began to talk even to the Greeks, announcing the good news of the Lord Jesus to them. [21] The hand of the Lord was with them and a great number of them believed and were converted to the Lord. [22] News of this eventually reached the ears of the church in Jerusalem, resulting in Barnabas' being sent to Antioch. [23] On his arrival he rejoiced to see the evidence of God's favor. He encouraged them all to remain firm in their commitment to the Lord, [24] since he himself was a good man filled with the Holy Spirit and faith. Thereby large numbers were added to the Lord. [25] Then Barnabas went off to Tarsus to look for Saul; [26] once he had found him, he brought him back to Antioch. For a whole year they met with the church and instructed great numbers. It was in Antioch that the disciples were called Christians for the first time.

Prediction of Agabus

[27] At about that time, certain prophets came down from Jerusalem to Antioch. [28] One of them named Agabus was inspired to stand up and proclaim that there was going to be a severe famine all over the world. (It did in fact occur while Claudius was emperor.) [29] This made the disciples determine to set something aside, each according to his means, and send it to the relief of the brothers who lived in Judea. [30] They did this, dispatching it to the presbyters in the care of Barnabas and Saul.

12

Herod Persecutes the Church

[1] During that period, King Herod started to harass some of the members of the church. [2] He beheaded James the brother of

---

11, 27-30: It is not clear whether the prophets from Jerusalem came to Antioch to request help in view of the coming famine or whether they received this insight during their visit there. The former supposition seems more likely. Suetonius and Tacitus speak of famines during the reign of Claudius (A. D. 41-54), while the Jewish historian Josephus records a famine in Judea in A. D. 46-48. Luke is interested, rather, in showing the charity of the Antiochean community toward the Judaeo-Christians of Jerusalem despite their differences on mixed communities.

12, 1-19: Herod Agrippa ruled Judea A. D. 41-44. While Luke does not assign a motive for his execution of James and his intended execution of Peter, the broad background lies in Herod's policy of conciliating his Jewish subjects. The Judaeo-Christians had lost the popularity they had had in Jerusalem (2, 47), perhaps because of suspicions against them traceable to the teaching of Stephen. The account of Peter's escape derives from his subjective visionary experience, making him aware essentially of what was happening to him. Exactly how divine power effected the release is not possible to determine. The events related in this narrative are probably to be dated before the occurrence of the famine mentioned in 11, 27-30.

John, ³ and when he saw that this pleased certain of the Jews, he took Peter into custody too. During the feast of Unleavened Bread ⁴ he had him arrested and thrown into prison, with four squads of soldiers to guard him. Herod intended to bring him before the people after the Passover. ⁵ Peter was thus detained in prison, while the church prayed fervently to God on his behalf. ⁶ During the night before Herod was to bring him to trial, Peter was sleeping between two soldiers, fastened with double chains, while guards kept watch at the door. ⁷ Suddenly an angel of the Lord stood nearby and light shone in the cell. He tapped Peter on the side and woke him. "Hurry, get up!" he said. With that, the chains dropped from Peter's wrists. ⁸ The angel said, "Put on your belt and your sandals!" This he did. Then the angel told him, "Now put on your cloak and follow me."

⁹ Peter followed him out, but with no clear realization that this was taking place through the angel's help. The whole thing seemed to him a mirage. ¹⁰ They passed the first guard, then the second, and finally came to the iron gate leading out to the city, which opened for them of itself. They emerged and made their way down a narrow alley, when suddenly the angel left him. ¹¹ Peter had recovered his senses by this time, and said, "Now I know for certain that the Lord has sent his angel to rescue me from Herod's clutches and from all that the Jews hoped for."

¹² After coming to realize this, he went to the house of Mary the mother of John (also known as Mark), where many others were gathered in prayer. ¹³ Peter knocked at the door and a maid named Rhoda came to answer it. ¹⁴ On recognizing his voice she was so overjoyed that she did not stop to open the door, but ran in and announced that Peter was outside. ¹⁵ "You're out of your wits," they said to her, but she insisted it was true. All they could say was "It must be his angel." ¹⁶ Through all this, Peter kept on knocking. They finally opened the door and were astonished to see him. ¹⁷ He motioned to them to be quiet, and explained how the Lord had brought him out of prison. "Report this to James and the brothers," he said, then left them to go off to another place. ¹⁸ At daybreak confusion broke out among the soldiers, who did not know what had happened to

---

12, 17: *He . . . left them to go off to another place:* the conjecture that Peter left for Rome at this time has nothing to recommend it. His chief responsibility was still the leadership of the Judaeo-Christian communities in Palestine: Gal 2, 7. The concept of the great missionary effort of the church was yet to come; cf 13, 1ff.

Peter. [19] Herod then initiated a search for him. When it proved unsuccessful, he had the guards tried and executed. Shortly after this, Herod left Judea to spend some time in Caesarea.

Herod's Death

[20] Herod had long been infuriated by the people of Tyre and Sidon, who now by common consent came before him in his court. They won over his royal chamberlain Blastus and attempted to placate him, because their country was supplied with food from the king's territory. [21] On an appointed day Herod, arrayed in royal robes, took his seat on the rostrum and publicly addressed them. [22] The assembled crowd shouted back, "This is the voice of a god, not a man!" [23] The angel of the Lord struck Herod down at once because he did not ascribe the honor to God, and he died eaten by worms.

[24] Meanwhile the word of the Lord continued to spread and increase.

V: MISSION OF BARNABAS AND SAUL

[25] Barnabas and Saul returned to Jerusalem upon completing the relief mission, taking with them John Mark.

13

[1] There were in the church at Antioch certain prophets and teachers: Barnabas, Symeon known as Niger, Lucius of Cyrene, Manaen (who had been brought up with Herod the tetrarch), and Saul. [2] On one occasion, while they were engaged in the liturgy of the Lord and were fasting, the Holy Spirit spoke to them: "Set apart Barnabas and Saul for me to do the work for which I have called them." [3] Then, after they had fasted and prayed, they imposed hands on them and sent them off.

First Mission Begins in Cyprus

[4] These two, sent forth by the Holy Spirit, went down to the port of Seleucia and set sail from there for Cyprus. [5] On their

---

12, 20-23: Josephus gives a similar account of Herod's death. Early Christian tradition considered the manner of it to be a divine punishment upon his evil life. See 2 Kgs 19, 35 for the figure of *the angel of the Lord* in such a context.

13, 1ff: The impulse for the first missionary effort in Asia Minor is ascribed to the prophets of the Antiochean community, under the inspiration of the Holy Spirit. The thinking behind the mission was perhaps that if the Jews of the disaspora could be converted as successfully as had been the case at Antioch, the Jews of Palestine would eventually lose their hostility toward Christian messianism.

13, 4—14, 27: The key event in Luke's account of the first missionary journey is the experience of Paul and Barnabas at Pisidian Antioch (14-52).

arrival in Salamis they proclaimed the word of God in the Jewish synagogues, John accompanying them as an assistant. ⁶ They traveled over the whole island as far as Paphos, where they came across a Jewish magician named Bar-Jesus who posed as a prophet. ⁷ He was attached to the court of the proconsular governor Sergius Paulus, a man of intelligence who had summoned Barnabas and Saul and was anxious to hear the word of God. ⁸ But Elymas—"the magician," for that is what his name means—opposed them and sought to turn the governor away from the faith. ⁹ Saul (also known as Paul) was filled with the Holy Spirit; he stared at him ¹⁰ and exclaimed: "You are an impostor and a thoroughgoing fraud, you son of Satan and enemy of all that is right! Will you never stop trying to make crooked the straight paths of the Lord? ¹¹ The Lord's hand is upon you even now! For a time you shall be blind, unable so much as to see the sun." At once a misty darkness came over him, and he groped about for someone to lead him by the hand. ¹² When the governor saw what had happened, he believed, so impressed was he by the teaching about the Lord.

Arrival at Antioch in Pisidia

¹³ From Paphos, Paul and his companions put out to sea and sailed to Perga in Pamphylia. There John left them and returned to Jerusalem. ¹⁴ They continued to travel on from Perga and came to Antioch in Pisidia. On the sabbath day they entered the synagogue and sat down. ¹⁵ After the reading of the law and of the prophets, the leading men of the synagogue

---

The Christian kerygma proclaimed by Paul in the synagogue was favorably received. Some Jews and "God-fearers" were effectively converted (42f—see note on 8, 26-40), and the congregation at large asked the missionaries to speak again on the following sabbath. By that time, however, the appearance of a large number of Gentiles from the city had so disconcerted the Jews that they became hostile toward the apostles (44f). Thus the Jews of Pisidian Antioch proved no less opposed to the mixed community than the Judaeo-Christians of Jerusalem. As long as Paul refused to incorporate the Gentiles into Judaism as the condition for their acceptance of Christ, the Jews continued to regard Christian messianism as destructive of their religious traditions and their culture. This fear of theirs appears in all three accounts of Paul's missionary journeys in Acts, the Jews of Iconium (14, 1f) and Beroea (17, 11) being notable exceptions.

13, 6: *A Jewish magician named Bar-Jesus who posed as a prophet:* again Luke takes the opportunity to dissociate Christianity from the magical arts of the time (7-11); cf 8, 18-24.

13, 11f: The temporary blindness symbolized the falsity of the man's teaching.

13, 13: *There John left them:* it has been conjected that John Mark objected to Paul's ascendancy over his cousin Barnabas, but it is more likely that that rugged country and alien culture had made Mark homesick for Jerusalem; cf 12, 12.

sent this message to them: "Brothers, if you have any exhortation to address to the people, please speak up."

Preaching in the Synagogue

[16] So Paul arose, motioned to them for silence, and began: "Fellow Israelites and you others who reverence our God, listen to what I have to say! [17] The God of the people Israel once chose our fathers. He made this people great during their sojourn in the land of Egypt, and with an outstretched arm he led them out of it. [18] For forty years he put up with them in the desert: [19] then he destroyed seven nations in the land of Canaan to give them that country as their heritage [20] at the end of some four hundred and fifty years. Later on he set up judges to rule them until the time of the prophet Samuel. [21] When they asked for a king, God gave them Saul son of Kish, of the tribe of Benjamin, who ruled for forty years. [22] Then God removed him and raised up David as their king; on his behalf God testified, 'I have found David son of Jesse to be a man after my own heart who will fulfill my every wish.'

[23] "According to his promise, God has brought forth from this man's descendants Jesus, a savior for Israel. [24] John heralded the coming of Jesus by proclaiming a baptism of repentance to all the people of Israel. [25] As John's career was coming to an end, he would say, 'What you suppose me to be I am not. Rather, look for the one who comes after me. I am not worthy to unfasten the sandals on his feet.' [26] My brothers, children of the family of Abraham and you others who reverence our God, it was to us that this message of salvation was sent forth. [27] The inhabitants of Jerusalem and their rulers failed to recognize him, and in condemning him they fulfilled the words of the prophets which we read sabbath after sabbath. [28] Even though they found no charge against him which deserved death, they begged Pilate to have him executed. [29] Once they had thus brought about all that had been written of him, they took him down from the tree and laid him in a tomb. [30] Yet God raised him from the dead, [31] and for many days thereafter Jesus appeared

13, 17: Ex 1, 1.
18: Ex 16, 3.
19: Jos 14, 2.
20: Jgs 3, 9.
21: 1 Sm 8, 5; 9, 16; 10, 1.
22: 1 Sm 13, 14; 16, 13; Ps 89, 21.
23: Is 11, 1.
24: Mt 3, 1; Mk 1, 4;
Lk 3, 2f.

25: Mt 3, 11; Mk 1, 7;
Jn 1, 20.
28: Mt 27, 20.23;
Mk 15, 13; Lk 23, 21.23;
Jn 19, 15.
30: Mt 28, 8ff.16-20;
Mk 16, 9.12-20;
Lk 24, 15-53;
Jn 20, 14-29.

to those who had come up with him from Galilee to Jerusalem. These are his witnesses now before the people.

³² "We ourselves announce to you the good news that what God promised our fathers ³³ he has fulfilled for us, their children, in raising up Jesus, according to what is written in the second psalm, 'You are my son; this day I have begotten you.' ³⁴ As a proof that the one whom he raised from the dead would never again see the decay of death, God declared, 'I will give you the benefits assured to David under the covenant.' ³⁵ That is why he said in still another place, 'You will not suffer your faithful one to undergo corruption.' ³⁶ Now David, after he had spent a life-time in carrying out God's will, fell asleep and joined his fathers, thereby undergoing corruption. ³⁷ But the one whom God has raised up did not undergo corruption. ³⁸ You must realize, my brothers, that it is through him that the forgiveness of sins is being proclaimed to you, including the remission of all those charges you could never be acquitted of under the law of Moses. ³⁹ In him, every believer is acquitted. ⁴⁰ Have a care, then, lest what was said by the prophets be realized in you: ⁴¹ 'Look on in amazement, you cynics, then disappear! For I am doing a deed in your days which you never would have believed even if you had been told.' "

⁴² As they were leaving, the people invited them to speak on this subject again on the following sabbath. ⁴³ When the congregation finally broke up, many Jews and devout Jewish converts followed Paul and Barnabas, who spoke to them and urged them to hold fast to the grace of God.

Address to the Gentiles

⁴⁴ The following sabbath, almost the entire city gathered to hear the word of God. ⁴⁵ When the Jews saw the crowds, they became very jealous and countered with violent abuse whatever Paul said. ⁴⁶ Paul and Barnabas spoke out fearlessly, nonetheless: "The word of God has to be declared to you first of all;

33: Ps 2, 7.
34: Is 55, 3.
35: Ps 16, 10.

36: 1 Kgs 2, 10.
39: Rom 3, 20.
41: Heb 1, 5.

13, 31: *These are his witnesses now before the people:* the prophetic rule of the Twelve concerning Jesus; see note on 10, 39.
13, 38: *Including the remission of all those charges you could never be acquitted of under the law of Moses:* a doctrinal statement of justification by faith, particularly appropriate to Paul; see note on 9, 1-19.
13, 46: *Unworthy of everlasting life:* the refusal to believe frustrates God's plan for his chosen people; however no adverse judgment is made here concerning their ultimate destiny.

but since you reject it and thus convict yourselves as unworthy of everlasting life, we now turn to the Gentiles. [47] For thus were we instructed by the Lord: 'I have made you a light to the nations, a means of salvation to the ends of the earth.' " [48] The Gentiles were delighted when they heard this and responded to the word of the Lord with praise. All who were destined for life everlasting believed in it. [49] Thus the word of the Lord was carried throughout that area.

[50] But some of the Jews stirred up their influential women sympathizers and the leading men of the town, and in that way got a persecution started against Paul and Barnabas. The Jews finally expelled them from their territory. [51] So the two shook the dust from their feet in protest and went on to Iconium. [52] The disciples could not but be filled with joy and the Holy Spirit.

14

Preaching at Iconium

[1] In Iconium likewise, they entered the Jewish synagogue and spoke in such a way as to convince a good number of Jews and Greeks. [2] But the Jews who remained unconvinced stirred up the Gentiles and poisoned their minds against the brothers. [3] Paul and Barnabas spent considerable time there and spoke out fearlessly, in complete reliance on the Lord. He for his part confirmed the message with his grace and caused signs and wonders to be done at their hands. [4] Most of the townspeople were divided over them, some siding with the Jews and others with the apostles. [5] A move was made by Gentiles and Jews, together with their leaders, to abuse and stone them. [6] When Paul and Barnabas learned of this, they fled to the Lycaonian towns of Lystra and Derbe and to the surrounding country, [7] where they continued to proclaim the good news.

A Cure in Lystra

[8] At Lystra there was a man who was lame from birth; he used to sit crippled, never having walked in his life. [9] On one occasion he was listening to Paul preaching, and Paul looked

---

51: Mt 10, 14; Mk 6, 11;   14, 3: Mk 16, 17-20.
    Lk 9, 5.   5: 2 Tm 3, 11.

14, 8-17: In an effort to convince his hearers that the divine power works through his word, Paul cures the cripple. However, the pagan tradition of the occasional appearance of gods among men leads the people astray in interpreting the miracle. The incident reveals the cultural difficulties with which the church had to cope.

directly at him and saw that he had the faith to be saved. [10] He called out to him in a loud voice, "Stand up! On your feet!" The man jumped up and began to walk around. [11] When the crowds saw what Paul had done, they cried out in Lycaonian, "Gods have come to us in the form of men!" [12] They named Barnabas Zeus; Paul they called Hermes, since he was the spokesman. [13] Even the priest of the temple of Zeus, which stood outside the town, brought oxen and garlands to the gates because he wished to offer sacrifice to them with the crowds.

[14] When the apostles Barnabas and Paul heard of this, they tore their garments and rushed out into the crowd. [15] "Friends, why do you do this?" they shouted frantically. "We are only men, human like you. We are bringing you the good news that will convert you from just such follies as these to the living God, 'the one who made heaven and earth and the sea and all that is in them.' [16] In past ages he let the Gentiles go their way. [17] Yet in bestowing his benefits, he has not hidden himself completely, without a clue. From the heavens he sends down rain and rich harvests; your spirits he fills with food and delight." [18] Yet even with a speech such as this, they could scarcely stop the crowds from offering sacrifice to them.

End of the First Mission

[19] Just at that point, some Jews from Antioch and Iconium arrived and won the people over. They stoned Paul and dragged him out of the town, leaving him there for dead. [20] His disciples quickly formed a circle about him, and before long he got up and went back into the town. The next day he left with Barnabas for Derbe. [21] After they had proclaimed the good news in that town and made numerous disciples, they retraced their steps to Lystra and Iconium first, then to Antioch. [22] They gave their disciples reassurances, and encouraged them to persevere in the faith with this instruction: "We must undergo many trials if we are to enter into the reign of God." [23] In each church they installed presbyters and, with prayer and fasting, commended them to the Lord in whom they had put their faith.

11: 28, 6.
15: 3, 12; 10, 26.
17: Wis 13, 1.

19f: 2 Cor 11, 25;
2 Tm 3, 11.

14, 23: *In each church they installed presbyters:* the communities are given their own religious leaders. Seemingly (cf Jas 5, 14), a part of their task is the performance of liturgical rites, especially the liturgy of the Eucharist; cf 2, 42. Paul's caution in organizing the communities is shown by the fact that they receive presbyters only after a period of testing.

Return to Antioch

[24] Then they passed through Pisidia and came to Pamphylia. [25] After preaching the message in Perga, they went down to Attalia. [26] From there they sailed back to Antioch, where they had first been commended to the favor of God for the task they had now completed. [27] On their arrival, they called the congregation together and related all that God had helped them accomplish, and how he had opened the door of faith to the Gentiles. [28] Then they spent some time there with the disciples.

15

Council of Jerusalem

[1] Some men came down to Antioch from Judea and began to teach the brothers: "Unless you are circumcised according to Mosaic practice, you cannot be saved." [2] This created dissension and much controversy between them and Paul and Barnabas. Finally it was decided that Paul, Barnabas, and some others should go up to see the apostles and presbyters in Jerusalem about this question.

[3] The church saw them off and they made their way through Phoenicia and Samaria, telling everyone about the conversion of the Gentiles as they went. Their story caused great joy among the brothers. [4] When they arrived in Jerusalem they were welcomed by that church, as well as by the apostles and the presbyters, to whom they reported all that God had helped them accomplish. [5] Some of the converted Pharisees then got up and demanded that such Gentiles be circumcised and told to keep the Mosaic law.

[6] The apostles and the presbyters, accordingly convened to

25: 13, 1ff.
15, 1-4: Gal 2, 1-9.

1: Gal 5, 2.

14, 26: The report of the missioners to the church at Antioch was not wholly encouraging. The attempt to create mixed communities after the Antiochean model had been essentially a failure; cf 13, 46.50f; 14, 2.4f.19. On the other hand, the receptivity among the Gentiles offered hope for the future.

15, 1-5: When some of the converted Pharisees of Jerusalem discover the results of the first missionary journey of Paul, they conclude that their worst fears over the Antiochean experiment of the mixed community have been realized. They urge that the lesson to be learned from Paul's failure to convert the Jews of the diaspora is that the Gentiles must be taught to adopt the religious traditions of Judaism, for only in this way will it be possible for the Jews of the diaspora to form a common church with the Gentiles.

15, 6-12: This gathering is probably the same as that recalled by Paul in Gal 2, 1-10. Note that in 15, 2 it is only the apostles and presbyters, a small group, with whom Paul and Barnabas are to meet. Here Luke gives the meeting a public character because he wishes to emphasize its doctrinal significance for the entire world; cf v 22.

look into the matter. [7] After much discussion, Peter took the floor and said to them: "Brothers, you know well enough that from the early days God selected me from your number to be the one from whose lips the Gentiles would hear the message of the gospel and believe. [8] God, who reads the hearts of men, showed his approval by granting the Holy Spirit to them just as he did to us. [9] He made no distinction between them and us, but purified their hearts by means of faith also. [10] Why, then, do you put God to the test by trying to place on the shoulders of these converts a yoke which neither we nor our fathers were able to bear? [11] Our belief is rather that we are saved by the favor of the Lord Jesus and so are they." [12] At that the whole assembly fell silent. They listened to Barnabas and Paul as the two described all the signs and wonders God had worked among the Gentiles through them.

James on Dietary Law

[13] When they concluded their presentation, James spoke up: "Brothers, listen to me. [14] Symeon has told you how God first concerned himself with taking from among the Gentiles a people to bear his name. [15] The words of the prophets agree with this, where it says in Scripture, [16] 'Hereafter I will return and rebuild the fallen hut of David: from its ruins I will rebuild it and set it up again, [17] so that all the rest of mankind and all the nations that bear my name may seek out the Lord. [18] Thus says the Lord who accomplishes these things known to him from of old.' [19] It is my judgment, therefore, that we ought

---

7: 10, 20.
8: 10, 44-47.
10: Mt 23, 4; Gal 5, 1.

11: Gal 3, 11.
16: Am 9, 11f.
19: 21, 25.

15, 7ff: Paul's refusal to impose the Mosaic law on the Gentile Christians is supported by Peter on the ground that within his own experience God bestowed the Holy Spirit upon Cornelius and his household without preconditions concerning the adoption of the Mosaic law; cf 10, 44-47.

15, 10: A devout Jew considered the law a blessing. For the Christian, however, who understood that in his regard its observance was not a condition for receiving the divine benefits, such observance could be only a burden; cf Gal 4, 31.

15, 11: In support of Paul, Peter formulates the fundamental meaning of the gospel: that all mankind is invited to be saved through faith in the salvific power of Christ; personal observance of the divine law is man's necessary response to God's saving action, though not the cause of it.

15, 13-35: Some scholars think that this apostolic decree requested by James, the immediate leader of the Jerusalem community, derives from another historical occasion than the meeting in question. This seems to be the case if the meeting is the same as the one related in Galatians 2, 1-10. According to that account, nothing was imposed upon Gentile Christians in respect to Mosaic law; whereas the decree instructs Gentile Christians of mixed communities to abstain from meats offered to idols and from bloodmeats, and to avoid marriage within forbidden degrees of kindred (Lv 18), all of which practices were especially abhorrent to Jews.

15, 14: *Symeon:* Simon Peter; cf 15, 7.

not to cause God's Gentile converts any difficulties. ²⁰ We should merely write to them to abstain from anything contaminated by idols, from illicit sexual union, from the meat of strangled animals, and from eating blood. ²¹ After all, for generations now Moses has been proclaimed in every town and has been read aloud in the synagogues on every sabbath."

Letter of the Apostles

²² It was resolved by the apostles and the presbyters, in agreement with the whole Jerusalem church, that representatives be chosen from among their number and sent to Antioch along with Paul and Barnabas. Those chosen were leading men of the community, Judas, known as Barsabbas, and Silas. ²³ They were to deliver this letter:

"The apostles and presbyters, your brothers, send greetings to the brothers of Gentile origin in Antioch, Syria, and Cilicia. ²⁴ We have heard that some of our number without any instructions from us have upset you with their discussions and disturbed your peace of mind. ²⁵ Therefore we have unanimously resolved to choose representatives and send them to you, along with our beloved Barnabas and Paul, ²⁶ who have dedicated themselves to the cause of our Lord Jesus Christ. ²⁷ Those whom we are sending you are Judas and Silas, who will convey this message by word of mouth: ²⁸ 'It is the decision of the Holy Spirit, and ours too, not to lay on you any burden beyond that which is strictly necessary, ²⁹ namely, to abstain from meat sacrificed to idols, from blood, from the meat of strangled animals, and from illicit sexual union. You will be well advised to avoid these things. Farewell.' "

Delegates to Antioch

³⁰ Thus were the representatives sent on their way to Antioch; and upon their arrival there they called the assembly together to deliver the letter. ³¹ When it was read there was great delight at the encouragement it gave. ³² Judas and Silas, who were themselves prophets, strengthened the community and gave them reassurance in a long discourse. ³³ After passing some time there, they were sent back with greetings from the brothers to those who had commissioned them. ³⁵ Paul and Barnabas continued in Antioch, along with many others, teaching and preaching the word of the Lord.

35: 14, 28.

VI: PAUL'S MISSION TO THE GENTILES

Paul and Barnabas Separate

[36] After a certain time Paul said to Barnabas, "Let us go back now and see how the brothers are getting on in each of the towns where we proclaimed the word of the Lord." [37] Barnabas wanted to take along John, called Mark. [38] But Paul insisted that, as he had deserted them at Pamphylia, refusing to join them on that mission, he was not fit to be taken along now. [39] The disagreement which ensued was so sharp that the two separated. Barnabas took Mark along with him and sailed for Cyprus.

[40] Paul, for his part, chose Silas to accompany him on his journey, and in this he was commended by the brothers to the favor of the Lord. [41] He traveled throughout Syria and Cilicia, giving the churches there renewed assurance.

16

In Lycaonia: Timothy

[1] Paul arrived first at Derbe; next he came to Lystra, where there was a disciple named Timothy, whose mother was Jewish and a believer, and whose father was a Greek. [2] Since the brothers in Lystra and Iconium spoke highly of him, [3] Paul was anxious to have him come along on the journey. Paul had him circumcised because of the Jews of that region, for they all knew that it was only his father who was Greek. [4] As they made their way from town to town, they transmitted to the people for observance the decisions which the apostles and presbyters had made in Jerusalem.

38: 13, 13.
16, 1: 1 Tm 1, 2; 2 Tm 1, 5.
2: Heb 13, 23.

15, 34: Certain codices add: "But Silas decided to remain there"; however, the verse is omitted in the Greek manuscripts.

15, 36—18, 22: This continuous narrative recounts Paul's second missionary journey. On the internal evidence of the Lucan account it lasted about three years. Paul first visited the communities he had established on his first journey (16, 1-5), then pushed on into Macedonia, where he established communities at Philippi, Thessalonica and Beroea (16, 6—17, 15). To escape the hostility of the Jews of Thessalonica he left for Greece, and while resident in Athens attempted, without success, to establish an effective Christian community there. From Athens he proceeded to Corinth, and after a stay of a year and a half, returned to Antioch by way of Ephesus and Jerusalem (17, 16—18, 22). Luke's narrative is colorful and lively. He does not concern himself with the structure or statistics of the communities but aims to show the general progress of the gospel in the Gentile world, as well as its continued failure to take root in the Jewish community.

16, 3: *Paul had him circumcised:* in order that Timothy might be able to socialize with the Jews and so perform a ministry among them. Paul did not object to the Judaeo-Christians' adherence to the law out of custom, as was the case in Palestine. But he insisted that the law could not be imposed on the Gentiles. Paul himself lived in accordance with the law, or as exempt from the law, according to particular circumstances; cf 1 Cor 9, 19-23.

⁵ Through all this, the congregations grew stronger in faith and daily increased in numbers.

Through Asia Minor

⁶ They next traveled through Phrygia and Galatian territory because they had been prevented by the Holy Spirit from preaching the message in the province of Asia. ⁷ When they came to Mysia they tried to go on into Bithynia, but again the Spirit of Jesus would not allow them. ⁸ Crossing through Mysia instead, they came down to Troas. ⁹ There one night Paul had a vision. A man of Macedonia stood before him and invited him, "Come over to Macedonia and help us."

¹⁰ After this vision, we immediately made efforts to get across to Macedonia, concluding that God had summoned us to proclaim the good news there.

Into Europe

¹¹ We put out to sea from Troas and set a course straight for Samothrace, and the next day on to Neapolis; ¹² from there we went to Philippi, a leading city in the district of Macedonia and a Roman colony. We spent some time in that city. ¹³ Once, on the sabbath, we went outside the city gate to the bank of the river, where we thought there would be a place of prayer. We sat down and spoke to the women who were gathered there. ¹⁴ One who listened was a woman named Lydia, a dealer in purple goods from the town of Thyatira. She already reverenced God, and the Lord opened her heart to accept what Paul was saying. ¹⁵ After she and her household had been baptized, she extended us an invitation: "If you are convinced that I believe in the Lord, come and stay at my house." She managed to prevail on us.

Philippi: Imprisonment

¹⁶ It was while we were on our way out to the place of

16, 6: The prohibition may have come through one of Paul's companions endowed with a prophetic charism; cf 11, 27f.

16, 10-17: This is the first of the so-called "we-sections" in Acts, where Luke writes as one of Paul's companions. The other passages are 20, 5-15; 21, 1-18; 27, 1—28, 16. Scholars debate whether Luke may not have used the first person plural simply as a literary device to lend color to the narrative. It is more probable, however, that the "we" includes Luke or another companion of Paul whose data Luke used as a source.

16, 11-40: The church at Philippi became a sufficiently flourishing community for Paul to honor it with one of his letters. Judging, however, from Luke's account of Paul's vicissitudes in the city, his personal success was minimal. Evidently the community grew considerably after his departure and, as is clear from Paul's letter to them, he reserved his greatest affection for the Christians of Philippi.

prayer that we met a slave girl who had a clairvoyant spirit. She used to bring substantial profit to her masters by fortune-telling. [17] The girl began to follow Paul and the rest of us shouting, "These men are servants of the Most High God; they will make known to you a way of salvation." [18] She did this for several days until finally Paul became annoyed, and turned around, and said to the spirit, "In the name of Jesus Christ I command you, come out of her!" Then and there the spirit left her.

[19] When her masters saw that their source of profit was gone, they seized Paul and Silas and dragged them into the main square before the local authorities. [20] They turned them over to the magistrates with this complaint: "These men are agitators disturbing the peace of our city! Furthermore, they are Jews, [21] which means they advocate customs which are not lawful for us Romans to adopt or practice." [22] The crowd joined in the attack on them, and the magistrates stripped them and ordered them to be flogged. [23] After receiving many lashes they were thrown into prison, and the jailer was given instructions to guard them well. [24] Upon receipt of these instructions he put them in maximum security, going so far as to chain their feet to a stake.

The Earthquake

[25] About midnight, while Paul and Silas were praying and singing hymns to God as their fellow prisoners listened, [26] a severe earthquake suddenly shook the place, rocking the prison to its foundations. Immediately all the doors flew open and everyone's chains were pulled loose. [27] The jailer woke up to see the prison gates wide open. Thinking that the prisoners had escaped, he drew his sword to kill himself; [28] but Paul shouted to him: "Do not harm yourself! We are all still here." [29] The jailer called for a light, then rushed in and fell trembling at the feet of Paul and Silas. [30] After a brief interval he led them out and said, "Men, what must I do to be saved?" [31] Their

---

17: Mt 8, 29.   1 Thes 2, 2.
18: Mk 1, 25f.   26: 12, 6-11.
19: 19, 24-27.   27: 12, 18f; 27, 42.
22: 2 Cor 11, 25;

16, 22: Apparently the attack on Paul and Silas was so violent that they were unable to invoke their Roman citizenship to avoid the scourging; cf 16, 37f.

16, 25f: The earthquake seems to have been a visionary experience that accompanied the opening of the doors and the unfastening of the chains. It is otherwise difficult to see why the jailer was so impressed; cf 16, 27-34.

answer was, "Believe in the Lord Jesus and you will be saved, and all your household." [32] They proceeded to announce the word of God to him and to everyone in his house. [33] At that late hour of the night he took them in and bathed their wounds; then he and his whole household were baptized. [34] He led them up into his house, spread a table before them, and joyfully celebrated with his whole family his newfound faith in God.

Release from Prison

[35] When it was day, the magistrates dispatched officers with orders to let these men go. [36] The jailer conveyed this information to Paul: "The magistrates have sent orders that you are to be released. Get started, now. On your way!" [37] Paul's response to this was, "They flogged us in public without even a trial, then they threw us into jail, although we are Roman citizens! Now they want to smuggle us out in secret. Not a bit of it! Let them come into the prison and escort us out." [38] The officers reported this to the magistrates, who were immediately alarmed at hearing they were Roman citizens. [39] They came along and tried to quiet them; then they escorted them out with the request that they leave the city. [40] Once outside the prison, however, the two first made their way to Lydia's house, where they saw and encouraged the brothers; afterward they departed.

17

Problems at Thessalonica

[1] Paul and Silas took the road through Amphipolis and Apollonia and came to Thessalonica, where there was a Jewish synagogue. [2] Following his usual custom, Paul joined the people there and conducted discussions with them about the Scriptures for three sabbaths. [3] He explained many things, showing that the Messiah had to suffer and rise from the dead: "This Jesus I am telling you about is the Messiah!" [4] Some of the Jews were convinced and threw in their lot with Paul and Silas. So, too, did a great number of Greeks sympathetic to Judaism, and numerous prominent women.

[5] This only aroused the resentment of the Jews, however, who engaged loafers from the public square to form a mob and

---

37: 22, 25.
38: 22, 29.

17, 3: Lk 24, 25ff.46.
5: Rom 16, 21.

start a riot in the town. They marched on the house of Jason in an attempt to bring Paul and Silas before the people's assembly. [6] When they could not find them there, they dragged Jason himself and some of the brothers to the town magistrates, shouting: "These men have been creating a disturbance all over the place. Now they come here [7] and Jason has taken them in. To a man, they disregard the Emperor's decrees and claim instead that a certain Jesus is king." [8] In this way they stirred up the crowd. When the town's magistrates heard the whole story, [9] they released Jason and the others on bail.

Paul in Beroea

[10] As soon as it was night, the brothers sent Paul and Silas off to Beroea. On their arrival, they went to the Jewish synagogue. [11] Its members were better disposed than those in Thessalonica, and welcomed the message with great enthusiasm. Each day they studied the Scriptures to see whether these things were so. [12] Many of them came to believe, as did numerous influential Greek women and men. [13] But when the Jews of Thessalonica learned that the word of God had been proclaimed by Paul in Beroea also, they hurried there to cause a commotion and stir up the crowds. [14] The brothers sent Paul off directly on his way to the sea, while Silas and Timothy stayed behind. [15] Paul was taken as far as Athens by his escort, who then returned with instructions for Silas and Timothy to join him as soon as possible.

Paul at Athens

[16] While Paul was waiting for them in Athens, he grew exasperated at the sight of idols everywhere in the city. [17] In the synagogue he used to hold discussions with the Jews and those sympathetic to Judaism, as well as daily debates in the public square with ordinary passersby. [18] Epicurean and Stoic philosophers disputed with him, some of them asking, "What is this magpie trying to say to us?" Others commented, "He sounds like a promoter of foreign gods," because he was heard to speak of "Jesus" and "the resurrection." [19] They then led him off the Areopagus, saying, "We are curious to know what this new teaching is that you propose. [20] You are introducing subjects unfamiliar to us and we should like to know what it is

---

7: Lk 23, 2; Jn 19, 12-15. 14: 1 Thes 3, 2.
11: Jn 5, 39. 19: 1 Cor 1, 22.

17, 7: *A certain Jesus is king:* a distortion into a political sense of the apostolic proclamation of Jesus' religious kingship.

all about." [21] (Indeed, all Athenian citizens, as well as the foreigners who live there, love nothing more than to tell about or listen to something new.)

Paul's Discourse

[22] Then Paul stood up in the Areopagus and delivered his address: "Men of Athens, I note that in every respect you are scrupulously religious. [23] As I walked around looking at your shrines, I even discovered an altar inscribed, 'To a God Unknown.' Now, what you are thus worshiping in ignorance I intend to make known to you. [24] For the God who made the world and all that is in it, the Lord of heaven and earth, does not dwell in sanctuaries made by human hands; [25] nor does he receive man's service as if he were in need of it. Rather, it is he who gives to all life and breath and everything else. [26] From one stock he made every nation of mankind to dwell on the face of the earth. It is he who set limits to their epochs and fixed the boundaries of their regions. [27] They were to seek God, yes to grope for him and perhaps eventually to find him—though he is not really far from any one of us. [28] 'In him we live and move and have our being,' as some of your own poets have put it, 'for we too are his offspring.' [29] If we are in fact God's offspring, we ought not to think of divinity as something like a statue of gold or silver or stone, a product of man's genius and his art. [30] God may well have overlooked bygone periods when men did not know him; but now he calls on all men everywhere to reform their lives. [31] He has set the day on which he is going to 'judge the world with justice' through a man he has appointed—one whom he has endorsed in the sight of all by raising him from the dead."

24: 7, 48ff; Gn 1, 1;
    Is 42, 5.
27: Wis 13, 6; Rom 1, 19.

29: 19, 26; Is 40, 18f;
    Rom 1, 22f.

17, 20f: According to ancient writers the Athenians' interest in novel ideas was proverbial.

17, 22-31: Paul's discourse appeals to the Greek world's belief in divinity as responsible for the origin and existence of the universe. It contests the common belief in a multiplicity of gods supposedly exerting their powers through their images (idol-worship). It acknowledges (17, 27) that mankind's attempt to understand God is one of the most anxious of all its endeavors. It declares, further, that the divine being is the judge of mankind, and concludes by hinting that the apostle has information on the latter subject concerning a man whom God raised from the dead and who is to be judge of all men. The speech reflects sympathy with pagan religiosity, handles the subject of idol-worship gently, and appeals for a new examination of divinity, not from the standpoint of creation but from the standpoint of judgment. It is possible that Luke intends to show in the whole incident the difficulties of the learned men of the time in accepting the Christian message; cf 17, 32ff; 1 Cor 1, 26f.

[32] When they heard about the raising of the dead, some sneered, while others said, "We must hear you on this topic some other time." [33] At that point, Paul left them. [34] A few did join him, however, to become believers. Among these were Dionysius, a member of the court of Areopagus, a woman named Damaris, and a few others.

18

Paul Founds the Church in Corinth

[1] After that, Paul left Athens and went to Corinth. [2] There he found a Jew named Aquila, a native of Pontus recently arrived from Italy with his wife Priscilla. An edict of Claudius had ordered all Jews to leave Rome. Paul went to visit the pair, [3] whose trade he had in common with them. He took up lodgings with them and they worked together as tentmakers. [4] Every sabbath, in the synagogue, Paul led discussions in which he persuaded certain Jews and Greeks.

[5] When Silas and Timothy came down from Macedonia, Paul was absorbed in preaching and giving evidence to the Jews that Jesus was the Messiah. [6] When they opposed him and insulted him, he would shake out his garments in protest and say to them: "Your blood be on your own heads. I am not to blame! From now on, I will turn to the Gentiles."

[7] Later, Paul withdrew and went to the house of a Gentile named Titus Justus, who reverenced God; his house was next door to the synagogue. [8] A leading man of the synagogue, Crispus, along with his whole household, put his faith in the Lord. Many of the Corinthians, too, who heard Paul believed and were baptized. [9] One night in a vision the Lord said to Paul: "Do not be afraid. Go on speaking and do not be silenced, [10] for I am with you. No one will attack you or harm you. There are many of my people in this city." [11] Paul ended by settling there for a year and a half, teaching them the word of God.

Paul Accused before Gallio

[12] During Gallio's proconsulship in Achaia, the Jews rose in

18, 1: Rom 16, 3. 8: 1 Cor 1, 14.
6: Mt 27, 24f. 10: Jer 1, 8.
7: 13, 46f.51; 28, 28.

18, 2: *Aquila . . . with his wife Priscilla:* if this couple were not already Christians they soon became such; cf 18, 26. According to 1 Cor 16, 19 their home became a Christian meeting place.

a body against Paul and brought him before the bench. [13] "This fellow," they charged, "is influencing people to worship God in ways that are against the law." [14] Paul was about to sepak in self-defense when Gallio said to the Jews: "If it were a crime or a serious fraud, I would give you Jews a patient and reasonable hearing. [15] But since this is a dispute about terminology and titles and your own law, you must see to it yourselves. I refuse to judge such matters." [16] With that, he dismissed them from the court. [17] Then they all pounced on Sosthenes, a leading man of the synagogue, and beat him in full view of the bench; but Gallio paid no attention to it.

Return to Antioch

[18] Paul stayed on in Corinth for quite a while; but eventually he took leave of the brothers and sailed for Syria, in the company of Priscilla and Aquila. At the port of Cenchreae he shaved his head because of a vow he had taken. [19] When they landed at Ephesus, he left Priscilla and Aquila behind and entered the synagogue to hold discussions with the Jews. [20] They asked him to stay on longer but he declined. [21] As he said goodbye he gave them his promise, "God willing, I will come back to you again." Then he set sail from Ephesus. [22] On landing at Caesarea, he went up and paid his respects to the congregation, and then went down to Antioch.

[23] After spending some time there he set out again, traveling systematically through the Galatian country and Phrygia to reassure all his disciples.

The Orator Apollos

[24] A Jew named Apollos, a native of Alexandria and a man of eloquence, arrived by ship at Ephesus. He was both an

---

18: Nm 6, 18.   24: 1 Cor 1, 12.

18, 23—21, 16: Luke's account of Paul's third missionary journey devotes itself mainly to his work at Ephesus (19, 1—20, 1) and to his farewell address to the elders of this community (20, 17-35). Throughout the narrative runs a theme reflecting a certain restlessness and uneasiness on Paul's part. He has a growing conviction that the Spirit bids him return to Jerusalem and prepare to go to Rome (19, 21). He senses that imprisonment and suffering will be his lot in Jerusalem (20, 22f) and that he has paid his last visit to the Ephesian community (20, 25). Arriving at Tyre, on the Phoenician coast, he is warned by Christian prophets not to proceed to Jerusalem (21, 4). When he reaches Caesarea on the way to Jerusalem, another Christian prophet utters the same warning (21, 10f).

18, 24f: Apollos became a celebrated Christian preacher in the Corinthian community; 1 Cor 1, 12; 3, 5. He made use of the teaching of Jesus but placed it in the context of John's baptism of repentance. Since the teaching of Jesus was already known in an oral form to Apollos, it seems evident that the Christian communities likewise possessed this teaching.

authority on Scripture ²⁵ and instructed in the new way of the Lord. Apollos was a man full of spiritual fervor. He spoke and taught accurately about Jesus, although he knew only of John's baptism. ²⁶ He too began to express himself fearlessly in the synagogue. When Priscilla and Aquila heard him, they took him home and explained to him God's new way in greater detail. ²⁷ He wanted to go on to Achaia, and so the brothers encouraged him by writing the disciples there to welcome him. When he arrived, he greatly strengthened those who through God's favor had become believers. ²⁸ He was vigorous in his public refutation of the Jewish party as he went about establishing from the Scriptures that Jesus is the Messiah.

19

Paul in Ephesus

¹ While Apollos was in Corinth, Paul passed through the interior of the country and came to Ephesus. There he found some disciples ² to whom he put the question, "Did you receive the Holy Spirit when you became believers?" They answered, "We have not so much as heard that there is a Holy Spirit." ³ "Well, how were you baptized?" he persisted. They replied, "With the baptism of John." ⁴ Paul then explained, "John's baptism was a baptism of repentance. He used to tell the people about the one who would come after him in whom they were to believe—that is, Jesus." ⁵ When they heard this, they were baptized in the name of the Lord Jesus. ⁶ As Paul laid his hands on them, the Holy Spirit came down on them and they began to speak in tongues and to utter prophecies. ⁷ There were in the company about twelve men in all.

⁸ Paul entered the synagogue, and over a period of three months debated fearlessly, with persuasive arguments, about the kingdom of God. ⁹ When some in their obstinacy would not believe, but chose to speak ill of the new way in the presence of the assembly, Paul simply left them. He took his disciples with him, and after that held his discussions from day to day in the lecture hall of Tyrannus. ¹⁰ This continued for two years, with the result that all the inhabitants of the province of Asia, Jews and Greeks alike, heard the word of the Lord.

19, 4: 1, 5; 11, 16; 13, 24f;   6: 8, 15ff.
   Mt 3, 11.

19, 1-4: Upon his arrival in Ephesus Paul discovers other men at the same religious stage as Apollos, though they seem to have considered themselves followers of Christ, not of the Baptizer.
19, 6: A pentecostal experience at Ephesus.

[11] Meanwhile God worked extraordinary miracles at the hands of Paul. [12] When handkerchiefs or cloths which had touched his skin were applied to the sick, their diseases were cured and evil spirits departed from them.

The Jewish Exorcists

[13] Some itinerant Jewish exorcists once tried to invoke the name of the Lord Jesus over those who were possessed by evil spirits, saying, "I adjure you by the Jesus whom Paul preaches." [14] Another time, when the seven sons of Sceva, a Jewish high priest, were doing this, [15] the evil spirit answered, "Jesus I recognize, Paul I know; but who are you?" [16] Then the man with the evil spirit sprang at them and overpowered them all. He dealt with them so violently that they fled from his house naked and bruised. [17] When this became known to the Jews and Greeks living in Ephesus, fear fell upon all, and the name of the Lord Jesus came to be held in great reverence. [18] Many who had become believers came forward and openly confessed their former practices. [19] A number who had been dealing in magic even collected their books and burned them in public. When the value of these was assessed, it came to fifty thousand silver pieces.

[20] Thus did the word of the Lord continue to spread with influence and power.

Future Plans

[21] When all this was concluded, Paul made up his mind to travel through Macedonia and Achaia again, and then go on to Jerusalem. "Once I have been there," he said, "I must visit Rome too." [22] So he sent two of his assistants, Timothy and Erastus, into Macedonia ahead of him, while he himself stayed on for a time in Asia.

Riot of the Silversmiths

[23] At about that time a serious disturbance broke out concerning the new way. [24] There was a silversmith named Demetrius who made miniature shrines of Artemis and brought in no little work for his craftsmen. [25] He called a meeting of these men and other workers in the same craft. "Men," he said, "you know that our prosperity depends on this work. [26] But as you can see and hear for yourselves, not only at Ephesus but throughout most of the province of Asia, this Paul has per-

12: Lk 8, 44-47.   21: Rom 15, 22-32.

suaded great numbers of people to change their religion. He tells them that man-made gods are no gods at all. [27] The danger grows, not only that our trade will be discredited, but even that the temple of the great goddess Artemis will count for nothing. In fact, she whom Asia and all the world revere may soon be stripped of her magnificence."

[28] When they heard this speech, they were overcome with fury and began to shout, "Long live Artemis of Ephesus!" [29] Before long, confusion spread throughout the city. People rushed together to the theater and dragged in Gaius and Aristarchus, Paul's traveling companions from Macedonia. [30] Paul wanted to go before this gathering but his disciples would not let him. [31] Even some of the Asiarchs who were friends of Paul sent word to him advising him not to venture into the theater. [32] Meanwhile, various people were shouting all sorts of things, with the whole assembly in chaos and the majority not even knowing why they had come together. [33] Some brought out of the crowd Alexander, as the Jews pushed him forward. He motioned for silence, indicating that he wanted to explain something to the gathering. [34] But when they recognized that he was a Jew, they started to chant in unison, "Long live Artemis of Ephesus!" and kept shouting for about two hours.

[35] Finally the town clerk quieted the mob. "Citizens of Ephesus," he said, "what man is there who does not know that Ephesus is the custodian of the temple of the great Artemis, and of her image which fell from the sky? [36] Since this is beyond question, you must calm yourselves and not do anything rash. [37] These men whom you have brought here are not temple-robbers. They have not insulted our goddess. [38] If Demetrius and his fellow craftsmen want to bring charges against anyone, there are courts in session for that. There are proconsuls. Let the parties argue their case. [39] If there is any further matter you want to investigate, it ought to be settled in the lawful assembly. [40] As it is, we run the risk of being accused of rioting because of today's conduct. We have no valid excuse for this wild demonstration." These words of his broke up the meeting.

20

Paul Departs for Greece

[1] When the disturbance was over, Paul brought his disciples

---

27: 17, 29.   29: Col 4, 10.   20, 1: 1 Cor 16, 5.

together to encourage them. ² Then he said goodbye and set out on his journey to Macedonia. He traveled throughout its regions, providing as he went many words of encouragement for the Christians there. Finally he arrived in Greece, ³ where he stayed for three months. As he was on the point of embarking for Syria, a plot was hatched against him by certain Jews; so he decided to return by way of Macedonia.

Return to Troas

⁴ Accompanying him were Sopater, son of Pyrrhus, from Beroea; Aristarchus and Secundus from Thessalonica; Gaius from Derbe; Timothy; Tychicus and Trophimus from Asia. ⁵ These companions went on ahead and waited for us in Troas. ⁶ We ourselves set sail from Philippi as soon as the festival of Unleavened Bread was over. Five days later we joined them in Troas, where we spent a week.

Eutychus Restored to Life

⁷ On the first day of the week when we gathered for the breaking of the bread, Paul preached to them. Because he intended to leave the next day, he kept on speaking until midnight. ⁸ As it happened, there were many lamps in the upstairs room where we were assembled. ⁹ Paul talked on and on, and a certain young lad named Eutychus who was sitting on the windowsill became drowsier and drowsier. He finally went sound asleep, and fell from the third story to the ground. When they picked him up he was dead. ¹⁰ Paul hurried down immediately and threw himself on him, clutching the boy to himself. "Don't be alarmed!" he said to them. "There is life in him." ¹¹ Afterward Paul went upstairs again, broke bread, and ate. Then he talked for a long while—until his departure at dawn. ¹² To the great comfort of the people, they were able to take the boy away alive.

Journey to Miletus

¹³ We ourselves went on ahead to the ship and set sail for Assos, where we were to pick Paul up. This was the arrange-

---

4: Rom 16, 21.
5: 21, 29; 2 Tm 4, 20.
10: 1 Kgs 17, 17-24;

2 Kgs 4, 30-37;
Mk 5, 39.

20, 7:. *The first day of the week:* the day after the sabbath, apparently chosen originally by the Jerusalem community for the celebration of the liturgy of the Eucharist in order to relate it to the resurrection of Christ. Thus, in view of the sacramental presence of Christ in the Eucharist, the liturgy of the Eucharist was an anticipated parousia; cf 1 Cor 10, 16.

ment he had made, since his plan was to travel overland. [14] When he met us at Assos we took him aboard and sailed to Mitylene. [15] From there we took off the next day, and reached a point opposite Chios; on the second day we crossed to Samos, and on the day after that we put in at Miletus. [16] Paul had decided to sail past Ephesus so as not to lose time in Asia, for he was eager to get to Jerusalem by the feast of Pentecost if at all possible.

Address to the Miletus Presbyters

[17] Paul sent word from Miletus to Ephesus, summoning the presbyters of that church. [18] When they came to him he delivered this address: "You know how I lived among you from the first day I set foot in the province of Asia—[19] how I served the Lord in humility through the sorrows and trials that came my way from the plottings of certain Jews. [20] Never did I shrink from telling you what was for your own good, or from teaching you in public or in private. [21] With Jews and Greeks alike I insisted solemnly on repentance before God and on faith in our Lord Jesus. [22] But now, as you see, I am on my way to Jerusalem, compelled by the Spirit and not knowing what will happen to me there—[23] except that the Holy Spirit has been warning me from city to city that chains and hardships await me. [24] I put no value on my life if only I can finish my race and complete the service to which I have been assigned by the Lord Jesus, bearing witness to the gospel of God's grace. [25] I know as I speak these words that none of you among whom I went about preaching the kingdom will ever see my face again. [26] Therefore I solemnly declare this day that I take the blame for no man's conscience, [27] for I have never shrunk from announcing to you God's design in its entirety.

[28] "Keep watch over yourselves, and over the whole flock the Holy Spirit has given you to guard. Shepherd the church of

---

28: Jn 21, 15ff.

20, 16-35: Apparently Paul was aware of difficulties in the Christian communities at Ephesus and neighboring areas, and felt that he would be long detained if he undertook to deal with them himself. He determined to remind the presbyters of the communities of their responsibility, calling them together for this purpose at Miletus, about thirty miles from Ephesus. Paul's moving discourse reminds them of his apostolic activity in their area and stresses his total dedication to the gospel (18-21); it describes his reaction to his presentiment that he is about to suffer for the gospel (22-27), and admonishes them to guard their communities against the teaching of false prophets, who he feels sure will arise upon his departure (20ff). He concludes by citing a saying of Jesus (35) not recorded in the gospel tradition but known to them. To the extent that Luke may be responsible for the discourse in this form, he portrays Paul as the model leader of the Christian community.

God, which he has acquired at the price of his own blood. [29] I know that when I am gone, savage wolves will come among you who will not spare the flock. [30] From your own number, men will present themselves distorting the truth and leading astray any who follow them. [31] Be on guard, therefore. Do not forget that for three years, night and day, I never ceased warning you individually even to the point of tears. [32] I commend you now to the Lord, and to that gracious word of his which can enlarge you, and give you a share among all who are consecrated to him. [33] Never did I set my heart on anyone's silver or gold or envy the way he dressed. [34] You yourselves know that these hands of mine have served both my needs and those of my companions. [35] I have always pointed out to you that it is by such hard work that you must help the weak. You need to recall the words of the Lord Jesus himself, who said, 'There is more happiness in giving than receiving.' "

[36] After this discourse, Paul knelt down with them all and prayed. [37] They began to weep without restraint, throwing their arms around him and kissing him, [38] for they were deeply distressed to hear that they would never see his face again. Then they escorted him to the ship.

21

Arrival in Tyre

[1] When we had finally taken leave of them, we put out to sea and sailed straight to Cos. On the following day we came to Rhodes and went on from there to Patara. [2] When we found a ship bound for Phoenicia, we boarded it and sailed off. [3] We caught sight of Cyprus but passed it by on our left as we continued on toward Syria. Finally we put in at Tyre, where the ship had to unload cargo. [4] We looked for the disciples there and stayed with them for a week. Under the Spirit's prompting, they tried to tell Paul that he should not go up to Jerusalem; but to no purpose. [5] Then, when our time was up, we continued our journey. All of them—wives and children included—came out of the city to see us off, and we knelt down on the beach and prayed. After we had said goodbye to one another, [6] we boarded the ship and they returned home.

29: 1 Pt 5, 1ff.   2 Thes 3, 8.
30: Mt 7, 15; 2 Pt 2, 1f.   35: Sir 4, 31.
34: 1 Cor 4, 12;

At Ptolemais and Caesarea

⁷ Continuing our voyage from Tyre we put in at Ptolemais, where we greeted the brothers and spent the day with them. ⁸ The next day we pushed on and came to Caesarea. There we entered the home of Philip the evangelist, one of the Seven, with whom we stayed. ⁹ This man had four unmarried daughters gifted with prophecy. ¹⁰ During our few days' stay a prophet named Agabus arrived from Judea. ¹¹ He came up to us, and taking Paul's belt, tied his own hands and feet with it. Then he said, "Thus says the Holy Spirit: 'This is how the Jews in Jerusalem will bind the owner of this belt and hand him over to the Gentiles.' " ¹² Upon hearing this, both we ourselves and the people of Caesarea urged Paul not to proceed to Jerusalem. ¹³ He answered with a question: "Why are you crying and breaking my heart in this way? For the name of the Lord Jesus I am prepared, not only for imprisonment, but for death, in Jerusalem." ¹⁴ Since he would not be dissuaded, we said nothing further except, "The Lord's will be done."

VII: PAUL THE PRISONER BEARS WITNESS TO THE RESURRECTION

Paul and James in Jerusalem

¹⁵ At the conclusion of our stay, we got ready and started up toward Jerusalem. ¹⁶ Some of the disciples from Caesarea came along to escort us to the house of Mnason, a Cypriot and an early disciple, with whom we were to stay. ¹⁷ On our arrival in Jerusalem, the brothers there gave us a warm welcome. ¹⁸ The next day, Paul and the rest of us paid a visit to James in the presence of all the presbyters. ¹⁹ Paul first greeted them, and then described in detail all that God had accomplished among the Gentiles through his ministry. ²⁰ When they heard it they praised God, and said to Paul:

"You see, brother, how many thousands of Jews have come to believe, all of them staunch defenders of the law. ²¹ Yet

---

21, 8: 6, 5; 8, 4f.
11: 11, 27; 20, 23.

13: 9, 15f.
14: Mt 6, 10; Lk 22, 42.

21, 8: *One of the Seven:* see note on 6, 1-11.
21, 17-26: The leaders of the Judaeo-Christians of Jerusalem inform Paul that the Jews there believe he has encouraged the Jews of the diaspora to abandon the Mosaic law. In reality, Paul had no objection to the retention of the law, according to custom, by the Judaeo-Christians of Jerusalem, and left the Jews of the diaspora who accepted Christian messianism free to follow the same practice. Perhaps this misunderstanding of Paul's position was supported by the fact that some Judaeo-Christians of the diaspora had abandoned the law.

they have been informed that you teach the Jews who live among the Gentiles to abandon Moses, to give up the circumcision of their children, and to renounce their customs. ²² What are we to do about your coming, of which they are sure to hear? ²³ Please do as we tell you. There are four men among us who have made a vow. ²⁴ Take them along with you and join with them in their rite of purification; pay the fee for the shaving of their heads. In that way, everyone will know that there is nothing in what they have been told about you, but that you follow the law yourself with due observance. ²⁵ As for the Gentile converts we sent them a letter with our decision that they were merely to avoid meat sacrificed to idols, blood, the flesh of strangled animals, and illicit sexual union."

²⁶ Accordingly, Paul gathered the men together and went through the rite of purification with them the next day. Then he entered the temple precincts to give notice of the day when the period of purification would be over, at which time the offering was to be made for each of them.

Riot in the Temple

²⁷ The seven-day period was nearing completion when some Jews from the province of Asia recognized Paul in the temple precincts and began to stir up the whole crowd there. They seized him, ²⁸ shouting: "Fellow Israelites, help us! This is the man who is spreading his teaching everywhere against our people, our law, and this sanctuary. He has even brought Greeks into the temple area and thus profaned this sacred place." ²⁹ They had seen Trophimus, an Ephesian, with him in the city earlier, so they now assumed that Paul had brought him into the temple.

³⁰ Before long the whole city was in turmoil. People came running from all sides. They seized Paul, dragged him outside the temple, and immediately closed its gates. ³¹ Attempts were being made on his life when a report reached the commander of the cohort that all Jerusalem was rioting. ³² Immediately

---

24: 18, 18; Nm 6, 18.
25: 15, 19f.28f.

28: Rom 15, 31.

21, 23f: The leaders of the community suggest that Paul, on behalf of four members of the Jerusalem community, make the customary payment for the sacrifices offered at the termination of the nazirite vow; cf Nm 6, 1-21. Since Paul himself had once made this vow (18, 18), his respect for the law would be on public record.

21, 25: The allusion to the apostolic decree (15, 13-29) was probably introduced here by Luke to remind his readers that the Gentile Christians themselves were asked to respect certain Jewish practices deriving from the law. Paul was not being asked to violate his conscience.

the commander took his soldiers and centurions and charged down on the rioters. As soon as the crowd caught sight of him and the soldiers, they stopped assaulting Paul. [33] Then, when the commander arrived on the scene, he arrested Paul and had him bound with double irons. He tried to find out who he was and what he had been doing, [34] but different people in the crowd shouted out different answers.

The commander could not get at the truth because of the uproar, so he ordered Paul to be led away to headquarters. [35] When Paul reached the steps, he actually had to be carried up by the soldiers because of the violence of the mob. [36] A crowd of people was following along shouting, "Kill him! Kill him!" [37] Just as Paul was about to be led into the headquarters, he said to the commander, "May I say something to you?" "So you know Greek!" the commander exclaimed. [38] "Aren't you that Egyptian who caused the riot some time ago and led a band of four thousand cutthroats out into the desert?" [39] Paul replied, "I am a Jew, a citizen of Tarsus in Cilicia—no mean city; I beg you, let me address these people." [40] With his permission Paul then stood on the steps and motioned the people to silence. A great hush fell on them as he began to speak to them in Hebrew.

22

Discourse to the Crowd

[1] "My brothers and fathers, listen to what I have to say to you in my defense." [2] "When they heard him addressing them in Hebrew, they grew quieter still. He went on: [3] "I am a Jew, born in Tarsus in Cilicia, but I was brought up in this city. Here I sat at the feet of Gamaliel and was educated strictly in the law of our fathers. I was a staunch defender of God, just as all of you are today. [4] Furthermore I persecuted this new way to the point of death. I arrested and imprisoned both men and women.

[5] "On this point the high priest and the whole council of elders can bear me witness, for it was from them that I received letters to our brother Jews in Damascus. I set out with the intention of bringing the prisoners I would arrest back to Jeru-

---

Gal 1, 13f; Phil 3, 5f.   **22,** 3: 5, 34; 26, 4f;
4: 8, 3; 9, 2.   2 Cor 11, 22;

21, 40: *In Hebrew:* more precisely, "Aramaic," which at this time was the Semitic tongue in common use. This indicates that Paul's audience was principally composed of native-born Palestinian Jews.

salem for punishment. ⁶ As I was traveling along, approaching Damascus around noon, a great light from the sky suddenly flashed all about me. ⁷ I fell to the ground and heard a voice say to me, 'Saul, Saul, why do you persecute me?' ⁸ I answered, 'Who are you, sir?' He said to me, 'I am Jesus the Nazorean whom you are persecuting.' ⁹ My companions saw the light but did not hear the voice speaking to me. ¹⁰ 'What is it I must do, sir?' I asked, and the Lord replied, 'Get up and go into Damascus. There you will be told about everything you are destined to do.' ¹¹ But since I could not see because of the brilliance of the light, I had to be taken by the hand and led into Damascus by my companions.

¹² "A certain Ananias, a devout observer of the law and well spoken of by all the Jews who lived there, ¹³ came and stood by me. 'Saul, my brother,' he said, 'recover your sight.' In that instant I regained my sight and looked at him. ¹⁴ The next thing he said was, 'The God of our fathers long ago designated you to know his will, to look upon the Just One, and to hear the sound of his voice; ¹⁵ before all men you are to be his witness to what you have seen and heard. ¹⁶ Why delay, then? Be baptized at once and wash away your sins as you call upon his name.'

¹⁷ "Upon my return to Jerusalem I was praying in the court of the temple, where I fell into a trance ¹⁸ and saw Jesus speaking to me. 'You must make haste' he said. 'Leave Jerusalem at once because they will not accept your testimony about me.' ¹⁹ I answered: 'Lord, it is because they know that I imprisoned those who believed in you and flogged them in every synagogue. ²⁰ While the blood of your witness Stephen was being shed, I stood by and approved it. I even guarded the cloaks of those who killed him! ²¹ At that he said to me: 'Be on your way. I mean to send you far from here, among the Gentiles.'"

Paul Imprisoned

²² Up to this point in his speech the crowd had been listening to Paul, but now they began to shout, "Kill him! Rid the earth

---

20: 7, 58.   21: 9, 15.

22, 6-16: See note on 9, 1-19.
22, 21: Paul endeavors to explain that his position on the law has not been identical with that of his audience because it has been his prophetic mission to preach to the Gentiles, to whom the law was not addressed and who had no faith in it as a way of salvation.
22, 22: Paul's suggestion that his prophetic mission to the Gentiles did not involve his imposing the law on them provokes the same opposition as occurred in Pisidian Antioch (13, 45f).

of the likes of him! He isn't worthy to live!" [23] They yelled and waved their cloaks and flung dirt through the air. [24] At that display, the commander directed Paul to be brought inside the headquarters. He issued orders that he be examined under the lash to find out why they made such an outcry against him. [25] No sooner had they bound Paul than he said to the centurion who was standing by, "Is it legal to flog a Roman citizen without a trial?" [26] On hearing this, the centurion ran to the commander and demanded, "Do you realize what you are doing? This man is a Roman citizen!" [27] The commander rushed in and asked Paul, "Is it true? Are you a Roman citizen?" "I am," Paul answered. [28] The commander then observed, "It cost me quite a sum to get my citizenship." "Ah," said Paul, "but I am a citizen by birth!" [29] At these words, those who were about to interrogate him backed away. The commander became alarmed because he realized that in restraining Paul he had restrained a citizen of Rome.

Paul before the Sanhedrin

[30] The next day the commander released Paul from prison, intending to look carefully into the charge which the Jews were bringing against him. He summoned the chief priests and the whole Sanhedrin to a meeting; then he brought Paul down and made him stand before them.

23

[1] Paul gazed intently at the Sanhedrin. Then he said, "Brothers, to this day I have lived my life with a clear conscience before God." [2] At that, the high priest Ananias ordered his attendants to strike Paul on the mouth. [3] Paul said to him in rebuttal: "You are the one God will strike, you whitewashed wall! You sit there judging men according to the law, yet you violate the law yourself by ordering me to be struck!" [4] At this, the attendants protested, "How dare you insult God's high priest?" [5] Paul answered: "My brothers, I did not know that he was the high priest. Indeed, Scripture has it, 'You shall not curse a prince of your people!'"

[6] Paul, it should be noted, was aware that some of them were

---

3: Ez 13, 10-15; Mt 23, 27.

22, 25: A Roman citizen could not be punished unless legally condemned. The tribune considers it his duty to be assured that Paul is not a seditionist.
23, 5: This was probably not said in sarcasm. Paul withdraws the epithet *whitewashed wall* when he is reminded of the rule in Ex 22, 27.

Sadducees and some Pharisees. Consequently he spoke out before the Sanhedrin: "Brothers, I am a Pharisee and was born a Pharisee. I find myself on trial now because of my hope in the resurrection of the dead." [7] At these words, a dispute arose between Pharisees and Sadducees which divided the whole assembly. [8] (The Sadducees, of course, maintain that there is no resurrection and that there are neither angels nor spirits, while the Pharisees believe in all these things.) [9] A loud uproar ensued. Finally, some scribes of the Pharisee party arose and declared emphatically: "We do not find this man guilty of any crime. If a spirit or an angel has spoken to him. . . ." [10] At this, the dispute grew worse and the commander feared they would tear Paul to pieces. He therefore ordered his troops to go down and rescue Paul from their midst and take him back to headquarters. [11] That night the Lord appeared at Paul's side and said: "Keep up your courage! Just as you have given testimony to me here in Jerusalem, so must you do in Rome."

Transfer to Caesarea

[12] When it was day, certain Jews formed a conspiracy in which they bound themselves by oath not to eat or drink until they had killed Paul. [13] (There were more than forty of them who took the oath together.) [14] They then went to the chief priests and the elders and said: "We have bound ourselves by oath to touch no food until we kill Paul. [15] Now, together with the Sanhedrin, you must suggest to the commander that he have Paul brought down to you on the pretext that you would like to examine his case more carefully. We are prepared to kill him before he gets there." [16] The son of Paul's sister heard about the plot, and when he did so he came to headquarters. They allowed him to enter, and he told Paul about it. [17] Paul then called for one of the centurions, to whom he said, "Take this young man to the commander; he has something to report to him." [18] The centurion took him in charge and led him to the commander, with the explanation, "The prisoner Paul called me and asked me to bring you this boy, who has something to tell you." [19] The commander took him by the hand and drew him aside to ask privately, "What do you have to report?" [20] The boy replied: "The Jews have agreed among themselves to ask you tomorrow to have Paul brought down to the San-

---

6: Phil 3, 5.   8: Mt 22, 23.

23, 11: The occurrence of the vision of Christ suggests that Paul's experiences may have placed him in a state of depression.

hedrin, on the pretext that they want to question him more carefully. [21] But don't be fooled by them. More than forty of them are lying in wait; they have bound themselves by oath not to eat or drink until they kill him. They are all ready now, waiting only for your consent." [22] The commander sent the boy away with the order, "Don't tell anyone that you gave me this information."

[23] Then the commander summoned two of his centurions and said to them, "Get ready to leave for Caesarea by nine o'clock tonight, with two hundred infantrymen, seventy cavalrymen, and two hundred spearmen. [24] Also provide horses for Paul's journey, so that you may give him safe conduct to Felix the governor." [25] He then wrote the governor a letter to this effect:

[26] "Claudius Lysias sends greetings to His Excellency Felix, Governor. [27] Here is a man whom the Jews seized and were about to murder. When I learned that he was a Roman citizen, I intervened with my troops and rescued him. I then had him brought before the Sanhedrin, [28] hoping to determine what their charge against him was. [29] I subsequently discovered that he was accused in matters of their own law and was in no way guilty of anything deserving death or imprisonment. [30] When I later came to be informed of a plot against this man's life, I decided at once to send him to you. I have also instructed his accusers to take the matter up with you."

[31] According to their orders, the infantry took Paul and escorted him that night as far as Antipatris. [32] The next day they returned to headquarters, leaving it to the cavalry to go on with him. [33] When the cavalrymen arrived in Caesarea, they delivered the letter to the governor and brought Paul before him. [34] The governor, upon reading the letter, asked Paul what province he came from, only to learn he was from Cilicia. [35] "I shall hear your case," he said, "when your accusers arrive." Then he ordered Paul to be kept under guard in Herod's praetorium.

24

Trial before Felix

[1] Five days later, the high priest Ananias came down to

27: 21, 31ff.   29: 18, 15; 25, 18f.

23, 26-30: The letter emphasizes the fact that Paul is a Roman citizen and asserts the lack of evidence that he is guilty of a crime against the empire. The tone of the letter implies that the commander became initially involved in Paul's case because of his Roman citizenship, but this is not an exact description of what really happened; cf 21, 31-33; 22, 25ff.

Caesarea with some of the elders and an attorney named Tertullus. They presented their case against Paul to the governor. [2] Following Paul's summons to the bar, Tertullus began his prosecution by addressing Felix: "Your Excellency, through your efforts we enjoy great peace. Many improvements have been made in this nation through your provident care. [3] Therefore we must always and everywhere acknowledge our deep gratitude to you. [4] But now, lest I impose on your time unduly, I beg your indulgence for a brief hearing of our case. [5] We have found that this man is a troublemaker who stirs up sedition among the Jews all over the world. He is a ringleader of the sect of Nazoreans. [6] He even tired to desecrate our temple, but we apprehended him in time. [8] Feel free now to question him about all this and learn for yourself why we are accusing him." [9] The Jews supported this indictment and maintained that these were the facts.

[10] The governor then gestured to Paul, who replied as follows: "I know that you have been a judge over this nation for many years. I am thus encouraged to make my defense before you, [11] since you are in position to understand. Not more than twelve days have passed since I went to Jerusalem to worship there. [12] Neither in the temple area, nor in the synagogue, nor anywhere else in the city, did my accusers find me debating with anyone or inciting a mob. [13] They cannot substantiate the charges they are making against me. [14] I admit to you that it is according to the new way—which they call a sect—that I worship the God of our fathers. At the same time, I believe all that is written in the law and the prophets, [15] and I have the same hope in God as these men have that there is to be a resurrection of the good and the wicked alike. [16] In this regard I too always strive to keep my conscience clear before God and man.

[17] "After several years' absence, I had come to bring alms to my own people and to make my offerings. [18] That is what I was doing when they found me in the temple court completing the rites of purification without any crowd around me or any disturbance. [19] Certain Jews from the province of Asia are

---

24, 5: Lk 23, 2.
15: Jn 5, 29.

18: 21, 26.

24, 5f: The charges leveled against Paul accurately reflect the portrait formed of him among the Jews.
24, 6b-7: This portion is not found in the best Greek MSS.
24, 11ff: Whereas the lawyer Tertullus referred to Paul's activities on his missionary journeys, the apostle narrowed the charges down to the riot connected with the incident in the temple; cf 21, 27-30; 24, 17-20.

the ones who found me. These are the men who should be here before you to make whatever charge they have against me. ²⁰ Let those who are here declare what crime they found me guilty of when I stood before the Sanhedrin, ²¹ unless it was what I called out as I stood in their presence: 'I am on trial before you today because of the resurrection of the dead.'"

Captivity at Caesarea

²² Felix was rather well informed about the new way, and when he heard these words he adjourned the trial, saying merely, "I will decide the case when Lysias the commander arrives." ²³ He gave orders to the centurion that Paul was to be kept in custody but allowed some freedom, and that no one was to be prevented from seeing to his wants.

²⁴ A few days later Felix came with his Jewish wife Drusilla, and sent for Paul to hear him speak about faith in Christ Jesus. ²⁵ As Paul talked on about uprightness, continence, and the coming judgment, Felix became frightened. Before long he exclaimed: "That's enough for now! You can go. I'll send for you again when I find time." ²⁶ At the same time, he hoped he would be offered a bribe by Paul, so he used to send for him frequently to converse with him.

²⁷ Two years passed, following which Felix was succeeded by Porcius Festus. The latter wanted to ingratiate himself with the Jews, so he left Paul in prison.

25

Appeal to the Emperor

¹ Three days after Festus had arrived in the province, he went up from Caesarea to Jerusalem. ² There the Jewish chief priests and the leaders presented him with their case against Paul, ³ requesting that he favor them rather than Paul, and urging Festus to send him to Jerusalem. Their plot was to kill

---

21: 23, 6.

24, 22: *Rather well informed about the new way:* he probably had learned from talking to Christians that Christianity posed no threat to the empire. He may have kept Paul in custody simply to forestall fresh trouble in Jerusalem.
24, 24f: The way of Christian discipleship greatly disquiets Felix, who has entered into an adulterous marriage with Drusilla, daughter of Herod Agrippa I.
24, 26: As time passed Felix began to hope that Paul would be willing to leave the country under Roman protection, which he would be prepared to arrange in exchange for a bribe.
25, 2: Even after two years the animosity toward Paul in Jerusalem has not subsided; cf 24, 27.

him on the way. [4] But Festus answered that Paul was being kept in custody at Caesarea, and that he himself would be returning there soon. [5] "Your leading men can come down with me," he said, "and if this man is at fault, they can prosecute him there."

[6] After spending eight or ten days in Jerusalem, Festus went down to Caesarea. On the following day he took his seat on the bench and ordered Paul to be brought in. [7] When Paul appeared, the Jews who had come down from Jerusalem surrounded him and leveled many serious charges against him, none of which they were able to prove. [8] Paul's defense was, "I have committed no crime either against the law of the Jews or against the temple or against the emperor." [9] But Festus, wishing to please the Jewish people, asked Paul, "Are you willing to go up to Jerusalem and stand trial before me there on these charges?" [10] Paul answered: "I stand before the imperial bench; that is where I must be tried. I have done the Jews no wrong, as you yourself realize. [11] If I am guilty, if I have committed a crime deserving death, I do not seek to escape that penalty. But if there is nothing to the charges these men bring against me, no one has a right to hand me over to them. I appeal to the emperor!" [12] Thereupon Festus conferred with his council and finally declared: "You have appealed to the emperor. To the emperor you shall go."

Agrippa Invited To Hear Paul

[13] A few days later King Agrippa and Bernice arrived in Caesarea and paid Festus a courtesy call. [14] Since they were to spend several days there, Festus referred Paul's case to the king. There is a prisoner here," he said, "whom Felix left behind in custody. [15] While I was in Jerusalem the chief priests and the elders of the Jews presented their case against this man and demanded his condemnation. [16] I replied that it was not the Roman practice to hand an accused man over before he had been confronted with his accusers and given a chance to defend himself against their charges. [17] When they came here with me, I did not delay the matter. The very next day

25, 11f: Paul uses his right as a Roman citizen to appeal his case to the jurisdiction of the emperor (Nero, c 60 A. D.). This move broke the deadlock between Roman protective custody of Paul and the plan of his enemies to kill him; cf 25, 3.

25, 13: *King Agrippa and Bernice:* brother and sister, children of Herod Agrippa I whose activities against the Jerusalem community are mentioned in 12, 1-19. Agrippa was a petty ruler over small areas in northern Palestine and some villages in Perea.

I took my seat on the bench and ordered the man brought in. [18] His accusers surrounded him but they did not charge him with any of the crimes I expected. [19] Instead they differed with him over issues in their own religion, and about a certain Jesus who had died but who Paul claimed is alive. [20] Not knowing how to decide the case, I asked whether the prisoner was willing to go to Jerusalem and stand trial there on these charges. [21] Paul appealed to be kept here until there could be an imperial investigation of his case, so I issued orders that he be kept in custody until I could send him to the emperor."

[22] Agrippa said to Festus, "I too should like to hear this man." "Tomorrow you shall hear him," replied Festus. [23] So the next day Agrippa and Bernice came with great pomp and entered the audience chamber in the company of military officers and prominent men of the city. At Festus' command Paul was brought in. [24] The governor began to speak: "King Agrippa and all you who are here present with us, look at this man! The whole Jewish community, both here and in Jerusalem, has appealed to me about him, clamoring that he should live no more. [25] But I did not find that he had done anything deserving of death, so when he appealed to His Majesty the Emperor, I determined to send him on. [26] The trouble is, I have nothing definite to write about him to our sovereign. That is why I have brought him before all of you, and in particular before you, King Agrippa, that from this investigation I may have something to set down in his regard. [27] It seems to me a senseless procedure to send on a prisoner without indicating the charges against him."

26

Agrippa Hears Paul

[1] Agrippa now spoke to Paul: "You have permission to state your case." So Paul stretched out his hand and began his defense.

[2] "Many charges have been leveled against me by the Jews, King Agrippa. I count myself fortunate to be able to make my defense today in your presence, [3] especially since you are expert in all the various Jewish customs and disputes. I beg you to listen to me patiently.

25, 27: Festus' difficulty of lacking a charge against Paul from the Roman jurisdiction is not solved by Agrippa; cf 26, 31f. One solution open to the governor would have been a statement similar to Lysias's letter (23, 26-30) with the addition of Paul's appeal to the emperor.

⁴ "The way I have lived since my youth, and the life I have led among my own people from the beginning and later at Jerusalem, is well known to all Jews. ⁵ They have been acquainted with me for a long time and can testify, if they wish, to my life lived as a Pharisee, the strictest sect of our religion. ⁶ But today I stand trial because of my hope in the promise made by God to our fathers. ⁷ The twelve tribes of our people fervently worship God day and night in the hope that they will see that promise fulfilled. It is because of this hope, Your Majesty, that I stand accused by the Jews. ⁸ Let me ask why you, above all, who are Jews, should find it hard to believe that God raises dead men to life.

⁹ "For my part, I once thought it my duty to oppose the name of Jesus the Nazorean in every way possible. ¹⁰ That is just what I did in Jerusalem. With the authority I received from the chief priests, I sent many of God's holy people to prison. When they were to be put to death I cast my vote against them. ¹¹ Many a time, in synagogue after synagogue, I compelled them by force to blaspheme. Indeed, so wild was my fury against them that I pursued them even to foreign cities. ¹² "On one such occasion I was traveling toward Damascus armed with the authority and commission of the chief priests. ¹³ On this journey, Your Majesty, I saw a light more brilliant than the sun shining in the sky at midday. It surrounded me and those who were traveling with me. ¹⁴ All of us fell to the ground and I heard a voice saying to me in Hebrew, 'Saul, Saul, why do you persecute me? It is hard for you to kick against the goad.' ¹⁵ I said, at that, 'Who are you, sir?' and the Lord answered: 'I am that Jesus whom you are persecuting. ¹⁶ Get up now and stand on your feet. I have appeared to you to designate you as my servant and as a witness to what you have seen of me and what you will see of me. ¹⁷ I have delivered you from this people and from the nations, ¹⁸ to open the eyes of those to whom I am sending you, to turn them from darkness to light and from the dominion of Satan to God; that through their faith in me they may obtain the forgiveness of their sins and a portion among God's people.'

¹⁹ "King Agrippa, I could not disobey that heavenly vision. ²⁰ I preached a message of reform and of conversion to God, first to the people of Damascus, then to the people of Jerusalem

---

26, 5: Gal 1, 14.

26, 9-18: See note on 9, 1-19.

and all the country of Judea; yes, even to the Gentiles. I urged them to act in conformity with their change of heart. [21] That is why the Jews seized me in the temple court and tried to murder me. [22] But I have had God's help to this very day, and so I stand here to testify to great and small alike. Nothing that I say differs from what the prophets and Moses foretold: namely, [23] that the Messiah must suffer, and that, as the first to rise from the dead, he will proclaim light to our people and to the Gentiles."

Reactions to Paul's Speech

[24] As Paul went on defending himself in this way, Festus interrupted with a shout, "Paul, you are mad! And your great learning is driving me mad!" [25] "No, Your Excellency," answered Paul, "I am not mad. The message I proclaim is the sober truth. [26] The king here is well acquainted with these matters. Before him I can speak freely. I am convinced that none of this escapes him—after all, it did not take place in a dark corner! [27] Do you believe the prophets, King Agrippa? I am sure you do." [28] At this, Agrippa said, "A little more, Paul, and you will make a Christian out of me!" [29] Paul replied, "Whether little more or much more, I would to God that not only you but all who listen to me today might become what I am—without these chains!"

[30] Then the king rose, and with him the governor and Bernice and the rest of the company. [31] After they had left the chamber, they talked matters over among themselves and admitted, "This man is doing nothing that deserves death or imprisonment." [32] Agrippa further remarked to Festus, "He could have been set at liberty if he had not appealed to the emperor!"

27

Departure for Rome

[1] When it was decided that we were to sail for Italy, Paul and

21: 21, 31.
23: 1 Cor 15, 20-23.

29: 28, 20.

26, 31: In recording the episode of Paul's appearance before Agrippa, Luke wishes to show that when Paul's case was judged impartially, no grounds for legal action against him were found.

27, 1—28, 15: Here Luke has written a stirring account of adventure on the high seas, incidentally to his main purpose of showing how well Paul got along with his captors and how his prophetic influence ultimately saved the lives of all on board. The recital also establishes the existence of Christian communities in Puteoli and Rome.

some other prisoners were handed over to a centurion named Julius from the cohort known as Augusta. [2] We boarded a ship from Adramyttium bound for ports in the province of Asia, and set sail. With us was a Macedonian, Aristarchus of Thessalonica. [3] The following day we put in at Sidon, where Julius kindly allowed Paul to visit some friends who cared for his needs. [4] Then, putting out from Sidon, we sailed the sheltered side of Cyprus because of strong headwinds. [5] We crossed the open sea off the coast of Cilicia and Pamphylia, and came to Myra in Lycia.

Storm and Shipwreck

[6] There the centurion discovered an Alexandrian vessel bound for Italy, and he ordered us aboard. [7] For many days we made little headway, arriving at Cnidus only with difficulty. Since the winds would not permit us to continue our course, we sailed for Salmone and the shelter of Crete. [8] Again with difficulty we moved along the coast to a place called Fair Havens, near the town of Lasea.

[9] Much time had now gone by. The autumn fast was over, and with the lateness of the year sailing had become hazardous. It was then that Paul uttered this warning: [10] "Men, I can see that this voyage is bound to meet with disaster and heavy loss, not only to ship and cargo, but to our own lives as well." [11] However, the centurion preferred listening to the pilot and the shipowner to listening to Paul.

[12] Since the harbor was not fit to pass the winter in, the majority preferred to put out to sea in the hope of making Phoenix and spending the winter there. This was a Cretan port exposed on the southwest and the northwest. [13] When a gentle south wind began to blow, they thought they had what they were looking for, so they weighed anchor and proceeded, hugging the coast of Crete. [14] It was not long before a hurricane struck, the kind called a "northeaster." [15] Since the ship was caught up in it and could not head into the wind, we yielded and ran before it. [16] We passed under the lee of a small island named Cauda and only with difficulty were we able to gain control of the ship's boat. [17] They hoisted it aboard and then made use of cables to brace the ship itself. Because of their fear that they would be driven on the reef of Syrtis, they lowered the small anchor used for moving the ship and the ship was

---

27, 2: 2 Cor 11, 25.   9-44: Jon 1, 4-16.

carried along. ¹⁸ We were being pounded by the storm so violently that the next day some of the cargo was thrown over the side. ¹⁹ On the third day they deliberately threw even the ship's gear overboard. ²⁰ For many days neither the sun nor the stars were to be seen, so savagely did the storm rage. Toward, the end, we abandoned any hope of survival.

²¹ All hands had gone without food for a long time when Paul stood up among them and said: "Men you should have taken my advice and not set sail from Crete. Then you would not have incurred this disastrous loss. ²² I urge you now to keep up your courage. None among you will be lost—only the ship. ²³ Last night a messenger of the God whose man I am and whom I serve, stood by me. ²⁴ 'Do not be afraid, Paul,' he said. 'You are destined to appear before the emperor. Therefore, as a favor to you, God has granted safety to all who are sailing with you.' ²⁵ So keep up your courage, men. I trust in God that it will all work out just as I have been told, ²⁶ though we still have to face shipwreck on some island."

²⁷ It was the fourteenth night of the storm, and we were still being driven across the Ionian sea. When toward midnight the sailors began to suspect that land was near. ²⁸ They took a sounding and found a depth of twenty fathoms; after sailing on a short distance they again took a sounding and found it to be fifteen. ²⁹ For fear that we should be dashed against some rocky coast, they dropped four anchors from the stern and prayed for daylight. ³⁰ Then the sailors tried to abandon ship. Pretending that they were going to run out anchors from the bow of the ship, they let the ship's boat down into the sea. ³¹ Paul alerted the centurion and the soldiers to this: "If these men do not stay with the ship, you have no chance to survive." ³² At this, the soldiers cut the ropes and let the boat drift.

³³ At dawn Paul urged all on board to take some food: "For fourteen days you have been in constant suspense; you have gone hungry—eaten nothing. ³⁴ Now I urge you to take some food, which will give you strength to survive. Not one of you shall lose a hair of his head." ³⁵ When he had said this he took some bread, gave thanks to God before all of them, broke it, and began to eat. ³⁶ This gave them new courage, and they too had something to eat. ³⁷ (In all, there were two hundred and seventy-six of us on board.) ³⁸ When they had had enough to eat, they lightened the ship further by throwing the wheat overboard.

³⁹ With the coming of daylight, they did not recognize the land they saw. They could make out a bay with a sandy beach,

however, so they planned to run the ship aground on it if possible. [40] They cut loose the anchors and abandoned them to the sea. At the same time they untied the guy-ropes of the rudders, hoisted the foresail into the wind, and made for the beach; [41] but the ship hit a sandbar and ran aground. The bow stuck fast and could not be budged, while the stern was shattered by the pounding of the sea. [42] The soldiers thought at first of killing the prisoners so that none might swim away and escape; [43] but because the centurion was anxious to save Paul, he opposed their plan. Instead, he ordered those who could swim to jump overboard first and make for land. [44] The rest were to follow, on planks, or on other debris from the ship. In this way all came safely ashore.

28

Winter in Malta

[1] Once on shore, we learned that the island was called Malta. [2] The natives showed us extraordinary kindness by lighting a fire and gathering us all around it, for it had begun to rain and was growing cold. [3] Paul had just fed the fire with a bundle of brushwood he had collected, when a poisonous snake, escaping from the heat, fastened itself on his hand. [4] At the sight of the snake hanging from his hand, the natives said to one another, "This man must really be a murderer if, after his escape from the sea, Justice will not let him live." [5] But Paul shook the snake off into the fire and suffered no ill effects from the bite. [6] They expected to see him swell up or suddenly fall dead. After waiting for some time, however, and seeing nothing unusual happen to him, they changed their minds and began to say that he was a god.

[7] In the vicinity of that place was the estate of Publius, the chief figure on the island. He took us in and gave us kind hospitality for three days. [8] It happened that Publius' father was sick in bed, laid up with chronic fever and dysentery. Paul went in to see the man and, praying, laid his hands on him and cured him. [9] After this happened, the rest of the sick on the island began to come to Paul and they too were healed. [10] They paid us much honor, and when we eventually set sail they brought us provisions for our needs.

42: 16, 27.   28, 6: 14, 11.

Arrival in Rome

¹¹ Three months later we set sail in a ship which had passed the winter at the island. It was a Alexandrian vessel with the "Heavenly Twins" as its figurehead. ¹² We put in at Syracuse and spent three days there. ¹³ Then we sailed around the toe and arrived at Rhegium. A day later a south wind began to blow which enabled us to reach Puteoli in two days. ¹⁴ Here we found some of the brothers, who urged us to stay on with them for a week.

This is how we finally came to Rome. ¹⁵ Certain brothers from Rome who heard about us came out as far as the Forum of Appius and the Three Taverns to meet us. When Paul saw them, he thanked God and took fresh courage. ¹⁶ Upon our entry into Rome Paul was allowed to take a lodging of his own, although a soldier was assigned to keep guard over him.

Testimony to Roman Jews

¹⁷ Three days later Paul invited the prominent men of the Jewish community to visit him. When they had gathered he said: "My brothers, I have done nothing against our people or our ancestral customs; yet in Jerusalem I was handed over to the Romans as a prisoner. ¹⁸ The Romans tried my case and wanted to release me because they found nothing against me deserving of death. ¹⁹ When the Jews objected, I was forced to appeal to the emperor, though I had no cause to make accusations against my own people. ²⁰ This is the reason, then, why I have asked to see you and speak with you. I wear these chains solely because I share the hope of Israel."

²¹ They replied: "We have had no letters from Judea about you, nor have any of the brothers arrived with a report or rumor to your discredit. ²² For our part, we are anxious to hear you present your views. We know very well that this sect is denounced everywhere."

²³ With that, they arranged a day with him and came to his

19: 25, 11.　　　　　　　　23: 13, 15-41.
22: 24, 5.14.

28, 16: The mild form of custody in which Paul is detained reflects, perhaps, the arrangements made for him by Festus; cf 25, 27.
28, 17-22: Paul's first act in Rome is to learn from the leaders of the Jewish community whether the Jews of Jerusalem plan to pursue their case against him before the Roman jurisdiction. He is informed that no such plan is afoot, but that the Jews of Rome have heard the Christian teaching denounced. Paul's offer to explain it to them is readily accepted.
28, 23-28: Some critics of Acts have expressed doubt that these meetings between Paul and the leading Jews of Rome took place; they incline to the

lodgings in great numbers. From morning to evening he laid the case before them, bearing witness to the reign of God among men. He sought to convince them about Jesus by appealing to the law of Moses and the prophets. ²⁴ Some, indeed, were convinced by what he said; others would not believe.

²⁵ Without reaching any agreement among themselves, they began to leave. Then Paul added one final word: "The Holy Spirit stated it well when he said to your fathers through the prophet Isaiah:

²⁶ 'Go to this people and say:
You may listen carefully yet you will never
    understand;
    you may look intently yet you will never see.
²⁷ The heart of this people has grown sluggish.
They have scarcely used their ears to listen;
    their eyes they have closed,
Lest they should see with their eyes,
    hear with their ears,
    understand with their minds,
And repent;
    and I should have to heal them.'

²⁸ Now you must realize that this salvation of God has been transmitted to the Gentiles—who will heed it!"

Summary

³⁰ For two full years Paul stayed on in his rented lodgings, welcoming all who came to him. ³¹ With full assurance, and without any hindrance whatever, he preached the reign of God and taught about the Lord Jesus Christ.

26: Is 6, 9; Mt 13, 14;   Jn 12, 40; Rom 11, 8.
    Mk 4, 12; Lk 8, 10;

---

view that Luke here created ideal scenes to show the final separation between Judaism and Christianity. The scenes, however, are historically plausible: Paul would naturally have been concerned that the Christian community of Rome be not embarrassed by charges against it if he were brought to trial; while the Jews of Rome stood to gain from an explanation of the new doctrines by a trained rabbi. The citation from Isaiah is probably introduced by Luke, who uses the unbelief of Israel as typical of the difficulty men meet when confronted with the prophetic word of God.
28, 29: This verse is not found in the Greek manuscripts.
28, 30f: Many attempts have been made to explain what seems to be the abrupt ending of Luke's Acts of the Apostles. The author has Paul still in detention, though he intimates a bright outcome for his case. Perhaps the most satisfactory explanation is that Luke does not regard the subsequent missionary activity of Paul or his martyrdom as necessary for his acount of the origin and development of the church.

THE EPISTLE OF PAUL
TO THE ROMANS

INTRODUCTION

Christians in Rome seem to have become numerous first among the Jewish population of the city. The Roman historian Suetonius mentions an edict of the Emperor Claudius (died c 49 A.D.) ordering the expulsion of Jews from Rome in connection with a certain "Chrestus," probably an error for "Christus." According to Acts 18, 2, Aquila and Priscilla (or Prisca, as in this epistle) were affected by this edict; cf Rom 16, 3. Since neither early Christian tradition nor Paul's letter to the Romans mentions a founder of the Christian community in Rome, it may be concluded that the Christian faith came to that city through members of the Jewish community of Jerusalem who were Christian converts. About 57 A.D., when Paul wrote the letter, most probably from Corinth, Christians in Rome were predominantly Gentile, with a Judaeo-Christian minority, a circumstance which the majority of scholars see reflected in the letter itself.

At this time Paul was considering a missionary journey to Spain and desired to make Rome his headquarters for the project (15, 22f.28). He was informed about the Roman community (14, 1-11), perhaps by Aquila and Prisca, and it may be assumed that he in turn was known to the Christians there. It would be difficult to explain why he should have written this lengthy letter to them unless they were aware of his apostolic role and his whole remarkable history, and would receive his reflections with corresponding interest.

The principal theme of the letter is the relationship between Judaism and Christianity, a topic which Paul judged to be much in the minds of the Roman Christians. Each of these religious faiths claimed to be the way of salvation which established a covenant between God and man and made man the beneficiary of divine gifts. But Christianity regarded itself as the prophetic development and fulfillment of the faith of the Old Testament, declaring that the preparatory Mosaic covenant must now give way to the new and more perfect covenant in Jesus Christ. Paul himself had been the implacable advocate of freedom from the laws of the Mosaic covenant, and he refused to impose them on Gentile converts to Christianity. He had witnessed the personal hostilities that developed between the adherents of the two faiths, and had written his strongly worded letter to the Galatians against those Judaeo-Christians who were persuading Gentile Christian communities to adopt the religious practices of Judaism. For him, the purity of the religious understanding of Jesus as the source of salvation would be seriously impaired if Gentile Christians were obliged to amalgamate the two religious faiths.

Although Paul expressed his grief over Israel's failure to accept Christian messianism (9, 1-8), he remained unsympathetic toward both Jewish and Gentile unbelievers (2 Thes 1, 8ff). This need not seem startling if Paul in fact considered the parousia or second coming of Christ to be a distinct possibility in his own lifetime. His attitude would thus reflect the urgency of conversion and the imminence of the judgment of the world. See notes on 1 Thessalonians 4, 13-18, and on Mark 13, 1-37.

The implication of Paul's exposition of justification by faith rather than by the law is that the divine plan of salvation works itself out on a broad theological plane to include the whole of humanity despite the differences in the content of the given religious system to which a human culture is heir.

The Epistle to the Romans contains a powerful exposition of the doctrine of the supremacy of Christ and of faith in him as the source of salvation. It is an implicit plea to the Christians of Rome to hold fast to that faith. They are to resist any pressure put on them to accept a doctrine of salvation through works of the law. At the same time they are not to exaggerate Christian freedom through repudiation of law itself.

Romans is a well-constructed epistle. It is divided as follows:

THE EPISTLE OF PAUL
TO THE ROMANS

I: INTRODUCTION

1

Greetings

¹ Greetings from Paul, a servant of Christ Jesus, called to be an apostle and set apart to proclaim the gospel of God ² which he promised long ago through his prophets, as the holy Scriptures record—³ the gospel concerning his Son, who was descended from David according to the flesh ⁴ but was made Son of God in power according to the spirit of holiness, by his resurrection from the dead: Jesus Christ our Lord. ⁵ Through him we have been favored with apostleship, that we may spread his name and bring to obedient faith all the Gentiles, ⁶ among whom are you who have been called to belong to Jesus Christ.

⁷ To all in Rome, beloved of God and called to holiness, grace and peace from God our Father and the Lord Jesus Christ.

Paul and the Romans

⁸ First of all, I give thanks to my God through Jesus Christ for all of you because your faith is heralded throughout the world. ⁹ The God I worship in the spirit by preaching the gospel of his Son will bear witness that I constantly mention you in prayer, ¹⁰ always pleading that somehow by God's will I may at last find my way clear to visit you. ¹¹ For I long to see you and share with you some spiritual gift to strenghten you— ¹² rather, what I wish is that we may be mutually encouraged by our common faith. ¹³ My brothers, I want you to know that I have often planned to visit you (though up to now I have been kept from it) in order to do some fruitful work among you, as I have among the other Gentiles. ¹⁴ I am under obligation to Greeks and non-Greeks, to learned and unintelligent alike.

1, 1: Gal 1, 15.
3: Rv 22, 16.
4: 10, 9.

8: 16, 19; 1 Thes 1, 8.
10: 1 Thes 2, 17.
13: Acts 19, 21.

1, 1-7: The address follows the epistolary style of Paul's time, naming the sender and the addressees and extending good wishes (1.7). Paul proclaims the Christian faith in the humanity of Jesus (v 3) and in his divine sanctifying power (v 4).

1, 4: *Was made Son of God in power:* other possible translations are "was declared" or "proclaimed the powerful Son of God." *by his resurrection from the dead:* the resurrection made Jesus a "life-giving spirit" (1 Cor 15, 45), able to communicate the Spirit to those who believe in him. This is the power which he now exercises as exalted Son of God.

1, 5: Paul recalls his apostolic office, implying that the Romans know something of his history.

[15] That is why I am eager to preach the gospel to you Romans as well.

God's Power for Salvation

[16] I am not ashamed of the gospel. It is the power of God leading everyone who believes in it to salvation, the Jew first, then the Greek. [17] For in the gospel is revealed the justice of God which begins and ends with faith; as Scripture says, "The just man shall live by faith."

II: HUMANITY WITHOUT CHRIST

Punishment of Idolatry

[18] The wrath of God is being revealed from heaven against the irreligious and perverse spirit of men who, in this perversity of theirs, hinder the truth. [19] In fact, whatever can be known about God is clear to them; he himself made it so. [20] Since the creation of the world, invisible realities, God's eternal power and divinity, have become visible, recognized through the things he has made. Therefore these men are inexcusable. [21] They certainly had knowledge of God, yet they did not glorify him as God or give him thanks; they stultified themselves through speculating to no purpose, and their senseless hearts were darkened. [22] They claimed to be wise, but turned into fools instead; [23] they exchanged the glory of the immortal God for images

---

17: Hb 2, 4; Gal 3, 11; Heb 10, 38.
20: Wis 13, 1-9; Acts 17, 24-29;

1 Cor 1, 21.
21: Is 5, 21; 1 Cor 1, 19f.
23: Jer 2, 11.

1, 16f: The principal theme of the letter is salvation through faith. *I am not ashamed of the gospel:* a reminder of the criticism which Jews and Gentiles leveled against the doctrine of the crucified Savior; cf 1 Cor 1, 23f. Paul affirms, however, that it is precisely through the crucifixion and resurrection of Jesus that God chose to manifest his saving will and power. The apostle appeals through Jesus and his teaching for a faith to be held by all the world.

1, 17: *In the gospel is revealed the justice of God which begins and ends with faith:* the gospel is concerned with Jesus, in whom God has made known his saving presence and justice in history. Through Jesus, God offers the gift of faith, which makes his saving action effective in man. It manifests God's supremacy over man and his destiny, and likewise moves man to respond to the divine generosity. Faith makes clear the purpose and meaning of the Old Testament, revealing through the history of Israel the inability of man to effect his salvation in terms of covenant law.

1, 18-32: The conversion of the Gentiles through the gospel preaching constituted the divine indictment against paganism, which error had benighted and moral depravity had corrupted. It was the evil will of the pagan world that provoked the divine anger and abandonment (v 18). Contrary to nature itself which provides evidence of God's existence, power, and divinity through creation (19f), pagan society misread the evidence, fashioned gods of its own that could not exert any moral restraint, and freely indulged its perverse desires through every kind of wickedness (21-32; cf Wis 13, 1—14, 31).

representing mortal man, birds, beasts, and snakes. [24] In consequence, God delivered them up in their lusts to unclean practices; they engaged in the mutual degradation of their bodies, [25] these men who exchanged the truth of God for a lie and worshiped and served the creature rather than the Creator—blessed be he forever, amen! [26] God therefore delivered them up to disgraceful passions. Their women exchanged natural intercourse for unnatural, [27] and the men gave up natural intercourse with women and burned with lust for one another. Men did shameful things with men, and thus received in their own persons the penalty for their perversity. [28] They did not see fit to acknowledge God, so God delivered them up to their own depraved sense to do what is unseemly. [29] They are filled with every kind of wickedness: maliciousness, greed, ill will, envy, murder, bickering, deceit, craftiness. They are gossips [30] and slanderers, they hate God, are insolent, haughty, boastful, ingenious in their wrongdoing and rebellious toward their parents. [31] One sees in them men without conscience, without loyalty, without affection, without pity. [32] They know God's just decree that all who do such things deserve death; yet they not only do them but approve them in others.

2

God's Just Judgment

[1] That is why every one of you who judges another is inexcusable. By your judgment you convict yourself, since you do the very same things. [2] "We know that God's judgment on men who do such things is just." [3] Do you suppose, then, that you will escape his judgment, you who condemn these things in others yet do them yourself? [4] Or do you presume on his kindness and forbearance? Do you not know that God's kindness

---

24: Wis 12, 24; 13, 10f;   **2,** 1: Mt 7, 1.
Eph 4, 19.

2, 1—3, 9: The key to this passage is in the final verse: *We have already brought the charge against Jews and Greeks alike that they are under the domination of sin.* This judgment is based on the doctrine of universal salvation through the redemptive death of Christ. The Jew cannot condemn the sins of Gentiles without implicitly condemning himself (2, 1-11). He cannot reasonably demand from them the standard of conduct inculcated in the Old Testament since God did not address its revelation to them. Rather, God gave the Gentile the law of reason and conscience by which he was to be judged (2, 12-16). Not mere possession of the law by Jew or Gentile, but observance of it, is evidence of virtue (2, 17-29). Paul responds to the objection that his teaching on the sinfulness of all humanity detracts from the religious privileges of Israel, by stressing that the Jew always remained the vehicle of God's revelation despite his sins. His privileges depend, not on his own attainments, but on the fidelity of God (3, 1-4).

is an invitation to you to repent? [5] In spite of this, your hard and impenitent heart is storing up retribution for that day of wrath when the just judgment of God will be revealed, [6] when he will repay every man for what he has done: [7] eternal life to those who strive for glory, honor, and immortality by patiently doing right; [8] wrath and fury to those who selfishly disobey the truth and obey wickedness. [9] Yes, affliction and anguish will come upon every man who has done evil, the Jew first, then the Greek. [10] But there will be glory, honor, and peace for everyone who has done good, likewise the Jew first, then the Greek. [11] With God there is no favoritism.

Judgment by the Interior Law

[12] Sinners who do not have the law will perish without reference to it; sinners bound by the law will be judged in accordance with it. [13] For it is not those who hear the law who are just in the sight of God; it is those who keep it who will be declared just. [14] When Gentiles who do not have the law keep it as by instinct, these men although without the law serve as a law for themselves. [15] They show that the demands of the law are written in their hearts. Their conscience bears witness together with that law, and their thoughts will accuse or defend them [16] on the day when, in accordance with the gospel I preach, God will pass judgment on the secrets of men through Christ Jesus.

Judgment by the Mosaic Law

[17] Let us suppose you bear the name of "Jew" and rely firmly on the law and pride yourself on God. [18] Instructed by the law, you know his will and are able to make sound judgments on disputed points. [19] You feel certain that you can guide the blind and enlighten those in darkness, [20] that you can discipline the foolish and teach the simple, because in the law you have at hand a clear pattern of knowledge and truth. [21] Now then, teacher of others, are you failing to teach yourself? You who preach against stealing, do you steal? [22] You who forbid adultery, do you commit adultery? You who abhor idols, do you rob temples? [23] You who pride yourself on the law, do you dishonor God by breaking the law? [24] As Scripture says, "On your account the name of God is held in contempt among the Gentiles."

5: Acts 7, 51.
11: Dt 10, 17; Acts 10, 34.
13: Lk 8, 21; Jas 1, 22-25.
21: Ps 50, 16-21; Mt 23, 3f.
24: Is 52, 5; Ez 36, 20.

²⁵ Circumcision, to be sure, has value if you observe the law, but if you break it you might as well be uncircumcised! ²⁶ Again, if an uncircumcised person keeps the precepts of the law, will he not be considered circumcised? ²⁷ If a man who is uncircumcised keeps the law, he will pass judgment on you who, with your written law and circumcision, break it. ²⁸ Appearance does not make a Jew. True circumcision is not a sign in the flesh. ²⁹ He is a real Jew who is one inwardly, and true circumcision is of the heart; its source is the spirit, not the letter. Such a one receives his praise, not from men, but from God.

3

Answers to Objections

¹ What is the advantage, then, of being a Jew, and what value is there in circumcision? ² The answer is, much in every respect. First of all, the Jews were entrusted with the words of God. ³ You may ask, what if some of them have not believed? Will not their unbelief put an end to God's faithfulness? ⁴ Of course not! God must be proved true even though every man be proved a liar, so that, as Scripture says,

"You shall be vindicated in what you say,
    and win out when you are judged."

⁵ But if our wrongdoing provides proof of God's justice, what are we to say? "Is not God unjust when he inflicts punishment?" (I speak in a merely human way.) ⁶ Assuredly not! If that were so, how could God judge the world? Another question: ⁷ If my falsehood brings to light God's truth and thus promotes his glory, why must I be condemned as a sinner? ⁸ Or why may we not do evil that good may come of it? This is the very thing that some slanderously accuse us of teaching; but they will get what they deserve.

Universal Bondage of Sin

⁹ Well, then, do we find ourselves in a position of superiority? Not entirely. We have already brought the charge against Jews and Greeks alike that they are under the domination of sin. ¹⁰ It is as Scripture says:

25: 1 Cor 7, 19; Gal 5, 3.
26: Jer 9, 24f.
29: Jer 4, 4.
3, 3: Ps 89, 30-37;
    2 Tm 2, 13.

4: Ps 116, 11.
5: Jb 34, 12-17.
8: 6, 1.15.
9: Sir 8, 5.

"There is no just man, not even one;
11 there is no one who understands,
no one in search of God.
12 All have taken the wrong course,
all alike have become worthless;
not one of them acts uprightly, no, not one.
13 Their throats are open tombs;
they use their tongues to deceive;
The venom of asps lies behind their lips.
14 Their mouths are full of curses and bitterness.
15 Swiftly run their feet to shed blood;
16 ruin and misery strew their course.
17 The path of peace is unknown to them;
18 the fear of God is not before their eyes."

19 We know that everything the law says is addressed to those who are under its authority. This means that every mouth is silenced and the whole world stands convicted before God, 20 since no one will be justified in God's sight through observance of the law; the law does nothing but point out what is sinful.

III: SALVATION THROUGH FAITH IN CHRIST

Justice apart from the Law

21 But now the justice of God has been manifested apart from the law, even though both law and prophets bear witness to it—22 that justice of God which works through faith in Jesus Christ for all who believe. 23 All men have sinned and are deprived of the glory of God. 24 All men are now undeservedly justified by the gift of God, through the redemption wrought in Christ Jesus. 25 Through his blood, God made him the means of expiation for all who believe. He did so to manifest his own justice, for the sake of remitting sins committed in the past— 26 to manifest his justice in the present, by way of forbearance,

---

11: Ps 14, 1ff.
13: Pss 5, 10; 140, 4.
14: Ps 10, 7.
15: Is 59, 7; Prv 1, 16.

18: Ps 36, 2.
20: 7, 7.
24: 5, 2.
25: Acts 17, 30; 1 Jn 4, 10.

3, 21-31: *The justice of God:* is his mercy whereby he declares guilty man innocent and makes him so. He does this, not as a result of the law, but *apart from it* (v 21); not because of any merit of man, but through forgiveness of his sins (v 24), in virtue of *the redemption wrought in Christ Jesus* for all who believe (22.24f). No man can boast of his own holiness, since it is God's free gift (v 27), both to the Jew who practices circumcision out of faith, and to the Gentile who accepts faith without the Old Testament religious culture symbolized by circumcision (29f).

so that he might be just and might justify those who believe in Jesus.

²⁷ What occasion is there then for boasting? It is ruled out. By what law, the law of works? Not at all! By the law of faith. ²⁸ For we hold that a man is justified by faith apart from observance of the law. ²⁹ Does God belong to the Jews alone? Is he not also the God of the Gentiles? Yes, of the Gentiles too. ³⁰ It is the same God who justifies the circumcised and the uncircumcised on the basis of faith. ³¹ Are we then abolishing the law by means of faith? Not at all! On the contrary, we are confirming the law.

4

Abraham Justified by Faith

¹ What, then, shall we say of Abraham, our ancestor according to the flesh? ² Certainly if Abraham was justified by his deeds he has grounds for boasting, but not in God's view; ³ for what does Scripture say? "Abraham believed God, and it was credited to him as justice." ⁴ Now, when a man works, his wages are not regarded as a favor but as his due. ⁵ But when a man does nothing, yet believes in him who justifies the sinful, his faith is credited as justice. ⁶ Thus David congratulates the man to whom God credits justice without requiring deeds:

⁷ "Blest are they whose iniquities are forgiven,
    whose sins are covered over.
⁸ Blest is the man to whom the Lord
    imputes no guilt."

⁹ Does this blessedness apply only to the circumcised, or to the uncircumcised as well? For we say that Abraham's faith was "credited as justice." ¹⁰ What were the circumstances in which it was credited? Was it after he was circumcised or before? It was before. ¹¹ In fact, he received the sign of circumcision as a seal attesting to the justice received through faith while he was still uncircumcised. Thus he was to be the father of all the

---

27: 1 Cor 1, 29.
28: 5, 1.
31: Mt 5, 17.
4, 1: Gal 3, 6-9.

3: Gn 15, 6;
    Jas 2, 14.20-24.
7: Ps 32, 1f.
11: Gn 17, 10f.

3, 31: *We are confirming the law:* placing it in its proper perspective. The Old Testament law, unable to effect salvation, was observed out of the motive of faith. Now, through the revelation of Christ, the importance of faith is manifest.

4, 1-25: This is an expanded treatment of the significance of Abraham's faith, which Paul discusses in Gal 3, 6-18; see notes there.

uncircumcised who believe, so that for them too faith might be credited as justice, [12] as well as the father of those circumcised who are not merely so but who follow the path of faith which Abraham walked while still uncircumcised.

Inheritance through Faith

[13] Certainly the promise made to Abraham and his descendants that they would inherit the world did not depend on the law; it was made in view of the justice that comes from faith. [14] If only those who observe the law are heirs, then faith becomes an empty word and the promise loses its meaning. [15] Indeed, the law serves only to bring down wrath, for where there is no law there is no transgression. [16] Hence, all depends on faith, everything is grace. Thus the promise holds true for all Abraham's descendants, not only for those who have the law but for all who have his faith. He is father of us all, [17] which is why Scripture says, "I have made you father of many nations." Yes, he is our father in the sight of God in whom he believed, the God who restores the dead to life and calls into being those things which had not been. [18] Hoping against hope, Abraham believed and so became the father of many nations, just as it was once told him, "Numerous as this shall your descendants be." [19] Without growing weak in faith he thought of his own body, which was as good as dead (for he was nearly a hundred years old), and of the dead womb of Sarah. [20] Yet he never questioned or doubted God's promise; rather, he was strengthened in faith and gave glory to God, [21] fully persuaded that God could do whatever he had promised. [22] Thus his faith was credited to him as justice.

[23] The words, "It was credited to him," were not written with him alone in view; [24] they were intended for us too. For our faith will be credited to us also if we believe in him who raised Jesus our Lord from the dead, [25] the Jesus who was handed over to death for our sins and raised up for our justification.

5

Faith, Hope and Love

[1] Now that we have been justified by faith, we are at peace with God through our Lord Jesus Christ. [2] Through him we

13: Gal 3, 16ff.
15: 5, 13.
17: Gn 17, 50.
18: Gn 15, 5.

20: Heb 11, 11.
25: Is 53, 6.11;
    1 Cor 15, 17; 1 Pt 1, 3.
5, 1: Eph 3, 12.

have gained access by faith to the grace in which we now stand, and we boast of our hope for the glory of God. ³ But not only that—we even boast of our afflictions! We know that affliction makes for endurance, ⁴ and endurance for tested virtue, and tested virtue for hope. ⁵ And this hope will not leave us disappointed, because the love of God has been poured out in our hearts through the Holy Spirit who has been given to us. ⁶ At the appointed time, when we were still powerless, Christ died for us godless men. ⁷ It is rare that anyone should lay down his life for a just man, though it is barely possible that for a good man someone may have the courage to die. ⁸ It is precisely in this that God proves his love for us: that while we were still sinners, Christ died for us. ⁹ Now that we have been justified by his blood, it is all the more certain that we shall be saved by him from God's wrath. ¹⁰ For if, when we were God's enemies, we were reconciled to him by the death of his Son, it is all the more certain that we who have been reconciled will be saved by his life. ¹¹ Not only that; we go so far as to make God our boast through our Lord Jesus Christ, through whom we have now received reconciliation.

Mankind's Sin through Adam

¹² Therefore, just as through one man sin entered the world and with sin death, death thus coming to all men inasmuch as all sinned—¹³ before the law there was sin in the the world, even though sin is not imputed when there is no law—¹⁴ I say, from Adam to Moses death reigned, even over those who had not sinned by breaking a precept as did Adam, that type of the man to come.

4: 2 Cor 12, 9f; Jas 1, 2ff;
   1 Pt 4, 13f.
5: 8, 14ff.
8: 1 Jn 4, 10.19.

9: 8, 32.
10: 2 Cor 5, 18.
12: Wis 2, 24.

5, 1-5: A development of the doctrine of justification by faith. It is God who effects man's justification through Christ. This gives the believer a firm confidence in his salvation (5, 1f). The hardships of life should merely teach him patience and strengthen his hope (3f), which will not disappoint him because the Holy Spirit dwells in his heart and infuses into it God's love (v 5).
5, 12-21: Paul reflects on the sin of Adam (Gn 3, 1-13) in the light of the redemptive mystery of Christ. Sin, i. e., man's guilt before God which merited the punishment of death and loss of grace, began with Adam and infected the entire human race (v 12). Through the Old Testament law the sinfulness of mankind, operative from the beginning (v 13), became abundantly manifest (v 20). The judgments in 5, 12ff are based on the mystery of man's redemption through the death of Christ. Paul contrasts the divergent effects of Adam and of Christ on the human race (15-21) to show the culmination in Christ of what is revealed concerning man's condition and destiny.

Grace and Life through Christ

[15] But the gift is not like the offense. For if by the offense of the one man all died, much more did the grace of God and the gracious gift of the one man, Jesus Christ, abound for all. [16] The gift is entirely different from the sin committed by the one man. In the first case, sentence followed upon one offense and brought condemnation, but in the second, the gift came after many offenses and brought acquittal. [17] If death began its reign through one man because of his offense, much more shall those who receive the overflowing grace and gift of justice live and reign through the one man, Jesus Christ.

[18] To sum up, then: just as a single offense brought condemnation to all men, a single righteous act brought all men acquittal and life. [19] Just as through one man's disobedience all became sinners, so through one man's obedience all shall become just.

Purpose of the Law

[20] The law came in order to increase offenses; but despite the increase of sin, grace has far surpassed it, [21] so that, as sin reigned through death, grace may reign by way of justice leading to eternal life, through Jesus Christ our Lord.

IV: JUSTIFICATION AND THE CHRISTIAN LIFE

6

Death to Sin, Life in God

[1] What, then, are we to say? "Let us continue in sin that grace may abound"? [2] Certainly not! How can we who died to sin go on living in it? [3] Are you not aware that we who were baptized into Christ Jesus were baptized into his death? [4] Through baptism into his death we were buried with him, so that, just as Christ was raised from the dead by the glory of the Father, we too might live a new life. [5] If we have been united with him through likeness to his death, so shall we be through a like resurrection. [6] This we know: our old self was crucified

---

19: Is 53, 11; Phil 2, 8f.
20: 7, 7f.
6, 1: 3, 8.

3: Gal 3, 27; Col 2, 12;
1 Pt 3, 21f.
5: Phil 3, 10f.

6, 1-11: Paul denies that sin calls forth the grace of God; it is rather the divine generosity that is the source of the gift of grace (3, 22; cf note on Mk 1, 9ff). Grace is bestowed at baptism and produces a true renewal. It makes the baptized person capable of responding effectively to the dictates of his conscience concerning faith and life. This renewal is the prelude to the Christian's bodily resurrection and admission to eternal life (5, 21).

with him so that the sinful body might be destroyed and we might be slaves to sin no longer. [7] A man who is dead has been freed from sin. [8] If we have died with Christ, we believe that we are also to live with him. [9] We know that Christ, once raised from the dead, will never die again; death has no more power over him. [10] His death was death to sin, once for all; his life is life for God. [11] In the same way, you must consider yourselves dead to sin but alive for God in Christ Jesus.

[12] Do not, therefore, let sin rule your mortal body and make you obey its lusts; [13] No more shall you offer the members of your body to sin as weapons for evil. Rather, offer yourselves to God as men who have come back from the dead to life, and your bodies to God as weapons for justice. [14] Sin will no longer have power over you; you are now under grace, not under the law.

[15] What does all this lead to? Just because we are not under the law but under grace, are we free to sin? By no means! [16] You must realize that, when you offer yourselves to someone as obedient slaves, you are the slaves of the one you obey, whether yours is the slavery of sin, which leads to death, or of obedience, which leads to justice. [17] Thanks be to God, though once you were slaves of sin, you sincerely obeyed that rule of teaching which was imparted to you; [18] freed from your sin, you became slaves of justice. [19] (I use the following example from human affairs because of your weak human nature.) Just as formerly you enslaved your bodies to impurity and licentiousness for their degradation, make them now the servants of justice for their sanctification. [20] When you were slaves of sin, you had freedom from justice. [21] What benefit did you then enjoy? Things you are now ashamed of, all of them tending toward death. [22] But now that you are freed from sin and have become slaves of God, your benefit is sanctification as you tend toward eternal life. [23] The wages of sin is death, but the gift of God is eternal life in Christ Jesus our Lord.

8: Acts 13, 34.
9: 1 Cor 15, 26;
   2 Tm 1, 10; Rv 1, 18.
13: Col 3, 5.

16: Jn 8, 31; 2 Pt 2, 19.
21: 8, 6; Prv 12, 28.
23: Gn 2, 17; Gal 6, 7ff;
   Jas 1, 15.

6, 12-19: While the Christian remains in this mortal life, the power of sin in him is not fully overcome; his personal effort under the influence of grace is required to surmount the weakness remaining in him.

6, 20-23: The two ways of life, intrinsically opposed, produce opposite results: false *freedom from justice* brings enslavement by sin and the punishment of death; freedom from sin begets sanctification and *eternal life in Christ Jesus.*

7

Freedom from the Law

¹ Are you not aware, my brothers (I am speaking to men who know what law is), that the law has power over a man only so long as he lives? ² For example, a married woman is bound to her husband by law while he lives, but if he dies she is released from the law regarding husbands. ³ She will be called an adulteress if, while her husband is still alive, she gives herself to another. But if her husband dies she is freed from that law, and does not commit adultery by consorting with another man. ⁴ In the same way, my brothers, you died to the law through the body of Christ, that you might belong to that Other who was raised from the dead, so that we might bear fruit for God. ⁵ When we were in the flesh, the sinful passions roused by the law worked in our members and we bore fruit for death. ⁶ Now we have been released from the law—for we have died to what bound us—and we serve in the new spirit, not the antiquated letter.

Knowledge of Sin through the Law

⁷ What follows from what I have said? That the law is the same as sin? Certainly not! Yet it was only through the law that I came to know sin. I should never have known what evil desire was unless the law had said, "You shall not covet." ⁸ Sin seized that opportunity; it used the commandment to rouse in me every kind of evil desire. Without law sin is dead, ⁹ and at first I lived without law. Then the commandment came; with it sin came to life, ¹⁰ and I died. The commandment that should have led to life brought me death. ¹¹ Sin found its opportunity and used the commandment: first to deceive me, then to kill me. ¹² Yet the law is holy and the commandment is holy and just and good.

7, 2: 1 Cor 7, 39.
6: 2 Cor 3, 6.
7: 3, 20; Ex 20, 17; Dt 5, 21.

8: 1 Cor 15, 56.
11: Gn 3, 13.
12: 1 Tm 1, 8.

7, 1-6: Paul reflects upon the fact that the Christian has a different understanding of the law because of his faith in Christ. Law binds the living, not the dead, as exemplified in marriage, which binds in life but is dissolved through death. Similarly the Christian, who through baptism has died with Christ to sin, is freed from the law that occasioned sin and its punishment of death. Having risen with Christ, he is joined to him in newness of life so as to *bear fruit for God*.
7, 7-12: The apostle defends himself against the charge of identifying law with sin. Sin does not exist in law but rather in man, whose sinful inclinations are not overcome by the mere proclamation of law.

Sin and Death

[13] Did this good thing then become death for me? Not that either! Rather, sin, in order to be seen clearly as sin, used what was good to bring about my death. It did so that, by misusing the commandment, sin might go to the limit of sinfulness. [14] We know that the law is spiritual, whereas I am weak flesh sold into the slavery of sin. [15] I cannot even understand my own actions. I do not do what I want to do but what I hate. [16] When I act against my own will, by that very fact I agree that the law is good. [17] This indicates that it is not I who do it but sin which resides in me. [18] I know that no good dwells in me, that is, in my flesh; the desire to do right is there but not the power. [19] What happens is that I do, not the good I will to do, but the evil I do not intend. [20] But if I do what is against my will, it is not I who do it, but sin which dwells in me. [21] This means that even though I want to do what is right, a law that leads to wrongdoing is always ready at hand. [22] My inner self agrees with the law of God, [23] but I see in my body's members another law at war with with the law of my mind; this makes me the prisoner of the law of sin in my members. [24] What a wretched man I am! Who can free me from this body under the power of death? [25] All praise to God, through Jesus Christ our Lord! So with my mind I serve the law of God but with my flesh the law of sin.

8

The Flesh and the Spirit

[1] There is no condemnation now for those who are in Christ Jesus. [2] The law of the spirit, the spirit of life in Christ Jesus, has freed you from the law of sin and death. [3] The law was powerless because of its weakening by the flesh. Then God sent his Son in the likeness of sinful flesh as a sin offering, thereby condemning sin in the flesh, [4] so that the just demands of the

---

13: 5, 20.   8, 3: 2 Cor 5, 21; Gal 3, 13.

7, 13-25: The man who does not experience the justifying grace of God recognizes a rift between his reasoned desire for the goodness of the law and his actual performance contrary to the law. These two are found to be basically opposed. Unable to free himself from the slavery of sin and the power of death, he can only be rescued from defeat in the conflict by the power of God's grace working through Jesus Christ.

8, 1-13: This is a reflection on the redemptive work of Christ mentioned in 7, 25. The Christian is freed from God's judgment of condemnation by reason of Christ's death for the sins of humanity (1-4). With *the just demands of the law* thus fulfilled, he must live now, not *according to the flesh, . . . at enmity with God,* threatened with death, but *according to the spirit* which dwells in him and leads to *life and peace* (5-17).

law might be fulfilled in us who live, not according to the flesh, but according to the spirit. [5] Those who live according to the flesh are intent on the things of the flesh, those who live according to the spirit, on those of the spirit. [6] The tendency of the flesh is toward death but that of the spirit toward life and peace. [7] The flesh in its tendency is at enmity with God; it is not subject to God's law. Indeed, it cannot be; [8] those who are in the flesh cannot please God. [9] But you are not in the flesh; you are in the spirit, since the Spirit of God dwells in you. If anyone does not have the Spirit of Christ, he does not belong to Christ. [10] If Christ is in you, the body is indeed dead because of sin, while the spirit lives because of justice. [11] If the Spirit of him who raised Jesus from the dead dwells in you, then he who raised Christ from the dead will bring your mortal bodies to life also, through his Spirit dwelling in you.

[12] We are debtors, then, my brothers—but not to the flesh, so that we should live according to the flesh. [13] If you live according to the flesh, you will die; but if by the spirit you put to death the evil deeds of the body, you will live.

Sons of God through Adoption

[14] All who are led by the Spirit of God are sons of God. [15] You did not receive a spirit of slavery leading you back into fear, but a spirit of adoption through which we cry out, "Abba!" (that is, "Father"). [16] The Spirit himself gives witness with out spirit that we are children of God. [17] But if we are children, we are heirs as well: heirs of God, heirs with Christ, if only we suffer with him so as to be glorified with him.

Destiny of Glory

[18] I consider the sufferings of the present to be as nothing compared with the glory to be revealed in us. [19] Indeed, the whole created world eagerly awaits the revelation of the sons of God. [20] Creation was made subject to futility, not of its own accord but by him who once subjected it; yet not without hope,

---

8: 1 Jn 2, 16.
9: 1 Cor 3, 16.

15: Jn 1, 12; Gal 4, 6.
16: Gal 3, 26-29.

8, 14-17: The Christian, by reason of the Spirit's presence within him, enjoys not only new life but also a new relationship to God, that of adopted son and heir through Christ, whose sufferings and glory he shares.

8, 18-27: The glory which the believer is destined to share with Christ far exceeds the sufferings of the present life. Paul considers the created world to be linked to human destiny through its solidarity with man. As it shares in man's penalty of corruption through sin, so also it will share in his benefits of redemption and future glory (19ff). At present both must suffer until they achieve through hope and patient endurance the full harvest of the Spirit's presence, of which they now possess the first fruits or guarantee.

21 because the world itself will be freed from its slavery to corruption and share in the glorious freedom of the children of God. 22 Yes, we know that all creation groans and is in agony even until now. 23 Not only that, but we ourselves, although we have the Spirit as first fruits, groan inwardly while we await the redemption of our bodies. 24 In hope we were saved. But hope is not hope if its object is seen; how is it possible for one to hope for what he sees? 25 And hoping for what we cannot see means awaiting it with patient endurance.

26 The Spirit too helps us in our weakness, for we do not know how to pray as we ought; but the Spirit himself makes intercession for us with groanings that cannot be expressed in speech. 27 He who searches hearts knows what the Spirit means, for the Spirit intercedes for the saints as God himself wills.

God's Love for Man

28 We know that God makes all things work together for the good of those who have been called according to his decree. 29 Those whom he foreknew he predestined to share the image of his Son, that the Son might be the first-born of many brothers. 30 Those he predestined he likewise called; those he called he also justified; and those he justified he in turn glorified. 31 What shall we say after that? If God is for us, who can be against us? 32 Is it possible that he who did not spare his own Son but handed him over for the sake of us all will not grant us all things besides? 33 Who shall bring a charge against God's chosen ones? God, who justifies? 34 Who shall condemn them? Christ Jesus, who died or rather was raised up, who is at the right hand of God and who intercedes for us?

Indomitable Love for Christ

35 Who will separate us from the love of Christ? Trial, or

21: 2 Pt 3, 12f;	32: Jn 3, 16.
Rv 21, 1.	33f: Is 50, 8f.
22: 2 Cor 5, 2-5.	34: Heb 7, 25.
28f: Eph 1, 4-14.	

8, 28ff: These verses outline the Christian vocation as it was designed by God: *to share the image of his Son, that the Son might be the first-born of many brothers.* In terms of God's initiative, the call in its totality consists in the exercise of the divine foreknowledge, God's predetermination, God's gift of the call, his sanctification and glorification of the Christian. Thus all that happens to one who loves God is directed by God toward the achievement of that *good* which is likeness to God's Son through grace and glory.

8, 31-39: The all-conquering power of God's love has overcome every obstacle to man's salvation and every threat of his separation from God. That power manifested itself fully when God delivered up to death even his own Son for our salvation. Through him, the Christian can overcome all his afflictions and trials.

distress, or persecution, or hunger, or nakedness, or danger, or the sword? ³⁶ As Scripture says: "For your sake we are being slain all the day long; we are looked upon as sheep to be slaughtered." ³⁷ Yet in all this we are more than conquerors because of him who has loved us. ³⁸ For I am certain that neither death nor life, neither angels nor principalities, neither the present nor the future, nor powers, ³⁹ neither height nor depth nor any other creature, will be able to separate us from the löve of God that comes to us in Christ Jesus, our Lord.

V: ISRAEL'S PRESENT REJECTION

9

Grief for the Jews

¹ I speak the truth in Christ: I do not lie. My conscience bears me witness in the Holy Spirit ² that there is great grief and constant pain in my heart. ³ Indeed, I could even wish to be separated from Christ for the sake of my brothers, my kins- men ⁴ the Israelites. Theirs were the adoption, the glory, the covenants, the law-giving, the worship, and the promises; ⁵ theirs were the patriarchs, and from them came the Messiah (I speak of his human origins). Blessed forever be God who is over all! Amen.

God's Free Choice

⁶ Not that God's word has failed. For not all Israelites are true Israelites ⁷ nor are all Abraham's descendants his children, but as Scripture says, "Through Isaac shall your descendants be called." ⁸ That means that it is not the children of the flesh who are the children of God; it is the children of the promise who are to be considered descendants. ⁹ And this was the

---

36: Ps 44, 23; 2 Tm 3, 12.
9, 6f: Gn 21, 12; Mt 3, 9.

9: Gn 18, 10.

9, 1—11, 36: Israel's unbelief and its rejection of Jesus as Savior aston- ished and puzzled Christians. It constituted a serious theological problem for them in view of God's specific preparation of Israel for the advent of the Messiah. Paul addresses himself here to the essential question of how the divine plan could be frustrated by Israel's unbelief.
9, 1-5: The apostle speaks in strong terms of the depth of his grief over the unbelief of his own people. He would willingly undergo a curse himself for the sake of their coming to the knowledge of Christ (v 3; cf Lv 27, 28f). His love of them derives from God's choice of them and the spiritual bene- fits he bestowed on them (4f).
9, 6-13: Israel's unbelief reflects the mystery of the divine election that was always operative within it. Mere natural descent from Abraham did not en- sure the full possession of the divine gifts; it was God's sovereign prerogative to bestow this fullness upon, or to withhold it from, whomsoever he wished; cf Mt 3, 9; Jn 3, 3f. The choice of Jacob over Esau is a case in point.

promise: "I will return at this time, and Sarah shall have a son." [10] Not only that; for when Rebekah had conceived twin children by one man, our father Isaac—[11] while they were yet unborn and had done neither good nor evil, in order that God's decree might stand fast [12] "not by works but by the favor of him who calls"—God said to her, "The older shall serve the younger." [13] It is just as Scripture says, "I have loved Jacob and hated Esau." [14] What are we to say, then? That God is unjust? Not at all! [15] He says to Moses, "I will show mercy to whomever I choose; I will have pity on whomever I wish." [16] So it is not a question of man's willing or doing but of God's mercy. [17] Scripture says to Pharaoh, "This is why I raised you up: that through you I might show my power, and my name might be proclaimed throughout all the earth." [18] In other words, God has mercy on whom he wishes, and whom he wishes he makes obdurate.

[19] You will say to me, "Why, then, does he find fault? For who can oppose his will?" [20] Friend, who are you to answer God back? Does something molded say to its molder, "Why did you make me like this?" [21] Does not a potter have the right to make from the same lump of clay one vessel for a lofty purpose and another for a humble one? [22] What if God, wishing to show his wrath and make known his power, has endured with much patience vessels fit for wrath, ready to be destroyed; [23] and in order to make known the riches of his glory toward the vessels for mercy which he prepared for glory—[24] I am speaking about us whom he called, not only from among the Jews, but from among the Gentiles.

Witness of the Old Testament

[25] As it says in the Book of Hosea: "Those who were not my people I will call 'my people,' and those who were not loved I

12: 11, 5f; Gn 25, 23f.
13: Mal 1, 3.
16: Ex 33, 19.
17: Ex 9, 16.
18: Ex 7, 3.

19: 3, 7; Wis 12, 12.
20f: Wis 15, 7; Is 29, 16;
    45, 9; Jer 18, 6.
22: Wis 12, 20f.
25: Hos 2, 25.

9, 14-18: The principle of divine election does not mean that God is unfair in his dealings with men. Rather, he reveals in this way that the gift of faith is the enactment of his mercy (v 16). God raised up Moses to display his mercy and Pharaoh to display his severity in punishing those who obstinately oppose him.

9, 19-29: The apostle responds to the objection that if God rules over faith through the principle of divine election, he cannot then accuse the unbelieving man of sin (v 19). For Paul, this objection is in the last analysis a manifestation of human insolence, and his "answer" is less an explanation of God's ways than the rejection of an argument which places man on the level of God.

will call 'Beloved'; ²⁶ in the very place where it was said to them, 'You are not my people,' they shall be called sons of the living God." ²⁷ Isaiah cries out, referring to Israel, "Though the number of the Israelites should be as the sands of the sea, only the remnant will be saved, ²⁸ for quickly and decisively will the Lord execute sentence upon the earth." ²⁹ It is just as Isaiah predicted: "Unless the Lord of hosts had left us a remnant, we should have become as Sodom, we should be like Gomorrah."

Israel's Unbelief

³⁰ How, then, shall we put it? That the Gentiles, who were not seeking justice, attained it—the justice which comes from faith—³¹ while Israel, seeking a law from which justice would come, did not arrive at that law? ³² And why did it not? Because justice comes from faith, not from works. They stumbled over the strumbling stone, ³³ as Scripture says: "Behold, I am placing in Zion a stone to make men stumble and a rock to make them fall; but he who believes in him will not be put to shame."

10

¹ Brothers, my heart's desire, my prayer to God for the Israelites, is that they may be saved. ² Indeed, I can testify that they are zealous for God though their zeal is unenlightened. ³ Unaware of God's justice and seeking to establish their own, they did not subject themselves to the justice of God. ⁴ Christ is the end of the law. Through him, justice comes to everyone who believes. ⁵ Moses writes of the justice that comes from the law, "The one who observes the law shall live by it." ⁶ But of the justice that comes from faith he says, "Do not say in your

---

26: 11, 5.
27: Is 10, 22f; Hos 2, 1.
29: Is 1, 9.
30: 10, 4.
32: Is 8, 14.

33: Is 28, 16; 1 Pt 2, 6ff.
10, 4: 2 Cor 3, 14.
    5: Gal 3, 12.
    6: Dt 30, 12.

9, 30-33: In the conversion of the Gentiles, and by contrast, of relatively few Jews, the Old Testament prophecies are seen to be fulfilled; cf 9, 25-29. Israel placed an unbalanced overemphasis on the literal observance of the law and was thus unwilling to accept the doctrine of justification by faith; the Gentiles were more open to this doctrine because to them the very idea of justification was new.

10, 1-4: Despite Israel's unbelief in Christ, Paul does not abandon hope for its salvation (v 1). Israel misunderstood the true nature of salvation (v 3), but retained its faith in God (v 4).

10, 5-13: In the past, Israel was promised particular benefits for observance of the law (v 5), but in Christ the law has been fulfilled (4f). It is faith in Jesus which is the source of God's saving action for Jew and Gentile alike (6-13).

heart, 'Who shall go up into heaven?' (that is, to bring Christ down), [7] or 'Who shall go down into the abyss?' (that is, to bring Christ up from the dead)." [8] What is it he does say? "The word is near you, on your lips and in your heart" (that is, the word of faith which we preach). [9] For if you confess with your lips that Jesus is Lord, and believe in your heart that God raised him from the dead, you will be saved. [10] Faith in the heart leads to justification, confession on the lips to salvation. [11] Scripture says, "No one who believes in him will be put to shame." [12] Here there is no difference between Jew and Greek; all have the same Lord, rich in mercy toward all who call upon him. [13] "Everyone who calls on the name of the Lord will be saved."

[14] But how shall they call on him in whom they have not believed? And how can they believe unless they have heard of him? And how can they hear unless there is someone to preach? [15] And how can men preach unless they are sent? Scripture says, "How beautiful are the feet of those who announce good news!" [16] But not all have believed the gospel. Isaiah asks, "Lord, who has believed what he has heard from us?" [17] Faith, then, comes through hearing, and what is heard is the word of Christ. [18] I ask you, have they not heard? Certainly they have, for "their voice has sounded over the whole earth, and their words to the limits of the world." [19] I put the question again, did Israel really not understand? First of all, Moses says, "I will make you jealous of those who are not even a nation; with a senseless nation I will make you angry." [20] Then Isaiah says boldly, "I was found by those who were not seeking me; to those who were not looking for me I revealed myself." [21] But of Israel he says, "All day long I stretched out my hands to an unbelieving and contentious people."

11

Partial Rejection of Israel

[1] I ask, then, has God rejected his people? Of course not! I

7: 1 Pt 3, 19.	15: Is 52, 7.
8: Dt 30, 14.	16: Is 53, 1.
9: 1 Cor 12, 3.	18: Ps 19, 5; Mt 24, 14.
11: 9, 33; Is 28, 16.	19: 11, 1; Dt 32, 21.
13: Jl 3, 5; Acts 2, 21.	20f: 9, 30; Is 65, 1f.
14: Acts 8, 31.	**11,** 1f: 1 Sm 12, 22; Ps 94, 14.

10, 14-21: The gospel has been sufficiently proclaimed to Israel, which has adequately understood it, but, as in the past, has not accepted the prophetic message; cf Acts 7, 51ff.

11, 1-10: Though Israel has been unfaithful to the prophetic message of the gospel (10, 14-21), God remains faithful to Israel. Proof of the divine

myself am an Israelite, descended from Abraham, of the tribe of Benjamin. [2] No, God has not rejected his people whom he foreknew. Do you not know what Scripture says about Elijah, how he pleaded with God against Israel? [3] "Lord, they have killed your prophets, they have torn down your altars; I alone am left and they are seeking my life." [4] How does God answer him? "I have left for myself seven thousand men who have not bowed the knee to Baal." [5] Just so, in the present time there is a remnant chosen by the grace of God. [6] But if the choice is by grace, it is not because of their works—otherwise grace would not be grace. [7] What then are we to say? Just this: Israel did not obtain what she was seeking, but those who were chosen did. The rest became blind, [8] as Scripture says: "God gave them a spirit of stupor; blind eyes and deaf ears, and it is so to this day." [9] David says: "Let their table become a snare and a trap, a stumbling stone and a retribution; [10] let their eyes be darkened so that they may not see. Bow down their back forever."

Israel's Fall the Gentiles' Salvation

[11] I further ask, does their stumbling mean that they are forever fallen? Not at all! Rather, by their transgression salvation has come to the Gentiles to stir Israel to envy. [12] But if their transgression and their diminishing have meant riches for the Gentile world, how much more their full number!

[13] I ask this now to you Gentiles: Inasmuch as I am the apostle of the Gentiles, I glory in my ministry, [14] trying to rouse my fellow Jews to envy and save some of them. [15] For if their rejection has meant reconciliation for the world, what will their acceptance mean? Nothing less than life from the dead! [16] If the first fruits are consecrated, so too is the whole mass of dough,

---

3: 1 Kgs 19, 10.14.
4: 1 Kgs 19, 18.
8: Dt 29, 3; Is 29, 10;

Mt 13, 14.
9f: Ps 69, 23f.

---

fidelity lies in the existence of the Judaeo-Christians like Paul himself. The unbelieving Jews have been blinded by the Christian teaching concerning the Messiah.

11, 11-15: The unbelief of Israel has paved the way for the preaching of the gospel to the Gentiles and for their easier acceptance of it outside the context of Jewish culture. In God's design it should follow that Israel's ultimate acceptance of the gospel message will benefit the world even more than its original unbelief.

11, 16-24: Israel remains holy in the eyes of God and stands as a witness to the faith of the Old Testament because of the *first fruits* which *are consecrated*, i. e., the converted remnant, and the *root* which *is consecrated*, i. e., the patriarchs (v 16). The Jews' failure to believe in Christ is a warning to Gentile Christians to be on guard lest they themselves fall through loss of faith.

and if the root is consecrated, so too are the branches. [17] If some of the branches were cut off and you, a branch of the wild olive tree, have been grafted in among the others and have come to share in the rich root of the olive, do not boast against the branches. [18] If you do boast, remember that you do not support the root; the root supports you. [19] You will say, "Branches were cut off that I might be grafted in." [20] Well and good. They were cut off because of unbelief and you are there because of faith. Do not be haughty on that account, but fearful. [21] If God did not spare the natural branches, he will certainly not spare you.

[22] Consider the kindness and the severity of God—severity toward those who fell, kindness toward you, provided you remain in his kindness; if you do not, you too will be cut off. [23] And if the Jews do not remain in their unbelief they will be grafted back on, for God is able to do this. [24] If you were cut off from the natural wild olive and, contrary to nature, were grafted into the cultivated olive, so much the more will they who belong to it by nature be grafted into their own olive tree.

Israel's Final Conversion

[25] Brothers, I do not want you to be ignorant of this mystery lest you be conceited: blindness has come upon part of Israel until the full number of Gentiles enter in, [26] and then all Israel will be saved. As Scripture says: "Out of Zion will come the deliverer who shall remove all impiety from Jacob; [27] and this is the covenant I will make with them when I take away their sins." [28] In respect to the gospel, the Jews are enemies of God for your sake; in respect to the election, they are beloved by him because of the patriarchs. [29] God's gifts and his call are irrevocable.

Triumph of God's Mercy

[30] Just as you were once disobedient to God and now have received mercy through their disobedience, [31] so they have become disobedient—since God wished to show you mercy—that they too may receive mercy. [32] God has imprisoned all in disobedience that he might have mercy on all.

18: 1 Cor 1, 31.   29: Nm 23, 19; Is 54, 10.
26f: Is 59, 20f.   32: Gal 3, 22.
27: Jer 31, 33.

11, 25-32: In God's design, Israel's unbelief is being utilized to grant the light of faith to the Gentiles. Meanwhile, Israel remains dear to God, still the object of his special providence, the mystery of which will one day be revealed.

[33] How deep are the riches and the wisdom and the knowledge of God! How inscrutable his judgments, how unsearchable his ways! [34] For "who has known the mind of the Lord? Or who has been his counselor? [35] Who has given him anything so as to deserve return?" [36] For from him and through him and for him all things are. To him be glory forever. Amen.

VI: THE DUTIES OF CHRISTIANS

12

Sacrifice of Body and Mind

[1] And now, brothers, I beg you through the mercy of God to offer your bodies as a living sacrifice holy and acceptable to God, your spiritual worship. [2] Do not conform yourselves to this age but be transformed by the renewal of your mind, so that you may judge what is God's will, what is good, pleasing and perfect.

Many Members in One Body

[3] Thus, in virtue of the favor given to me, I warn each of you not to think more highly of himself than he ought. Let him estimate himself soberly, in keeping with the measure of faith that God has apportioned him. [4] Just as each of us has one body with many members, and not all the members have the same function, [5] so too we, though many, are one body in Christ and individually members one of another. [6] We have gifts that differ according to the favor bestowed on each of us. One's gift may be prophecy; its use should be in proportion to his faith. [7] It may be the gift of ministry; it should be used for service. One who is a teacher should use his gift for teaching; [8] one with the power of exhortation should exhort. He who gives alms

33: Ps 139, 6.17f.
34f: Wis 9, 13; Is 40, 13;
    1 Cor 2, 11.
  36: 1 Cor 8, 6; Col 1, 16f.
12, 3: Phil 2, 3.

4: 1 Cor 12, 9.
5: 1 Cor 12, 12.
6f: 1 Cor 12, 8ff.28ff;
    Eph 4, 7-12;
    1 Pt 4, 10.

11, 33-36: This final reflection celebrates the wisdom of God's plan of salvation. As Paul has indicated throughout these chapters, both Jew and Gentile, despite the religious recalcitrance of each, have received the gift of faith. Thus the divine plan of salvation has become open and comprehensible to the whole human race.

12, 1—13, 14: This moral teaching expresses the necessary response to the gift of justification through faith. It is the Christian's personal sacrificial way of serving God (12, 1f). It consists in the humble use of one's gifts for the benefit of the community (12, 3-13); it is marked by love of enemies (12, 14-21), and by the acceptance of legitimate civil authority (13, 1-7). The commandments of the Mosaic covenant (Ex 20, 13-17) remain its norm, and the hope of salvation in Christ its incentive (13, 11-14).

should do so generously; he who rules should exercise his authority with care; he who performs works of mercy should do so cheerfully.

Fraternal Charity

[9] Your love must be sincere. Detest what is evil, cling to what is good. [10] Love one another with the affection of brothers. Anticipate each other in showing respect. [11] Do not grow slack but be fervent in spirit; he whom you serve is the Lord. [12] Rejoice in hope, be patient under trial, persevere in prayer. [13] Look on the needs of the saints as your own; be generous in offering hospitality. [14] Bless your persecutors; bless and do not curse them. [15] Rejoice with those who rejoice, weep with those who weep. [16] Have the same attitude toward all. Put away ambitious thoughts and associate with those who are lowly. Do not be wise in your own estimation. [17] Never repay injury with injury. See that your conduct is honorable in the eyes of all. [18] If possible, live peaceably with everyone. [19] Beloved, do not avenge yourselves; leave that to God's wrath, for it is written: " 'Vengeance is mine; I will repay,' says the Lord." [20] But "if your enemy is hungry, feed him; if he is thirsty, give him something to drink; by doing this you will heap burning coals upon his head." [21] Do not be conquered by evil but conquer evil with good.

13

Obedience to Authority

[1] Let everyone obey the authorities that are over him, for there is no authority except from God, and all authority that exists is established by God. [2] As a consequence, the man who opposes authority rebels against the ordinance of God; those who resist thus shall draw condemnation down upon themselves. [3] Rulers cause no fear when a man does what is right but only when his conduct is evil. Do you wish to be free from the fear of authority? Do what is right and you will gain its approval, [4] for the ruler is God's servant to work for your good. Only if you do wrong ought you to be afraid. It is not without purpose that the ruler carries the sword; he is God's servant, to inflict

---

9: Am 5, 15.
10: Jn 13, 34.
14-21: Mt 5, 38-48.
15: Sir 7, 34.
16: Prv 3, 7.
17: 1 Thes 5, 15.

19: Lv 19, 18; Dt 32, 35;
　　1 Cor 6, 6f.
20: Prv 25, 21f.
13, 1: Ti 3, 1.
　　2: Prv 8, 15.

his avenging wrath upon the wrongdoer. [5] You must obey, then, not only to escape punishment but also for conscience' sake. [6] You pay taxes for the same reason, magistrates being God's ministers who devote themselves to his service with unremitting care. [7] Pay each one his due: taxes to whom taxes are due; toll to whom toll is due; respect and honor to everyone who deserves them.

Love Fulfills the Law

[8] Owe no debt to anyone except the debt that binds us to love one another. He who loves his neighbor has fulfilled the law. [9] The commandments, "You shall not commit adultery; you shall not murder; you shall not steal; you shall not covet," and any other commandment there may be are all summed up in this, "You shall love your neighbor as yourself." [10] Love never wrongs the neighbor, hence love is the fulfillment of the law.

Christian Use of Time

[11] Take care to do all these things, for you know the time in which we are living. It is now the hour for you to wake from sleep, for our salvation is closer than when we first accepted the faith. [12] The night is far spent; the day draws near. Let us cast off deeds of darkness and put on the armor of light. [13] Let us live honorably as in daylight; not in carousing and drunkenness, not in sexual excess and lust, not in quarreling and jealousy. [14] Rather, put on the Lord Jesus Christ and make no provision for the desires of the flesh.

14

To Live and Die for Christ

[1] Extend a kind welcome to those who are weak in faith. Do not enter into disputes with them. [2] A man of sound faith knows he can eat anything, while one who is weak in faith eats only vegetables. [3] The man who will eat anything must not ridicule

---

7: Mt 22, 21.
9: Ex 20, 13-17; Dt 5, 17-21
10: 1 Cor 13, 4-7.
11: Eph 5, 8-16.
12: Jn 8, 12; 1 Thes 5, 4-8;

1 Jn 2, 8.
14: Gal 3, 27; 5, 16; Eph 6, 11.
14, 2: 1 Cor 8, 1-13; 10, 14-33.
3: Col 2, 16.

14, 1—15, 6: Paul applies the principle of love of neighbor to a certain conflict existing within the Roman community over clean and unclean foods. Although he acknowledges that in principle no food is a source of moral contamination (14, 14), he recommends that the consciences of Christians who are scrupulous in this regard be respected by other Christians (14, 21).

him who abstains from certain foods; the man who abstains must not sit in judgment on him who eats. After all, God himself has made him welcome. [4] Who are you to pass judgment on another's servant? His master alone can judge whether he stands or falls. And stand he will, for the Lord is able to make him stand. [5] One man regards this day as better than that; someone else considers all days alike. Each should be certain of his own conscience. [6] The man who observes the day does so to honor the Lord. The man who eats does so to honor the Lord, and he gives thanks to God. The man who does not eat abstains to honor the Lord, and he too gives thanks to God. [7] None of us lives as his own master and none of us dies as his own master. [8] While we live we are responsible to the Lord, and when we die we die as his servants. Both in life and in death we are the Lord's. [9] That is why Christ died and came to life again, that he might be Lord of both the dead and the living. [10] But you, how can you sit in judgment on your brother? Or you, how can you look down on your brother? We shall all have to appear before the judgment seat of God. [11] It is written, "As surely as I live, says the Lord, every knee shall bend before me and every tongue shall give praise to God."

Peace and Joy in the Holy Spirit

[12] Every one of us will have to give an account of himself before God. [13] Therefore we must no longer pass judgment on one another. Instead you should resolve to put no stumbling block or hindrance in your brother's way. [14] I know with certainty on the authority of the Lord Jesus that nothing is unclean in itself; it is only when a man thinks something unclean that it becomes so for him. [15] If, then, your brother feels remorse for the food he has eaten, you have ceased to follow the rule of love. You must not let the food you eat bring to ruin him for whom Christ died; [16] neither may you allow your privilege to become an occasion for blasphemy. [17] The kingdom of God is not a matter of eating or drinking, but of justice, peace, and the joy that is given by the Holy Spirit. [18] Whoever serves Christ in this way pleases God and wins the esteem of men. [19] Let us, then, make it our aim to work for peace and to strengthen one another.

[20] Take care not to destroy God's work for the sake of some-

4: Jas 4, 12.
9: Acts 10, 42.
11: Is 45, 23f; Phil 2, 10f.
14: Acts 10, 15; 1 Tm 4, 4.

17: 1 Cor 8, 8.
20f: 1 Cor 8, 11ff; 10, 28f;
Ti 1, 15.

thing to eat. True, all foods are clean; but it is wrong for a man to eat when the food offends his conscience. [21] You would be acting nobly if you abstained from eating meat, or drinking wine, or anything else that offers your brother an occasion for stumbling or scandal, or that weakens him in any way. [22] Use the faith you have as your rule of life in the sight of God. Happy the man whose conscience does not condemn what he has chosen to do! [23] But if a man eats when his conscience has misgivings about eating, he is already condemned, because he is not acting in accordance with what he believes. Whatever does not accord with one's belief is sinful.

15

Patience and Self-denial

[1] We who are strong in faith should be patient with the scruples of those whose faith is weak; we must not be selfish. [2] Each should please his neighbor so as to do him good by building up his spirit. [3] Thus, in accord with Scripture, Christ did not please himself: "The reproaches they uttered against you fell on me." [4] Everything written before our time was written for our instruction, that we might derive hope from the lessons of patience and the words of encouragement in the Scriptures. [5] May God, the source of all patience and encouragement, enable you to live in perfect harmony with one another according to the spirit of Christ Jesus, [6] so that with one heart and voice you may glorify God, the Father of our Lord Jesus Christ.

God's Fidelity and Mercy

[7] Accept one another, then, as Christ accepted you, for the glory of God. [8] Yes, I affirm that Christ became the servant of the Jews because of God's faithfulness in fulfilling the promises to the patriarchs, [9] whereas the Gentiles glorify God because of his mercy. As Scripture has it, "Therefore I will praise you among the Gentiles and I will sing to your name." [10] Again, "Rejoice, O Gentiles, with his people." [11] And, "Praise the Lord, all you Gentiles and sing his glory, all you peoples." [12] Once more, Isaiah says, "The root of Jesse will appear, he who will rise up to rule the Gentiles; in him the Gentiles will find hope." [13] So may God, the source of hope, fill you with

15, 3: Ps 69, 10.
    4: 2 Tm 3, 16.
    8: Mt 15, 24; Acts 3, 25.
9: Ps 18, 50.
11: Ps 117, 1.
12: Is 11, 1.10.

all joy and peace and believing so that through the power of the Holy Spirit you may have hope in abundance.

VII: CONCLUSION

Apostle of the Gentiles

[14] I am convinced, my brothers, that you are filled with goodness, that you have complete knowledge, and that you are able to give advice to one another. [15] Yet I have written to you rather boldly in parts of this letter by way of reminder. I take this liberty because God has given me the grace [16] to be a minister of Christ Jesus among the Gentiles, with the priestly duty of preaching the gospel of God so that the Gentiles may be offered up as a pleasing sacrifice, consecrated by the Holy Spirit. [17] This means I can take glory in Christ Jesus for the work I have done for God. [18] I will not dare to speak of anything except what Christ has done through me to win the Gentiles to obedience by word and deed, [19] with mighty signs and marvels, by the power of God's Spirit. As a result, I have completed preaching the gospel of Christ from Jerusalem all the way around to Illyria. [20] It has been a point of honor with me never to preach in places where Christ's name was already known, for I did not want to build on a foundation laid by another [21] but rather to fulfill the words of Scripture, "They who received no word of him will see him, and they who have never heard will understand."

Paul's Plans; Need for Prayers

[22] That is why I have so often been hindered from visiting you. [23] Now I have no more work to do in these regions, and I continue to cherish the desire to visit you which I have had for many years. [24] As soon as I can set out for Spain, I hope to see you in passing; I trust that you will send me on my journey only after I have had the joy of being with you for a little while. [25] Just now I am leaving for Jerusalem to bring assistance to the saints. [26] Macedonia and Achaia have kindly decided to make a contribution for those in need among the saints in Jerusalem. [27] They did so of their own accord, yet they are also under obligation. For if the Gentiles have shared in the spiritual belssings of the Jews, they ought to contribute to their temporal needs in return. [28] When I have finished my task and have safely handed over this contribution to them,

---

21: Is 52, 15.   23: Acts 19, 21f.   26: 1 Cor 16, 1.

I shall set out for Spain, passing through your midst on the way. ²⁹ I am certain that when I do visit you, I shall come with Christ's full blessing.

³⁰ I beg you, brothers, for the sake of our Lord Jesus Christ and the love of the Spirit, join me in the struggle by your prayers to God on my behalf. ³¹ Pray that I may be kept safe from the unbelievers in Judea, and that the offerings I bring to Jerusalem may be well received by the saints there; ³² so that, God willing, I may come to you with joy and be refreshed in spirit by your company. ³³ May the God of peace be with you all. Amen.

16

Phoebe Commended

¹ I commend to your our sister Phoebe, who is a deaconess of the church of Cenchreae. ² Please welcome her in the Lord, as saints should. If she needs help in anything, give it to her, for she herself has been of help to many including myself.

Paul's Greetings

³ Give my greetings to Prisca and Aquila; they were my fellow workers in the service of Christ Jesus ⁴ and even risked their lives for the sake of mine. Not only I but all the churches of the Gentiles are grateful to them. ⁵ Remember me also to the congregation that meets in their house. Greetings to my beloved Epaenetus; he is the first offering that Asia made to Christ. ⁶ My greetings to Mary, who has worked hard for you, ⁷ and to Andronicus and Junias, my kinsmen and fellow prisoners; they are outstanding apostles, and they were in Christ even before I was. ⁸ Greetings to Ampliatus, who is dear to me in the Lord; ⁹ to Urbanus, our fellow worker in the service of Christ; and to my beloved Stachys. ¹⁰ Greetings to Apelles, who proved himself in Christ's service, and to all who belong to the household of Aristobulus. ¹¹ Greetings to my kinsman Herodion and to the members of the household of Narcissus who are in the Lord. ¹² Greetings, too, to Tryphaena and Tryphosa, who have worked hard for the Lord; and also to dear Persis, who has labored long in the Lord's service. ¹³ Greetings to Rufus, a chosen servant of the Lord, and to his mother, who has been

---

16, 3: Acts 18, 2.26.

16, 1-23: Some authorities regard these verses as a later addition to Paul's letter, but in general the evidence favors the view that they were included in the original.

a mother to me as well. ¹⁴ Greetings to Asyncritus, Phlegon, Hermes, Patrobas, Hermas, and the brothers who are with them; ¹⁵ to Philologus and Julia, to Nereus and his sister, to Olympas, and all the saints who are with them. ¹⁶ Greet one another with a holy kiss. All the churches of Christ send you greetings.

Against Dissenters

¹⁷ Brothers, I beg you to be on the watch against those who cause dissension and scandal, contrary to the teaching you have received. Avoid their company. ¹⁸ Such men serve, not Christ our Lord, but their own bellies, and they deceive the simple-minded with smooth and flattering speech. ¹⁹ Your obedience is known to all, and so I am delighted with you. I want you to be wise in regard to what is good and innocent of all evil. ²⁰ Then the God of peace will quickly crush Satan under your feet. May the grace of our Lord Jesus Christ be with you.

Greetings from Corinth

²¹ Timothy, my fellow worker, sends you his greetings; so, too, do my kinsmen Lucius, Jason, and Sosipater. ²² I, Tertius, who have written this letter, send you my greetings in the Lord. ²³ Greetings also from Gaius, who is host to me and to the whole church. ²⁴ Erastus, the city treasurer, and our brother Quartus wish to be remembered to you.

Doxology

²⁵ Now to him who is able to strengthen you in the gospel which I proclaim when I preach Jesus Christ, the gospel which reveals the mystery hidden for many ages ²⁶ but now manifested through the writings of the prophets, and, at the command of the eternal God, made known to all the Gentiles that they may believe and obey—²⁷ to him, the God who alone is wise, may glory be given through Jesus Christ unto endless ages. Amen.

18: Phil 3, 19.
19: Mt 10, 16;
      1 Cor 14, 20.
20: Gn 3, 15.

25: Eph 3, 3; Col 1, 26.
27: Gal 1, 5; Eph 3, 21;
      Phil 4, 20; 1 Tm 1, 17.

16, 25: *The gospel which reveals the mystery hidden for many ages:* justification and salvation through faith, with all the implications for Jew and Gentile that Paul has developed in this letter.

THE FIRST EPISTLE OF PAUL TO THE CORINTHIANS

INTRODUCTION

St. Paul established a Christian community in Corinth about the year 50, on his second missionary journey. According to his own testimony in this epistle (written c 56), he began his work in Corinth in "fear and trepidation" (2, 3) because of the city's extreme moral depravity and its pagan cult, which included the practice of religious prostitution. Moderate success attended his efforts among the Jewish Corinthians at first, but they soon turned against him (Acts 18, 1-8). More fruitful was his year-and-a-half mission among the Gentiles (Acts 18, 11), which won to the faith many of the city's poor and unprivileged (1, 26). After his departure, the eloquent and fervent Apollos, an Alexandrian Judaeo-Christian, rendered great service to the Corinthian community. He expounded "from the Scriptures that Jesus is the Messiah" (Acts 18, 27f).

While Paul was in Ephesus on his third missionary journey (16, 8; Acts 19, 1-20), he received disquieting news about Corinth. The community there was displaying open factionalism, certain members identifying themselves with, respectively, the teaching of Paul, of Apollos, of Cephas and others apparently claiming a relationship with Jesus peculiar to themselves alone (1, 12). Christian teaching was being interpreted as a superior wisdom for the initiated few, rather than as the divine means for the humble opening of all hearts to the prophetic word of God in Christ (1, 10—4, 21). The community lacked the moral power to take appropriate action against one of its members who was living publicly in an incestuous union (5, 1-13). Other members engaged in legal conflicts, presenting in pagan courts of law a disedifying portrait of their fellows (6, 1-11); still others had even revived the old practice of religious prostitution (6, 13-20) and participated in sacrifices in the temples of the gods (10, 14-22). Some in the community questioned Paul's apostolic authority and pressed the point that, unlike the other apostles, he did not use the rights of apostleship since he did not accept financial support from the community (9, 15-18). Women appeared at the liturgical assembly without the customary head-covering (11, 2-16), and quarreled over their right to address the assembly (14, 34f).

The community's ills were reflected in the celebration of the eucharistic liturgy itself, when some members behaved clannishly, drank too freely at the agape, and denied Christian social courtesies to the poor among the membership (11, 17-22). Charisms such as ecstatic prayer and messages, attributed freely to the impulse of the Holy Spirit, were more highly prized than works of charity (13, 1f.8), and were used at times in a disordered and even ridiculous way (14, 1-40). There were also members who despite their belief in the resurrection of Christ, had accepted the opinion of certain peripatetic philosophers against the possibility of general bodily resurrection (15, 1-57).

The lesser problems Paul had to deal with in this epistle concerned matters of conscience discussed among the faithful members of the community: the eating of meats that had been offered to idols (8, 1-13); the use of sex in marriage (7, 1-7); and the attitude to be taken by the unmarried toward marriage in view of the possible nearness of Christ's second coming (7, 8-40). The introductory section of the epistle shows that this general group was in the majority (1, 19), and that it was actually on its behalf that Paul wrote against the threat posed to the community by the views and conduct of the minority.

The epistle illustrates well the mind and character of Paul. He does not stigmatize people by mentioning names. He always treats the questions at issue on the level of the purity of Christian teaching and conduct. Though impelled to insist on his God-given office as founder of the community, and generously including Apollos in this labor, he nevertheless evaluates his own leading role as that of a servant of God (3, 5-8). On the other hand, he does not hesitate to exercise his authority accordingly as his judgment dictates in every situation, even going so far as to promise a direct confrontation with the recalcitrant should the abuses he scores remain uncorrected (4, 18-21).

Paul writes with confidence in the authority of his apostolic mission. He presumes that the Corinthians will recognize and accept it, despite the deficiencies of their faith. Certain passages in the epistle are of the greatest importance for an understanding of the early Christian teaching on the Eucharist (10, 14-22; 11, 17-34) and on the resurrection of the body (15, 1-57).

The First Epistle to the Corinthians is divided as follows:

THE FIRST EPISTLE OF PAUL
TO THE CORINTHIANS
I: INTRODUCTION

1

Greeting to the Church

¹ Paul, called by God's will to be an apostle of Christ Jesus, and Sosthenes our brother, ² send greetings to the church of God which is in Corinth; to you who have been consecrated in Christ Jesus and called to be a holy people, as to all those who, wherever they may be, call on the name of our Lord Jesus Christ, their Lord and ours. ³ Grace and peace from God our Father and the Lord Jesus Christ.

Thanksgiving

⁴ I continually thank my God for you because of the favor he has bestowed on you in Christ Jesus, ⁵ in whom you have been richly endowed with every gift of speech and knowledge. ⁶ Likewise, the witness I bore to Christ has been so confirmed among you ⁷ that you lack no spiritual gift as you wait for the revelation of our Lord Jesus Christ. ⁸ He will strengthen you to the end, so that you will be blameless on the day of our Lord Jesus [Christ]. ⁹ God is faithful, and it was he who called you to fellowship with his Son, Jesus Christ our Lord.

II: CONDEMNATION OF DISORDERS
IN THE CORINTHIAN CHURCH

Factions

¹⁰ I beg you, brothers, in the name of our Lord Jesus Christ, to agree in what you say. Let there be no factions; rather, be united in mind and judgment. ¹¹ I have been informed, my brothers, by certain members of Chloe's household that you are quarreling among yourselves. ¹² This is what I mean: One of you will say, "I belong to Paul," another, "I belong to Apollos,"

1, 1: Rom 1, 1.
7: Ti 2, 13.
8: Phil 1, 6.

9: 1 Jn 1, 3.
10: Phil 2, 2.
12: 3, 4.22; Acts 18, 24.

1, 1-9: After the customary salutation (1ff), Paul commends the Christian community of Corinth (4-7), and reminds its members of their expectation of Christ's second coming (8f; cf note on 1 Thes 4, 13-18).
1, 10-16: The presence in the community of factions due to particular attachments to Paul, Apollos, and Cephas (the reference to Christ may well be ironically intended) is an indication both of the enthusiasm for the new-found faith and the imperfect understanding of it among some of the Corinthians. We can merely conjecture about the divisions and the groups to which the apostle refers.

still another, "Cephas has my allegiance," and the fourth, "I belong to Christ." [13] Has Christ, then, been divided into parts? Was it Paul who was crucified for you? Was it in Paul's name that you were baptized? [14] Thank God, I baptized none of you except Crispus and Gaius, [15] so there are none who can say that you were baptized in my name. [16] Oh, and I baptized the household of Stephanas. Beyond that, I am not aware of having baptized anyone else. [17] For Christ did not send me to baptize, but to preach the gospel—not with wordy "wisdom," however, lest the cross of Christ be rendered void of its meaning!

The Wisdom and Folly of the Cross

[18] The message of the cross is complete absurdity to those who are headed for ruin, but to us who are experiencing salvation it is the power of God. [19] Scripture says,

> "I will destroy the wisdom of the wise,
>   and thwart the cleverness of the clever."

[20] Where is the wise man to be found? Where the scribe? Where is the master of worldly argument? Has not God turned the wisdom of this world into folly? [21] Since in God's wisdom the world did not come to know him through "wisdom," it pleased God to save those who believe through the absurdity of the preaching of the gospel. [22] Yes, Jews demand "signs" and Greeks look for "wisdom," [23] but we preach Christ crucified— a stumbling block to Jews, and an absurdity to Gentiles; [24] but to those who are called, Jews and Greeks alike, Christ the power of God and the wisdom of God. [25] For God's folly is wiser than men, and his weakness more powerful than men.

The Case of the Corinthians

[26] Brothers, you are among those called. Consider your situa-

---

14: Acts 18, 8.
16: 16, 15ff.
17: 2, 4.
18: 2, 14.

19: Is 29, 14.
20: Is 19, 12.
22: Mt 12, 38; 16, 1;
     Acts 17, 18.

1, 17-25: From the allusions here to *wisdom* (17) and the *wise* (19), it seems the Christians mentioned in v 12 were attempting unsuccessfully to align their faith with the philosophies of the day. Paul points out that the Christian message of redemption through the crucifixion of Christ (17f) lies outside the ken of philosophical speculation. It is God, not man, who controls human destiny beyond this life.

1, 26-31: God's choice of the foolish, the weak, the lowborn and the despised among the Corinthians to bestow on them the gift of faith in Christ, while shaming the wise and the strong of this world and reducing to nothing those who were something, is a sign that man receives life and attains to God in Christ Jesus, not by his own effort, but by God's act.

tion. Not many of you are wise, as men account wisdom; not many are influential; and surely not many are wellborn. [27] God chose those whom the world considers absurd to shame the wise; he singled out the weak of this world to shame the strong. [28] He chose the world's lowborn and despised, those who count for nothing, to reduce to nothing those who were something; [29] so that mankind can do no boasting before God. [30] God it is who has given you life in Christ Jesus. He has made him our wisdom and also our justice, our sanctification, and our redemption. [31] This is just as you find it written, "Let him who would boast, boast in the Lord."

2

Paul's Preaching

[1] As for myself, brothers, when I came to you I did not come proclaiming God's testimony with any particular eloquence or "wisdom." [2] No, I determined that while I was with you I would speak of nothing but Jesus Christ and him crucified. [3] When I came among you it was in weakness and fear, and with much trepidation. [4] My message and my preaching had none of the persuasive force of "wise" argumentation, but the convincing power of the Spirit. [5] As a consequence, your faith rests not on the wisdom of men but on the power of God.

True Wisdom

[6] There is, to be sure, a certain wisdom which we express among the spiritually mature. It is not a wisdom of this age, however, nor of the rulers of this age, who are men headed for destruction. [7] No, what we utter is God's wisdom: a mysterious, a hidden wisdom. God planned it before all ages for our glory. [8] None of the rulers of this age knew the mystery; if they had known it, they would never have crucified the Lord of glory. [9] Of this wisdom it is written:

28: Jas 2, 5.
30: Eph 2, 9.
31: Jer 9, 23f;
   2 Cor 10, 17.
2, 1: 1, 17.

2: Gal 6, 14.
4: 1 Thes 1, 5.
7: Rom 16, 25f.
9: Is 64, 3.

2, 1-5: In Paul's preaching at Corinth, he proclaimed the crucified Jesus as God's message of salvation to mankind. He is not denying here that he employed human eloquence, but rather pointing out that he presented himself as a man commissioned by God; cf Gal 4, 14. Thus the Corinthians believed in the gospel message on God's authority rather than on its intrinsic appeal to human reason.
2, 6-9: The Christian message is rightly termed a "wisdom," but a God-given wisdom pertaining to man's ultimate destiny through God's power. It is completely unknown to the rulers and great minds of the world (v 8).

"Eye has not seen, ear has not heard,
        nor has it so much as dawned on man
    what God has prepared for those who love him."

[10] Yet God has revealed this wisdom to us through the Spirit. The Spirit scrutinizes all matters, even the deep things of God. [11] Who, for example, knows a man's innermost self but the man's own spirit within him? Similarly, no one knows what lies at the depths of God but the Spirit of God. [12] The Spirit we have received is not the world's spirit but God's Spirit, helping us to recognize the gifts he has given us. [13] We speak of these, not in words of human wisdom but in words taught by the Spirit, thus interpreting spiritual things in spiritual terms. [14] The natural man does not accept what is taught by the Spirit of God. For him, that is absurdity. He cannot come to know such teaching because it must be appraised in a spiritual way. [15] The spiritual man, on the other hand, can appraise everything, though he himself can be appraised by no one. [16] For, "Who has known the mind of the Lord so as to instruct him?" But we have the mind of Christ.

3

Immaturity of the Corinthians

[1] Brothers, the trouble was that I could not talk to you as spiritual men but only as men of flesh, as infants in Christ. [2] I fed you with milk, and did not give you solid food because you were not ready for it. You are not ready for it even now, [3] being still very much in a natural condition. For as long as there are jealousy and quarrels among you, are you not of the flesh? And is not your behavior that of ordinary men? [4] When someone says, "I belong to Paul," and someone else, "I belong to Apollos," is it not clear that you are still at the human level?

10: Jn 14, 26; 16, 13.   Rom 11, 34.
16: Wis 9, 13; Is 40, 13;   **3, 3:** 1, 10ff; Jas 3, 16.

2, 10-16: Just as the individual is the only one cognizant of his own thoughts, which he alone can reveal, so it is with God and his plans for the salvation of humanity (10f). The Christian message expresses the secret thoughts, not of men, but of God (12f). It applies those thoughts to the innermost recesses of the mind and soul of man. By his acceptance or rejection of the gospel, a person shows himself to be affected or unaffected by the presence of God in the gospel (14ff).

3, 1-9: Here Paul seems to address himself to those who were more impressed by Apollos' preaching than by his own. His teaching had to be elementary, since it was the Corinthians' first confrontation with the demands of the Christian message. However, comparison between Apollos and himself is irrelevant, for they performed different tasks for the community, whose actual success was due to the presence of God.

The Office of God's Ministers

⁵ After all, who is Apollos? And who is Paul? Simply ministers through whom you became believers, each of them doing only what the Lord assigned him. ⁶ I planted the seed and Apollos watered it, but God made it grow. ⁷ This means that neither he who plants nor he who waters is of any special account, only God, who gives the growth. ⁸ He who plants and he who waters work to the same end. Each will receive his wages in proportion to his toil. ⁹ We are God's co-workers, while you are his cultivation, his building.

The Work of God's Ministers

¹⁰ Thanks to the favor God showed me I laid a foundation as a wise master-builder might do, and now someone else is building upon it. Everyone, however, must be careful how he builds. ¹¹ No one can lay a foundation other than the one that has been laid, namely Jesus Christ. ¹² If different ones build on this foundation with gold, silver, precious stones, wood, hay or straw, ¹³ the work of each will be made clear. The Day will disclose it. That day will make its appearance with fire, and fire will test the quality of each man's work. ¹⁴ If the building a man has raised on this foundation still stands, he will receive his recompense; ¹⁵ if a man's building burns, he will suffer loss. He himself will be saved, but only as one fleeing through fire.

¹⁶ Are you not aware that you are the temple of God, and that the Spirit of God dwells in you? ¹⁷ If anyone destroys God's temple, God will destroy him. For the temple of God is holy, and you are that temple.

¹⁸ Let no one delude himself. If any one of you thinks he

6: Acts 18, 8.11.24.
9: Eph 2, 20; 1 Pt 2, 4ff.
13: Mt 3, 11f.

16: 6, 19; 2 Cor 6, 16; Eph 2, 20ff.

3, 10-15: Paul's work was to found the community on Christ (10f). The work of others for the spiritual good of the community is to be evaluated in terms of enhancing faith in Christ, and of this, God is ultimately the judge (12-15).

3, 16f: *You are the temple of God . . . dwells in you:* God's Spirit sanctifies the Christian community, making it a fit abode for God. *If anyone destroys . . . God will destroy him:* the sudden vehemence seems strange in the context. Some scholars believe Paul has in mind those guilty of corrupting the community morally; cf 5, 1-13; 6, 12-20. However, he may now wish to stress the importance of the Christian teacher's work (10-15), since he previously subordinated this role (5-19) to the effective action of God.

3, 18-23: The Corinthians will prove themselves fools, no better than "the wise" of this world, if they continue *boasting about men.* But since through their faith they belong to Christ, and through him to God, all things, *life* and *death* themselves, can assist them in attaining their end.

is wise in a worldly way, he had better become a fool. In that way he will really be wise, [19] for the wisdom of this world is absurdity with God. Scripture says, "He catches the wise in their craftiness"; [20] and again, "The Lord knows how empty are the thoughts of the wise." [21] Let there be no boasting about men. All things are yours, [22] whether it be Paul, or Apollos, or Cephas, or the world, or life, or death, or the present, or the future: all these are yours, [23] and you are Christ's, and Christ is God's.

4

Christ Judges His Ministers

[1] Men should regard us as servants of Christ and administrators of the mysteries of God. [2] The first requirement of an administrator is that he prove trustworthy. [3] It matters little to me whether you or any human court pass judgment on me. I do not even pass judgment on myself. [4] Mind you, I have nothing on my conscience. But that does not mean that I am declaring myself innocent. The Lord is the one to judge me, [5] so stop passing judgment before the time of his return. He will bring to light what is hidden in darkness and manifest the intentions of hearts. At that time, everyone will receive his praise from God.

Corinthians Contrasted with Apostles

[6] Brothers, I have applied all this to myself and Apollos by way of example for your benefit. May you learn from us not to go beyond what is set down, so that none of you will grow self-important by reason of his association with one person rather than another. [7] Who confers any distinction on you? Name something you have that you have not received. If, then, you have received it, why are you boasting as if it were your own? [8] At the moment you are completely satisfied. You have

---

19: Jb 5, 13;
Ps 94, 11.
4, 1: Ti 1, 7.

4: 2 Cor 5, 10.
5: 3, 13.
6: Rom 12, 13.

4, 1-5: Paul and his associates are to be regarded as assistants and managers in God's household, charged with administering the mysteries in complete dependence upon him. It is his truth which they preach and his interests which they serve. Therefore they are accountable only to him, not to the judgments of men.

4, 6-13: The example of Paul and Apollos is offered as a norm or pattern of conduct for the Corinthians. The sufferings of the apostles, their humiliations and lowly condition, contrast sharply with the self-satisfaction and boastfulness of the Corinthians. And yet all the benefits the latter enjoy are gifts from God, and, as such, should preclude their boasting as if they had not received them.

grown rich! You have launched upon your reign with no help from us. Would that you had really begun to reign, that we might be reigning with you!

⁹ As I see it, God has put us apostles at the end of the line, like men doomed to die in the arena. We have become a spectacle to the universe, to angels and men alike. ¹⁰ We are fools on Christ's account. Ah, but in Christ you are wise! We are the weak ones, you the strong! They honor you, while they sneer at us! ¹¹ Up to this very hour we go hungry and thirsty, poorly clad, roughly treated, wandering about homeless. ¹² We work hard at manual labor. When we are insulted we respond with a blessing. Persecution comes our way; we bear it patiently. ¹³ We are slandered, and we try conciliation. We have become the world's refuse, the scum of all; that is the present state of affairs.

¹⁴ I am writing you in this way not to shame you but to admonish you as my beloved children. ¹⁵ Granted you have ten thousand guardians in Christ, you have only one father. It was I who begot you in Christ Jesus through my preaching of the gospel. ¹⁶ I beg you, then, be imitators of me. ¹⁷ This is why I have sent you Timothy, my beloved and faithful son in the Lord. He will remind you of my ways in Christ, just as I teach them in all the churches.

¹⁸ Some have grown full of self-importance, thinking that I will not come to you. ¹⁹ But I shall come to you soon, the Lord willing, and find out, not what they say, but what they can do. ²⁰ The kingdom of God does not consist in talk but in power. ²¹ Which do you prefer, that I come to you with a rod, or with love and a gentle spirit?

III: MORAL DISORDERS

5

An Incestuous Man

¹ It is actually reported that there is lewd conduct among you

---

9: Rom 8, 36;
2 Cor 4, 8-12.
10: 2 Cor 13, 9.
11: 2 Cor 11, 23-27.
12: Acts 18, 3; 20, 34;
1 Thes 2, 9.

16: 11, 1; 2 Thes 3, 7.
17: Acts 16, 1.
20: 2, 4; 1 Thes 1, 5.
21: 2 Cor 10, 2.
5, 1: Lv 18, 7f; Dt 23, 10.

4, 14-21: Paul tempers his severity by reminding them that, as the founder of their community, he has a certain right to display his feelings. Moreover, he reserves the further right to confront personally in the future those who may remain recalcitrant.

5, 1-13: Two deviations of the community are considered here: the toler-

of a kind not even found among the pagans—a man living with his father's wife. [2] Still you continue to be self-satisfied, instead of grieving, and getting rid of the offender! [3] As for me, though absent in body I am present in spirit, and have already passed sentence in the name of our Lord Jesus Christ on the man who did this deed. [4] United in spirit with you and empowered by our Lord Jesus, [5] I hand him over to Satan for the destruction of his flesh, so that his spirit may be saved on the day of the Lord.

[6] This boasting of yours is an ugly thing. Do you not know that a little yeast has its effect all through the dough? [7] Get rid of the old yeast to make of yourselves fresh dough, unleavened loaves, as it were; Christ our Passover has been sacrificed. [8] Let us celebrate the feast not with the old yeast, that of corruption and wickedness, but with the unleavened bread of sincerity and truth.

[9] I wrote you in my letter not to associate with immoral persons. [10] I was not speaking of association with immoral people in this world, or the covetous or thieves or idolaters. To avoid them, you would have to leave the world! [11] What I really wrote about was your not associating with anyone who bears the title "brother" if he is immoral, covetous, an idolater, an abusive person, a drunkard, or a thief. It is clear that you must not eat with such a man. [12] What business is it of mine to judge outsiders? Is it not those inside the community you must judge? [13] God will judge the others. "Expel the wicked man from your midst."

6

Lawsuits before Pagans

[1] How can anyone with a case against another dare bring it for judgment to the wicked and not to God's holy people?

3: Col 2, 5.
5: 1 Tm 1, 20.
7: 1 Pt 1, 19.
9: 2 Thes 3, 14.

10: Jn 17, 15.
11: Mt 18, 17; 2 Thes 3, 6;
    2 Jn 10.
13: Dt 13, 6.

---

ation of the incestuous union of a man with his stepmother (1-8); and the misunderstanding of Paul's admonition against associating with fellow Christians guilty of sexual immorality (9-13). In the first case, Paul (impelled perhaps by his belief in the imminence of the parousia) recommends the ecclesial penalty of separating the offender from the unity of the faithful and handing him over to Satan, i. e., for medicinal punishment through bodily affliction, even death (1 Tm 1, 20), so that the incestuous relationship may be destroyed and the path to repentance and reunion laid open.

6, 1-8: The apostle expresses his dismay that the image of mutual charity among Christians is being tarnished by their lawsuits in Roman courts. This

[2] Do you not know that the believers will judge the world? If the judgment of the world is to be yours, are you to be thought unworthy of judging in minor matters? [3] Do you not know that we are to judge angels? Surely, then, we are up to deciding everyday affairs. [4] If you have such matters to decide, do you accept as judges those who have no standing in the church? [5] I say this in an attempt to shame you. Can it be that there is no one among you wise enough to settle a case between one member of the church and another? [6] Must brother drag brother into court, and before unbelievers at that? [7] Why, the very fact that you have lawsuits against one another is disastrous for you. Why not put up with injustice, and let yourselves be cheated? [8] Instead, you yourselves injure and cheat your very own brothers. [9] Can you not realize that the unholy will not fall heir to the kingdom of God? Do not deceive yourselves: no fornicators, idolaters, or adulterers, no sodomites, [10] thieves, misers, or drunkards, no slanderers or robbers will inherit God's kingdom. [11] And such were some of you; but you have been washed, consecrated, justified in the name of our Lord Jesus Christ and in the Spirit of our God.

Against Sexual Immorality

[12] "Everything is lawful for me"—but that does not mean that everything is good for me. "Everything is lawful for me" —but I will not let myself be enslaved by anything. [13] "Food is for the stomach and the stomach for food, and God will do away with them both in the end"—but the body is not for immorality; it is for the Lord, and the Lord is for the body. [14] God, who raised up the Lord, will raise us also by his power.

[15] Do you not see that your bodies are members of Christ? Would you have me take Christ's members and make them the members of a prostitute? God forbid! [16] Can you not see that the man who is joined to a prostitute becomes one body

---

6, 3: Wis 3, 8; Mt 19, 28;
Rv 20, 4.
7: Mt 5, 28-42;
Rom 12, 17ff;
1 Thes 5, 15.
9: Gal 5, 19ff; Eph 5, 5.

10: 15, 50.
11: Ti 3, 3-7; 1 Jn 2, 12.
14: Rom 8, 11; 2 Cor 4, 14.
15: Rom 6, 12f.
16: Gn 2, 24; Eph 5, 30.

---

is all the more deplorable since Christians are to share with Christ the judgment of the world, and ought therefore to be capable of settling one another's minor cases within the society of believers; cf Dn 7, 22.27.
6, 9-20: Paul insists that the Christian give evidence of the reality of his faith in Christ by living according to a high moral standard. The gravity of the sins mentioned in vv 9f can be gauged from the fact that they exclude the offender from inheriting the kingdom of God. In 6, 12-20 the fornication referred to is probably that of religious prostitution, an accepted part of pagan culture in Rome.

with her? Scripture says, "The two shall become one flesh." [17] But whoever is joined to the Lord becomes one spirit with him. [18] Shun lewd conduct. Every other sin a man commits is outside his body, but the fornicator sins against his own body. [19] You must know that your body is a temple of the Holy Spirit, who is within—the Spirit you have received from God. You are not your own. [20] You have been purchased, and at a price. So glorify God in your body.

7

Advice to the Married

[1] Now for the matters you wrote about. A man is better off having no relations with a woman. [2] But to avoid immorality, every man should have his own wife and every woman her own husband. [3] The husband should fulfill his conjugal obligations toward his wife, the wife hers toward her husband. [4] A wife does not belong to herself but to her husband; equally, a husband does not belong to himself but to his wife. [5] Do not deprive one another, unless perhaps by mutual consent for a time, to devote yourselves to prayer. Then return to one another, that Satan may not tempt you through your lack of self-control. [6] I say this by way of concession, not as a command. [7] Given my preference, I should like you to be as I am. Still, each one has his own gift from God, one this and another that.

Advice to the Unmarried

[8] To those not married and to widows I have this to say: It would be well if they remain as they are, even as I do myself; [9] but if they cannot exercise self-control, they should marry. It is better to marry than to be on fire. [10] To those now married, however, I give this command (though it is not mine; it is the Lord's): a wife must not separate from her husband. [11] If she does separate, she must either remain single or be-

---

17: Rom 8, 9f; 2 Cor 3, 17.   7, 7: Mt 19, 12.
19: 3, 16f; Rom 5, 5.   9: 1 Tm 5, 11-14.
20: 3, 23; Phil 1, 20.   10: Mt 5, 32; 19, 9.

7, 1-11: Paul's teaching concerning marriage and the celibate state is placed in the framework of the second coming of Christ (26.28f); see note on 1 Thes 4, 13-18. The apostle commends sexual asceticism in marriage provided it is agreed to by both parties, spiritually motivated, and not carried beyond either party's limits of control (1-7). The existing practice within the community of widows and widowers remaining unmarried is also commended, without, however, any implication against the freedom to remarry should sexual attraction prove irresistible. Christ's teaching against divorce and remarriage must be strictly adhered to in marriages between Christians; cf Mk 10, 9.

come reconciled to him again. Similarly, a husband must not divorce his wife.

Obligation of the Believing Partner

[12] As for the other matters, although I know of nothing the Lord has said, I say: If any brother has a wife who is an unbeliever but is willing to live with him, he must not divorce her. [13] And if any woman has a husband who is an unbeliever but is willing to live with her, she must not divorce him. [14] The unbelieving husband is consecrated by his believing wife; the unbelieving wife is consecrated by her believing husband. If it were otherwise, your children should be unclean; but as it is, they are holy.

[15] If the unbeliever wishes to separate, however, let him do so. The believing husband or wife is not bound in such cases. God has called you to live in peace. [16] Wife, how do you know that you will not save your husband; or you, husband, that you will not save your wife?

No Change To Be Sought

[17] The general rule is that each one should lead the life the Lord has assigned him, continuing as he was when the Lord called him. This is the rule I give in all the churches. [18] Was someone called after he had been circumcised? He should not try to hide his circumcision. Did the call come to another who had never been circumcised? He is not to be circumcised. [19] Circumcision counts for nothing, and its lack makes no difference either. What matters is keeping God's commandments. [20] Everyone ought to continue as he was when he was called. [21] Were you a slave when your call came? Give it no thought. Even supposing you could go free, you would be better off making the most of your slavery. [22] The slave called in the Lord is a freedman of the Lord, just as the freeman who has been called is a slave of Christ. [23] You have been bought at a

12: 1 Pt 3, 1.   22: Eph 6, 5-9; Phlm 16.
14: Rom 11, 16.   23: 6, 20.
19: Rom 2, 25; Gal 5, 6.

7, 12-16: In the case of marriage between Christians and non-Christians, there must be no divorce as long as the unbelieving partner is willing to live peacefully with the Christian spouse (12f). But if the non-believer wishes to separate, or refuses to live peacefully with the Christian, the latter is no longer bound (15f).

7, 17-24: A degree of importance is attached to the circumstances that basically condition one's life at the time of conversion. Normally, everyone, whether Jew or Gentile, slave or free, should expect to retain his particular state.

price! Do not enslave yourselves to men. [24] Brothers, each of you should continue before God in the condition of life that was his when he was called.

The State of Virginity

[25] With respect to virgins, I have not received any commandment from the Lord, but I give my opinion as one who is trustworthy, thanks to the Lord's mercy. [26] It is this: In the present time of stress it seems good to me for a person to continue as he is. [27] Are you bound to a wife? Then do not seek your freedom. Are you free of a wife? If so, do not go in search of one. [28] Should you marry, however, you will not be committing sin. Neither does a virgin commit a sin if she marries. But such people will have trials in this life, and these I should like to spare you.

[29] I tell you, brothers, the time is short. From now on those with wives should live as though they had none; [30] those who weep should live as though they were not weeping, and those who rejoice should live as though they were not rejoicing; buyers should conduct themselves as though they owned nothing, [31] and those who make use of the world as though they were not using it, for the world as we know it is passing away.

[32] I should like you to be free of all worries. The unmarried man is busy with the Lord's affairs, concerned with pleasing the Lord; [33] but the married man is busy with this world's demands and occupied with pleasing his wife. [34] This means he is divided. The virgin—indeed, any unmarried woman—is concerned with things of the Lord, in pursuit of holiness in body and spirit. The married woman, on the other hand, has the cares of this world to absorb her and is concerned with pleasing her husband. [35] I am going into this with you for your own good. I have no desire to place restrictions on you, but I do want to promote what is good, what will help you to devote yourselves entirely to the Lord.

33: Lk 14, 20.   35: Lk 10, 39.42.

7, 25-31: The above principle of retention of one's state applies also to both the unmarried and the married because, in the light of the second coming of Christ, it is not the state that is important but rather the use of it in a spirit of sacrifice, i. e., as though not using it. In this way all things are made subservient to the supreme end of preparedness for Christ's coming in judgment.

7, 32-35: Those who were unmarried at the time of conversion should realize that their celibate state relieves them of the responsibilities of marriage and family, and the resulting involvement in worldly affairs. They are more free to engage directly in the service of the Lord (32ff). This does not, however, contradict the individual's freedom to marry (v 35; cf 7, 8f.28).

A Question of Marriage

³⁶ If anyone thinks he is behaving dishonorably toward his virgin because a critical moment has come and it seems that something should be done, let him do as he wishes. He commits no sin if there is a marriage. ³⁷ The man, however, who stands firm in his resolve, who while without constraint and free to carry out his will makes up his mind to keep his virgin, also acts rightly. ³⁸ To sum up: the man who marries his virgin, acts fittingly; the one who does not, will do better.

Widows

³⁹ A wife is bound to her husband as long as he lives. If her husband dies she is free to marry, but on one condition, that it be in the Lord. ⁴⁰ She will be happier, though, in my opinion, if she stays unmarried. I am persuaded that in this I have the Spirit of God.

8

Meats Offered to Idols

¹ Now about meats that have been offered to idols. Of course we all "know" about that. But whereas "knowledge" inflates, love upbuilds. ² If a man thinks he knows something, that means he has never really known it as he ought. ³ But if anyone loves God, that man is known by him. ⁴ So then, about this matter of eating meats that have been offered to idols: we know that an idol is really nothing, and that there is no God but one. ⁵ Even though there are so-called gods in the heavens and on the earth—there are, to be sure, many such "gods" and "lords"—⁶ for us there is one God, the Father, from whom all things come and for whom we live; and one Lord Jesus Christ, through whom everything was made and through whom we live.

Practical Rules

⁷ Not all, of course, possess this "knowledge." Because some

39: Rom 7, 2.
8, 2: Gal 6, 3.
4: 10, 19.

6: Mal 2, 10; Jn 1, 3;
Col 1, 16.
7: 10, 28; Rom 14, 23.

7, 36ff: These verses may mean either that a) a man living chastely with virgin may marry her; or b) a father may give his daughter in marriage, or a guardian his ward. However, dedicated celibacy and virginity anticipate he life of glory after the resurrection, when marriage will no longer exist; cf Mt 22, 30.
7, 39f: Widows who choose to remarry should prefer Christian husbands.
8, 1-13: See note on Romans 14, 1—15, 6.

were so recently devoted to idols, they eat meat, fully aware that it has been sacrificed, and because their conscience is weak, it is defiled by the eating. [8] Now food does not bring us closer to God. We suffer no loss through failing to eat, and we gain no favor by eating. [9] Take care, however, lest in exercising your right you become an occasion of sin to the weak. [10] If someone sees you, with your "knowledge," reclining at table in the temple of an idol, may not his conscience in its weak state be influenced to the point that he eats the idol-offering? [11] Because of your "knowledge" the weak one perishes, that brother for whom Christ died. [12] When you sin thus against your brothers and wound their weak consciences, you are sinning against Christ. [13] Therefore, if food causes my brother to sin I will never eat meat again, so that I may not be an occasion of sin to him.

9

Paul's Rights as an Apostle

[1] Am I not free? Am I not an apostle? Have I not seen Jesus our Lord? And are you not my work in the Lord? [2] Although I may not be an apostle for others, I certainly am one for you. You are the very seal of my apostolate in the Lord.

[3] My defense against those who criticize me is this: [4] Do we not have the right to eat and drink? [5] Do we not have the right to marry a believing woman like the rest of the apostles and the brothers of the Lord and Cephas? [6] Is it only myself and Barnabas who are forced to work for a living? [7] What soldier in the field pays for his rations? Who plants a vineyard and does not eat of its yield? What shepherd does not nourish himself with the milk of his flock? [8] You may think the reasons I am giving are merely human ones, but does not the law itself speak of these things? [9] It is written in the law of Moses, "You

---

8: Rom 14, 17; Col 2, 21f.   12: Acts 9, 5.
9: Rom 14, 20.   13: Rom 14, 21.
11: Rom 14, 15.   **9,** 1: Acts 26, 16.

9, 1-23: Behind this passage lies some objection within the Corinthian community to Paul's apostolic role. Since he does not accept material support from the community or make use of a woman servant, like the other apostles, he is apparently not to be considered their equal. Paul replies that he is quite aware of his right to do these things, but that he has made a free, personal decision not to exercise this right. He feels that his preaching of the gospel is a duty laid upon him by God, which he must fulfill by presenting the gospel to men as gratuitously as God gave it to him (15-18) He cannot be accused of pride, for his apostolic life is proof that he has conquered his pride; he adapts himself to the customary observances of the law when residing among Judaeo Christians, and to its non-observance when he shares the life of Gentile Christians (19-23).

shall not muzzle an ox while it treads out grain." Is God concerned here for oxen, [10] or does he not rather say this for our sakes? You can be sure it was written for us, for the plowman should plow in hope and the harvester expect a share in the grain. [11] If we have sown for you in the spirit is it too much to expect a material harvest from you? [12] If others have this right over you, is not our right even greater? But we have not used this right. On the contrary, we put up with all sorts of hardships so as not to place any obstacle in the way of the gospel of Christ. [13] Do you not realize that those who work in the temple are supported by the temple, and those who minister at the altar share the offerings of the altar? [14] Likewise the Lord himself ordered that those who preach the gospel should live by the gospel.

Reason for Not Using Rights

[15] As for me, I have not used any of these rights, nor do I write this now to see to it that anything should be done for me. I would rather die than let anyone rob me of my boast! [16] Yet preaching the gospel is not the subject of a boast; I am under compulsion and have no choice. I am ruined if I do not preach it! [17] If I do it willingly, I have my recompense; if unwillingly, I am nonetheless entrusted with a charge. [18] And this recompense of mine? It is simply this, that when preaching I offer the gospel free of charge and do not make full use of the authority the gospel gives me.

All Things to All Men

[19] Although I am not bound to anyone, I made myself the slave of all so as to win over as many as possible. [20] I became like a Jew to the Jews in order to win the Jews. To those bound by the law I became like one who is bound (although in fact I am not bound by it), that I might win those bound by the law. [21] To those not subject to the law I became like one not subject to it (not that I am free from the law of God, for I am subject to the law of Christ), that I might win those not subject to the law. [22] To the weak I became a weak person with a view to winning the weak. I have made myself all things to all men in order to save at least some of them. [23] In fact, I

9: Dt 25, 4; 1 Tm 5, 18.
11: Rom 15, 27.
12: 2 Cor 11, 9.
13: Nm 18, 8.31; Dt 18, 1ff.
14: Lk 10. 7.

15: 2 Cor 11, 9.
16: Acts 4, 20; 22, 14f.
18: 2 Cor 11, 7.
19: Mt 20, 26.
22: 2 Cor 11, 29.

do all that I do for the sake of the gospel in the hope of having a share in its blessings.

²⁴ You know that while all the runners in the stadium take part in the race, the award goes to one man. In that case, run so as to win! ²⁵ Athletes deny themselves all sorts of things. They do this to win a crown of leaves that withers, but we a crown that is imperishable.

²⁶ I do not run like a man who loses sight of the finish line. I do not fight as if I were shadowboxing. ²⁷ What I do is discipline my own body and master it, for fear that after having preached to others I myself should be rejected.

10

Against Overconfidence

¹ Brothers, I want you to remember this: our fathers were all under the cloud and all passed through the sea; ² by the cloud and the sea all of them were baptized into Moses. ³ All ate the same spiritual food. ⁴ All drank the same spiritual drink (they drank from the spiritual rock that was following them, and the rock was Christ), ⁵ yet we know that God was not pleased with most of them, for "they were struck down in the desert."

⁶ These things happened as an example to keep us from wicked desires such as theirs. ⁷ Do not become idolaters, as some of them did. Scripture says, "The people sat down to eat and drink, and arose to take their pleasure." ⁸ Let us not indulge in lewdness as some of them did, so that in one day twenty-three thousand perished. ⁹ Let us not test the Lord as some of them did, only to be destroyed by snakes. ¹⁰ Nor are you to grumble as some them did, to be killed by the destroying angel. ¹¹ The things that happened to them serve as an example. They have been written as a warning to us, upon whom the end of the ages has come. ¹² For all these reasons, let anyone who thinks he is standing upright watch out lest he

24: 2 Tm 4, 7f.
25: Jas 1, 12.
27: Rom 8, 13.
10, 1: Ex 13, 21; 14, 19-22.
3: Ex 16, 4-35.
4: Ex 17, 6; Nm 20, 7-11.

5: Nm 14, 16; Jude 5.
7: Ex 32, 6.
8: Nm 25, 1-9.
9: Nm 21, 5f.
10: Nm 14, 2.36.

10, 1-13: Paul approaches the question of participation in the sacrificial worship of pagan temples (14-22) by invoking Old Testament traditions from the history of Israel in the desert, especially Israel's forbidden worship of the golden calf (Ex 32, 1-29). Christians, in their turn, possess the spiritual gifts of God but this does not free them from the danger of yielding to temptation.

fall! [13] No test has been sent you that does not come to all men. Besides, God keeps this promise. He will not let you be tested beyond your strength. Along with the test he will give you a way out of it so that you may be able to endure it.

The Eucharist versus Pagan Sacrifices

[14] I am telling you, whom I love, to shun the worship of idols, [15] and I address you as one addresses sensible people. You may judge for yourselves what I am saying. [16] Is not the cup of blessing we bless a sharing in the blood of Christ? And is not the bread we break a sharing in the body of Christ? [17] Because the loaf of bread is one, we, many though we are, are one body, for we all partake of the one loaf.

[18] Look at Israel according to the flesh and see if those who eat the sacrifices do not share in the altar! [19] What am I saying —that meat offered to an idol is really offered to that idol, or that an idol is a reality? [20] No, I mean that the Gentiles sacrifice to demons and not to God, and I do not want you to become sharers with demons. [21] You cannot drink the cup of the Lord and also the cup of demons. You cannot partake of the table of the Lord and likewise the table of demons. [22] Do we mean to provoke the Lord to jealous anger? Surely we are not stronger than he!

Concerning Idol Offerings

[23] "All things are lawful," but not all are advantageous. "All things are lawful"—which does not mean that everything is constructive. [24] No man should seek his own interest but rather that of his neighbor. [25] Eat whatever is sold in the market without raising any question of conscience. [26] "The earth and its fullness are the Lord's." [27] If an unbeliever invites you to his table and you want to go, eat whatever is placed before you, without raising any question of conscience. [28] But if someone should say to you, "This was offered an idol worship," do not eat it, both for the sake of the one who called attention to it

---

13: Mt 6, 13; Jas 1, 13f.
16: Mt 26, 26f; Acts 2, 42.
17: 12, 7; Rom 12, 5;
    Eph 4, 4.
20: Dt 32, 17;

2 Cor 6, 14ff.
23: 6, 12.
24: Rom 15, 2; Phil 2, 4.
26: Ps 24, 1.

10, 14-22: Paul repudiates idol-worship on the ground of the meaning of the Eucharist: it is the Christian sacrifice that effects union with the living Christ. Although the pagan sacrifices aim at a union with the gods, in the light of Christian teaching they are seen to serve only the cause of evil.
10, 23—11, 1: See note on Romans 14, 1—15, 6.

and on account of the conscience issue—[29] not your own conscience but your neighbor's. You may ask, Why should my liberty be restricted by another man's conscience? [30] And why is it, if I partake thankfully, that I should be blamed for the food over which I gave thanks?

Conclusion

[31] The fact is that whether you eat or drink—whatever you do—you should do all for the glory of God. [32] Give no offense to Jew or Greek or to the church of God, [33] just as I try to please all in any way I can by seeking, not my own advantage, but that of the many, that they may be saved.

11

[1] Imitate me as I imitate Christ.

IV: CONDUCT AT PUBLIC WORSHIP

Headdress of Women

[2] I praise you because you always remember me and are holding fast to the traditions just as I handed them on to you. [3] I want you to know that the head of every man is Christ; the head of a woman is her husband; and the head of Christ is the Father. [4] Any man who prays or prophesies with his head covered brings shame upon his head. [5] Similarly, any woman who prays or prophesies with her head uncovered brings shame upon her head. It is as if she had had her head shaved. [6] Indeed, if a woman will not wear a veil, she ought to cut off her hair. If it is shameful for a woman to have her hair cut off or her head shaved, it is clear that she ought to wear a veil. [7] A man, on the other hand, ought not to cover his head, because he is the image of God and the reflection of his glory. Woman, in turn, is the reflection of man's glory. [8] Man was not made from woman but woman from man. [9] Neither was man created for woman but woman for man. [10] For this reason a woman ought to have a sign of submission on her head, because of the angels. [11] Yet, in the Lord, woman

---

30: Rom 14, 6; 1 Tm 4, 3f.   7: Gn 1, 27; 5, 1.
11, 1: 4, 16; Phil 3, 17.   9: Gn 2, 21ff.
   3: Eph 5, 23.   10: 14, 34.

11, 2-16: The apostle regards the independence of the Corinthian women who participate in worship with unveiled heads as a lack of humility, since a woman's veil is regarded as a sign of dependence on the authority of her husband. Paul's argument is based on his view of nature and on propriety, i. e., the custom of the earliest Christian communities.

is not independent of man nor man independent of woman. [12] In the same way that woman was made from man, so man is born of woman; and all is from God. [13] I will let you judge for yourselves. Is it proper for a woman to pray to God unveiled? [14] Does not nature itself teach you that it is dishonorable for a man to wear his hair long, [15] while the long hair of a woman is her glory? Her hair has been given her for a covering. [16] If anyone wants to argue about this, remember that neither we nor the churches of God recognize any other usage.

The Lord's Supper

[17] What I now have to say is not said in praise, because your meetings are not profitable but harmful. [18] First of all, I hear that when you gather for a meeting there are divisions among you, and I am inclined to believe it. [19] There may even have to be factions among you for the tried and true to stand out clearly. [20] When you assemble it is not to eat the Lord's Supper, [21] for everyone is in haste to eat his own supper. One person goes hungry while another gets drunk. [22] Do you not have homes where you can eat and drink? Would you show contempt for the church of God, and embarrass those who have nothing? What can I say to you? Shall I praise you? Certainly not in this matter!

[23] I received from the Lord what I handed on to you, namely, that the Lord Jesus on the night in which he was betrayed took bread, [24] and after he had given thanks, broke it and said, "This is my body, which is for you. Do this in remembrance of me." [25] In the same way, after the supper, he took the cup, saying, "This cup is the new covenant in my blood. Do this, whenever you drink it, in remembrance of me." [26] Every time, then, you eat this bread and drink this cup, you proclaim the death of the Lord until he comes! [27] This means that whoever eats the bread or drinks the cup of the Lord unworthily sins against the body and blood of the Lord. [28] A

18: 1, 10ff.
22: Jas 2, 5ff.
23: 10, 16f; Mt 26, 26-29;

Mk 14, 22-25;
Lk 22, 14-20.
25: Ex 24, 8; Heb 8, 6-13.

11, 17-34: Paul concerns himself with the proper celebration of the eucharistic liturgy (33f). He has become aware that at the agape preceding the celebration of the Eucharist, the mutual charity of sharing food and companionship is being violated through discrimination against the needy (21f). Moreover, even drunkenness has not been unknown (21). In this earliest written account of the Lord's Supper Paul emphasizes its sacrificial aspect, i. e., the proclamation of Jesus' death in atonement for sin (23-26). Participation in this mystery requires a clean conscience (27ff). Abuse of the mystery on the part of some is the cause of their punishment through illness and death (30ff).

man should examine himself first; only then should he eat of the bread and drink of the cup. [29] He who eats and drinks without recognizing the body eats and drinks a judgment on himself. [30] That is why many among you are sick and infirm, and why so many are dying. [31] If we were to examine ourselves, we would not be falling under judgment in this way; [32] but since it is the Lord who judges us, he chastens us to keep us from being condemned with the rest of the world. [33] Therefore, my brothers, when you assemble for the meal, wait for one another. [34] If anyone is hungry let him eat at home, so that your assembly may not deserve condemnation. As for other matters, I shall give instructions when I come.

V: SPIRITUAL GIFTS

12

Variety and Unity

[1] Now, brothers, I do not want to leave you in ignorance about spiritual gifts. [2] You know that when you were pagans you were led astray to mute idols, as impulse drove you. [3] That is why I tell you that nobody who speaks in the Spirit of God ever says, "Cursed be Jesus." And no one can say: "Jesus is Lord," except in the Holy Spirit.

[4] There are different gifts but the same Spirit; [5] there are different ministries but the same Lord; [6] there are different works but the same God who accomplishes all of them in everyone. [7] To each person the manifestation of the Spirit is given for the common good. [8] To one the Spirit gives wisdom in discourse, to another the power to express knowledge. [9] Through the Spirit one receives faith; by the same Spirit another is

32: Dt 8, 5; Heb 12, 5ff.
12, 2: Heb 2, 18f.
3: Mk 9, 39; 1 Jn 4, 2f.

4: Rom 12, 6; Eph 4, 4.
5: 12, 28; Eph 4, 11.

12, 1—14, 40: Here Paul speaks of special spiritual gifts (charisms) enabling individuals to exercise an office or function within the community. He provides a list of charisms in 12, 8ff (cf Rom 12, 6ff; Eph 4, 11) which he wishes to be recognized as a manifestation of the presence of the Holy Spirit (3-11), each contributing in its own way to the good of the whole community (12-30). (Paul does not value the charisms for their own sake, since Christian love is the only enduring gift of God; cf 12, 31—13, 13). Corinthians may lawfully desire to possess the charisms, but they should aspire especially to the gift of prophecy (probably, the gift of directing the community in new situations, and of revealing what could not otherwise be known; cf 14, 3.30; Acts 13, 1f). The apostle criticizes the overstressing of the gift of tongues (probably ecstatic utterances requiring an interpreter; cf 14, 1-25), and directs that this gift be employed only when an interpreter is present. At the assembly no more than three persons, not including women, are to act on the basis of a charism (26-40).

given the gift of healing, [10] and still another miraculous powers. Prophecy is given to one; to another power to distinguish one spirit from another. One receives the gift of tongues, another that of interpreting the tongues. [11] But it is one and the same Spirit who produces all these gifts, distributing them to each as he will.

Analogy of the Body

[12] The body is one and has many members, but all the members, many though they are, are one body; and so it is with Christ. [13] It was in one Spirit that all of us, whether Jew or Greek, slave or free, were baptized into one body. All of us have been given to drink of the one Spirit. [14] Now the body is not one member, it is many. [15] If the foot should say, "Because I am not a hand I do not belong to the body," would it then no longer belong to the body? [16] If the ear should say, "Because I am not an eye I do not belong to the body," would it then no longer belong to the body? [17] If the body were all eye, what would happen to our hearing? If it were all ear, what would happen to our smelling? [18] As it is, God has set each member of the body in the place he wanted it to be. [19] If all the members were alike, where would the body be? [20] There are, indeed, many different members, but one body. [21] The eye cannot say to the hand, "I do not need you," any more than the head can say to the feet, "I do not need you." [22] Even those members of the body which seem less important are in fact indispensable. [23] We honor the members we consider less honorable by clothing them with greater care, [24] thus bestowing on the less presentable a propriety which the more presentable already have. God has so constructed the body as to give greater honor to the lowly members, [25] that there may be no dissension in the body, but that all the members may be concerned for one another. [26] If one member suffers, all the members suffer with it; if one member is honored, all the members share its joy.

The One Body of Christ

[27] You, then are the body of Christ. Every one of you is a member of it. [28] Furthermore, God has set up in the church first apostles, second prophets, third teachers, then miracle

---

10: 14, 5; Acts 2, 4.
11: 7, 7; Eph 4, 7.
12: 10, 17; Rom 12, 4f;
    Col 3, 15.

13: Gal 3, 28; Eph 2, 13.16;
    Col 3, 11.
27: Rom 12, 5-8; Eph 5, 20.
28: Eph 4, 11.

workers, healers, assistants, administrators, and those who speak in tongues. [29] Are all apostles? Are all prophets? Are all teachers? Do all work miracles [30] or have the gift of healing? Do all speak in tongues, all have the gift of interpretation of tongues? [31] Set your hearts on the greater gifts.

13

Excellence of the Gift of Love

[1] Now I will show you the way which surpasses all the others. If I speak with human tongues and angelic as well, but do not have love, I am a noisy gong, a clanging cymbal. [2] If I have the gift of prophecy and, with full knowledge, comprehend all mysteries, if I have faith great enough to move mountains, but have not love, I am nothing. [3] If I give everything I have to feed the poor and hand over my body to be burned, but have not love, I gain nothing.

[4] Love is patient; love is kind. Love is not jealous, it does not put on airs, it is not snobbish. [5] Love is never rude, it is not self-seeking, it is not prone to anger; neither does it brood over injuries. [6] Love does not rejoice in what is wrong but rejoices with the truth. [7] There is no limit to love's forbearance, to its trust, its hope, its power to endure.

[8] Love never fails. Prophecies will cease, tongues will be silent, knowledge will pass away. [9] Our knowledge is imperfect and our prophesying is imperfect. [10] When the perfect comes, the imperfect will pass away. [11] When I was a child I used to talk like a child, think like a child, reason like a child. When I became a man I put childish ways aside. [12] Now we see indistinctly, as in a mirror; then we shall see face to face. My knowledge is imperfect now; then I shall know even as I am known. [13] There are in the end three things that last: faith, hope, and love, and the greatest of these is love.

14

Gift of Prophecy

[1] Seek eagerly after love. Set your hearts on spiritual gifts —above all, the gift of prophecy. [2] A man who speaks in a

---

13, 2: Mt 7, 22; 17, 20;
Jas 2, 14-17.
3: Mt 6, 2.
4: Rom 13, 8ff.

5: Rom 12, 9f.
7: Prv 10, 12; Gal 6, 2.
12: 2 Cor 5, 7; 1 Jn 3, 2.
13: 1 Thes 1, 3.

13, 1-13: See notes on 1 John 4, 7—5, 5.

tongue is talking not to men but to God. No one understands him, because he utters mysteries in the Spirit. ³ The prophet, on the other hand, speaks to men for their upbuilding, their encouragement, their consolation. ⁴ He who speaks in a tongue builds up himself, but he who prophesies builds up the church. ⁵ I should like it if all of you spoke in tongues, but I much prefer that you prophesy. The prophet is greater than one who speaks in tongues, unless the speaker can also interpret for the upbuilding of the church.

Interpretation of Tongues

⁶ Just suppose, brothers, that I should come to you speaking in tongues. What good will I do you if my speech does not have some revelation, or knowledge, or prophecy, or instruction for you? ⁷ Even in the case of lifeless things which produce a sound, such as a flute or a harp, how will anyone know what is being played if there is no distinction among the notes? ⁸ If the bugle's sound is uncertain, who will get ready for battle? ⁹ Similarly, if you do not utter intelligble speech because you are speaking in a tongue, how will anyone know what you are saying? You will be talking to the air. ¹⁰ There are many different languages in the world and all are marked by sound; ¹¹ but if I do not know the meaning, I shall be a foreigner to the speaker and he a foreigner to me. ¹² Since you have set your hearts on spiritual gifts, try to be rich in those that build up the church.

¹³ This means that the man who speaks in a tongue should pray for the gift of interpretation. ¹⁴ If I pray in a tongue my spirit is at prayer but my mind contributes nothing. ¹⁵ What is my point here? I want to pray with my spirit, and also to pray with my mind. I want to sing with my spirit and with my mind as well. ¹⁶ If your praise of God is solely with the spirit, how will the one who does not comprehend be able to say "Amen" to your thanksgiving? He will not know what you are saying. ¹⁷ You will be uttering praise very well indeed, but the other man will not be helped. ¹⁸ Thank God, I speak in tongues more than any of you, ¹⁹ but in the church I would rather say five intelligible words to instruct others than ten thousand words in a tongue.

Function of These Gifts

²⁰ Brothers, do not be childish in your outlook. Be like chil-

---

14, 15: Eph 5, 19.   20: Mt 10, 16; Rom 16, 19; Eph 4, 14.

dren as far as evil is concerned, but in mind be mature. [21] It is written in the law, "In strange tongues and in alien speech I will speak to this people, and even so they will not heed me, says the Lord." [22] The gift of tongues is a sign, not for those who believe but for those who do not believe, while prophecy is not for those who are without faith but for those who have faith. [23] If the uninitiated or unbelievers should come in when the whole church is assembled and everyone is speaking in tongues, would they not say that you are out of your minds? [24] But if an unbeliever or an uninitiate enters while all are uttering prophecy, he will be taken to task by all and called to account by all, [25] and the secret of his heart will be laid bare. Falling prostrate, he will worship God, crying out, "God is truly among you."

Rules of Order

[26] What do we propose, brothers? When you assemble, one has a psalm, another some instruction to give, still another a revelation to share; one speaks in a tongue, another interprets. All well and good, so long as everything is done with a constructive purpose. [27] If any are going to talk in tongues let it be at most two or three, each in turn, with another to interpret what they are saying. [28] But if there is no one to interpret, there should be silence in the assembly, each one speaking only to himself and to God. [29] Let no more than two or three prophets speak, and let the rest judge the worth of what they say. [30] If another, sitting by, should happen to receive a revelation, the first ones should then keep quiet. [31] You can all speak your prophecies, but one by one, so that all may be instructed and encouraged. [32] The spirits of the prophets are under the prophets' control, [33] since God is a God, not of confusion, but of peace.

According to the rule observed in all the assemblies of believers, [34] women should keep silent in such gatherings. They may not speak. Rather, as the law states, submissiveness is indicated for them. [35] If they want to learn anything, they should ask their husbands at home. It is a disgrace when a woman speaks in the assembly. [36] Did the preaching of God's word originate with you? Are you the only ones to whom it has come?

[37] If anyone thinks he is a prophet or a man of the Spirit,

23: Acts 2, 6.13.
25: Is 45, 14; Zec 8, 23.

34: 1 Tm 2, 11f.

he should know that what I have written you is the Lord's commandment. [38] If anyone ignores it, he in turn should be ignored. [39] Set your hearts on prophecy, my brothers, and do not forbid those who speak in tongues, [40] but make sure that everything is done properly and in order.

VI: THE RESURRECTION

15

Christ's Resurrection

[1] Brothers, I want to remind you of the gospel I preached to you, which you received and in which you stand firm. [2] You are being saved by it at this very moment if you hold fast to it as I preached it to you. Otherwise you have believed in vain. [3] I handed on to you first of all what I myself received, that Christ died for our sins in accordance with the Scriptures; [4] that he was burried and, in accordance with the Scriptures, rose on the third day; [5] that he was seen by Cephas, then by the Twelve. [6] After that he was seen by five hundred brothers at once, most of whom are still alive, although some have fallen asleep. [7] Next he was seen by James; then by all the apostles. [8] Last of all he was seen by me, as one born out of the normal course. [9] I am the least of the apostles; in fact, because I persecuted the church of God, I do not even deserve the name. [10] But by God's favor I am what I am. This favor of his to me has not proved fruitless. Indeed, I have worked harder than all the others, not on my own but through the favor of God. [11] In any case, whether it be I or they, this is what we preach and this is what you believed.

The Resurrection and Faith

[12] Tell me, if Christ is preached as raised from the dead,

15, 4: Acts 2, 23.   Lk 24, 34-43.
    5: Mk 16, 14;   9: Eph 3, 8; 1 Tm 1, 15.

15, 1-58: This exposition of the Christian doctrine of the resurrection of the dead in Christ was prompted by the belief among some of the Corinthians that the resurrection of the body was impossible (12, 35), though apparently they did not deny the resurrection of Christ (v 12). Paul takes up the issue by listing the divinely appointed witnesses to the resurrection (1-11). He develops its significance as revealing God's plan to raise the dead (12-28), belief in which has been a basic Christian incentive. It encourages the apostles in the face of the hardships of their ministry, and has even occasioned the practice in Corinth of baptism on behalf of the dead (29-34). Those who reject the doctrine of resurrection because of the fact of bodily corruption fail to understand the mystery of God's creative activity, which provides the kind of body suited to the new life after death (35-49). The risen body of man will be a body so changed by the power of God as to be immortal (50-53). Christ died for sin, which is the cause of man's death

how is it that some of you say there is no resurrection of the dead? [13] If there is no resurrection of the dead, Christ himself has not been raised. [14] And if Christ has not been raised, our preaching is void of content and your faith is empty too. [15] Indeed, we should then be exposed as false witnesses of God, for we have borne witness before him that he raised up Christ; but he certainly did not raise him up if the dead are not raised. [16] Why? Because if the dead are not raised, then Christ was not raised; [17] and if Christ was not raised, your faith is worthless. You are still in your sins, [18] and those who have fallen asleep in Christ are the deadest of the dead. [19] If our hopes in Christ are limited to this life only, we are the most pitiable of men.

Christ, the First Fruits

[20] But as it is, Christ is now raised from the dead, the first fruits of those who have fallen asleep. [21] Death came through a man; hence the resurrection of the dead comes through a man also. [22] Just as in Adam all die, so in Christ all will come to life again, [23] but each one in proper order: Christ the first fruits and then, at his coming, all those who belong to him. [24] After that will come the end, when, after having destroyed every sovereignty, authority, and power, he will hand over the kingdom to God the Father. [25] Christ must reign until God has put all enemies under his feet, [26] and the last enemy to be destroyed is death. [27] Scripture reads that God "has placed all things under his feet." But when it says that everything has been made subject, it is clear that he who has made everything subject to Christ is excluded. [28] When, finally, all has been subjected to the Son, he will then subject himself to the One who made all things subject to him, so that God may be all in all.

Practical Faith

[29] If the dead are not raised, what about those who have themselves baptized on behalf of the dead? If the raising of the dead is not a reality, why be baptized on their behalf? [30] And

15: Acts 5, 32.	24: Eph 1, 22.
18: Rom 10, 9.	25: Ps 110, 1.
20: Rom 8, 11; Col 1, 18;	26: Rom 6, 9; 2 Tm 1, 10;
1 Thes 4, 14.	Rv 20, 14.
21: Gn 3, 17ff;	27: Ps 8, 7; Phil 3, 21.
Rom 5, 12-18.	28: Eph 4, 6; Col 3, 11.
23: 1 Thes 4, 16.	30: 2 Cor 4, 10ff.

(Gn 3, 19); he rose from the dead to be the cause of man's resurrection (54-58).

why are we continually putting ourselves in danger? [31] I swear to you, brothers, by the very pride you take in me, which I cherish in Christ Jesus our Lord, that I face death every day. [32] If I fought those beasts at Ephesus for purely human motives, what profit was there for me? If the dead are not raised, "Let us eat and drink, for tomorrow we die!" [33] Do not be led astray any longer. "Bad company corrupts good morals." Return to reason, as you ought, and stop sinning. [34] Some of you are quite ignorant of God; I say it to your shame.

Manner of the Resurrection

[35] Perhaps someone will say, "How are the dead to be raised up? What kind of body will they have?" [36] A nonsensical question! The seed you sow does not germinate unless it dies. [37] When you sow, you do not sow the full-blown plant, but a kernel of wheat or some other grain. [38] God gives body to it as he pleases—to each seed its own fruition. [39] Not all bodily nature is the same. Men have one kind of body, animals another. Birds are of their kind, fish are of theirs. [40] There are heavenly bodies and there are earthly bodies. The splendor of the heavenly bodies is one thing, that of the earthly another. [41] The sun has a splendor of its own, so has the moon, and the stars have theirs. Even among the stars, one differs from another in brightness. [42] So is it with the resurrection of the dead. What is sown in the earth is subject to decay, what rises is incorruptible. [43] What is sown is ignoble, what rises is glorious. Weakness is sown, strength rises up. [44] A natural body is put down and a spiritual body comes up.

The Natural and the Spiritual Body

If there is a natural body, be sure there is also a spiritual body. [45] Scripture has it that Adam, the first man, became a living soul; the last Adam has become a life-giving spirit. [46] Take note, the spiritual was not first; first came the natural and after that the spiritual. [47] The first man was of earth, formed from dust, the second is from heaven. [48] Earthly men are like the man of earth, heavenly men are like the man of heaven. [49] Just as we resemble the man from earth, so shall we bear the likeness of the man from heaven.

31: Rom 8, 36.
32: Is 22, 13; 1 Cor 4, 9;
    2 Cor 1, 8.
36: Jn 12, 24.
38: Gn 1, 11.

43: Phil 3, 20.
45: Gn 2, 7; Jn 5, 21;
    2 Cor 3, 6f.
48: Rom 8, 29; Phil 3, 21.

Glorification of the Body

[50] This is what I mean, brothers: flesh and blood cannot inherit the kingdom of God; no more can corruption inherit incorruption. [51] Now I am going to tell you a mystery. Not all of us shall fall asleep, but all of us are to be changed—[52] in an instant, in the twinkling of an eye, at the sound of the last trumpet. The trumpet will sound and the dead will be raised incorruptible, and we shall be changed. [53] This corruptible body must be clothed with incorruptibility, this mortal body with immortality. [54] When the corruptible frame takes on incorruptibility and the moral immortality, then will the saying of Scripture be fulfilled: "Death is swallowed up in victory." [55] "O death, where is your victory? O death, where is your sting?" [56] The sting of death is sin, and sin gets its power from the law. [57] But thanks be to God who has given us the victory through our Lord Jesus Christ. [58] Be steadfast and persevering, my beloved brothers, fully engaged in the work of the Lord. You know that your toil is not in vain when it is done in the Lord.

VII: CONCLUSION

16

The Collection

[1] About the collection for the saints, follow the instructions I gave the churches of Galatia. [2] On the first day of each week everyone should put aside whatever he has been able to save, so that the collection will not have to be taken up after I arrive. [3] When I come I shall give letters of introduction to those whom you have chosen to take your gift to Jerusalem. [4] If it seems fitting that I should go myself, they will accompany me.

Paul's Plans

[5] I shall come to you after I have passed through Macedonia.

49: Gn 5, 3.
50: Jn 3, 3-6.
51: 1 Thes 4, 14.
52: Jl 2, 1; Zec 9, 14;
    Mt 24, 31.
53: 2 Cor 5, 4.

55: Is 25, 8; Hos 13, 14.
56: Rom 4, 15; 7, 7.13
57: Jn 16, 33.
16, 1: Gal 2, 10.
    5: Acts 19, 21.

16, 1: This collection taken up for the poor Christians of Jerusalem is elsewhere referred to (Acts 24, 17; Rom 15, 26ff; 2 Cor 8, 1—9, 15; Gal 2, 10). Paul is especially interested in it as an opportunity to break down the barriers between Jew and Gentile.

[6] If it is at all possible, I should like to remain with you for some time—even to spend the winter with you— that you may provide me with what I need for the rest of my journey. [7] I do not want to see you just in passing. I hope to spend some time with you, if the Lord permits. [8] I intend to stay in Ephesus until Pentecost. [9] A door has been opened wide for my work, but at the same time there are many opposed. [10] If Timothy should come, be sure to put him at ease among you. He does the Lord's work just as I do, [11] so let no one treat him disdainfully. Rather, help him come to me by sending him on his way in peace. I am expecting him with the brothers. [12] As for our brother Apollos, I urged him strongly to go to you with the brothers, but he did not wish to go at this time. He will go when circumstances are more favorable.

Directions and Greetings

[13] Be on your guard, stand firm in the faith, and act like men. In a word, be strong. [14] Do everything with love. [15] You know that the household of Stephanas is the first fruits of Achaia and is devoted to the service of the saints. [16] I urge you to serve under such men and under everyone who cooperates and toils with them. [17] I was very happy at the arrival of Stephanas, Fortunatus, and Achaicus, because they made up for your absence. [18] They have refreshed my spirit as they did yours. You should recognize the worth of such men.

[19] The churches of Asia send you greetings. Aquila and Prisca, together with the assembly that meets in their house, send you cordial greetings in the Lord. [20] All the brothers greet you. Greet one another with a holy kiss.

[21] It is I, Paul, who send you this greeting in my own hand. [22] If anyone does not love the Lord, let a curse be upon him. O Lord, come! [23] The favor of the Lord Jesus be with you. [24] My love to all of you in Christ Jesus.

7: Acts 18, 21.
8: Acts 19, 1.10.
9: Acts 14, 27.
10: 4, 17; Acts 19, 22;
    Phil 2, 20ff.
12: Acts 18, 24.
15: 1, 16.
18: 1 Thes 5, 12.

19: Acts 18, 2.18.26;
    Rom 16, 3.5.
20: Rom 16, 16;
    2 Cor 13, 12;
    1 Pt 5, 14.
21: Col 4, 18; 2 Thes 3, 17.
22: Gal 1, 8f.

16, 22: *O Lord, come!: Maranatha:* an Aramaic expression, reflected also in Rv 22, 20, probably used in the Christian liturgy of the time. It may be read as a prayer for the arrival of the second coming of Christ: *Marana tha,* "Lord, come"; or as an expression of hope in the proximity of the parousia, *Maran atha,* "The Lord is coming." See note on 1 Thes 4, 13-18.

THE SECOND EPISTLE OF PAUL
TO THE CORINTHIANS
INTRODUCTION

This epistle contains Paul's reflections on events that occurred after his first letter had been sent to the Corinthians. He had changed his plan to stay with that community, an intention he had previously announced (1 Cor 16, 5ff), and was criticized by the Corinthian Christians for this; one of them had even publicly reviled him (2, 5). Their attitude caused Paul much anxiety (2, 3f) and greatly strained the relationship between himself and the community he had founded and knew so well (6, 11f; Acts 18, 11). It indirectly impeded his work of ministry at Troas, where he was to be joined by Titus (2, 12f) to receive his personal report on the state of the church at Corinth. Not finding him there, Paul left Troas for Macedonia in search of him. When they finally met, he was greatly relieved, for the letter of reproof Titus had carried to the Corinthians from Paul had won the day at Corinth (7, 5-9). Accordingly, Paul wrote the present letter to confirm the Corinthians' renewed acceptance of his apostolic authority and to prepare them for his coming visit (12, 14; 13, 1).

Although these data do not constitute a complete reconstruction of events in Corinth between the writing of the two Corinthian letters, they are adequate to account for the nature of this second letter, the most subjective of all the Pauline epistles.

The themes of the epistle must be understood in terms of this general background: Paul's suffering and consolation (1, 3-11); his sincerity (1, 12ff); his honesty (1, 15—2, 4); his forgiveness of the offender (2, 5-11); his past anxiety and present relief (2, 12-17); his confidence in the apostolic office despite its hardships (3, 1—6, 10); his plea for frankness (6, 11ff; 7, 2ff); Titus' report upon the effect of the reproachful letter he had brought to the community from Paul (7, 5-16); the appeal concerning the collection for the poor Christians of Jerusalem, delayed because of the troubles within the community (8, 1—9, 15); the reaffirmation of Paul's apostolic authority (10, 1—13, 10).

Many scholars have felt that the lack of continuity in the Second Epistle to the Corinthians and the repetition of material on the same topic (e.g., 2, 14—6, 3 and 10, 1—13, 10; 8, 1-24 and 9, 1-15) are evidence that the epistle was formed from several Pauline letters, including perhaps the letter to the Corinthians written before First Corinthians (1 Cor 5, 9), and the second, severe letter which preceded Second Corinthians (2 Cor 7, 8). However, no theory fragmenting Second Corinthians into several letters has proved entirely convincing. A partial explanation of the degree of discontinuity and repetition in the letter would be Paul's own state of mind when he composed it. As new thoughts on the themes of his letter occurred to him, he recorded them in the hope that the outpouring of his own heart (6, 11) would ensure the community's faithfulness to him.

The Second Epistle to the Corinthians was written in Macedonia (2 Cor 2, 12f; 7, 5f; 8, 1-4; 9, 2ff), probably in the autumn of 57 A.D., during the course of Paul's third missionary journey (Acts 20, 1f).

THE SECOND EPISTLE OF PAUL
TO THE CORINTHIANS

1

Greeting to the Church

¹ Paul, by God's will an apostle of Jesus Christ, and Timothy his brother, to the church of God that is at Corinth and to all the holy ones of the church who live in Achaia. ² Grace and peace from God our Father and the Lord Jesus Christ.

Thanksgiving after Affliction

³ Praised be God, the Father of our Lord Jesus Christ, the Father of mercies, and the God of all consolation! ⁴ He comforts us in all our afflictions and thus enables us to comfort those who are in trouble, with the same consolation we have received from him. ⁵ As we have shared much in the suffering of Christ, so through Christ do we share abundantly in his consolation. ⁶ If we are afflicted it is for your encouragement and salvation, and when we are consoled it is for your consolation, so that you may endure patiently the same sufferings we endure. ⁷ Our hope for you is firm because we know that just as you share in the sufferings, so you will share in the consolation.

⁸ Brothers, we do not wish to leave you in the dark about the trouble we had in Asia; we were crushed beyond our strength, even to the point of despairing of life. ⁹ We were left to feel like men condemned to death so that we might trust, not in ourselves, but in God who raises the dead. ¹⁰ He rescued us from that danger of death and will continue to do so. We have put our hope in him who will never cease to deliver us. ¹¹ But you must help us with your prayers, so that on our behalf God may be thanked for the gift granted us through the prayers of so many.

Paul's Sincerity

¹² Conscience gives testimony to the boast that in our behavior toward all and especially toward you we have always acted from

---

1, 3: Eph 1, 3; 1 Pt 1, 3.
8: Acts 20, 19.

9: 4, 7; Rom 4, 17.
11: 4, 15; 9, 12.

1, 1f: See note on Rom 1, 1-7.
1, 3-11: Paul gives thanks to God, as he informs the Corinthians that he has been relieved of the serious troubles he experienced in the province of Asia Minor, and is now at peace. The community was evidently aware of the apostle's difficulties, but their nature is now unknown.
1, 5: The sufferings of Paul are identified with those of Christ, for whom they are endured; the consolation he receives is shared with the Christians at Corinth.
1, 12—2, 4: Paul answers the criticism leveled against him for having

God-given holiness and candor; this has been prompted, not by debased human wisdom, but by God's goodness. [13] We never write anything that you cannot read and understand. I hope that, just as you know us to a certain degree already, you will in time come to know us well, [14] and will recognize that we shall be your boast, and you ours, on the day of our Lord Jesus.

[15] Confident as I am about this, I wanted to visit you first so that a double grace might be yours. [16] I planned to visit you, both on my way to Macedonia and on my return, that I might receive your help on my journey to Judea. [17] Do you suppose that in making those plans I was acting insincerely? Or that my plans are so determined by self-interest that I change my mind from one minute to the next? [18] As God keeps his word, I declare that my word to you is not "yes" one minute and "no" the next. [19] Jesus Christ, whom Silvanus, Timothy, and I preached to you as Son of God, was not alternately "yes" and "no"; he was never anything but "yes." [20] Whatever promises God has made have been fulfilled in him; therefore it is through him that we address our Amen to God when we worship together. [21] God is the one who firmly establishes us along with you in Christ; it is he who anointed us [22] and has sealed us, thereby depositing the first payment, the Spirit, in our hearts.

[23] I call on God as my witness that it was out of consideration for you that I did not come to Corinth again. [24] Domineering over your faith is not my purpose. I prefer to work with you toward your happiness. As regards faith, you are standing firm.

2

[1] I did decide, however, not to visit you again in painful circumstances. [2] For if I cause you pain, who can make me happy again but the ones I grieved? [3] I wrote as I did so that when I come I may not be saddened by those who should rejoice my heart. I know you all well enough to be convinced that my happiness is yours. [4] That is why I wrote you in great sorrow and anguish, with copious tears—not to make you sad but to help you realize the great love I bear you.

15: Phil 2, 16; 1 Thes 2, 19f.   17: Mt 5, 37. 22: Rom 5, 5; Eph 1, 13f; 1 Jn 2, 20.

---

twice planned and twice failed to visit the Corinthians (1, 15f). He denies that his original plan failed for any but apostolic reasons (1, 17-22), namely, lack of favorable circumstances to discharge his office peaceably. Instead of visiting the Corinthians he sent them a severe letter which caused them distress (2, 3; cf 7, 8), for it was weighted with his own anguish over the situation in their community (2, 4).

1, 22: *First payment:* on full messianic benefits; cf Eph 1, 13f.

Forgiveness for the Offender

⁵ If anyone has given offense he has hurt not only me, but in some measure, to say no more, every one of you. ⁶ The punishment already inflicted by the majority on such a one is enough; ⁷ you should now relent and support him so that he may not be crushed by too great a weight of sorrow. ⁸ I therefore beg you to reaffirm your love for him. ⁹ The reason I wrote you was to test you and learn whether you are obedient in all matters. ¹⁰ If you forgive a man anything, so do I. Any forgiving I have done has been for your sakes and, before Christ, ¹¹ to prevent Satan—whose guile we know too well—from outwitting us.

Paul's Anxiety and Relief

¹² When I came to Troas to preach the gospel of Christ, the door of opportunity was opened wide for me by the Lord. ¹³ Yet I was inwardly troubled because I did not find my brother Titus there. So I said good-bye to them and went off to Macedonia. ¹⁴ Thanks be to God, who unfailingly leads us on in Christ's triumphal train, and employs us to diffuse the fragrance of his knowledge everywhere! ¹⁵ We are an aroma of Christ for God's sake, both among those who are being saved and those on the way to destruction; ¹⁶ to the latter an odor dealing death, to the former a breath bringing life. For such a mission as this, is anyone really qualified? ¹⁷ We at least are not like so many who trade on the word of God. We speak in Christ's name, pure in motivation, conscious of having been sent by God and of standing in his presence.

3

Ministers of the New Covenant

¹ Am I beginning to speak well of myself again? Or do I need

2, 7: Col 3, 13.
11: Eph 4, 27.

13: 7, 6; Ti 1, 3.
16: 1 Cor 1, 18.

2, 5-11: Some scholars believe that the person alluded to here rejected Paul's authority, thereby scandalizing many in the community. It is clear that these latter took action against him, and the apostle now recommends that the punishment be terminated.

2, 14—4, 18: Paul wishes to convince the Corinthians that his actions toward them were motivated, not by selfish reasons, but by apostolic concern. This leads him to a series of reflections on the apostolic office: his effectiveness as an apostle derives from Christ (2, 14-17); his achievements are supported by the Holy Spirit (3, 1ff); his qualifications for the apostolate are gifts of God; and his ministry of the justifying power of God is superior to that of the Mosaic covenant (3, 4-11). The apostle knows that his work is to result in the permanent presence of Christ among men through the power of the Holy Spirit (3, 13-18).

letters of recommendation to you or from you as others might? ² You are my letter, known and read by all men, written on your hearts. ³ Clearly you are a letter of Christ which I have delivered, a letter written not with ink but by the Spirit of the living God, not on tablets of stone but on tablets of flesh in the heart.

⁴ This great confidence in God is ours, through Christ. ⁵ It is not that we are entitled of ourselves to take credit for anything. Our sole credit is from God, ⁶ who has made us qualified ministers of a new covenant, a covenant not of a written law but of spirit. The written law kills, but the Spirit gives life.

⁷ If the ministry of death, carved in writing on stone, was inaugurated with such glory that the Israelites could not look on Moses' face because of the glory that shone on it (even though it was a fading glory), ⁸ how much greater will be the glory of the ministry of the Spirit? ⁹ If the ministry of the covenant that condemned had glory, greater by far is the glory of the ministry that justifies. ¹⁰ Indeed, when you compare that limited glory with this surpassing glory, the former should be declared no glory at all. ¹¹ If what was destined to pass away was given in glory, greater by far is the glory that endures.

¹² Our hope being such, we speak with full confidence. ¹³ We are not like Moses, who used to hide his face with a veil so that the Israelites could not see the final fading of that glory. ¹⁴ Their minds, of course, were dulled. To this very day, when the old covenant is read the veil remains unlifted; it is only in Christ that it is taken away. ¹⁵ Even now, when Moses is read a veil covers their understanding. ¹⁶ "But whenever he turns to the Lord, the veil will be removed." ¹⁷ The Lord is the Spirit, and where the Spirit of the Lord is there is freedom. ¹⁸ All of us, gazing on the Lord's glory with unveiled faces, are being transformed from glory to glory into his very image by the Lord who is the Spirit.

4

Treasure in Earthen Vessels

¹ Because we possess this ministry through God's mercy, we

3, 3: Ex 24, 12; Jer 31, 33;
  Ez 11, 19; 36, 26.
5: Jn 3, 27.
6: Eph 3, 7.

7: Ex 32, 15f; 34, 29-35.
15: Rom 11, 7-10.
18: 4, 6; Rom 8, 29;
  1 Jn 3, 2.

4, 1-6: The power of the gospel is divine; the apostle, therefore, has no need to modify it to make it acceptable to men (1f). It is men who blind themselves to the light of Christ (3-6).

do not give in to discouragement. ² Rather, we repudiate shameful, underhanded practices. We do not resort to trickery or falsify the word of God. We proclaim the truth openly and commend ourselves to every man's conscience before God. ³ If our gospel can be called "veiled" in any sense, it is such only for those who are headed toward destruction. ⁴ Their unbelieving minds have been blinded by the god of the present age so that they do not see the splendor of the gospel showing forth the glory of Christ, the image of God. ⁵ It is not ourselves we preach but Christ Jesus as Lord, and ourselves as your servants for Jesus' sake. ⁶ For God, who said, "Let light shine out of darkness," has shone in our hearts, that we in turn might make known the glory of God shining on the face of Christ. ⁷ This treasure we possess in earthen vessels to make it clear that its surpassing power comes from God and not from us. ⁸ We are afflicted in every way possible, but we are not crushed; full of doubts, we never despair. ⁹ We are persecuted but never abandoned; we are struck down but never destroyed. ¹⁰ Continually we carry about in our bodies the dying of Jesus, so that in our bodies the life of Jesus may also be revealed. ¹¹ While we live we are constantly being delivered to death for Jesus' sake, so that the life of Jesus may be revealed in our mortal flesh. ¹² Death is at work in us, but life in you. ¹³ We have that spirit of faith of which the Scripture says, "Because I believed, I spoke out." We believe and so we speak, ¹⁴ knowing that he who raised up the Lord Jesus will raise us up along with Jesus and place both us and you in his presence. ¹⁵ Indeed, everything is ordered to your benefit, so that the grace bestowed in abundance may bring greater glory to God because they who give thanks are many.

Lving by Faith

¹⁶ We do not lose heart, because our inner being is renewed

4, 2: 1 Thes 2, 4f.
4: 2 Thes 2, 10; 1 Tm 1, 11.
6: Gn 1, 3; Jn 8, 12;
Heb 1, 3.
8: 6, 4-10 1 Cor 4, 9-13.

10: Col 1, 24.
11: 1 Cor 15, 31.
13: Ps 116, 10.
14: Rom 8, 11.

4, 7-12: The apostle's sufferings reenact the life of Jesus, both as a sign and as an instrument of the divine life he ministers to men.

4, 13f: Paul lives through faith in his own future resurrection and that of his fellow Christians. *He . . . will raise us up:* this may imply that Paul did not expect to be alive at the parousia; cf 1 Cor 15, 51-55.

4, 16ff: Though the apostle's physical forces are being spent, his soul is renewed daily through living the Christ life and meriting that transformation of soul and body after death in which transitory realities are exchanged for those that are eternal; cf 1 Cor 15, 42ff.

each day even though our body is being destroyed at the same time. [17] The present burden of our trial is light enough, and earns for us an eternal weight of glory beyond all comparison. [18] We do not fix our gaze on what is seen but on what is unseen. What is seen is transitory; what is unseen lasts forever.

5

[1] Indeed, we know that when the earthly tent in which we dwell is destroyed we have a dwelling provided for us by God, a dwelling in the heavens, not made by hands but to last forever. [2] We groan while we are here, even as we yearn to have our heavenly habitation envelop us. [3] This it will, provided we are found clothed and not naked. [4] While we live in our present tent we groan; we are weighed down because we do not wish to be stripped naked but rather to have the heavenly dwelling envelop us, so that what is mortal may be absorbed by life. [5] God has fashioned us for this very thing and has given us the Spirit as a pledge of it.

[6] Therefore we continue to be confident. We know that while we dwell in the body we are away from the Lord. [7] We walk by faith, not by sight. [8] I repeat, we are full of confidence and would much rather be away from the body and at home with the Lord. [9] This being so, we make it our aim to please him whether we are with him or away from him. [10] The lives of all of us are to be revealed before the tribunal of Christ so that each one may receive his recompense, good or bad, according to his life in the body.

Ministry of Reconciliation

[11] Standing in awe of the Lord we try to persuade men, but what we are is known to God. I hope that it is also known to you in your consciences. [12] We shall not begin to recommend

---

17: Mt 5, 11f; Rom 8, 18.
18: Rom 8, 24f; Heb 11, 1.
5, 1: Is 38, 12.
2: Rom 8, 23; Col 3, 3f.
3: 1 Cor 15, 51ff;
1 Thes 4, 15.

5: 1, 22.
8: Rom 8, 24; Phil 1, 21ff.
9: Mt 25, 31f.
10: Rom 14, 10.
12: Phil 1, 26.

5, 6-9: Paul comforts himself with the thought that his present existence is in a sense an exile from Christ, whereas death brings life with Christ through the possession of heavenly glory.

5, 11—6, 14: Paul trusts that his dispositions, known to God, may also be recognized by the Corinthians whom he serves, so that they in turn can answer his critics (5, 11f). In his dealings with people, he is motivated by love for Christ (5, 14). To delve into his past might reveal that he once entertained mistaken ideas about the Savior (5, 16). This may be the meaning of looking upon Christ *in terms of mere human judgment*. But the apostle, like other Christians, is also a new man; reconciled to God through

ourselves to you again, but we are giving you an opportunity to boast about us so that you may have something to say to those who take pride in external appearances, and not in what lies in the heart. [13] Indeed, if we are ever caught up out of ourselves, God is the reason; and when we are brought back to our senses, it is for your sakes. [14] The love of Christ impels us who have reached the conviction that since one died for all, all died. [15] He died for all so that those who live might live no longer for themselves, but for him who for their sakes died and was raised up.

[16] Because of this we no longer look on anyone in terms of mere human judgment. If at one time we so regarded Christ, we no longer know him by this standard. [17] This means that if anyone is in Christ, he is a new creation. The old order has passed away; now all is new! [18] All this has been done by God, who has reconciled us to himself through Christ and has given us the ministry of reconciliation. [19] I mean that God, in Christ, was reconciling the world to himself, not counting men's transgressions against them, and that he has entrusted the message of reconciliation to us. [20] This makes us ambassadors for Christ, God as it were appealing through us. We implore you, in Christ's name: be reconciled to God! [21] For our sakes God made him who did not know sin, to be sin, so that in him we might become the very holiness of God.

6

[1] As your fellow workers we beg you not to receive the grace of God in vain. [2] For he says, "In an acceptable time I have heard you; on a day of salvation I have helped you." Now is the acceptable time! Now is the day of salvation! [3] We avoid giving anyone offense, so that our ministry may not be blamed. [4] On the contrary, in all that we do we strive to present ourselves as ministers of God, acting with patient endurance amid

---

15: Rom 6, 4-11; 14, 9.
17: Is 43, 19; Eph 2, 10;
     Rv 21, 5.
19: Jn 3, 17.
21: Is 53, 6-9; Gal 3, 13;

1 Pt 2, 24; 1 Jn 3, 5.
6, 2: Is 49, 8.
3: 8, 21.
4: 4, 8ff; 1 Cor 4, 9-13.

Christ, he is given the special mission of serving as Christ's ambassador, the essential purpose of his own personal renewal by God (5, 17-21). His mission is to appeal to men to accept God's salvation in Christ (6, 1f), a task he tries to perform with the greatest possible discretion. The attempt nevertheless produces personal hardships and social upheavals, even though all that he strives to offer is God's word and power (6, 3-10). In conclusion, Paul asks of the Corinthians that they be as open to him in acceptance of his ministry as he has been frank and loving toward them (6, 11ff; cf 7, 2).

trials, difficulties, distresses, [5] beatings, imprisonments, and riots; as men familiar with hard work, sleepless nights, and fastings; [6] conducting ourselves with innocence, knowledge, and patience, in the Holy Spirit, in sincere love; [7] as men with the message of truth and the power of God; wielding the weapons of righteousness with right hand and left, [8] whether honored or dishonored, spoken of well or ill. We are called imposters, yet we are truthful; [9] nobodies who in fact are well known; dead, yet here we are, alive; punished, but not put to death; [10] sorrowful, though we are always rejoicing; poor, yet we enrich many. We seem to have nothing, yet everything is ours!

[11] Men of Corinth, we have spoken to you frankly, opening our hearts wide to you. [12] There is no lack of room for you in us; the narrowness is in you. [13] In fair exchange, then (I speak as a father to his children), open wide your hearts!

The Temple of the Living God

[14] Do not yoke yourselves in a mismatch with unbelievers. After all, what do righteousness and lawlessness have in common, or what fellowship can light have with darkness? [15] What accord is there between Christ and Belial, what common lot between believer and unbeliever? [16] Tell me what agreement there is between the temple of God and idols. You are the temple of the living God, just as God has said:

> "I will dwell with them and walk among them.
> I will be their God
> and they shall be my people.
> [17] Therefore, 'Come out from among them
> and separate yourselves from them,' says the Lord;
> 'and touch nothing unclean.
> I will welcome you [18] and be a father to you
> and you will be my sons and daughters,'
> says the Lord Almighty."

7

[1] Since we have these promises, beloved, let us purify ourselves from every defilement of flesh and spirit, and in the fear of God strive to fulfill our consecration perfectly.

6: Gal 5, 22.
7: Eph 6, 11.
9: 4, 11.
11: 7, 3.
13: Gal 4, 19.
16: Lv 26, 12; Ez 37, 27;
1 Cor 3, 17; 6, 19.
17: Is 52, 11.
18: Jer 31, 9.

6, 14—7, 1: It is difficult to account for this passage in the present context. It has similarities with the Qumran literature, and may be an excerpt of a lost Pauline epistle.

Joy over Repentance

2 Make room for us in your hearts! We have injured no one, we have corrupted no one, we have cheated no one. 3 I do not condemn you. I have already said that you are in our hearts, even to the sharing of death and life together. 4 I speak to you with utter frankness and boast much about you. I am filled with consolation, and despite my many afflictions my joy knows no bounds.

5 When I arrived in Macedonia I was restless and exhausted. I was under all kinds of stress—quarrels with others and fears within myself. 6 But God, who gives heart to those who are low in spirit, gave me strength with the arrival of Titus. 7 This he did, not only by his arrival but by the reinforcement Titus had already received from you; for he reported your longing, your grief, and your ardent concern for me, so that my joy is greater still. 8 If I saddened you by my letter I have no regrets. Or if I did feel some regret (because I understand that the letter caused you grief for a time), 9 I am happy once again; not because you were saddened, but because your sadness led to repentance. You were filled with a sorrow that came from God; thus you did not suffer any loss from us. 10 Indeed, sorrow for God's sake produces a repentance without regrets, leading to salvation, whereas worldly sorrow brings death. 11 Just look at the fruit of this sorrow which stems from God. What a measure of holy zeal it has brought you, not to speak of readiness to defend yourselves! What indignation, fear, and longing! What ardent desire to restore the balance of justice! In every way you have displayed your innocence in this matter. 12 Therefore, my writing to you was not intended for the man who had given the offense or for the one offended, but to make plain in the sight of God the devotion you have for us. 13 This done, we are comforted.

Beyond this consolation, we have rejoiced even more at the joy of Titus because his mind has been set at rest by all of you. 14 For though I had boasted to him about you, I was not put to shame. Rather, just as everything I ever said to you was true, so my boasting to Titus has been proved equally true. 15 His

---

7, 3: 6, 11-13.   8: Heb 12, 11.

7, 5-16: Paul resumes the thought from which he had digressed in 2, 13, completing the account of his meeting with Titus to discuss the community's reaction to his severe letter; see note on 1, 12—2, 4. He expresses genuine satisfaction over the steps they have taken to correct what he had found objectionable in their conduct. The joy of Titus over their response to the apostle's admonitions pleases Paul all the more and justifies his complete trust in them.

heart embraces you with an expanding love as he recalls the obedience you showed to God when you received him in fear and trembling. [16] I rejoice because I trust you utterly.

8

Liberal Giving

[1] Brothers, I should like you to know of the grace of God conferred on the churches of Macedonia. [2] In the midst of severe trial their overflowing joy and deep poverty have produced an abundant generosity. [3] According to their means—indeed I can testify even beyond their means—and voluntarily, [4] they begged us insistently for the favor of sharing in this service to members of the church. [5] Beyond our hopes they first gave themselves to God and then to us by the will of God. [6] That is why I have exhorted Titus, who had already begun this work of charity among you, to bring it to successful completion: [7] that just as you are rich in every respect, in faith and discourse, in knowledge, in total concern, and in the love we bear you, so may you abound in this charity.

[8] I am not giving an order but simply testing your generous love against the concern which others show. [9] You are well acquainted with the favor shown you by our Lord Jesus Christ: how for your sake he made himself poor though he was rich, so that you might become rich by his poverty. [10] I am about to give you some advice on this matter of rich and poor. It will help you who began this good work last year, not only to carry it through, but to do so willingly. [11] Carry it through now to a successful completion, so that your ready resolve may be matched by giving according to your means. [12] The willingness to give should accord with one's means, not go beyond them. [13] The relief of others ought not to impoverish you; there should be a certain equality. [14] Your plenty at the present time should supply their need so that their surplus may one day supply your need, with equality as the result. [15] It is written, "He who

---

8, 1: 11, 8f.	9: Mt 8, 20; Phil 2, 6f.
7: 1 Cor 1, 5.	15: Ex 16, 18.

8, 1—9, 15: See note on 1 Corinthians 16, 1 concerning the collection spoken of here. No doubt the conflicts in Corinth to which this letter alludes were responsible for delaying this collection (8, 10). Paul here presents certain motives to the community for completing it: they are to emulate the generosity of the Macedonians (8, 1-5) and imitate the poverty of Christ (8, 9); they too may at some time need the charity of others (8, 14). Paul plans to visit them and convey the generous fruit of their charity to the community in Jerusalem. Not only will it supply the needs of that church; it will be the cause of their giving thanks and glory to God and of obtaining God's favor for themselves (9, 6-15).

gathered much had no excess and he who gathered little had no lack."

Titus and His Companions

[16] Thanks be to God, who has put an equal zeal for you in the heart of Titus! [17] Not only did he welcome our appeal, but being very eager he has gone to you freely. [18] We have sent along with him that brother whom all the churches praise for his preaching of the gospel. [19] He has been appointed our traveling companion by the churches, as we willingly carry on this work of charity for the glory of the Lord. [20] There is one thing I wish to avoid, namely any blame over my handling of this generous collection. [21] We are concerned not only for God's approval but also for the good esteem of men. [22] We have sent along that brother whose eagerness has been proved to us in many ways. He is now more eager than ever for this work because of his great trust in you. [23] As for Titus, he is my companion and fellow worker in your behalf; our brothers too are apostles of the churches, the glory of Christ. [24] Therefore, show these men the proof of your love, and why we boast about you, for all the churches to see.

9

The Offering for the Saints

[1] There is really no need for me to write you about this collection for the members of the church. [2] I already know your willingness, and boast about you to the Macedonians with respect to it, saying that Achaia has been ready since last year. Your zeal has stirred up most of them. [3] I nonetheless send the brothers so that our claims for you in this regard may not be shown empty. I do so that you may be ready, as I have been saying you are, [4] lest any Macedonians come with me and find you unready; then I should be put to shame—to say nothing of you—for having had this trust. [5] I have thought it necessary to exhort the brothers to go to you and arrange in advance for the bountiful gift you have already promised. It should be ready as a gracious gift, nor as an exaction.

[6] Let me say this much: He who sows sparingly will reap sparingly, and he who sows bountifully will reap bountifully. [7] Everyone must give according to what he has inwardly decided; not sadly, not grudgingly, for God loves a cheerful

---

18: 12, 18.   21: Rom 12, 17.   9, 6: Prv 11, 24f.

giver. [8] God can multiply his favors among you so that you may always have enough of everything and even a surplus for good works, [9] as it is written:

> "He scattered abroad and gave to the poor,
> his justice endures forever."

[10] He who supplies seed for the sower and bread for the eater will provide in abundance; he will multiply the seed you sow and increase your generous yield. [11] In every way your liberality is enriched; through us it results in thanks offered to God. [12] The administering of this public benefit not only supplies the needs of the members of the church but also overflows in much gratitude to God. [13] Because of your praiseworthy service they are glorifying God for your obedient faith in the gospel of Christ, and for your generosity in sharing with them and with all. [14] They pray for you longingly because of the surpassing grace God has given you. [15] Thanks be to God for his indescribable gift!

10

Paul Defends His Ministry

[1] I, Paul, exhort you by the meekness and kindness of Christ, I who (you say) when present in your midst am lowly, but when absent am bold toward you. [2] I beg you that when I am there, I may not have to act boldly, with that assurance I might dare to use courageously against certain ones who accuse us of weak human behavior. [3] We do indeed live in the body but we do not wage war with human resources. [4] The weapons of our warfare are not merely human. They possess God's power for the destruction of strongholds. We demolish sophistries [5] and every proud pretension that raises itself against the knowledge of God; we likewise bring every thought into captivity to make it obedient to Christ. [6] We are ready to punish disobedience in anyone else once your own obedience is perfect.

9: Ps 112, 9.
10, 2: 1 Cor 4, 21.

4: 1 Cor 1, 25; Eph 6, 11.

10, 1-18: Since Paul's previous tone of gentleness changes in chapters 10 through 13 to one of aggressive criticism, some scholars conclude that these chapters belong to a lost Pauline epistle, probably the severe letter; see note on 2 Corinthians 7, 5-16. The background to these chapters is the criticism directed against Paul by people whom he names *super-apostles* (11, 5; 12, 11). He appeals to the community to take the proper steps to safeguard his authority; otherwise he will exercise it personally and fully (10, 1-11). He observes that the disturbers of the community are self-praisers, boasting of work which not they, but others, have accomplished. To be approved requires recommendation by God, not by oneself (10, 12-18).

7 You view things superficially. If anyone is convinced that he belongs to Christ, let him reflect on this: he may belong to Christ but just as much do we. 8 If I find I must make a few further claims about the power the Lord has given us for your upbuilding and not for your destruction, this will not embarrass me in the least. 9 At the same time, I do not wish to intimidate you with my letters. 10 His letters, they say, are severe and forceful, but when he is here in person he is unimpressive and his word makes no great impact. 11 Well, let such people give this some thought, that what we are by word, in the letters during our absence, that we mean to be in action when we are present.

12 We are not so bold, of course, as to classify or compare ourselves with certain people who recommend themselves. Since people like that are their own appraisers, comparing themselves with one another, they only demonstrate their ignorance. 13 When we make claims we will not go over the mark but will stay within the bounds the God of moderation has set for us—leading us to you. 14 We are not over-reaching ourselves, as we should be doing if we have not bothered to come to you. But indeed we did get as far as you with the gospel of Christ. 15 We do not boast immoderately of the work of others; we hope that as your faith grows our influence may also grow among you and overflow. 16 Following the rule laid down for us, we hope to preach the gospel even beyond your borders without having to boast of work already done by another in his allotted territory. 17 "Let him who would boast, boast in the Lord." 18 It is not the man who recommends himself who is approved but the man whom the Lord recommends.

11

Paul and the False Apostles

1 You must endure a little of my folly. Put up with me, I beg you! 2 I am jealous of you with the jealousy of God himself, since I have given you in marriage to one husband, presenting you as a chaste virgin to Christ. 3 My fear is that, just as the serpent seduced Eve by his cunning, your thoughts may be

---

8: 13, 10.
12: 3, 1.
17: 1 Cor 1, 31.

11, 2: Eph 5, 27.
3: Gn 3, 4.

11, 1-15: Paul sees in the work of the *super-apostles* a threat to the purity of the gospel as he preached it to Corinthians (1-6). He regards his own selflessness in the ministry as worthy of a hearing against the conduct of those whom he now designates as false apostles (7-15).

corrupted and you may fall away from your sincere and complete devotion to Christ. ⁴ I say this because, when someone comes preaching another Jesus than the one we preached, or when you receive a different spirit than the one you have received, or a gospel other than the gospel you accepted, you seem to endure it quite well. ⁵ I consider myself inferior to the "super-apostles" in nothing. ⁶ I may be unskilled in speech but I know that I am not lacking in knowledge. We have made this evident to you in every conceivable way.

⁷ Could I have done wrong when I preached the gospel of God to you free of charge, humbling myself with a view to exalting you? ⁸ I robbed other churches, I accepted support from them in order to minister to you. ⁹ When I was with you and in want I was a burden to none of you, for the brothers who came from Macedonia supplied my needs. In every way possible I kept myself from being burdensome to you, and I shall continue to do so. ¹⁰ I swear by the Christ who is in me that this boast of mine will not cease in the regions of Achaia! ¹¹ Why? Because I do not love you? God knows I do. ¹² What I am doing I shall continue to do, depriving at every turn those who look for a chance to say that in their much-vaunted ministry they work on the same terms as we do. ¹³ Such men are false apostles. They practice deceit in their disguise as apostles of Christ. ¹⁴ And little wonder! For even Satan disguises himself as an angel of light. ¹⁵ It comes as no surprise that his ministers disguise themselves as ministers of the justice of God. But their end will correspond to their deeds.

Paul's Sufferings as an Apostle

¹⁶ I repeat: let no one think me foolish. But if you do, then accept me as a fool all the way and let me do a little boasting. ¹⁷ What I am about to say in this self-assured boasting, I speak not as the Lord desires but after the manner of a fool. ¹⁸ Since many are bragging about their human distinctions, I too will boast. ¹⁹ Being wise yourselves, you gladly put up with fools.

4: Gal 1, 6-9.
5: 12, 11.
6: 1 Cor 2, 1-5.

7: Acts 18, 3; 1 Cor 9, 18.
8: 1 Cor 9, 15.
19: 3, 1.

11, 16—12, 10: Since the false apostles have thrilled the community with accounts of their achievements, Paul will boast of his sufferings and humiliations (16-33). If they seek from Paul evidence of unique religious experiences, his have been so extraordinary as to be incapable of expression in words (12, 1-5). To keep him humble despite his unique visions, God gave Paul a special affliction, *a thorn in the flesh* (12, 7)—whether a disease or a spiritual affliction is not certain (12, 7-10). If his phrase is an echo of Nm 33, 55 or Ez 28, 24, the thorn is the "super-apostles."

[20] You even put up with those who exploit you, who impose upon you and put on airs, with those who slap your face. [21] To my shame I must confess that we have been too weak to do such things. But what anyone else dares to claim—I speak with absolute foolishness now—I, too, will dare. [22] Are they Hebrews? So am I! Are they Israelites? So am I! Are they the seed of Abraham? So am I! [23] Are they ministers of Christ? Now I am really talking like a fool—I am more: with my many more labors and imprisonments, with far worse beatings and frequent brushes with death. [24] Five times at the hands of the Jews I received forty lashes less one; [25] three times I was beaten with rods; I was stoned once, shipwrecked three times; I passed a day and a night on the sea. [26] I traveled continually, endangered by floods, robbers, my own people, the Gentiles; imperiled in the city, in the desert, at sea, by false brothers; [27] enduring labor, hardship, many sleepless nights; in hunger and thirst and frequent fastings, in cold and nakedness. [28] Leaving other sufferings unmentioned, there is that daily tension pressing on me, my anxiety for all the churches. [29] Who is weak that I am not affected by it? Who is scandalized that I am not aflame with indignation? [30] If I must boast, I will make a point of my weaknesses. [31] The God and Father of the Lord Jesus knows—blessed be he forever—that I do not lie. [32] In Damascus the ethnarch of King Aretas was keeping a close watch on the city in order to arrest me, [33] but I was lowered in a basket through a window in the wall and escaped his hands.

12

Visions and Revelations

[1] I must go on boasting, however useless it may be, and speak of visions and revelations of the Lord. [2] I know a man in Christ who, fourteen years ago, whether he was in or outside his body I cannot say, only God can say—a man who was snatched up to the third heaven. [3] I know that this man—whether in or outside his body I do not know, God knows—[4] was snatched up to Paradise to hear words which cannot be uttered, words which no man may speak. [5] About this man I will boast; but I will do no boasting about myself unless it be about my weaknesses. [6] And even if I were to boast it would not be folly in me because I would only be telling the truth.

22: Acts 22, 3; Rom 11, 1.
24: Dt 25, 2f;
    Acts 16, 22.
25: Acts 14, 19.
27: 1 Cor 4, 11.
29: 1 Cor 9, 22.
32: Acts 9, 24.
12, 2: Acts 9, 3.

⁷ But I refrain, lest anyone think more of me than what he sees in me or hears from my lips. As to the extraordinary revelations, in order that I might not become conceited I was given a thorn in the flesh, an angel of Satan to beat me and keep me from getting proud. ⁸ Three times I begged the Lord that this might leave me. ⁹ He said to me, "My grace is enough for you, for in weakness power reaches perfection." And so I willingly boast of my weaknesses instead, that the power of Christ may rest upon me.

¹⁰ Therefore I am content with weakness, with mistreatment, with distress, with persecutions and difficulties for the sake of Christ; for when I am powerless, it is then that I am strong.

Concern for the Corinthian Church

¹¹ What a fool I have become! You have driven me to it. You are the ones who should have been commending me. Even though I am nothing, I am in no way inferior to the "super-apostles." ¹² Indeed, I have performed among you with great patience the signs that show the apostle, signs and wonders and deeds of power. ¹³ In what way are you inferior to the other churches except in this, that I was no burden to you? Forgive me this injustice! ¹⁴ This is the third time that I am about to visit you, and I am not going to burden you; for I do not want what you have, I only want you. Children should not save up for their parents, but parents for children. ¹⁵ I will gladly spend myself and be spent for your sakes. If I love you too much, will I be loved the less for that? ¹⁶ Granted that I did not burden you—but being crafty, you say, I caught you by guile. ¹⁷ Did I ever take advantage of you through any of the men I sent to you? ¹⁸ I urged Titus to go to you, and I sent the other brother with him. Did Titus take advantage of you in any way? Did we not act in the one spirit, walk in the same footsteps?

¹⁹ Do you think throughout this recital that I am defending myself to you? Before God I tell you, in Christ, I have done everything to build you up, my dear ones. ²⁰ I fear that when I come I may not find you to my liking, nor may you find me

---

7: Nm 33, 55; Ez 28, 24;
   Mt 26, 39.42.44.
8: 4, 7.

10: Phil 4, 13.
12: Rom 15, 19;
    1 Thes 1, 5.

12, 11-21: Paul recalls to the minds of the Corinthians the kind of apostle he showed himself in their midst (11-15). He indicates the absurdity of the false apostles' suggestion that he and Titus took no support from the community in order to gain control of it more easily (16ff). His aim has been, not to defend himself, but to keep the community faithful to the teaching of Christ (19ff).

to yours. I fear I may find discord, jealousy, outbursts of anger, selfish ambitions, slander and gossip, self-importance, disorder. [21] I fear that when I come again my God may humiliate me before you, and I may have to mourn over the many who sinned earlier and have not repented of the uncleanness, fornication, and sensuality they practiced.

13

Final Warnings

[1] This is the third time I shall be coming to you. "A judicial fact shall be established only on the testimony of two or three witnesses." [2] I said before when I was there the second time—and I repeat it now in my absence—to those who sinned before and to all the rest, that if I come again I shall not spare you. [3] You are, after all, looking for a proof of the Christ who speaks in me. He is not weak in dealing with you, but is powerful in you. [4] It is true he was crucified out of weakness, but he lives by the power of God. We too are weak in him, but we live with him by God's power in us. [5] Test yourselves to see whether you are living in faith; examine yourselves. Perhaps you yourselves do not realize that Christ Jesus is in you—unless, of course, you have failed the challenge. [6] I hope you will understand that we have not failed. [7] We pray God that you may do no evil—not in order that we may appear approved but simply that you may do what is good, even though we may seem to have failed. [8] We cannot do anything against the truth, but only for the sake of the truth. [9] We even rejoice when we are weak and you are strong. Our prayer is that you may be built up to completion.

Farewell

[10] I am writing in this way while away from you, so that when I am with you I may not have to exercise with severity the authority the Lord has given me—authority to build up rather than to destroy. [11] And now, brothers, I must say good-bye. Mend your ways. Encourage one another. Live in harmony and peace, and the God of love and peace will be with you. [12] Greet one

---

13, 1: Dt 19, 15; Mt 18, 16; Jn 8, 17; Heb 10, 28.
4: Rom 8, 11.

10: 10, 8.
12: 1 Cor 16, 20.

13, 1-10: The apostle's final appeal is that the community correct the evils within it through an examination of its own conscience. This will preclude the disagreeable necessity of his taking severe action against them.

another with a holy kiss. All the holy ones send greetings to you. [13] The grace of the Lord Jesus Christ, and the love of God, and the fellowship of the Holy Spirit be with you all!

THE EPISTLE OF PAUL
TO THE GALATIANS
INTRODUCTION

Until the nineteenth century it was assumed that the Epistle to the Galatians was addressed to Christian communities which Paul founded in the interior of Asia Minor on his second missionary journey (Acts 16, 6) and visited on his third (Acts 18, 23). The epistle would then have been written at some time during these journeys between the years 52 and 57. Since the last century, however, many scholars have advanced what is called the South Galatian theory, contending that the epistle was actually written to the communities founded on Paul's first missionary journey in the area of Asia Minor extending from the seacoast inland (Acts 13, 13—14, 27). This premise has also been adopted here. If valid, it places the epistle among Paul's earliest writings, possibly in 48 A.D., or even before, but more probably after the Council of Jerusalem, 49 or 50 A.D. The meeting with James, Cephas, and John on which Paul reports in 2, 1-10 would then be the meeting described by Luke in Acts 15 as the Council itself.

The background facts regarding the Epistle to the Galatians provide a needed explanation of the complex data relative to it in the epistle itself and in Acts. They help to account for the passionate intensity with which Galatians is written.

Paul shows no knowledge of any limitation of the freedom of Gentile Christians in respect to Mosaic law (2, 9). This suggests that Luke's account of the Council of Jerusalem in which that freedom is limited by the provisions of the apostolic decree (Acts 15, 23-29) is a theological construct. After Paul had left Galatia, Judaeo-Christians from Jerusalem came there, and urged the Galatian communities to adopt the practices of the Mosaic law. The "false claimants to the title of brother" (2, 4), as Paul names these preachers who followed him, did not reject Christ as Savior in favor of the law. But, holding to the Christian doctrine of his central role, they nevertheless advocated the law as a highly beneficial addition to Christian living, and appealed for precedent to the actual practice in Palestine under Cephas (2, 1-10). They made light of Paul's apostolic role, holding him to be less informed than the Twelve (1, 11-24) because he had not been a disciple of Jesus during the ministry. They succeeded in disturbing and confusing the consciences of the Galatians, who were tending more and more to follow their teaching as a surer way of salvation (3, 1).

This subtle form of religiosity evoked from Paul a resounding declaration of the true nature of justification by faith in Christ, which frees the conscience from the Mosaic law as a principle of man's justice before God. The process thus begun in Galatians, of reflecting intensively on the meaning of the Christian gospel, eventually led Paul to his more far-reaching and profound exposition in the Epistle to the Romans.

The Epistle to the Galatians is divided as follows:

THE EPISTLE OF PAUL
TO THE GALATIANS
I: INTRODUCTION

1

Greetings

¹ Paul, an apostle sent, not by men or by any man, but by Jesus Christ and God his Father who raised him from the dead —² I and my brothers who are with me send greetings to the churches in Galatia. ³ We wish you the favor and peace of God our Father and of the Lord Jesus Christ, ⁴ who gave himself for our sins, to rescue us from the present evil age, as our God and Father willed—⁵ to him be glory for endless ages. Amen.

Reproof for Disloyalty

⁶ I am amazed that you are so soon deserting him who called you in accord with his gracious design in Christ, and are going over to another gospel. ⁷ But there is no other. Some who wish to alter the gospel of Christ must have confused you. ⁸ For even if we, or an angel from heaven, should preach to you a gospel not in accord with the one we delivered to you, let a curse be upon him! ⁹ I repeat what I have just said: if anyone preaches a gospel to you other than the one you received, let a curse be upon him!

¹⁰ Whom would you say I am trying to please at this point —men or God? Is this how I seek to ingratiate myself with men? If I were trying to win man's approval, I would surely not be serving Christ!

1, 1: 1, 11f.
4: 2, 20; 1 Tm 2, 6.

6: 2 Cor 11, 4.
10: 1 Thes 2, 4.

1, 1-5: Together with his customary greeting (see note on Rom 1, 1-7), Paul abruptly introduces the two main topics of the epistle: the authenticity of his apostolic office (1ff) and the doctrine of justification through faith rather than through observance of the law. Alluding to the Judaizers, i. e, Judaeo-Christians who have attempted to introduce traditional Jewish observances into the Galatian churches (cf 2, 4), he reminds the Galatians of his direct appointment to the office of apostle by Christ (v 1). He reaffirms what he had previously preached to them, that Christ's sacrificial death alone saves from sin (v 4).

1, 6-10: To impress upon the Galatians the doctrinal seriousness of their inclination to combine the practices of Judaism as saving acts with their faith in Christ, Paul calls this teaching *another gospel,* i. e., a doctrine of salvation substantially different from authentic Christian teaching (v 6), and declares that the Judaeo-Christians responsible for introducing it into the Galatian communities are to be condemned (v 9). The Judaizers have alleged that Paul originally refrained from teaching the Galatians the practices of Judaism in order to win them over more easily; the charge is now refuted, for he has made it clear that he will not compromise even with his fellow Jewish-Christians (v 10).

II: PAUL'S DEFENSE OF
HIS AUTHORITY AND DOCTRINE

Called by Christ

[11] I assure you, brothers, the gospel I proclaimed to you is no mere human invention. [12] I did not receive it from any man, nor was I schooled in it. It came by revelation from Jesus Christ. [13] You have heard, I know, the story of my former way of life in Judaism. You know that I went to extremes in persecuting the church of God and tried to destroy it; [14] I made progress in Jewish observance far beyond most of my contemporaries, in my excess of zeal to live out all the traditions of my ancestors.

[15] But the time came when he who had set me apart before I was born and called me by his favor [16] chose to reveal his Son to me, that I might spread among the Gentiles the good tidings concerning him. Immediately, without seeking human advisers [17] or even going to Jerusalem to see those who were apostles before me, I went off to Arabia; later I returned to Damascus. [18] Three years after that I went up to Jerusalem to get to know Cephas, with whom I stayed fifteen days. [19] I did not meet any other apostles except James, the brother of the Lord. [20] I declare before God that what I have just written is true.

[21] Thereafter I entered the regions of Syria and Cilicia. [22] The communities of Christ in Judea had no idea what I looked like; [23] they had only heard that "he who was formerly persecuting us is now preaching the faith he tried to destroy," [24] and they gave glory to God on my account.

2

The Council of Jerusalem

[1] Then, after fourteen years, I went up to Jerusalem again

11: 1, 1.
12: Eph 3, 3.
13: Acts 8, 1ff.
14: Acts 26, 4f.

15: Is 49, 1; Lk 1, 15.
16: 2, 7; Acts 9, 3-19.
18: Acts 9, 23-30.

1, 11-24: *The gospel I proclaimed:* this is shown to be the common possession of all the apostles including himself (see note on v 4). It was an understanding of the meaning of Christ's death in the order of salvation, divinely granted to Paul (11f), which led him to surrender his early career in Judaism (13f). Once he received this understanding of Christ and the apostolic office, he deemed it unnecessary to confer with the other apostles. Instead he went into retirement for a time (15ff). When, three years later, he spent two weeks with Peter in Jerusalem, he did not compare his understanding of Christ with that of the other apostles (18f). He is speaking truthfully, for the Judaeo-Christian churches near Jerusalem also recognized that he had abandoned Judaism for Christ as the way of salvation (20-24).

with Barnabas, this time taking Titus with me. [2] I went prompted by a revelation, and I laid out for their scrutiny the gospel as I present it to the Gentiles—all this in private conference with the leaders, to make sure the course I was pursuing, or had pursued, was not useless. [3] Not even Titus, who was with me, was ordered to undergo circumcision, despite his being a Greek. [4] Certain false claimants to the title of brother were smuggled in; they wormed their way into the group to spy on the freedom we enjoy in Christ Jesus and thereby to make slaves of us, [5] but we did not submit to them for a moment. We resisted so that the truth of the gospel might survive intact for your benefit.

[6] Those who were regarded as important, however (and it makes no difference to me how prominent they were—God plays no favorites), made me add nothing.

[7] On the contrary, recognizing that I had been entrusted with the gospel for the uncircumcised, just as Peter was for the circumcised (for he who worked through Peter as his apostle among the Jews had been at work in me for the Gentiles), [9] and recognizing, too, the favor bestowed on me, those who were the acknowledged pillars, James, Cephas, and John, gave Barnabas and me the handclasp of fellowship, signifying that we should go to the Gentiles as they to the Jews. [10] The only stipulation was that we should be mindful of the poor—the one thing that I was making every effort to do.

Peter and the Judaizers

[11] When Cephas came to Antioch I directly withstood him,

2, 5: 3, 1.
6: Dt 10, 17; Rom 2, 11;
Eph 6, 9.

9: Eph 3, 8.
11ff: Acts 15, 1.

2, 1-10: The *private conference with the leaders* is probably the same described by Luke in Acts 15; see note on Acts 15, 6-12. The first time Paul discussed the nature of the Christian gospel with other apostles was some fourteen years after his conversion (v 1), and then in consequence of a prophetic inspiration (v 2). The misgivings about Paul entertained at that time did not pertain to his doctrine, but probably to his persistence in establishing Christian communities among the Gentiles despite Jewish opposition (v 2; cf Acts 13, 13f.27). When it was suggested by Judaeo-Christians who opposed him that the Gentile Christian Titus be circumcised so as to display Paul's respect for Judaism, he refused to comply lest such a concession be turned against him (2, 3ff). James, Cephas, and John, far from objecting to his stand, even conceded that he possessed a God-given mission to the Gentiles, just as Peter was founder and leader of the Judaeo-Christian communities of Palestine. It was agreed then that Gentile Christians would not adopt the practices of Judaism, even though the Judaeo-Christian communities continued to retain them for cultural reasons (6-9). Paul readily acceded to the idea of organizing a collection among the Gentile communities for the poor Christians of Jerusalem (v 10), for he saw in it an occasion to develop unity of faith despite the prevailing diversity of culture; cf 2 Cor 9, 13.

2, 11-14: This incident, which probably occurred after the meeting of 2,

because he was clearly in the wrong. [12] He had been taking his meals with the Gentiles before others came who were from James. But when they arrived he drew back to avoid trouble with those who were circumcised. [13] The rest of the Jews joined in his dissembling, till even Barnabas was swept away by their pretense. [14] As soon as I observed that they were not being straightforward about the truth of the gospel, I had this to say to Cephas in the presence of all: "If you who are a Jew are living according to Gentile ways rather than Jewish, by what logic do you force the Gentiles to adopt Jewish ways?"

Paul's Basic Teaching

[15] We are Jews by birth, not sinners of Gentile origin. [16] Nevertheless, knowing that a man is not justified by legal observance but by faith in Jesus Christ, we too have believed in him in order to be justified by faith in Christ, not by observance of the law; for by works of the law no one will be justified. [17] But if, in seeking to be justified in Christ, we are shown to be sinners, does that mean that Christ is encouraging sin? Unthinkable! [18] If, however, I were to build up the very things I had demolished, I should then indeed be a transgressor. [19] It was through the law that I died to the law, to live for God. I have been crucified with Christ, [20] and the life I live now is not my own; Christ is living in me. I still live my human life, but it is a life of faith in the Son of God, who loved me and gave himself for me. [21] I will not treat God's gracious gift as point-

---

16: Rom 3, 20.22; Phil 3, 9.   21: 5, 2.
20: Rom 8, 10f; Col 3, 3f.

1-10, is more understandable if the policy then arrived at was not publicly promulgated to the Judaeo-Christians of Jerusalem (see note on Acts 15, 6-12). When Peter realized that sharing the agape-meal (see note on 1 Cor 11, 17-34) with Gentile Christians wounded the sensibilities of Judaeo-Christians, he abandoned the practice out of deference to their presence (11f). Other Judaeo-Christians in Antioch followed suit, thereby placing in jeopardy the unity of the Antiochean church (v 13). Paul publicly criticized Peter's conduct because it implied that, although in theory the Judaeo-Christian could eat with Gentile Christians, in practice the Gentile Christians should not eat with Judaeo-Christians (v 14).

2, 15-21: Although the Judaeo-Christian enjoys a certain religious privilege by birth (v 15), he knows that he is not justified by the Mosaic law but by faith in Christ (v 16). If he insists on his privilege as a Jew (v 11-14), he implies that Christ has misled him (a probable sense of v 17), and that he has sinned in abandoning his privilege by accepting Christ (v 18). The Judaeo-Christian, like Paul, knows that his privileged position occasioned his transgression of the law and revealed him to be a sinner in need of the redemptive death of Christ (v 19). Therefore, disregarding his privileged status as a Jew, he values only the new condition received from Christ, the source of his holiness (v 20). He seeks no privileged status in the Christian community—*I will not treat God's gracious gift as pointless* (v 21)—lest his justification seem to come from the law and not from the sacrifice of Christ.

less. If justice is available through the law, then Christ died to no purpose!

III: CHRISTIAN FAITH AND LIBERTY

3

Justification through Faith

[1] You senseless Galatians! Who has cast a spell over you—you before whose eyes Jesus Christ was displayed to view upon his cross? [2] I want to learn only one thing from you: how did you receive the Spirit? Was it through observance of the law or through faith in what you heard? [3] How could you be so stupid? After beginning in the spirit, are you now to end in the flesh? [4] Have you had such remarkable experiences all to no purpose—if indeed they were to no purpose? [5] Is it because you observe the law or because you have faith in what you heard that God lavishes the Spirit on you and works wonders in your midst? [6] Consider the case of Abraham: he "believed God, and it was credited to him as justice." [7] This means that those who believe are sons of Abraham. [8] Because Scripture saw in advance that God's way of justifying the Gentiles would be through faith, it foretold this good news to Abraham: "All nations shall be blessed in you." [9] Thus it is that all who believe are blessed along with Abraham, the man of faith.

No Justification from the Law

[10] All who depend on observance of the law, on the other hand, are under a curse. It is written, "Cursed is he who does

---

3, 6: Gn 15, 6; Rom 4, 3; Jas 2, 23.
7: Sir 44, 19ff.

8: Gn 12, 3.
10: Dt 27, 26; Rom 7, 7.

3, 1-5: Paul suggests that the Galatians must be under an evil spell to have forgotten the redemptive meaning of Jesus' crucifixion (v 1). He asks them to recall the reason for their conversion: the reception of the Spirit, not the works of the law (2-5).

3, 6-9: Probably in response to the argument of the Judaizers that if a Christian wishes to benefit fully from the promises made to Abraham he should embrace Judaism, Paul cites Gn 15, 6 to the effect that Abraham won God's favor because of his faith. Christians too have already won God's favor through their faith in Christ; cf 3, 2-5. They therefore may expect the fullness of the benefits promised Abraham for the Gentile nations (7-9).

3, 10-14: To seek salvation through observance of the law is to subject oneself to divine retribution (v 10), for the law is not the source of justification (v 11). It is associated with justification only if it is observed through faith (v 12). Christ removed the threat of divine retribution which came with non-observance of the law (v 13) in order that the Gentiles might receive through faith the blessings promised to Abraham on their behalf. Thus they are freed of the continual threat of divine punishment (v 14).

not abide by everything written in the book of the law and carry it out." [11] It should be obvious that no one is justified in God's sight by the law, for "the just man shall live by faith." [12] But the law does not depend on faith. Its terms are: "Whoever does these things shall live by them." [13] Christ has delivered us from the power of the law's curse by himself becoming a curse for us, as it is written: "Accursed is anyone who is hanged on a tree." [14] This has happened so that through Christ Jesus the blessing bestowed on Abraham might descend on the Gentiles in Christ Jesus, thereby making it possible for us to receive the promised Spirit through faith.

Promise Not Nullified by the Law

[15] Brothers, let me give you an everyday example. You cannot add anything to a man's will or set it aside once it is legally validated. [16] There were promises spoken to Abraham and to his "descendant." Scripture does not say "and to your descendants," as if it applied to many, but as if it applied only to one, "and to your descendant"; that is, to Christ. [17] My point is this: a covenant formally ratified by God is not set aside as invalid by any law that came into being four hundred and thirty years later, nor is its promise nullified. [18] Clearly, if one's inheritance comes through the law, it is no longer conferred in virtue of the promise. Yet it was by way of promise that God granted Abraham his privilege.

True Function of the Law

[19] What is the relevance of the law, in such case? It was given

---

11: Hb 2, 4; Rom 1, 17.
12: Lv 18, 5.
13: Dt 21, 23.

15: Heb 9, 17.
16: Gn 12, 7; Mt 1, 1.
19: Rom 5, 20.

3, 15-18: The example of the promise to Abraham derives its force from a certain continuity in the divine plan of salvation. Abraham, on whom the law that came only centuries later was not imposed, is the type or figure of God's gift of salvation to the Gentiles as well as to Israel. Hence to impose the law upon men as a means of salvation would be to deface the image of Abraham in Genesis as the spiritual father of all nations; cf Gn 12, 3.

3, 19-22: Though not the source of justification and salvation (3, 11), the Mosaic law fulfilled the purpose of revealing through Israel's history, illumined by the sacrifice of Christ, the sinfulness of all humanity (v 19; cf Rom 3, 9-20). Through the coming of Christ, this divine revelation is now fully grasped by those who believe in him (v 22). The fact that the law was delivered through Moses as mediator indicates that the law is not the fulfillment of the promise to Abraham concerning the Gentiles (v 19; cf Gn 12, 3). It is God alone who fulfills this promise of his for their salvation (v 20; cf Rom 3, 24). He could have imposed a law upon man that would justify him through its observance (v 21); instead he used the Mosaic law to reveal the sinfulness of man, and thus prepare him for salvation from sin through faith in Christ (v 22).

in view of transgressions and promulgated by angels, at the hands of a mediator; it was to be valid only until that descendant or offspring came to whom the promise had been given. ²⁰ Now, there can be no mediator when only one person is involved; and God is one. ²¹ Does this mean that the law is opposed to the promises [of God]? Again, unthinkable! If the law that was given was such that it could impart life, then justice would be a consequence of the law. ²² In fact, however, Scripture has locked all things in under the constraint of sin. Why? So that the promise might be fulfilled in those who believe, in consequence of faith in Jesus Christ.

The Benefit of Faith

²³ Before faith came we were under the constraint of the law, locked in until the faith that was coming should be revealed. ²⁴ In other words, the law was our monitor until Christ came to bring about our justification through faith. ²⁵ But now that faith is here, we are no longer in the monitor's charge. ²⁶ Each one of you is a son of God because of your faith in Christ Jesus. ²⁷ All of you who have been baptized into Christ have clothed yourselves with him. ²⁸ There does not exist among you Jew or Greek, slave or freeman, male or female. All are one in Christ Jesus. ²⁹ Furthermore, if you belong to Christ you are the descendants of Abraham, which means you inherit all that was promised.

4

Free Sons of God in Christ

¹ Brothers: as long as a designated heir is not of age his condition is no different from that of a slave, even though in

---

22: Rom 3, 9-20.23.
26: 4, 5ff; Jn 1, 12;
    Rom 8, 14f.
27: Rom 6, 4; Eph 4, 24.

28: Rom 10, 12;
    1 Cor 12, 13; Col 3, 11.
29: Heb 6, 12; Jas 2, 5.

3, 23-29: Paul here summarizes his previous thought. The purpose of the Mosaic law was to keep man aware of his own sinfulness—*locked in*—that he might realize his need of justification through an act of God accepted in faith (v 23). The value of the law lay in its role of leading to an understanding of the absolute necessity of faith in Christ (v 24). This having been accomplished, its function is fulfilled (v 25). The Galatian Christians, whether Jew or Gentile, slave or free, men or women, all walk the same path of salvation through faith in Christ. In this they are the true descendants of Abraham, the man of faith (23-29).

4, 1-7: Paul draws on the culture of the time to indicate to the Galatians their status in the history of salvation. They have reached a point in the religious history of humanity comparable to the state of a child in a Roman family who has attained his majority. From that moment he enjoys the goods, rights and privileges of an adult (1-3). The Galatians have been

name he is master of all his possessions; [2] for he is under the supervision of guardians and administrators until the time set by his father. [3] In the same way, while we were not yet of age we were like slaves subordinated to the elements of the world; [4] but when the designated time had come, God sent forth his Son born of a woman, born under the law, [5] to deliver from the law those who were subjected to it, so that we might receive our status as adopted sons. [6] The proof that you are sons is the fact that God has sent forth into our hearts the spirit of his Son which cries out "Abba!" ("Father!") [7] You are no longer a slave but a son! And the fact that you are a son makes you an heir, by God's design.

No Return to Slavery

[8] In the past, when you did not acknowledge God, you served as slaves to gods who are not really divine. [9] Now that you have come to know God—or rather, have been known by him—how can you return to those powerless, worthless, natural elements to which you seem willing to enslave yourselves once more? [10] You even go so far as to keep the ceremonial observance of days and months, seasons and years! [11] I fear for you; all my efforts with you may have been wasted.

Former Devotion of the Galatians

[12] I beg you, brothers, to become like me as I became like you. (Understand, you have not done me any wrong.) [13] You are aware that it was a bodily ailment that first occasioned my bringing you the gospel. [14] My physical condition was a challenge which you did not despise or brush aside in disgust. On the contrary, you took me to yourselves as an angel of God, even as if I had been Christ Jesus! [15] What has happened to your openhearted spirit? I can testify on your behalf that if it were possible you would have plucked out your eyes and given them

---

4, 3: 3, 23.
  5: 3, 13.26.
  6: Rom 8, 15ff.

8: 1 Cor 12, 2.
10: Col 2, 16-20.

---

freed through Christ from the tutelage of the law, which kept humanity conscious of its slavery to sin. As a result they have experienced the power of the Holy Spirit, who has recreated them as God's sons and enabled them to live their lives according to the sense and spirit of this new relationship (4-7).

4, 8-11: Referring to the conversion of the Galatians, Paul presses his argument against their adoption of practices of the law by showing that, if they were to accept Judaism as a partial principle of salvation, it would be no less futile than to return to polytheism.

4, 12-20: The apostle appeals to their personal loyalty to him through whom Christ was formed in them.

to me. [16] Have I become your enemy just because I tell you the truth?

[17] The people I have referred to are not courting your favor in any generous spirit. What they really want is to exclude you so that you may court their favor. [18] It would be well for you to be courted for the right reasons at all times, and not only when I happen to be with you. [19] You are my children, and you put me back in labor pains until Christ is formed in you. [20] If only I could be with you now and speak to you differently! You have me at a complete loss!

Allegory on Freedom

[21] You who want to be subject to the law, tell me: do you know what the law has to say? [22] There it is written that Abraham had two sons, one by the slave girl, the other by his freeborn wife. [23] The son of the slave girl had been begotten in the course of nature, but the son of the free woman was the fruit of the promise. [24] All this is an allegory: the two women stand for the two covenants. One is from Mount Sinai, and brought forth children to salvery: this is Hagar. [25] The mountain Sinai [Hagar] is in Arabia and corresponds to the Jerusalem of our time, which is likewise in slavery with her children. [26] But the Jerusalem on high is freeborn, and it is she who is our mother. [27] That is why Scripture says:

"Rejoice, you barren one who bear no children;
> break into song, you stranger to the pains of
> childbirth!
For many are the children of the wife deserted—
> far more than of her who has a husband!"

[28] You, my brothers, are children of the promise, as Isaac was. [29] But just as in those days the son born in nature's course persecuted the one whose birth was in the realm of spirit, so do

17: 1, 7.
19: 1 Cor 4, 14f;
    2 Cor 6, 13;
    1 Thes 2, 7f.
22: Gn 16, 15; 21, 2.

23: Gn 17, 16.
24: 5, 1.
27: Is 54, 1.
28: Rom 9, 8.

4, 21-31: Paul creates an allegory out of the story of Sarah and Hagar (Gn 21, 8-21; cf Gn 16, 1-16). The two women represent two covenants: Hagar, the slave girl, represents the covenant of Sinai. The children of this covenant are sons of Abraham *begotten in the course of nature*. By the covenant of Sinai they were enslaved to the law like Hagar's offspring, who were born into slavery. Sarah, the freewoman, represents the covenant made by God with Abraham. The children of this covenant, also sons of Abraham, are *the fruit of the promise*. Like the offspring of Sarah, born to freedom, these are free from the slavery of the Mosaic law.

we find it now. [30] What does Scripture say on the point? "Cast out slave girl and son together; for the slave girl's son shall never be an heir on equal terms with the son" of the one born free.

[31] Therefore, my brothers, we are not children of a slave girl but of a mother who is free.

IV: EXHORTATION TO CHRISTIAN LIVING

5

Basic Import of Faith

[1] It was for liberty that Christ freed us. So stand firm, and do not take on yourselves the yoke of slavery a second time! [2] Pay close attention to me, Paul, when I tell you that if you have yourselves circumcised, Christ will be of no use to you! [3] I point out once more to all who receive circumcision that they are bound to the law in its entirety. [4] Any of you who seek your justification in the law have severed yourselves from Christ and fallen from God's favor! [5] It is in the spirit that we eagerly await the justification we hope for, and only faith can yield it. [6] In Christ Jesus neither circumcision nor the lack of it counts for anything; only faith, which expresses itself through love.

Against Being Misled

[7] You were progressing so very well; who diverted you from the path of truth? [8] Such enticement does not come from him who calls you. [9] "A little yeast can affect the entire dough." [10] I trust that, in the Lord, you will not adopt a different view. May condemnation fall on whoever it is that is unsettling you! [11] As for me, brothers, if I am still preaching circumcision, why do the attacks on me continue? If I were, the cross would be a stumbling block no more. [12] Would that those who are troubling you might go the whole way, and castrate themselves!

Proper Use of Freedom

[13] My brothers, remember that you have been called to live in freedom—but not a freedom that gives free rein to the flesh.

30: Gn 21, 10.
31: 3, 29; Jn 8, 35.
5, 2: 2, 21; Acts 15, 1ff.
6: 6, 15; 1 Cor 7, 19.

8: 1, 6.
9: 1 Cor 5, 6.
11: 1 Cor 1, 23.
13: Rom 6, 15; 1 Pt 2, 16.

5, 7-12: A strongly worded appeal that they will reject the teachers who are misleading them.
5, 13-26: Since the teaching of the Judaizers has apparently provoked dissension within the community, Paul urges upon all the Christian law of love

Out of love, place yourselves at one another's service. [14] The whole law has found its fulfillment in this one saying: "You shall love your neighbor as yourself." [15] If you go on biting and tearing one another to pieces, take care! You will end up in mutual destruction!

[16] My point is that you should live in accord with the spirit and you will not yield to the cravings of the flesh. [17] The flesh lusts against the spirit and the spirit against the flesh; the two are directly opposed. This is why you do not do what your will intends. [18] If you are guided by the spirit, you are not under the law. [19] It is obvious what proceeds from the flesh: lewd conduct, impurity, licentiousness, [20] idolatry, sorcery, hostilities, bickering, jealousy, outbursts of rage, selfish rivalries, dissensions, factions, [21] envy, drunkenness, orgies, and the like. I warn you, as I have warned you before: those who do such things will not inherit the kingdom of God!

[22] In contrast, the fruit of the spirit is love, joy, peace, patient endurance, kindness, generosity, faith, [23] mildness, and chastity. Against such there is no law! [24] Those who belong to Christ Jesus have crucified their flesh with its passions and desires. [25] Since we live by the spirit, let us follow the spirit's lead. [26] Let us never be boastful, or challenging, or jealous toward one another.

6

The Demands of Conscience

[1] My brothers, if someone is detected in sin, you who live by the spirit should gently set him right, each of you trying to avoid falling into temptation himself. [2] Help carry one another's burdens; in that way you will fulfill the law of Christ. [3] If anyone thinks he amounts to something, when in fact he is nothing, he is only deceiving himself. [4] Each man should look to his conduct; if he has reason to boast of anything, it will be because the achievement is his and not another's. [5] Everyone should bear his own responsibility.

[6] The man instructed in the word should share all he has

14: Lv 19, 18; Mt 22, 39; Rom 13, 9.
16: 1 Pt 2, 11.
21: 1 Cor 6, 10.
22: 1 Cor 13, 4-7;

1 Tm 4, 12.
24: Rom 6, 6; Col 3, 5.
6, 1: Mt 18, 15; 2 Tm 2, 25.
3: 1 Cor 3, 18.

---

of neighbor (13ff). He forestalls the accusation that his doctrine of justification by faith opens the way to a life of moral irresponsibility (16-26).

with his instructor. [7] Make no mistake about it, no one makes a fool of God! A man will reap only what he sows. [8] If he sows in the field of the flesh, he will reap a harvest of corruption; but if his seed-ground is the spirit, he will reap everlasting life. [9] Let us not grow weary of doing good; if we do no relax our efforts, in due time we shall reap our harvest. [10] While we have the opportunity, let us do good to all men—but especially those of the household of the faith.

V: CONCLUSION

The Cross, Our True Boast

[11] See, I write to you in my own large handwriting! [12] Those who are trying to force you to be circumcised are making a play for human approval—with an eye to escaping persecution for the cross of Christ. [13] The very ones who accept circumcision do not follow the law themselves. They want you to be circumcised only that they may boast about your bodily observance.

[14] May I never boast of anything but the cross of our Lord Jesus Christ! Through it, the world has been crucified to me and I to the world. [15] It means nothing whether one is circumcised or not. All that matters is that one is created anew. [16] Peace and mercy on all who follow this rule of life, and on the Israel of God.

[17] Henceforth, let no man trouble me, for I bear the brand marks of Jesus in my body.

[18] Brothers, may the favor of our Lord Jesus Christ be with your spirit. Amen.

7: Hos 8, 7.
8: Prv 11, 18.
9: 2 Thes 3, 13.
10: 1 Thes 5, 15.

11: 1 Cor 16, 21.
12: 5, 11.
15: 5, 6; 2 Cor 5, 17.

6, 11-18: Paul asserts that the Judaizers wish the Gentile Christians to observe the laws of Judaism only in order that they themselves may escape persecution by the Jews. He observes that he already bears the scars of such persecution, but this has not prevented him from reaffirming the true doctrine in the present epistle.

THE EPISTLE OF PAUL
TO THE EPHESIANS
INTRODUCTION

Early Christian tradition, beginning with Irenaeus and Clement of Alexandria in the late second century, unhesitatingly ascribed this epistle to St. Paul. Since the early nineteenth century, however, critical scholarship has considered the word-usage, style, comparison with Colossians, the epistle's concept of the church, as well as the doctrine put forward by the writer, to be the basis for strong doubts about its Pauline authorship. This divergence between the two capital sources of opinion on the origin of Ephesians makes it impossible to give a categorical pronouncement for or against authorship by Paul. He was probably not the author of Ephesians in the same sense as of other epistles such as Romans, Galatians, 1 and 2 Corinthians. Whatever the epistle's literary origin, however, the author considered its teachings to be in the Pauline tradition (1, 1; 3, 1); and for purposes of interpreting the text itself, it is practical to adopt the clear implication therein that Paul is its author. If Ephesians is analyzed within the context of Pauline writings, the question of its relationship to the thought of Colossians and other letters of Paul may be fruitfully studied.

It seems certain that this epistle was not specifically addressed to the Christians of Ephesus. Paul had labored there for well over two years (Acts 19, 10), and would hardly have written so impersonally to a community with which he was intimately acquainted. Important early manuscripts (Vaticanus and Sinaiticus) omit the words *at Ephesus* in 1, 1. If Ephesians is the letter referred to in Colossians 4, 16, it may well have been addressed to a number of Christian communities, a possibility that would account for its impersonal character. What is called the letter to the Ephesians is traditionally regarded as having been written by Paul from prison—Colossians, Philippians, Philemon, and Ephesians are in fact known as the "captivity epistles." If the letter is authentically Pauline, it was probably written, as tradition has held, during Paul's first (?) Roman imprisonment, 61-63 A.D.

Ephesians consists of a greeting (1, 1f); a doxology of the greatest importance for the cosmic significance it attaches to Christ (1, 3-14); reflections on the Christian mystery of salvation (1, 15-22) as well as the mystery of the church (2, 22—3, 13); a prayer for the Christian community (3, 14-21); a discussion of the practical implications of the Christian mysteries (4, 1—6, 20), with special attention to family life and a famous reflection on the theology of Christian marriage (5, 22-23); and a friendly conclusion (6, 21-24).

THE EPISTLE OF PAUL
TO THE EPHESIANS

1

Greeting

[1] Paul, by the will of God an apostle of Jesus Christ, to the holy ones [at Ephesus], believers in Christ Jesus. [2] Grace and peace to you from God our Father and the Lord Jesus Christ.

The Father's Plan of Salvation

[3] Praised be the God and Father of our Lord Jesus Christ, who has bestowed on us in Christ every spiritual blessing in the heavens! [4] God chose us in him before the world began, to be holy and blameless in his sight, to be full of love; [5] he likewise predestined us through Christ Jesus to be his adopted sons—such was his will and pleasure—[6] that all might praise the glorious favor he has bestowed on us in his beloved.

Fulfillment through Christ

[7] It is in Christ and through his blood that we have been redeemed and our sins forgiven, [8] so immeasurably generous is God's favor to us. [9] God has given us the wisdom to understand fully the mystery, the plan he was pleased to decree in Christ, [10] to be carried out in the fullness of time: namely, to bring all things in the heavens and on earth into one under Christ's headship.

Blessing for Jew and Gentile

[11] In him we were chosen; for in the decree of God, who administers everything according to his will and counsel, [12] we were predestined to praise his glory by being the first to hope in

---

1, 1: Rom 1, 7; 1 Cor 1, 2; Col 1, 1.
2: Col 1, 2.
3: 2, 6.
4: 5, 27; Jn 45, 16; 17, 24; Rom 8, 29.
5: Jn 1, 12; 1 Jn 3, 1.
6: Mt 3, 17.
7: 2, 7; Rom 3, 24; Col 1, 14.20.
8: Col 1, 9.
9: 3, 9; Rom 16, 25.
11: Is 46, 10; Rom 8, 28; Col 1, 12; Rv 4, 11.

1, 3-14: This prayer of thanksgiving, similar in its opening words to Colossians 1, 12, is better understood if the later vertes also (Col 1, 15-20) are taken into consideration. The exalted Christology of the second passage of Colossians is at one with this prayer which reflects upon the divine plan of salvation centering in Christ and revealed to Christians as fully at work in themselves. The spiritual blessings the Christians communities have received through Christ (v 3) are gratefully enumerated: the call to faith and holiness (v 4; cf Rom 3, 30); the gift of divine adoptive sonship establishing a unique spiritual relationship with God the Father through Christ (v 5; cf Rom 8, 14-17); the liberation from sin through Christ's sacrificial death (v 7); the revelation of God's plan of salvation in Christ (v 9; cf Rom 16, 25; Eph 3, 3f); the gift of faith in Christ bestowed upon Jews (11f);

Christ. [13] In him you too were chosen; when you heard the glad tidings of salvation, the word of truth, and believed in it, you were sealed with the Holy Spirit who had been promised. [14] He is the pledge of our inheritance, the first payment against the full redemption of a people God has made his own, to praise his glory.

Fulfillment in the Church

[15] For my part, from the time I first heard of your faith in the Lord Jesus and your love for all the members of the church, [16] I have never stopped thanking God for you and recommending you in my prayers. [17] May the God of our Lord Jesus Christ, the Father of glory, grant you a spirit of wisdom and insight to know him clearly. [18] May he enlighten your innermost vision that you may know the great hope to which he has called you, the wealth of his glorious heritage to be distributed among the members of the church, [19] and the immeasurable scope of his power in us who believe. It is like the strength [20] he showed in raising Christ from the dead and seating him at his right hand in heaven, [21] high above every principality, power, virtue, and domination, and every name that can be given in this age or in the age to come.

[22] He has put all things under Christ's feet and has made him, thus exalted, head of the church, [23] which is his body; the fullness of him who fills the universe in all its parts.

2

Generosity of God's Plan

[1] You were dead because of your sins and offenses, [2] as

13: 4, 30; Col 1, 5f;
   Acts 2, 33.
14: 2 Cor 1, 22; 5, 5.
15: Col 1, 3f; Phlm 4f.
17: 3, 14.16; 1 Jn 5, 20.
19: 2 Cor 13, 4; Col 1, 11.
20: Ps 110, 1.

21: Phil 2, 9; 1 Pt 3, 22.
22: Ps 8, 6; Mt 28, 18;
   Col 1, 18.
23: 4, 10; Rom 12, 5;
   1 Cor 12, 27; Col 1, 19.
2, 1: Col 1, 21; 2, 13.
   2: 6, 12; Jn 12, 31; Col 1, 13.

---

and finally, the same gift granted to Gentiles (v 13). In the christological faith of the Christian communities the apostle sees the predetermined plan of God (4.11) to bring all creation under the final rule of Christ (v 10). The Christian community has the initial understanding of the gifts God has so freely given to men for the sake of Christ (6.8f), which all humanity will eventually possess.

1, 15-23: Paul prays that the blessings of the faith imparted by God the Father (v 3) to the Ephesians will be strengthened in them through the message of the gospel (1, 17ff). Those blessings are to be measured by his power in establishing the sovereignty of Christ over all other creatures (1, 20f) and in appointing him head of the church (1, 22f). For the allusion to angelic spirits, see the note on Colossians 1, 15.20.

2, 1-10: The recipients of Paul's letter have experienced, in their redemption

you gave allegiance to the present age and to the prince of the air, that spirit who is even now at work among the rebellious. [3] All of us were once of their company; we lived at the level of the flesh, following every whim and fancy, and so by nature deserved God's wrath like the rest. [4] But God is rich in mercy; because of his great love for us [5] he brought us to life with Christ when we were dead in sin. By this favor you were saved. [6] Both with and in Christ Jesus he raised us up and gave us a place in the heavens, [7] that in the ages to come he might display the great wealth of his favor, manifested by his kindness to us in Christ Jesus. [8] I repeat, it is owing to his favor that salvation is yours through faith. This is not your own doing, it is God's gift; [9] neither is it a reward for anything you have accomplished, so let no one pride himself on it. [10] We are truly his handiwork, created in Christ Jesus to lead the life of good deeds which God prepared for us in advance.

All United in Christ

[11] You men of Gentile stock—called "uncircumcised" by those who, in virtue of a hand-executed rite on their flesh, call themselves "circumcised"—[12] remember that, in former times, you had no part in Christ and were excluded from the community of Israel. You were strangers to the covenant and its promise; you were without hope and without God in the world. [13] But now in Christ Jesus you who once were far off have been brought near through the blood of Christ. [14] It is

---

3: Col 3, 6.
5: Rom 5, 8; 6, 13;
　　Col 2, 13.
6: Rom 8, 10f; Phil 3, 20;
　　Col 2, 12.
8: Gal 2, 16.

9: 1 Cor 1, 29.
10: 2 Cor 5, 17.
12: Rom 9, 4; Col 1, 21.27.
13: Is 57, 19; Col 1, 20.
14: Gal 3, 28.

---

from sin, the effect of Christ's supremacy (1f), the power of which over-came the evil force of demons. (In Jewish thought these were considered to dwell in the air.) Both Jew and Gentile have experienced, through Christ, God's generosity, his free gift of salvation which already marks them for a heavenly destiny (3-6). In Christ, God reveals the wealth of his kind-ness (v 7), saving men through faith and not by any works of their own (8f). Christians are a newly created people in Christ, fashioned by God for a new life of goodness (v 10).

　2, 11-22: The Gentiles were without Israel's messianic expectation, without the various covenants God made with Israel, without hope of salvation and knowledge of the true God (11f); but through Christ, all these religious barriers between Jew and Gentile have been transcended (13f) by the aboli-tion of the Mosaic covenant-law (v 15) for the sake of uniting Jew and Gentile into a single religious community (15ff), imbued with the same Holy Spirit and worshiping the same Father (v 18). The Gentiles are now within the pale of God's revelation (v 19) as it derives from the apostles, assisted by those endowed with the prophetic charism, the preachers of Christ (v 20; cf Acts 8, 4f; 1 Cor 12, 28). With Christ as the capstone (v 20), they are being built into the holy temple of God's people where the divine presence dwells (21f).

he who is our peace, and who made the two of us one by breaking down the barrier of hostility that kept us apart. [15] In his own flesh he abolished the law with its commands and precepts, to create in himself one new man from us who had been two and to make peace, [16] reconciling both of us to God in one body through his cross, which put that enmity to death. [17] He came and "announced the good news of peace to you who were far off, and to those who were near"; [18] through him we both have access in one Spirit to the Father.

[19] This means that you are strangers and aliens no longer. No, you are fellow citizens of the saints and members of the household of God. [20] You form a building which rises on the foundation of the apostles and prophets, with Christ Jesus himself as the capstone. [21] Through him the whole structure is fitted together and takes shape as a holy temple in the Lord; [22] in him you are being built into this temple, to become a dwelling place for God in the Spirit.

3

Commission To Preach God's Plan

[2] I am sure you have heard of the ministry which God in his goodness gave me in your regard. [1] That is why to me, Paul, a prisoner for Christ Jesus on behalf of you Gentiles, [3] God's secret plan as I have briefly described it was revealed. [4] When you read what I have said, you will realize that I know what I am talking about in speaking of the mystery of Christ, [5] unknown to men in former ages but now revealed by the Spirit to the holy apostles and prophets. [6] It is no less than this: in

---

15: 2 Cor 5, 17; Col 2, 14.
16: Col 1, 20.22.
17: Is 57, 19; Zec 9, 10.
18: 3, 12.
19: Heb 12, 22f.
20: Is 28, 16; Rv 21, 14.

21: Col 2, 19; 1 Cor 3, 16.
22: 1 Pt 2, 5.
3, 1: Phif 1, 7.13;
    Col 1, 24-29;
    2 Tm 2, 9.
5: Col 1, 26.

3, 1: *A prisoner for Christ Jesus:* see the Introduction.
3, 1-13: Paul reflects on his mission to the Gentiles. He alludes to his conversion and appointment to the apostolic office (2f) and observes that his own apostolic experience, as well as that of the other apostles and charismatic prophets in the church (4f), has deepened his understanding of God's plan of salvation in Christ. Paul is the special herald (v 7) of a new revelation to the world (v 6): that the divine plan includes the Gentiles in the spiritual benefits promised to Israel. Not only does he enjoy this unique apostolic role, but he also has been given the task of explaining to all men the divine plan of salvation (8f). Through the church, God's plan of salvation in Christ becomes manifest to angelic beings (v 10), a plan which God had kept hidden from all creatures (v 11). The fulfillment of the plan in Christ gives the whole church more confidence in God (v 12). The readers of this epistle are also encouraged to greater confidence despite Paul's imprisonment (v 13).

Christ Jesus the Gentiles are now co-heirs with the Jews, members of the same body and sharers of the promise through the preaching of the gospel.

Mission to the Gentiles

⁷ Through the gift God in his goodness bestowed on me by the exercise of his power, I became a minister of the gospel. ⁸ To me, the least of all believers, was given the grace to preach to the Gentiles the unfathomable riches of Christ ⁹ and to enlighten all men on the mysterious design which for ages was hidden in God, the Creator of all. ¹⁰ Now, therefore, through the church, God's manifold wisdom is made known to the principalities and powers of heaven, ¹¹ in accord with his age-old purpose, carried out in Christ Jesus our Lord. ¹² In Christ and through faith in him we can speak freely to God, drawing near him with confidence. ¹³ Hence, I beg you not to be disheartened by the trials I endure for you; they are your glory.

Prayer for the Readers

¹⁴ That is why I kneel before the Father ¹⁵ from whom every family in heaven and on earth takes its name; ¹⁶ and I pray that he will bestow on you gifts in keeping with the riches of his glory. May he strengthen you inwardly through the working of his Spirit. ¹⁷ May Christ dwell in your hearts through faith, and may charity be the root and foundation of your life. ¹⁸ Thus you will be able to grasp fully, with all the holy ones, the breadth and length and height and depth of Christ's love, ¹⁹ and experience this love which surpasses all knowledge, so that you may attain to the fullness of God himself.

²⁰ To him whose power now at work in us can do immeasurably more than we ask or imagine—²¹ to him be glory in the church

7: Col 1, 25.29;
  1 Thes 2, 4.
8: 1 Cor 15, 8f;
  Gal 1, 16; 2, 8.
9: Rom 16, 25; Col 1, 26f.
10: 1 Pt 1, 12.
12: Rom 5, 1f; Heb 4, 16.
13: Col 1, 22.24;

  2 Tm 1, 8.
16: 6, 10; Col 1, 11;
  2 Pt 1, 3.
17: Jn 14, 23; Rom 7, 22;
  Col 1, 23; 2, 7.
18: Col 2, 2.
19: Col 2, 3.9.
20: Rom 16, 25f; Col 1, 29.

3, 14-21: The apostle prays that those he is addressing may, like the rest of the church, deepen their understanding of God's plan of salvation in Christ. It is a plan which affects the whole universe: this is the sense of *the breadth and length and height and depth* (v 18). The apostle prays further that they may perceive the redemptive love of Christ for them and be completely immersed in the mystery of Christ in God (14-19). The prayer concludes with a doxology to God the Father (20f).

and in Christ Jesus through all generations, world without end. Amen.

4

Unity in the Mystical Body

[1] I plead with you, then, as a prisoner for the Lord, to live a life worthy of the calling you have received, [2] with perfect humility, meekness, and patience, bearing with one another lovingly. [3] Make every effort to preserve the unity which has the Spirit as its origin and peace as its binding force. [4] There is but one body and one Spirit, just as there is but one hope given all of you by your call. [5] There is one Lord, one faith, one baptism; [6] one God and Father of all, who is over all, and works through all, and is in all.

Diversity of Graces

[7] Each of us has received God's favor in the measure in which Christ bestows it. [8] Thus you find Scripture saying:

"When he ascended on high, he took a host of captives
    and gave gifts to men."

[9] "He ascended"—what does this mean but that he had first descended into the lower regions of the earth? [10] He who descended is the very one who ascended high above the heavens, that he might fill all men with his gifts.

[11] It is he who gave apostles, prophets, evangelists, pastors and teachers [12] in roles of service for the faithful to build up the body of Christ, [13] till we become one in faith and in the

---

4, 1: Col 1, 10.
2: Col 3, 12.
3: Col 3, 14f.
4: Rom 12, 15;
    1 Cor 10, 17.
5: 1 Cor 8, 6.

6: 1 Cor 12, 6.
7: Rom 12, 6;
    1 Cor 12, 28.
8: Ps 68, 19; Col 2, 15.
11: 1 Cor 12, 28.
13: Col 1, 28.

4, 1-16: A general plea for unity in the churches. Christians have been fashioned through the Spirit into a single harmonious religious community (*one body*), distinguished by a single Lord in contrast to the many gods of the pagan world, and by one way of salvation through faith, brought out especially by the significance of baptism (1-6; cf Rom 6, 1-11). But Christian unity is more than adherence to a common belief. It works itself out functionally through Christ's gifts to individuals to rule and teach so as to make the community ever more Christlike (11-16). This teaching on Christ as the source of the charisms is introduced by a citation of Psalm 68, 18 which depicts Yahweh triumphantly leading Israel to salvation in Jerusalem. It is here understood of Christ, the God-man, head of the church; through his redemptive death, resurrection and ascension he has become the source of the church's spiritual gifts. The "descent" of Christ (9f) refers more probably to the incarnation than to Christ's presence after his death in the abode of the dead.

knowledge of God's Son, and form that perfect man who is Christ come to full stature.

[14] Let us, then, be children no longer, tossed here and there, carried about by every wind of doctrine that originates in human trickery and skill in proposing error. [15] Rather, let us profess the truth in love and grow to the full maturity of Christ the head. [16] Through him the whole body grows, and with the proper functioning of the members joined firmly together by each supporting ligament, builds itself up in love.

Renewal in Christ

[17] I declare and solemnly attest in the Lord that you must no longer live as the pagans do—their minds empty, [18] their understanding darkened. They are estranged from a life in God because of their ignorance and their resistance; [19] without remorse they have abandoned themselves to lust and the indulgence of every sort of lewd conduct. [20] That is not what you learned when you learned Christ! [21] I am supposing, of course, that he has been preached and taught to you in accord with the truth that is in Jesus: [22] namely, that you must lay aside your former way of life and the old self which deteriorates through illusion and desire, [23] and acquire a fresh, spiritual way of thinking. [24] You must put on that new man created in God's image, whose justice and holiness are born of truth.

Vices To Be Avoided

[25] See to it, then, that you put an end to lying; let everyone speak the truth to his neighbor, for we are members of one another. [26] If you are angry, let it be without sin. The sun must not go down on your wrath; [27] do not give the devil a chance to work on you. [28] The man who has been stealing must steal no longer; rather, let him work with his hands at honest labor so that he will have something to share with those in need. [29] Never let evil talk pass your lips; say only the good things men need to hear, things that will really help them.

14: 1 Cor 14, 20;
   Col 2, 4.8; Heb 13, 9.
15: Col 1, 18; 2, 19.
17: Rom 1, 21.
18: Col 1, 21; 1 Pt 1, 14.
19: Col 3, 5.
22: Rom 8, 13; Col 3, 9.

23: Rom 12, 2.
24: Col 3, 10.
25: Zec 8, 16.
26: Mt 5, 22.
27: 2 Cor 2, 11.
28: 1 Thes 4, 11.
29: 5, 4; Col 3, 16; 4, 6.

4, 17—5, 20: For similar exhortations to a morally good life in response to God's gift of faith, see notes on Romans 12, 1—13, 14 and Galatians 5, 13-26.

³⁰ Do nothing to sadden the Holy Spirit with whom you were sealed against the day of redemption. ³¹ Get rid of all bitterness, all passion and anger, harsh words, slander, and malice of every kind. ³² In place of these, be kind to one another, compassionate, and mutually forgiving, just as God has forgiven you in Christ.

5

¹ Be imitators of God as his dear children. ² Follow the way of love, even as Christ loved you. He gave himself for us as an offering to God, a gift of pleasing fragrance.

³ As for lewd conduct or promiscuousness or lust of any sort, let them not even be mentioned among you; your holiness forbids this. ⁴ Nor should there be any obscene, silly, or suggestive talk; all that is out of place. Instead, give thanks. ⁵ Make no mistake about this: no fornicator, no unclean or lustful person—in effect an idolater—has any inheritance in the kingdom of Christ and of God. ⁶ Let no one deceive you with worthless arguments. These are sins that bring God's wrath down on the disobedient; ⁷ therefore have nothing to do with them.

Duty To Live in the Light

⁸ There was a time when you were darkness, but now you are light in the Lord. Well, then, live as children of light. ⁹ Light produces every kind of goodness and justice and truth. ¹⁰ Be correct in your judgment of what pleases the Lord. ¹¹ Take no part in vain deeds done in darkness; rather, condemn them. ¹² It is shameful even to mention the things these people do in secret; ¹³ but when such deeds are condemned they are seen in the light of day, and all that then appears is light. ¹⁴ That is why we read:

> "Awake, O sleeper,
>   arise from the dead,
>   and Christ will give you light."

¹⁵ Keep careful watch over your conduct. Do not act like fools, but like thoughtful men. ¹⁶ Make the most of the present

---

31: Col 3, 8.
32: Mt 6, 14; Col 3, 12f.
5, 1: Mt 5, 48.
2: 1 Jn 3, 16.
3: Gal 5, 19;
   Col 3, 5.
5: 1 Cor 6, 9f;
   Gal 5, 21.

6: Rom 1, 18;
   Col 2, 4.8.
8: 4, 18; Jn 12, 36;
   Col 1, 12f.
11: 1 Thes 5, 4-8.
13: Jn 3, 20f.
14: Is 60, 1.
15: Col 4, 5.

opportunity, for these are evil days. [17] Do not continue in ignorance, but try to discern the will of the Lord. [18] Avoid getting drunk on wine; that leads to debauchery. Be filled with the Spirit, [19] addressing one another in psalms and hymns and inspired songs. Sing praise to the Lord with all your hearts. [20] Give thanks to God the Father always and for everything in the name of our Lord Jesus Christ. [21] Defer to one another out of reverence for Christ.

Christian Wives and Husbands

[22] Wives should be submissive to their husbands as if to the Lord [23] because the husband is head of his wife just as Christ is head of his body the church, as well as its savior. [24] As the church submits to Christ, so wives should submit to their husbands in everything.

[25] Husbands, love your wives, as Christ loved the church. He gave himself up for her [26] to make her holy, purifying her in the bath of water by the power of the word, [27] to present to himself a glorious church, holy and immaculate, without stain or wrinkle or anything of that sort. [28] Husbands should love their wives as they do their own bodies. He who loves his wife loves himself. [29] Observe that no one ever hates his own flesh; no, he nourishes it and takes care of it as Christ cares for the church—[30] for we are members of his body.

> [31] "For this reason a man shall leave his father
> and mother,
> and shall cling to his wife,
> and the two shall be made into one.".

[32] This is a great foreshadowing; I mean that it refers to Christ and the church. [33] In any case, each one should love his wife

---

18: Lk 21, 34.
19: Col 3, 16.
20: Col 3, 17.
22: Col 3, 18—4, 1;
    1 Pt 3, 1-7.
23: 1 Cor 11, 3;
    Col 1, 18.

25: Col 3, 19.
26: Rom 6, 4; Ti 3, 5ff.
27: 2 Cor 11, 2;
    Col 1, 22.
30: 1 Cor 6, 15.
31: Gn 2, 24; Mt 19, 5;
    Mk 10, 7f.

5, 21-33: The apostle exhorts married Christians to a strong mutual love. Holding with Genesis 2, 24 that marriage is a divine institution (v 31), he sees Christian marriage as taking on a new meaning symbolic of the intimate relationship of love between Christ and the church. The wife should serve her husband in the same spirit as that of the church's service to Christ (22ff), and the husband should care for his wife with the devotion of Christ to the church (25-30). In his conclusion Paul gives to the Genesis passage its highest meaning in the light of the union of Christ and the church, of which Christlike loyalty and devotion in Christian marriage is a clear reflection (31ff).

.as he loves himself, the wife for her part showing respect for her husband.

6

Children and Parents

[1] Children, obey your parents in the Lord, for that is what is expected of you. [2] "Honor your father and mother" is the first commandment to carry a promise with it—[3] "that it may go well with you, and that you may have long life on the earth."

[4] Fathers, do not anger your children. Bring them up with the training and instruction befitting the Lord.

Slaves and Masters

[5] Slaves, obey your human masters with the reverence, the awe, and the sincerity you owe to Christ. [6] Do not render service for appearance only and to please men, but do God's will with your whole heart as slaves of Christ. [7] Give your service willingly, doing it for the Lord rather than men. [8] You know that each one, whether slave or free, will be repaid by the Lord for whatever good he does.

[9] Masters, act in a similar way toward your slaves. Stop threatening them. Remember that you and they have a Master in heaven who plays no favorites.

Christian Warfare

[10] Finally, draw your strength from the Lord and his mighty power. [11] Put on the armor of God so that you may be able to stand firm against the tactics of the devil. [12] Our battle is not against human forces but against the principalities and powers, the rulers of this world of darkness, the evil spirits in regions above. [13] You must put on the armor of God if you are to resist on the evil day; do all that your duty requires, and hold your ground. [14] Stand fast, with the truth as the belt

---

6, 1: Prv 6, 20; Sir 3, 1-6;
    Col 3, 20.
  2: Ex 20, 12.
  4: Col 3, 21f.
  5: Col 3, 22-25;
    Ti 2, 9f.
  6: 1 Pt 2, 18.

  9: Col 4, 1.
  11: 2 Cor 6, 7; 10, 4;
    Jas 4, 7.
  12: Col 1, 13.
  14: Wis 5, 17-20; Is 11, 5;
    Lk 12, 35;
    1 Thes 5, 8.

6, 1-9: See note on Colossians 3, 18—4, 1.

6, 10-20: A general exhortation to courage and prayer. Drawing upon the imagery and ideas of Isaiah 11, 5; 59, 16ff and Wisdom 5, 17-23, Paul describes the Christian in terms of the dress and equipment of the Roman soldier. He observes, however, that the Christian's readiness for combat is not directed against men but against the spiritual powers of evil (10-17). Observe the unique importance he places on prayer (18ff).

around your waist, justice as your breastplate, [15] and zeal to propagate the gospel of peace as your footgear. [16] In all circumstances hold faith up before you as your shield; it will help you extinguish the fiery darts of the evil one. [17] Take the helmet of salvation and the sword of the spirit, the word of God.

Assiduous Prayer

[18] At every opportunity pray in the Spirit, using prayers and petitions of every sort. Pray constantly and attentively for all in the holy company. [19] Pray for me that God may put his word on my lips, that I may courageously make known the mystery of the gospel—[20] that mystery for which I am an ambassador in chains. Pray that I may have courage to proclaim it as I ought.

Conclusion

[21] Tychicus, my dear brother and faithful minister in the Lord, will keep you informed as to how I am and what I am doing. [22] I have sent him to you for the very purpose of giving you news about me for your hearts' consolation.

[23] May God the Father and the Lord Jesus Christ grant the brothers peace and love and faith. [24] Grace be with all who love our Lord Jesus Christ with unfailing love.

15: Is 52, 7.
16: 1 Pt 5, 9.
17: Is 59, 17;
1 Thes 5, 8.
18: Mt 26, 41;
Col 4, 2f.

19: Acts 4, 29;
Col 4, 3;
2 Thes 3, 1.
20: 2 Cor 5, 20.
21: Acts 20, 4; Col 4, 7; 2 Tm 4, 12.

6, 21-24: Tychicus is the bearer of the letter. On the assumption that Ephesians was addressed to several Christian communities (see the Introduction), it is understandable that no greetings to individual members of these communities should have been included in it.

THE EPISTLE OF PAUL
TO THE PHILIPPIANS

INTRODUCTION

The Christian community at Philippi dates from about 50 A.D., when Paul, apparently in the company of Luke (Acts 16, 10-40), visited the city on his second missionary journey. On his third journey he again visited Philippi (Acts 20, 1). The city had a proud history. It was founded by Philip of Macedonia, father of Alexander the Great, and was the scene of the defeat of Mark Antony by Octavian in 42 B.C. After this event it became a Roman colony, and its citizens were granted the right of Roman citizenship. Their esteem for this privilege is reflected in Luke's account of Paul's treatment in Philippi (Acts 16, 35-40).

Describing himself in the present epistle as a prisoner (1, 7.17) facing a possibly unfavorable outcome to his trial (1, 19-26), he three times warns the Philippians against the enemies of their faith (1, 28; 3, 2.18f). He also gives them news of Epaphroditus, one of their number, who had become extremely ill while attending to Paul's needs (2, 25-30). He expresses his own deep affection for the Philippians (1, 3-11), and thanks them warmly for the donations they have sent him (4, 11-20). He exhorts them to be faithful to their vocation (2, 12-18), and to maintain their present unity of belief (2, 1f; 3, 15f; 4, 1), mentioning only one instance of disharmony (4, 2). He ponders the favorable effect his imprisonment has had on the spread of the gospel (1, 12-26), and points to the disinterested sacrifice of Christ as the transcendent formative rule for every Christian action (2, 1-11); proposing his own complete abnegation for the sake of Christ as the example to be followed against the false teaching of the Judaizers (3, 3-18).

The somewhat rambling quality of the epistle has led certain scholars to suggest that several brief letters of Paul to the Philippians were formed into this single composition. The alternative view is that the apostle dictated portions of the letter on separate occasions. Traditionally, Philippians has been assigned to the period of Paul's first Roman imprisonment (61-63 A.D.). In recent years Ephesus has been proposed by a growing number of scholars as the place of composition. It is known to have had a praetorian guard (alluded to in Philippians 4, 22), and therefore probably a judicial authority. It can readily be assumed that Luke did not record all of Paul's imprisonments in Acts; cf 2 Cor 6, 5. Others, however, consider the prison at Caesarea to have been the place (Acts 23, 23.31ff). If the epistle was written in Ephesus, it is to be dated about the year 53; if in Caesarea, about five years later; if in Rome, about 62. Its famous passage on the *kenosis* or emptying of Christ (2, 5-11), probably taken from a Christian hymn, was of inestimable value for the early Christian understanding of the mystery of the incarnation.

The Epistle to the Philippians is divided as follows:

THE EPISTLE OF PAUL TO THE PHILIPPIANS

1

Greeting

¹ Paul and Timothy, servants of Christ Jesus, to all the holy ones at Philippi, with their bishops and deacons in Christ Jesus. ² Grace and peace be yours from God our Father and from the Lord Jesus Christ!

I: THE EXAMPLE OF PAUL

Gratitude and Hope

³ I give thanks to my god every time I think of you—⁴ which is constantly, in every prayer I utter—rejoicing, as I plead on ·your behalf, ⁵ at the way you have all continually helped promote the gospel from the very first day.

⁶ I am sure of this much: that he who has begun the good work in you will carry it through to completion, right up to the day of Christ Jesus. ⁷ It is only right that I should entertain such expectations in your regard since I hold all of you dear—you who, to a man, are sharers of my gracious lot when I lie in prison or am summoned to defend the solid grounds on which the gospel rests. ⁸ God himself can testify how much I long for each of you with the affection of Christ Jesus! ⁹ My prayer is that your love may more and more abound, both in understanding and wealth of experience, ¹⁰ so that with a clear conscience and blameless conduct you may learn to value the things that really matter, up to the very day of Christ. ¹¹ It is my wish that you may be found rich in the harvest of justice which Jesus Christ has ripened in you, to the glory and praise of God.

1, 3: 1 Thes 1, 2.
  6: 1 Cor 1, 6ff.
  9: Col 1, 9f; Phlm 6.

10: Rom 2, 18.
11: Jn 15, 8.

1, 1f: See note on Romans 1, 1-7, *Bishops and deacons:* literally, "overseers and assistants." This structure of the Christian community is similar to that found in the Pastoral Epistles.

1, 3-11: The Philippians' devotion to their faith and to Paul made them his pride and joy. Here he is possibly alluding to their monetary gifts (5f; cf 4, 14ff), and surely to their sufferings for the faith (1, 29f), and he expresses his conviction that the characteristics thus manifested are evidence of the community's preparation for the Lord's parousia (5f). He feels keenly (v 8) their concern for his apostolic work, which has created a special relationship between them and himself (v 7). He prays that the love they have shown for him may also affect other phases of their lives so as to prepare them perfectly for the parousia (9ff; see note on 1 Thes 4, 13-18).

The Spreading Gospel

[12] My brothers, I want you to know that my situation has worked out to the furtherance of the gospel. [13] My imprisonment in Christ's cause has become well known throughout the praetorium here, and to others as well; [14] most of my brothers in Christ, taking courage from my chains, have been further emboldened to speak the word of God fearlessly. [15] It is true, some preach Christ from motives of envy and rivalry, [16] but others do so out of good will. Some act from unaffected love, aware that my circumstances provide an opportunity to defend the gospel's cause; [17] others promote Christ, not from pure motives but as an intrigue against me, thinking that it will make my imprisonment even harsher.

[18] What of it? All that matters is that in any and every way, whether from specious motives or genuine ones, Christ is being proclaimed! That is what brings me joy. Indeed, I shall continue to rejoice, [19] in the conviction that this will turn out to my salvation, thanks to your prayers and the support I receive from the Spirit of Jesus Christ. [20] I firmly trust and anticipate that I shall never be put to shame for my hopes; I have full confidence that now as always Christ will be exalted through me, whether I live or die. [21] For, to me, "life" means Christ; hence dying is so much gain. [22] If, on the other hand, I am to go on living in the flesh, that means productive toil for me— and I do not know which to prefer. [23] I am strongly attracted by both: I long to be freed from this life and to be with Christ, for that is the far better thing; [24] yet it is more urgent that I remain alive for your sakes. [25] This fills me with confidence that I will stay with you, and persevere with you all, for your joy and your progress in the faith. [26] My being with you once again should make you even prouder of me in Christ.

12f: Eph 3, 1; 6, 20f;
    2 Tm 2, 9.
19: Jb 13, 16.

20: 1 Cor 6, 20; 1 Pt 4, 16.
21: Gal 2, 20.
23: 2 Cor 5, 8.

1, 12-26: Knowing their concern for his apostolate, Paul informs the Philippians of the positive effect his imprisonment has had upon the spread of the gospel (12ff). He notes, however, that some Christian preachers have been hostile to him personally (15f), a fact that pains him until he recalls that in any case Christ is being made known (v 18) and that his own pain will contribute to his salvation (v 19). Facing the possibility of a death sentence, he reflects that for him both life and death take their meaning from Christ (20f). In life he can bear witness to him (v 22), in death, which he prefers as the outcome of his imprisonment, he will be finally united to him (v 23). But the Philippians' need of him makes him confident that he will be released from his imprisonment (24ff).

II: PLEAS FOR CHRISTIAN HEROISM

Courage in Professing the Faith

27 Conduct yourselves, then, in a way worthy of the gospel of Christ. If you do, whether I come and see you myself or hear about your behavior from a distance, it will be clear that you are standing firm in unity of spirit and exerting yourselves with one accord for the faith of the gospel. 28 Do not be intimidated by your opponents in any situation. Their opposition foreshadows downfall for them, but salvation for you. All this is as God intends, 29 for it is your special privilege to take Christ's part—not only to believe in him but also to suffer for him. 30 Yours is the same struggle as mine, the one in which you formerly saw me engaged and now hear that I am caught up.

2

Imitating Christ's Humility

1 In the name of the encouragement you owe me in Christ, in the name of the solace that love can give, of fellowship in spirit, compassion, and pity, I beg you: 2 make my joy complete by your unanimity, possessing the one love, united in spirit and ideals. 3 Never act out of rivalry or conceit; rather let all parties think humbly of others as superior to themselves, 4 each of you looking to others' interests rather than his own. 5 Your attitude must be that of Christ:

27: Col 1, 10; 1 Thes 2, 12.
29: Mt 5, 10ff; Acts 5, 41.
2, 2: Rom 15, 5.
3: Rom 12, 3;

1 Cor 1, 10f;
Gal 5, 26.
4: 1 Cor 10, 33; 13, 5.

1, 27-30: He encourages them to hold fast, in the face of opposition, to their faith in the gospel.

2, 1-11: This passage is composed of two parts: introductory exhortations pleading for unity in the Philippian church and for the elimination of differences that are harmful to the community (1-4); and a panegyric hymn (6-11) which reflects the self-effacement of Christ, the model for Christian service (v 5). The hymn begins by invoking Christian faith in Jesus' divinity (*Though he was in the form of God*), and by recalling that, paradoxically, his divinity was concealed throughout his mortal life (v 6). Divesting himself of his divine prerogatives, not indeed of the divinity itself but of the state of glory rightfully his, and assuming the role of a servant, he presented himself simply as a man (v 7; cf Is 52, 13-53; 42, 1). Having fully accepted the human condition, he followed it in obedience to the Father even to death on a cross (v 8). The Father responded by raising him from the dead and placing him at his right hand. The resurrection and ascension are the theological sense of *hypsoun,* the Greek verb used; cf also Acts 2, 33. God endowed him with his own name (v 9), so that the name JESUS (Savior) would be identified in the knowledge of every creature with the very same name (KYRIOS "Lord") that is addressed to God the Father (2, 10f).

⁶ Though he was in the form of God,
    he did not deem equality with God
    something to be grasped at.

⁷ Rather, he emptied himself
    and took the form of a slave,
    being born in the likeness of men.

He was known to be of human estate,
    ⁸ and it was thus that he humbled himself,
    obediently accepting even death,
    death on a cross!

⁹ Because of this,
    God highly exalted him
    and bestowed on him the name
    above every other name,

¹⁰ So that at Jesus' name
    every knee must bend
    in the heavens, on the earth,
    and under the earth,
¹¹ and every tongue proclaim
    to the glory of God the Father:
    JESUS CHRIST IS LORD!

Innocence of the Children of God

¹² So then, my dearly beloved, obedient as always to my urging, work with anxious concern to achieve your salvation, not only when I happen to be with you but all the more now that I am absent. ¹³ It is God who, in his good will toward you, begets in you any measure of desire or achievement. ¹⁴ In everything you do, act without grumbling or arguing; ¹⁵ prove yourselves innocent and straightforward, children of God be-

---

6: Jn 1, 1f; 17, 5;
Heb 1, 3.
7: Is 53, 3; 2 Cor 8, 9;
Gal 4, 4;
Heb 2, 14.17.
8: Mt 26, 39; Heb 5, 8;
12, 2.

9: Is 52, 12; Mt 23, 12;
Eph 1, 20-23.
10: Is 45, 23f; Jn 5, 23;
Rom 14, 11; Rv 5, 13.
11: Acts 2, 36; Rom 10, 9.
15: Mt 10, 16.

2, 12-18: Paul exhorts his readers further through a reminder that the goal of their endeavors within the community is their salvation (v 12); this is the whole purpose of the divine activity within them (v 13). Consequently, all complaints and disputes harmful to the community should be avoided so that the Philippians may be a shining light to pagans everywhere (14f). They should transmit to the world the life of the gospel and thus become a source of pride for him at the parousia (v 16). If they achieve this, he can rejoice in the sufferings of his imprisonment and they in turn can be happy because of his joy (17f).

yond reproach in the midst of a twisted and depraved generation—among whom you shine like the stars in the sky [16] while
holding fast to the word of life. As I look to the Day of Christ,
you give me cause to boast that I did not run the race in vain
or work to no purpose. [17] Even if my life is to be poured out
as a libation over the sacrificial service of your faith, I am glad
of it and rejoice with all of you. [18] May you be glad on the
same score, and rejoice with me!

III: PAUL'S ASSISTANTS AND PLANS

Timothy

[19] I hope, in the Lord Jesus, to send Timothy to you very
soon, that I may derive courage from learning how things go
with you. [20] I have no one quite like him for genuine interest
in whatever concerns you. [21] Everyone is busy seeking his own
interests rather than those of Christ Jesus. [22] You know from
experience what Timothy's qualities are, how he was like a
son at his father's side serving the gospel along with me. [23] I
hope to send him as soon as I see how things go with me. [24] In
fact, I am confident in the Lord that I myself will be coming
soon.

Epaphroditus

[25] I have decided, too, that I must send you Epaphroditus,
my brother, co-worker, and comrad in arms, whom you sent
to take care of my needs. [26] He has been longing for all of you,
and was distressed that you heard about his illness. [27] He was,
in fact, sick to the point of death, but God took pity on him;
not just on him, I should say, but on me, too, so as to spare
me one sorrow after another. [28] I have been especially eager
to send him so that you may renew your joy on seeing him,

16: Is 49, 4.   21: 1 Cor 13, 5.
17: Rom 15, 16.   25: Phil 4, 18.
19: 1 Cor 4, 17; 16, 10.

2, 19—3, 1: To show his concern for the Philippians, Paul announces his
intention of sending them his most trusted assistant in his apostolate—Timothy, whom they already know (cf Acts 16, 1-15). If Paul is released, as
he anticipates, he himself plans to visit to them (19-24). He commends
Epaphroditus, whom they had sent to aid him in his imprisonment. He is
relieved that Epaphroditus' recovery from a critical illness spares him, Paul,
the sorrow of a death in the midst of this display of the Philippians' charity; indicating that as soon as Epaphroditus is well enough to make the
journey, he will return to them (25-30). 3, 1 seems to be the beginning of a
conclusion to the letter, interrupted by Paul's second thought of adding a
strong warning against the teaching of the Judaizers (see notes on Gal 1,
1-5 and 1, 6-10). Some scholars think the verse implies a previous letter to
the Philippians, now lost.

and my own anxieties may be lessened. [29] Welcome him joyously in the Lord and hold men like him in esteem, [30] for he came near to death for the sake of Christ's work. He risked his life in an effort to render me those services you could not render.

IV: CHRISTIAN DEDICATION

3

Breaking with the Past

[1] For the rest, my brothers, rejoice in the Lord. I find writing you these things no burden, and for you it is a safeguard. [2] Beware of unbelieving dogs. Watch for workers of evil. Be on guard against those who mutilate. [3] It is we who are the circumcision, who worship in the spirit of God and glory in Christ Jesus rather than putting our trust in the flesh—[4] though I can be confident even there. If anyone thinks he has a right to put his trust in external evidence, all the more can I! [5] I was circumcised on the eighth day, being of the stock of Israel and the tribe of Benjamin, a Hebrew of Hebrew origins; in legal observance I was a Pharisee, [6] and so zealous that I persecuted the church. I was above reproach when it came to justice based on the law.

[7] But those things I used to consider gain I have now re-

3, 2: 2 Cor 11, 13;
  Rv 22, 15.
  3: Rom 2, 29.
  4: 2 Cor 11, 18.21f;

Col 2, 11.
5: Acts 22, 3; 26, 5.
6: Acts 23, 6.

3, 2—4, 1: The Judaizers are called *unbelieving dogs* (the customary Jewish term at the time for Gentiles, here applied ironically) and *workers of evil*. Their urging of the religious rite of circumcision upon Christians is regarded as mutilation (v 2). The apostle declares that Christians, who possess the true worship prefigured by circumcision, have no need of this religious rite (v 3). He offers himself an example of one reared in the Jewish tradition of circumcision and the law, which he thought it his duty to defend by persecuting the Christian communities (4ff). Because of his faith in Christ he has now abandoned this religious tradition of salvation (7f). He relies solely on Christ for his justice before God, not on his own efforts to observe the law (v 9). He conforms his life to the sufferings of Christ, that he may know him alone, and experience bodily resurrection through him (10f). This adherence to Christ in faith does not mean that Paul has already ensured his own salvation by arriving at perfect spiritual maturity (v 12). He strives for still greater perfection, mindful of the meaning of God's call in Christ (13f).

Paul's prayer is that God may correct the Philippians if their attitude in this regard is different, though he sincerely believes they have no need except to make still greater progress (15f). His way and that of his followers are the model for their study (v 17). He mourns for those in the Christian community who fail to perceive that salvation lies in the cross of Christ, not in food regulations or circumcision (18f). Salvation does not lie in the body but in Christ, who at his second coming, will transform the body (20f). Paul begs the Philippians, in terms of great affection, to adhere firmly to what he has taught (4, 1).

appraised as loss in the light of Christ. [8] I have come to rate all as loss in the light of the surpassing knowledge of my Lord Jesus Christ. For his sake I have forfeited everything; I have accounted all else rubbish so that Christ may be my wealth [9] and I may be in him, not having any justice of my own based on observance of the law. The justice I possess is that which comes through faith in Christ. It has its origin in God and is based on faith. [10] I wish to know Christ and the power flowing from his resurrection; likewise to know how to share in his sufferings by being formed into the pattern of his death. [11] Thus do I hope that I may arrive at resurrection from the dead.

[12] It is not that I have reached it yet, or have already finished my course; but I am racing to grasp the prize if possible, since I have been grasped by Christ [Jesus]. Brothers, [13] I do not think of myself as having reached the finish line. I give no thought to what lies behind but push on to what is ahead. [14] My entire attention is on the finish line as I run toward the prize to which God calls me—life on high in Christ Jesus. [15] All of us who are spiritually mature must have this attitude. If you see it another way, God will clarify the difficulty for you. [16] It is important that we continue on our course, no matter what stage we have reached.

Christ Our Goal

[17] Be imitators of me, my brothers. Take as your guide those who follow the example that we set. [18] Unfortunately, many go about in a way which shows them to be enemies of the cross of Christ. I have often said this to you before; this time I say it with tears. [19] Such as these will end in disaster! Their god is their belly and their glory is in their shame. I am talking about those who are set upon the things of this world. [20] As you well know, we have our citizenship in heaven; it is from there that we eagerly await the coming of our Savior, the Lord Jesus Christ. [21] He will give a new form to this lowly body of ours and remake it according to the pattern of his glorified body, by his power to subject everything to himself.

9: Rom 3, 21f.
10: Rom 6, 3ff; 8, 17; Gal 6, 17.
11: Rv 20, 4-6.
12: 1 Tm 6, 12.
14: 1 Cor 9, 24f; 2 Tm 4, 7.
17: 1 Cor 11, 1; 1 Pt 5, 3.
18: 1 Cor 1, 17.23; Gal 6, 12.
19: Rom 16, 18.
20: Eph 2, 6; Col 3, 1f; Heb 12, 22.
21: Rom 8, 23.29; 2 Cor 15, 43ff.

V: EXHORTATIONS TO VIRTUE

4

Christian Concord

¹ For these reasons, my brothers, you whom I so love and long for, you who are my joy and my crown, continue, my dear ones, to stand firm in the Lord. ² I plead with Evodia just as I do with Syntyche: come to some mutual understanding in the Lord. ³ Yes, and I ask you, too, my dependable fellow worker, to go to their aid; they have struggled at my side in promoting the gospel, along with Clement and the others who have labored with me, whose names are in the book of life.

Joy and Peace

⁴ Rejoice in the Lord always! I say it again. Rejoice! ⁵ Everyone should see how unselfish you are. The Lord is near. ⁶ Dismiss all anxiety from your minds. Present your needs to God in every form of prayer and in petitions full of gratitude. ⁷ Then God's own peace, which is beyond all understanding, will stand guard over your hearts and minds, in Christ Jesus.

⁸ Finally, my brothers, your thoughts should be wholly directed to all that is true, all that deserves respect, all that is honest, pure, admirable, decent, virtuous, or worthy of praise. ⁹ Live according to what you have learned and accepted, what you have heard me say and seen me do. Then will the God of peace be with you.

Generosity

¹⁰ It gave me great joy in the Lord that your concern for me bore fruit once more. You had been concerned all along, of

---

4, 1: 2 Cor 1, 14;
1 Thes 2, 19f.
3: Ex 32, 32; Ps 69, 29;
Lk 10, 20; Rv 3, 5.

5: Ti 3, 2.
6: Mt 6, 25-34; 1 Pt 5, 7.
8: Rom 12, 17.
9: 1 Thes 4, 1.

4, 2-9: The apostle appeals personally to these two women to reconcile their differences (v 2) and adds an appeal to his *syzygos* to aid them in achieving a reconciliation. This word means "comrade, yoke-fellow," and may be a proper name, though no evidence has been found of its use as such (v 3). Paul wishes the Philippians to be a model community, marked by a joy that will have its effect also upon non-Christians (4f). Mindful of the possible nearness of the parousia (see note on 1 Thes 4, 13-18), the Philippians are not to be overly concerned about their troubles but instead are to resolve them in prayer (5f). Thus they will always be at peace (v 7). Their thoughts and lives should reflect only what is true, pure, admirable, virtuous or worthy of praise, as exemplified by his own life among them (8f).

4, 10-20: Paul thanks the Philippians for their monetary contribution, brought by Epaphroditus (v 18). He accepts it gratefully, though not be-course, but lacked the opportunity to show it. [11] I do not say this because I am in want, for whatever the situation I find myself in I have learned to be self-sufficient. [12] I am experienced in being brought low, yet I know what it is to have an abundance. I have learned how to cope with every circumstance —how to eat well or go hungry, to be well provided for or do without. [13] In him who is the source of my strength I have strength for everything.

[14] Nonetheless, it was kind of you to want to share in my hardships. [15] You yourselves know, my dear Philippians, that at the start of my evangelizing, when I left Macedonia, not a single congregation except yourselves shared with me by giving me something for what it had received. [16] Even when I was at Thessalonica you sent something for my needs, not once but twice. [17] It is not that I am eager for the gift; rather, my concern is for the ever-growing balance in your account. [18] Herewith is my receipt, which says that I have been fully paid and more. I am well supplied because of what I received from you through Epaphroditus, a fragrant offering, a sacrifice acceptable and pleasing to God.

[19] My God in turn will supply your needs fully, in a way worthy of his magnificent riches in Christ Jesus. [20] All glory to our God and Father for unending ages! Amen.

Farewell

[21] Give my greetings in Christ Jesus to every member of the church. My brothers here send you theirs, [22] as do all those who believe, particularly those in Caesar's service. [23] May the favor of the Lord Jesus Christ be with your spirit. Amen.

11: 2 Cor 11, 9; 1 Tm 6, 6.
12: 1 Cor 4, 11;
    2 Cor 6, 10; 11, 27;
    12, 9f; Col 1, 29.

13: 2 Cor 12, 10;
    2 Tm 4, 17.
17: 1 Tm 6, 19.
18: Eph 5, 2; Heb 13, 16.

---

cause he needs the money, for with God's help he always manages to provide for his wants (10-13); rather, he appreciates their sharing with him, noting that they are the only community from which he has taken such a gift (14ff). His joy in accepting the gift, more than he actually needed, comes from his certainty that God will reward their charity by fulfilling all their needs in turn (17-20).

4, 21ff: The final greetings, extended to all the members of the Philippian community individually, come not only from Paul but also from the Christians of the place where the letter originated (see Introduction).

THE EPISTLE OF PAUL TO THE COLOSSIANS

INTRODUCTION

The Christian community at Colossae was not established by Paul, who had never visited there (1, 4; 2, 1), but by Epaphras (1, 7; 4, 12; Phlm 23), to whom Paul refers as a member of the Colossian group. He was probably one of Paul's Ephesian converts. A second likely inference is that he had requested the apostle's aid in the matter of certain religious tenets of non-Christian origin which were influencing the Colossian community. The epistle's two christological passages (1, 15-20; 2, 9-15) are set in contexts suggesting that certain doctrines having to do with angelic spirits (1, 16) and ascetical practices (2, 16) were being advocated at Colossae in a way that detracted from the person of Christ (1, 17.20) and distorted the nature of the Christian life (2, 16-23).

Without entering into debate over the existence of angelic spirits or their function, Paul simply affirms that Christ possesses the sum total of redemptive power (1, 19) and that the spiritual renewal of the human person occurs through contact in baptism with the person of Christ, who died and rose again for man's justification (2, 9-14). It is unnecessary for the Christian to be concerned about placating spirits (2, 15) or avoiding imagined defilement through ascetical practices in regard to food and drink (2, 20-23). True Christian asceticism consists in the conquering of personal sins (3, 5-10) and the practice of love of neighbor in accordance with the standard set by Christ (3, 12-16).

Paul commends the community as a whole (1, 3-8), which seems to indicate that, though the Colossians have been under a certain pressure to adopt the false doctrines, they have not yet succumbed. The apostle expresses his prayerful concern for them (1, 9-14). His preaching has cost him persecution, suffering, and imprisonment, but he regards these as the completion of the sufferings of Christ (i.e., the church?), a required discipline for the sake of the gospel (1, 24—2, 4). His instructions to the Christian family and to slaves and masters require a new spirit of reflection and action. Love, obedience, and service are to be rendered *in the Lord* (3, 18—4, 1).

Paul wrote the letter to the Colossians while in prison, but his several imprisonments leave the specific place and date of composition uncertain On this point the same problem of determination exists as with Ephesians and Philippians (see the Introductions to these epistles). The highly developed Christology of Colossians would seem to indicate a later imprisonment, most likely the traditional Roman house arrest in which he enjoyed a certain restricted freedom in preaching (61-63 A.D.).

The Epistle to the Colossians is divided as follows:

THE EPISTLE OF PAUL
TO THE COLOSSIANS
I: INTRODUCTION

1

Greeting

[1] Paul, an apostle of Christ Jesus by the will of God, and Timothy our brother, [2] to the holy ones at Colossae, faithful brothers in Christ. May God our Father give you grace and peace.

Thanksgiving

[3] We always give thanks to God, the Father of our Lord Jesus Christ, in our prayers for you [4] because we have heard of your faith in Christ Jesus and the love you bear toward all the saints—moved as you are by the hope held in store for you in heaven. [5] You heard of this hope through the message of truth, the gospel, [6] which has come to you, has borne fruit, and has continued to grow in your midst, as it has everywhere in the world. This has been the case from the day you first heard it and comprehended God's gracious intention [7] through the instructions of Epaphras, our dear fellow slave, who represents us as a faithful minister of Christ. [8] He it was who told us of your love in the Spirit.

Prayer for Continued Progress

[9] Ever since we heard this we have been praying for you unceasingly and asking that you may attain full knowledge of his will through perfect wisdom and spiritual insight. [10] Then you

---

1, 3: Eph 1, 15f.
5: Eph 1, 13.

9: Eph 5, 17; Phil 1, 9.

1, 1f: For the epistolary form used by Paul at the beginning of his letters, see note on Romans 1, 1-7. The apostle frequently designates the members of the Christian community as *holy ones* (literally, "saints"), a term that includes the Old Testament idea of the people of God, and now expresses a relation to Christ. They have been called by God to union with Christ and have experienced the spiritual benefits of this union. The awareness of it helps them to be *faithful brothers in Christ*, i. e., dedicated to the tasks implied in their calling.

1, 3-8: Recalling his prayers for them and the deeply satisfying account of them he has received, the apostle congratulates the Colossians upon their acceptance of Christ and their faithful efforts to live his gospel (3ff). For their encouragement he mentions the success of the gospel elsewhere (v 6), and assures them that his knowledge of their community is accurate since he has been in personal contact with Epaphras, their presumed founder (7f).

1, 9-14: Moved by Epaphras' account, the apostle has prayed fervently for the Colossians that their response to the gospel may bring the fullest knowledge of God's will, *through perfect wisdom and spiritual insight* (v 9; cf 3, 10). He expects a mutual interaction between their life according to the gospel and this knowledge (v 10), which will reveal the power of God's

will lead a life worthy of the Lord and pleasing to him in every way. You will multiply good works of every sort and grow in the knowledge of God. [11] By the might of his glory you will be endowed with the strength needed to stand fast, even to endure joyfully whatever may come, [12] giving thanks to the Father for having made you worthy to share the lot of the saints in light. [13] He rescued us from the power of darkness and brought us into the kingdom of his beloved Son. [14] Through him we have redemption, the forgiveness of our sins.

II: THE PREEMINENCE OF CHRIST

Fullness and Reconciliation

[15] He is the image of the invisible god, the first-born of all creatures. [16] In him everything in heaven and on earth was created, things visible and invisible, whether thrones or dominations, principalities or powers; all were created through him, and for him. [17] He is before all else that is. In him everything continues in being. [18] It is he who is head of the body, the church; he who is the beginning, the first-born of the dead, so that primacy may be his in everything. [19] It pleased God to make absolute fullness reside in him [20] and, by means of him, to reconcile everything in his person, both on earth and in the heavens, making peace through the blood of his cross.

12: Jn 8, 12; Acts 26, 18;
1 Pt 2, 9.
15: Ps 89, 28; Jn 1, 3.18.
16: 1 Cor 8, 6;

18: Eph 1, 10.21.
1 Cor 15, 20;
Eph 1, 22f; Rv 1, 5.
20: Eph 2, 14.16.

---

presence among them, inspire them to courage and calm determination (v 11), and result in grateful love of the Father for his saving gifts (v 12). For he conquers the power of evil over men by offering them the power of his Son, who is his love in person (v 13) and has already forgiven their sins (v 14).

1, 15-20: Scholars raise the question whether Paul may not have adapted these verses from a Christian hymn or a Hellenistic wisdom poem. Whatever the case, the passage with all its lyricism is probably Paul's. Its exalted Christology synthesizes the growing awareness in New Testament times of Christ as man, Son of God, king and judge of the world, endowed with divine redemptive power, and containing in himself the fullness of that effective presence of God among men which was first manifested in the Old Testament (cf Jn 1, 1-18). Whereas man is patterned after the image of God, being given a certain likeness to him (Gn 1, 26f), Christ is the actual likeness of God. Through faith, the remote reality of the Deity is rendered discernibly present in him and comprehensible to men. *He is the image of the invisible God* (v 15), in the sense that as a person he is supreme in every way over all creation. Christ's supremacy requires not only that nothing appear in creation except in relation to him but also that he himself share in the creation of all things (v 16). Such is his supremacy that he existed before creation came into being. It is to him that creation owes all that it has been, is, and will be (v 17).

Christ cannot be anything but supreme over the church, which in any case is unthinkable and unrealizable without him (his *body*). Furthermore, because of his supremacy he was the first to be raised by God from the

²¹ You yourselves were once alienated from him; you nourished hostility in your hearts because of your evil deeds. ²² But now Christ has achieved reconciliation for you in his mortal body by dying, so as to present you to God holy, free of reproach and blame. ²³ But you must hold fast to faith, be firmly grounded and steadfast in it, unshaken in the hope promised you by the gospel you have heard. It is the gospel which has been announced to every creature under heaven, and I, Paul, am its servant.

The Mystery: Christ in Us

²⁴ Even now I find my joy in the suffering I endure for you. In my own flesh I fill up what is lacking in the sufferings of Christ for the sake of his body, the church. ²⁵ I became a minister of this church through the commission God gave me to preach among you his word in its fullness, ²⁶ that mystery hidden from ages and generations past but now revealed to his holy ones. ²⁷ God has willed to make known to them the glory beyond price which this mystery brings to the Gentiles—the mystery of Christ in you, your hope of glory. ²⁸ This is the Christ we proclaim while we admonish all men and teach them in the full measure of wisdom, hoping to make every man complete in Christ. ²⁹ For this I work and struggle, impelled by that energy of his which is so powerful a force within me.

2

¹ I want you to know how hard I am struggling for you and

26: Rom 16, 25.   27: 3, 4.   29: Phil 4, 13.

---

dead; and his resurrection placed him in full possession of headship over the community which he brought into being (v 18). Since, as is clear from Christ's role in creation (v 16), the cosmos is dependent on him (v 19), his death upon the cross has its effect on the whole of creation without exception, pacifying it and uniting it to God (v 20). Paul's clear exposition of the supremacy of Christ was occasioned by the Colossians' difficulties concerning the relationship of angelic spirits to the world (see Introduction).

1, 21ff: Paul reminds them that they have experienced the reconciling effect of Christ's death, and appeals to them to adhere firmly to him as their only conciliator with God.

1, 24f—2,5: As the community at Colossae is not personally known to Paul (see Introduction), he here invests his recommendations with greater authority by presenting a brief sketch of his apostolic ministry and sufferings as they reflect those of Christ in behalf of the church (v 24). The preaching of God's word (v 25) manifests the divine will to sanctify the Gentiles (v 26) by revealing God's saving presence among them in Christ (v 27). It teaches men the God-given wisdom about Christ (v 28), whose power works mightily in the apostle (v 29). Even in those communities which do not know him personally (2, 1), he can increase the perception of God in Christ, unite the faithful more firmly in love, and so bring spiritual comfort to them (v 2). He hopes that his apostolic authority will make the Colossians perceive more readily the defects in the teaching of others who have sought to delude them (4f).

for the Laodiceans and the many others who have never seen me in the flesh. [2] I wish their hearts to be strengthened and themselves to be closely united in love, enriched with full assurance by their knowledge of the mystery of God—namely Christ—[3] in whom every treasure of wisdom and knowledge is hidden.

III: WARNINGS AGAINST FALSE TEACHERS

A General Admonition

[4] I tell you all this so that no one may delude you with specious arguments. [5] I may be absent in body but I am with you in spirit, happy to see good order among you and the firmness of your faith in Christ. [6] Continue, therefore, to live in Christ Jesus the Lord, in the spirit in which you received him. [7] Be rooted in him and built up in him, growing ever stronger in faith, as you were taught, and overflowing with gratitude. [8] See to it that no one deceives you through an empty, seductive philosophy that follows mere human traditions, a philosophy based on cosmic powers rather than on Christ.

Sovereign Role of Christ

[9] In Christ the fullness of deity resides in bodily form. Yours is a share of this fullness, in him [10] who is the head of every

---

2, 2: 2 Eph 3, 18f.   7: Eph 3, 17.
      3: Prv 2, 4f.   8: Gal 4, 3.
      4: Eph 4, 14.   9: Eph 3, 19.
      5: Phil 1, 27.

2, 6—3, 4: The Colossians are admonished to adhere to the gospel as it was first preached to them (v 6), steeping themselves in it with grateful hearts (v 7). They must reject religious teachings originating in any source except the gospel (v 8) because in Christ alone will they have access to the divinity (v 9). So fully has he enlightened them that they need no other source of religious knowledge or virtue (v 10). They do not require circumcision (v 11), for in baptism their whole being has been affected by Christ (v 12) through forgiveness of sin and restoration to a new life (v 13; cf Rom 6, 1-11).

On the cross Christ canceled the bond that stood against us, with all its claims; i. e., he eliminated the law (cf Eph 2, 15), which men could not observe—and which could not save them. He forgave sins against the law (v 14), and exposed as false and misleading (v 15) all other powers which offer salvation to men. Therefore the Colossians are not to judge food and drink or the keeping of religious festivals according to the rule of other religious powers, including angelic spirits (16ff), for they thereby risk severing themselves from Christ (v 19). If, when they accepted the gospel, they believe in Christ as their Savior, they must be convinced that their salvation cannot be achieved by appeasing ruling spirits through dietary practices, or through a wisdom gained simply in virtue of harsh asceticism (20-23). By retaining the message of the gospel that the risen, living Christ is the source of their salvation, they will be free from false religious evaluations of the things of the world, 3, 1f). The Colossians, it is true, will not have the personal satisfaction that material religious practices offer. They have died to these; but one day they will live with Christ in the presence of God (3f).

principality and power. [11] You were also circumcised in him, not with the circumcision administered by hand but with Christ's circumcision which strips off the carnal body completely. [12] In baptism you were not only buried with him but also raised to life with him because you believed in the power of God who raised him from the dead. [13] Even when you were dead in sin and your flesh was uncircumcised, God gave you new life in company with Christ. He pardoned all our sins. [14] He canceled the bond that stood against us with all its claims, snatching it up and nailing it to the cross. [15] Thus did God disarm the principalities and powers. He made a public show of them and, leading them off captive, triumphed in the person of Christ.

Practices contrary to Faith

[16] No one is free, therefore, to pass judgment on you in terms of what you eat or drink or what you do on yearly or monthly feasts, or on the sabbath. [17] All these were but a shadow of things to come; the reality is the body of Christ. [18] Let no one rob you of your prize by insisting on servility in the worship of angels. Such a one takes his stand on his own experience; he is inflated with empty pride by his human reflections [19] when he should be in close touch with the head. The whole body, mutually supported and upheld by joints and sinews, achieves a growth from this source which comes from God.

[20] If with Christ you have died to cosmic forces, why should you be bound by rules that say, [21] "Do not handle! Do not taste! Do not touch!" as though you were still living a life bounded by this world? [22] Such prescriptions deal with things that perish in their use. They are based on merely human precepts and doctrines. [23] While these make a certain show of wisdom in their affected piety, humility, and bodily austerity, their chief effect is that they indulge men's pride.

IV: THE IDEAL CHRISTIAN LIFE IN THE WORLD

3

Mystical Death and Resurrection

[1] Since you have been raised up in company with Christ,

11: Jer 4, 4; Rom 2, 25-29;
    Phil 3, 3.
12: Rom 6, 3f.
13: Eph 2, 1.
14: Eph 2, 15.
15: 2 Cor 2, 14.

16: Rom 14, 3f;
    1 Tm 4, 3.
17: Heb 10, 1.
18: Mt 24, 4.
3, 1: Phil 3, 20.

set your heart on what pertains to higher realms where Christ is seated at God's right hand. [2] Be intent on things above rather than on things of earth. [3] After all, you have died! Your life is hidden now with Christ in God. [4] When Christ our life appears, then you shall appear with him in glory.

Renunciation of Vices

[5] Put to death whatever in your nature is rooted in earth: fornication, uncleanness, passion, evil desires, and that lust which is idolatry. [6] These are the sins which provoke God's wrath. [7] Your own conduct was once of this sort, when these sins were your very life. [8] You must put that aside now: all the anger and quick temper, the malice, the insults, the foul language. [9] Stop lying to one another. What you have done is put aside your old self with its past deeds [10] and put on a new man, one who grows in knowledge as he is formed anew in the image of his Creator. [11] There is no Greek or Jew here, circumcised or uncircumcised, foreigner, Scythian, slave, or freeman. Rather, Christ is everything in all of you.

The Practice of Virtues

[12] Because you are God's chosen ones, holy and beloved, clothe yourselves with heartfelt mercy, with kindness, humility, meekness, and patience. [13] Bear with one another; forgive whatever grievances you have against one another. Forgive as the Lord has forgiven you. [14] Over all these virtues put on love, which binds the rest together and makes them perfect. [15] Christ's peace must reign in your hearts, since as members of the one body you have been called to that peace. Dedicate yourselves to thankfulness. [16] Let the word of Christ, rich as it is, dwell in you. In wisdom made perfect, instruct and admonish one another. Sing gratefully to God from your hearts in psalms,

---

5: Eph 5, 3.
6: Rom 1, 18.
8: Eph 4, 31.
9: Rom 6, 4.6;
   Eph 4, 22-25;
   Heb 12, 1; 1 Pt 2, 1;
   4, 2.
11: 1 Cor 12, 13;
   Gal 3, 27f.

12: Eph 4, 1f.32;
   1 Thes 5, 15.
13: Mt 6, 14; 18, 21-35;
   Eph 4, 32.
14: Rom 13, 8ff.
15: 1 Cor 12, 12;
   Eph 2, 16; 4, 3f.
16: Eph 5, 19f.

3, 5-17: In lieu of false asceticism and superstitious festivals, the apostle reminds the Colossians of the moral life that is to characterize their response to God through Christ. He urges their participation in the liturgical hymns and prayers that center upon God's plan of salvation in Christ (16f).

hymns, and inspired songs. [17] Whatever you do, whether in speech or in action, do it in the name of the Lord Jesus. Give thanks to God the Father through him.

The Christian Family

[18] You who are wives, be submissive to your husbands. This is your duty in the Lord. [19] Husbands, love your wives. Avoid any bitterness toward them. [20] You children, obey your parents in everything as the acceptable way in the Lord. [21] And fathers, do not nag your children lest they lose heart.

Slaves and Masters

[22] To slaves I say, obey your human masters perfectly, not with the purpose of attracting attention and pleasing men but in all sincerity and out of reverence for the Lord. [23] Whatever you do, work at it with your whole being. Do it for the Lord rather than for men, [24] since you know full well you will receive an inheritance from him as your reward. Be slaves of Christ the Lord. [25] Whoever acts unjustly will be repaid for the wrong he has done. No favoritism will be shown. [1] You slave-owners, deal justly and fairly with your slaves, realizing that you too have a master in heaven.

4

Prayer and Apostolic Spirit

[2] Pray perseveringly, be attentive to prayer, and pray in a spirit of thanksgiving. [3] Pray for us, too, that God may provide us with an opening to proclaim the mystery of Christ, for which I am a prisoner. [4] Pray that I may speak it clearly, as I must. [5] Be prudent in dealing with outsiders; make the most of every opportunity. [6] Let your speech be always gracious and in good taste, and strive to respond properly to all who address you.

17: 1 Cor 10, 31.
18: Eph 5, 22; Ti 2, 5;
    1 Pt 3, 1.
20: Eph 6, 1.
21: Eph 6, 4.
22: Eph 6, 5; 1 Tm 6, 1;
    Ti 2, 9f; 1 Pt 2, 18.

25: Rom 2, 5.
4, 2: Lk 18, 1; Rom 12, 12;
    Eph 6, 18-20;
    1 Thes 5, 17.
3: Rom 15, 30; Eph 6, 19;
    2 Thes 3, 1.
5: Eph 5, 15f.

3, 18—4, 18: After general recommendations which connect family life and the social condition of slavery with the service of Christ (3, 18—4, 1), Paul requests prayers for himself, especially in view of his imprisonment (2f), and recommends friendly relations and meaningful discussions of Christian teaching with non-Christians (5f). He concludes with greetings and information concerning various Christians known to the Colossians (7-18).

V: CONCLUSION

Tychicus and Onesimus

[7] Tychicus, our dear brother, our faithful minister and fellow slave in the Lord, will give you all the news about me. [8] I am sending him to you for this purpose, and to comfort your hearts. [9] With him is Onesimus, our dear and faithful brother, who is one of you. They will tell you all that has happened here.

From Paul's Co-workers

[10] Aristarchus, who is a prisoner along with me, sends you greetings. So does Mark, the cousin of Barnabas. You have received instructions about him: if he comes to you, make him welcome. [11] Jesus known also as Justus sends greetings. These are the only circumcised ones among those who are working with me for the kingdom of God. They have been a great comfort to me. [12] Epaphras, who is one of you, sends greetings. He is a servant of Christ Jesus who is always pleading earnestly in prayer that you stand firm, that you be perfect and have full conviction about whatever pertains to God's will. [13] I can certainly testify how solicitous he is for you and for those at Laodicea and Hierapolis. [14] Luke, our dear physician, sends you greetings. So does Demas.

A Message for the Laodiceans

[15] Give our best wishes to the brothers at Laodicea and to Nymphas and the assembly that meets at his house. [16] Once this letter has been read to you, see that it is read in the assembly of the Laodiceans as well, and that you yourselves read the letter that is coming from Laodicea. [17] To Archippus say, "Take care to discharge the ministry you have received in the Lord."

[18] This greeting is from Paul—in my own hand! Remember my chains. Grace be with you.

7: Acts 20, 4; Eph 6, 21.
9: Phlm 10f.
10: Acts 19, 29.
12: Rom 15, 30.

14: 2 Tm 4, 11.
18: 1 Cor 16, 21;
2 Thes 3, 17.

4, 16: The reference is perhaps to a letter Paul wrote to be read in a number of Christian communities in the area of the Lycus Valley, that eventually became known as the letter to the Ephesians (see Ephesians Introduction).

THE FIRST EPISTLE OF PAUL
TO THE THESSALONIANS
INTRODUCTION

Paul's formation of a Christian community at Thessalonica on his second missionary journey (Acts 17, 1-9) produced a considerable disturbance among the Jews residing there. To prevent further disorder he and his companion, Silas, agreed to leave the city (Acts 17, 10). However, he revisited the community on his third journey (Acts 20, 1f). Indications from 1 Thessalonians itself and from Acts permit the almost certain conclusion that the epistle was written only a short time after Paul's departure from Thessalonica (1 Thes 2, 17). In that interval he had been in Athens (3, 1; Acts 17, 16), and from there had sent Timothy to the Thessalonians (3, 2). He now writes to them from Corinth (1, 7; Acts 18, 1-18). Gallio is mentioned as proconsul of Achaia (Acts 18, 12-17) during Paul's Corinthian sojourn of more than a year; and since Gallio assumed the office in 51 or 52 A.D., the letter is to be dated at that time.

Paul writes after receiving Timothy's report on the Thessalonian community (3, 6). Deeply grateful for the information it conveys (1, 2f), he is also moved to declare how valuable to his own work the news of their conversion has been (1, 4-10). Probably to offset slanders uttered against him from outside the community after his departure from Thessalonica, he recalls his undemanding manner of life among them (2, 1-12). He reminds them of the prophetic character of the Christian message and relates it to the harassment they continue to suffer at the hands of the Jews (2, 14ff). He is satisfied of their firm adherence to the gospel, and prays that he may be able to visit them soon (3, 6-10). He exhorts them to greater care in carrying out the gospel precepts, particularly those pertaining to right sexual conduct (4, 1-8). He urges them to live peaceably and to avoid idleness (4, 11f).

Paul next turns his attention to the most serious problem which Timothy's visit to the community has brought to light: their excessive sorrow over the death of members of the community, who are thought to be deprived thereby of the joy of the second coming of Christ. Paul appeals to his own knowledge of Christ's teaching to affirm that the resurrection of the dead is to occur before the parousia, so that Christians living at the time are to have no advantage over those who have died (4, 13-18). He reminds them of Christ's words on the suddenness of the parousia and on the need of constant spiritual readiness for it (5, 1-11). He concludes with a request that they esteem those who occupy positions of authority in the community (5, 12f), and show the proper attitude toward one another in the Christian spirit (5, 14f). His final words are a prayer that they may be ready at the glorious coming of Christ (5, 23f).

The epistle is of great doctrinal value, revealing as it does the faith of the community. It also manifests the care and labor which were expended in instructing the Christian communities in New Testament times.

The principal divisions of 1 Thessalonians are as follows:

THE FIRST EPISTLE OF PAUL
TO THE THESSALONIANS

I: INTRODUCTION

1

Greeting

¹ Paul, Silvanus, and Timothy, to the church of the Thessalonians who belong to God the Father and the Lord Jesus Christ. Grace and peace be yours.

A Model for Believers

² We keep thanking God for all of you and we remember you in our prayers, ³ for we constantly are mindful before our God and Father of the way you are proving your faith, and laboring in love, and showing constancy of hope in our Lord Jesus Christ. ⁴ We know, too, brothers beloved of God, how you were chosen. ⁵ Our preaching of the gospel proved not a mere matter of words for you but one of power; it was carried on in the Holy Spirit and out of complete conviction. You know as well as we do what we proved to be like when, while still among you, we acted on your behalf. ⁶ You, in turn, became imitators of us and of the Lord, receiving the word despite great trials, with the joy that comes from the Holy Spirit. ⁷ Thus you became a model for all the believers of Macedonia and Achaia. ⁸ The word of the Lord has echoed forth from you resoundingly. This is true not only in Macedonia and Achaia; throughout every region your faith in God is celebrated, which makes it needless for us to say anything more. ⁹ The people of those parts are reporting what kind of reception we had from you, and how you turned to God from idols, to serve him who is the living and true God ¹⁰ and to await from heaven the Son he raised from the dead— Jesus, who delivers us from the wrath to come.

1, 1: Acts 15, 40; 16, 19;
  2 Thes 1, 1f.
2: 2 Thes 1, 3.
6: Acts 13, 52; 17, 1-9.

7: 2 Thes 1, 4.
9: Acts 14, 15; Gal 4, 8.
10: Acts 17, 31; Rom 5, 9.

1, 1: For Paul's use of the conventional epistolary form, see note on Romans 1, 1-7.
1, 2-10: The apostle expresses his satisfaction that the three principal Christian characteristics, faith, hope and love, are at work in the Thessalonian community (2f). Unhesitatingly he places its members among those specially beloved and chosen by God (v 4); recalling that his preaching of the gospel to them was not received as a mere intellectual exercise but had made a strong actual impact on their lives (v 5) which not even the opposition of unbelievers could dispel (v 6). Their faith has been an inspiration to Christians elsewhere (7f), who have been impressed especially by the Thessalonians' complete abandonment of idolatry for the worship of the true God, and by their profound orientation toward the second coming of Jesus (9f).

II: RELATIONS WITH THE THESSALONIANS

2

Paul's Sincerity

[1] You know well enough, brothers, that our coming among you was not without effect. [2] Fresh from the humiliation we had suffered at Philippi—about which you know—we drew courage from our God to preach his good tidings to you in the face of great opposition. [3] The exhortation we deliver does not spring from deceit or impure motives or any sort of trickery; [4] rather, having met the test imposed on us by God, as men entrusted with the good tidings, we speak like those who strive to please God, "the tester of our hearts," rather than men.

[5] We were not guilty, as you well know, of flattering words or greed under any pretext, as God is our witness! [6] Neither did we seek glory from men, you or any others, [7] even though we could have insisted on our own importance as apostles of Christ.

On the contrary, while we were among you we were as gentle as any nursing mother fondling her little ones. [8] So well disposed were we to you, in fact, that we wanted to share with you not only God's tidings but our very lives, so dear had you become to us. [9] You must recall, brothers, our efforts and our toil: how we worked day and night all the time we preached God's good tidings to you in order not to impose on you in any way. [10] You are witnesses, as is God himself, of how upright, just, and irreproachable our conduct was toward you who are believers. [11] You likewise know how we exhorted every one of you, as a father does his children—[12] how we encouraged and pleaded with you to make your lives worthy of the God who calls you to his kingship and glory. [13] That is why we thank God constantly that in receiving his message from us you took it, not as

---

2, 2: Acts 16, 19-40.
    4: Gal 1, 10.
    6: Jn 5, 41.44.
    9: Acts 20, 34;

2 Thes 3, 7-9.
11: Acts 20, 31.
12: Phil 1, 27;
    1 Pt 5, 10.

2, 1-12: Paul had experienced such great opposition in Thessalonica that he had to be secretly escorted from the city (Acts 17, 1-10). It is probably the memory of this which underlies the present words recalling his selflessness in preaching the gospel to them (1-7), his affection for them (8f), and the pleasant relationships he established with them (10ff).

2, 13-16: The apostle is grateful because the Thessalonians accepted his preaching as a message from God and not as a mere human communication (v 13). This perception has enabled them, as well as the Judaeo-Christians of Jerusalem, to be steadfast in the face of persecution (v 14). Paul condemns the active Jewish opposition to the gospel, branding it as sinful and worthy of divine punishment (15f).

the word of men, but as it truly is, the word of God at work within you who believe.

Partnership in Suffering

¹⁴ Brothers, you have been made like the churches of God in Judea which are in Christ Jesus. You suffered the same treatment from your fellow countrymen as they did from the Jews ¹⁵ who killed the Lord Jesus and the prophets, and persecuted us. Displeasing to God and hostile to all mankind, ¹⁶ they try to keep us from preaching salvation to the Gentiles. All this time they have been "filling up their quota of sins," but the wrath has descended upon them at last.

¹⁷ Brothers, when we were orphaned by separation from you for a time—in sight, not in mind—we were seized with the greatest longing to see you. ¹⁸ So we tried to come to you—I, Paul, tried more than once—but Satan blocked the way. ¹⁹ Who, after all, if not you, will be our hope or joy, or the crown we exult in, before our Lord Jesus Christ at his coming? ²⁰ You are our boast and our delight.

3

Mission of Timothy

¹ That is why, when we could endure it no longer, we decided to remain alone at Athens ² and send you Timothy. He is our brother and God's fellow worker in preaching the gospel of Christ, and so we sent him to strengthen and encourage you in regard to your faith ³ lest any one of you be shaken by these trials. You know well enough that such trials are our common lot. ⁴ When we were still with you, we used to warn you that we would undergo trial; now it has happened, and you know what we meant. ⁵ That is why I sent to find out about your faith when I could stand the suspense no longer, fearing that the tempter had put you to the test and all our labor might have

---

15: Acts 2, 23;
    7, 52.
16: 2 Mc 6, 14.
17: 3, 10; Rom 1, 10f.
19: 2 Cor 1, 14.

3, 1: Acts 17, 14f.
2: Acts 16, 1f.
4: Acts 14, 22;
    2 Tm 3, 12.

2, 17-20: Twice had Paul made an effort to visit the community at Thessalonica, only to be "blocked by Satan"—an expression which probably refers to the situation in Thessalonica itself; cf 3, 5.
3, 1-10: Troubled by the lack of news concerning the Thessalonians, Paul had sent Timothy to them as his representative. Timothy's report was reassuring (6ff) except as regards certain possible *shortcomings* in their faith (v 10). Paul is probably dealing with these defects concretely in chapters 4 and 5 of the epistle.

gone for nothing. [6] But now, brothers, since Timothy has returned to us from you reporting the good news of your faith and love, and telling us that you constantly remember us and are as desirous to see us as we are to see you, [7] we have been much consoled by your faith throughout our distress and trial —[8] so much so that we shall continue to flourish only if you stand firm in the Lord!

Plea for Growth in Holiness

[9] What thanks can we give to God for all the joy we feel in his presence because of you, [10] as we ask him fervently night and day that we may see you face to face and remedy any shortcomings in your faith? [11] May God himself, who is our Father, and our Lord Jesus make our path to you a straight one! [12] And may the Lord increase you and make you overflow with love for one another and for all, even as our love does for you. [13] May he strengthen your hearts, making them blameless and holy before our God and Father at the coming of our Lord Jesus with all his holy ones.

4

Chastity and Charity

[1] Now, my brothers, we beg and exhort you in the Lord Jesus that, even as you learned from us how to conduct yourselves in a way pleasing to God—which you are indeed doing—so you must learn to make still greater progress. [2] You know the instructions we gave you in the Lord Jesus. [3] It is God's will that you grow in holiness: that you abstain from immorality, [4] each of you guarding his member in sanctity and honor, [5] not in passionate desire as do the Gentiles who know not God; [6] and that each refrain from overreaching or cheating his brother in the matter at hand; for the Lord is an avenger of all such things, as we once indicated to you by our testimony. [7] God

---

12: 2 Thes 1, 3.   13: 5, 23; 1 Cor 1, 8.

3, 11ff: The theme of this prayer is solidarity: between Paul and the Thessalonian Christians (his prospective visit); among themselves; between them and all men (Christian love); and between them and God (holiness).

4, 1-12: To conserve their holiness they are to recall what the apostle taught them in the name of Christ at the time of their conversion (1f). Fornication and all sexual misconduct are to be avoided (3-6), in consideration of the truth that God sanctifies his faithful by the presence of the Holy Spirit (7f). They have heeded Christ's message of love of neighbor and should improve it within the community (9f). He urges that they concern themselves with their own affairs, each laboring faithfully to earn his own living and all presenting a good example to the outside world (11f; cf 5, 14; 2 Thes 3, 10ff).

has not called us to immorality but to holiness; [8] hence, whoever rejects these instructions rejects, not man, but God who sends his Holy Spirit upon you.

[9] As regards brotherly love, there is no need for me to write you. God himself has taught you to love one another, [10] and this you are doing with respect to all the brothers throughout Macedonia. Yet we exhort you to even greater progress, brothers. [11] Make it a point of honor to remain at peace and attend to your own affairs. Work with your hands as we directed you to do, [12] so that you will give good example to outsiders and want for nothing.

III: THE LORD'S SECOND COMING

Witnessed by the Dead

[13] We would have you be clear about those who sleep in death, brothers; otherwise you might yield to grief, like those who have no hope. [14] For if we believe that Jesus died and rose, God will bring forth with him from the dead those also who have fallen asleep believing in him. [15] We say to you, as if the Lord himself had said it, that we who live, who survive until his coming, will in no way have an advantage over those who have fallen asleep. [16] No, the Lord himself will come down from heaven at the word of command, at the sound of the archangel's voice and God's trumpet; and those who have died in Christ will rise first. [17] Then we, the living, the survivors, will be caught up with them in the clouds to meet the Lord in the air. Thenceforth we shall be with the Lord unceasingly. [18] Console one another with this message.

4, 9: Jn 6, 45; 13, 34;
1 Jn 4, 7.
11: 2 Thes 3, 6-12.
14: 1 Cor 15, 3f.12.20.

15: 1 Cor 15, 51.
16: Mt 24, 31;
1 Cor 15, 23.52.

4, 13-18: Here Paul takes up the practice among the Thessalonians of mourning excessively for their dead (v 13), a reaction deriving from the stress placed by the community on the proximity of the parousia; cf 1, 10. The apostle reminds them of the Christian doctrine of the resurrection of the dead in Christ (v 14). On the basis of Christ's teaching, he affirms that the resurrection of the dead is to precede the second coming. Those who are alive at the time of the latter will not have the advantage over the dead of being the first witnesses to it (v 15), for the Lord will first command the dead to rise (v 16); the living will then join them and both groups will be witnesses of the parousia (v 17; this and the preceding verse reflect the traditional apocalyptic imagery for an act of God).

The doctrine spoken of here is to be recalled when future bereavements overtake the community (v 18). Since Paul does not know the time of the parousia (5, 2; Mt 24, 43) he aligns himself with the Thessalonians (*we . . . who survive*, v 15) in the hope of living until that day, i. e., within the first Christian generation. In his mind such a possibility seems not to have been excluded by the teaching of Jesus himself.

5

The Need for Preparation

[1] As regards specific times and moments, brothers, we do not need to write you; [2] you know very well that the day of the Lord is coming like a thief in the night. [3] Just when people are saying, "Peace and security," ruin will fall on them with the suddenness of pains overtaking a woman in labor, and there will be not escape. [4] You are not in the dark, brothers, that the day should catch you off guard, like a thief. [5] No, all of you are children of light and of the day. We belong neither to darkness nor to night; [6] therefore let us not be asleep like the rest, but awake and sober! [7] Sleepers sleep by night and drunkards drink by night. [8] We who live by day must be alert, putting on faith and love as a breastplace and the hope of salvation as a helmet. [9] God has not destined us for wrath but for acquiring salvation through our Lord Jesus Christ. [10] He died for us, that all of us, whether awake or asleep, together might live with him. [11] Therefore, comfort and upbuild one another, as indeed you are doing.

Christian Conduct

[12] We beg you, brothers, respect those among you whose task it is to exercise authority in the Lord and admonish you; [13] esteem them with the greatest love because of their work. Remain at peace with one another. [14] We exhort you to admonish the unruly; cheer the fainthearted; support the weak; be patient toward all. [15] See that no one returns evil to any other; always seek one another's good and, for that matter, the good of all.

[16] Rejoice always, [17] never cease praying, [18] render constant thanks; such is God's will for you in Christ Jesus.

5, 1-3: Mt 24, 36-45.
2: 2 Pt 3, 10.
4: Eph 5, 8f.
5: Jn 8, 12.
6: Mt 24, 42;
   Rom 13, 12f; 1 Pt 5, 8.

8: Eph 6, 11.14-17;
   Is 59, 17.
15: Prv 20, 22; Mt 5, 38;
    Rom 12, 17.
18: Eph 5, 20.

5, 1-11: Paul does not wish his criticism of the Thessalonians' grief over their dead to de-emphasize the doctrine of the parousia itself; he commends the importance they accord it and its influence over their lives. They know how unexpected, sudden, and certain it will be (1ff); therefore they are to live in constant anticipation of it, for it will determine their salvation (4-11).

5, 12-22: Respect and love are due to those who hold positions of authority in the community (12f); possibly the presbyters are meant; cf Acts 14, 23. It is the duty of all to reprove and strengthen those who fail in their Christian duty and to show patience toward nonbelievers, especially by quenching the spirit of revenge (14f). The spirit of joy, prayer, and thanksgiving must prevail (16ff). Due respect is to be shown to the charism of prophecy, but its authentic presence is not to be admitted uncritically (19ff), as evil may make its entrance even by this door (v 22).

¹⁹ Do not stifle the Spirit. ²⁰ Do not despise prophecies. ²¹ Test everything; retain what is good. ²² Avoid any semblance of evil.

Blessing and Greeting

²³ May the God of peace make you perfect in holiness. May he preserve you whole and entire, spirit, soul, and body, irreproachable at the coming of our Lord Jesus Christ. ²⁴ He who calls us is trustworthy, therefore he will do it.

²⁵ Brothers, pray for us too.

²⁶ Greet all the brothers with a holy embrace. ²⁷ I adjure you by the Lord that this letter be read to them all.

²⁸ May the grace of our Lord Jesus Christ be with you.

23: 2 Thes 3, 16.

5, 23ff: The burden of the apostle's prayer is the sanctification of the community (cf 3, 13—4, 12) in preparation for the second coming of Christ.

5, 27: The public reading of the Pauline letters is the method to be employed for insuring their acceptance by the Christian assembly as the word of God.

THE SECOND EPISTLE OF PAUL TO THE THESSALONIANS

INTRODUCTION

Most scholars accept the authenticity of the second letter to the Thessalonians, as being written in Paul's characteristic language and style. Both letters were written from Corinth, and within a short time of each other, since they show that the apostle is still accompanied by his companions of the second missionary journey, Silas and Timothy (2 Thes 1, 1; Acts 18, 5).

Despite the remarkable literary similarities in the letters, however, the second is the more impersonal, its approach to the subject being somewhat set and formal in tone. The explanation may well lie in the apostle's own less serene circumstances and state of mind, as well as in the disturbing news he had received from Thessalonica after the first letter was written.

He himself is experiencing the difficulties caused by *confused and evil men* (2 Thes 3, 1ff). Meanwhile, persecution against the Thessalonian Christians has intensified (2 Thes 1, 3-10), and the situation among them is worsened by idleness due to the spreading expectation of the parousia (2 Thes 3, 6-12), despite Paul's admonitions in his first letter. He now repeats that the community's life is not to be guided by the false belief that the second coming is imminent, i.e., a day-to-day possibility, whether the alleged source of the belief be the oracular utterance of a self-styled prophet or a letter supposedly written by himself (2 Thes 2, 1ff). He originally taught the Thessalonians, he reminds them, that certain religious events must occur before the parousia can be expected (2 Thes 2, 3-12). Finally, he knows that the community has its refractory members from whom he cannot anticipate simple acquiescence to his teaching, and he gives directions regarding them (2 Thes 3, 14).

The letters to the Thessalonians present incontrovertible evidence that the expectation of the parousia played a capital role in the development of New Testament thought. There is no evidence that this expectation attained in other communities the strength it came to exert in Thessalonica; but the data of 1 and 2 Thessalonians compel its recognition as a conditioning element in the presentation of doctrine while the literature of the New Testament developed.

The principal divisions of 2 Thessalonians are as follows:

I: Introduction (1, 1-12)
II: The Lord's Second Coming (2, 1-17)
III: Exhortation (3, 1-18)

THE SECOND EPISTLE OF PAUL
TO THE THESSALONIANS
I: INTRODUCTION

1

Greeting

¹ Paul, Silvanus, and Timothy, to the church of the Thessalonians who belong to God our Father and the Lord Jesus Christ. ² Grace and peace be yours from God the Father and the Lord Jesus Christ.

Praise for the Church at Thessalonica

³ It is no more than right that we thank God unceasingly for you, brothers, because your faith grows apace and your mutual love increases; ⁴ so much so that in God's communities we can boast of your constancy and your faith in persecution and trial. You endure these ⁵ as an expression of God's just judgment, in order to be found worthy of his kingdom—it is for his kingdom you suffer—⁶ even if strict justice would require that God visit hardships on those who visit them on you. ⁷ He will provide relief to you who are sorely tried, as well as to us, when the Lord Jesus is revealed from heaven with his mighty angels; ⁸ when "with flaming power he will inflict punishment on those who do not acknowledge God nor heed" the good news of our Lord Jesus. ⁹ Such as these will suffer the penalty of eternal ruin apart from the presence of the Lord and the glory of his might ¹⁰ on the Day when he comes, to be glorified in his holy ones and adored by all who have believed—for you already have our witness to you.

Prayer for Their Progress

¹¹ We pray for you always that our God may make you worthy of his call, and fulfill by his power every honest intention and work of faith. ¹² In this way the name of our Lord Jesus may

---

1, 1: 1 Thes 1, 1.
  3: 1 Thes 1, 2.
  5: 1 Thes 3, 4.
  8: Ps 79, 6; Is 66, 15;

Jer 10, 25.
  10: Ps 89, 8.
  11: Phil 2, 13.

1, 1f: On the address and greeting, see note on Romans 1, 1-7.
1, 3-12: The Thessalonian community is encouraged to stand fast under the severe trial they are experiencing (3ff). *God's just judgment* will bring relief to the afflicted as well as punishment to the persecutors (6-10). The harrassment of the community seems to have intensified during the interval between the writing of 1 and 2 Thessalonians; cf 1 Thes 2, 14ff. This plight may well have contributed to the notion that the parousia was near. Paul considers this question in 2, 1-12.

be glorified in you and you in him, in accord with the gracious gift of our God and of the Lord Jesus Christ.

II: THE LORD'S SECOND COMING

2

Adversary Restrained

¹ On the question of the coming of our Lord Jesus Christ and our being gathered to him, we beg you, brothers, ² not to be so easily agitated or terrified, whether by an oracular utterance, or rumor, or a letter alleged to be ours, into believing that the day of the Lord is here.

³ Let no one seduce you, no matter how. Since the mass apostasy has not yet occurred nor the man of lawlessness been revealed—that son of perdition ⁴ and adversary who exalts himself above every so-called god proposed for worship, he who seats himself in God's temple and even declares himself to be God—⁵ do you not remember how I used to tell you about these things when I was still with you? ⁶ You know what restrains him until he shall be revealed in his own time. ⁷ The secret force of lawlessness is already at work, mind you, but there is one who holds him back until that restrainer shall be taken from the scene. ⁸ Thereupon the lawless one will be revealed, and the Lord Jesus will destroy him with the breath of his mouth and annihilate him by manifesting his own presence. ⁹ This lawless one will appear as part of the workings of Satan, accompanied by all the power and signs and wonders at the

---

2, 1: 1 Thes 4, 13-17.   8: Is 11, 4; Rv 19, 15.
7: Acts 20, 29.   9: Mt 24, 24.

2, 1-12: Though the parousia is certain (v 1), the Thessalonians are not to expect it to occur at almost any time in the immediate future. No appeal to an utterance of a self-styled prophet, or to any supposed letter of Paul justifies such an expectation (v 2). They should not allow themselves to be duped into this way of thinking, for a religious apostasy is destined to precede the Lord's second coming. It will be embodied in *the man of lawlessness*, a personage totally dedicated to evil, *that son of perdition* marked for eternal doom (vv 3f); cf Jn 17, 12. In the epistles of John he is usually identified with the antichrist (1 Jn 2, 18.22; 4, 3; 2 Jn 7). He will be anti-God and will himself lay claim to divine honors (v 4).

During Paul's stay at Thessalonica (Acts 17, 1-9) he instructed the people on this subject (v 5). Now he wishes to add that there is a restraining power which prevents the man of lawlessness from coming into his own (v 6). *The secret force of lawlessness,* though *already at work,* is held down now by a restraining power (v 7), the nature of which Paul does not explain. While the restraint continues, the parousia cannot occur; but when it is removed, *the lawless one* will make his appearance accompanied by all the panoply of satanic power (vv 8f). He will bring some to ruin (v 10), but is destined to be destroyed by Jesus' coming (v 8). God acts toward the impious in such a way as to allow them to become confirmed in evil (v 11); cf Rom 1, 24f) through their deliberate rejection of the truth (v 12).

disposal of falsehood—[10] by every seduction the wicked can devise for those destined to ruin because they have not opened their hearts to the truth in order to be saved. [11] Therefore God is sending upon them a perverse spirit which leads them to give credence to falsehood, [12] so that all who have not believed the truth but have delighted in evildoing will be condemned.

Encouraging Words

[13] We are bound to thank God for you always, beloved brothers in the Lord, because you are the first fruits of those whom God has chosen for salvation, in holiness of spirit and fidelity to truth. [14] He called you through our preaching of the good news so that you might achieve the glory of our Lord Jesus Christ.

[15] Therefore, brothers, stand firm. Hold fast to the traditions you received from us, either by our word or by letter. [16] May our Lord Jesus Christ himself, may God our Father who loved us and in his mercy gave us eternal consolation and hope, [17] console your hearts and strengthen them for every good work and word.

III: EXHORTATION

3

Request for Prayers

[1] For the rest, brothers, pray for us that the word of the Lord may make progress and be hailed by many others, even as it has been by you. [2] Pray that we may be delivered from confused and evil men. For not every man has faith, [3] but the Lord keeps faith; he it is who will strengthen you and guard you against the evil one. [4] In the Lord we are confident that you are doing and

---

13: 1 Thes 2, 13; 1 Pt 1, 2.
14: 1 Thes 4, 7; 5, 9.
3, 1: Eph 6, 19; Col 4, 3.

3: Mt 6, 13; 1 Thes 5, 34.
4: 2 Cor 7, 16.

2, 13-17: The Christian faithful are on the path of salvation. They have received, through the medium of Paul's preaching, the divine gift of sanctification that flows from faith in the gospel (v 13); it is the first step toward ultimate participation in Christ's glory (v 14). They are not to depart from the instructions given them at the time of their conversion (cf Acts 17, 1-9) nor from those contained in Paul's previous letter (1 Thes 2, 15). The apostle's prayer is that God may comfort and strengthen them as they strive to live out the gospel in their own lives (16f).
3, 1-5: Paul requests prayers that his preaching of the gospel may continue to be successful (v 1), and he himself may be free from hindrance by the wicked (v 2). He is confident that the Lord will preserve the faith of the community (v 3) and help them to carry out faithfully all that has been enjoined upon them (v 4). A second prayer reminds them that the goal of their efforts is to love God through patient acceptance of trials, inspired by the example of Christ (v 5).

will continue to do whatever we enjoin. [5] May the Lord rule your hearts in the love of God and the constancy of Christ.

Dealing with the Idle

[6] We command you, brothers, in the name of the Lord Jesus Christ, to avoid any brother who wanders from the straight path and does not follow the tradition you received from us. [7] You know how you ought to imitate us. We did not live lives of disorder when we were among you, [8] nor depend on anyone for food. Rather, we worked day and night, laboring to the point of exhaustion so as not to impose on any of you. [9] Not that we had no claim on you, but that we might present ourselves as an example for you to imitate. [10] Indeed, when we were with you we used to lay down the rule that anyone who would not work should not eat.

[11] We hear that some of you are unruly, not keeping busy but acting like busybodies. [12] We enjoin all such, and we urge them strongly in the Lord Jesus Christ, to earn the food they eat by working quietly.

[13] You must never grow weary of doing what is right, brothers.

[14] If anyone will not obey our injunction, delivered through this letter, single him out to be ostracized that he may be ashamed of his conduct. [15] But do not treat him like an enemy; rather, correct him as you would a brother.

Final Blessing and Greeting

[16] May he who is the Lord of peace give you continued peace in every possible way. The Lord be with you all.

[17] This greeting is in my own hand—Paul's. I append this signature to every letter I write.

[18] May the grace of our Lord Jesus Christ be with you all.

8: 1 Thes 2, 9.
9: Mt 10, 10.
10: 1 Thes 4, 11.
11: 1 Thes 5, 14.

15: 2 Cor 2, 7; Gal 6, 1.
16: Jn 14, 27.
17: Gal 6, 11.

3, 6-15: Some members of the community, whether in good or bad faith, have ceased to work for a living; they claim to regard money as useless in view of the imminence of the parousia (cf 2, 1-12), and consequently depend upon others for sustenance (8.10). This result of their false expectation has posed a perplexing problem to the charitable of the community. Stringent measures are to be taken against them: avoidance of voluntary association with them (v 6); refusal to support them gratuitously (v 10); and a gradual but firm exclusion of them from the community (v 14).

3, 17: The apostle takes up the pen himself, evidence that he normally engaged a secretary in the composition of his epistles. Out of fear of possible forgeries composed in his name (2 Thes 2, 2), he points to the unusually large Greek letters that characterize his handwriting.

THE FIRST EPISTLE OF PAUL TO TIMOTHY

INTRODUCTION

The three letters, 1 and 2 Timothy, and Titus, were first named "pastoral epistles" in the eighteenth century. From the late second century to the nineteenth, their Pauline authorship went unchallenged. Since then, discussion of that question has reached an impasse. Some scholars are convinced that Paul could not have been responsible for the vocabulary and style of the letters, their concept of church organization, or the theological expressions found in them. Others believe just as firmly that, on the basis of statistical evidence, the vocabulary and style are Pauline, even if at first sight the contrary appears to be the case; that the concept of church organization in these epistles is not as advanced as the opponents of Pauline authorship make it out to be, the notion of a hierarchical order in a religious community having existed among the Jews even before the time of Christ, as the scrolls of Qumran indicate; and, finally, that there are affinities between the theological thought of the pastorals and that of unquestionably genuine letters of Paul. A third group, while conceding a degree of validity to the position of the other two, suggests that either the apostle made use of a secretary (possibly Luke; see 2 Tm 4, 11) who was responsible for the composition of the letters, or that they are the work of an anonymous writer compiling traditions about Paul in his later years.

The problem of the literary authorship of the pastorals has not disproved the authenticity of their content. If Paul is considered their more immediate author, they are to be dated between the end of his first Roman imprisonment (Acts 28, 16) and his execution under Nero (63-67 A.D.); if they are regarded as only more remotely Pauline, their date may be as late as the early second century.

The first of the pastorals, 1 Timothy is presented as having been written from Macedonia. Timothy, whom Paul converted, was of mixed Jewish and Gentile parentage (Acts 16, 1ff). He was the apostle's companion on both the second and third missionary journeys (Acts 16, 3; 19, 22), and was often sent by him on special missions (1 Thes 3, 2; 1 Cor 4, 17; Acts 19, 22). In 1 Timothy (1, 3) he is described as the administrator of the entire Ephesian community. The epistle instructs him on his duty to restrain false and useless teaching (1, 3-11; 4, 1-5; 6, 3-16); proposes principles pertaining to his relationship to the older members of the community (5, 1f) and to the presbyters (5, 17-25); gives rules for aid to widows (5, 3-8), and their selection for charitable ministrations (5, 9-16); deals with liturgical celebrations (2, 1-15), the selection of men for the offices of bishop and deacon (3, 1-13), the relations of slaves and their masters (6, 1f), and the obligations of the wealthier members of the community (6, 17ff). It also reminds Timothy of the prophetic character of his office (1, 12-18), and encourages him in his exercise of it (4, 6-16). The central passage of the letter (3, 14ff) expresses the chief motive that should guide the conduct of Timothy—preservation of the purity of the church's doctrine. On this same note the epistle concludes (6, 20-21).

THE FIRST EPISTLE OF PAUL
TO TIMOTHY

1

¹ Paul, an apostle of Christ Jesus by command of God our savior and Christ Jesus our hope, ² to Timothy, my own true child in faith. May grace, mercy, and peace be yours from God the Father and Christ Jesus our Lord.

On Holding Fast to Sound Doctrine

³ I repeat the directions I gave you when I was on my way to Macedonia: stay on in Ephesus in order to warn certain people there against teaching false doctrines ⁴ and busying themselves with interminable myths and genealogies, which promote idle speculations rather than that training in faith which God requires.
⁵ What we are aiming at in this warning is the love that springs from a pure heart, a good conscience, and sincere faith. ⁶ Some people have neglected these and instead have turned to meaningless talk, ⁷ wanting to be teachers of the law but actually not understanding the words they are using, much less the matters they discuss with such assurance.
⁸ We know that the law is good, provided one uses it in the way law is supposed to be used—⁹ that is, with the understanding that it is aimed, not at good men but at the lawless and unruly, the irreligious and the sinful, the wicked and the godless, men who kill their fathers or mothers, murderers, ¹⁰ fornicators, sexual perverts, kidnapers, liars, perjurers, and those who in other ways flout the sound teaching ¹¹ that pertains to the glorious gospel of God—blessed be he—with which I have been entrusted.
¹² I thank Christ Jesus our Lord, who has strengthened me, that he has made me his servant and judged me faithful. ¹³ I was once a blasphemer, a persecutor, a man filled with arrogance; but because I did not know what I was doing in my un-

---

1, 2: Acts 16, 1.
4: 6, 4.20;
    2 Tm 2, 14.16;
Ti 3, 9.
8: Rom 7, 12.
13: Acts 8, 3.

1, 1f: For Pauline use of the conventional epistolary form, see note on Romans 1, 1-7.
1, 3-7: Here Timothy's initial task in Ephesus (cf Acts 20, 17-35) is outlined: to suppress the idle religious speculations, probably about Old Testament figures (3f), which do not contribute to the development of love within the community (v 5) but rather encourage others to similar useless conjectures (1, 6f).
1, 8-11: Those responsible for the empty surmises which are to be suppressed by Timothy do not present the Old Testament from the Christian viewpoint. The Christian values the Old Testament, not as a system of law, but as the first stage in God's revelation of his saving plan, which is brought to fulfillment in the good news of salvation through faith in Jesus Christ.

belief, I have been treated mercifully, [14] and the grace of our Lord has been granted me in overflowing measure, along with the faith and love which are in Christ Jesus. [15] You can depend on this as worthy of full acceptance: that Christ Jesus came into the world to save sinners. Of these I myself am the worst. [16] But on that very account I was dealt with mercifully, so that in me, as an extreme case, Jesus Christ might display all his patience, and that I might become an example to those who would later have faith in him and gain everlasting life. [17] To the King of ages, the immortal, the invisible, the only God, be honor and glory forever and ever! Amen.

[18] I have a solemn charge to give you, Timothy, my child. This charge is in accordance with the prophecies made in your regard, and I give it to you so that under the inspiration of these prophecies you may fight the good fight [19] and hold fast to faith and a good conscience. Some men, by rejecting the guidance of conscience, have made shipwreck of their faith, [20] among them Hymenaeus and Alexander; these I have turned over to Satan so that they may learn not to blaspheme.

2

Conduct of Men and Women

[1] First of all, I urge that petitions, prayers, intercessions, and thanksgivings be offered for all men, [2] especially for kings and those in authority, that we may be able to lead undisturbed and tranquil lives in perfect piety and dignity. [3] Prayer of this kind is good, and God our savior is pleased with it, [4] for he wants all men to be saved and come to know the truth. [5] And the truth is this:

15: 3, 1; 4, 9; Mt 9, 13;
      Mk 2, 17.
17: Ps 145, 13.

18: 4, 14.
20: 2 Tm 2, 17; 4, 14.

1, 12-17: Present gratitude for the Christian apostleship leads to a recalling of the earlier time when Paul was a fierce persecutor of the Christian communities (cf Acts 26, 9ff), until his conversion by intervention of the divine mercy. This and his subsequent apostolic experience testify to the saving purpose of Jesus' incarnation. The fact of his former ignorance of the truth has not kept the apostle from regarding himself as having been the worst of sinners (v 15). Yet he was chosen to be an apostle, that God might manifest his firm will to save sinful humanity through Jesus Christ (v 16). The recounting of so great a mystery of mercy leads to a spontaneous outpouring of adoration (v 17).

1, 18ff: Timothy is to be mindful of his calling, which is here compared to that of Barnabas and Saul; cf Acts 13, 1ff. Such is probably the sense of the allusion to *the prophecies* (v 18). His task is not to yield, whether in doctrine or in conduct, to erroneous opinions, taking warning from what has already happened at Ephesus in the case of Hymenaeus and Alexander (19f). For the error of Hymenaeus, cf 2 Tm 2, 17f.

2, 1-8: This marked insistence that the liturgical prayer of the community concern itself with the needs of all men, whether Christian or not,

"God is one.
One also is the mediator between God and men,
   the man Christ Jesus,
[6] who gave himself as a ransom for all."

This truth was attested at the fitting time. [7] I have been made its herald and apostle (believe me, I am not lying but speak the truth), the teacher of the nations in the true faith.

[8] It is my wish, then, that in every place the men shall offer prayers with blameless hands held aloft, and be free from anger and dissension. [9] Similarly, the women must deport themselves properly. They should dress modestly and quietly, and not be decked out in fancy hair styles, gold ornaments, pearls, or costly clothing; [10] rather, as becomes women who who profess to be religious, their adornment should be good deeds. [11] A woman must learn in silence and be completely submissive. [12] I do not permit a woman to act as a teacher, or in any way to have authority over a man; she must be quiet. [13] For Adam was created first, Eve afterward; [14] moreover, it was not Adam who was deceived but the woman. It was she who was led astray and fell into sin. [15] She will be saved through childbearing, provided she continues in faith and love and holiness—her chastity, of course, being taken for granted.

3

Qualifications of Various Ministers

[1] You can depend on this: whoever wants to be a bishop

2, 5: Heb 8, 6.
    6: Mt 20, 28; Gal 1, 4.
    7: Gal 2, 7; 2 Tm 1, 11.
    9: 1 Pt 3, 3.

    12: 1 Cor 14, 34.
    13: Gn 1, 27.
    14: Gn 3, 6.
3, 1: 1, 15.

---

and especially of those in authority, may imply that a disposition existed at Ephesus to refuse prayer for pagans. In actuality, such prayer aids the community to achieve peaceful relationships with non-Christians (v 2) and contributes to their salvation, since it derives its value from the presence within the community of Christ who is the one and only Savior of all men (3-6). The vital apostolic mission to the Gentiles concerning Christ's purpose of the universal salvation should be reflected in the prayer of the community (v 7), which should be unmarred by internal dissension (v 8); cf Mt 5, 23ff.

2, 9-13: At the liturgical assembly the dress of women should be appropriate to the occasion (v 9); their chief adornment is to be their reputation for good works (v 10). Women are not to take part in the charismatic activity of the assembly (11f; cf 1 Cor 14, 34); their conduct there should not reflect authority but the role of man's helpmate (v 13; cf Gn 2, 18), thus reversing the relationship of Eve to Adam (v 14; cf Gn 3, 6f). As long as women perform their role as wives and mothers in faith and love, their salvation is assured (v 15).

3, 1-7: The passage begins by commending those who aspire to the office of bishop within the community (v 1), and proceeds to list the qualifications required: personal stability and graciousness; talent for teaching (v 2);

aspires to a noble task. ² A bishop must be irreproachable, married only once, of even temper, self-controlled, modest, and hospitable. He should be a good teacher. ³ He must not be addicted to drink. He ought not to be contentious but, rather, gentle, a man of peace. Nor can he be someone who loves money. ⁴ He must be a good manager of his own household, keeping his children under control without sacrificing his dignity; ⁵ for if a man does not know how to manage his own house, how can he take care of the church of God? ⁶ He should not be a new convert, lest he become conceited and thus incur the punishment once meted out to the devil. ⁷ He must also be well thought of by those outside the church, to ensure that he does not fall into disgrace and the devil's trap. ⁸ In the same way, deacons must be serious, straightforward, and truthful. They may not overindulge in drink or give in to greed. ⁹ They must hold fast to the divinely revealed faith with a clear conscience. ¹⁰ They should be put on probation first; then, if there is nothing against them, they may serve as deacons. ¹¹ The women, similarly, should be serious, not slanderous gossips. They should be temperate and entirely trustworthy. ¹² Deacons may be married but once and must be good managers of their children and their households. ¹³ Those who serve well as deacons gain a worthy place for themselves and much assurance in their faith in Christ Jesus.

¹⁴ Although I hope to visit you soon, I am writing you about these matters ¹⁵ so that if I should be delayed you will know what kind of conduct befits a member of God's household, the

---

2: Ti 1, 7.   8: Acts 6, 1-6.

---

moderation in habits and temperament (v 3); managerial ability (v 4), and experience in Christian living (3, 5f). Moreover the candidate's life before his conversion should provide no grounds for the charge that he did not previously practice what he now preaches.

3, 8-13: Deacons, besides possessing the virtue of moderation (v 8), are to be outstanding for their faith (v 9) and well respected within the community (v 10). Women in this same role (cf Rom 16, 1) must be of serious mien, temperate, and dedicated, and not given to malicious talebearing (v 11). Deacons must have shown stability in marriage and have a good record as family men (v 12), for such experience prepares them well for the exercise of their ministry in behalf of the community (v 13).

3, 14ff: Lest there be some delay in the visit planned for the near future to Timothy at Ephesus, the present letter is being sent on ahead to arm and enlighten him in his task of preserving sound Christian conduct in the Ephesian church (14f). The care he must exercise over this community is required by the profound nature of Christianity. It centers in Christ, preexistent but appearing in human flesh; the goodness of his mortal existence was verified by the Holy Spirit; the mystery of his Person was revealed to the angels, announced to the Gentiles, and accepted by them in faith. He himself was returned (through his resurrection and ascension) to the divine glory that is properly his (v 16). This passage apparently includes part of a liturgical hymn used among the Christian communities in and around Ephesus, and directed against the cult of Artemis.

church of the living God, the pillar and bulwark of truth. ¹⁶ Wonderful, indeed, is the mystery of our faith, as we say in professing it:

"He was manifested in the flesh,
    vindicated in the Spirit;
Seen by the angels;
    preached among the Gentiles,
Believed in throughout the world,
    taken up into glory."

4

False Asceticism

¹ The Spirit distinctly says that in later times some will turn away from the faith and will heed deceitful spirits and things taught by demons ² through plausible liars—men with seared consciences ³ who forbid marriage and require abstinence from foods which God created to be received with thanksgiving by believers who know the truth. ⁴ Everything God created is good; nothing is to be rejected when it is received with thanksgiving, ⁵ for it is made holy by God's word and by prayer.

Counsel to Timothy

⁶ If you put these instructions before the brotherhood you will be a good servant of Christ Jesus, reared in the words of faith and the sound doctrine you have faithfully followed. ⁷ Have nothing to do with profane myths or old wives' tales. Train yourself for the life of piety, ⁸ for while physical training is to some extent valuable, the discipline of religion is incalculably more so, with its promise of life here and hereafter. ⁹ You can depend on this as worthy of complete acceptance.

¹⁰ This explains why we work and struggle as we do; our hopes are fixed on the living God who is the savior of all men, but especially of those who believe.

16: Mk 16, 19; Jn 1, 14;
    Acts 1, 2.
4, 1: Acts 20, 29f;
    2 Tm 3, 1; 2 Pt 3, 3.
3: Gn 9, 3; Col 2, 16-23.

4: Gn 1, 31;
    1 Cor 10, 25.30.
7: 1, 4; 2 Tm 2, 23;
    Ti 3, 9.

4, 1-11: Doctrinal deviations within the church from the true Christian message have been prophesied, though the origin of the prophecy is not specified (1f); cf Acts 20, 29f. The letter warns against a false asceticism which prohibits marriage and regards certain foodstuffs as morally contaminating (v 3). Timothy is urged to reiterate the Christian teaching that neither salvation nor damnation is to be found in material creation (4-8). Man is saved only by the action of God (9ff).

¹¹ Such are the things you must urge and teach. ¹² Let no one look down on you because of your youth, but be a continuing example of love, faith, and purity to believers. ¹³ Until I arrive, devote yourself to the reading of Scripture, to preaching and teaching. ¹⁴ Do not neglect the gift you received when, as a result of prophecy, the presbyters laid their hands on you. ¹⁵ Attend to your duties; let them absorb you, so that everyone may see your progress. ¹⁶ Watch yourself and watch your teaching. Persevere at both tasks. By doing so you will bring to salvation yourself and all who hear you.

5

¹ Never censure an older man, but appeal to him as to a father. You should treat younger men as brothers, ² older women as mothers, and younger women as sisters, with absolute purity.

Rules for Widows

³ Honor the claims of widows who are real widows—that is, who are alone and bereft. ⁴ If a widow has any children or grandchildren, let these learn that piety begins at home and that they should fittingly support their parents and grandparents; this is the way God wants it to be. ⁵ The real widow, left destitute, is one who has set her hope on God and continues night and day in supplications and prayers. ⁶ A widow who gives herself up to selfish indulgence, however, leads a life of living death.

⁷ Make the following rules about widows, so that no one may incur blame. ⁸ If anyone does not provide for his own relatives and especially for members of his immediate family, he has denied the faith; he is worse than an unbeliever. ⁹ To be on the church's roll of widows, a widow should be not less than sixty years of age. She must have been married only once.

12: 1 Cor 16, 11.
14: 1, 18.

5, 1: Ti 2, 2.
10: Jn 13, 14.

4, 12-16: Timothy is urged to preach and teach with confidence, relying on the gifts and the mission that God has bestowed on him.

5, 1-16: After a few words of general advice based on common sense (1f), the letter takes up, in its several aspects, the subject of widows. The first responsibility for their care belongs to the family circle, not to the Christian community as such (3f.16). The widow left without the aid of relatives may benefit the community by her prayer, and the community should consider her material sustenance its responsibility (5f). Widows who wish to work directly for the Christian community should not be accepted unless they are well beyond the probability of marriage, i. e., sixty years of age, married only once, and with a reputation for good works (9f). Younger widows are apt to be troublesome and should be encouraged to re-marry (11-15).

[10] Her good character will be attested to by her good deeds. Has she brought up children? Has she been hospitable to strangers? Has she washed the feet of Christian visitors? Has she given help to those in distress? In a word, has she been eager to do every possible good work?

[11] Refuse to enroll the younger widows, for when their passions estrange them from Christ they will want to marry. [12] This will bring them condemnation for breaking their first pledge. [13] Besides, they learn to be ladies of leisure, who go about from house to house—becoming not only timewasters but gossips and busybodies as well, talking about things they ought not. [14] That is why I should like to see the younger ones marry, have children, keep house, and in general give our enemies no occasion to speak ill of us. [15] Already, some have turned away to follow Satan. [16] If a woman church member has relatives who are widows, she must assist them. She should not let them become a burden to the church, which ought to be free to give help to the widows who are really in need.

[17] Presbyters who do well as leaders deserve to be paid double, especially those whose work is preaching and teaching. [18] The Scripture says, "You shall not put a muzzle on an ox when he is threshing the grain," and also, "The worker deserves his wages."

[19] Pay no attention to an accusation against a presbyter unless it is supported by two or three witnesses. [20] The ones who do commit sin, however, are to be publicly reprimanded, so that the rest may fear to offend. [21] I charge you before God, Christ Jesus, and the chosen angels: apply these rules without prejudice, act with complete impartiality! [22] Never lay hands hastily

---

11-16: 1 Cor 7, 8f.39f.
17: 1 Thes 5, 12.
18: Dt 25, 4; Lk 10, 17;

1 Cor 9, 9.
19: Dt 19, 15; Mt 18, 16.

5, 17-25: The function of *presbyters* is not exactly the same as that of the "*episkopos,*" *bishop* (3, 1); in fact, the relation of the two at the time of this epistle is obscure. The pastorals seem to reflect a transitional stage that developed into the monarchical episcopate of the second century (v 17). The presbyters possess the responsibility of preaching and teaching, for which functions they are supported by the community (17f). The realization that their position subjects them to adverse criticism is implied in the direction to Timothy (19f) to make sure of the truth of any accusation against them before public reproof is given. He must be as objective as possible in weighing charges against presbyters (v 21), learning from his experience both to take care in selecting them (v 22) and to judge prudently any criticism of them. The letter now sounds an informal note of personal concern in its advice to Timothy not to take his task so strenuously that he even avoids table wine (v 23).

Judgment concerning the fitness of candidates to serve as presbyters is easy with persons of open conduct, more difficult and prolonged with those of greater reserve (24f).

on anyone, or you may be sharing in the misdeeds of others. Keep yourself pure.

²³ Stop drinking water only. Take a little wine for the good of your stomach, and because of your frequent illnesses.

²⁴ Some men's sins are flagrant and cry out for judgment now, while other men's sins will appear only later. ²⁵ Similarly, some good deeds stand out clearly as such; even inconspicuous ones cannot be hidden forever.

6

¹ All under the yoke of slavery must regard their masters as worthy of full respect; otherwise the name of God and the church's teaching suffer abuse. ² Those slaves whose masters are brothers in the faith must not take liberties with them on that account. They must perform their tasks even more faithfully, since those who will profit from their work are believers and beloved brothers. These are the things you must teach and preach. ³ Whoever teaches in any other way, not holding to the sound doctrines of our Lord Jesus Christ and the teaching proper to true religion, ⁴ should be recognized as both conceited and ignorant, a sick man in his passion for polemics and controversy. From these come envy, dissension, slander, evil suspicions—⁵ in a word, the bickering of men with twisted minds who have lost all sense of truth. Such men value religion only as a means of personal gain. ⁶ There is, of course, great gain in religion—provided one is content with a sufficiency. ⁷ We brought nothing into this world, nor have we the power to take anything out. ⁸ If we have food and clothing we have all that we need. ⁹ Those who want to be rich are falling into temptation and a trap. They are letting themselves be captured by foolish and harmful desires which drag men down to ruin and destruction. ¹⁰ The love of money is the root of all evil. Some men in their passion for it have strayed from the faith, and have come to grief amid great pain.

¹¹ Man of God that you are, flee from all this. Instead, seek

---

6, 1: 1 Cor 7, 21f;   **7:** Jb 1, 21; Ps 49, 17.
Eph 6, 5-8;   **11:** 2 Tm 2, 22; 4, 1f.
Col 3, 22-25.

6, 1f: Domestic relationships derive supernatural value from the Christian faith.

6, 3-10: Timothy is exhorted to maintain steadfastly the position outlined in this letter, not allowing himself to be pressured into any other course. He must realize that false teachers can be discerned by their pride, envy, quarrelsomeness, and their greed for material gain.

6, 11-16: Timothy's position demands total dedication to God and faultless witness to Christ (11-14) operating from an awareness, through faith, of the coming revelation of Jesus as King, Lord, and God (15f).

after integrity, piety, faith, love, steadfastness, and a gentle spirit. [12] Fight the good fight of faith. Take firm hold on the everlasting life to which you were called when, in the presence of many witnesses, you made your noble profession of faith. [13] Before God, who gives life to all, and before Christ Jesus, who in bearing witness made his noble profession before Pontius Pilate, [14] I charge you to keep God's command without blame or reproach until our Lord Jesus Christ shall appear. [15] This appearance God will bring to pass at his chosen time. He is the blessed and only ruler, the King of kings and Lord of lords [16] who alone has immortality and who dwells in unapproachable light, whom no human being has ever seen or can see. To him be honor and everlasting rule! Amen.

[17] Tell those who are rich in this world's goods not to be proud, and not to rely on so uncertain a thing as wealth. Let them trust in the God who provides us richly with all things for our use. [18] Charge them to do good, to be rich in good works and generous, sharing what they have. [19] Thus will they build a secure foundation for the future, for receiving that life which is life indeed.

[20] O Timothy, guard what has been committed to you. Stay clear of worldly, idle talk and the contradictions of what is falsely called knowledge. [21] In laying claim to such knowledge, some men have missed the goal of faith. Grace be with you.

12: 2 Tm 4, 7.
13: Mt 27, 11; Jn 18, 33.37.
15: Dt 10, 17; Rv 17, 14;
    19, 16.
16: Jn 1, 18; 1 Jn 4, 12.
17: Lk 12, 17-21.
19: Mt 6, 20.
20: 2 Tm 1, 14.

6, 17ff: Timothy is directed to instruct the rich, advising them to make good use of their wealth by aiding the poor.

6, 20f: The final words reflect the chief concern of this letter: that Timothy take every means to preserve the traditional Christian faith.

THE SECOND EPISTLE OF PAUL TO TIMOTHY

INTRODUCTION

The authorship and date of this epistle are discussed in the Introduction to the First Epistle of Paul to Timothy. The letter portrays Paul as a prisoner (1, 8.16; 2, 9) in Rome (1, 17), and indicates that Timothy is in Ephesus (4, 12). It reveals that, with rare exceptions, Christians have not rallied to Paul's support (1, 15-18), and takes a pessimistic view of the outcome of his case (4, 16). It describes Paul as fully aware of what impends, looking to God, not to men, for his deliverance (4, 3-8.18). It recalls with affectionate remembrance his mission days with Timothy (1, 3ff; cf Acts 16, 1-4). It points to his preaching of the gospel as the reason for his imprisonment and offers Timothy as a motive of steadfastness his own example of firmness in faith despite adverse circumstances (1, 6-14). The epistle suggests that Timothy should prepare others to replace himself as Paul has prepared him for his own replacement (2, 1f), urging him not to desist out of fear from preserving and spreading the Christian message (2, 3-7). It presents the resurrection of Jesus and his messianic role as the heart of the gospel for which Paul has been ready to lay down his life (2, 8f), not only to express fully his own conviction but to support the conviction of others (2, 10-13).

This letter, like the preceding one, urges Timothy to protect the community from the inevitable impact of false teaching (2, 14—3, 9), without fear of the personal attacks which may result (3, 10-14). It recommends that he rely on the power of the Scriptures and on the positive proposal of doctrine (3, 15—4, 2) without being troubled by those who do not accept him (4, 3ff). The epistle observes in passing that Paul has need of his reading materials and his cloak (4, 13), and what will be best of all, a visit from Timothy.

THE SECOND EPISTLE OF PAUL
TO TIMOTHY

1

¹ Paul, by the will of God an apostle of Christ Jesus sent to proclaim the promise of life in him, ² to Timothy, my child whom I love. May grace, mercy, and peace from God the Father and from Christ Jesus our Lord be with you.

Thanksgiving and Prayer

³ I thank God, the God of my forefathers whom I worship with a clear conscience, whenever I remember you in my prayers —as indeed I do constantly, night and day. ⁴ Recalling your tears when we parted, I yearn to see you again. That would make my happiness complete. ⁵ I find myself thinking of your sincere faith—faith which first belonged to your grandmother Lois and to your mother Eunice, and which (I am confident) you also have.

Exhortation to Faithfulness

⁶ For this reason, I remind you to stir into flame the gift of God bestowed when my hands were laid on you. ⁷ The Spirit God has given us is no cowardly spirit, but rather one that makes us strong, loving, and wise. ⁸ Therefore, never be ashamed of your testimony to our Lord, nor of me, a prisoner for his sake; but with the strength which comes from God bear your share of the hardship which the gospel entails.

⁹ God has saved us and has called us to a holy life, not because of any merit of ours but according to his own design— the grace held out to us in Christ Jesus before the world began ¹⁰ but now made manifest through the appearance of our Savior. He has robbed death of its power and has brought life and

---

1, 5: 3, 14f;
Acts 16, 1.
7: Rom 8, 15.
8: Lk 9, 26; Rom 5, 3.

9: Mt 10, 10; Lk 10, 7;
Ti 3, 5.
10: Rom 6, 9.

1, 1f: For the formula of address and greeting, see note on Romans 1, 1-7. *The promise of life in him:* which God grants to men through union with Christ in faith and love; cf Col 3, 4; 1 Tm 4, 8.

1, 4f: Purportedly written from prison in Rome (1, 8; 4, 6ff) shortly before the writer's death, the letter recalls the earlier sorrowful parting from Timothy, commending him for his faith and expressing the longing to see him again.

1, 6: *The gift of God bestowed when my hands were laid on you:* the grace of ordination, signified by the laying on of hands; cf 1 Tm 4, 14.

1, 8: *Never be ashamed of your testimony to our Lord:* i. e., of preaching and suffering for the sake of the gospel.

1, 9f: Redemption from sin and the call to holiness of life are not won by personal deeds but gratuitously bestowed through the incarnation according to God's eternal plan; cf Eph 1, 4.

immortality into clear light through the gospel. ¹¹ In the service of this gospel I have been appointed preacher and apostle and teacher, ¹² and for its sake I undergo present hardships. But I am not ashamed, for I know him in whom I have believed, and I am confident that he is able to guard what has been entrusted to me until that Day. ¹³ Take as a model of sound teaching what you have heard me say, in faith and love in Christ Jesus. ¹⁴ Guard the rich deposit of faith with the help of the Holy Spirit who dwells within us.

¹⁵ You know that all in Asia, including even Phygelus and Hermogenes, have turned their backs on me. ¹⁶ May the Lord have mercy on the family of Onesiphorus, because he has often given me new heart and has not been ashamed of me, even in my chains. ¹⁷ When he was in Rome, he sought me out earnestly and found me. ¹⁸ When he stands before the Lord on the great Day, may the Lord grant him mercy! And the many services he has performed for Christ in Ephesus you know even better than I.

2

The Gospel versus Empty Fables

¹ So you, my son, must be strong in the grace which is ours in Christ Jesus. ² The things which you have heard from me through many witnesses you must hand on to trustworthy men who will be able to teach others. ³ Bear hardship along with me as a good soldier of Christ Jesus. ⁴ No soldier becomes entangled in the affairs of civilian life; he avoids this in order to please his commanding officer. ⁵ Similarly, if one takes part in

---

11: 1 Tm 2, 7.   2, 5: 1 Cor 9, 25.

1, 12: *He is able to guard . . . until that Day:* the deposit of faith (or, less likely, the reward of Christian ministry) until the second coming of Christ.

1, 15: Keen disappointment is expressed, here and later (4, 16), that the Christians of the province of Asia, especially Phygelus and Hermogenes, should have *abandoned* the writer and done nothing to defend his *case in court.*

1, 16ff: *The family of Onesiphorus, because he . . . even in my chains:* Onesiphorus seems to have died before this letter was written. His family is mentioned twice (v 16 and 4, 19), though it was Onesiphorus himself who was helpful to Paul in prison and rendered much service to the community of Ephesus (16ff). Because the apostle complains of abandonment by *all in Asia* during his second imprisonment and trial, the assistance of Onesiphorus is understood as having been given to Paul during his first Roman imprisonment (61-63 A. D.).

2, 1-7: This passage manifests a characteristic deep concern for safeguarding the deposit of faith and faithfully transmitting it through *trustworthy men* (1f; cf 1, 14; 1 Tm 6, 20; Ti 1, 9). Comparisons to the soldier's loyalty, the athlete's fidelity, and the farmer's arduous work as the price of reward (4ff) emphasize the need of singleness of purpose in preaching the word, even at the cost of hardship, for the sake of Christ (v 3).

an athletic contest, he cannot receive the winner's crown unless he has kept the rules. [6] The hardworking farmer is the one who should have the first share of the crop. [7] Reflect on what I am saying, for the Lord will make my meaning fully clear.

[8] Remember that Jesus Christ, a descendant of David, was raised from the dead. This is the gospel I preach; [9] in preaching it I suffer as a criminal, even to the point of being thrown into chains—but there is no chaining the word of God! [10] Therefore I bear with all of this for the sake of those whom God has chosen, in order that they may obtain the salvation to be found in Christ Jesus and with it eternal glory.

[11] You can depend on this:

> If we have died with him
>> we shall also live with him;
> [12] If we hold out to the end
>> we shall also reign with him.

But if we deny him he will deny us. [13] If we are unfaithful he will still remain faithful, for he cannot deny himself.

[14] Keep reminding people of these things and charge them before God to stop disputing about mere words. This does no good and can be the ruin of those who listen. [15] Try hard to make yourself worthy of God's approval, a workman who has no cause to be ashamed, following a straight course in preaching the truth. [16] Avoid worldly, idle talk, for those who indulge in it become more and more godless, [17] and the influence of their talk will spread like the plague. This is the case with Hymenaeus and Philetus, [18] who have gone far wide of the truth in saying that the resurrection has already taken place. They are upsetting some people's faith. [19] But the foundation God has laid stands firm. It bears this inscription: "The Lord knows those who are

---

8: Acts 13, 22f; Rom 1, 3f.
9: Phil 1, 13-18.
10: Col 1, 24.
11: Rom 6, 5.
12: Mt 10, 33; Mk 8, 38;

Rom 8, 17.
13: Rom 3, 3.
15: 1 Tm 4, 6f.
18: 1 Tm 1, 20.
19: Nm 16, 5; Eph 2, 20.

2, 8-13: Through baptism, Christians die spiritually with Christ and *live with him* in the hope of reigning with him forever, but not without giving witness to him through suffering in the present life, even as the apostle has been imprisoned for preaching the gospel (v 9). His sufferings are helpful to the elect in attaining salvation and glory in Christ (v 10), who will reward the faithful and disown the unfaithful (12f).

2, 14-19: For those who dispute about mere words (cf 2, 23f) and indulge in irreligious talk to the detriment of their listeners (14.16-19), see note on 1 Tm 1, 3f. *Hymenaeus and Philetus* (v 17), while accepting the Christian's mystical death and resurrection in Christ through baptism, deny the resurrection of the body and eternal glory.

his"; and, "Let everyone who professes the name of the Lord abandon evil."

[20] In every large household there are vessels not only of gold and silver but also of wood and clay, some for distinguished and others for common use. [21] The lesson is that if a person will but cleanse himself of evil things he may be a distinguished vessel, dedicated and useful to the master of the house and ready for every noble service. [22] So, turn from youthful passions and pursue integrity, faith, love, and peace, along with those who call on the Lord in purity of heart. [23] Have nothing to do with senseless, ignorant disputations. As you well know, they only breed quarrels, [24] and the servant of the Lord must not be quarrelsome but must be kindly toward all. He must be an apt teacher, patiently, [25] and gently correcting those who contradict him, in the hope always that God will enable them to repent and know the truth. [26] Thus, taken captive by God to do his will, they shall escape the devil's trap.

3

Against False Teachers

[1] Do not forget this: there will be terrible times in the last days. [2] Men will be lovers of self and of money, proud, arrogant, abusive, disobedient to their parents, ungrateful, profane, [3] inhuman, implacable, slanderous, licentious, brutal, hating the good. [4] They will be treacherous, reckless, pompous, lovers of pleasure rather than of God [5] as they make a pretense of religion but negate its power. Stay clear of them. [6] It is such as these who worm their way into homes and make captives of silly women burdened with sins and driven by desires of many kinds, [7] always learning but never able to reach a knowledge of the truth. [8] Just as Jannes and Jambres opposed Moses, so these men also oppose the truth; with perverted minds they falsify the faith. [9] But they will not get very far; as with those two men, the stupidity of these will be plain for all to see.

22: 1 Tm 6, 11.
23: 1 Tm 1, 4; Ti 3, 9.
24: 1 Tm 3, 2; Ti 1, 7.
25: Mt 12, 20; Gal 6, 1.

3, 1: 1 Tm 4, 1; 2 Pt 3, 3;
Jude 18.
2: Rom 1, 29.
8: Ex 7, 11; Jn 8, 32.

2, 22: *Those who call on the Lord:* those who believe in Christ and worship him as Lord, i. e., Christians (Acts 9, 14ff.20f; Rom 10, 12 f).
3, 1-9: The moral depravity and false teachings of men that will prevail in the last days are already at work (1-5). Frivolous and superficial women too, devoid of the true spirit of religion, will be easy victims of those who pervert them by falsifying the truth (6ff), just as Jannes and Jambres, the magicians of Egypt (Ex 7, 11f.22), discredited the truth in Moses' time.

Paul's Example and Teaching

[10] You have followed closely my teaching and my conduct. You have observed my resolution, fidelity, patience, love, and endurance, [11] through persecutions and sufferings in Antioch, Iconium, and Lystra. You know what persecutions I have had to bear, and you know how the Lord saved me from them all. [12] Anyone who wants to live a godly life in Christ Jesus can expect to be persecuted. [13] But all the while evil men and charlatans will go from bad to worse, deceiving others, themselves deceived. [14] You, for your part, must remain faithful to what you have learned and believed, because you know who your teachers were. [15] Likewise, from your infancy you have known the sacred Scriptures, the source of the wisdom which through faith in Jesus Christ leads to salvation. [16] All Scripture is inspired of God and is useful for teaching—for reproof, correction, and training in holiness [17] so that the man of God may be fully competent and equipped for every good work.

4

Apostolic Charge

[1] In the presence of God and of Christ Jesus, who is coming to judge the living and the dead, and by his appearing and his kingly power, [2] I charge you to preach the word, to stay with this task whether convenient or inconvenient—correcting, reproving, appealing—constantly teaching and never losing patience. [3] For the time will come when people will not tolerate sound doctrine, but, following their own desires, will surround themselves with teachers who tickle their ears. [4] They will stop listening to the truth and will wander off to fables. [5] As for you, be steady and self-possessed; put up with hardship, perform your work as an evangelist, fulfill your ministry.

11: Acts 14, 1-5.22.
13: 1 Thes 3, 4f.
15: 1, 5.
16: Rom 15, 4; 1 Cor 10, 6;

2 Pt 1, 20f.
4, 1: Acts 10, 42;
1 Tm 6, 14.
4: 1 Tm 1, 4.

3, 15ff: The Scriptures are the source of wisdom, i. e., of belief in and loving fulfillment of God's word revealed in Christ, through whom man finds salvation. *All Scripture is inspired of God:* has God as its principal author, with the writer as the human collaborator. Thus the Scriptures are the word of God in human language. *Useful for teaching . . . every good work:* because as God's word the Scriptures share his divine authority. It is exercised through those who are ministers of the word.

4, 1-5: The gravity of the obligation incumbent on Timothy to preach the word can be gauged from the solemn adjuration: *in the presence of God,* and of Christ coming as universal judge *and by his appearing and his kingly power* (v 1). Patience, courage, constancy, and endurance are required despite the opposition, hostility, indifference, and defection of many to whom the truth has been preached (2-5).

Reward for Fidelity

⁶ I for my part am already being poured out like a libation. The time of my dissolution is near. ⁷ I have fought the good fight, I have finished the race, I have kept the faith. ⁸ From now on a merited crown awaits me; on that Day the Lord, just judge that he is, will award it to me—and not only to me, but to all who have looked for his appearing with eager longing.

Paul's Loneliness

⁹ Do your best to join me soon, ¹⁰ for Demas, enamored of the present world, has left me and gone to Thessalonica. Crescens has gone to Galatia and Titus to Dalmatia. ¹¹ I have no one with me but Luke. Get Mark and bring him with you, for he can be of great service to me. ¹² Tychicus I have sent to Ephesus. ¹³ When you come, bring the cloak I left in Troas with Carpus, and the books, especially the parchments.

Comfort in Trial

¹⁴ Alexander the coppersmith did me a great deal of harm; the Lord will repay him according to his deeds. ¹⁵ Meanwhile, you too had better be on guard, for he has strongly resisted our preaching. ¹⁶ At the first hearing of my case in court, no one took my part. In fact, everyone abandoned me. May it not

---

6: Phil 2, 17.
7: Acts 20, 24;
   1 Tm 1, 18.
10: Phlm 4, 14.

11: Col 4, 10.
13: Ti 3, 10.
14: Pss 28, 4; 62, 13;
    Prv 24, 12; 1 Tm 1, 20.

4, 6: The apostle recognizes his death through martyrdom to be imminent. He regards it, like the death of Christ, as an act of worship in which his blood will be poured out in sacrifice; cf Ex 29, 40.

4, 7: *I have fought the good fight, I have finished the race:* at the close of his life Paul could testify to the accomplishment of what Christ himself had foretold concerning him at the time of his conversion: *I myself shall indicate to him how much he will have to suffer for my name* (Acts 9, 16). *I have kept the faith:* preserved the true teaching concerning Christ, both in his personal adherence to it, and in his ministry.

4, 8: When the world is judged at the parousia all who have eagerly *looked for his appearing,* i. e., lived according to his teaching, will be rewarded. *A merited crown:* a reference to the laurel wreath placed on the heads of conquerors and winners of various contests; cf 2, 5; 1 Cor 9, 25.

4, 10-13: *Demas* either abandoned the work of the ministry for worldly affairs or, perhaps, gave up the faith itself (v 10). *Luke* may have accompanied Paul on part of his second and third missionary journeys (Acts 16, 10-18; 20, 5—21, 19). *Mark,* once rejected by Paul (Acts 13, 13; 15, 39-40), is now to render him *great service* (v 11); cf Col 4, 10; Phlm 24. *Tychicus I have sent to Ephesus:* see Eph 6, 21; cf also Acts 20, 4; Col 4, 7 (12f).

4, 14-18: *Alexander:* an opponent of Paul's preaching (14f), perhaps the same who is mentioned in 1 Tm 1, 20. Despite Paul's abandonment by his friends in the province of Asia (cf 1, 15f), the divine assistance brought this first trial to a successful issue—even to the point of making the gospel message known to those who participated in or witnessed the trial (16f). Though Paul was not released from prison, he was made ready for the *heavenly kingdom* (v 18).

be held against them! [17] But the Lord stood by my side and
gave me strength, so that through me the preaching task might
be completed and all the nations might hear the gospel. That
is how I was saved from the lion's jaws. [18] The Lord will continue to rescue me from all attempts to do me harm and will
bring me safe to his heavenly kingdom. To him be glory forever and ever. Amen.

Greetings

[19] Greet Prisca and Aquila and the family of Onesiphorus.
[20] Erastus has stayed in Corinth, while Trophimus I had to
leave ill at Miletus. [21] Get here before winter if you can. Eubu-
lus, Pudens, Linus, Claudia, and all the brothers send greetings.
[22] The Lord be with your spirit. Grace be with you.

17: Ps 22, 22; Mt 10, 19.
18: Rom 16, 27.
19: 1, 16.

20: Acts 18, 2; 19, 22;
Rom 16, 23.

4, 19-22: *Prisca and Aquila* assisted Paul in his ministry in Corinth (Acts
18, 2f) and Ephesus (Acts 18, 19.26; 1 Cor 16, 19). They risked death
to save his life, and all the Gentile communities are indebted to them (Rom
16, 3ff), (v 19). *Erastus:* treasurer of the city of Corinth (Rom 16, 23); cf
also Acts 19, 22. *Trophimus:* from the province of Asia, who accompanied Paul from Greece to Troas (Acts 20, 4f). *Linus:* possibly to be identified with Linus, the supposed successor of Peter as Bishop of Rome.
Claudia: in the Constitutio Apostolica 7.46, 17-19, she is called mother of
Linus, Bishop of Rome.

THE EPISTLE OF PAUL TO TITUS
INTRODUCTION

The authorship and date of the Epistle to Titus are discussed in the Introduction to 1 Timothy. Titus was a Gentile Christian, apparently from Antioch (Gal. 2, 1). According to 2 Corinthians (2, 13; 7, 6.13f), he was with Paul on his third missionary journey; there is, however, no mention of him in Acts. Besides being the bearer of Paul's severe letter to the Corinthians (2 Cor 7, 6ff), he had the responsibility of taking up the collection in Corinth for the Christian community of Jerusalem (2 Cor 8, 6.16.23). In the present letter (1, 5), he is mentioned as the administrator of the Christian community in Crete, charged with the task of organizing it through the appointment of presbyters and bishops (1, 5-9; here the two terms refer to the same personages).

The letter instructs Titus about the character of the men he is to choose in view of the pastoral difficulties peculiar to Crete (1, 5-16). It suggests the special individual and social virtues which the various age groups and classes in the Christian community should be encouraged to acquire (2, 1-10). The motives for improving one's personal character are to be found preeminently in the mysteries of the incarnation and the second coming of Christ (2, 11-15; 3, 5ff). The community is to be fashioned into a leaven for Christianizing the social world about it (3, 1ff). Good works are to be the evidence of their faith in God (3, 8); those who engage in religious controversy are, after suitable warning, to be ignored (3, 9ff).

The material in Titus is similar to that in 1 Timothy; it is, however, differently oriented.

The principal divisions of the Epistle to Titus are as follows:
I: Introduction (1, 1-4)
II: Pastoral Charge (1, 5-16)
III: Teaching the Christian Life (2, 1—3, 15)

THE EPISTLE OF PAUL TO TITUS

I: INTRODUCTION

1

Greeting

¹ Paul, a servant of God, sent as an apostle of Jesus Christ for the sake of the faith of those whom God has chosen, and to promote their knowledge of the truth as our religion embodies it, ² in the hope of that eternal life which God, who cannot lie, promised in endless ages past. ³ This he has now manifested in his own good time as his word, in the preaching entrusted to me by the command of God our Savior. ⁴ Paul to Titus, my own true child in our common faith: May grace and peace from God our Father, and Christ Jesus our Savior, be with you.

II: PASTORAL CHARGE

Qualities of a Presbyter

⁵ My purpose in leaving you in Crete was that you might accomplish what had been left undone, especially the appointment of presbyters in every town. As I instructed you, ⁶ a presbyter must be irreproachable, married only once, the father of children who are believers and are know not to be wild and insubordinate. ⁷ The bishop as God's steward must be blameless. He my not be self-willed or arrogant, a drunkard, a violent or greedy man. ⁸ He should, on the contrary, be hospitable and a lover of goodness; steady, just, holy, and self-controlled. ⁹ In his teaching he must hold fast to the authentic message, so that he will be able both to encourage men to follow sound doctrine and to refute those who contradict it. ¹⁰ There are many irresponsible teachers, especially from among the Jewish converts —men who are empty talkers and deceivers. ¹¹ These must be silenced. They are upsetting whole families by teaching things

---

1, 2: Nm 23, 19.
   3: 1 Tm 1, 1.
   6: Rom 12, 8; 1 Tm 3, 2.

7: 1 Pt 5, 2.
11: 1 Tm 6, 10.

1, 1-4: On the epistolary form, see note on Romans 1, 1-7. The apostolate is the divinely appointed mission to lead others to the true faith, and through it to eternal salvation (1ff).

1, 5-9: This instruction on the selection and appointment of presbyters, substantially identical in 1 Timothy 3, 1-7 (see note), was aimed at strengthening the authority of Titus by apostolic mandate; cf 2, 15. In Titus 1, 6f and Acts 20, 17.28 the terms *episkopos* and *presbyteros* ("bishop" and "presbyter") refer to the same persons. As they did not exercise the functions reserved to the apostle Paul and his legates, such as Timothy and Titus, they were not bishops in the later sense familiar to us.

1, 10-16: This adverse criticism of the defects within the community is directed especially against certain Judaeo-Christians, who busy themselves with

they have no right to teach—and all for sordid gain! ¹² A man of Crete, one of their own prophets, has testified,

"Cretans have ever been liars, beasts, and lazy gluttons,"

¹³ and that is the simple truth!

Admonish them sharply, in an attempt to keep them close to sound faith, ¹⁴ and unaffected by Jewish myths or rules invented by men who have swerved from the truth. ¹⁵ To the clean all things are clean, but to those defiled unbelievers nothing is clean. Their very minds and consciences are tainted. ¹⁶ They claim to "know God," but by their actions they deny that he exists. They are disgusting—intractable and thoroughly incapable of any decent action.

III: TEACHING THE CHRISTIAN LIFE

2

Various Counsels

¹ As for yourself, let your speech be consistent with sound doctrine. ² Tell the older men that they must be temperate, serious-minded, and self-controlled; likewise sound in the faith, loving, and steadfast. ³ Similarly, the older women must behave in ways that befit those who belong to God. They must not be slanderous gossips or slaves to drink. ⁴ By their good example they must teach the younger women to love their husbands and children, ⁵ to be sensible, chaste, busy at home, kindly, submissive to their husbands. Thus the word of God will not fall into disrepute. ⁶ Tell the young men to keep themselves completely under control—⁷ nor may you yourself fail to set them good example. ⁸ Your teaching must have the integrity of serious, sound words to which no one can take exception. If it does, no opponent will be able to find anything bad to say about us, and hostility will yield to shame.

⁹ Slaves are to be submissive to their masters. They should try to please them in every way, not contradicting them ¹⁰ nor

---

14: 1 Tm 1, 4.
15: Rom 14, 14-20.
2, 5: Eph 5, 22; Col 3, 18.

7: 1 Tm 4, 12.
9: Eph 6, 5; Col 3, 22;
1 Pt 2, 18.

---

useless speculations over persons mentioned in the Old Testament and insist on the observance of Jewish ritual purity regulations, thereby *upsetting whole families by teaching things they have no right to teach;* cf 3, 9; 1 Tm 1, 3-10; 4, 1-10; 6, 3-10. One of Titus' main tasks in Crete is to become acquainted with the national character of the Cretans and thereby learn to cope with its deficiencies (cf 1, 12, the citation from the sixth-century B. C. Cretan poet Epimenides).

stealing from them, but expressing a constant fidelity by their conduct, so as to adorn in every way possible the doctrine of God our Savior.

Transforming of Life

[11] The grace of God has appeared, offering salvation to all men. [12] It trains us to reject godless ways and worldly desires, and live temperately, justly, and devoutly in this age [13] as we await our blessed hope, the appearing of the glory of the great God and of our Savior Christ Jesus. [14] It was he who sacrificed himself for us, to redeem us from all unrighteousness and to cleanse for himself a people of his own, eager to do what is right.

[15] These are the things you are to say. Make our appeals and corrections with the authority of command. Let no one look down on you.

3

[1] Remind people to be loyally subject to the government and its officials, to obey the laws, to be ready to take on any honest employment. [2] Tell them not to speak evil of anyone or be quarrelsome. They must be forbearing and display a perfect courtesy toward all men. [3] We ourselves were once foolish, disobedient, and far from true faith; we were the slaves of our passions and of pleasures of various kinds. We went our way in malice and envy, hateful ourselves and hating one another. [4] But when the kindness and love of God our savior appeared, [5] he saved us; not because of any righteous deeds we had done, but because of his mercy. He saved us through the baptism of new birth and renewal by the Holy Spirit. [6] This Spirit he lavished on us through Jesus Christ our Savior, [7] that we might be justified by his grace and become heirs, in hope, of eternal life. [8] You can depend on this to be true.

11: 3, 4.
14: Ex 19, 5; Ps 130, 8;
    1 Tm 2, 6.
15: 1 Tm 4, 12.
3, 1: Rom 13, 1-7;
    1 Pt 2, 13f.
3: Eph 2, 3-10; Col 3, 7;

1 Pt 1, 3.
4: 2, 11.
5: Jn 3, 5; Rom 5, 5;
    6, 4 Eph 5, 26;
    2 Tm 1, 9.
7: Rom 3, 24.

2, 11-15: The moving force in the moral improvement outlined in 2, 1-10 is to be the constant appeal to God's revelation of salvation in Christ, with its demand for transformation of life.

3, 1-7: The spiritual renewal of the Cretans, signified in God's merciful gift of baptism (4-7), should be reflected in their improved attitude toward civil authority and in their Christian relationship with all (1ff).

3, 8-11: In matters of good conduct and religious doctrine Titus is to show himself uncompromising.

Advice to Titus

I want you to lay great weight on the things I have been saying, so that those who have committed themselves to God may be careful to do what is right. This is what is good and advantageous for men. [9] See to it that you abstain from stupid arguments and genealogies, and from all controversies and quarrels about the law. They are useless and have no point. [10] Warn a heretic once and then a second time; after that, have nothing to do with him. [11] You must recognize such a person as perverted and sinful; he stands self-condemned.

Directives, Greetings, and Blessing

[12] When I send Artemas to you, or perhaps Tychicus, hurry to me at Nicopolis; I have decided to spend the winter there. [13] Speed Zenas the lawyer and Apollos on their journey, having first seen to it that they have everything they need. [14] Let our people devote themselves to honest work in order to take care of their needs, so that they may be in position to live fruitful lives.

[15] All who are with me send their greetings. Greet those who love us in the faith.

May grace be with you all!

9: 1 Tm 4, 7; 2 Tm 2, 23.   13: Acts 18, 24.
12: Acts 20, 4.

3, 12-15: Artemas or Tychicus (2 Tm 4, 12) is to replace Titus, who will join Paul in his winter sojourn at Nicopolis in Epirus, on the western coast of Greece. Titus will no doubt report on his efforts in Crete, and perhaps also assist in preaching the gospel.

THE EPISTLE OF PAUL TO PHILEMON
INTRODUCTION

The date of this epistle is discussed in the Introduction to Ephesians. Its Pauline authorship is considered to be incontestable. The interesting fact is that this very personal and undoubtedly private letter was conserved and made public by the second century in a society in which human slavery was an accepted part of the culture.

The letter concerns Onesimus, slave of Philemon, a well-to-do Christian of Colossae (Col 4, 9). Onesimus escaped Philemon's service (v 15), and was guilty of theft in the process (v 18). Paul converted Onesimus to the gospel (v 10) and persuaded him to return to his former condition (v 12); this had been his teaching concerning slaves from the first; cf 1 Cor 7, 21. Evidently Onesimus was fearful of the possible punishment that would be meted out to him, but Paul was confident both of Philemon's understanding of Christian teaching (15f) and of his own influence over Philemon (19f). The apostle promised to visit Philemon, meanwhile placing him under a telling kind of moral pressure to accede to his request and receive back his slave with nothing but kindness.

The delicate tone of this letter reflects, against the legal fact of slavery at the time, the incipient Christian insight into its injustice. Paul does not attack the institution, for the small Christian communities were in no position to raise such an issue in a dictatorial political structure. Also, the fact that they regarded the second coming of Christ as an occurrence possible within their lifetime lessened the impulse to any abrupt and widespread change. That Onesimus the slave was "brother" to Philemon, his legal master (v 16), was a revolutionary idea in the context of the times.

THE EPISTLE OF PAUL TO PHILEMON

Greeting

¹ Paul, a prisoner of Christ Jesus, and Timothy our brother, to our beloved friend and fellow worker Philemon, ² to Apphia our sister, to our fellow soldier Archippus, and to the church that meets in your house. ³ Grace to you and peace from God our Father and from the Lord Jesus Christ.

Philemon's Faith and Charity

⁴ I thank God always, my brother, as I commend you in my prayers, ⁵ for I keep hearing of your love and faith toward the Lord Jesus and all God's people. ⁶ And my prayer is that your sharing of the faith with others may enable you to know all the good which is ours in Christ. ⁷ I find great joy and comfort in your love, because through you the hearts of God's people have been refreshed.

Plea for Onesimus

⁸ Therefore, although I feel that I have every right to command you to do what ought to be done, ⁹ I prefer to appeal in the name of love. Yes, I, Paul, ambassador of Christ and now a prisoner for him, ¹⁰ appeal to you for my child, whom I have begotten during my imprisonment. He has become in truth Onesimus [Useful], for he who was formerly useless to you is now useful indeed both to you and to me. ¹² It is he I am sending back to you—and that means I am sending my heart! ¹³ I had wanted to keep him with me, that he might serve me in your place while I am in prison for the gospel; ¹⁴ but I did not want to do anything without your consent, that kind-

---

2: Col 4, 17.
4: Eph 1, 15f.
6: Col 1, 9ff.

9: Eph 3, 1.
10: Gal 4, 19; Col 4, 9.

1ff: It is the prisoner and friend appealing, rather than the apostle commanding with authority, who greets Philemon, Apphia, Archippus, and the assembly that meets in Philemon's house.

4-7: Philemon's faith and love for the Lord and the people of God whom he refreshes have urged him to share these blessings with others (5.7). Paul prays that as a result Philemon himself will benefit by a deepening knowledge and appreciation of the endless good they possess in common in possessing Christ (4.6).

10-22: *Appeal to you for my child:* Onesimus, Philemon's runaway slave, whom Paul the prisoner converted to the Christian faith (v 10), and whom he now asks Philemon to receive back as *a beloved brother* (16f), rather than as a slave liable to punishment for theft and damage and for escape (18). The name Onesimus means "useful" or profitable. Paul realizes that his convert has shown himself "useless" by his previous conduct; but he is confident that Onesimus will now live up to his name and be useful both to Philemon and to Paul himself (11.20). He would even prefer to have the service of Onesimus for the work of the ministry, but recognizes Philemon's prior right (13ff).

ness might not be forced on you but might be freely bestowed. [15] Perhaps he was separated from you for a while for this reason: that you might possess him forever, [16] no longer as a slave but as more than a slave, a beloved brother, especially dear to me; and how much more than a brother to you, since now you will know him both as a man and in the Lord.

[17] If then you regard me as a partner, welcome him as you would me. [18] If he has done you an injury or owes you anything, charge it to me. [19] I, Paul, write this in my own hand: I agree to pay—not to mention that you owe me your very self! [20] You see, brother, I want to make you "useful" to me in the Lord. Refresh this heart of mine in Christ.

Farewell Blessing

[21] Confident of your compliance, I write you, knowing that you will do more than I say. [22] And get a room ready for me; I hope that through your prayers I shall be restored to you.

[23] Epaphras, my fellow prisoner in Christ Jesus, greets you, [24] as do Mark, Aristarchus, Demas, and Luke, my fellow workers. [25] The grace of our Lord Jesus Christ be with your spirit.

22: Heb 13, 19.   24: Col 4, 10.

23f: *Epaphras:* a Colossian who founded the church in Colossae (Col 1, 7) and perhaps also in Laodicea and Hierapolis (Col 2, 1; 4, 12f). *Aristarchus:* a native of Thessalonica and fellow worker of Paul (Acts 19, 29; 20, 4; 27, 2). For Mark, Demas, and Luke, see 2 Timothy 4, 10-13 and note.

THE EPISTLE TO THE HEBREWS
INTRODUCTION

There are numerous features of this epistle that indicate authorship other than that of St. Paul the apostle. There is the high quality of its style, which makes Hebrews one of the distinguished works of the New Testament. Its literary structure intermingles doctrinal teaching and moral exhortation. The manner of citing the Old Testament is different, and the system of exegesis it follows reflects Hellenistic rather than Palestinian Judaism.

As early as the end of the second century the Eastern churches had accepted Hebrews as an inspired work composed by Paul, but until the second half of the fourth century the churches of the West questioned its Pauline authorship. Since the letter of Clement of Rome to the Corinthians, written about 96 A.D., cites the Epistle to the Hebrews, it is necessary to date the letter before that time. The identity of its author is a matter of pure speculation. Among those considered, Apollos seems more likely than Luke and Barnabas (cf Acts 18, 24), although nothing is know of his history beyond his activity in Corinth (1 Cor 1, 12; 3, 5). The data of the epistle indicate that its author wrote to a specific Christian community, or at least to communities in a particular area (13, 23; 6, 11f; 10, 19-25), but the allusions are insufficient to permit a judgment on their location. Commentators today are sharply divided on whether the addressees of the epistle were Judaeo-Christian or predominantly Gentile Christian, although the latter view is regarded with slightly more favor. The title "To the Hebrews" may merely represent an inference of the late second century: that the epistle's extensive use of the Old Testament points to its having been addressed to Judaeo-Christians.

The letter seeks to strengthen the practical faith of its recipients, and appeals to them for perseverance (6, 11f) despite harassment (12, 7-13) from forces outside the community (13, 3). Their knowledge and love of Christ hardly support the opinion of those who, on the basis of 6, 4-8, consider them to have been Judaeo-Christians on the point of reversion to Judaism.

The author begins with a reminder of the mysteries of the incarnation and exaltation of Jesus (1, 3), which proclaimed him the culminator of God's word to humanity (1, 1ff). He dwells upon the dignity of the Person of Christ, superior to the angels, who according to Old Testament tradition appeared in order to make God's plans known to men (1, 4—2, 2). Christ is God's final word of salvation communicated (in association with accredited witnesses to his teaching: 2, 3f; cf Acts 1, 21ff) not merely by word but through the suffering humanity common to Jesus and to the rest of men (2, 5-16). This enactment of salvation went beyond the pattern known to Moses, faithful prophet though he was of God's word; for Jesus as high priest personally expiated sin and was faithful to God with the fidelity of God's own Son (2, 17—3, 6).

Just as the infidelity of the people thwarted Moses' effort to save them all, so the infidelity of any Christian thwarts God's plan in Christ (3, 6—4, 13). Christians are to reflect that it is their humanity which

Jesus assumed, with all its defects except its sinfulness, and that he bore the burden of it to his death out of obedience to God. This work of his Son God declared to be the cause of salvation for all (4, 14—5, 10). Although Christians recognize this fundamental doctrine, they may grow weary of its repetition and therefore require other reflections to stimulate their faith (5, 11—6, 20).

The author of Hebrews presents to his Christian readers for their reflection the everlasting priesthood of Christ (7, 1-28), a priesthood which fulfills the promise of the Old Testament (8, 1-13). It also provides the meaning God ultimately intended in the sacrifices of the Old Testament (9, 1-28): these were symbols of the unique sacrifice of Christ which alone obtains forgiveness of the sins of mankind (10, 1-18). Any trial of faith the readers of the epistle may have should resolve itself through consideration of the reality of Jesus' actual existence in the heavenly sanctuary, his foreordained parousia, and the fruits they have already enjoyed through their faith (11, 19-39). It is in the nature of faith to trust the intangible (11, 1ff) which in God's providence one day becomes reality, as the Old Testament itself demonstrates (11, 4-40). This truth shines forth throughout the life of Christ. Despite the afflictions of his ministry, he remained confident of God's final intervention to ensure his resurrection and triumph (12, 1ff). Life's difficulties have meaning when they are accepted as God's discipline (12, 4-13). The message of the gospel is the word of Christ (12, 18-29), advocating peace among men (12, 14-17) and reverence toward all (13, 1-4), respect for authority (13, 7f), and complete reliance upon Christ for holiness of life (13, 9-17).

The principal divisions of the Epistle to the Hebrews are as follows:

THE EPISTLE TO THE HEBREWS

I: INTRODUCTION

1

[1] In times past, God spoke in fragmentary and varied ways to our fathers through the prophets; [2] in this, the final age, he has spoken to us through his Son, whom he has made heir of all things and through whom he first created the universe. [3] This Son is the reflection of the Father's glory, the exact representation of the Father's being, and he sustains all things by his powerful word. When he had cleansed us from our sins, he took his seat at the right hand of the Majesty in heaven, [4] as far superior to the angels as the name he has inherited is superior to theirs.

II: THE SON HIGHER THAN THE ANGELS

Messianic Enthronement

[5] To which of the angels did God ever say,

"You are my son; today I have begotten you"?

Or again,

"I will be his father, and he shall be my son"?

[6] And again, when he leads his first-born into the world, he says,

"Let all the angels of God worship him."

[7] Of the angels he says,

1, 2: Jn 1, 3; Gal 4, 4.
3: Ps 110, 1; Wis 7, 26;
Mk 16, 19; Col 1, 15.
4: Phil 2, 9ff; Col 1, 14.

5: 2 Sm 7, 14; Ps 2, 7;
Acts 13, 33.
6: Rv 1, 5.
7: Ps 104, 4.

1, 1-4: The letter opens with a reflection on the climax of God's revelation to mankind in his Son (v 3). The divine communication with men was initiated and maintained during Old Testament times through chosen men, the prophets (v 1). But now in messianic times, the final period of man's religious history, God the Son, creator and end of all things, is the communicator with men (v 2). He is the perfect and *exact representation of the Father's being*—even to the divine creative power—who entered human existence to destroy the power of sin. After accomplishing this he returned, through his resurrection and ascension, to his natural place with the Father (v 3). No creature, not even angels, can match the unique dignity of his Person (v 4).

1, 5-14: The citations from the psalms in v 5 (Ps 2, 7) and v 13 (Ps 110, 1) were traditionally used of Jesus' messianic sonship (cf Acts 13, 33) through his resurrection and ascension (cf Acts 2, 33ff); those in v 8 (Ps 45, 6f) and vv 10ff (Ps 102, 25ff) are concerned with his divine kingship and his creative function. The author states that, in the Christian understanding of Christ, the Old Testament elevates him above the angels. At best the angels can only be servants at the disposal of the creator (v 7, citing Ps 104, 4) and consequently they are *sent to serve those who are to inherit salvation* (v 14).

> "He makes his angels winds, and his ministers
> flaming fire";

[8] but of the Son,

> "Your throne, O God, stands forever and ever;
> a righteous scepter is the scepter of your kingdom.
> [9] You have loved justice and hated wickedness,
> therefore God, your God, has anointed you
> with the oil of gladness above your fellow kings."

[10] And,

> "Lord, of old you established the earth,
> and the heavens are the work of your hands.
> [11] They will perish, but you remain;
> all of them will grow old like a garment.
> [12] You will roll them up like a cloak;
> like a garment they will be changed.
> But you are the same, and your years will have
> no end."

[13] To which of the angels has God ever said,

> "Sit at my right hand till I make your enemies
> your footstoo"?

[14] Are they not all ministering spirits, sent to serve those who
are to inherit salvation?

2

Exhortation to Faithfulness

[1] In view of this, we must attend all the more to what we have
heard, lest we drift away. [2] For if the word spoken through
angels stood unchanged, and all transgression and disobedience
received its due punishment, [3] how shall we escape if we ignore
a salvation as great as ours? Announced first by the Lord, it

---

8: Ps 45, 7f.
10ff: Ps 102, 26ff.
13: Ps 110, 1.

14: Ps 91, 11; Dn 7, 10.
2, 1: 2 Pt 3, 17.
2: Acts 7, 53; Gal 3, 19.

2, 1-4: The absolute supremacy of Christ should greatly strengthen
Christians against abandoning their faith (v 1). If, according to Jewish
tradition (Gal 3, 19), angels played the role of intermediaries for the
Mosaic covenant, the violation of which was divinely punished (v 2), an
even severer punishment awaits those who knowingly neglect the salvation
offered in Christ's own word, proclaimed by witnesses whom God appointed (Lk 1, 1f; Acts 1, 21f) and confirmed by divine power through
signs and *miracles* (3f).

was confirmed to us by those who had heard him. ⁴ God then gave witness to it by signs, miracles, varied acts of power, and distribution of the gifts of the Holy Spirit as he willed.

Exaltation through Abasement

⁵ For he did not make the world to come—that world of which we speak—subject to angels. ⁶ Somewhere this is testified to, in the passage that says:

"What is man that you should be mindful of him,
  or the son of man that you should care for him?
⁷ You made him for a little while lower than the angels;
  You crowned him with glory and honor,
  ⁸ and put all things under his feet."

In subjecting all things to him, God left nothing unsubjected. At present we do not see all things thus subject, ⁹ but we do see Jesus crowned with glory and honor because he suffered death: Jesus, who was made for a little while lower than the angels, that through God's gracious will he might taste death for the sake of all men. ¹⁰ Indeed, it was fitting that when bringing many sons to glory God, for whom and through whom all things exist, should make their leader in the work of salvation perfect through suffering. ¹¹ He who consecrates and those who are consecrated have one and the same Father. Therefore he is not ashamed to call them brothers, ¹² saying,

"I will announce your name to my brothers,
  I will sing your praise in the midst of the
      assembly";

¹³ and,

4: Mk 16, 20; Acts 14, 3; 19, 11.
6: Ps 8, 5ff.
8: Mt 28, 18; 1 Cor 15, 25-28. Eph 1, 20-23;

Phil 3, 21.
9: Phil 2, 6-11.
10: 12, 2; Is 53, 4; Rom 11, 36; 1 Cor 8, 6.
12: Ps 22, 23.
13: 2 Sm 22, 3; Is 8, 17f.

2, 5-18: The humanity and the suffering of Jesus do not constitute a valid reason for relinquishing the Christian faith. The thought of the psalmist (Ps 8, 4ff in the Septuagint) concerning man's glory and splendor despite his subordination to the angels (6f) is perfectly reflected in the history of Jesus, who lived a truly human existence during his mortal life but is now in full possession of the divine kingly glory (v 9). It was altogether fitting that God should direct him along the path of suffering (v 10), since in the spirit of the Old Testament (Ps 22, 22; Is 8, 17f) he identified himself entirely with those for whom he obtained sanctification (11-15). He deliberately allied himself with the descendants of Abraham (v 16) in order to function as an authentic high priest, expiating the sins of the people (v 17) as one who experienced the same tests as they (v 18).

"I will put my trust in him";

and again,

"Here am I, and the children God has given me!"

[14] Now, since the children are men of blood and flesh, Jesus likewise had a full share in ours, that by his death he might rob the devil, the prince of death, of his power, [15] and free those who through fear of death had been slaves their whole life long. [16] Surely he did not come to help angels, but rather the children of Abraham; [17] therefore he had to become like his brothers in every way, that he might be a merciful and faithful high priest before God on their behalf, to expiate the sins of the people. [18] Since he was himself tested through what he suffered, he is able to help those who are tempted.

III: JESUS, FAITHFUL AND COMPASSIONATE HIGH PRIEST

3

Jesus, Superior to Moses

[1] Therefore, holy brothers who share a heavenly calling, fix your eyes on Jesus, the apostle and high priest whom we acknowledge in faith, [2] who was faithful to him who appointed him. Moses, too, "was faithful in all God's household," [3] but Jesus is more worthy of honor than he, as the founder of a house is more honorable than the house itself. [4] Every house is founded by someone, but God is the founder of all. [5] Moses "was faithful in all God's household" as a servant charged with the task of witnessing to what would be spoken; [6] but Christ was faithful as the Son placed over God's house. It is we who are that house if we hold fast to our confidence and the hope of which we boast.

14: Is 25, 8; Hos 13, 14;
   Jn 12, 31; Rom 6, 9;
   1 Cor 15, 54.
15: Rom 8, 15.
17: 4, 15; Phil 2, 7.
3, 2: 10, 23; Nm 12, 7.

3: Mt 12, 41f; 16, 18;
   2 Cor 3, 7.
5: Dt 18, 18.
6: 10, 21; Eph 2, 19-22;
   1 Tm 3, 15.

3, 1-6: Christians must have full confidence in Jesus, whom their faith recognizes as the one sent by God (*the apostle*) to be the high priest of the Christian community (v 1). Like Moses, the leader of the people of Israel, Jesus was faithful to the task assigned to him (v 2). Moses, however, was faithful *in* the house of God, i. e., he was himself but a member of God's chosen people (3ff), whereas Jesus possesses the fidelity of God's Son *over* the new people of God (v 6).

Israel's Infidelity, a Warning

⁷ Wherefore, as the Holy Spirit says:

"Today, if you should hear his voice,
⁸ harden not your hearts as at the revolt
in the day of testing in the desert,
⁹ When your fathers tested and tried me,
and saw my works ¹⁰ for forty years.
Because of this I was angered with that generation
and I said, 'They have always been of erring heart,
and have never known my ways.'

¹¹ "Thus I swore in my anger,
'They shall never enter into my rest.'"

¹² Take care, my brothers, lest any of you have an evil and
unfaithful spirit and fall away from the living God. ¹³ Encourage one another daily while it is still "today," so that no one
grows hardened by the deceit of sin. ¹⁴ We have become partners of Christ only if we maintain to the end that confidence
with which we began. ¹⁵ When Scripture says,

"Today, if you should hear his voice,
harden not your hearts as at the revolt,"

¹⁶ who were those that revolted when they heard that voice?
Was it not all whom Moses had led out of Egypt? ¹⁷ With whom
was God angry for forty years? Was it not those who had
sinned, whose corpses fell in the desert? ¹⁸ To whom but to the
disobedient did he swear that they would not enter into his
rest? ¹⁹ We see, moreover, that it was their unbelief that kept
them from entering.

4

¹ Therefore, while the promise of entrance into his rest still

---

7: Nm 14, 21ff.
Ps 95, 8-11.
14: Rom 8, 17.

17: Nm 14, 29.
18: Nm 14, 23; Dt 1, 35.

3, 7—4, 11: The author appeals for steadfastness of faith in Jesus. Citing
the Old Testament warning (Ps 95, 7-11) against hardness of heart, i. e.,
practical disregard of the divine message (7-11), he urges the community
to watchfulness and mutual encouragement (12ff). They are to remember
the example of Israel's revolt in the desert which cost a whole generation
the loss of the promised land (15-19; cf Nm 14, 20-29). The promised land,
designated here under the concept of *rest*, is the author's symbol for final
union with Christ. He concludes his appeal, developing the idea that his
Christian audience is experiencing a test of faith similar to that of Israel
in the desert, and one which could have the same unfortunate results (4,
1-11).

holds, we ought to be fearful of disobeying lest any one of you be judged to have lost his chance of entering. [2] We have indeed heard the good news, as they did. But the word which they heard did not profit them, for they did not receive it in faith. [3] It is we who have believed who enter into that rest, just as God said:

> "Thus I swore in my anger,
> 'They shall never enter into my rest.'"

Yet God's work was finished when he created the world, [4] for in reference to the seventh day Scripture somewhere says, "And God rested from all his work on the seventh day"; [5] and again, in the place we have referred to, God says, "They shall never enter into my rest." [6] Therefore, since it remains for some to enter, and those to whom it was first announced did not because of unbelief, [7] God once more set a day, "today," when long afterward he spoke through David the words we have quoted:

> "Today, if you should hear his voice,
> harden not your hearts."

[8] Now if Joshua had led them into the place of rest, God would not have spoken afterward of another day. [9] Therefore a sabbath rest still remains for the people of God. [10] And he who enters into God's rest, rests from his own work as God did from his. [11] Let us strive to enter into that rest, so that no one may fall, in imitation of the example of Israel's unbelief.

[12] Indeed, God's word is living and effective, sharper than any two-edged sword. It penetrates and divides soul and spirit, joints and marrow; it judges the reflections and thoughts of the heart. [13] Nothing is concealed from him; all lies bare and exposed to the eyes of him to whom we must render an account.

Jesus, Compassionate High Priest

[14] Since, then, we have a great high priest who has passed

4, 3: Ps 95, 11.
4: Gn 2, 2.
7: 3, 7f; Ps 95, 7f.
8: Dt 31, 7.
12: Jos 22, 4; Wis 18, 15f;

Is 49, 2; Eph 6, 17;
Rv 1, 16; 19, 15.
13: Jb 34, 21f; Pss 90, 8;
139, 2f.
14: 9, 11.24.

4, 12-15: The word of God, i. e., the divine message of salvation in Jesus, lays open to God man's real intentions and purposes in this life (v 12) so that there is no escaping the manifestation of his conscience (v 13). But the Christian who holds fast to his faith in Jesus as high priest (v 14; 2, 17) need have no fear even of his own weakness (16), for his appeal is to a high priest who understands the human condition from his own experience of suffering and temptation, sin excepted (v 15).

through the heavens, Jesus, the Son of God, let us hold fast to our profession of faith. [15] For we do not have a high priest who is unable to sympathize with our weakness, but one who was tempted in every way that we are, yet never sinned. [16] So let us confidently approach the throne of grace to receive mercy and favor and to find help in time of need.

5

[1] Every high priest is taken from among men and made their representative before God, to offer gifts and sacrifices for sins. [2] He is able to deal patiently with erring sinners, for he himself is beset by weakness [3] and so must make sin offerings for himself as well as for the people. [4] One does not take this honor on his own initiative, but only when called by God as Aaron was. [5] Even Christ did not glorify himself with the office of high priest; he received it from the One who said to him,

> "You are my son;
>> today I have begotten you";

[6] just as he says in another place,

> "You are a priest forever,
>> according to the order of Melchizedek."

[7] In the days when he was in the flesh, he offered prayers and supplications with loud cries and tears to God, who was able to save him from death, and he was heard because of his reverence. [8] Son though he was, he learned obedience from what he suffered; [9] and when perfected, he became the source of eternal salvation for all who obey him, [10] designated by God as high priest according to the order of Melchizedek.

15: 2, 17f; 5, 7.
16: 10, 19; Eph 3, 12.
5, 3: Lv 9, 7; 16, 17.
4: Ex 28, 1.
5: Ps 2, 7; Jn 8, 54.

6: Ps 110, 4.
7: Mt 26, 38ff.
8: Phil 2, 8.
9: 7, 28.
10: 6, 20.

5, 1-10: The true humanity of Jesus (see note on 2, 5-18) makes him a more rather than a less effective high priest to the Christian community. In Old Testament tradition the high priest was identified with the people, guilty of personal sin just as they were (1ff). Even so, the office was of divine appointment (v 4), as was also the case with the sinless (4. 15) Christ (v 5). For v 6, see note on Ps 110, 4. Although Jesus was Son of God, he was destined as man to learn obedience by accepting the suffering he had to endure (v 8). Because of his perfection through this experience of human suffering he is the cause of salvation for all (v 9), a *high priest according to the order of Melchizedek* (v 10; cf 7, 3).

IV: JESUS' ETERNAL PRIESTHOOD
AND ETERNAL SACRIFICE

Exhortation to Spiritual Renewal

[11] About this we have much to say, and it is difficult to explain, for you have become deaf. [12] Although by this time you should be teaching others, you need to have someone teach you again the basic elements of the oracles of God; you need milk, not solid food. [13] Everyone whose food is milk alone is ignorant of the word that sanctifies, for he is a child. [14] Solid food is for the mature, for those whose faculties are trained by practice to distinguish good from evil.

6

[1] Let us, then, go beyond the initial teaching about Christ and advance to maturity, not laying the foundation all over again: repentance from dead works, faith in God, [2] instruction about baptisms and laying-on of hands, resurrection of the dead, and eternal judgment. [3] And, God permitting, we shall advance!

[4] For when men have once been enlightened and have tasted the heavenly gift and become sharers in the Holy Spirit, [5] when they have tasted the good word of God and the powers of the age to come, [6] and then have fallen away, it is impossible to make them repent again, since they are crucifying the Son of God for themselves and holding him up to contempt. [7] Ground which drinks in the rain falling on it again and again, and brings forth vegetation useful to those for whom it is cultivated, receives the blessing of God. [8] But if it bears thorns and thistles, it is worthless; it is soon cursed, and finally is burned.

[9] Beloved, even though we speak in this way, we are persuaded of better things in your regard, things pointing to your

---

12: 1 Cor 3, 1ff.
6, 1: 9, 14.
4: 10, 26; Mt 12, 45;

2 Pt 2, 20.
6: 1 Jn 5, 16.
8: Gn 3, 17f.

5, 11-14: By way of preparation for his reflections on the priesthood of Christ, in chapter 7, the author deliberately arouses his audience by provocation, observing that they are not really prepared to assimilate advanced theological reflection.
6, 1-8: The author judges that the community's faith will benefit more from profound theological reflection than from a reretition of traditional catechesis (1ff). He will make no effort to address himself to apostates, for their very hostility to the Christian message cuts them off completely from Christ (4-8).
6, 9-20: To balance his criticism of the community (1ff.9), the author expresses his confidence that its members are living truly Christian lives, and that God will justly reward their efforts (v 10). He is concerned especially

salvation. [10] God is not unjust; he will not forget your work and the love you have shown him by your service, past and present, to his holy people. [11] Our desire is that each of you show the same zeal till the end, fully assured of that for which you hope. [12] Do not grow lazy, but imitate those who, through faith and patience, are inheriting the promises.

[13] When God made his promise to Abraham, he swore by himself, having no one greater to swear by, [14] and said, "I will indeed bless you, and multiply you." [15] And so, after patient waiting, Abraham obtained what God had promised. [16] Men swear by someone greater than themselves; an oath gives firmness to a promise and puts an end to all argument. [17] God, wishing to give the heirs of his promise even clearer evidence that his purpose would not change, guaranteed it by oath, [18] so that, by two things that are unchangeable, in which he could not lie, we who have taken refuge in him might be strongly encouraged to seize the hope which is placed before us. [19] Like a sure and firm anchor, that hope extends beyond the veil [20] through which Jesus, our forerunner, has entered on our behalf, being made high priest forever according to the order of Melchizedek.

7

Melchizedek a Type of Christ

[1] This Melchizedek, king of Salem and priest of the Most High God, met Abraham returning from his defeat of the kings and blessed him. [2] And Abraham apportioned to him one tenth of all his booty. His name means "king of justice"; he was also king of Salem, that is, "king of peace." [3] Without father, mother or ancestry, without beginning of days or end of life, like the Son of God he remains a priest forever.

[4] See the greatness of this man to whom Abraham the

11: 3, 14.
12: Gal 3, 14; Eph 1, 13f.
14: Gn 22, 16.
15: Rom 4, 20.
18: Nm 23, 19; 2 Tm 2, 13.

19: 10, 20; Lv 16, 2; Jn 14, 3.
20: 5, 10; Ps 110, 4.
7, 1: Gn 14, 17-20.

---

about their persevering (11f), and cites in this regard the achievement of Abraham, who relied on God's promise and on God's oath (13-18; cf Gn 22, 16). The author proposes to them a firm anchor of Christian hope, the high priesthood of Christ now living with God (19f).

7, 1ff: Recalling the meeting between Melchizedek and Abraham described in Genesis 14, 17-20, the author enhances the significance of this priest by providing the etymological meaning of his name and that of the city over which he ruled (v 2). Since Genesis gives no information on the parentage or the death of Melchizedek, he is seen here as a type of Christ, representing a priesthood that is unique and eternal (v 3).

7, 4-10: The tithe which Abraham gave to Melchizedek (v 4), a practice

patriarch gave one tenth of his booty! [5] The law provides that the priests of the tribe of Levi should receive tithes from the people, their brother Israelites, even though all of them are descendants of Abraham; [6] but Melchizedek, who was not of their ancestry, received tithes of Abraham and blessed him who had received God's promises. [7] It is indisputable that a lesser person is blessed by a greater. [8] And whereas men subject to death receive tithes, Scripture testifies that this man lives on. [9] Levi, who receives tithes, was, so to speak, tithed in the person of his father, [10] for he was still in his father's loins when Melchizedek met Abraham.

[11] If, then, perfection had been achieved through the levitical priesthood (on the basis of which the people received the law), what need would there have been to appoint a priest according to the order of Melchizedek, instead of choosing a priest according to the order of Aaron? [12] When there is a change of priesthood, there is necessarily a change of law. [13] Now he of whom these things are said was of a different tribe, none of whose members ever officiated at the altar. [14] It is clear that our Lord rose from the tribe of Judah, regarding which Moses said nothing about priests. [15] The matter is clearer still if another priest is appointed according to the likeness of Melchizedek: [16] one who has become a priest, not in virtue of a law expressed in a commandment concerning physical descent, but in virtue of the power of a life which cannot be destroyed. [17] Scripture testifies: "You are a priest forever according to the order of Melchizedek."

5: Nm 18, 21.   Mt 1, 1f; 2, 6;
11: Ps 110, 4.   Rom 1, 3; Rv 5, 5.
14: Gn 49, 10; Is 11, 1;   17: Ps 110, 4.

---

later followed by the levitical priesthood (v 5), was a gift (v 6) acknowledging a certain superiority in Melchizedek, the foreign priest (v 7). This is further indicated by the fact that the institution of the levitical priesthood was sustained by hereditary succession in the tribe of Levi, whereas the absence of any mention of Melchizedek's death in Genesis implies that his personal priesthood is permanent (v 8). The levitical priesthood itself, through Abraham, its ancestor, paid tithes to Melchizedek, thus acknowledging the superiority of his priesthood over its own (9f).

7, 11-14: The levitical priesthood was not typified by the priesthood of Melchizedek, for Psalm 110, 4 speaks of a priesthood of a new order, the order of Melchizedek, to arise in messianic times (v 11). Since the levitical priesthood served the Mosaic law, a new priesthood (v 12) would not come into being without a change in the law itself. Thus Jesus was not associated with the Old Testament priesthood, for he was a descendant of the tribe of Judah, which had never exercised the priesthood (13f).

7, 15-19: Jesus does not exercise a priesthood through family lineage but through his immortal existence (15f), fulfilling Psalm 110, 4 (v 17; cf 7, 3). Thus he abolishes forever both the levitical priesthood and the law it serves, because neither could effectively sanctify men (v 18) by leading them into direct communication with God (v 19).

[18] The former commandment has been annulled because of its weakness and uselessness, [19] for the law brought nothing to perfection. But a better hope has supervened, and through it we draw near to God. [20] This has been confirmed by an oath. The priests of the old covenant became priests without an oath, [21] unlike Jesus to whom God said:

"The Lord has sworn, and he will not repent:
    'You are a priest forever, according to the
    order of Melchizedek.' "

[22] Thus has Jesus become the guarantee of a better covenant. [23] Under the old covenant there were many priests because they were prevented by death from remaining in office; [24] but Jesus, because he remains forever, has a priesthood which does not pass away. [25] Therefore he is always able to save those who approach God through him, since he forever lives to make intercession for them.

[26] It was fitting that we should have such a high priest: holy, innocent, undefiled, separated from sinners, higher than the heavens. [27] Unlike the other high priests, he has no need to offer sacrifice day after day, first for his own sins and then for those of the people; he did that once for all when he offered himself. [28] For the law sets up as high priests men who are weak, but the word of the oath which came after the law appoints as priest the Son, made perfect forever.

8

The Heavenly Priesthood of Jesus

[1] The main point in what we are saying is this: we have

18: 10, 1.
21: Ps 110, 4.
25: Rom 8, 34; 1 Jn 2, 1.
27: 5, 3; 9, 12.25-28;

10, 11-14; Lv 16, 6.17;
    Rom 6, 10.
28: 5, 9.

7, 20-25: As was the case with the promise to Abraham (6, 13)—but not with levitical priesthood—the eternal priesthood of the order of Melchizedek was confirmed by God's oath (20f); cf Ps 110, 4. Thus Jesus becomes the guarantee of a permanent covenant (v 22) that does not require a succession of priests as did the levitical priesthood (v 23), because his high priesthood is eternal and unchangeable (v 24). Jesus, therefore, is able to save all who draw near to God through him since he is their ever-living intercessor (v 25).

7, 26-28: Jesus is precisely the high priest whom mankind requires, holy and sinless, installed far above humanity (v 26); one having no need to offer his sacrifice daily for the sins of men, but making a single offering of himself (v 27) once and for all. The law could only appoint high priests with human limitations, but the fulfillment of God's oath regarding the priesthood of Melchizedek (Ps 110, 4) makes the Son of God the perfect priest forever (v 28).

8, 1-5: The Christian community has in Jesus the kind of high priest

such a high priest, who has taken his seat at the right hand of the throne of the Majesty in heaven, [2] minister of the sanctuary and of that true tabernacle set up, not by man, but by the Lord. [3] Now every high priest is appointed to offer gifts and sacrifices; hence the necessity for this one to have something to offer. [4] If he were on earth he would not be a priest, for there are priests already offering the gifts which the law prescribes. [5] They offer worship in a sanctuary which is only a copy and shadow of the heavenly one, for Moses, when about to erect the tabernacle, was warned, "See that you make everything according to the pattern shown you on the mountain." [6] Jesus has obtained a more excellent ministry now, just as he is mediator of a better covenant, founded on better promises.

The Old and the New Covenants

[7] If that first covenant had been faultless, there would have been no place for a second one. [8] But God, finding fault with them, says:

"Days are coming, says the Lord,
　　when I will make a new covenant with the
　　　　house of Israel
　　and with the house of Judah.
[9] It will not be like the covenant I made with
　　　　their fathers
　　the day I took them by the hand
　　to lead them forth from the land of Egypt;
For they broke my covenant
　　and I grew weary of them, says the Lord.
[10] But this is the covenant I will make with the
　　　　house of Israel
　　after those days, says the Lord:

8, 2: Ex 33, 7.　　　　　　　6: 7, 22.
　4: 7, 13.　　　　　　　　　　8: Jer 31, 31-34;
　5: 9, 23; Ex 25, 40;　　　　　　Mt 26, 28.
　　Acts 7, 44; Col 2, 17.　　　10: 10, 16f.

---

described in 7, 26ff. In virtue of his ascension Jesus has taken his place at God's right hand in accordance with Psalm 110, 1 (v 1), where he presides over the heavenly sanctuary established by God himself (v 2). Like every high priest, he has his offering to make (v 3; cf 9, 12.14), but it differs from that of the levitical priesthood in which he had no share (v 4), and which was in any case but a shadowy reflection of the true offering in the heavenly sanctuary (v 5).

8, 6-13: Jesus' ministry in the heavenly sanctuary is that of mediator of a superior covenant which accomplishes what it signifies (v 6). Since the first covenant was deficient in this respect, it had to be replaced (v 7), as Jeremiah (31, 31-34) had prophesied (8-12). Even in the time of Jeremiah, the first covenant was antiquated (v 13).

I will place my laws in their minds
    and I will write them upon their hearts;
I will be their God
    and they shall be my people.
11 And they shall not teach their fellow citizens
    or their brothers, saying, 'Know the Lord,'
    for all shall know me, from least to greatest.
12 I will forgive their evildoing,
    and their sins I will remember no more."

13 When he says, "a new covenant," he declares the first one obsolete. And what has become obsolete and has grown old is close to disappearing.

9

The Worship of the Old Covenant

1 The first covenant had regulations for worship and an earthly sanctuary. 2 For a tabernacle was constructed, the outer one, in which were the lampstand, the table, and the showbread; this was called the holy place. 3 Behind the second veil was the tabernacle called the holy of holies, 4 in which were the golden altar of incense and the ark of the covenant entirely covered with gold. In the ark were the golden jar containing the manna, the rod of Aaron which had blossomed, and the tablets of the covenant. 5 Above the ark were the cherubim of glory overshadowing the place of expiation. We cannot speak now of each of these in detail. 6 These were the arrangements for worship. In performing their service the priests used to go into the outer tabernacle constantly, 7 but only the high priest went into the inner one, and that but once a year, with the blood which he

---

9, 2: Ex 25, 23-30.
3: Ex 26, 31ff.
4: Lv 16, 12f; Ex 16, 33;

25, 10; Nm 17, 2-7.
5: Ex 25, 16-22; 26, 34.
7: Ex 30, 10.

9, 1-14: The regulations for worship under the old covenant permitted all the priests to enter the holy place (2, 6), but only the high priest to enter the holy of holies and then only once a year (3ff.7). The description of the sanctuary and its furnishing is taken essentially from Exodus 25-26. This exclusion of the people from the holy of holies signified that they were not allowed to stand in God's presence (v 8) because their offerings and sacrifices, which were merely symbols of their need of spiritual renewal (v 10), could not obtain forgiveness of their sins (v 9). But Christ, the high priest of the spiritual blessings foreshadowed in the Old Testament sanctuary, has actually entered the true sanctuary of heaven that is not of man's makng (v 11). His place there is permanent, and his offering is his own blood which won man's eternal redemption (v 12). If the sacrifice of animals could bestow legal purification (v 13), how much more effective is the blood of the sinless, divine Christ who spontaneously offered himself to purge man of his sins and to render him fit for the service of God (v 14)!

offered for himself and for the sins of the people. [8] The Holy Spirit was showing thereby that while the first tabernacle was still standing, the way into the sanctuary had not yet been revealed. [9] This is a symbol of the present time, in which gifts and sacrifices are offered that can never make perfect the conscience of the worshiper, [10] but can only cleanse in matters of food and drink and various ritual washings: regulations concerning the flesh, imposed until the time of the new order.

The Sacrifice of Jesus

[11] But when Christ came as high priest of the good things which have come to be, he entered once for all into the sanctuary, passing through the greater and more perfect tabernacle not made by hands, that is, not belonging to this creation. [12] He entered, not with the blood of goats and calves, but with his own blood, and achieved eternal redemption. [13] For if the blood of goats and bulls and the sprinkling of a heifer's ashes can sanctify those who are defiled so that their flesh is cleansed, [14] how much more will the blood of Christ, who through the eternal spirit offered himself up unblemished to God, cleanse our consciences from dead works to worship the living God!

[15] This is why he is mediator of a new covenant: since his death has taken place for deliverance from transgressions committed under the first covenant, those who are called may receive the promised eternal inheritance. [16] Where there is a testament, it is necessary that the death of the testator be confirmed. [17] For a testament comes into force only in the case of death; it has no force while the testator is alive. [18] Hence,

---

10: Col 2, 16.
12: 7, 27; Mt 26, 28.
13: 10, 4; Lv 16, 6.16;
Nm 19, 17-18.

14: 10, 10; Ti 2, 14;
1 Pt 1, 18f; 1 Jn 1, 7;
Rv 1, 5.
15: 1 Tm 2, 5.

9, 15-28: Jesus' role as mediator of the new covenant resulted in his death, which freed men from the sins committed under the Mosaic covenant and made them instead inheritors of the benefits of the new covenant (v 15). This effect of his work follows the human pattern whereby a last will and testament becomes effective only with the death of the testator (16f). The Mosaic covenant was also associated with death, for Moses made use of blood to seal the pact between God and the people (18-21). In Old Testament tradition guilt could normally not be remitted without the use of blood (v 22; cf Lv 17, 11). Since inevitably the blood of animals became a cleansing symbol among Old Testament prefigurements, it was necessary that the realities foreshadowed be brought into being by a shedding of blood that was infinitely more effective by reason of its worth (v 23). Christ did not simply prefigure the heavenly realities (v 24) by performing an annual sacrifice with a blood not his own (v 25), but offered the single sacrifice of himself as the final annulment of sin (v 26). Just as death is the unrepeatable act which ends man's life, so Christ's offering of himself for all men is the unrepeatable sacrifice which has once and for all achieved redemption (27f).

not even the first covenant was inaugurated without blood. [19] When Moses had read all the commandments of the law to the people, he took the blood of goats and calves, together with water and crimson wool and hyssop, and sprinkled the book and all the people, [20] saying, "This is the blood of the covenant which God has enjoined upon you." [21] He also sprinkled the tabernacle and all the vessels of worship with blood. [22] According to the law almost everything is purified by blood, and without the shedding of blood there is no forgiveness.

[23] It was necessary that the copies of the heavenly models be purified in this way, but the heavenly realities themselves called for better sacrifices. [24] For Christ did not enter into a sanctuary made by hands, a mere copy of the true one; he entered heaven itself that he might appear before God now on our behalf. [25] Not that he might offer himself there again and again, as the high priest enters year after year into the sanctuary with blood that is not his own; [26] if that were so, he would have had to suffer death over and over from the creation of the world. But now he has appeared at the end of the ages to take away sins once for all by his sacrifice. [27] Just as it is appointed that men die once, and after death be judged, [28] so Christ was offered up once to take away the sins of many; he will appear a second time not to take away sin but to bring salvation to those who eagerly await him.

10

One Sacrifice instead of Many

[1] Since the law had only a shadow of the good things to come, and no real image of them, it was never able to perfect the worshipers by the same sacrifices offered continually year after year. [2] Were matters otherwise, the priests would have

---

20: Ex 24, 6ff; Mt 26, 28.
22: Lv 17, 11.
24: 1 Jn 2, 1f.
26: 7, 27; Jn 1, 29;

Gal 4, 4.
27: Gn 3, 19.
28: 10, 10; Is 53, 12.
10, 1: 8, 5; Col 2, 17.

10, 1-10: Christian faith now realizes that the Old Testament sacrifices did not effect the spiritual benefits to come, but only prefigured them (v 1). For if the sacrifices actually effected the forgiveness of sin, there would have been no reason for their constant repetition (v 2). They were rather a continual reminder of the people's sins (v 3). It is not reasonable to suppose that human sins could be removed by the blood of animal sacrifices (v 4). Christ, therefore, is here shown to understand his mission in terms of Psalm 40, 6ff, cited according to the Septuagint (5-7). Jesus acknowledged that the Old Testament sacrifices did not remit the sins of the people and so, perceiving the will of God, offered his own body for this purpose (8ff).

stopped offering them, for the worshipers, once cleansed, would have had no sin on their conscience. ³ But through those sacrifices there came only a yearly recalling of sins, ⁴ because it is impossible for the blood of bulls and goats to take sins away. ⁵ Wherefore, on coming into the world, Jesus said:

"Sacrifice and offering you did not desire,
    but a body you have prepared for me;
⁶ Holocausts and sin offerings you took no delight in.
⁷ Then I said, 'As is written of me in the book,
    I have come to do your will, O God.' "

⁸ First he says,

"Sacrifices and offerings, holocausts and sin offerings,
    you neither desired nor delighted in."

(These are offered according to the prescriptions of the law.)
⁹ Then he says,

"I have come to do your will."

In other words, he takes away the first covenant to establish the second.
¹⁰ By this "will," we have been sanctified through the offering of the body of Jesus Christ once for all. ¹¹ Every other priest stands ministering day by day, and offering again and again those same sacrifices which can never take away sins. ¹² But Jesus offered one sacrifice for sins and took his seat forever at the right hand of God; ¹³ now he waits until his enemies are placed beneath his feet. ¹⁴ By one offering he has forever perfected those who are being sanctified. ¹⁵ The Holy Spirit attests this to us, for after saying,

¹⁶ "This is the covenant I will make with them
    after those days, says the Lord:
I will put my laws in their hearts
    and I will write them on their minds,"

3: Lv 16, 21.   9: Mt 26, 38; Jn 6, 38.
4: Mi 6, 6ff.   10: 9, 14.
5: Ps 40, 7f.   12f: Ps 110, 1.
8: 1 Sm 15, 22.   16: 8, 8.10; Jer 31, 33f.

10, 11-18: Whereas the levitical priesthood offered daily sacrifices that were ineffectual in remitting sin (v 11), Jesus offered a single sacrifice which won him a permanent place at God's right hand. There he has only to await the final outcome of his work (12f; cf Ps 110, 1). Thus he has brought into being in his own person the new covenant prophesied by Jeremiah (31, 33f) which has rendered meaningless all other offerings for sin (14-18).

¹⁷ he also says,

> "Their sins and their transgressions
> I will remember no more."

¹⁸ Once these have been forgiven, there is no further offering for sin.

Recalling the Past

¹⁹ Brothers, since the blood of Jesus assures our entrance into the sanctuary ²⁰ by the new and living path he has opened up for us through the veil (the "veil" meaning his flesh), ²¹ and since we have a great priest who is over the house of God, ²² let us draw near in utter sincerity and absolute confidence, our hearts sprinkled clean from the evil which lay on our conscience and our bodies washed in pure water. ²³ Let us hold unswervingly to our profession which gives us hope, for he who made the promise deserves our trust. ²⁴ We must consider how to rouse each other to love and good deeds. ²⁵ We should not absent ourselves from the assembly, as some do, but encourage one another; and this all the more because you see that the Day draws near.

²⁶ If we sin willfully after receiving the truth, there remains for us no further sacrifice for sin—²⁷ only a fearful expectation of judgment and a flaming fire to consume the adversaries of God. ²⁸ Anyone who rejects the law of Moses is put to death without mercy on the testimony of two or three witnesses. ²⁹ Do you not suppose that a much worse punishment is due

---

19: 4, 16.
20: 6, 19f; 9, 8.11f.
22: Ez 36, 25; 1 Pt 3, 21.
26: 6, 4.

27: Zep 1, 18.
28: Dt 17, 6.
29: 6, 6.

10, 19-39: Practical consequences from these reflections on the priesthood and the sacrifice of Christ should make it clear that Christians may now have direct and confident access to God through the person of Jesus (19f), who rules God's house as high priest (v 21). They should approach God with sincerity and faith, in the knowledge that through baptism their sins have been remitted (v 22), reminding themselves of the hope they expressed in Christ at that event (v 23). They are to encourage one another to Christian love and activity (v 24), not refusing, no matter what the reason, to participate in the community's assembly especially in view of the parousia (v 25; cf 1 Thes 4, 13-18). If refusal to participate in the assembly indicates rejection of Christ, no sacrifice exists to obtain forgiveness for so great a sin (v 26); only the dreadful judgment of God remains (v 27). For if violation of the Mosaic law could be punished by death, how much worse will be the punishment of those who have turned their backs on Christ by despising his sacrifice and disregarding the gifts of the Holy Spirit (28f)! Judgment belongs to the Lord, and he enacts it by his living presence (30f). There was a time when the spirit of their community caused them to welcome and share their sufferings (32ff). To revitalize that spirit is to share in the courage of the Old Testament prophets (cf Is 26, 20; Hab 2, 3f), the kind of courage that must distinguish the faith of the Christian (35-39).

the man who disdains the Son of God, thinks the covenant-blood by which he was sanctified to be ordinary, and insults the Spirit of grace? [30] We know who said,

> "Vengeance is mine; I will repay,"

and

> "The Lord will judge his people."

[31] It is a fearful thing to fall into the hands of the living God. [32] Recall the days gone by when, after you had been enlightened, you endured a great contest of suffering. [33] At times you were publicly exposed to insult and trial; at other times you associated yourselves with those who were being so dealt with. [34] You even joined in the sufferings of those who were in prison and joyfully assented to the confiscation of your goods, knowing that you had better and more permanent possessions. [35] Do not, then, surrender your confidence; it will have great reward. [36] You need patience to do God's will and receive what he has promised.

> [37] For, just a brief moment,
>   and he who is to come will come; he will not delay.
> [38] My just man will live by faith,
>   and if he draws back
>   I take no pleasure in him.

[39] We are not among those who draw back and perish, but among those who have faith and live.

V: EXAMPLES, DISCIPLINE, DISOBEDIENCE

11

Faith of the Ancients

[1] Faith is confident assurance concerning what we hope for, and conviction about things we do not see. [2] Because of faith

---

30: Dt 32, 35f; Rom 12, 19.
33: 1 Cor 4, 9.
34: Mt 6, 20.
36: Lk 21, 19.

37: Hb 2, 3.
38: Hb 2, 4; Rom 1, 17.
11, 1: Rom 4, 20; 2 Cor 4, 18.

11, 1-40: This chapter draws upon the people and events of the Old Testament to paint an inspiring portrait of religious faith, firm and unyielding in the face of any obstacles that confront it. In the opinion of some authorities, these pages rank among the most eloquent and lofty to be found in the Bible. They expand the author's theme, broached in 6, 12, to which he now returns (10, 39).

The material of the chapter is consistently developed. Verses 3-7 draw upon the first nine chapters of Genesis; 8-22, upon the period of the patriarchs;

the men of old were approved by God. [3] Through faith we perceive that the worlds were created by the word of God, and that what is visible came into being through the invisible. [4] By faith Abel offered God a sacrifice greater than Cain's. Because of this he was attested to be just, God himself having borne witness to him on account of his gifts; therefore, although Abel is dead, he still speaks. [5] By faith Enoch was taken away without dying, and "he was seen no more because God took him." Scripture testifies that, before he was taken up, he was pleasing to God—[6] but without faith, it is impossible to please him. Anyone who comes to God must believe that he exists, and that he rewards those who seek him. [7] By faith Noah, warned about things not yet seen, revered God and built an ark that his household might be saved. He thereby condemned the world and inherited the justice which comes through faith. [8] By faith Abraham obeyed when he was called, and went forth to the place he was to receive as a heritage; he went forth, moreover, not knowing where he was going. [9] By faith he sojourned in the promised land as in a foreign country, dwelling in tents with Isaac and Jacob, heirs of the same promise; [10] for he was looking forward to the city with foundations, whose designer and maker is God. [11] By faith Sarah received power to conceive though she was past the age, for she thought that the One who had made the promise was worthy of trust. [12] As a result of this faith, there came forth from one man, who was himself as good as dead, descendants as numerous as the stars in the sky and the sands of the seashore.

[13] All of these died in faith. They did not obtain what had been promised but saw and saluted it from afar. By acknowl-

---

3: Gn 1, 3; Jn 1, 3.
4: 12, 24; Gn 4, 4.
5: Gn 5, 24.
7: Gn 6, 8-22; Sir 44, 17; Mt 24, 37ff; 1 Pt 3, 20.
8: Gn 12, 1-4; Sir 44, 19-23; Acts 7, 2-8;

Rom 4, 16-22.
9: Gn 23, 4; 26, 3.
10: 13, 14; Rv 21, 10-22.
11: Gn 17, 19; 21, 2; Rom 4, 19-21.
12: Gn 15, 5; 22, 17; 32, 12; Ex 32, 13.

23-31, upon the time of Moses; 32-38, upon the history of the judges, the prophets and the Maccabean martyrs. The author gives the most extensive description of faith provided in the New Testament, though his interest does not lie in a technical, theological definition. In view of the needs of his audience he describes what authentic faith does, not what it is in itself. Through faith God guarantees the blessings to be hoped for from him, providing evidence in the gift of faith that what he promises will eventually come to pass (v 1). Because they accepted in faith God's guarantee of the future, the biblical personages discussed in 3-38 were themselves commended by God (v 2). Christians have even greater reason to remain firm in faith, since they, unlike the Old Testament men of faith, have perceived the beginning of God's fulfillment of his messianic promises (39f).

edging themselves to be strangers and foreigners on the earth, [14] they showed that they were seeking a homeland. [15] If they had been thinking back to the place from which they had come, they would have had the opportunity of returning there. [16] But they were searching for a better, a heavenly home. Wherefore God is not ashamed to be called their God, for he has prepared a city for them. [17] By faith Abraham, when put to the test, offered up Isaac; he who had received the promises was ready to sacrifice his only son, [18] of whom it was said, "Through Isaac shall your descendants be called." [19] He reasoned that God was able to raise from the dead, and so he received Isaac back as a symbol. [20] By faith Isaac invoked for Jacob and Esau blessings that were still to be.

[21] By faith Jacob, when dying, blessed each of the sons of Joseph, and worshiped God, leaning on the head of his staff. [22] By faith Joseph, near the end of his life, spoke of the Exodus of the Israelites, and gave instructions about his burial. [23] By faith Moses' parents hid him for three months after his birth, thereby disregarding the king's edict, because they saw that he was a beautiful child.

[24] By faith Moses, when he had grown up, refused to be known as the son of Pharaoh's daughter; [25] he wished to be ill-treated along with God's people rather than enjoy the fleeting rewards of sin. [26] Moses considered the reproach borne by God's Anointed greater riches than the treasures of Egypt, for he was looking to the reward. [27] By faith he left Egypt, not fearing the king's wrath, for he persevered as if he were looking on the invisible God. [28] By faith he kept the Passover and sprinkled the lamb's blood, that the destroying angel might not touch the first-born of Israel. [29] By faith the Israelites crossed the Red Sea as if it were dry land, but when the Egyptians attempted the same thing they were drowned. [30] Because of Israel's faith, the walls of Jericho fell after being encircled for seven days. [31] By faith Rahab the harlot escaped from being destroyed with the unbelievers, for she had peacefully received the spies.

14: Ps 39, 13.
16: 13, 14; Ex 3, 6; Phil 3, 20.
17: Gn 22, 1-10; 1 Mc 2, 52; Jas 2, 21.
18: Gn 21, 12; Rom 9, 7.
19: Rom 4, 17-21.
20: Gn 27, 27-40.
21: Gn 48, 15.

22: Gn 50, 23ff.
23: Ex 2, 2; Acts 7, 20.
24: Ex 2, 10-15.
27: Ex 2, 15.
28: Ex 12, 21ff.
29: Ex 14, 21ff.
30: Jos 6, 12-21.
31: Jos 2, 1-21; 6, 22-25; Jas 2, 25.

³² What more shall I recount? I have no time to tell of Gideon, Barak, Samson, Jephthah, of David and Samuel and the prophets, ³³ who by faith conquered kingdoms, did what was just, obtained the promises; they broke the jaws of lions, ³⁴ put out raging fires, escaped the devouring sword; though weak they were made powerful, became strong in battle, and turned back foreign invaders. ³⁵ Women received back their dead through resurrection. Others were tortured and would not receive deliverance, in order to obtain a better resurrection. ³⁶ Still others endured mockery, scourging, even chains and imprisonment. ³⁷ They were stoned, sawed in two, put to death at sword's point; they went about garbed in the skins of sheep or goats, needy, afflicted, tormented. ³⁸ The world was not worthy of them. They wandered about in deserts and on mountains, they dwelt in caves and in holes of the earth. ³⁹ Yet despite the fact that all of these were approved because of their faith, they did not obtain what had been promised. ⁴⁰ God had made a better plan, a plan which included us. Without us, they were not to be made perfect.

12

God's Treatment of His Sons

¹ Therefore, since we for our part are surrounded by this cloud of witnesses, let us lay aside every encumbrance of sin which clings to us and persevere in running the race which lies ahead; ² let us keep our eyes fixed on Jesus, who inspires and perfects our faith. For the sake of the joy which lay before him he endured the cross, heedless of its shame. He has taken his seat at the right of the throne of God. ³ Remember how he endured the opposition of sinners; hence do not grow despondent or abandon the struggle. ⁴ In your fight against sin you have not yet resisted to the point of shedding blood. ⁵ Moreover, you have forgotten the encouraging words addressed to you as sons:

32: Jgs 4, 6; 6, 11; 11, 1.
33: Dn 6, 22.
34: Dn 3, 22-25.
35: 1 Kgs 17, 23;
    2 Mc 6, 18—7, 42.

36: Jer 20, 2; 37, 15.
38: 1 Mc 2, 28ff.
12, 2: 2, 10; Ps 110, 1;
    Phil 2, 6ff.
5: Prv 3, 11f.

12, 1-4: Christian life is to be inspired not only by the Old Testament men of faith (v 1), but above all by Jesus. As the architect of Christian faith, he had himself to endure the cross before receiving the glory of his triumph (v 2). Reflection on his sufferings should give his followers courage to continue the struggle, if necessary even to the shedding of blood (3f).

12, 5-13: Christians should regard their own sufferings as the affectionate correction of the Lord, who loves them as a father loves his children.

"My sons, do not disdain the discipline of the Lord
  nor lose heart when he reproves you;
⁶ For whom the Lord loves, he disciplines;
  he scourges every son he receives."

⁷ Endure your trials as the discipline of God, who deals with you as sons. For what son is there whom his father does not discipline? ⁸ If you do not know the discipline of sons, you are not sons but bastards. ⁹ If we respected our earthly fathers who corrected us, should we not all the more submit to the Father of spirits, and live? ¹⁰ They disciplined us as seemed right to them, to prepare us for the short span of mortal life; but God does so for our true profit, that we may share his holiness. ¹¹ At the time it is administered, all discipline seems a cause for grief and not for joy, but later it brings forth the fruit of peace and justice to those who are trained in its school. ¹² So strengthen your drooping hands and your weak knees. ¹³ Make straight the paths you walk on, that your halting limbs may not be dislocated but healed.

Penalties of Disobedience

¹⁴ Strive for peace with all men, and for that holiness without which no one can see the Lord. ¹⁵ See to it that no man falls away from the grace of God; that no bitter root springs up through which many may become defiled; ¹⁶ that there be among you no fornicator or godless person like Esau, who sold his birthright for a meal. ¹⁷ You know that afterward he wanted to inherit his father's blessing, but he was rejected because he had no opportunity to alter his choice, even though he sought the blessing with tears.

¹⁸ You have not drawn near to an untouchable mountain and a blazing fire, nor gloomy darkness and storm ¹⁹ and

---

7: Prv 13, 24; Sir 30, 1.
12: Is 35, 3.
13: Prv 4, 26.
14: Rom 12, 18.
15: Dt 29, 18.
16: Gn 25, 33.
17: Gn 27, 38.
18: Ex 19, 12.
19: Ex 19, 16.19; 20, 19.

12, 14-17: The example of Esau's conduct should warn the community against apostasy from Christ.

12, 18-29: As a final appeal for adherence to Christian teaching, the two covenants, of Moses and of Christ, are compared. The Mosaic covenant is shown to have orginated in fear of God and threats of divine punishment (18-21). The covenant in Christ gives men direct access to God (v 22), makes them members of the Christian community, God's sons, a sanctified people (v 23) who have Jesus as mediator to speak for them (v 24). Not to heed the voice of the risen Christ is a sin more grave by far than the rejection of the word of Moses (25ff). Though men fall away, God's kingdom in Christ will remain, and his justice will punish those guilty of deserting it (28f).

trumpet blast, nor a voice speaking words such that those who heard begged that they be not addressed to them, [20] for they could not bear to hear the command: "If even an animal touches the mountain, it must be stoned to death." [21] Indeed, so fearful was the spectacle that Moses said, "I am terrified and trembling." [22] No, you have drawn near to Mount Zion and the city of the living God, the heavenly Jerusalem, to myriads of angels in festal gathering, [23] to the assembly of the first-born enrolled in heaven, to God the judge of all, to the spirits of just men made perfect, [24] to Jesus, the mediator of a new covenant, and to the sprinkled blood which speaks more eloquently than that of Abel.

[25] Do not refuse to hear him who speaks. For if the Israelites did not escape punishment when they refused to listen as God spoke to them on earth, how much greater punishment will be ours if we turn away from him who speaks from heaven! [26] His voice then shook the earth, but now he has promised, "I will once more shake not only earth but heaven!" [27] And that "once more" shows that shaken, created things will pass away, so that only what is unshaken may remain. [28] Wherefore, we who are receiving the unshakable kingdom should hold fast to God's grace, through which we may offer worship acceptable to him in reverence and awe. [29] For our God is a consuming fire.

VI: FINAL EXHORTATION, BLESSING, GREETINGS

13

[1] Love your fellow Christians always. [2] Do not neglect to show hospitality, for by that means some have entertained angels without knowing it. [3] Be as mindful of prisoners as if you were sharing their imprisonment, and of the ill-treated

20: Ex 19, 13.
21: Dt 9, 19.
23: Lk 10, 20.
24: 8, 6; Gn 4, 10.
26: Ex 19, 18; Jgs 5, 4f;

Ps 68, 9; Hg 2, 6.
27: Mt 24, 35.
29: Dt 4, 24; Is 33, 14.
13, 2: Gn 18, 3; 19, 2f;
Jgs 6, 11-22; Tb 5, 4.

13, 1-16: After recommendations on social and moral matters (1-6), the letter turns to doctrinal issues. The fact that the original leaders are dead should not cause the recipients of this letter to lose their faith (v 7), for Christ still lives and he remains always the same (v 8). They must not rely for their personal sanctification on regulations concerning foods (v 9), nor should they entertain the notion that Judaism and Christianity can be intermingled (v 10; cf note on Gal 2, 11-14; 15-21). As Jesus died separated from his own people, so must the Christian community remain apart from the religious doctrines of Judaism (11-14). Christ must be the heart and center of the community (15-16).

as of yourselves, for you may yet suffer as they do. [4] Let marriage be honored in every way and the marriage bed be kept undefiled, for God will judge fornicators and adulterers. [5] Do not love money but be content with what you have, for God has said, "I will never desert you, nor will I forsake you." [6] Thus we may say with confidence:

> "The Lord is my helper,
>   I will not be afraid;
> What can man do to me?"

[7] Remember your leaders who spoke the word of God to you; consider how their lives ended, and imitate their faith. [8] Jesus Christ is the same yesterday, today, and forever.

[9] Do not be carried away by all kinds of strange teaching. It is good to have our hearts strengthened by the grace of God and not by foods which are useless to those who take them as a standard for living. [10] We have an altar from which those who serve the tabernacle have no right to eat. [11] The bodies of the animals whose blood is brought into the sanctuary by the high priest as a sin offering are burned outside the camp. [12] Therefore Jesus died outside the gate, to sanctify the people by his own blood. [13] Let us go to him outside the camp, bearing the insult which he bore. [14] For here we have no lasting city; we are seeking one which is to come. [15] Through him let us continually offer God a sacrifice of praise, that is, the fruit of lips which acknowledge his name.

[16] Do not neglect good deeds and generosity; God is pleased by sacrifices of that kind. [17] Obey your leaders and submit to them, for they keep watch over you as men who must render an account. So act that they may fulfill their task with joy, not with sorrow, for that would be harmful to you. [18] Pray for us; we are confident that we have a good conscience, wishing, as we do, to act rightly in every respect. [19] I especially ask your prayers that I may be restored to you very soon.

[20] May the God of peace, who brought up from the dead the

3: Mt 25, 36.
5: Dt 31, 6; Jos 1, 5.
6: Pss 27, 1ff; 118, 6.
9: Rom 14, 17; 1 Cor 8, 8;
    Eph 4, 14.
11: Ex 29, 14; Lv 16, 27.

12: Mt 21, 39; Jn 19, 17.
14: 11, 10.
15: Is 57, 19; Hos 14, 2.
20: Is 63, 11; Zec 9, 11;
    Jn 10, 11; Acts, 2, 24;
    Rom 15, 33.

13, 17ff: Recommending obedience to the leaders of the community, the author observes that he has done his best not to give cause for objection to himself.
13, 20-25: The letter concludes with a prayer (20f): a final request for the

great Shepherd of the sheep by the blood of the eternal covenant, Jesus our Lord, [21] furnish you with all that is good, that you may do his will. Through Jesus Christ may he carry out in you all that is pleasing to him. To Christ be glory forever! Amen.

[22] My brothers, I beg you to bear with this word of encouragement, for I have written to you rather briefly. [23] I must let you know that our brother Timothy has been set free. If he is able to join me soon, he will be with me when I see you. [24] Greetings to all your leaders, and to all the people of God. [25] Grace be with you all.

acceptance of its message (v 22); casual information regarding Timothy; and general greetings (23ff).

THE EPISTLE OF JAMES

INTRODUCTION

The title "catholic" gradually came into use to designate seven New Testament epistles: JAMES; 1, 2 and 3 JOHN; 1 and 2 PETER; and JUDE. It first appears in reference to 1 John in the writings of Apollonius about 197 A.D., and later in reference to all these epistles in the church historian Eusebius (260-340 A.D.). The title supposes the epistles in question to lack specific addressees and therefore to be directed to the whole church. This, however, is not the case for 2 and 3 John. With the exception of 1 Peter and 1 John, the inspired character of these catholic epistles was disputed in the early church, and finally settled in their favor only at the beginning of the fifth century.

The Epistle of James has a general addressee: *To the twelve tribes in the dispersion* (1, 1). Its content, however, affords no evidence that the author wrote to non-Christian Jews outside Palestine. Scholarly opinion concerning addressees is undecided between Judaeo-Christian communities outside Palestine and Christians generally. The author concerns himself entirely with Christian conduct. He writes in the spirit of Old Testament wisdom literature (Proverbs, Sirach, Wisdom) and of the moral teaching of Tobit. He is influenced by the tradition of moral exhortation within Judaism, as is indicated by similarities between his letter and extracanonical Jewish literature, e.g., *The Testament of the Twelve Patriarchs; 1 Enoch; The Manual of Discipline* discovered at Qumran.

Some forty-eight verses in James reveal the influence of sayings of Jesus, especially those in Matthew's Sermon on the Mount. However, except for two allusions to Jesus (1, 1; 2, 1) and one to the parousia (5, 7), the epistle does not relate its moral exhortation to Christology or to the authoritative teaching of Jesus. The force of its teaching is made to rest on the reputation of its author, *James, a servant of God and of the Lord Jesus Christ* (1, 1). The author is a known figure and possesses a standing enabling him to speak with authority.

Of the various personages in the New Testament bearing this name, the James mentioned by Paul in Galatians 2, 9 as one of the pillars of the church in Palestine well meets the requirements for the authorship of this epistle. He is designated by Paul, not as one of the Twelve, but as *the brother of the Lord* (Gal 1, 19). The risen Christ made a significant appearance to him (1 Cor 15, 7). James was the administrator of the Jerusalem community (Acts 12, 17), and for this reason played a leading role in the apostolic Council (Acts 15, 13-21). He was the adviser of Paul on the latter's arrival in Jerusalem after the third missionary journey (Acts 21, 17-25). He is probably to be identified as one of the relatives of Jesus who did not believe in him during the ministry; cf Mk 6, 13; Jn 7, 2-5.

Though not all scholars are satisfied that James, leader of the Jerusalem community, is the author, it must be conceded that the epistle is datable before 62 A.D., when, according to Josephus, James was executed in Jerusalem. Nevertheless, scholars who do not admit James of

Jerusalem as the author of the epistle select a date for it toward the end of the first century.

The Epistle of James has acquired special prominence in Christendom because of Martin Luther's claim that its emphasis on good works does not agree with St. Paul's doctrine of justification by faith, and because the Council of Trent declared that James 5, 14f pertains to the promulgation of the sacrament of the Anointing of the Sick.

THE EPISTLE OF JAMES

1

¹ To the twelve tribes in the dispersion, James a servant of God and of the Lord Jesus Christ, sends greeting.

Endurance

² My brothers, count it pure joy when you are involved in every sort of trial. ³ Realize that when your faith is tested this makes for endurance. ⁴ Let endurance come to its perfection so that you may be fully mature and lacking in nothing.

Prayer for Wisdom

⁵ If any of you is without wisdom, let him ask it from the God who gives generously and ungrudgingly to all, and it will be given him. ⁶ Yet he must ask in faith, never doubting, for the doubter is like the surf tossed and driven by the wind. ⁸ A man of this sort, devious and erratic in all that he does, ⁷ must not expect to receive anything from the Lord.

Humility

⁹ Let the brother in humble circumstances take pride in his eminence ¹⁰ and the rich man be proud of his lowliness, for he will disappear "like the flower of the field." ¹¹ When the sun comes up with its scorching heat it parches the meadow, the field flowers droop, and with that the meadow's loveliness is gone. Just so will the rich man wither away amid his many projects.

Temptation

¹² Happy the man who holds out to the end through trial!

1, 1: Acts 26, 7; Jn 7, 35.
2: Rom 5, 3ff; 1 Pt 1, 6; 4, 13f.
5: Prv 2, 3-6; Wis 8, 21.
6: Mt 21, 21; Mk 11, 24.

9: 2, 5.
10: Is 40, 6ff.
12: Wis 5, 15f; 1 Cor 9, 25; 2 Tm 4, 8; 1 Pt 5, 4; Rv 2, 10.

1, 1: *James, a servant of God and of the Lord Jesus Christ:* a declaration of authority for instructing the Christian communities; cf Rom 1, 1. Regarding the identity of the author, see the Introduction.

1, 2: *Count it pure joy . . . every sort of trial:* a frequent teaching of the New Testament derived from the words and sufferings of Christ (Mt 5, 10ff; Jn 10, 11; 15, 12f; Acts 5, 41).

1, 3-8: The gradation of testing, endurance, and perfection indicates the manner of achieving spiritual maturity and full preparedness for the coming of Christ (3f; cf Rom 5, 3ff; 1 Pt 1, 6f). To sustain trials, to achieve endurance and perfection, require wisdom which God readily grants to believing petitioners but withholds from those who doubt (5-8; cf Sir 4, 7).

1, 9ff: From the religious standpoint, the lot of the poor and the lowly as opposed to that of the proud rich is, here and elsewhere in the epistle, found to have value in inverse ratio to circumstance (2, 5.13; 4, 10.13-16; 5, 1-6).

1, 12: *The crown of life:* the ultimate and eternal reward for fidelity and

Once he has been proved, he will receive the crown of life the Lord has promised to those who love him. [13] No one who is tempted is free to say, "I am being tempted by God." Surely God, who is beyond the grasp of evil, tempts no one. [14] Rather, the tug and lure of his own passion tempt every man. [15] Once passion has conceived, it gives birth to sin, and when sin reaches maturity it begets death.

Response to God's Gift

[16] Make no mistake about this, my dear brothers. [17] Every worthwhile gift, every genuine benefit comes from above, descending from the Father of the heavenly luminaries, who cannot change and who is never shadowed over. [18] He wills to bring us to birth with a word spoken in truth so that we may be a kind of first fruits of his creatures. [19] Keep this in mind, dear brothers.

Let every man be quick to hear, slow to speak, slow to anger; [20] for a man's anger does not fulfill God's justice. [21] Strip away all that is filthy, every vicious excess. Humbly welcome the word that has taken root in you, with its power to save you. [22] Act on this word. If all you do is listen to it, you are deceiving yourselves.

[23] A man who listens to God's word but does not put it into practice is like a man who looks into a mirror at the face he was born with; [24] he looks at himself, then goes off and promptly forgets what he looked like. [25] There is, on the other hand, the man who peers into freedom's ideal law and abides by it. He is no forgetful listener, but one who carries out the law in practice. Blest will this man be in whatever he does.

13: Sir 15, 11-20;
  1 Cor 10, 13.
17: 1 Jn 1, 5.
18: 1 Pt 1, 23; 1 Jn 1, 12f.
19: Prv 14, 17; Sir 5, 13.

20: Eph 4, 26.
21: Col 3, 8.
22: Mt 7, 24-27; Rom 2, 13.
25: Ps 19, 8; Jn 13, 17.

---

perseverance in following the law of Christ; cf Rom 8, 28; 2 Tm 4, 8; 1 Pt 5, 4: Rv 2, 10.
1, 13ff: It is contrary to the nature of God for him to be the author of man's temptation (v 13). In the genesis of sin, man is first beguiled by passion (v 14), then gives his consent, which in turn begets the act of sin. As sin grows, it incurs the ultimate penalty of death (v 15).
1, 18: *He wills to bring us to birth . . . truth:* acceptance of the gospel message constitutes a new birth and makes the recipient the first fruits of a new creation: cf Jn 3, 5f: Rom 8, 23.
1, 19-25: To *be quick to hear* the gospel is to accept it readily and to act in conformity with it, removing from one's soul whatever opposes it so that it may take root and effect salvation (19-22). To listen to and not practice the gospel message is to misunderstand religion (23f). Only conformity of life to the ideal law of true freedom brings happiness (v 25).

²⁶ If a man who does not control his tongue imagines that he is devout, he is self-deceived; his worship is pointless. ²⁷ Looking after orphans and widows in their distress and keeping oneself unspotted by the world make for pure worship without stain before our God and Father.

2

Against Favoritism

¹ My brothers, your faith in our glorious Lord Jesus Christ must not allow of favoritism. ² Suppose there should come into your assembly a man fashionably dressed, with gold rings on his fingers, and at the same time a poor man in shabby clothes. ³ Suppose further that you were to take notice of the well-dressed man and say, "Sit right here, please," whereas you were to say to the poor man, "You can stand!" or "Sit over there by my footrest." ⁴ Have you not in a case like this discriminated in your hearts? Have you not set yourselves up as judges handing down corrupt decisions?

⁵ Listen, dear brothers. Did not God choose those who are poor in the eyes of the world to be rich in faith and heirs of the kingdom he promised to those who love him? ⁶ Yet you treated the poor man shamefully. Are not the rich exploiting you? They are the ones who hale you into the courts ⁷ and who blaspheme that noble name which has made you God's own.

⁸ You are acting rightly, however, if you fulfill the law of the kingdom. Scripture has it, "You shall love your neighbor as yourself." ⁹ But if you show favoritism, you commit sin and are convicted by the law as transgressors. ¹⁰ Whoever falls into sin on one point of the law, even though he keeps the entire remainder, has become guilty on all counts. ¹¹ For he who said,

26: 3, 2f; Ps 33, 14.
27: Ex 22, 21.
2, 5: 1, 12; 1 Cor 1, 26-29; Rv 2, 9.
7: 1 Pt 4, 14.

8: Lv 19, 18; Mt 22, 39; Rom 13, 9.
9: Dt 1, 17.
10: Mt 5, 19; Gal 3, 10.
11: Ex 20, 13f; Dt 5, 17f.

1, 26: For control of the tongue, see note on 3, 1-12.
1, 27: *Orphans and widows:* the defenseless and oppressed; cf Acts 6, 1ff.
2, 1-13: In the Christian community there must be no discrimination against the poor, or favoritism toward the rich based on a mistaken exaltation of status or wealth (2ff); cf Mt 23, 6. Divine favor rather consists in God's promises, his election, and his rewards elicited by man's faith and response to his love (v 5); cf Mt 5, 3; 11, 5; 1 Cor 1, 17-29. The impious rich who oppress the poor dishonor the name of Christ. By violating the law of love of neighbor, they offend against the whole law (6f.9ff). On the other hand, abiding consciousness of the final judgment helps the faithful to fulfill the whole law (v 12).

"You shall not commit adultery," also said, "You shall not kill." If therefore you do not commit adultery but do commit murder, you have become a transgressor of the law.

¹² Always speak and act as men destined for judgment under the law of freedom. ¹³ Merciless is the judgment on the man who has not shown mercy; but mercy triumphs over judgment.

Faith and Good Works

¹⁴ My brothers, what good is it to profess faith without practicing it? Such faith has no power to save one, has it? ¹⁵ If a brother or sister has nothing to wear and no food for the day, ¹⁶ and you say to them, "Goodbye and good luck! Keep warm and well fed," but do not meet their bodily needs, what good is that? ¹⁷ So it is with the faith that does nothing in practice. It is thoroughly lifeless.

¹⁸ To such a person one might say, "You have faith and I have works—is that it?" Show me your faith without works, and I will show you the faith that underlies my works! ¹⁹ Do you believe that God is one? You are quite right. The demons believe that, and shudder. ²⁰ Do you want proof, you ignoramus, that without works faith is idle? ²¹ Was not our father Abraham justified by his works when he offered his son Isaac on the altar? ²² There you see proof that faith was both assisting his works and implemented by his works. ²³ You also see how the Scripture was fulfilled which says, "Abraham believed God, and it was credited to him as justice"; for this he received the title "God's friend."

²⁴ You must perceive that a person is justified by his works and not by faith alone. ²⁵ Rahab the harlot will illustrate the point. Was she not justified by her works when she harbored the messengers and sent them out by a different route? ²⁶ Be assured, then, that faith without works is as dead as a body without breath.

12: 1, 25.
13: Mt 5, 7; 6, 14f;
    18, 29-34.
14: Gal 5, 6.
15: Mt 25, 41-44.
16: 1 Jn 3, 17.

21: Gn 22, 9-12; Rom 4, 1;
    Heb 11, 17.
23: Gn 15, 6; Rom 4, 3;
    Gal 3, 6.
25: Jos 2, 4-16; 6, 17;
    Heb 11, 31.

2, 14-26: The theme of these verses is the relationship of faith and good works. Neither can merit salvation without the other, as even the demons, who believe that God exists (v 19), can testify (14-20). The faith that justified Abraham was accompanied by his willingness, at the divine behest, to sacrifice his son Isaac (21ff). A living faith works through love, as opposed to a dead faith that lacks good works (24.26).

3

Restraining the Tongue

[1] Not many of you should become teachers, my brothers; you should realize that those of us who do so will be called to the stricter account. [2] All of us fall short in many respects. If a person is without fault in speech he is a man in the fullest sense, because he can control his entire body. [3] When we put bits into the mouths of horses to make them obey us, we guide the rest of their bodies. [4] It is the same with ships: however large they are, and despite the fact that they are driven by fierce winds, they are directed by very small rudders on whatever course the steersman's impulse may select. [5] The tongue is something like that. It is a small member, yet it makes great pretensions.

See how tiny the spark is that sets a huge forest ablaze! [6] The tongue is such a flame. It exists among our members as a whole universe of malice. The tongue defiles the entire body. Its flames encircle our course from birth, and its fire is kindled by hell. [7] Every form of life, four-footed or winged, crawling or swimming, can be tamed, and has been tamed, by mankind; [8] the tongue no man can tame. It is a restless evil, full of deadly poison. [9] We use it to say, "Praised be the Lord and Father"; then we use it to curse men, though they are made in the likeness of God. [10] Blessing and curse come out of the same mouth. This ought not to be, my brothers! [11] Does a spring gush forth fresh water and foul from the same outlet? [12] A fig tree, brothers, cannot produce olives, or a grapevine figs; no more can a brackish source yield fresh water.

True Wisdom

[13] If one of you is wise and understanding, let him show this in practice through a humility filled with good sense. [14] Should

---

3, 2: 1, 26; Prv 10, 19;
　　　13, 3; Sir 14, 1;
　　　28, 13-26.
6: Prv 26, 18ff.

8: Ps 140, 4.
12: Mt 7, 16ff.
13: Eph 4, 1f.

3, 1-12: The use and abuse of the important role of teaching in the church are here (v 1) related to the good or bad use of the tongue (9-12), the instrument through which teaching was chiefly conveyed; cf Sir 5, 13—6, 1; 28, 12-26. The bit and the rudder are figures of the tongue's control (2ff), just as the spark and destroying flames portray the evils of unbridled speech. The tongue is *a whole universe of malice*, a defiler of the body (v 6), *a restless evil, full of deadly poison* (5-8).
3, 13-18: This discussion on true wisdom is related to the previous reflection on the role of the teacher as one who is in control of his speech.

you instead nurse bitter jealousy and selfish ambition in your hearts, at least refrain from arrogant and false claims against the truth. [15] Wisdom like this does not come from above. It is earthbound, a kind of animal, even devilish, cunning. [16] Where there are jealousy and strife, there also are inconstancy and all kinds of vile behavior. [17] Wisdom from above, by contrast, is first of all innocent. It is also peaceable, lenient, docile, rich in sympathy and the kindly deeds that are its fruits, impartial and sincere. [18] The harvest of justice is sown in peace for those who cultivate peace.

4

Worldly Desires

[1] Where do the conflicts and disputes among you originate? Is it not your inner cravings that make war within your members? [2] What you desire you do not obtain, and so you resort to murder. You envy and you cannot acquire, so you quarrel and fight. You do not obtain because you do not ask. [3] You ask and you do not receive because you ask wrongly, with a view to squandering what you receive on your pleasures. [4] O you unfaithful ones, are you not aware that love of the world is enmity to God? A man is marked out as God's enemy if he chooses to be the world's friend. [5] Do you suppose it is to no purpose that Scripture says, "The spirit he has implanted in us tends toward jealousy"? [6] Yet he bestows a greater gift, for the sake of which it is written,

"God resists the proud
but bestows his favor on the lowly."

[7] Therefore submit to God; resist the devil and he will take

---

15: 1, 5.17.
17: Wis 7, 22.
18: Mt 5, 9.
4, 1: Rom 7, 23.
   3: Mt 6, 5-13; Rom 8, 26.

4: Mt 6, 24; 1 Jn 2, 15ff.
6: Jb 22, 29; Prv 3, 34;
   Mt 23, 12; 1 Pt 5, 5.
7: Eph 6, 12; 1 Pt 5, 8f.

The qualities of the wise man endowed from above (17f) are: innocence, peace, docility, sincerity, impartiality, sympathy and kindly deeds (cf Gal 5, 22f): all this in contrast to earthbound wisdom with its cunning, jealousy, strife, inconstancy, arrogance and endless variety of vile behavior (14ff); cf 2 Cor 12, 20.

4, 1-12: The concern here is with the origin of conflicts in the Christian community. These are occasioned by misuse of the tongue (cf 3, 2-16), and false wisdom shown by *love of the world* which *is enmity to God* (v 4). Further, the conflicts are bound up with failure to pray properly (cf Mt 7, 7-11; Jn 6, 33)—that is, not petitioning God at all or using his kindness only for the petitioner's pleasure (2f). In contrast, the proper dispositions are submission to God, repentance, humility, and resistance to evil (7-10).

flight. **8** Draw close to God, and he will draw close to you. Cleanse your hands, you sinners; purify your hearts, you backsliders. **9** Begin to lament, to mourn, and to weep; let your laughter be turned into mourning and your joy into sorrow. **10** Be humbled in the sight of the Lord and he will raise you on high.

Judging One's Fellows

11 Do not, my brothers, speak ill of one another. The one who speaks ill of his brother or judges his brother is speaking against the law. It is the law he judges. If, however, you judge the law you are no observer of the law, you are its judge. **12** There is but one Lawgiver and Judge, one who can save and destroy. Who then are you to judge your neighbor?

Against Presumption

13 Come now, you who say, "Today or tomorrow we shall go to such and such a town, spend a year there, trade, and come off with a profit!" **14** You have no idea what kind of life will be yours tomorrow. You are a vapor that appears briefly and vanishes. **15** Instead of saying, "If the Lord wills it, we shall live to do this or that," **16** all you can do is make arrogant and pretentious claims. All such boasting is reprehensible. **17** When a man knows the right thing to do and does not do it, he sins.

5

Warning to the Rich

1 As for you, you rich, weep and wail over your impending miseries. **2** Your wealth has rotted, your fine wardrobe has grown motheaten, **3** your gold and silver have corroded, and their corrosion shall be a testimony against you; it will devour your

---

8: Is 1, 16; Zec 1, 13.
10: Mt 23, 12; Lk 14, 11; 18, 14; 1 Pt 5, 6.
12: Mt 7, 1; Rom 2, 1.
13: Prv 27, 1; Lk 12, 19f.

14: Ps 39, 6f.
17: Lk 12, 47.
5, 1: Lk 6, 24.
2: Sir 29, 10ff; Mt 6, 19.
3: Prv 11, 4.28.

4, 13-17: The uncertainty of life (v 14), its complete dependence on God, the necessity of submitting to his will (v 15), all help man to know and to do *the right* (v 17). To disregard this standard is to live arrogantly and presumptuously (v 16), i. e., without God. This is sin (v 17).

5, 1-6: Continuing with the theme of the transitory character of life on earth, the epistle traces the impending ruin of the godless. It denounces the unjust rich, whose victims cry to heaven for judgment on their exploiters (4ff). The decay and corrosion of the costly garments and metals, which here signalize *wealth,* prove them worthless and portend the destruction of their possessors (2f).

flesh like a fire. See what you have stored up for yourselves against the last days. ⁴ Here, crying aloud, are the wages you withheld from the farmhands who harvested your fields. The cries of the harvesters have reached the ears of the Lord of hosts. ⁵ You lived in wanton luxury on the earth; you fattened yourselves for the day of slaughter. ⁶ You condemned, even killed, the just man; he does not resist you.

Patience

⁷ Be patient, therefore, my brothers, until the coming of the Lord. See how the farmer awaits the precious yield of the soil. He looks forward to it patiently while the soil receives the winter and the spring rains. ⁸ You, too, must be patient. Steady your hearts, because the coming of the Lord is at hand. ⁹ Do not grumble against one another, my brothers, lest you be condemned. See! The judge stands at the gate. ¹⁰ As your models in suffering hardship and in patience, brothers, take the prophets who spoke in the name of the Lord. ¹¹ Those who have endured we call blessed. You have heard of the steadfastness of Job, and have seen what the Lord, who is compassionate and merciful, did in the end.

¹² Above all else, my brothers, you must not swear an oath, any at all, either "by heaven" or "by earth." Rather, let it be "yes" if you mean yes and "no" if you mean no. In this way you will not incur condemnation.

Anointing and Prayer

¹³ If anyone among you is suffering hardship, he must pray.

4: Ex 22, 22; Lv 19, 13;
   Dt 24, 14f; Mal 3, 5.
5: Lk 16, 19.25.
6: Wis 2, 10-20.
7: Dt 11, 14; Lk 21, 19;

Heb 10, 36.
10: Mt 5, 12.
11: Jb 1, 21f; Ps 103, 8.
12: Mt 5, 34ff.

5, 7-11: Those oppressed by the unjust rich are reminded of the need for patience, both in bearing the sufferings of human life (v 9) and in their expectation of the coming of the Lord. It is then that they will receive their reward (7f.10f; cf Heb 10, 25; 1 Jn 2, 18).

5, 12: This is a threat of condemnation for the abuse of an oath; cf Mt 5, 33-37. *By heaven* and *by earth* were substitutes for the original form of an oath, to circumvent its binding force, and to avoid pronouncing the holy name of Yahweh; cf Ex 22, 10.

5, 14: *Is there anyone sick . . . Lord:* in case of the serious, even if not extreme, illness of a member of the community, *he should ask for the presbyters,* i. e., those who have authority in the church (Acts 15, 2.22f; 1 Tm 5, 17; Ti 1, 5). *They . . . are to pray over him* (cf Sir 38, 9), *anointing him with oil:* oil was used for medicinal purposes in Oriental medicine (cf Is 1, 6; Lk 10, 34). In Mark 6, 13 it is also the medium through which miraculous healing is effected *in the Name* [*of the Lord*], i. e., by the power of Jesus Christ.

If a person is in good spirits, he should sing a hymn of praise. [14] Is there anyone sick among you? He should ask for the presbyters of the church. They in turn are to pray over him, anointing him with oil in the Name [of the Lord]. [15] This prayer uttered in faith will reclaim the one who is ill, and the Lord will restore him to health. If he has committed any sins, forgiveness will be his. [16] Hence, declare your sins to one another, and pray for one another, that you may find healing.

The fervent petition of a holy man is powerful indeed. [17] Elijah was only a man like us, yet he prayed earnestly that it would not rain and no rain fell on the land for three years and six months. [18] When he prayed again, the sky burst forth with rain and the land produced its crop.

[19] My brothers, the case may arise among you of someone straying from the truth, and of another bringing him back. [20] Remember this: the person who brings a sinner back from his way will save his soul from death and cancel a multitude of sins.

14: Mk 6, 13.   18: 1 Kgs 18, 42.
16: Prv 28, 13.   19: Mt 18, 15; Gal 6, 1.
17: 1 Kgs 17, 1; Lk 4, 25.   20: Prv 10, 12.

5, 15: *This prayer uttered in faith . . . to health:* though other passages in James speak of saving or salvation in reference to the soul (1, 21; 2, 14; 4, 12; 5, 20), here the reference is to bodily health: *the Lord will restore him to health,* literally "raise him up" (Mk 1, 31; 9, 27). *If he has committed any sins, forgiveness will be his:* in the public ministry of Jesus, bodily cures and forgiveness of sins are often closely related (Mt 9, 1-8; Mk 2, 1-12; Jn 5, 14). The Council of Trent (Sess. 14) declared the Anointing of the Sick to be a sacrament "instituted by Christ our Lord and promulgated by blessed James the apostle."

5, 16ff: *Declare . . . sins:* as a sign of repentance (cf Lv 5, 5; Ps 31, 5; Ezr 9, 6-15; Mt 3, 6; Acts 19, 18); *to one another:* probably in connection with liturgical prayer to make the public confession more efficacious, as witness the *Didache. Pray for one another:* cf Col 3, 4; 1 Thes 5, 25; Heb 13, 18.

5, 19f: This passage is reminiscent of the parable of the Good Shepherd (Lk 15, 3-7).

5, 20: *Will save his soul from death:* the soul of the sinner will be saved from eternal condemnation.

THE FIRST EPISTLE OF PETER

INTRODUCTION

There is abundant evidence in this epistle that *scattered strangers* in 1, 1 refers to Gentile Christian communities (1, 14.18; 2, 9f; 4, 3f; cf Introduction to James). They are envisioned as the new people of God, aliens in the pagan world. The place-names in 1, 1 indicate that the epistle was intended for Christian communities in Asia Minor, but it is uncertain whether those founded by Paul are also included.

Early Christian tradition, starting with Irenaeus at the beginning of the third century, unhesitatingly ascribed the epistle to Peter. Since the early nineteenth century, however, many scholars have considered it a pseudonymous work. Those who defend its Petrine authorship hold that certain data in the epistle favor the traditional view: its allusions to the sufferings of Jesus (2, 21-24; 3, 18; 4, 1); its recollections of his sayings (1, 6-12; Jn 1, 10f; 16, 20; Mt 5, 10; 13, 17); and its relationship to the kerygmatic speeches attributed to Peter in Acts (1, 16-22; 2, 14-36; 3, 12-26; 4, 8-12). Such evidence, though valuable, is not conclusive for Petrine authorship since other Christians of the first century familiar with the church's teachings could have been responsible for these formulations. For those who believe Peter wrote the epistle, it must be dated before 64-67 A.D., the period within which his execution under Nero took place. Those who regard it as pseudonymous work date it at 90-95 A.D. It is generally conceded that its place of composition was Rome—the *Babylon* referred to in 5, 13.

Unlike the Epistle of James, this letter presents the moral exhortation which is its dominant feature in close relationship to Christian doctrine: the Trinity of persons in God (1, 2f.12; 4, 14); the redemptive value of Jesus' death and resurrection (1, 3; 3, 21f); the sinfulness of man (1, 18; 2, 24), whom God destined to be holy (1, 15f). Some scholars are of the opinion that 1 Peter 1, 3—2, 10 is taken substantially from an early Christian baptismal liturgy. Whether this view is correct or not, the passages in question are among the clearest expositions on the meaning of Christian baptism to be found in the New Testament.

THE FIRST EPISTLE OF PETER

1

Greeting

¹ Peter, an apostle of Jesus Christ, to those who live as strangers scattered throughout Pontus, Galatia, Cappadocia, Asia, and Bithynia; to men chosen ² according to the foreknowledge of God the Father, consecrated by the Spirit to a life of obedience to Jesus Christ and purification with his blood. Favor and peace be yours in abundance.

Thanksgiving

³ Praised be the God and Father
of our Lord Jesus Christ,
he who in his great mercy
gave us new birth;
a birth unto hope which draws its life
from the resurrection of Jesus Christ from the dead;
⁴ a birth to an imperishable inheritance,
incapable of fading or defilement,
which is kept in heaven for you
⁵ who are guarded with God's power through faith;
a birth to a salvation which stands ready
to be revealed in the last days.

⁶ There is cause for rejoicing here. You may for a time have to suffer the distress of many trials; ⁷ but this is so that your faith, which is more precious than the passing splendor of fire-tried gold, may by its genuineness lead to praise, glory, and honor when Jesus Christ appears. ⁸ Although you have

---

1, 1: Jas 1, 1.
    2: Rom 8, 29.
    3: Jn 3, 5; 1 Jn 2, 29.
    4: Mt 6, 19f; Col 1, 5.

6: Jas 1, 2f.
7: Prv 17, 3; 1 Cor 3, 13.
8: 2 Cor 5, 7.

1, 1f: The introductory formula names Peter as the writer (see Introduction). He is Simon, son of John (Mt 16, 18; Jn 21, 15ff), whom Christ called Cephas, meaning Peter, "rock" (Jn 1, 42): an apostle (Mt 10, 2) and fellow elder (1 Pt 5, 1). In his office of apostle he addresses himself to the Gentile converts of Asia Minor. Their privileged status of a *chosen, consecrated,* and purified people makes them worthy of God's peace and favor. In contrast is their actual existence as pilgrims and strangers, scattered among pagans, far from their true country.
1, 3ff: A prayer of praise and thanksgiving to God who bestows the gift of new life and hope that derive from the resurrection of his Son. It contains the promise, not of an earthly land, but of *an imperishable inheritance . . . in heaven,* for those *guarded with God's power through faith,* and it is *to be revealed in the last days.*
1, 6-9: As the glory of Christ's resurrection was preceded by his sufferings and death, the new life of faith which it bestows is to be subjected to *many trials* (v 6) while achieving its goal: the glory of the fullness of salvation (v 9) at the coming of Christ (v 8).

never seen him, you love him, and without seeing you now believe in him, and rejoice with inexpressible joy touched with
glory [9] because you are achieving faith's goal, your salvation.
[10] This is the salvation which the prophets carefully searched
out and examined. They prophesied the divine favor that was
destined to be yours. [11] They investigated the times and the
circumstances which the Spirit of Christ within them was pointing to, for he predicted the sufferings destined for Christ and
the glories that would follow. [12] They knew by revelation that
they were providing, not for themselves but for you, what has
now been proclaimed to you by those who preach the gospel
to you, in the power of the Holy Spirit sent from heaven. Into
these matters angels long to search.

Filial Obedience and Fear

[13] So gird the loins of your understanding; live soberly; set
all your hope on the gift to be conferred on you when Jesus
Christ appears. [14] As obedient sons, do not yield to the desires
that once shaped you in your ignorance. [15] Rather, become holy
yourselves in every aspect of your conduct, after the likeness
of the holy One who called you; [16] remember, Scripture says,
"Be holy, for I am holy." [17] In prayer you call upon a Father
who judges each one justly on the basis of his actions. Since
this is so, conduct yourselves reverently during your sojourn in
a strange land. [18] Realize that you were delivered from the
futile way of life your fathers handed on to you, not by any
diminishable sum of silver or gold, [19] but by Christ's blood

---

11: Is 52, 13, 53, 12.   Rom 2, 11.
15: Mt 5, 48; 1 Jn 3, 3.
16: Lv 19, 2.   18: Is 52, 3; 1 Cor 6, 20.
17: Dt 10, 17; Mal 1, 6;   19: Jn 1, 29; Heb 9, 14.

1, 10ff: *The Spirit of Christ* (v 11) is here shown to have been present
in both the prophets and the apostles: in the prophets moving them to
search out, examine, investigate, and predict the divine favor of salvation
that was to come (v 10); in the apostles impelling them to preach the
fulfillment of salvation in the mystery of Christ's sufferings and glory
(v 12).

1, 13-25: These verses are concerned with the call of God's people to
holiness and to fraternal love by reason of their relationship with him, a
covenant sealed with the blood of his Son.

1, 13: *Gird the loins of your understanding:* a figure reminiscent of the
rite of Passover when the Israelites were in flight from their oppressors
(Ex 12, 11), and suggesting also the vigilance of the Christian people in expectation of the second coming of Christ (Lk 12, 35f).

1, 14-17: The *ignorance* here referred to (v 14) was their former lack
of knowledge of God, leading inevitably to godless conduct; holiness (15f),
on the contrary, is the result of their call to the knowledge and love of
God as the *Father who judges each one justly* (v 17).

1, 18f: The deliverance or ransom of Israel foretold by Isaiah (52, 3) is
here fulfilled in behalf of the Christian people at the cost of the blood
(i. e., the life) of the spotless lamb (Is 53, 7.10; Rom 3, 24f; 1 Cor 6, 20;
cf Ex 12, 5).

beyond all price: the blood of a spotless, unblemished lamb
[20] chosen before the world's foundation and revealed for your
sake in these last days. [21] It is through him that you are believers in God, the God who raised him from the dead and
gave him glory. Your faith and hope, then, are centered in God.

Brotherly Love

[22] By obedience to the truth you have purified yourselves for
a genuine love of your brothers; therefore, love one another
constantly from the heart. [23] Your rebirth has come, not from
a destructible but from an indestructible seed, through the
living and enduring word of God.
[24] For,

> "All mankind is grass
>   and the glory of men is like the flower of the field.
> The grass withers, the flowers wilts,
>   but the word of the Lord endures forever."

[25] Now this "word" is the gospel which was preached to you.

2

Growth in Holiness

[1] So strip away everything vicious, everything deceitful; pre-
tenses, jealousies, and disparaging remarks of any kind. [2] Be
as eager for milk as newborn babies—pure milk of the spirit
to make you grow unto salvation, [3] now that you have tasted
that the Lord is good.

[4] Come to him, a living stone, rejected by men but approved,
nonetheless, and precious in God's eyes. [5] You too are living

---

22: Rom 12, 9.
23: 1 Jn 3, 9.
24: Is 40, 6ff.
2, 1: Jas 1, 21.

3: Ps 34, 9.
4: Mt 21, 42; Acts 4, 11.
5: Eph 2, 21f.

1, 23ff: The rebirth of Christians (v 23) derives from Christ, the *indestructible seed* effecting a new and lasting existence in those who accept
the gospel (24f), and making them brothers with the duty of loving one
another (v 22).

2, 1ff: Growth *unto salvation* (v 2) is here considered negatively, as a
stripping away of all that is contrary to the new life received from Christ;
and positively, as the taking of the *pure milk,* i. e., the nourishment which
the newly baptized *have tasted* and found *good* (1f).

2, 4-8: *Come to him:* to Christ, *a living stone, rejected by men but approved* by God because of his death and resurrection (v 4). Believers joined
by the Spirit (1 Cor 3, 16) to Christ the *cornerstone* (v 7) themselves become *living stones* and constitute the spiritual edifice of the Christian
community. They are *a holy priesthood* whose function is to offer *spiritual
sacrifices acceptable to God through Jesus Christ* (5f). To unbelievers,
Christ is *an obstacle and a stumbling stone* on which they are destined
to fall (v 8); cf Rom 11, 11.

stones, built as an edifice of spirit, into a holy priesthood, offering spiritual sacrifices acceptable to God through Jesus Christ. [6] For Scripture has it:

"See, I am laying a cornerstone in Zion,
an approved stone, and precious.
He who puts his faith in it shall not be shaken."

[7] The stone is of value for you who have faith. For those without faith, it is rather,

"A stone which the builders rejected
that became a cornerstone."

[8] It is likewise "an obstacle and a stumbling stone." Those who stumble and fall are the disbelievers in God's word; it belongs to their destiny to do so.

[9] You, however, are "a chosen race, a royal priesthood, a holy nation, a people he claims for his own to proclaim the glorious works" of the One who called you from darkness into his marvelous light. [10] Once you were no people, but now you are God's people; once there was no mercy for you, but now you have found mercy.

Good Example

[11] Beloved, you are strangers and in exile; hence I urge you not to indulge your carnal desires. By their nature they wage war on the soul. [12] Though the pagans may slander you as

6: Is 28, 16; Rom 9, 33.
7: Ps 118, 22; Mt 21, 42.
8: Is 8, 14.
9: Ex 19, 6.
10: Hos 1, 6.9; 2, 3.
11: Gal 5, 24.

2, 9: The prerogatives of ancient Israel here mentioned are now more fully and fittingly applied to the Christian people: *a chosen race* (cf Is 44, 1ff) indicates their divine election (Eph 1, 4ff); *a royal priesthood* (cf *a kingdom of priests*, Ex 19, 6) to serve and worship God in Christ, thus continuing the priestly functions of his life, passion, and resurrection; *a holy nation* (Ex 19, 6) reserved for God; *a people he claims for his own* (cf Mal 3, 17) in virtue of their baptism into his death and resurrection. This transcends all natural and national divisions, and unites the people into one community to glorify him who led them from the darkness of paganism to the light of faith in Christ. From being "no people," deprived of all mercy, they have become the very people of God, the chosen recipients of his mercy; cf Hos 1, 9; 2, 25.
2, 11—3, 12: After explaining the doctrinal basis for the Christian community, the letter traces practical applications in terms of the virtues that should prevail in all the social relationships of the members of the community: good example to pagan neighbors (2, 11f); respect for human authority (2, 13-17); obedience, patience, and endurance of hardship in domestic relations (2, 18-25); Christian behavior of husbands and wives (3, 1-7); mutual charity (3, 8-12).
2, 11: *You are strangers and in exile:* no longer signifying absence from one's native land (Gn 23, 4), this denotes rather their estrangement from this world during their earthly pilgrimage in search of the city *which is to come* (Heb 13, 14).

troublemakers, conduct yourselves blamelessly among them. By observing your good works they may give glory to God on the day of visitation.

For the Citizen

¹³ Because of the Lord, be obedient to every human institution, whether to the emperor as sovereign ¹⁴ or to the governors he commissions for the punishment of criminals and the recognition of the upright. ¹⁵ Such obedience is the will of God. You must silence the ignorant talk of foolish men by your good behavior. ¹⁶ Live as free men, but do not use your freedom as a cloak for vice. In a word, live as servants of God. ¹⁷ You must esteem the person of every man. Foster love for the brothers, reverence for God, respect for the emperor.

For the Slave

¹⁸ You household slaves, obey your masters with all deference, not only the good and reasonable ones but even those who are harsh. ¹⁹ When a man can suffer injustice and endure hardship through his awareness of God's presence, this is the work of grace in him. ²⁰ If you do wrong and get beaten for it, what credit can you claim? But if you put up with suffering for doing what is right, this is acceptable in God's eyes. ²¹ It was for this you were called, since Christ suffered for you in just this way and left you an example, to have you follow in his footsteps. ²² He did no wrong; no deceit was found in his mouth. ²³ When he was insulted, he returned no insult. When he was made to suffer, he did not counter with threats. Instead, he delivered himself up to the One who judges justly. ²⁴ In his own body he brought your sins to the cross, so that all of us, dead to sin, could live in accord with God's will. By his wounds you were

---

13: Rom 13, 1-7.
16: Gal 5, 13.
17: Jude 4; Prv 24, 21;
    Mt 22, 21.

18: Eph 6, 5.
21: Mt 16, 24.
22: Is 53, 9; Mt 5, 39.
24: Is 53, 5f; Rom 6, 11.

2, 13: *Be obedient to every human institution:* the text could also mean, though less probably, "every human creature." This obedience is enjoined *because of the Lord,* i. e., because it conforms to his will (v 15).

2, 16f: *Live as free men . . . vice:* the freedom of the Christian is that which derives from right order, i. e., service of God and *reverence* toward him, besides *esteem* for *every man* (v 17).

2, 18-25: The author's concern for *household slaves* was not aimed at overthrowing the institution of slavery, but was meant rather to indicate how those in servitude should accept it through the power of grace as a means of imitating the suffering Christ. They are reminded that his willing endurance of insult, suffering, and death delivered men from the bondage of sin and won for them the freedom of living according to God's will; cf Is 53, 1-12; Gal 3, 13.

healed. ²⁵ At one time you were straying like sheep, but now you have returned to the Shepherd, the Guardian of your souls.

3

For Wife and Husband

¹ You married women must obey your husbands, so that any of them who do not believe in the word of the gospel may be won over apart from preaching, through their wives' conduct. ² They have only to observe the reverent purity of your way of life. ³ The affection of an elaborate hairdress, the wearing of golden jewelry, or the donning of rich robes is not for you. ⁴ Your adornment is rather the hidden character of the heart, expressed in the unfading beauty of a calm and gentle disposition. This is precious in God's eyes. ⁵ The holy women of past ages used to adorn themselves in this way, reliant on God and obedient to their husbands—⁶ for example, Sarah, who was subject to Abraham and called him her master. You are her children when you do what is right and let no fears alarm you.

⁷ You husbands, too, must show consideration for those who share your lives. Treat women with respect as the weaker sex, heirs just as much as you to the gracious gift of life. If you do so, nothing will keep your prayers from being answered.

In Christian Charity

⁸ In summary, then, all of you should be like-minded, sympathetic, loving toward one another, kindly disposed, and humble. ⁹ Do not return evil for evil or insult for insult. Return a

---

7: Eph 5, 25.
9: Mt 5, 44; Lk 6, 28;
     Rom 12, 14.

3, 1: 1 Cor 7, 12-16;
        Eph 5, 22-24; Col 3, 18.
3: 1 Tm 2, 9-15.

2, 25: *The Shepherd, the Guardian of your souls:* the familiar shepherd-and-flock figures express the care, vigilance, and love of God for his people in the Old Testament (Ps 23; Is 23, 3f; 40, 11; Ez 34, 11-16), and of Christ for all men in the New (Mt 18, 10-14; Lk 15, 3-6; Jn 10, 11; Heb 13, 20). In Acts (20, 28), St. Paul calls the elders of the church of Ephesus, shepherds and guardians of the flock.

3, 1-7: This passage outlines, on the one hand, the marital duties of wives: reverence, chaste conduct, and obedience to their husbands; and on the other, the love and consideration husbands owe their wives (cf Eph 5, 21-28). At the same time, attention is called to the opportunity of wives for winning over their pagan husbands to belief in the gospel by their own Christian conduct. In imitation of the pious women of the past, they are to cultivate the virtues of the interior life instead of indulging in the display of robes and jewelry. The fulfillment of these duties by husbands and wives is the surest guarantee of God's response to their prayers.

3, 8-12: To the proper ordering of Christian life in its various aspects as described in 2, 11—3, 9 there is promised the blessing expressed in Psalm 34, 13-17. In the Old Testament, this referred to the temporal benefits of longevity and prosperity; in the New, it refers to eternal life.

blessing instead. This you have been called to do, that you may receive a blessing as your inheritance.

> [10] "He who cares for life
> and wants to see prosperous days
> must keep his tongue from evil
> and his lips from uttering deceit.
> [11] He must turn from evil and do good,
> seek peace and follow after it,
> [12] because the Lord has eyes for the just
> and ears for their cry;
> but against evildoers the Lord sets his face."

In Christian Suffering

[13] Who indeed can harm you if you are committed deeply to doing what is right? [14] Even if you should have to suffer for justice' sake, happy will you be. "Fear not and do not stand in awe of what this people fears." [15] Venerate the Lord, that is, Christ, in your hearts. Should anyone ask you the reason for this hope of yours, be ever ready to reply, [16] but speak gently and respectfully. Keep your conscience clear, so that, whenever you are defamed, those who libel your way of life in Christ may be shamed. [17] If it should be God's will that you suffer, it is better to do so for good deeds than for evil ones.

[18] The reason why Christ died for sins once for all, the just man for the sake of the unjust, was that he might lead you to God. He was put to death insofar as fleshly existence goes, but was given life in the realm of the spirit. [19] It was in the spirit also that he went to preach to the spirits in prison. [20] They had disobeyed as long ago as Noah's day, while God patiently waited until the ark was built. At that time, a few persons, eight in all, escaped in the ark through the water. [21] You are now saved by a baptismal bath which corresponds to this exactly.

10-12: Ps 34, 13-17.
14: Is 8, 12.
18: Rom 5, 6.

20: Gn 7, 7.17; 2 Pt 2, 5.
21: Eph 5, 26.

3, 13-22: This exposition, centering on verse 17, runs as follows: By his suffering and death Christ the just One saved the unjust (v 18); by his resurrection he acquired new life in the spirit, which he communicates to believers through the baptismal bath that cleanses their consciences from sin. As the ark saved Noah's family, so baptism saves sinners from the flood waters that would destroy them (19-22). Hence they need not share the fear of sinners; they should rather rejoice in suffering because of their hope in Christ. Thus their innocence disappoints their accusers (13-16; Mt 10, 28; Rom 8, 35-39).

3, 19: There are various interpretations of this verse. It probably refers to the risen Christ making known to imprisoned souls his victory over sin and death.

This baptism is no removal of physical stain, but the pledge to God of an irreproachable conscience through the resurrection of Jesus Christ. [22] He went to heaven and is at God's right hand, with angelic rulers and powers subjected to him.

4

In Christian Faithfulness

[1] Christ suffered in the flesh; therefore, arm yourselves with his same mentality. He who has suffered in the flesh has broken with sin. [2] You are not to spend what remains of your earthly life on human desires but on the will of God. [3] Already you have devoted enough time to what the pagans enjoy, living lives of debauchery, evil desires, drunkenness, orgies, carousing, and wanton idolatry. [4] It is no wonder that those blasphemers are surprised when you do not plunge into the same swamp of profligacy as they. [5] They shall give an accounting to him who stands ready to judge the living and the dead. [6] The reason the gospel was preached even to the dead was that, although condemned in the flesh in the eyes of men, they might live in the spirit in the eyes of God.

Mutual Charity

[7] The consummation of all is close at hand. Therefore do not be perturbed; remain calm so that you will be able to pray. [8] Above all, let your love for one another be constant, for love covers a multitude of sins. [9] Be mutually hospitable without complaining. [10] As generous distributors of God's manifold grace, put your gifts at the service of one another, each in the measure he has received. [11] The one who speaks is to deliver

---

22: Eph 1, 20f.
4, 3: Eph 4, 17f.
5: Acts 10, 42; Rom 14, 9f; 1 Tm 4, 1.
8: Prv 10, 12.

9: Heb 13, 2.
10: Rom 12, 6ff;
     1 Cor 12, 4-11.
11: Rom 12, 7.

4, 1-6: Willingness to suffer with Christ equips the Christian with the power to conquer sin. Christ is here portrayed as the judge to whom those guilty of pagan vices must render an account; cf Jn 5, 22-27; Acts 10, 42; 2 Tm 4, 1.

4, 6: *The gospel was preached even to the dead:* this may refer to bringing the benefits of salvation to the "spirits" in prison (cf 3, 19), or to the preaching of the gospel to Christians who have since died.

4, 7-11: The author outlines the means to be used in preparing for *the consummation of all* at the parousia (7): calmness, prayer, and constant love for one another through unfeigned hospitality and the generous use of one's gifts for the glory of God and of Christ (8-11); cf Lk 21, 34ff; I Cor 7, 29ff; Jas 5, 7-12.

4, 8: *Love covers a multitude of sins:* a favorite maxim of the apostles, based on Proverbs 10, 12. Fraternal love will overcome such evils as occur (cf Lk 7, 47; Jas 5, 20).

4, 11: *God is to be glorified . . . throughout the ages. Amen:* this

God's message. The one who serves is to do it with the strength provided by God. Thus, in all of you God is to be glorified through Jesus Christ: to him be glory and dominion throughout the ages. Amen.

Blessings of Persecution

[12] Do not be surprised, beloved, that a trial by fire is occurring in your midst. It is a test for you, but it should not catch you off guard. [13] Rejoice instead, in the measure that you share Christ's sufferings. When his glory is revealed, you will rejoice exultantly. [14] Happy are you when you are insulted for the sake of Christ, for then God's Spirit in its glory has come to rest on you. [15] See to it that none of you suffers for being a murderer, a thief, a malefactor, or a destroyer of another's rights. [16] If anyone suffers for being a Christian, however, he ought not to be ashamed. He should rather glorify God in virtue of that name. [17] The season of judgment has begun, and begun with God's own household. If it begins this way with us, what must be the end for those who refuse obedience to the gospel of God? [18] And if the just man is saved only with difficulty, what is to become of the godless and the sinner? [19] Accordingly, let those who suffer as God's will requires continue in good deeds, and entrust their lives to a faithful Creator.

5

For the Ministry

[1] To the elders among you I, a fellow elder, a witness of

12: 1, 6f; 3, 14.
13: Rom 5, 3-5; 8, 17;
     2 Tim 2, 12.
14: Is 11, 2; Acts 5, 41;

Col 3, 4.
17: Lk 23, 31; 2 Thes 1, 8.
18: Prv 11, 31.
5, 1: Rv 1, 9.

---

doxology concludes the portion of 1 Peter begun in 1, 3. The source of the letter here used seems to have been a sermon of exhortation on the sacrament of baptism, to which numerous references are made.

4, 12-19: A trial of suffering faces the followers of Christ (12). If it is inflicted on them for the sake of his name, i. e., because of their being Christians (16), they are to rejoice in thus sharing the sufferings of the Christ whose glorification they will also share (13f; cf Rom 8, 17). If the trial is inflicted because of sins and misdeeds (v 15), the present judgment, though severe even for those of *God's own household,* is but the beginning of punishment for those *who refuse obedience to the gospel of God* (17f). The watchword is perseverance in the good and trust in God's fidelity (19).

4, 12: *A trial by fire:* severe affliction—in the form of slander (2, 12), insult (4, 14), and persecution from pagan neighbors; cf 3, 14.17.

4, 14: *God's Spirit in its glory has come to rest on you:* the Spirit both strengthens Christians to endure suffering and then glorifies them because they suffer for Christ; even as the glorificaton of Christ consisted, not only in his resurrection and ascension, but in his passion as well (Jn 13, 31f).

5, 1: *Elders: "presbyteroi"*—those to whom the task, both of governing

Christ's sufferings and sharer in the glory that is to be revealed, make this appeal. ² God's flock is in your midst; give it a shepherd's care. Watch over it willingly as God would have you do, not under constraint; and not for shameful profit either, but generously. ³ Be examples to the flock, not lording it over those assigned to you, ⁴ so that when the chief Shepherd appears you will win for yourselves the unfading crown of glory.

Counsel to the Laity

⁵ In the same way, you younger men must be obedient to the elders. In your relations with one another, clothe yourselves with humility, because God "is stern with the arrogant but to the humble he shows kindness." ⁶ Bow humbly under God's mighty hand, so that in due time he may lift you high. ⁷ Cast all your cares on him because he cares for you. ⁸ Stay sober and alert. Your opponent the devil is prowling like a roaring lion looking for someone to devour. ⁹ Resist him, solid in your faith, realizing that the brotherhood of believers is undergoing the same sufferings throughout the world. ¹⁰ The God of all grace, who called you to his everlasting glory in Christ, will himself restore, confirm, strengthen, and establish those who have suffered a little while. ¹¹ Dominion be his throughout the ages! Amen.

2: Acts 20, 28;
   1 Tm 3, 2-7; Ti 1, 7.
4: 2 Tm 4, 8.
5: Prv 3, 34; Mt 23, 12.
6: Jb 22, 29; Jas 4, 10.
7: Ps 54, 23; Mt 6, 25;

Phil 4, 6.
8: 1 Thes 5, 6.
9: Eph 6, 11ff.
10: Rom 8, 18; 2 Cor 4, 17;
    1 Thes 5, 24.

---

the faithful and of conducting worship for them, was entrusted; cf 1 Tm 5, 17f; Ti 1, 5.7f; Jas 5, 14. Peter, here called *a fellow elder*, nevertheless admonishes the others as one exercising authority over them.

5, 2ff: In imitation of Christ, *the chief Shepherd*, those charged with the pastoral office are to shepherd the flock by their care, by their solicitude for what pertains to doctrine and discipline, and by their example. They are to render this service, *not under constraint, and not for shameful profit*, nor to lord it over the flock, but out of generosity and kindness, as God would have them do, thus meriting *the unfading crown of glory;* cf Acts 20, 17-31 and note on 2, 25.

5, 5-11: The laity are to be obedient toward the elders, and to show humility toward one another and complete trust in God's loving care (5ff). By sobriety, alertness, and firm faith, they must ward off the evil one who seeks to destroy their souls. Their sufferings are shared with Christians everywhere (8ff). As a reward for their faith and trust in God, they will be strengthened and attain to *everlasting glory in Christ* (10).

5, 8: *Your opponent the devil . . . someone to devour:* the synonymous Greek terms "antidikos" (*opponent*) and "diabolos" (*accuser*) are used to designate those who persecute Christians. In the manner of Satan they prowl about *like a roaring lion* seeking to destroy their victims (Ps 22, 14).

Farewell

¹² I am writing briefly through Silvanus, whom I take to be a faithful brother to you. Herewith are expressed my encouragement and my testimony that this is the true grace of God. Be steadfast in it. ¹³ The church that is in Babylon, chosen together with you, sends you greeting, as does Mark my son. ¹⁴ Greet one another with the embrace of true love. Peace to all of you who are in Christ.

13: Acts 12, 12.25;
2 Tm 4, 11.

14: 1 Cor 16, 20.

5, 12ff: *Silvanus:* Paul's companion (2 Cor 1, 19; 1 Thes 1, 1; 2 Thes 1, 1). *This is the true grace of God:* a possible reference to the trials which the Christians were enduring, regarded from the standpoint of their salutary effects. *Babylon:* Rome which, like ancient Babylon, conquered Jerusalem and destroyed its temple. *Mark my son:* cf Acts 12, 25; 13, 5; Col 4, 10.

THE SECOND EPISTLE OF PETER

INTRODUCTION

Early Christian tradition was not so impressed by the claim of Petrine authorship of this epistle (1, 1.14.16ff; 3, 1.15f) as to concede its authenticity without question. Both Origen (185-254) and St. Jerome (342-420) found it debatable. In the early fifth century the epistle was accepted into the canon of the Scriptures.

The chief reason for concluding that 2 Peter was not composed by the chief of the apostles is its discussion of the parousia (3, 1-13). The main purpose of the epistle was to meet the difficulty caused in many minds by the non-fulfillment of the expectation of Christ's second coming. This difficulty could not have arisen in the lifetime of Peter, who died between the years 64 and 67 A.D. Only after the destruction of Jerusalem, in 70 A.D., did Christians begin slowly to realize that the parousia was reserved for a date in the more remote future. The epistle was written at a time when Christian teaching was placing less emphasis on the proximity of the parousia, and therefore not while Peter was still living. Scholars add other arguments against Petrine authorship from the epistle's vocabulary and theology, and from its clear relationship to Jude—without, however, removing all doubt on the question.

It is not unreasonable to conclude that 2 Peter was written by an unknown author who followed the pseudonymous convention of the time in order to attract readers to his work. The date of composition is conjectural. Some think that the author was close enough to the tradition of Petrine teaching to assume the important name Peter, but it is probable that he was a third- or fourth-generation Christian who wrote in the period between 100 and 125. The letter is addressed to Christians generally (1, 1), without giving any indication of its place of composition.

The epistle is well composed, leading gradually to its discussion of the parousia. It reminds its readers of the divine authenticity of Christ's teaching (1, 3f), continues reflections on Christian conduct (1, 5-15), then returns to the exalted dignity of Jesus by incorporating in the text the apostolic witness to his transfiguration (1, 16ff). It takes up the question of the interpretation of Scripture by pointing out that it is possible to misunderstand the sacred writings (1, 19—2, 1) and that divine punishment will be visited upon false teachers (2, 2-22). It explains that the parousia is the doctrine of Jesus and of the apostles and is therefore an eventual certainty (3, 1-13); at the same time it warns that the meaning of St. Paul's writing on this question should not be distorted (3, 14-18).

THE SECOND EPISTLE OF PETER

1

Greeting

¹ Simeon Peter, servant and apostle of Jesus Christ, to those who have been given a faith like ours in the justifying power of our God and Savior Jesus Christ: ² may grace be yours and peace in abundance through your knowledge of God and of Jesus, our Lord.

Christian Virtue

³ That divine power of his has freely bestowed on us everything necessary for a life of genuine piety, through knowledge of him who called us by his own glory and power. ⁴ By virtue of them he has bestowed on us the great and precious things he promised, so that through these you who have fled a world corrupted by lust might become sharers of the divine nature. ⁵ This is reason enough for you to make every effort to undergird your virtue with faith, your discernment with virtue, ⁶ and your self-control with discernment; this self-control, in turn, should lead to perseverance, and perseverance to piety, ⁷ and piety to care for your brother, and care for your brother, to love.

⁸ Qualities like these, made increasingly your own, are by no means ineffectual; they bear fruit in true knowledge of our Lord Jesus Christ. ⁹ Any man who lacks these qualities is shortsighted to the point of blindness. He forgets the cleansing of his long-past sins. ¹⁰ Be solicitous to make your call and election permanent, brothers; surely those who do so will never

---

1, 3: 2 Cor 4, 6; 1 Pt 2, 9.
   4: 2 Cor 7, 1; 1 Jn 2, 15.
   5: Gal 5, 22f.

7: Gal 6, 10.
9: 1 Jn 2, 9.11.

1, 1: *Simeon Peter, servant and apostle of Jesus Christ:* on the question of authorship of 2 Peter, see the Introduction. *To those who have been given a faith . . . Jesus Christ:* it is *the justifying power* of Jesus, *God and Savior,* which causes the faith of the apostles and of succeeding believers to be one and the same.

1, 3f: Christian life in its fullness is a gift of divine power to those who are called. This power effects in them a knowledge of Christ and fulfills the divine promises in their regard, making them shares of the divine nature, safe from a *world corrupted by lust;* cf 1, 2.8; 3, 18; Jn 17, 22; Rom 8, 14-17; 1 Jn 3, 2.

1, 5-9: Note the climactic gradation of qualities, beginning with faith and leading to the fullness of Christian life which is love (5-7); cf Rom 5, 3ff; 10, 14f. Their fruit is the knowledge of Christ (v 8) referred to in 1, 3; their absence is spiritual blindness (v 9).

1, 10f: Perseverance in the Christian vocation is the best preventative against losing it and the safest provision for attaining its goal, entrance *into the everlasting kingdom,* identified here as the *kingdom of our Lord and Savior Jesus Christ.*

be lost. [11] On the contrary, your entry into the everlasting kingdom of our Lord and Savior Jesus Christ will be richly provided for.

Witness to Christ

[12] I intend to recall these things to you constantly, even though you already understand and are firmly rooted in the truth you possess. [13] I consider it my duty, as long as I live, to prompt you with this reminder. [14] I know, by the indications our Lord Jesus Christ has given me, how close is the day when I must fold my tent. [15] I shall press to have you recall these things frequently after my departure. [16] It was not by way of cleverly concocted myths that we taught you about the coming in power of our Lord Jesus Christ, [17] for we were eyewitnesses of his sovereign majesty. He received glory and praise from God the Father when that unique declaration came to him out of the majestic splendor: "This is my beloved Son, on whom my favor rests." [18] We ourselves heard this said from heaven while we were in his company on the holy mountain. [19] Besides, we possess the prophetic message as something altogether reliable. Keep your attention closely fixed on it, as you would on a lamp shining in a dark place until the first streaks of dawn appear and the morning star rises in your hearts.

The Nature of Prophecy

[20] First you must understand this: there is no prophecy contained in Scripture which is a personal interpretation. [21] Prophecy has never been put forward by man's willing it. It is rather that men impelled by the Holy Spirit have spoken under God's influence.

14: Is 38, 12; Jn 21, 18f.   17: Ps 2, 7; Mt 17, 4-6.
16: Jn 1, 14.   19: Lk 1, 78; Rv 2, 28.

1, 12-19: Alive to his responsibility even when faced with the proximity of death, the apostle bequeaths to his readers a perpetual reminder of the teachings of the faith (12-15) and of the certainty of Christ's coming in power (v 16). As motives for belief in the parousia, he offers the prophetic message of Scripture and also his own testimony as eyewitness to the transfiguration of Christ in glory and majesty, confirmed by the voice of God the Father (18-22). These serve as a shining light amid the darkness to those preparing for the parousia. The value of continual reminders and repeated instructions, for preserving the truths of the faith and the historic facts surrounding them, is insisted on in the New Testament (12f.15; 3, 1f; 1 Cor 11, 2; 15, 1).

2

False Teachers

[1] In times past there were false prophets among God's people, and among you also there will be false teachers who will smuggle in pernicious heresies. They will go so far as to deny the Master who acquired them for his own, thereby bringing on themselves swift disaster. [2] Their lustful ways will lure many away. Through them, the true way will be made subject to contempt.

Warning from the Past

[3] They will deceive you with fabricated tales, in a spirit of greed. Their condemnation has not lain idle all this time, however; their destruction is not asleep. [4] Did God spare even the angels who sinned? He did not! He held them captive in Tartarus —consigned them to pits of darkness, to be guarded until judgment. [5] Nor did he spare the ancient world—even though he preserved Noah as a preacher of holiness, with seven others, when he brought down the flood on that godless earth. [6] He blanketed the cities of Sodom and Gomorrah in ashes and condemned them to destruction, thereby showing what would happen in the future to the godless. [7] He did deliver Lot,

---

2, 1: Mt 24, 11; 1 Tm 4, 1;
Jude 4.
2: Is 52, 5.
3: Rom 16, 18;

1 Thes 2, 5.
4: Jude 6.
5: Gn 8, 18; Heb 11, 7.
6: Gn 19, 25; Jude 7.

2, 1-22: This account of the false teachers and evildoers and the dire punishments which threaten them finds a parallel in Jude 4-13. The present passage is generally considered by scholars to be dependent on Jude, despite modifications and omissions.

2, 1ff: The pattern of false teaching in the Old Testament recurs in apostolic times among the people of the New, and will be repeated (10-22) before the final cataclysm at the end of the world (Mt 24, 11). It is accompanied by denial of faith in Christ, immorality, scandal, and contempt for the way of salvation.

2, 3-9: *Their condemnation . . . ; their destruction is not asleep:* the interventions of the divine chastisement are exemplified in the case of the rebellious angels (v 4; Jude 6), the deluge (v 6; Jude 7), and the destruction of Sodom and Gomorrah.

2, 4: *Tartarus:* a term borrowed from Greek mythology to indicate the infernal regions, *pits of darkness* where sinners, especially fallen angels, are punished.

2, 5: The deluge is described as marking the end of *the ancient world* and the beginning of the new. Noah, the preacher of holiness, is the type of new life initiated through Christian baptism and made comformable to God's sanctity (1 Pt 3, 20f).

2, 6: The destruction of the cities of Sodom and Gomorrah stands for all time as a warning of punishment of sin. The association of this catastrophe with that of the deluge is also found in Wisdom 10, 4ff and in Christ's prediction concerning the signs of the coming of the kingdom of God (Lk 17, 26-29).

however, a just man oppressed by the conduct of men un-principled in their lusts. [8] (Day after day that just one, good as he was, felt himself tormented by seeing and hearing about the lawless deeds of those among whom he lived.) [9] The Lord, indeed, knows how to rescue devout men from trial, and how to continue the punishment of the wicked up to the day of judgment.

Punishment of Evildoers

[10] He knows, especially, how to treat those who live for the flesh in their desire for whatever corrupts, and who despise authority. These bold and arrogant men have no qualms whatever about reviling celestial beings, [11] on whom angels, though greater than men in strength and power, pass no opprobrious sentence in the Lord's presence. [12] These men pour abuse on things of which they are ignorant. They act like creatures of instinct, brute animals born to be caught and destroyed. Because of their decadence they too will be destroyed, suffering the reward of their wickedness. [13] Thinking daytime revelry a de-light, they are stain and defilement as they share your feasts in a spirit of seduction. [14] Constantly on the lookout for a woman, theirs is a never-ending search for sin. They lure the weaker types. Their hearts are trained in greed. An accursed lot are they! [15] They have abandoned the straight road and wander off on the path taken by Balaam, son of Beor. He was a man attracted to dishonest gain, [16] but he was rebuked for his evil-doing. A mute beast spoke with a human voice to restrain the prophet's madness.

[17] These men are waterless springs, mists whipped by the gale. The darkest gloom has been reserved for them. [18] They talk empty bombast while baiting their hooks with passion,

---

9: 1 Cor 10, 13; Rv 3, 10.
10: Jude 8.
11: Jude 9.
12: Ps 49, 13-15; Jude 10.
13: Jude 12.

15: Nm 22, 2; Jude 4.
16: Nm 22, 28-33.
17: Jude 12f.
18: Jude 16.

2, 10-22: These verses portray in detail the conduct of the false teachers. They are slaves of the flesh and its passions; they despise true sovereignty, that of Christ and his church (v 10); they even revile the *celestial beings* considered to be fallen angels (cf 2, 4) in comparison to the angels in 2, 11. Abusive in their ignorance, imitating brute animals in their irrational-ity, decadent in their instincts, they deserve, like animals, *to be caught and destroyed* (v 12). In their day-long revelries they seduce others (v 13), even those who *have just come free of a life of errors* (v 18), making their new condition of return to corruption and rejection of Christ worse than the first (18-22). In their greed they abandon righteousness, like Balaam of old, for the sake of material gain (14ff).

with the lustful ways of the flesh, to catch those who have just come free of a life of errors. [19] They promise them freedom though they themselves are slaves of corruption—for surely anyone is the slave of that by which he has been overcome. [20] When men have fled a polluted world by recognizing the Lord and Savior Jesus Christ, and then are caught up and overcome in pollution once more, their last condition is worse than their first. [21] It would have been better for them not to have recognized the road to holiness than to have turned their backs on the holy law handed on to them, once they had known it. [22] How well the proverb fits them: "The dog returns to its vomit," and, "A sow bathes by wallowing in the mire."

3

Christ Will Come in Judgment

[1] I am writing you this second letter, dear friends, intending them both as reminders urging you to sincerity of outlook. [2] Recall the teaching delivered long ago by the holy prophets, as well as the new command of the Lord and Savior preached to you by the apostles.

[3] Note this first of all: In the last days, mocking, sneering men who are ruled by their passions will arrive on the scene. [4] They will ask: "Where is that promised coming of his? Our forefathers have been laid to rest, but everything stays just as it was when the world was created." [5] In believing this, they do

---

19: Jn 8, 34; Rom 6, 16f.
20: Mt 12, 45.
21: Ez 3, 20.
22: Prv 26, 11.

3, 2: Jude 17.
3: 1 Tm 4, 1; Jude 18.
4: Is 5, 19.
5: Gn 1, 2.6.8; Ps 24, 2.

3, 1-4: The false teachers not only flout Christian morality (cf Jude 18f), they also deny the second coming of Christ and eternal retribution. They seek to justify their licentiousness, arguing that the promised return of Christ has not been realized and the world is the same, no better than it was before (3f). The author wishes to strengthen the faithful against this pernicious error by reminding them of the instruction in his letters (1 and 2 Peter), and of the teaching of the prophets and of Christ, conveyed through the apostles (1f); cf 1 Pt 1, 10ff. 16-21; Eph 2, 20.

3, 4: *Our forefathers have been laid to rest:* the death of the apostolic fathers indicates a date after that time for the composition of 2 Peter.

3, 5-10: The scoffers' objection (v 4) is refuted by showing that the power of God's word, which called the world into being, also destroyed it by the waters of a flood, and will destroy it again by fire on the day of judgment (5ff). The delay of the Lord is not an indication of failure to fulfill his word but rather of his *generous patience* in giving time for repentance before the final judgment (8ff; 1 Thes 5, 2). The New Testament writers used the deluge as a figure of eschatological events; cf Mt 24, 37ff; Lk 17, 26f. The effect of Christian baptism is compared to the radical action of fire which purifies metal of dross. For Old Testament examples of God's judgment described by the imagery of fire, see Is 66, 15f; Mi 1, 4; Dn 7, 9ff; Zep 1, 18; 3, 8; Ps 97, 3. Acceptance of the truths of faith does not require acceptance of the popular imagery used to describe them.

not take into account that of old there were heavens and an earth drawn out of the waters and standing between the waters, all brought into being by the word of God. ⁶ By water that world was then destroyed; it was overwhelmed by the deluge. ⁷ The present heavens and earth are reserved by God's word for fire; they are kept for the day of judgment, the day when godless men will be destroyed.

⁸ This point must not be overlooked, dear friends. In the Lord's eyes, one day is as a thousand years and a thousand years are as a day. ⁹ The Lord does not delay in keeping his promise —though some consider it "delay." Rather, he shows you generous patience, since he wants none to perish but all to come to repentance. ¹⁰ The day of the Lord will come like a thief, and on that day the heavens will vanish with a roar; the elements will be destroyed by fire, and the earth and all its deeds will be made manifest.

¹¹ Since everything is to be destroyed in this way, what sort of men must you not be! How holy in your conduct and devotion, ¹² looking for the coming of the day of God and trying to hasten it! Because of it, the heavens will be destroyed in flames and the elements will melt away in a blaze. ¹³ What we await are new heavens and a new earth where, according to his promise, the justice of God will reside.

Preparation for the Coming

¹⁴ So, beloved, while waiting for this, make every effort to be found without stain or defilement, and at peace in his sight. ¹⁵ Consider that our Lord's patience is directed toward salva-

---

6: Gn 7, 21.
7: Is 51, 6; Mt 3, 12.
8: Ps 90, 4.
9: Ez 18, 23; 1 Tm 2, 4.
10: Is 66, 15f;
    Mt 24, 29.43;

1 Thes 5, 2f.
11: Acts 3, 19f.
12: Is 34, 4; Heb 12, 27.
13: Is 65, 17; 66, 22;
    Rom 8, 21; Rv 21, 1.27.
15: Rom 8, 19; Jude 24.

3, 9: *He shows you generous patience:* the longsuffering of God is a sign of his mercy toward man, who is so slow to change. God wills all men to be saved and to come to the knowledge of the truth; cf Wis 11, 23-26; Ez 18, 23; 33, 11; Rom 11, 32; 1 Tm 2, 4.

3, 11-15: The coming of Christ and the judgment of the world are the doctrinal bases here and elsewhere in the New Testament for the moral exhortation to preparedness through vigilance and a virtuous life (Mt 24, 42.51; Lk 12, 40; 1 Thes 5, 1-11; Jude 20f).

3, 12: *Trying to hasten it:* i. e., the day of God, by advancing his kingdom through holiness of life; cf v 9.

3, 13: *New heavens and a new earth:* the fulfillment of the divine promises after the day of judgment will have passed and the universe will be transformed by the reign of perfect justice; cf Is 65, 17; 66, 22; Acts 3, 21; Rom 8, 19ff; Rv 21, 1.

3, 15f: The teachings of this epistle—the Lord's salvific will toward mankind (Rom 2, 4; 9, 22f; 1 Cor 1, 7f); preparedness for the judgment (Eph

tion. Paul, our beloved brother, wrote you this in the spirit of wisdom that is his, [16] dealing with these matters as he does in all his letters. There are certain passages in them hard to understand. The ignorant and the unstable distort them (just as they do the rest of Scripture) to their own ruin.

[17] You are forewarned, beloved brothers. Be on your guard lest you be led astray by the error of the wicked, and forfeit the security you enjoy. [18] Grow rather in grace, and in the knowledge of our Lord and Savior Jesus Christ. Glory be to him now and to the day of eternity! Amen.

17: Mk 13, 5; Heb 2, 1.   18: Rom 16, 27.

1, 4-14; 4, 30; 5, 5.14ff; Col 1, 22f); the coming of Christ (1 Thes 4, 16f; 1 Cor 15, 23.52)—are further confirmed by the letters of Paul. He is called here *our beloved brother*, i. e., a fellow apostle of Peter, after whom this letter is named.

The rest of Scripture: the sacred writings inspired by the Holy Spirit to regulate the religious life of the people. The writings of Paul are thus recognized as having the same quality and authority as the books of the Old Testament.

3, 17f: To avoid the danger of error and loss of security, the faithful are exhorted to persevere in the principles of the Christian life through growth *in the knowledge* of Christ. The final doxology recalls that of I Pt 4, 11.

THE FIRST EPISTLE OF JOHN

INTRODUCTION

Early Christian tradition attributed this letter to John the apostle. Subsequently, the majority of scholars have concluded, from its resemblance to the fourth gospel in style, vocabulary, and ideas, that one author actually was responsible for both works. These resemblances are not so compelling as absolutely to exclude the possibility of separate authors, as some critics have shown. But it is very probable that the person who composed the fourth gospel also wrote 1 John. On the identity of this author, see the Introduction to the gospel itself.

The opening of the epistle does not state to whom it is addressed, but the data indicate that it was written to specific Christian communities some of whose members were advocating false doctrines (2, 18f.26; 3. 7). These errors are here recognized and rejected (4, 4); although their advocates have left the community (2, 19), the threat posed by them remains (3, 11). They have refused to acknowledge that Jesus is the Christ (2, 22) the Son of God (2, 23) who came into the world as true man (4, 2). They are difficult people to deal with, claiming special knowledge of God but disregarding the divine commandments (2, 4), particularly the commandment of love of neighbor (4, 8), and refusing to accept faith in Christ as the source of sanctification (1, 6; 2, 6.9). Thus they are denying the redemptive value of Jesus' death (5, 6). Scholars generally agree that the group so stigmatized had adopted some form of Gnosticism, but as yet it has not been identified with any specific body of heretical teaching.

The epistle is of particular value for its declaration of the humanity and divinity of Christ as apostolic teaching (1, 1-4), and for its development of the intrinsic connection between Christian moral conduct and Christian doctrine. Although the author recognizes that Christian doctrine presents intangible mysteries of faith about Christ, he insists that the concrete Christian life brings to light the deeper realities of the gospel. The epistle is generally held to date at the same time as the fourth gospel, c 90-100 A.D.

THE FIRST EPISTLE OF JOHN

Prologue

1

¹ This is what we proclaim to you:
what was from the beginning,
what we have heard,
what we have seen with our eyes,
what we have looked upon
and our hands have touched—
we speak of the word of life.
² (This life became visible;
we have seen and bear witness to it,
and we proclaim to you the eternal life
that was present to the Father
and became visible to us.)
³ What we have seen and heard
we proclaim in turn to you
so that you may share life with us.
This fellowship of ours is with the Father
and with his Son, Jesus Christ.
⁴ Indeed, our purpose in writing you this
is that our joy may be complete.

The Light of God

⁵ Here, then, is the message
we have heard from him
and announce to you:
that God is light;
in him there is no darkness.

1, 1: 2, 13; Jn 1, 1.14;
20, 20.25.27.
2: Jn 15, 27; 17, 5.

3: Jn 17, 21; Acts 4, 20.
4: Jn 15, 11; 2 Jn 12.

1, 1-4: There is a striking parallel between this prologue and that of the
gospel of John (1, 1-16). The substance of the apostles' teaching is their
experience of the historic Christ and the witness they bear to him (v 1; cf
Jn 1, 7f.15). He is *the word of life* (v 1; cf Jn 1, 4), *eternal life that was
present to the Father and became visible* to the apostles (v 2; cf Jn 1, 1.14).
The purpose of their teaching is to share that *life,* called *fellowship . . . with
the Father and with his Son Jesus Christ,* with those who receive their witness (v 3; Jn 1, 14.16), and thus to make the joy of the apostles complete
(v 4).
1, 5ff: *Light* is to be understood here as truth and goodness; *darkness,* as
error and depravity; cf Jn 3, 19ff; 17, 17; Eph 5, 8f; 1 Thes 5, 5. To walk
in light or darkness is to live according to truth or error, not merely intellectual but moral as well; that is, in accordance with, or contrary to, God's
will. Thus, fellowship with God (v 6) and with one another (v 7) consists
in a life according to truth and goodness as found in God and in Christ,
their source. This is made possible through the redemptive work of Christ,
who cleanses us from our sins; cf Jn 8, 12; 12, 35f.

Claims of Flase Teachers

[6] If we say, "We have fellowship with him,"
while continuing to walk in darkness,
we are liars and do not act in truth.
[7] But if we walk in light,
as he is in the light,
we have fellowship with one another,
and the blood of his Son Jesus cleanses us
  from all sin.
[8] If we say, "We are free of the guilt of sin,"
we deceive ourselves; the truth is not
  to be found in us.
[9] But if we acknowledge our sins,
he who is just can be trusted
to forgive our sins
and cleanse us from every wrong.
[10] If we say, "We have never sinned,"
we make him a liar
and his word finds no place in us.

2

[1] My little ones,
I am writing this to keep you from sin.
But if anyone should sin,
we have, in the presence of the Father,
Jesus Christ, an intercessor who is just.
[2] He is an offering for our sins,
and not for our sins only,
but for those of the whole world.

6: Jn 12, 35.
7: Mt 26, 28; Rom 3, 24f;
   Heb 9, 14; 1 Pt 1, 19;
   Rv 1, 5.
8: 2 Chr 6, 36; Prv 20, 9.

9: Prv 28, 13; Jas 5, 16.
10: Jn 5, 38.
2, 1: Jn 14, 16; Heb 7, 25.
2: 4, 10.

1, 8ff: One is never entirely free from sin. To claim the contrary would be self-deception and would even contradict divine revelation (v 10; cf 1 Kgs 8, 46; Prv 24, 16). There is the continual possibility of sin's recurrence. Forgiveness and deliverance from sin through Christ are assured provided the sin is acknowledged through repentance. Such acknowledgment refers probably to a rite of confession; cf Mt 16, 19; 18, 18; Jn 20, 23; Jas 5, 16.

2, 1f: Believers are here addressed as *little ones* (v 1), elsewhere as *children* (2, 18) or *dearly beloved* (2, 7), to express the pastoral love and devotion of the apostles toward those entrusted to their care; cf Jn 13, 33; 21, 5; 1 Cor 4, 15; Gal 4, 19. After exhorting Christians to keep free from sin, the author returns to the thought of 1, 9: the assurance of forgiveness of sin through the power of Christ's intercession. *He is an offering for our sins:* literally, "propitiation," i. e., a permanent office exercised by Christ on behalf of sinners.

Keeping the Commandments

³ The way we can be sure of our knowledge of him
is to keep his commandments.
⁴ The man who claims, "I have known him,"
without keeping his commandments,
is a liar; in such a one there is no truth.
⁵ But whoever keeps his word,
truly has the love of God been made perfect in him.
The way we can be sure we are in union with him
⁶ is for the man who claims to abide in him
to conduct himself just as he did.

⁷ Dearly beloved,
it is no new commandment that I write to you,
but an old one which you had from the start.
The commandment, now old, is the word you
have already heard.
⁸ On second thought, the commandment that I
write you is new,
as it is realized in him and you,
for the darkness is over
and the real light begins to shine.
⁹ The man who claims to be in light,
hating his brother all the while,
is in darkness even now.
¹⁰ The man who continues in the light
is the one who loves his brother;
there is nothing in him to cause a fall.
¹¹ But the man who hates his brother is in darkness.
He walks in shadows,

3: Jn 14, 15; 15, 10.
4: 4, 20.
5: Jn 14, 23.
7: 3, 11; Dt 6, 5;
    Mt 22, 37-40.

8: Jn 1, 5; 13, 34;
    Rom 13, 12.
9: Jn 8, 12.
10: Eccl 2, 14; Jn 11, 10.

2, 3-6: *The way we can be sure of our knowledge . . . commandments:*
not mere intellectual knowledge of Christ but a life conformable to the divine will revealed to mankind through his teaching and example (v 6; cf
Jn 14, 21-24; 17, 3). Thus *love of God* is *made perfect* (v 5) and those who
live in this manner abide in Christ (v 6) and achieve union with him; cf 3,
2f. Disparity between moral life and doctrinal teaching was the error of the
Gnostics.

2, 7-11: The law of fraternal charity is based on human nature itself
and is confirmed by the divine positive command to the Israelites (Lv 19,
18). Through Christ, however, a new and higher relationship with neighbor
(vv 8.10) is achieved as a result of the new relationship with the Father:
that of sons of God (cf Jn 1, 12) and brothers of Christ (Lk 8, 21). Note
here and elsewhere the characteristic Johannine polemic in which a positive
assertion is further emphasized by the negative statement of its opposite
(9ff).

not knowing where he is going,
since the dark has blinded his eyes.

Members of the Community

[12] Little ones, I address you,
for through his Name your sins have been forgiven.
[13] Fathers, I address you,
for you have known him who is from the beginning.
Young men, I address you,
for you have conquered the evil one.
[14] I address you, children,
for you have known the Father.
I address you, fathers,
for you have known him who is from the beginning.
I address you, young men,
for you are strong,
and the word of God remains in you,
and you have conquered the evil one.

Against the World

[15] Have no love for the world,
nor the things that the world affords.
If anyone loves the world,
the Father's love has no place in him,
[16] for nothing that the world affords
comes from the Father.
Carnal allurements,
enticements for the eye,
the life of empty show—
all these are from the world.
[17] And the world with its seductions is passing away
but the man who does God's will
endures forever.

12: 1 Cor 6, 11.
13: 1, 1; Jn 1, 1.
15: Rom 8, 7f; Jas 4, 4;

2 Pt 1, 4.
17: Is 40, 8; Mt 7, 21;
1 Cor 7, 31; 1 Pt 4, 2.

2, 12-17: The Christian community, which has experienced the grace of God through forgiveness of sin and knowledge of Christ, i. e., practice of the faith, is thereby armed against *the evil one* and protected from the world with its allurements; cf 3, 7-10; 5, 18f.
2, 15: *The world:* men subject to sin and therefore hostile toward God. Love of the world and love of God are mutually exclusive; cf Jas 4, 4.
2, 16: *Carnal allurements:* inordinate desire for sensuality (cf Eph 2, 3; 1 Pt 2, 11; 2 Pt 2, 10.18); *enticements for the eye:* avarice; the eyes are regarded as the windows of the soul (cf Jb 31, 1; Ez 23, 12-17; Mt 5, 27ff); *the life of empty show:* ostentation, pride and arrogance, independence of God, in the temporal existence of man.

Against Antichrists

[18] Children, it is the final hour;
just as you heard that the antichrist was coming,
so now many such antichrists have appeared.
This makes us certain that it is the final hour.
[19] It was from our ranks that they took their leave—
not that they really belonged to us;
for if they had belonged to us,
they would have stayed with us.
It only served to show that none of them
was ours.

[20] But you have the anointing that comes from the
Holy one,
so that all knowledge is yours.
[21] My reason for having written you
is not that you do not know the truth
but that you do,
and that no lie has anything in common with the
truth.
[22] Who is the liar?
He who denies that Jesus is the Christ.
He is the antichrist,
denying the Father and the Son.
[23] Anyone who denies the Son

18: 1 Tm 4, 1.   22: 2 Thes 2, 4.
20: Jn 14, 26.   23: Jn 14, 7-9.
21: 3, 19; 2 Pt 1, 12.

2, 18: *The final hour:* the time between the first and second coming of
Christ. *The antichrist:* the opponent or adversary of Christ; one who denies
the Father and the Son (v 22). The term is found in 1 and 2 John; cf Mt
24, 23f; Mk 3, 21f. Paul calls him *the man of lawlessness, that son of perdition and adversary* (2 Thes 2, 3.8; cf Rv 13; 17, 7-14). Matthew, Mark, and
Revelation seem to refer to a collectivity of persons. *Many such antichrists
have appeared:* the reference is to all the false teachers who afflict the church
in *the final hour.* The early Christian community was familiar with this doctrine and expected an early return or second coming of Christ.

2, 19: *If they had belonged to us, . . . stayed with us:* the anti-christs,
apostate teachers, have always lacked the true spirit of the community of
God's people.

2, 20f.27: *The anointing that comes from the Holy One:* the Spirit of
God which the faithful received. It preserves them against the errors of the
antichrists. The *Holy One* may refer to Christ, whose name (*Christos,*
"anointed one") and mission are in a real sense shared by his followers. *All
knowledge is yours:* one of the gifts of the Holy Spirit (Is 11, 2) by which
the faithful could distinguish truth from falsehood (Jn 16, 13ff). The auth-
or's purpose is to reassure rather than instruct (v 21), because his readers
have already received knowledge through their anointing (v 27).

2, 22f: To deny the Son is to deny the Father since only in and through
the Son has God fully revealed his fatherhood; cf M. 11, 27; Lk 10, 22; Jn
5, 23; 10, 30; 14, 7.9.

has no claim on the Father,
but he who acknowledges the Son
can claim the Father as well.

Life for God's Anointed

24 As for you,
let what you heard from the beginning
remain in your hearts,
If what you heard from the beginning
does remain in your hearts,
then you in turn will remain in the Son and in
the Father.
25 He himself made us a promise
and the promise is no less than this:
eternal life.
26 I have written you these things
about those who try to deceive you.
27 As for you,
the anointing you received from him
remains in your hearts.
This means you have no need
for anyone to teach you.
Rather, as his anointing teaches you about all things
and is true—free from any lie—
remain in him
as that anointing taught you.

Children of God

28 Remain in him now, little ones,
so that, when he reveals himself,
we may be fully confident
and not retreat in shame at his coming.
29 If you consider the holiness that is his,
you can be sure that everyone who acts in holiness
has been begotten by him.

24: Jn 14, 23.   25: Jn 5, 24; 10, 28; 17, 2.

2, 25: *The promise is no less than this: eternal life:* the only passage of the Johannine writings in which *eternal life* has the exclusively eschatological sense of the life of glory, the object of Christian hope and striving. Elsewhere the term is invariably used of the present life of grace leading to glory.

2, 28f: A renewed exhortation to Christians to *remain* in Christ, i. e., to live the Christ-life and thus enjoy the assurance of acceptance by him at his second coming. The verses prepare them for the transition to the theme of their divine sonship and the duties flowing from it: *Everyone who acts in holiness has been begotten by him.*

3

¹ See what love the Father has bestowed on us
in letting us be called children of God!
Yet that is what we are.
The reason the world does not recognize us
is that it never recognized the Son.
² Dearly beloved,
we are God's children now;
what we shall later be has not yet come to light.
We know that when it comes to light
we shall be like him,
for we shall see him as he is.
³ Everyone who has this hope based on him
keeps himself pure, as he is pure.

Avoiding Sin

⁴ Everyone who sins acts lawlessly,
for sin is lawlessness.
⁵ You know well that the reason he revealed himself
was to take away sins;
in him there is nothing sinful.
⁶ The man who remains in him does not sin.
The man who sins has not seen him
or known him.
⁷ Little ones,
let no one deceive you;
the man who acts in holiness is holy indeed,
even as the Son is holy.
⁸ The man who sins belongs to the devil,

3, 1: Jn 1, 12; 15, 21;
17, 25; Eph 1, 5.
2: Phil 3, 21.
3: 2, 6.

5: Is 53, 9; Jn 1, 29; 8, 46;
1 Pt 2, 22.
8: Jn 8, 44; 12, 31f.

3, 1ff: **The greatest proof of God's love for men** is the gift of his Son, through whom they are not only called, but are in reality, God's sons; cf Jn 3, 16. This condition is true of their present life and, in the fullest sense, of the life to come when the divine filiation will result in their being like God and in seeing him *as he is*. They prepare for it by leading a life like that of God's Son, keeping themselves *pure, as he is pure* (v 3). Since the world never recognized the Father in the Son, neither will it recognize those who are children of the Father.

3, 4-10: The two contrary states, of sin and of holiness, are shown here in their intrinsic opposition. Release from sin establishes union and fellowship with Christ; adherence to sin, fellowship with the devil, who is *a sinner from the beginning.* Thus virtue and sin are the two opposite characteristics for distinguishing the children of God from the children of the devil.

3, 4: *Lawlessness:* hostility toward God and rejection of Christ, the standard of holiness.

because the devil is a sinner from the beginning.
It was to destroy the devil's works
that the Son of God revealed himself.
⁹ No one begotten of God acts sinfully
because he remains of God's stock;
he cannot sin
because he is begotton of God.
¹⁰ That is the way to see who are God's children
and who are the devil's.
No one whose actions are unholy belongs to God,
nor anyone who fails to love his brother.

Keeping the Commandments

¹¹ This, remember, is the message
you heard from the beginning:
we should love one another.
¹² We should not follow the example of Cain
who belonged to the evil one
and killed his brother.
Why did he kill him?
Because his own deeds were wicked
while his brother's were just.
¹³ No need, then, brothers, to be surprised
if the world hates you.
¹⁴ That we have passed from death to life we know
because we love the brothers.
The man who does not love is among the living dead.
¹⁵ Anyone who hates his brother is a murderer,
and you know that eternal life
abides in no murderer's heart.
¹⁶ The way we came to understand love
was that he laid down his life for us;
we too must lay down our lives for our brothers.
¹⁷ I ask you, how can God's love survive in a man
who has enough of this world's goods
yet closes his heart to his brother

11: 2, 7; Jn 13, 34;
    15, 12.17.
12: Gn 4, 8; Jude 11.
13: Mt 24, 9; Jn 15, 18;
    17, 14.

14: Lv 19, 17; Jn 5, 24.
15: Jn 8, 44.
16: 2, 6; Mt 20, 28;
    Jn 10, 11; 15, 13.
17: Dt 15, 7.11; Jas 2, 15f.

3, 11-24: The virtue of charity, even to the point of giving up one's life
for his neighbor as Christ did (v 16), is the fulfillment of the commandments (22ff), the guarantee of life and union with God through the presence of the Spirit (21.24).

when he sees him in need?
¹⁸ Little children,
let us love in deed and in truth
and not merely talk about it.
¹⁹ This is our way of knowing we are committed
   to the truth
and are at peace before him
²⁰ no matter what our consciences may charge
   us with;
for God is greater than our hearts
and all is known to him.
²¹ Beloved,
if our consciences have nothing to charge us with,
we can be sure that God is with us
²² and that we will receive at his hands
whatever we ask.
Why? Because we are keeping his commandments
and doing what is pleasing in his sight.
²³ His commandment is this:
we are to believe in the name of his Son, Jesus Christ,
and are to love one another as he commanded us.
²⁴ Those who keep his commandments remain in him
and he in them.
And this is how we know that he remains in us:
from the Spirit that he gave us.

4

Testing the Spirits

¹ Beloved,
do not trust every spirit,
but put the spirits to a test
to see if they belong to God,
because many false prophets have appeared in the
   world.

18: Jas 1, 22.
22: 5, 15; Mt 7, 7-11;
   21, 22; Jn 14, 13f.

23: Jn 13, 34; 15, 17.
24: 4, 13; Jn 14, 21-23.
4, 1: 2, 18; Mt 24, 24.

4, 1-6: Delusion and deception are invariably possible in matters of spiritual phenomena. Discernment between a true and false spirit of prophecy depends on acceptance or rejection of sound doctrine; cf 1 Cor 12, 3.10. Thus, acknowledgment or denial of the central truth of Christianity, the incarnation of Jesus Christ, the Son of God, is proof of whether one belongs to God or to antichrist (1ff). A power greater than that of the world abides in those who belong to God and who heed the teaching of the apostles (2.6). It conquers the false prophets (v 4) who belong to the world, speak its language and receive its attention (v 5; cf 2, 12-17.22-27).

2 This is how you can recognize God's Spirit:
every spirit that acknowledges Jesus Christ come
   in the flesh
belongs to God,
3 while every spirit that fails to acknowledge him
does not belong to God.
Such is the spirit of the antichrist
which, as you have heard, is to come;
in fact, it is in the world already.
4 You are of God, you little ones,
and thus you have conquered the false prophets.
For there is One greater in you
than there is in the world.
5 Those others belong to the world;
that is why theirs is the language of the world
and why the world listens to them.
6 We belong to God
and anyone who has knowledge of God gives us a
   hearing,
while anyone who is not of God refuses to hear us.
Thus do we distinguish the spirit of truth
from the spirit of deception.

God's Love and Ours

7 Beloved,
let us love one another
because love is of God;
everyone who loves is begotten of God
and has knowledge of God.
8 The man without love has known nothing of God,
for God is love.
9 God's love was revealed in our midst in this way:
he sent his only Son to the world
that we might have life through him.

2: 1 Cor 12, 3;
  1 Thes 5, 21.
3: 2, 22.

5: Jn 15, 19.
6: Jn 8, 47; 10, 16.
9: Jn 3, 16.

4, 7-21: These verses explain the nature of love as revealed by God and
accepted by man through faith.
4, 7f: *Love is of God:* therefore one who loves shows that he is begotten of God. *God is love:* love is his very being. To love God is to know
him and to share his life.
4, 9: *God's love . . . in this way:* the revelation of God's being consists
in sending the Son of his love *to the world* as our Savior (cf v 14) that
we might have life through him; cf Jn 3, 16.

¹⁰ Love, then, consists in this:
not that we have loved God,
but that he has loved us
and has sent his Son as an offering for our sins.
¹¹ Beloved,
if God has loved us so,
we must have the same love for one another.
¹² No one has ever seen God.
Yet if we love one another
God dwells in us,
and his love is brought to perfection in us.
¹³ The way we know we remain in him
and he in us
is that he has given us of his Spirit.
¹⁴ We have seen for ourselves, and can testify,
that the Father has sent the Son as savior of
     the world.
¹⁵ When anyone acknowledges that Jesus is
     the Son of God,
God dwells in him
and he in God.
¹⁶ We have come to know and to believe
in the love God has for us.

God is love,
and he who abides in love
abides in God,
and God in him.
¹⁷ Our love is brought to perfection in this,
that we should have confidence on the day
     of judgment;
for our relation to this world is just like his.
¹⁸ Love has no room for fear;
rather, perfect love casts out all fear.
And since fear has to do with punishment,
love is not yet perfect in one who is afraid.

10: Rom 5, 8.   12: Jn 1, 18; 1 Tm 6, 16.   17: 2, 28.

4, 10: *Love . . . consists in this: not that we have loved God but that he has loved us:* man has not merited God's love. It has been given freely and its value consists in sharing and continuing that love which is in God; cf v 19. *He . . . has sent his Son as an offering for our sins:* an act of his mercy and forgiveness manifested through the death of Christ; cf 2, 2. This is the motive of our love for one another.

4, 11f: Through love for one another we can be certain that *God dwells in us* and brings *his love . . . to perfection* in us. Thus we are able to "see," i. e., to know, the invisible God.

[19] We, for our part, love
because he first loved us.
[20] If anyone says, "My love is fixed on God,"
yet hates his brother,
he is a liar.
One who has no love for the brother he has seen
cannot love the God he has not seen.
[21] The commandment we have from him is this:
whoever loves God must also love his brother.

5

[1] Everyone who believes that Jesus is the Christ has been
begotten of God.

Now, everyone who loves the father
loves the child he has begotten.
[2] We can be sure that we love God's children
when we love God
and do what he has commanded.
[3] The love of God consists in this:
that we keep his commandments—
and his commandments are not burdensome.
[4] Everyone begotten of God conquers the world,
and the power that has conquered the world
is this faith of ours.
[5] Who, then, is conqueror of the world?
The one who believes that Jesus is the Son of God.

[6] Jesus Christ it is who came through water
and blood—
not in water only,
but in water and in blood.
It is the Spirit who testifies to this,

20: 2, 4.
21: Jn 13, 34; 14, 15.21;
    15, 17.
5, 1: Jn 8, 42; 1 Pt 1, 23.

3: Jn 14, 15.
4: Jn 16, 33.
5: 1 Cor 15, 57.
6: Jn 15, 26; 19, 34.

5, 1-5: To become a child of God it is necessary to believe in the divine
sonship of Jesus Christ, the only-begotten Son of the Father. It is through
him that we receive our sonship. The proof of love for God consists in
keeping his commandments (cf 2, 3-6; 3, 24), the greatest of which, after
love for God, is love of the brethren, i. e., those begotten of God; cf 4, 21;
Mt 22, 37-40; Mk 12, 30f; Lk 10, 27f. Practical faith of this kind confers
a power that conquers the world of evil, even as Christ overcame the world
(Jn 16, 33).
5, 6: *Jesus Christ it is who came through water and blood:* references to
the Father's testimony: *This is my beloved Son* (Mt 3, 17) when Jesus was
baptized in the waters of the Jordan, and to Jesus' office of Savior through
the shedding of his blood on the cross (Jn 19, 34).

and the Spirit is truth.
[7] Thus there are three that testify,
[8] the Spirit and the water and the blood—
and these three are of one accord.
[9] Do we not accept human testimony?
The testimony of God is much greater:
it is the testimony God has given
on his own Son's behalf.
[10] Whoever believes in the Son of God
possesses that testimony within his heart.
Whoever does not believe God
has made God a liar
by refusing to believe in the testimony
he has given on his own Son's behalf.
[11] The testimony is this:
God gave us eternal life,
and this life is in his Son.
[12] Whoever possesses the Son
possesses life;
whoever does not possess the Son of God
does not possess life.

[13] I have written this to you to make you realize that you possess eternal life—you who believe in the name of the Son of God.

Prayer for Sinners

[14] We have this confidence in God: that he hears us whenever we ask for anything according to his will. [15] And since we

---

7: Jn 5, 32.36; 15, 26.
9: Jn 5, 32.37.
10: Jn 3, 33.
11: 1, 2; Jn 1, 4; 5, 21.26;

17, 3.
13: Jn 1, 12; 20, 31.
14: 3, 22; Mt 7, 7;
Jn 14, 13f.

5, 7ff: The testimony to Christ, the Son of God and Savior (v 5), is confirmed by divine witness, greater by far than the two legally required human witnesses (Dt 17, 6) to substantiate truth; cf Jn 8, 17f. There is probably a symbolic reference here to baptism and the Eucharist whose existence and efficacy, like that of all the sacraments, derive from the death of Christ; cf Jn 19, 34.

5, 10: Through man's belief in the divine sonship of Christ, God dwells in man through Christ. Thus he becomes the witness to this truth. Unbelief in the divine sonship of Jesus means rejecting the divine testimony, thereby making God the author of a lie.

5, 11f: By accepting Christ as Son of God through faith, we receive Christ himself who becomes in us the source of eternal life.

5, 13: This summary of the epistle recalls the epilogue of the gospel of John (20, 30f).

5, 14f: The intimate relationship between God and those begotten of him creates in his children conformity to the divine will which gives them confident assurance of receiving what they ask for; cf 2, 28; 4, 17; 3, 21f.

know that he hears us whenever we ask, we know that what we have asked him for is ours. ¹⁶ Anyone who sees his brother sinning, if the sin is not deadly, should petition God, and thus life will be given to the sinner. This is only for those whose sin is not deadly. There is such a thing as a deadly sin; I do not say that one should pray about that. ¹⁷ True, all wrongdoing is sin, but not all sin is deadly.

¹⁸ We know that no one begotten of God commits sin; rather, God protects the one begotten by him, and so the evil one cannot touch him. ¹⁹ We know that we belong to God, while the whole world is under the evil one. ²⁰ We know, too, that the Son of God has come and has given us discernment to recognize the One who is true. And we are in the One who is true, for we are in his Son Jesus Christ. He is the true God and eternal life.

²¹ My little children, be on your guard against idols.

| 16: Mt 12, 31. | | 20: Jer 24, 7; Jn 17, 3; Eph 1, 17. |

5, 16f: The prayer of Christians for their erring brethren is in conformity to the will of God, who in turn will restore life to the sinners. *Deadly sin:* probably apostasy or final impenitence.

5, 18-21: The epistle concludes with the solemn reaffirmation and summary of the great truths contained therein as well as the false doctrines which these truths condemn. There is again the sharp antithesis between, on the one hand, God, his Son, and those begotten of God through faith, and on the other, the evil one and the world of those enslaved by him. The Son reveals the God of truth in himself and in those who accept him. He conquers the evil one, and by dwelling in his followers and giving them eternal life, preserves them from the sin of the world and from the *idols* of false teachings that threaten the Christian community.

THE SECOND EPISTLE OF JOHN
INTRODUCTION

The Second and Third Epistles of John are of the same length (probably determined by the practical consideration of the writing space on one piece of papyrus). Each is in the usual letter format, and treats a specific problem. In each, the writer calls himself "the elder"; and their common authorship is further evidenced internally by similarities in style and wording, especially in the introductions and conclusions. The mention in each of an impending visit by the elder to the respective community (2 Jn 12; 3 Jn 14) has led to the suggestion that they were written about the same time and perhaps carried by the same messenger to the two localities, both on the elder's proposed route of travel. The traditionally assigned place and date of composition, Ephesus in the 90's, are plausible.

The identity of the elder is a problem. Certainly, more than age is implied in the use of the title. If the man was simply one of the group of elders or presbyters who were officials in Christian churches by the latter part of the first century (Jas 5, 14; 1 Pt 5, 1; 1 Tm 5, 17), the absence of a proper name that would distinguish him from the other elders is curious. Seemingly, the title "elder" was also applicable to an apostle (1 Pt 1, 5); and it was certainly applicable to the disciple of an apostle, as we learn from Papias and Irenaeus. It is doubtful that the elder who wrote 3 John was an apostle, for he admits that the leader of the community involved in the letter ignores his authority. One can scarcely believe that a member of the Christian community, even a leader, could resist an apostle, especially at this time toward the close of the century, when the Twelve were venerated as the foundation of the church (Rv 21, 14).

On the other hand, the elder is important enough to exercise a certain authority over communities other than his own, to teach authoritatively and brand others as heretical, to send out missionary preachers, etc. The most probable supposition is that the elder was the disciple of an apostle, with a claim to some of the apostolic prestige and authority —a claim not, however, accepted by all. The traditional association with John, son of Zebedee, may mean that the elder was one of John's prominent disciples. Whether or not he is the same disciple who was the fourth evangelist is disputed; see the Introduction to the Gospel according to John.

The Second Epistle is addressed to "a Lady who is elect and to her children." Since the contents of the letter are scarcely appropriate to an individual, scholars assume that the elder was using an accepted literary device by personifying a Christian community as a woman.

Love and truth are the great themes of the letter. The elder encourages the Christians of this community to let their Christianity show forth in their daily lives in two ways: first, by truly adhering to the great commandment of mutual love; and second, by adhering to the truth about Jesus. There is critical need for this admonition because heretical missionaries are about to descend upon the community. The heresy in question is apparently the one referred to in 1 Jn 4, 2—a denial of the reality of the incarnation of Jesus. The elder urgently insists that no hospitality be shown to these false teachers lest they use the opportunity to infiltrate the community.

THE SECOND EPISTLE OF JOHN

[1] The elder to a lady who is elect and to her children.

In truth I love each of you—and not only I but also all those who have come to know the truth. [2] This love is based on the truth that abides in us and will be with us forever. [3] In truth and love, then, we shall have grace, mercy, and peace from God the Father and from Jesus Christ, the Father's Son.

[4] It has given me great joy to find some of your children walking in the path of truth, just as we were commanded by the Father. [5] But now, my Lady, I would make this request of you (not as if I were writing you some new commandment; rather, it is a commandment we have had from the start): let us love one another. [6] This love involves our walking according to the commandments, and as you have heard from the beginning, the commandment is the way in which you should walk.

[7] Many deceitful men have gone out into the world, men who do not acknowledge Jesus Christ as coming in the flesh. Such is the deceitful one! This is the antichrist! [8] Look out that you yourselves do not lose what you have worked for; you must receive your reward in full. [9] Anyone who is so "progressive" that he does not remain rooted in the teaching of Christ does not possess God, while anyone who remains rooted in the teaching possesses both the Father and the Son. [10] If anyone comes

---

1: Jn 8, 32.
4: 3 Jn 3.
5: Jn 13, 34; 15, 12.
6: Jn 14, 15; 1 Jn 5, 3.
7: 1 Jn 2, 22; 4, 2f.
9: Jn 8, 31; 1 Jn 2, 24.

1: *A lady who is elect:* the adjective *elect* ("chosen by God") is applied to Christians at the beginning of some other New Testament epistles (1 Pt 1, 1; Ti 1, 1). In 1 Peter 5, 13, a Christian community (in Rome under the name *Babylon*) is referred to as *chosen together with you* the Christians of the dispersion; 1 Pt 1, 1). *The truth:* the revelation of God in Jesus, which Christians accept through faith.

3. *Grace, mercy, and peace:* like 1 and 2 Tm, this letter adds *mercy* to the *grace and peace* salutation that is common in the Pauline letters. *The Father's Son:* This title embodies the substance of the entire New Testament, and close variations of it occur; cf, e. g., Jn 1, 14.18; 3, 35; 5, 20. However, the precise wording used here is not found elsewhere in the New Testament. It is echoed in the hymn "Glory to God" of the Roman Mass.

4: *To find some of your children:* those whom he met. There is no necessary indication that others were not *walking in the path* of truth, literally "walking in truth": a Semitic expression used in Johannine writing to describe a way of living in which the Christian faith comes to expression. *Commanded:* either the commandment of brotherly love is meant (Jn 13, 34; 15, 12; 1 Jn 2, 7-11; 4, 21), or the twofold commandment of love and of orthodox belief about Jesus Christ (1 Jn 3, 23). Love is stressed in 2 Jn 4ff, belief in 7ff.

7: *Such is the deceitful one:* another title of antichrist and of those associated with antichrist; cf 1 Jn 2, 18f.22; 4, 2f.

8: *You:* it is not certain whether this means the elder (3 Jn 9f.12) or the Christians as above in vv 2-4. Some MSS have "we."

9. *Anyone who is so "progressive":* literally "Everyone who moves ahead." The elder does not condemn all theological devolpment but only that which departs from Jesus' teaching.

10f: The attitude inculcated here reflects the life-and-death struggle be-to you who does not bring this teaching, do not receive him into your house; do not even greet him, [11] for whoever greets him shares in the evil he does.

[12] While there is much more that I could write you, I do not intend to put it down on paper; instead, I hope to visit you and talk with you face to face, so that our joy may be full.

[13] The children of your elect sister send you their greetings.

12: Jn 15, 11; 17, 13; 1 Jn 1, 4.

---

tween Christianity and Docetism at the end of the first century. To imitate this attitude in the changed circumstances of our own times would be to misuse Scripture and to fail to understand its time-conditioned aspect. The love that the elder inculcates above (5f) requires in our times that we extend kindness to one another in a divided Christianity.

12: *Our joy:* other textual witnesses read "your joy."
13: *Your elect sister:* the community where the elder resides.

THE THIRD EPISTLE OF JOHN
INTRODUCTION

General questions concerning format and authorship are adverted to in the Introduction to 2 John. The main purpose of the letter is to secure hospitality and support for missionaries approved by the elder and perhaps sent out by him. Although the missionaries preach to the pagans, it is possible also that they embody the elder's influence and doctrinal authority over communities. Perhaps this is why Diotrephes, the ambitious leader of the community who rejects the elder's authority, refuses to receive the missionaries and tries to force others within the community to follow the same policy. The exact position of Diotrephes himself is not clear; for example, is he a monarchical bishop, as we might conceive the office nowadays, or one of the elders who by force of personality has taken over leadership?

To gain his purpose despite Diotrephes' opposition, the elder writes to Gaius, seemingly a man of position and wealth within the community. The elder praises Gaius' past hospitality, emphasizing that this attitude represents the true exercise of Christianity—"walking in the path of truth." He urges Gaius to continue to extend hospitality and to help outfit the missionaries for further travels. He recommends Demetrius to Gaius, perhaps for the double reason that Demetrius is the head of the missionary band and yet is unknown to Gaius. The elder also mentions a forthcoming visit of his own. This visit, during which he will also rebuke Diotrephes, may be meant to assure Gaius of support if Diotrephes seeks to expel Gaius from the church for granting the hospitality the elder requests. Despite its brevity and the inadequacy of its details, 3 John furnishes an extremely important insight into the problem of authority and influence in Christianity at the end of the first century.

THE THIRD EPISTLE OF JOHN

[1] The elder to the beloved Gaius, whom indeed I love.

[2] Beloved, I hope you are in good health—may you thrive in all other ways as you do in the spirit. [3] For it has given me great joy to have the brothers bear witness to how truly you walk in the path of truth. [4] Nothing delights me more than to hear that my children are walking in this path.

[5] Beloved, you demonstrate fidelity by all that you do for the brothers even though they are strangers; [6] indeed, they have testified to your love before the church. And you will do a good thing if, in a way that pleases God, you help them to continue their journey. [7] It was for the sake of the Name that they set out, and they are accepting nothing from the pagans. [8] Therefore, we owe it to such men to support them and thus to have our share in the work of truth.

[9] I did write to the church; but Diotrephes, who enjoys being their leader, ignores us. [10] Therefore, if I come I will speak publicly of what he is doing in spreading evil nonsense about us. And that is not all. Not only does he refuse to welcome the brothers himself but he even hinders those who wish to do so and expels them from the church!

[11] Beloved, do not imitate what is evil but what is good. Whoever does what is good belongs to God; whoever does what is

---

3: 2 Jn 4.

1: *Gaius:* although influential, he does not seem to have had an office in the community. He is referred to as one of the elder's spiritual children (v 4); whether this means he was converted by the elder, or simply that he accepted the elder's leadership, is uncertain. Gaius is called *beloved,* a frequent form of address for fellow Christians in New Testament epistolary literature.

3. *The brothers:* a designation of fellow Christians; cf Jn 21, 23. In this letter it refers to Christians who have been on a missionary enterprise, visiting Gaius and receiving hospitality from him, even though they had been previously unknown to him (v 5).

5: *Demonstrate fidelity by all that you do:* literally, "Whatever work you do for the brothers, you are doing something faithful." Gaius' hospitality is a manifestation of his true Christian faith.

6: *Help them to continue:* besides asking for maintenance for the missionaries while they are in Gaius' community, the elder asks him to equip them for their further travels.

7: *The Name:* Jesus, referred to in this manner in the New Testament (Acts 5, 41) and in later Christian works. *Accepting nothing:* not expecting support from the pagans to whom they preach the gospel, in contrast to some of the devotees of pagan gods who were constantly begging money.

9: *I did write:* a letter probably destroyed by Diotrephes. *Enjoys being their leader:* the elder does not deny that Diotrephes is the leader of the community but implicitly criticizes his ambition to be independent of the elder's influence.

10: *Spreading evil nonsense:* probably Diotrephes is accusing the elder of dictatorial interference in the community on account of his sending the missionaries.

11: *What is evil:* Gaius should not be influenced by Diotrephes but should maintain his previous policy of hospitality.

evil has never seen God. [12] Demetrius is one who gets a good testimonial from all, even from truth itself. We give our testimonial as well, and you know that our testimony is true.

[13] There is much more that I had in mind to write you, but I do not wish to write it out with pen and ink. [14] Rather, I hope to see you soon, when we can talk face to face.

[15] Peace be with you. The beloved here send you their greetings; greet the beloved there, each by name.

12: Jn 19, 35; 21, 24.

12: *Testimonial:* because of the danger of heretical teachers (2 Jn), strange missionaries needed recommendation from someone who could vouch for them; cf 2 Cor 3, 1; Rom 16, 1f; Col 4, 7f. *From truth itself:* refers probably to the way Demetrius lived this external witness to the truth that was in him (2 Jn 2).

15: *Beloved:* the Greek word *philos* in the Johannine vocabulary is probably a synonym for *agapetos,* "beloved," which appears in vv 1, 2, 5 and 11. Every Christian was a *philos* of Jesus and of every other Christian: "I no longer speak of you as slaves, . . . Instead I call you friends (*philous*)," i. e., beloved (Jn 15, 15). See note on Jn 15, 13.

THE EPISTLE OF JUDE
INTRODUCTION

The epistle purports to have been written by *Jude, a servant of Jesus Christ and brother of James* (see Introduction to James). Since this claimant is not identified as one of the Twelve, he is presumably not Jude the apostle (Lk 6, 16), but that relative of Jesus who doubted him during the ministry (Mk 6, 3). Nearly all scholars agree on this point of identification. However, some hold that the epistle itself cannot be dated early enough to make the superscription anything but pseudonymous. They instance the allusion to the apostles as men of a past time (v 17; cf v 3), and assert, in addition, that the characterization of the false teachers (v 18) and the use of a Greek translation of 1 Enoch (14f) point to the date of approximately 100 A.D.

These arguments, however, should be viewed with caution. Though the allusion to the apostles cited above does indicate that the author of Jude was thinking of a second-generation Christian community, the reference point need not have been the end of that generation; it could equally well have been its beginning, therefore not long after 70 A.D. Moreover, the author of Jude might have so described false teachers about 80 A.D., and might also have had access to a Greek translation of 1 Enoch. The date of about 80 A.D. for the epistle remains entirely possible. For this reason many other scholars accept Jude, the relative of Jesus and brother of James of Jerusalem, as its author. Nothing is known of this Jude's history, nor does his epistle provide information on the location of the Christians to whom it is addressed. Since he invokes the name of James by way of introducing himself, he seems not to have been very well known among the Christians to whom he wrote.

The epistle warns its recipients against the false brethren who have infiltrated their community (v 4). These persons are to be identified by their exaggerated doctrine of Christian freedom, for they encourage sensuality (v 4) and reject authority (v 8). The community must be alert to this threat in its midst, mindful of the divine judgments against those who fail to live according to faith or to Christian standards of conduct (5ff.11; 14ff).

On the foundation of faith, supported by prayer, the Christian is preserved in the love of God, and awaits a merciful judgment and eternal life (20f). This common faith delivered to the saints is the criterion of right belief (v 3). What is contrary to it is *destined for condemnation* because it turns the grace of God into wantonness and denies Jesus Christ, the *only Master and Lord* (v 4).

The energetic and picturesque style of this epistle is reminiscent of that of the early prophets.

St. Jerome acknowledges that some rejected the epistle because of its citation of the apocryphal Book of Enoch, but states that the ancient authority it enjoyed and its use in the churches assured its place in the canon of the inspired writings.

Scholars agree that the author of 2 Peter drew upon the Epistle of Jude.

THE EPISTLE OF JUDE

Greeting

¹ Jude, a servant of Jesus Christ and brother of James, to those who have been called by God; who have found love in God the Father and have been guarded safely in Jesus Christ. ² May mercy, peace, and love be yours in ever greater measure.

Exhortation to Steadfastness

³ I was already fully intent on writing you, beloved, about the salvation we share. But now I feel obliged to write and encourage you to fight hard for the faith delivered once for all to the saints. ⁴ Certain individuals have recently wormed their way into your midst, godless types, long ago destined for the condemnation I shall describe. They pervert the gracious gift of our God to sexual excess and deny Jesus Christ, our only master and Lord.

Against False Teachers

⁵ I wish to remind you of certain things, even though you may already be very well aware of them. The Lord first rescued his people from the land of Egypt but later destroyed those who refused to believe. ⁶ There were angels, too, who did not keep to their own domain, who deserted their dwelling place. These the Lord has kept in perpetual bondage, shrouded in murky darkness against the judgment of the great day. ⁷ Sodom, Gomorrah, and the towns thereabout indulged in lust, just as those angels did; they practiced unnatural vice. They are set before us to dissuade us, as they undergo a punishment of eternal fire.

⁸ Similarly, these visionaries pollute the flesh; they spurn

1: Mt 13, 55.
3: 2 Pt 2, 1.
4: 2 Jn 10.

5: Nm 14, 35; 1 Cor 6, 3; 10, 5.
6: 2 Pt 2, 4.

1f: *Jude, . . . brother of James:* for the identity of the author of this letter, see the Introduction. *To those who have been called by God:* the vocation to the Christian faith is God's free gift to those whom he loves and whom he safely protects in Christ until the Lord's second coming.

3f: *The salvation we share:* the teachings of the Christian faith *delivered once for all to the saints:* i. e., handed down in their entirety and accepted by the Christian community. They are not to be perverted by haterodoxy; cf 1 Cor 3, 11; 15, 1; Gal 1, 6-19; 1 Tm 1, 3; 6, 3. *Certain individuals . . . destined for the condemnation:* false teachers within the community who deny Christ as Lord and Savior and seduce the people by advocating sexual lawlessness. Their punishment is already foreshadowed in Old Testament examples of unfaithful ones among the angels and among God's people (5ff). There is also reference here to the apocryphal Book of Enoch (14f), which was highly regarded in the early centuries of the Christian era.

5: *Destroyed those who refused to believe:* see note on Nm 14, 28f.

6: See note on Gn 6, 1-4; cf also 2 Pt 2, 4-6.

7: *Sodom, Gommorrah:* frequently used in the Scriptures as examples of sin and punishment; cf Is 1, 9; Jer 50, 40; Lam 4, 6; Ez 16, 56; Mt 10, 15; 11, 24 Lk 17, 29. See note on Gn 19, 25.

8: *Visionaries:* victims of hallucination, or self-authorized prophets of rev-

God's dominion and revile the angelic beings. [9] Even the arch-angel Michael, when his case with the devil was being judged—a dispute over Moses' body—did not venture to charge him with blasphemy. He simply said, "May the Lord punish you." [10] These people, however, not only revile what they have no knowledge of but are corrupted through the very things they know by instinct, like brute animals. [11] So much the worse for them! They have taken the road Cain took. They have abandoned themselves to Balaam's error for pay, and like Korah they perish in rebellion. [12] These men are blotches on your Christian banquets. They join your solemn feasts without shame and only look after themselves. They are blown on the wind like clouds that bring no rain. Like trees at the year's end they bear no fruit, being dead and uprooted. [13] They are wild ocean waves, splashing their shameless deeds abroad like foam, or shooting stars for whom the thick gloom of darkness has been reserved forever. [14] It was about these that Enoch, who was of the seventh generation descended from Adam, prophesied when he said, "See, the Lord has come with his countless holy ones about him [15] to pass judgment on all men, indicting the godless for every evil deed they have done, and convicting those godless sinners of every harsh word they have uttered against him."

[16] These men are grumblers and whiners. They live by their passions, uttering bombast. Whenever it is expedient, they resort

---

9: Zec 3, 2.
11: Gn 4, 8; Nm 16, 22; 31, 16.
12: Prv 25, 14.

13: Is 57, 20.
14: Gn 5, 21; Dt 33, 24.
15: Mal 3, 13.

---

elation (cf 2 Pt 2, 10.18) who distort and debase Christian revelation to the detriment of the community.

Revile the angelic beings: i. e., probably by attributing their own disorders to the angels whom they invoke as their patrons.

9. *The archangel Michael . . . blasphemy:* an apparent reference to the story concerning the dispute between Michael and the devil over Moses' body, as described in the apocryphal *Assumption of Moses.* If Michael did not accuse even the devil but left the judgment of him to God, how much less should men presume to revile the angels! Michael was regarded as the protector of ancient Israel and of the new Israel, the church cf Rv 12, 7; Dan 10, 13.20f; 13, 1ff.

11: *Cain . . . Balaam . . . Korah:* examples of rebillious leaders and of the punishments their conduct incurred; cf Gn 4, 8-16; Nm 16, 1-35; 31, 16.

12f: *Blotches on your Christian banquets:* scandalous conduct in connection with the eucharistic celebrations (cf 2 Pt 2, 13) which in apostolic times were associated with a community meal; cf Acts 2, 46; 1 Cor 11, 20-34.

Clouds that bring no rain; trees . . . dead and uprooted; wild ocean waves; shooting stars: empty display of force and beauty and splendor devoid of any genuine source to sustain them. Shooting stars were considered by the ancients to forebode catastrophe. Here they symbolize Christians who have withdrawn far from God as they plunge into exterior darkness; cf Enoch 18-21.

14f: A reference to Enoch (1, 9). For the description of Christ the universal judge of mankind, surrounded by his angels, cf Dn 7, 10; Mt 25, 21; Heb 12, 22.

to flattery. [17] Remember, beloved, all of you, the prophetic words of the apostles of our Lord Jesus Christ; [18] how they kept telling you, "In the last days there will be impostors living by their godless passions." [19] These sensualists, devoid of the Spirit, are causing divisions among you.

Christian Admonitions

[20] But you, beloved, grow strong in your holy faith through prayer in the Holy Spirit. Persevere in God's love, [21] and welcome the mercy of our Lord Jesus Christ which leads to life eternal. [22] Correct those who are confused; the others you must rescue, snatching them from the fire. [23] Even with those you pity, be on your guard; abhor so much as their flesh-stained clothing.

Doxology

[24] There is One who can protect you from a fall and make you stand unblemished and exultant in the presence of his glory. [25] Glory be to this only God our savior, through Jesus Christ our Lord. Majesty, too, be his, might and power from ages past, now and for ages to come. Amen.

17: 2 Pt 3, 2f.   Jas 5, 19f.
20: 1 Cor 3, 9-17.   24: 2 Pt 3, 14.
23: Am 4, 11; Zec 3, 2;

17ff: The prophetic utterances of the apostles concerning the last days are repeated here to help Christians prepare themselves for the struggle against the enemies of their faith.

18: *In the last days . . . godless passions:* the substance rather than the direct quotation of the many New Testament passages, such as Mk 13, 22; Acts 20, 30; 1 Tm 4, 1ff; 2 Pt 3, 3. *The last* refers not to the imminent proximity of the second coming of Christ, as thought by many in the early Christian community, but to various stages in messianic times.

20f: These verses contain the trinitarian doctrine: God (the Father) who loves us, *the Holy Spirit* who prays in us, and *our Lord Jesus Christ* who *leads* us to *life eternal.* They also sum up the Christian life in terms of the theological virtues (faith, hope, charity) and the practice of prayer.

24f: *There is One who can protect you:* God through Jesus Christ. The purpose of the epistle is brought back into focus at its conclusion: perseverance of Christians in the faith amid the many evils that threaten to destroy it; cf 1 Pt 3, 17f. Verse 25 contains an illustrious New Testament doxology; cf also Rom 16, 27; Eph 3, 20; 1 Pt 4, 11; 2 Pt 3, 18.

THE BOOK OF REVELATION
INTRODUCTION

The Book of Revelation, or the Apocalypse, is the last book of the Bible, and perhaps the least read. It is also one of the most difficult to understand because it abounds in unfamiliar and extravagant symbolism, which at best appears unusual to the modern reader. Symbolic language, however, is one of the chief characteristics of apocalyptic literature, of which this book is an outstanding example. Such literature enjoyed wide popularity in both Jewish and Christian circles from 200 B.C. to 200 A.D.

This book contains an account of visions in symbolic and allegorical language borrowed in part from the Old Testament, especially Ezekiel, Zechariah, and the apocalyptic Book of Daniel. Whether these visions were real experiences of the author or simply literary conventions employed by him is an open question, the solution of which in no way adds to, or detracts from, the divine inspiration of the book.

Symbolic descriptions are not to be taken as literal descriptions, nor is the symbolism capable of being pictured realistically. One would find it both difficult and repulsive to visualize a lamb with seven horns and seven eyes; yet Christ our Lord is described in precisely such words (5, 6). The author used these images to suggest Christ's universal power (seven horns) and knowledge (seven eyes). Another significant feature of apocalyptic writing is the use of symbolic colors (1, 13-16; 3, 18; 4, 4; 6, 1-8; 17, 4; 19, 8) and numbers (*four* signifies the world; *six,* imperfection; *seven,* totality or perfection; *twelve,* Israel's tribes or the Apostles; *thousand,* immensity). Finally, the vindictive language in the book (6, 9f; 18, 1—19, 4) is also to be understood symbolically, and not literally. The cries for vengeance that sound so harsh on the lips of Christian martyrs are in fact literary devices the author employed to evoke in the reader and hearer a feeling of horror for apostasy and rebellion, which will be severely punished by God.

The Book of Revelation cannot be adequately comprehended except against the historical background which occasioned its writing. Like the Book of Daniel and other apocalypses, it was composed as resistance literature to meet a crisis. The book itself suggests that the crisis was ruthless persecution of the early Church by the Roman authorities; the harlot Babylon symbolizes pagan Rome, the city on seven hills (17, 9). The book is, then, an exhortation and admonition to the Christian to stand firm in the faith and to avoid compromise with paganism, despite the threat of adversity and martyrdom; he is to await patiently the fulfillment of God's mighty promises. The triumph of God in the world of men remains a mystery, to be accepted in faith and longed for in hope. It is a triumph that unfolded in the history of Jesus of Nazareth, and continues to unfold in the history of the individual Christian who follows the way of the cross, even, if necessary, to a martyr's death.

Though the perspective is eschatological—ultimate salvation and victory are said to take place at the end of the present age when Christ will come in glory at the Parousia—the book presents the decisive struggle of Christ and his followers against Satan and his cohorts as already over. Christ's overwhelming defeat of the kingdom of Satan has ushered in the everlasting reign of God (11, 15; 12, 10). Even the forces of evil unwittingly carry out the divine plan (17, 17), for God is the sovereign Lord of history.

The Book of Revelation had its origin in a time of crisis, but it remains valid for Christians of all time. In the face of evils from within and without, the Christian can confidently trust in God's promise to be with the church forever.

The author of the book calls himself John (1, 1.4.9; 22, 8), who because of his Christian faith had been exiled to the rocky island of Patmos. Although he never claims to be the apostle of the same name, many of the early church Fathers so identified him. This identification is not altogether certain. Vocabulary, grammar, and style make it doubtful that the book could have been put into its present form by the person(s) responsible for the fourth gospel. Nevertheless, there are definite linguistic and theological affinities between the two books. The tone of the letters to the seven churches (1, 4—3, 22) is indicative of the great authority the writer enjoyed over the Christian communities in Asia. It is quite likely, therefore, that he was at least a disciple of the apostle John, who also lived in that part of the world. The date of composition is probably near the end of the reign of Domitian (81-96 A.D.), a fierce persecutor of the Christians.

The principal divisions of the Book of Revelation are the following:
   I: Prologue (1, 1-3)
  II: Letters to the Churches of Asia (1, 4—3, 22)
 III: Preparation for the Day of the Lord (4, 1—16, 21)
  IV: Punishment of Babylon (17, 1—19, 10)
   V: Destruction of Pagan Nations (19, 11—20, 15)
  VI: New Creation (21, 1—22, 5)
 VII: Epilogue (22, 6-21)

THE BOOK OF REVELATION
I: PROLOGUE

1

¹ This is the revelation God gave to Jesus Christ, that he might show his servants what must happen very soon. He made it known by sending his angel to his servant John, ² who in reporting all he saw bears witness to the word of God and the testimony of Jesus Christ. ³ Happy is the man who reads this prophetic message, and happy are those who hear it and heed what is written in it, for the appointed time is near!

II: LETTERS TO THE CHURCHES OF ASIA

Greeting

⁴ To the seven churches in the province of Asia: John wishes you grace and peace—from him who is and who was and who is to come, and from the seven spirits before his throne, ⁵ and from Jesus Christ the faithful witness, the first-born from the dead and ruler of the kings of earth. To him who loves us and freed us from our sins by his own blood, ⁶ who has made us a royal nation of priests in the service of his God and Father— to him be glory and power forever and ever! Amen.

⁷ See, he comes amid the clouds!
    Every eye shall see him,
      even of those who pierced him.
  All the peoples of the earth
    shall lament him bitterly.
So it is to be! Amen!

⁸ The Lord God says, "I am the Alpha and the Omega, the One who is and who was and who is to come, the Almighty!"

1, 5: 1 Cor 15, 20; Col 1, 18;
    Heb 9, 14; 1 Pt 1, 19;
    1 Jn 1, 7.

7: Zec 12, 10; Mt 24, 30;
    Jn 19, 37.
8: 21, 6; 22, 13; Is 44, 6.

1, 3: *Happy is the man:* the first of seven beatitudes in this book; the others are in 14, 13; 16, 15; 19, 9; 20, 6; 22, 7.14. *Those who hear it:* in the liturgical assembly. *The appointed time:* when Jesus will return in glory; cf 1, 7; 3, 11; 22, 7.10.12.20.

1, 4: *Seven churches . . . Asia:* in western Asia Minor (modern Turkey). These representative churches are mentioned by name in 1, 11; each is the recipient of a message (2, 1—3, 22). *Seven* is the biblical number suggesting fullness and completeness; thus John is writing for the whole church.

1, 5: *Freed us:* other ancient MSS read "washed us."

1, 8: *The Alpha and the Omega:* the first and last letters of the Greek alphabet. In 22, 13 the same words occur, together with the expressions *the First and the Last, the Beginning and the End;* cf 1, 17; 2, 8; 21, 6; Is 44, 6.

First Vision

⁹ I, John, your brother, who share with you the distress and the kingly reign and the endurance we have in Jesus, found myself on the island called Patmos because I proclaimed God's word and bore witness to Jesus. ¹⁰ On the Lord's day I was caught up in ecstasy, and I heard behind me a piercing voice like the sound of a trumpet, ¹¹ which said, "Write on a scroll what you now see and send it to the seven churches: to Ephesus, Smyrna, Pergamum, Thyatira, Sardis, Philadelphia, and Laodicea." ¹² I turned around to see whose voice it was that spoke to me. When I did so I saw seven lampstands of gold, ¹³ and among the lampstands One like a Son of Man wearing an ankle-length robe, with a sash of gold about his breast. ¹⁴ The hair of his head was as white as snow-white wool and his eyes blazed like fire. ¹⁵ His feet gleamed like polished brass refined in a furnace, and his voice sounded like the roar of rushing waters. ¹⁶ In his right hand he held seven stars. A sharp, two-edged sword came out of his mouth, and his face shone like the sun at its brightest.

¹⁷ When I caught sight of him I fell down at his feet as though dead. He touched me with his right hand and said: "There is nothing to fear. I am the First and the Last ¹⁸ and the One who lives. Once I was dead but now I live—forever and ever. I hold the keys of death and the nether world. ¹⁹ Write down, therefore, whatever you see in visions—what you see now and will see in time to come. ²⁰ This is the secret meaning of the seven stars you saw in my right hand, and of the seven

---

13: Dn 7, 13; 10, 5.
16: Ez 43, 2; Heb 4, 12.

17: Is 41, 4; Dn 8, 18.
19: Is 44, 6; 48, 12.

1, 9: *Island called Patmos:* in the Aegean Sea, southwest of Ephesus.
1, 10: *The Lord's day:* Sunday.
1, 12-16: A symbolic description of Christ in glory; cf Introduction.
1, 13: *Son of Man:* see note on Mt 8, 20. *Angle-length robe:* Christ is priest; cf Ex 28, 4; 29, 5. *Sash of gold:* Christ is king; cf 1 Mc 10, 89; 11, 58.
1, 14: *Hair . . . white as snow-white wool:* Christ is eternal (v 18; Dn 7, 9). *His eyes blazed like fire:* Christ is omniscient; cf 2, 23; Ps 7, 10; Jer 17, 10.
1, 15: *His feet . . . furnace:* Christ is immutable; cf Ez 1, 27; Dn 10, 6. *His voice . . . waters:* Christ speaks with divine authority; cf Ez 1, 24.
1, 16: *A sharp, two-edged sword:* the word of God (Eph 6, 17; Heb 4, 12), which will destroy unrepentant sinners (2, 16; 19, 15). *His face . . . brightest:* the divine majesty of Christ; cf 21, 23; Is 60, 19.
1, 17: It was an Old Testament belief that for sinful man to see God was to die (Ex 19, 21; 33, 20; Is 6, 5).
1, 18: *Nether world:* the abode of the dead (20, 13).
1, 20: *Presiding spirits:* literally, angels. Angels were thought to be in charge of the physical world (7, 1; 16, 5), as well as of nations (Dn 10, 13; 12, 1), communities (the seven churches), and individuals (Mt 18, 10; Acts 12, 15).

lampstands of gold: the seven stars are the presiding spirits of the seven churches, and the seven lampstands are the seven churches.

2

To Ephesus

[1] "To the presiding spirit of the church in Ephesus, write this:

" 'The One who holds the seven stars in his right hand and walks among the seven lampstands of gold has this to say: [2] I know your deeds, your labors, and your patient endurance. I know you cannot tolerate wicked men; you have tested those self-styled apostles who are nothing of the sort, and discovered that they are impostors. [3] You are patient and endure hardship for my cause. Moreover, you do not become discouraged. [4] I hold this against you, though: you have turned aside from your early love. [5] Keep firmly in mind the heights from which you have fallen. Repent, and return to your former deeds. If you do not repent I will come to you and remove your lampstand from its place. [6] But you have this much in your favor: you detest the practices of the Nicolaitans, just as I do.

[7] " 'Let him who has ears heed the Spirit's word to the churches! I will see to it that the victor eats from the tree of life which grows in the garden of God.'

To Smyrna

[8] "To the presiding spirit of the church in Smyrna, write this:

" 'The First and the Last who once died but now lives has this to say: [9] I know of your tribulation and your poverty, even though you are rich. I know the slander you endure from self-styled Jews who are nothing other than members of Satan's assembly. [10] Have no fear of the sufferings to come. The devil

2, 7: 13, 9; 22, 2; Gn 2, 9.   9: Jas 2, 5.

2, 1—3, 22: Each of the seven letters follows the same pattern: address; description of the exalted Christ; blame and/or praise for the church addressed; threat and/or admonition; final exhortation and promise to all Christians.

2, 1: *Ephesus:* capital of the Roman province of Asia. *Walks among the seven lampstands:* Christ is always present in the church; see note on 1, 4.

2, 2: *Self-styled apostles . . . impostors:* unauthorized and perverse missionaries; cf Acts 20, 29f.

2, 6: *Nicolaitans:* perhaps the impostors of v 2; see note on vv 14f.

2, 7: *The tree of life . . . garden of God:* reference to the tree in the primeval paradise (Gn 2, 9); cf 22, 2.14.19.

2, 8: *Smyrna:* modern Izmir, north of Ephesus.

2, 9f: The church in Smyrna was materially poor but spiritually rich. Accusations made by Jews occasioned the persecution of Christians; cf Acts 14, 2.19; 17, 5.13.

will indeed cast some of you into prison to put you to the test; you will be tried over a period of ten days. Remain faithful until death and I will give you the crown of life.

[11] " 'Let him who has ears heed the Spirit's word to the churches! The victor shall never be harmed by the second death.'

To Pergamum

[12] "To the presiding spirit of the church in Pergamum, write this:

" 'The One with the sharp, two-edged sword has this to say: [13] I know you live in the very place where Satan's throne is erected; and I know you hold fast to my name and have not denied the faith you have in me, not even at the time when Antipas, my faithful witness, was martyred in your city where Satan has his home. [14] Nevertheless I hold a few matters against you: there are some among you who follow the teaching of Balaam, who instructed Balak to throw a stumbling block in the way of the Israelites by tempting them to eat food sacrificed to idols and to practice fornication. [15] Yes, you too have those among you who hold to the teaching of the Nicolaitans. [16] Therefore repent! If you do not, I will come to you soon and fight against them with the sword of my mouth.

[17] " 'Let him who has ears heed the Spirit's word to the churches! To the victor I will give the hidden manna; I will also give him a white stone upon which is inscribed a new name, to be known only by him who receives it.'

To Thyatira

[18] "To the presiding spirit of the church in Thyatira, write this:

" 'The Son of God, whose eyes blaze like fire and whose feet gleam like polished brass, has this to say: [19] I know your deeds —your love and faith and service—as well as your patient

---

11: 20, 6.14; 21, 8;   14: Nm 24, 3; 25, 2.
    1 Cor 9, 25.   17: Is 62, 2; 65, 15.

2, 11: *The second death:* when sinners will receive their final punishment (20, 6.14f; 21, 8).
2, 12: *Pergamum:* modern Bergama, north of Smyrna.
2, 13: *Satan's throne:* reference to emperor worship and other pagan practices that flourished in the city.
2, 14f: Like Balaam, the biblical prototype of religious compromisers (Nm 25, 1ff; 31, 16; 2 Pt 2, 15; Jude 11), the Nicolaitans in Pergamum and Ephesus (v 6) accommodated their Christian faith to paganism. They misused the law of liberty enunciated by St. Paul (1 Cor 9, 19-23).
2, 17: *The hidden manna:* the food of life; cf Ps 78, 24f. *White stone:* symbol of victory and joy; cf 3, 4f. *New name:* reference to the Christian's rebirth in Christ; cf 3, 12; 19, 12; Is 62, 2; 65, 15.
2, 18: *Thyatira:* modern Akhisar, southeast of Pergamum.

endurance; I know also that your efforts of recent times are greater than ever. ²⁰ Nevertheless I hold this against you: you tolerate a Jezebel—that self-styled prophetess who seduces my servants by teaching them to practice lewdness and to eat food sacrificed to idols. ²¹ I have given her a chance to repent but she refuses to turn from her lewdness. ²² I mean to cast her down on a bed of pain; her companions in sin I will plunge into intense suffering unless they repent of their sins with her, ²³ and her children I will put to death. Thus shall all the churches come to know that I am the searcher of hearts and minds, and that I will give each of you what your conduct deserves. ²⁴ And now I address myself to you others in Thyatira who do not uphold this teaching and know nothing of the so-called "deep secrets" of Satan; on you I place no further burden. ²⁵ In any case, hold fast to what you have until I come.

²⁶ " 'To the one who wins the victory, who keeps to my ways till the end, I will give authority over the nations—²⁷ the same authority I received from my Father. He shall rule them with a rod of iron and shatter them like crockery; ²⁸ and I will give him the morning star.

²⁹ " 'Let him who has ears heed the Spirit's word to the churches!'

3

To Sardis

¹ "To the presiding spirit of the church in Sardis, write this:

" 'The One who holds the seven spirits of God, the seven stars, has this to say: I know your conduct; I know the reputation you have of being alive, when in fact you are dead! ² Wake up, and strengthen what remains before it dies. I find that the sum of your deeds is less than complete in the sight of my God. ³ Call to mind how you accepted what you heard; keep to it,

---

23: 1 Sm 16, 7; Ps 7, 10;
   Jer 17, 10.
26: Ps 2, 8f.
29: 2 Pt 1, 19.

3, 3: Mt 24, 42-44;
   Mk 13, 33; 1 Thes 5, 2;
   2 Pt 3, 10.

2, 20: The scheming and treacherous Jezebel of old (1 Kgs 21, 1-14; 2 Kgs 9, 22.30-34) introduced pagan customs into the religion of Israel; this new Jezebel was doing the same to Christianity.

2, 24: *The so-called "deep secrets" of Satan:* a scathing reference to the perverse teaching of the Nicolaitans (v 15).

2, 26ff: The Christian who perseveres in faith will share in Christ's messianic authority and victory over death, symbolized by *the morning star* (22, 16); cf Ps 2, 8f.

3, 1f: *Sardis*, south and east of Thyatira, is reproached for the feverish activity of its Christians (*the reputation you have of being alive*), since such activity could not substitute for a living faith.

and repent. If you do not rouse yourselves I will come upon you like a thief, at a time you cannot know. [4] I realize that you have in Sardis a few persons who have not soiled their garments; these shall walk with me in white because they are worthy.

[5] " 'The victor shall go clothed in white. I will never erase his name from the book of the living, but will acknowledge him in the presence of my Father and his angels.

[6] " 'Let him who has ears heed the Spirit's word to the churches!'

To Philadelphia

[7] "To the presiding spirit of the church in Philadelphia, write this:

" 'The holy One, the true,
    who wields David's key,
who opens and no one can close,
who closes and no one can open,

has this to say:

[8] " 'I know your deeds; that is why I have left an open door before you which no one can close. I know that your strength is limited; yet you have held fast to my word and have not denied my name. [9] I mean to make some of Satan's assembly, those self-styled Jews who are not really Jews but frauds, come and fall down at your feet; they will learn of my love for you in that way. [10] Because you have kept my plea to stand fast, I will keep you safe in the time of trial which is coming on the whole world, to test all men on earth. [11] I am coming soon. Hold fast to what you have lest someone rob you of your crown.

[12] " 'I will make the victor a pillar in the temple of my God and he shall never leave it. I will inscribe on him the name of my God and the name of the city of my God, the new Jerusalem

---

4: 1 Thes 5, 2.
6: Ps 69, 29; Mt 10, 32.
7: Is 22, 22; Mt 16, 19.

9: Is 45, 14; 60, 14.
12: Ez 48, 35.

3, 4f: *In white:* the sign of victory and joy; see note on 2, 17. *The book of the living:* where the names of the redeemed are kept (21, 27); cf 13, 8; 17, 8; 20, 12.15; Phil 4, 3; Dn 12, 1. They will be acknowledged by Christ in heaven (Mt 10, 32).

3, 7: *Philadelphia,* modern Alasehir, southeast of Sardis. Destroyed by earthquake in 17 A. D. and rebuilt with money from the Emperor Tiberius, the city was renamed Neocaesarea, "New Caesar City." *David's key:* to the heavenly City of David, the new Jerusalem (v 12), over which Christ has supreme authority; cf Is 22, 22.

3, 8: *An open door:* opportunities for sharing and proclaiming the faith; cf 1 Cor 16, 19; 2 Cor 2, 12.

3, 12: *A pillar:* allusion to the rebuilding of the city; see note on v 7. *New Jerusalem:* describe in 21, 10—22, 5.

which he will send down from heaven, and my own name which is new.

[13] " 'Let him who has ears heed the Spirit's word to the churches!'

To Laodicea

[14] "To the presiding spirit of the church in Laodicea, write this:

" 'The Amen, the faithful Witness and true, the Source of God's creation, has this to say: [15] I know your deeds; I know you are neither hot nor cold. How I wish you were one or the other—hot or cold! [16] But because you are lukewarm, neither hot nor cold, I will spew you out of my mouth! [17] You keep saying, "I am so rich and secure that I want for nothing." Little do you realize how wretched you are, how pitiable and poor, how blind and naked! [18] Take my advice, Buy from me gold refined by fire if you would be truly rich. Buy white garments in which to be clothed, if the shame of your nakedness is to be covered. Buy ointment to smear on your eyes, if you would see once more. [19] Whoever is dear to me I reprove and chastise. Be earnest about it, therefore. Repent!

[20] " 'Here I stand, knocking at the door. If anyone hears me calling and opens the door, I will enter his house and have supper with him, and he with me. [21] I will give the victor the right to sit with me on my throne, as I myself won the victory and took my seat beside my Father on his throne.

[22] " 'Let him who has ears heed the Spirit's word to the churches.' "

III: PREPARATION FOR THE DAY OF THE LORD

4

Vision of Heavenly Worship

[1] After this I had another vision: above me there was an

14: 1, 5; Jn 1, 3. 19: Prv 3, 12; Heb 12, 6.

3, 14: *Laodicea*, southeast of Philadelphia, was a wealth commercial center. *The Amen:* a divine title applied to Christ; cf Is 65, 16; 2 Cor 1, 20: *Source of God's creation:* a concept found also in Jn 1, 3; Col 1, 16f; Heb 1, 2; cf Wis 9, 1f.
3, 15f: Halfhearted commitment to the faith is nauseating to Christ.
3, 17: Material well-being occasioned spiritual bankruptcy.
3, 18: *Gold . . . fire:* God's grace. *White garments:* symbol of an upright life (the city was noted for its black woolen cloth). *Ointment . . . eyes:* to remove spiritual blindness (one of the city's exports was eye ointment).
3, 20: Christ invites all men to the messianic banquet in heaven (Lk 14, 15; 22, 30); cf Is 25, 6.
4, 1: The ancients viewed heaven as a solid vault, entered by way of actual doors.

open door to heaven, and I heard the trumpetlike voice which had spoken to me before. It said, "Come up here and I will show you what must take place in time to come." [2] At once I was caught up in ecstasy. A throne was standing there in heaven, and on the throne was seated One [3] whose appearance had a gemlike sparkle as of jasper and carnelian. Around the throne was a rainbow as brilliant as emerald. [4] Surrounding this throne were twenty-four other thrones upon which were seated twenty-four elders; they were clothed in white garments and had crowns of gold on their heads. [5] From the throne came flashes of lightning and peals of thunder; before it burned seven flaming torches, the seven spirits of God. [6] The floor around the throne was like a sea of glass that was crystal-clear.

At every center, around the throne itself, stood four living creatures covered with eyes front and back. [7] The first creature resembled a lion, the second an ox; the third had the face of a man, while the fourth looked like an eagle in flight. [8] Each of the four living creatures had six wings and eyes all over, inside and out.

Day and night, without pause, they sing:

"Holy, holy, holy, is the Lord God Almighty,
He who was, and who is, and who is to come!"

[9] Whenever these creatures give glory and honor and praise to the One seated on the throne, who lives forever and ever, [10] the twenty-four elders fall down before the One seated on the throne, and worship him who lives forever and ever. They throw down their crowns before the throne and sing:

[11] "O Lord our God, you are worthy
to receive glory and honor and power!
For you have created all things;
by your will they came to be and were made!"

4, 2: Dn 2, 28.
3: Ex 24, 10; Ez 1, 26-28.
6: Ex 24, 10; Ez 1, 5-21;
10, 14.
8: 1, 4; Is 6, 3; Ez 1, 5-21.

4, 2-8: Much of the imagery here is taken from Ez 1 and 10.
4, 4: *Twenty-four elders:* representing the twelve tribes of Israel and the twelve apostles; cf 21, 12ff.
4, 5: *Flashes of lightning and peals of thunder:* as in other descriptions of God's appearances or activity (8, 5; 11, 19; 16, 18; Ex 19, 16; Ez 1, 13).
4, 6ff: *A sea of glass . . . crystal-clear:* image adapted from Ez 1, 22-26. *Four living creatures:* symbols taken from Ez 1, 5-21; they are identified as cherubim in Ez 10, 20. *Covered with eyes:* suggesting God's knowledge and concern. *Six wings:* like the seraphim of Is 6, 2.

5

The Scroll and the Lamb

¹ In the right hand of the One who sat on the throne I saw a scroll. It had writing on both sides and was sealed with seven seals. ² Then I saw a mighty angel who proclaimed in a loud voice: "Who is worthy to open the scroll and break its seals?" ³ But no one in heaven or on earth or under the earth could be found to open the scroll or examine its contents. ⁴ I wept bitterly because no one could be found worthy to open or examine the scroll. ⁵ One of the elders said to me: "Do not weep. The Lion of the tribe of Judah, the Root of David, has won the right by his victory to open the scroll with the seven seals."

⁶ Then, between the throne with the four living creatures and the elders, I saw a Lamb standing, a Lamb that had been slain. He has seven horns and seven eyes; these eyes are the seven spirits of God, sent to all parts of the world. ⁷ The Lamb came and received the scroll from the right hand of the One who sat on the throne. ⁸ When he had taken the scroll, the four living creatures and the twenty-four elders fell down before the Lamb. Along with their harps, the elders were holding vessels of gold filled with aromatic spices, which were the prayers of God's holy people. ⁹ This is the new hymn they sang:

"Worthy are you to receive the scroll
　　and break open its seals,
　　for you were slain.
With your blood you purchased for God
　　men of every race and tongue,
　　of every people and nation.
¹⁰ You made of them a kingdom,
　　and priests to serve our God,
　　and they shall reign on the earth."

5, 1: Is 29, 11.
5: Is 11, 1.10.

6: Jn 1, 29.
10: Ex 19, 6.

5, 1: *A scroll:* containing the list of afflictions reserved for sinful men; cf Ez 2, 9f. *Sealed with seven seals:* totally hidden from all but God. Only the Lamb (vv 7ff) has the right to carry out the divine plan.
5, 5: *The Lion of the tribe of Judah, the Root of David:* messianic titles applied to Christ (22, 16; Gn 49, 9; Is 11, 1.10).
5, 6: Christ is the Paschal Lamb without blemish, whose blood saved the new Israel from sin and death (Jn 1, 29.36; 1 Pt 1, 18f; Acts 8, 32); cf Ex 12; Is 53, 7. *Seven horns and seven eyes:* Christ has the fullness (see note on 1, 4) of power and knowledge. *Seven spirits:* as in 1, 4 and 4, 5.

¹¹ As my vision continued, I heard the voices of many angels who surrounded the throne and the living creatures and the elders. They were countless in number, thousands and tens of thousands, ¹² and they all cried out:

"Worthy is the Lamb that was slain
to receive power and riches, wisdom and strength,
honor and glory and praise!"

¹³ Then I heard the voices of every creature in heaven and on earth and under the earth and in the sea; everything in the universe cried aloud:

"To the One seated on the throne, and to the Lamb,
be praise and honor, glory and might,
forever and ever!"

¹⁴ The four living creatures answered, "Amen," and the elders fell down and worshiped.

6

The First Six Seals

¹ Then I watched while the Lamb broke open the first of the seven seals, and I heard one of the four living creatures cry out in a voice like thunder, "Come forward!" ² To my surprise I saw a white horse; its rider had a bow, and he was given a crown. He rode forth victorious, to conquer yet again.

³ When the Lamb broke open the second seal, I heard the second living creature cry out, "Come forward!" ⁴ Another horse came forth, a red one. Its rider was given power to rob the earth of peace by allowing men to slaughter one another. For this he was given a huge sword.

⁵ When the Lamb broke open the third seal, I heard the third living creature cry out, "Come forward!" This time I saw a black horse, the rider of which held a pair of scales in his hand. ⁶ I heard what seemed to be a voice coming from in

---

11: Dn 7, 10.
13: Ps 150, 6.
6, 2: Zec 1, 8-10; 6, 1-3.

4: Ez 21, 14-16.
6: Lv 26, 26; Ez 4, 16f.

6, 1-8: Each of the four horsemen symbolizes a particular woe connected with war and destruction. The imagery is adapted from Zec 1, 8ff; 6, 1-8.
6, 2: *White horse . . . bow:* symbolizing the Parthians on the eastern border of the Roman empire. Expert in the use of the bow, they constantly harassed the Romans.
6, 4: *Huge sword:* symbol of war and violence.
6, 5: *Black horse:* symbol of famine, the usual accompaniment of war in antiquity.
6, 6: *A day's pay:* literally, "denarius," a silver coin. Famine brought

among the four living creatures. It said: "A day's pay for a ration of wheat and the same for three of barley! But spare the olive oil and the wine!"

[7] When the Lamb broke open the fourth seal, I heard the voice of the fourth living creature cry out, "Come forward!" [8] Now I saw a horse sickly green in color. Its rider was named Death, and the nether world was in his train. These four were given authority over one quarter of the earth, to kill with sword and famine and plague and the wild beasts of the earth.

[9] When the Lamb broke open the fifth seal, I saw under the altar the spirits of those who had been martyred because of the witness they bore to the word of God. [10] They cried out at the top of their voices: "How long will it be, O Master, holy and true, before you judge our cause and avenge our blood among the inhabitants of the earth?" [11] Each of the martyrs was given a long white robe, and they were told to be patient a little while longer until the quota was filled of their fellow servants and brothers to be slain, as they had been.

[12] When I saw the Lamb break open the sixth seal, there was a violent earthquake; the sun turned black as a goat's-hair tentcloth and the moon grew red as blood. [13] The stars in the sky fell crashing to earth like figs shaken loose by a mighty wind. [14] Then the sky disappeared as if it were a scroll being rolled up; every mountain and island was uprooted from its base. [15] The kings of the earth, the nobles and those in command, the wealthy and the powerful, the slave and the free— all hid themselves in caves and mountain crags. [16] They cried out to the mountains and rocks, "Fall on us! Hide us from the face of the One who sits on the throne and from the wrath of the Lamb! [17] The great day of their vengence has come. Who can withstand it?"

7

Sealing of the Thousands

[1] After this I saw four angels standing at the four corners

---

8: Ez 14, 21.
12: Jl 3, 4; Mt 24, 29.
13: Is 34, 4.

15f: Is 2, 19; Hos 10, 8;
    Lk 23, 30.
7, 1: Jer 49, 36; Zec 6, 5.

---

about the rationing of supplies, and the prices were exorbitant. *Barley:* food of the poor.

6, 8: *Sickly green:* symbol of death.

6, 12ff: Symbolic rather than literal description of the cosmic upheavals attending the day of the Lord, when the martyrs' prayer for vindication (v 10) would be answered; cf Mt 24, 29; Am 8, 8f; Is 34, 4; Jl 2, 10; 3, 3f.

7, 1-17: Two scenes precede the breaking of the seventh seal. In the first

of the earth; they held in check the earth's four winds so that no wind blew on land or sea or through any tree. ² I saw another angel come up from the east holding the seal of the living God. He cried out at the top of his voice to the four angels who were given power to ravage the land and the sea, ³ "Do no harm to the land or the sea or the trees until we imprint this seal on the foreheads of the servants of our God." ⁴ I heard the number of those who were so marked— one hundred and forty-four thousand from every tribe of Israel: ⁵ twelve thousand from the tribe of Judah, twelve thousand from the tribe of Reuben, twelve thousand from the tribe of Gad, ⁶ twelve thousand from the tribe of Asher, twelve thousand from the tribe of Naphtali, twelve thousand from the tribe of Manasseh, ⁷ twelve thousand from the tribe of Simeon, twelve thousand from the tribe of Levi, twelve thousand from the tribe of Issachar, ⁸ twelve thousand from the tribe of Zebulun, twelve thousand from the tribe of Joseph, and twelve thousand from the tribe of Benjamin.

Triumph of the Elect

⁹ After this I saw before me a huge crowd which no one could count from every nation and race, people and tongue. They stood before the throne and the Lamb, dressed in long white robes and holding palm branches in their hands. ¹⁰ They cried out in a loud voice, "Salvation is from our God, who is seated on the throne, and from the Lamb!" ¹¹ All the angels who were standing around the throne and the elders and the four living creatures fell down before the throne to worship God. They said: ¹² "Amen! Praise and glory, wisdom and thanksgiving and honor, power and might, to our God forever and ever. Amen!"

¹³ Then one of the elders asked me, "Who are these people all dressed in white? And where have they come from?" ¹⁴ I said to him, "Sir, you should know better than I." He then told me, "These are the ones who have survived the great

---

3: 14, 1f; Ez 9, 4.

(vv 1-8), the elect receive *the seal of the living God;* cf Ez 9, 4ff. The second scene (vv 9-17) portrays the victorious martyrs before God's throne.

7, 4-8: *One hundred and forty-four thousand:* the square of twelve (the number of Israel's tribes) multiplied by a thousand, symbolic of the new Israel that embraces men *from every nation and race, people and tongue* (v 9); cf Gal 6, 16; Jas 1, 1.

7, 9: *Long white robes . . . palm branches:* symbols of joy and victory; see note on 3, 4f.

7, 14: *Great period of trial:* fierce persecution by the Romans; cf Introduction.

period of trial; they have washed their robes and made them white in the blood of the Lamb.

¹⁵ "It was this that brought them before God's throne:
    day and night they minister to him in his temple;
    he who sits on the throne will give them shelter.
¹⁶ Never again shall they know hunger or thirst,
    nor shall the sun or its heat beat down on them,
    ¹⁷ for the Lamb on the throne will shepherd them.
He will lead them to springs of life-giving water,
    and God will wipe every tear from their eyes."

8

The Seven Trumpets

¹ When the Lamb broke open the seventh seal, there was silence in heaven for about half an hour. ² Then, as I watched, the seven angels who minister in God's presence were given seven trumpets.

The Gold Censer

³ Another angel came in holding a censer of gold. He took his place at the altar of incense and was given large amounts of incense to deposit on the altar of gold in front of the throne, together with the prayers of all God's holy ones. ⁴ From the angel's hand the smoke of the incense went up before God, and with it the prayers of God's people. ⁵ Then the angel took the censer, filled it with live coals from the altar, and hurled it down to the earth. Peals of thunder and flashes of lightning followed, and the earth trembled.

First Four Trumpets

⁶ The seven angels with the seven trumpets made ready to blow them.
⁷ When the first angel blew his trumpet, there came hail and

16: 49, 10.
17: 21, 4; Is 25, 8.
8, 1: Hb 2, 20; Zec 2, 17.

4: Ps 141, 2.
5: Lv 16, 12; Ps 11, 6; Ez 10, 2.
6: 16, 1-9.

7, 17: *Life-giving water:* God's grace, which flows from Christ (21, 6; 22, 1.17; Jn 4, 10.14).

8, 1: *Silence in heaven:* as in Zep 1, 7, a prelude to the eschatological woes that are to follow.

8, 2: The breaking of the seventh seal brings not one, but seven, symbolic disasters, each to be announced by the blowing of a trumpet (8, 6ff); see note on 6, 12ff.

8, 7: This woe resembles the seventh plague of Egypt (Ex 9, 23f; cf Jl 3, 3.

then fire mixed with blood, which was hurled down to the earth. A third of the land was scorched, along with a third of the trees and every green plant.

⁸ When the second angel blew his trumpet, something like a huge mountain all in flames was cast into the sea. ⁹ A third of the sea turned to blood, a third of the creatures living in the sea died, and a third of the ships were wrecked.

¹⁰ When the third angel blew his trumpet, a huge star burning like a torch crashed down from the sky. It fell on a third of the rivers and the springs. ¹¹ The star's name was "Wormwood" because a third part of all the water turned to wormwood. Many people died from this polluted water.

¹² When the fourth angel blew his trumpet, a third of the sun, a third of the moon, and a third of the stars were hit hard enough to be plunged into darkness. The day lost a third of its light, as did the night.

¹³ As my vision continued, I heard an eagle flying in mid-heaven cry out in a loud voice, "Woe, woe, and again woe to the inhabitants of earth from the trumpet blasts the other three angels are about to blow!"

9

The Fifth Trumpet

¹ Then the fifth angel blew his trumpet, and I saw a star fall from the sky to the earth. The star was given the key to the shaft of the abyss; ² he opened it and smoke poured out of the shaft like smoke from an enormous furnace. The sun and the air were darkened by the smoke from the shaft. ³ Out of the smoke, onto the land, came locusts as powerful as scorpions in their sting. ⁴ The locusts were commanded to do no harm to the grass in the land or to any plant or tree but only to those men who had not the seal of God on their foreheads. ⁵ The

---

9: Ex 7, 20.   3: Ex 10, 12.15;
10: Is 14, 12; Jer 9, 14.   Wis 16, 9.
9, 2: Gn 19, 28.

8, 8-11: The background of these two woes is the first plague of Egypt (Ex 7, 20f).

8, 11: *Wormwood:* a bitter plant symbolizing the punishment God inflicts on the ungodly; cf Jer 9, 12ff; 23, 15.

8, 13: *Woe, woe, and again woe:* each of the three woes pronounced by the angel represents a separate disaster; cf 9, 12; 11, 14. The final woe, released by the seventh trumpet blast, includes the plagues of chapter 16.

9, 1: *A star:* an angel. *The abyss:* where Satan and the fallen angels are kept for a thousand years, to be cast afterward into the pool of fire (20, 7-10).

9, 2-6: This woe combines elements from the eighth and ninth plagues of Egypt (Ex 10, 12-15.21ff); cf Jl 1, 4—2, 10.

locusts were not allowed to kill them but only to torture them for five months; the pain they inflicted was like that of a scorpion's sting. ⁶ During that time these men will seek death but will not find it; they will yearn to die but death will escape them.

⁷ In appearance the locusts were like horses equipped for battle. On their heads they wore something like gold crowns; their faces were like men's faces ⁸ but they had hair like women's hair. Their teeth were the teeth of lions, ⁹ their chests like iron breastplates. Their wings made a sound like the roar of many chariots and horses charging into battle. ¹⁰ They had tails with stingers like scorpions; in their tails was enough venom to harm men for five months. ¹¹ Acting as their king was the angel in charge of the abyss, whose name in Hebrew is Abaddon and in Greek Apollyon.

The Sixth Trumpet

¹² The first woe is past, but beware! There are two more to come. ¹³ Then the sixth angel blew his trumpet, and I heard a voice coming from between the horns of the altar of gold in God's presence. ¹⁴ It said to the sixth angel, who was still holding his trumpet, "Release the four angels who are tied up on the banks of the great river Euphrates!" ¹⁵ So the four angels were released; this was precisely the hour, the day, the month, and the year for which they had been prepared, to kill a third of mankind. ¹⁶ Their cavalry troops, whose count I heard, were two hundred million in number—a number I heard myself. ¹⁷ Now, in my vision, this is how I saw the horses and their riders. The breastplates they wore were fiery red, deep blue, and pale yellow. The horses' heads were like heads of lions, and out of their mouths came fire and sulphur and smoke. ¹⁸ By these three plagues—the smoke and sulphur and fire which shot out of their mouths—a third of mankind was slain. ¹⁹ The deadly power of the horses was not only in their mouths but in their tails; for their tails were like snakes with heads poised to strike.

²⁰ That part of mankind which escaped the plagues did not

6: Jb 3, 21. 7: Wis 16, 9. 20: Ps 135, 15-17.

---

repent of the idols they had made. They did not give up the worship of demons, or of gods made from gold and silver, from bronze and stone and wood, which cannot see or hear or walk. [21] Neither did they repent of their murders or their sorcery, their fornication or their thefts.

10

Angel with the Scroll

[1] Then I saw another mighty angel come down from heaven wrapped in a cloud, with a rainbow about his head; his face shone like the sun and his legs like pillars of fire. [2] In his hand he held a little scroll which had been opened. He placed his right foot on the sea and his left foot on the land, [3] and then gave a loud cry like the roar of a lion. When he cried out, the seven thunders raised their voices too. [4] I was about to start writing when the seven thunders spoke, but I heard a voice from heaven say, "Seal up what the seven thunders have spoken and do not write it down!" [5] Then the angel whom I saw standing on the sea and on the land raised his right hand to heaven [6] and took an oath by the One who lives forever and ever, who created heaven and earth and sea along with everything in them: "There shall be no more delay. [7] When the time comes for the seventh angel to blow his trumpet, the mysterious plan of God, which he announced to his servants the prophets, shall be accomplished in full."

[8] Then the voice which I heard from heaven spoke to me again and said, "Go, take the open scroll from the hand of the angel standing on the sea and on the land." [9] I went up to the angel and said to him, "Give me the little scroll." He said to me, "Here, take it and eat it! It will be sour in your stomach, but in your mouth it will taste as sweet as honey." [10] I took the little scroll from the angel's hand and ate it. In my mouth it

---

10, 3: Am 3, 8.
6: Dn 12, 7; Dt 32, 40;
Ez 12, 28.

7: Am 3, 7.
10: Ez 3, 1-3.

10, 1—11, 14: An interlude in two scenes (10, 1-11 and 11, 1-14) precedes the sounding of the seventh trumpet; cf 7, 1-17.
10, 3f: *The seven thunders:* God's voice announcing judgment and doom; cf Ps 29, 3-9.
10, 6: *Heaven and earth and sea:* the three parts of the universe.
10, 7: *The mysterious plan of God:* the end of the present age, when the forces of evil will be put down (17, 1—19, 4.11-21; 20, 7-10; cf 2 Thes 2, 6-12; Rom 16, 25f), and the establishment of the reign of God, when all creation will be made anew (21, 1—22, 5).
10, 9f: The little scroll was sweet because it predicted the final victory of God's holy people; it was sour because it also announced the sufferings they are to endure; cf Ez 3, 1ff.

tasted as sweet as honey, but when I swallowed it my stomach turned sour. [11] Then someone said to me, "You must prophesy again for many peoples and nations, languages and kings."

11

The Two Witnesses

[1] Someone gave me a measuring rod and said: "Come and take the measurements of God's temple and altar, and count those who worship there. [2] Exclude the outer court of the temple, however; do not measure it, for it has been handed over to the Gentiles, who will crush the holy city for forty-two months. [3] I will commission my two witnesses to prophesy for those twelve hundred and sixty days, dressed in sackcloth."

[4] These are the two olive trees and the two lampstands which stand in the presence of the Lord of the earth. [5] If anyone tries to harm them, fire will come out of the mouths of these witnesses to devour their enemies. Anyone attempting to harm them will surely be slain in this way. [6] These witnesses have power to close up the sky so that no rain will fall during the time of their mission. They also have power to turn water into blood and to afflict the earth at will with any kind of plague.

[7] When they have finished giving their testimony, the wild beast that comes up from the abyss will wage war against them and conquer and kill them. [8] Their corpses will lie in the streets

---

11, 1: Zec 2, 5-9.
4: Zec 4, 3.14.

6: Ex 7, 17.
8: Dn 7, 21.

10, 11: This further prophecy is contained in chapters 12—22.

11, 1: The temple and altar symbolize the new Israel; see note on 7, 4-8. The worshipers represent Christians; cf Ez 40, 3—42, 20; 47, 1-12; Zec 2, 5f. The measuring of the temple suggests that God will preserve the faithful remnant who continue true to Christ (14, 1-5); cf Is 4, 2f.

11, 2: *The outer court:* the court of the Gentiles. *Crush . . . forty-two months:* the duration of the vicious persecution of the Jews by Antiochus IV Epiphanes (Dn 7, 25; 12, 7). This persecution of three and a half years (1260 days: v 3; 12, 6) became the prototype of periods of trial for God's people; cf Lk 4, 25; Jas 5, 17. The reference here is to the persecution by the Romans; cf Introduction.

11, 3f: The two witnesses who are *dressed in sackcloth,* symbolizing lamentation and repentance, are perhaps the apostles Peter and Paul, who represent all Christian martyrs. *The two olive trees and the two lampstands:* the martyrs who stand *in the presence of the Lord.* The imagery is taken from Zec 4, 1-3.11-14, where the olive trees refer to Joshua and Zerubbabel.

11, 5f: These details are derived from stories of Moses, who turned *water into blood* (Ex 7, 17-20), and of Elijah, who called down fire from heaven (1 Kgs 18, 36-40; 2 Kgs 1, 10) and closed up the sky (1 Kgs 17, 1).

11, 7: *The wild beast . . . from the abyss:* the Roman emperor Nero, who symbolizes the forces of evil, or the Antichrist (13, 1.8; 17, 8); cf Introduction; Dn 7, 2-8.11f.19-22.

11, 8: *"Sodom"* or *"Egypt":* symbols of immorality and oppression of God's people; cf Ex 1, 11-14; Is 1, 10. *Where also their Lord was crucified:*

of the great city, which has the symbolic name "Sodom" or "Egypt," where also their Lord was crucified. ⁹ Men from every people and race, language and nation, stare at their corpses for three and a half days but refuse to bury them. ¹⁰ The earth's inhabitants gloat over them and in their merriment exchange gifts, because these two prophets harassed everyone on earth. ¹¹ But after the three and a half days, the breath of life which comes from God returned to them. When they stood on their feet sheer terror gripped those who saw them. ¹² The two prophets heard a loud voice from heaven say to them, "Come up here!" So they went up to heaven in a cloud as their enemies looked on. ¹³ At that moment there was a violent earthquake and a tenth of the city fell in ruins. Seven thousand persons were killed during the earthquake; the rest were so terrified that they worshiped the God of heaven.

¹⁴ The second woe is past, but beware! The third is coming very soon.

The Seventh Trumpet

¹⁵ Then the seventh angel blew his trumpet. Loud voices in heaven cried out, "The kingdom of the world now belongs to our Lord and to his Anointed One, and he shall reign forever and ever." ¹⁶ The twenty-four elders who were enthroned in God's presence fell down to worship God ¹⁷ and said:

"We praise you, the Lord God Almighty
    who is and who was.
You have assumed your great power,
    you have begun your reign.
¹⁸ The nations have raged in anger,
    but then came your day of wrath
    and the moment to judge the dead:
The time to reward your servants the prophets
    and the holy ones who revere you,
    the great and the small alike;
The time to destroy those who lay the earth waste."

11: Ez 37, 10.   18: Ps 2, 1.5.

---

not the geographical, but the symbolic, Jerusalem which rejects God and his witnesses—Rome, called Babylon in chapters 16—19; see note on 17, 9 and Introduction.
11, 9-12: Over the martyrdom (v 7) of the two witnesses, now called prophets, the ungodly rejoice *for three and a half days,* a symbolic period of time; see note on v 2. Afterward they go in triumph to heaven, as did Elijah (2 Kgs 2, 11).
11, 15-19: The seventh trumpet proclaims the coming of God's reign; see note on 10, 7.

¹⁹ Then God's temple in heaven opened and in the temple could be seen the ark of his covenant. There were flashes of lightning and peals of thunder, an earthquake, and a violent hailstorm.

12

The Woman and the Dragon

¹ A great sign appeared in the sky, a woman clothed with the sun, with the moon under her feet, and on her head a crown of twelve stars. ² Because she was with child, she wailed aloud in pain as she labored to give birth. ³ Then another sign appeared in the sky: it was a huge dragon, flaming red, with seven heads and ten horns; on his heads were seven diadems. ⁴ His tail swept a third of the stars from the sky and hurled them down to the earth. Then the dragon stood before the woman about to give birth, ready to devour her child when it should be born. ⁵ She gave birth to a son—a boy destined to shepherd all the nations with an iron rod. Her child was caught up to God and to his throne. ⁶ The woman herself fled into the desert, where a special place had been prepared for her by God; there she was taken care of for twelve hundred and sixty days.

⁷ Then war broke out in heaven; Michael and his angels battled against the dragon. Although the dragon and his angels fought back, ⁸ they were overpowered and lost their place in heaven. ⁹ The huge dragon, the ancient serpent known as the devil or Satan, the seducer of the whole world, was driven out; he was hurled down to earth and his minions with him.

¹⁰ Then I heard a loud voice in heaven say:

"Now have salvation and power come,
the reign of our God and the authority

12, 1: Gn 37, 9.
3: Dn 7, 7.
4: Dn 8, 10.

5: Ps 2, 9; Is 66, 7.
7: Dn 10, 13.

12, 1f.4-6: The woman adorned with the sun, the moon, and the stars symbolizes God's people in the Old and the New Testament; cf Gn 37, 9f. The Israel of old gave birth to the Messiah (v 5) and then became the new Israel, the church, which suffers persecution by the dragon (vv 6.13-17).
12, 2: Because of Eve's sin, the woman gives birth in distress and pain (Gn 3, 16).
12, 3: *Huge dragon:* symbol of the forces of evil (v 9).
12, 5: *Shepherd . . . iron rod:* fulfilled in 19, 15; cf Ps 2, 9. *Was caught up to God:* a reference to Christ's ascension.
12, 6: God protects the persecuted church; see note on 11, 2.
12, 7: *Michael:* the archangel, guardian and champion of Israel; cf Dn 10, 13.21; 12, 1; Jude 9.
12, 9: *The ancient serpent* who seduced Eve (Gn 3, 1-6), mother of mankind; cf 20, 2; Eph 6, 12.
12, 10: *The accuser:* the meaning of the Hebrew word "Satan," found in v 9; Jb 1—2; Zec 3, 1; and 1 Chr 21, 1.

of his Anointed One.
For the accuser of our brothers is cast out,
who night and day accused them before our God.
[11] They defeated him by the blood of the Lamb
and by the word of their testimony;
love for life did not deter them from death.
[12] So rejoice, you heavens,
and you that dwell therein!
But woe to you, earth and sea,
for the devil has come down upon you!
His fury knows no limits,
for he knows his time is short."

[13] When the dragon saw that he had been cast down to the earth, he pursued the woman who had given birth to the boy. [14] But the woman was given the wings of a gigantic eagle so that she could fly off to her place in the desert, where, far from the serpent, she could be taken care of for a year and for two and a half years more. [15] The serpent, however, spewed a torrent of water out of his mouth to search out the woman and sweep her away. [16] The earth then came to the woman's rescue by opening its mouth and swallowing the flood which the dragon spewed out of his mouth. [17] Enraged at her escape, the dragon went off to make war on the rest of her offspring, on those who keep God's commandments and give witness to Jesus. He took up his position by the shore of the sea.

13

The First Beast

[1] Then I saw a wild beast come out of the sea with ten horns and seven heads; on its horns were ten diadems and on its heads blasphemous names. [2] The beast I saw was like a leopard, but it had paws like a bear and the mouth of a lion. The dragon gave it his own power and throne, together with great

---

14: Gn 3, 15; Ex 19, 4.   **13,** 2: Dn 7, 3-6.
17: 2, Thes 2, 3-12.

12, 14: *Gigantic eagle:* symbol of the power and swiftness of divine help; cf Ex 19, 4; Dt 32, 11; Is 40, 13.
12, 15: The serpent is depicted as the sea monster; cf 13, 1; Is 27, 1; Ez 32, 2; Ps 74, 13.
12, 17: Though the church is protected by God's special providence (v 16), the individual Christian is to expect persecution and suffering.
13, 1-8: This wild beast, combining features of the four beasts in Dn 7, 2-28, symbolizes the Roman empire; the seven heads represent the emperors; see notes on 17, 9f.12ff.
13, 2: Satan (12, 9), the prince of this world (Jn 12, 31), commissioned the beast to persecue the church (vv 5ff).

authority. ³ I noticed that one of the beast's heads seemed to have been mortally wounded, but this mortal wound was healed. In wonderment, the whole world followed after the beast. ⁴ Men worshiped the dragon for giving his authority to the beast; they also worshiped the beast and said, "Who can compare with the beast, or come forward to fight against it?"

⁵ The beast was given a mouth for uttering proud boasts and blasphemies, but the authority it received was to last only forty-two months. ⁶ It began to hurl blasphemies against God, reviling him and the members of his heavenly household as well. ⁷ The beast was allowed to wage war against God's people and conquer them. It was likewise granted authority over every race and people, language and nation. ⁸ The beast will be worshiped by all those inhabitants of earth who did not have their names written at the world's beginning in the book of the living, which belongs to the Lamb who was slain.

⁹ Let him who has ears heed these words! ¹⁰ If one is destined for captivity, into captivity he goes! If one is destined to be slain by the sword, by the sword he will be slain! Such is the faithful endurance that distinguishes God's holy people.

The Second Beast

¹¹ Then I saw another wild beast come up out of the earth; it had two horns like a ram and it spoke like a dragon. ¹² It used the authority of the first beast to promote its interests by making the world and all its inhabitants worship the first beast, whose mortal wound had been healed. ¹³ It performed great prodigies; it could even make fire come down from heaven to earth as men looked on. ¹⁴ Because of the prodigies it was allowed to perform by authority of the first beast, it led astray the earth's inhabitants, telling them to make an idol in honor of the beast that had been wounded by the sword

---

5: Dn 11, 36.
10: Jer 15, 2; Mt 13, 9.

13: Dt 13, 2-4; Mt 24, 24;
    2 Thes 2, 9f.

13, 3: This is perhaps a reference to the popular legend that Nero would come back to life and rule again after his death (which occurred in 68 A.D. from a self-inflicted wound in the throat); cf v 14; 17, 8. Domitian (81-96 A.D.) embodied all the cruelty and impiety of Nero; cf Introduction.
13, 4: *Worshiped the dragon:* allusion to emperor worship, which Domitian insisted upon and ruthlessly enforced.
13, 5f: Domitian, like Antiochus IV (Dn 7, 8.11.25), demanded that he be called by divine titles such as "our lord and god" and "Jupiter"; see note on 11, 2.
13, 11-17: The second beast is described in terms of the false prophets; cf 16, 13; 19, 20, 10; they accompany the false messiahs (the first beast) foretold by Jesus (Mt 34, 24; Mk 13, 22; 2 Thes 2, 9); cf Dt 13, 2ff. Christians had either to worship the emperor and his image or to suffer martyrdom.

and yet lived. [15] The second wild beast was then permitted to give life to the beast's image, so that the image had the power of speech and of putting to death anyone who refused to worship it. [16] It forced all men, small and great, rich and poor, slave and free, to accept a stamped image on their right hand or their forehead. [17] Moreover, it did not allow a man to buy or sell anything unless he was first marked with the name of the beast or with the number that stood for its name.

[18] A certain wisdom is needed here; with a little ingenuity anyone can calculate the number of the beast, for it is a number that stands for a certain man. The man's number is six hundred sixty-six.

14

Companions of the Lamb

[1] Then the Lamb appeared in my vision. He was standing on Mount Zion, and with him were the hundred and forty-four thousand who had his name and the name of his Father written on their foreheads. [2] I heard a sound from heaven which resembled the roaring of the deep, or loud peals of thunder; the sound I heard was like the melody of harpists playing on their harps. [3] They were singing a new hymn before the throne, in the presence of the four living creatures and the elders. This hymn no one could learn except the hundred and forty-four thousand who had been ransomed from the world. [4] These are men who have never been defiled by immorality with women. They are pure and follow the Lamb wherever he goes. They have been ransomed as the first fruits of mankind for God and the Lamb. [5] On their lips no deceit has been found; they are indeed without flaw.

14, 1: Jl 3, 5; Ob 17;
    Acts 2, 21.

3: Ps 33, 3; Is 42, 10.
5: Zep 3, 13.

13, 18: Each of the letters of the alphabet in Hebrew as well as in Greek has a numerical value. Many possible combinations of letters will add up to the total *six hundred sixty-six*, and many candidates have been nominated for this infamous number. The most likely, however, is the emperor Caesar Nero (see note on v 3), whose name in Hebrew letters gives the required sum. Nero personifies the emperors who viciously persecuted the church.

14, 1: *Mount Zion:* Jerusalem, the traditional place where the true remnant, the Israel of faith, is to be gathered together in the messianic reign of Christ; cf 2 Kgs 19, 30f; Mi 4, 6ff; Ob 17; Jl 3, 5; Zep 3, 12-20. *His name . . . foreheads:* in contrast to the pagans who were marked with the name or number of the beast (13, 17); cf note on 7, 4-8.

14, 4: *Pure:* literally, virgins, because they never indulged in any idolatrous practices, which are considered to be adultery and fornication (2, 14f. 20ff; 17, 1-7; cf Ez 16, 1-58; ch 23).

14, 5: *No deceit:* because they did not deny Christ or do homage to the beast.

The Three Angels

⁶ Then I saw another angel flying in mid-heaven, the herald of everlasting good news to the whole world, to every nation and race, language and people. ⁷ He said in a loud voice: "Honor God and give him glory, for his time has come to sit in judgment. Worship the Creator of heaven and earth, the Creator of the sea and the springs."

⁸ A second angel followed and cried out:

> "Fallen, fallen is Babylon the great,
>   which made all the nations drink
>   the poisoned wine of her lewdness!"

⁹ A third angel followed the others and said in a loud voice: "If anyone worships the beast or its image, or accepts its mark on his forehead or hand, ¹⁰ he too will drink the wine of God's wrath, poured full strength into the cup of his anger. He will be tormented in burning sulphur before the holy angels and before the Lamb, ¹¹ and the smoke of their torment shall rise forever and ever. There shall be no relief day or night for those who worship the beast or its image or accept the mark of its name." ¹² This is what sustains the holy ones, who keep the commandments of God and their faith in Jesus.

¹³ I heard a voice from heaven say to me: "Write this down: Happy now are the dead who die in the Lord!" The Spirit added, "Yes, they shall find rest from their labors, for their good works accompany them."

The Harvest of the Earth

¹⁴ Then, as I watched, a white cloud appeared, and on the cloud sat One like a Son of Man wearing a gold crown on his head and holding a sharp sickle in his hand. ¹⁵ Another angel

---

8: 18, 2f; Is 21, 9;
    Jer 25, 15; 51, 8.
13: Heb 4, 10.

14: Dn 7, 13.
15: Mt 13, 36-43; Jl 4, 13.

14, 6: *Everlasting good news:* that God's eternal reign is about to begin; see note on 10, 7.

14, 8: This verse anticipates the lengthy dirge over Babylon (Rome) in chapter 18.

14, 10f: *The wine of God's wrath:* image taken from Is 51, 17; Jer 25, 15f; 49, 12; 51, 7; Ez 23, 31-34. Eternal punishment in the fiery pool of burning sulphur is also reserved for the devil, the beast, and the false prophet (19, 20; 20, 10; 21, 8).

14, 12f: In addition to *faith in Jesus* John insists upon the necessity and value of *good works, as in* 2, 23; 20, 12f; 22, 12; see note on 1, 3.

14, 14-20: The cutting down of the harvest as well as the gathering and treading of the grapes symbolize the doom of the ungodly which will come (19, 11-21); cf Jl 4, 12f; Is 63, 1-6.

came out of the temple and in a loud voice cried out to him who sat on the cloud, "Use your sickle and cut down the harvest, for now is the time to reap; the earth's harvest is fully ripe." [16] So the one sitting on the cloud wielded his sickle over all the earth and reaped the earth's harvest.

[17] Then out of the temple in heaven came another angel, who likewise held a sharp sickle. [18] A second angel, who was in charge of the fire at the altar of incense, cried out in a loud voice to the one who held the sharp sickle, "Use your sharp sickle and gather the grapes from the vines of the earth, for the clusters are ripe." [19] So the angel wielded his sickle over the earth and gathered the grapes of the earth. He threw them into the huge winepress of God's wrath. [20] The winepress was trodden outside the city, and so much blood poured out of the winepress that for two hundred miles around, it reached as high as a horse's bridle.

15

The Seven Last Plagues

[1] I saw in heaven another sign, great and awe-inspiring: seven angels holding the seven final plagues which would bring God's wrath to a climax.

[2] I then saw something like a sea of glass mingled with fire. On the sea of glass were standing those who had won the victory over the beast and its image, and also the number that signified its name. They were holding the harps used in worshiping God, [3] and they sang the song of Moses, the servant of God, and the song of the Lamb:

> "Mighty and wonderful are your works,
>   Lord God Almighty!
> Righteous and true are your ways,
>   O King of the nations!
> [4] Who would dare refuse you honor,
>   or the glory due your name, O Lord?
> Since you alone are holy,

19: Is 63, 1-6.
15, 2: 7, 9.14; 13, 15-18.

3: Pss 92, 5; 98, 1; 145, 17.
4: Jer 10, 7.

14, 20: *Two hundred miles:* literally, 1600 stadia. The stadion, a Greek unit of measurement, was about 6071 feet in length.

15, 1-4: A vision of the victorious martyrs precedes the vision of woe in 15, 5—16, 21; cf 7, 9-12.

15, 3: *The song of Moses:* which Moses and the Israelites sang after their escape from the oppression of Egypt (Ex 15, 1-19). The martyrs have escaped from the oppression of the devil.

all nations shall come
and worship in your presence.
Your mighty deeds are clearly seen."

⁵ After this I had another vision. The heavenly sanctuary which is the tent of witness opened up, ⁶ and out of it came the seven angels holding the seven plagues. The angels were dressed in pure white linen, each with a sash of gold about his breast. ⁷ One of the four living creatures gave to the seven angels seven golden bowls filled with the wrath of the God who lives forever and ever. ⁸ Then the sanctuary became so filled with the smoke which arose from God's glory and might that no one could enter it until the seven plagues of the seven angels had come to an end.

16

The Seven Bowls

¹ I heard a mighty voice from the sanctuary say to the seven angels, "Go and pour out upon the earth the seven bowls of God's wrath!"

² The first angel went out, and when he poured out his bowl on the earth, severe and festering boils broke out on the men who had accepted the mark of the beast or worshiped its image.

³ The second angel poured out his bowl on the sea. The sea turned to blood like that of a corpse, and every creature living in the sea died.

⁴ The third angel poured out his bowl on the rivers and springs. These also turned to blood. ⁵ Then I heard the angel in charge of the waters cry out:

"You are just, O holy One
who is and who was,
in passing this sentence!
⁶ To those who shed the blood of saints and prophets,
you have given blood to drink;
they deserve it."

8: Is 6, 4.   **16,** 4: Ex 7, 14-24.   6: Ez 35, 6; Mt 23, 35.

15, 5: *The tent of witness:* the name of the meeting tent in the Greek text of Ex 40.
16, 1-21: These seven bowls, like the seven seals (6, 1-17; 8, 1) and the seven trumpets (8, 2—9, 21; 11, 15-19), bring on a succession of disasters modeled in part on the plagues of Egypt (Ex 7—12); see note on 6, 12ff.
16, 2: Like the sixth Egyptian plague (Ex 9, 8-11).
16, 3f: Like the first Egyptian plague (Ex 7, 20f). The same woe followed the blowing of the second trumpet (8, 8f).

[7] Then I heard the altar cry out:

"Yes, Lord God Almighty,
    your judgments are true and just!"

[8] The fourth angel poured out his bowl on the sun. He was commissioned to burn men with fire. [9] Those who were scorched by the intense heat blasphemed the name of God who had power to send these plagues, but they did not repent or give him due honor.

[10] The fifth angel poured out his bowl on the throne of the beast. Its kingdom was plunged into darkness; men bit their tongues in pain [11] and blasphemed the God of heaven because of their suffering and their boils. But they did not turn away from their wicked deeds.

[12] The sixth angel poured out his bowl on the great river Euphrates. Its water was dried up to prepare the way for the kings of the East. [13] I saw three unclean spirits like frogs come from the mouth of the dragon, from the mouth of the beast, and from the mouth of the false prophet; [14] these spirits were devils who worked prodigies. They went out to assemble all the kings of the earth for battle on the great day of God the Almighty. [15] (Be on your guard! I come like a thief. Happy the man who stays wide awake and fully clothed for fear of going naked and exposed for all to see!) [16] The devils then assembled the kings in a place called in Hebrew "Armageddon."

[17] Finally, the seventh angel poured out his bowl upon the empty air. From the throne in the sanctuary came a loud voice which said, "It is finished!" [18] There followed lightning flashes and peals of thunder, then a violent earthquake. Such was its violence that there has never been one like it in all the time men have lived on the earth. [19] The great city was split into three parts, and the other Gentile cities also fell. God remembered Babylon the great, giving her the cup filled with the

---

7: Dn 3, 27.
10: Ex 10, 21-23.
11: Ex 9, 8-11; Jer 5, 3.

15: 3, 3; Mt 24, 43;
    Lk 12, 39.

16, 10: *The throne of the beast:* symbol of the forces of evil. *Darkness:* like the ninth Egyptian plague (Ex 10, 21ff); cf 9, 2.
16, 12: *The kings of the East:* Parthians; see notes on 6, 2 and 17, 12ff.
16, 15: *Like a thief:* as in 3, 3; cf Mt 24, 42ff; I Thes 5, 2. *Happy:* see note on 1, 3. *Fully clothed:* see note on 3, 18.
16, 16: *Armageddon:* "Mountain of Megiddo." Since Megiddo was the scene of many decisive battles in antiquity (Jgs 5, 19f; 2 Kgs 9, 27; 2 Chr 35, 20-24), the town became the symbol of the final disastrous rout of the forces of evil; see note on v 19.
16, 19: *The great city:* Rome and the empire.

blazing wine of his wrath. ²⁰ Every island fled and mountains disappeared. ²¹ Giant hailstones like huge weights came crashing down on mankind from the sky, and men blasphemed God for the plague of hailstones, because this plague was so severe.

IV: PUNISHMENT OF BABYLON

17

Babylon the Great

¹ Then one of the seven angels who were holding the seven bowls came to me and said: "Come, I will show you the judgment in store for the great harlot who sits by the waters of the deep. ² The kings of the earth have committed fornication with her, and the earth's inhabitants have grown drunk on the wine of her lewdness." ³ The angel then carried me away in spirit to a desolate place where I saw a woman seated on a scarlet beast which was covered with blasphemous names. This beast had seven heads and ten horns. ⁴ The woman was dressed in purple and scarlet and adorned with gold and pearls and other jewels. In her hand she held a gold cup that was filled with the abominable and sordid deeds of her lewdness. ⁵ On her forehead was written a symbolic name, "Babylon the great, mother of harlots and all the world's abominations." ⁶ I saw that the woman was drunk with the blood of God's holy ones and the blood of those martyred for their faith in Jesus.

The Meaning of Beast and Harlot

When I saw her I was greatly astonished. ⁷ The angel said to me: "Why are you so taken aback? I will explain to you the symbolism of the woman and of the seven-headed and ten-horned beast carrying her. ⁸ The beast you saw existed once but now exists no longer. It will come up from the abyss once more before going to final ruin. All the men of the earth

---

21: Ex 9, 22-26.　　　　　　　　　　　　17, 1: Jer 51, 13.
3: Jer 51, 7.

16, 20f: See note on 6, 12ff. *Hailstones:* as in the seventh Egyptian plague (Ex 9, 23f); cf 8, 7.
17, 1-6: Babylon, *a symbolic name* (v 5) of Rome, is graphically described as *the great harlot.*
17, 2: *Fornication . . . lewdness:* see note on 14, 4. The pagan kings subject to Rome adopted the cult of the emperor.
17, 3: *Scarlet beast:* see note on 13, 1-8. *Blasphemous names:* divine titles assumed by the Roman emperors; see note on 13, 5f.
17, 4: Reference to the great wealth of Rome.
17, 8: Allusion to the belief that the dead Nero would return to power (v 11); see note on 13, 3.

whose names have not been written in the book of the living from the creation of the world shall be amazed when they see the beast, for it existed once and now exists no longer, and yet it will exist again. [9] Here is the clue for one who possesses wisdom! The seven heads are seven hills on which the woman sits enthroned. They are also seven kings: [10] five have already fallen, one lives now, and the last has not yet come; but when he does come he will remain only a short while. [11] The beast which existed once but now exists no longer, even though it is an eighth king, is really one of the seven and is on its way to ruin. [12] The ten horns you saw represent ten kings who have not yet been crowned; they will possess royal authority along with the beast, but only for an hour. [13] Then they will come to agreement and bestow their power and authority on the beast. [14] They will fight against the Lamb but the Lamb will conquer them, for he is the Lord of lords and the King of kings; victorious, too, will be his followers—the ones who were called: the chosen and the faithful."

[15] The angel then said to me: "The waters on which you saw the harlot enthroned are large numbers of peoples and nations and tongues. [16] The ten horns you saw on the beast will turn against the harlot with hatred; they will strip off her finery and leave her naked; they will devour her flesh and set her on fire. [17] For God has put it into their minds to carry out his plan, by making them agree to bestow their sovereignty on the beast until his will is accomplished. [18] The woman you saw is the great city which has sovereignty over the kings of the earth."

18

The Fall of Babylon

[1] After this I saw another angel coming down from heaven.

12: Dn 7, 24.
14: 19, 16; Rom 6, 15;

1 Tm 6, 15.
18, 1: Jer 50, 39.

17, 9: *Seven hills:* of Rome.
17, 10: There is little agreement as to the identity of the Roman emperors alluded to here. The number *seven* (v 9) suggests that all the emperors are meant; see note on 1, 4.
17, 11: *The beast:* Nero; see note on v 8.
17, 12ff: *Ten kings . . . not yet . . . crowned:* perhaps Parthian satraps who are to accompany the revived Nero (*the beast*) in his march on Rome to regain power; see note on 13, 3. In 19, 11ff, *the Lamb* and *his followers* will conquer them.
17, 16ff: The ten pagan kings (v 12) unwittingly fulfill God's will against *the harlot* Rome, *the great city;* cf Ex 16, 37.
18, 1—19, 4: A stirring dirge over the fall of Babylon-Rome. The perspective is prophetic—as if the fall of Rome had already taken place. The

His authority was so great that all the earth was lighted up by his glory. ² He cried out in a strong voice:

"Fallen, fallen is Babylon the great!
    She has become a dwelling place for demons.
She is a cage for every unclean spirit,
    a cage for every filthy and disgusting bird;
   ³ For she has made all the nations drink
    the poisoned wine of her lewdness.
The kings of the earth committed fornication with her,
    and the world's merchants grew rich from her wealth
    and wantonness."

⁴ Then I heard another voice from heaven say:

"Depart from her, my people,
    for fear of sinning with her
    and sharing the plagues inflicted on her!
 ⁵ For her sins have piled up as high as heaven,
    and God keeps count of her crimes.
 ⁶ Pay her back as she has paid others;
    pay her double for her deeds!
Pour into her cup twice the amount she concocted!
   ⁷ In proportion to her boasting and sensuality,
    repay her in torment and grief!
For she said to herself,
    'I sit enthroned as a queen.
No widow am I,
    and never will I go into mourning!'
 ⁸ Therefore her plagues will come all at once,
    death and mourning and famine.
She shall be consumed by fire,
    for mighty is the Lord God who condemns her."

⁹ The kings of the earth who committed fornication with her and wallowed in her sensuality will weep and lament over her when they see the smoke arise as she burns. ¹⁰ They will keep their distance for fear of the punishment inflicted on her, and will say:

2: 14, 8; Is 21, 9;
    Jer 51, 8.
4: Jer 50, 8.

5: Jer 51, 9.
7: Is 47, 8.

---

imagery here, as elsewhere in this book, is not to be taken literally. The vindictiveness of some of the language is meant to portray symbolically the inexorable demands of God's holiness and justice.

18, 3.24: Rome is condemned for *her lewdness,* symbol of idolatry (see note on 14, 4), and for persecuting the church; cf 19, 2.

> "Alas, alas, great city that you are,
>> Babylon the mighty!
>> In a single hour your doom has come!"

[11] The merchants of the world will weep and mourn over her too, for there will be no more market for their imports —[12] their cargoes of gold and silver, precious stones and pearls; fine linen and purple garments, silk and scarlet cloth; fragrant wood of every kind, all sorts of ivory pieces and expensive wooden furniture; bronze, iron and marble; [13] cinnamon and amomum, perfumes, myrrh and frankincense; wine and olive oil, fine flour and grain; cattle and sheep, horses and carriages; slaves and human lives.

> [14] "The fruit your appetite craved
>> has deserted you.
>> All your luxury and splendor are gone;
>> you shall never find them again!"

[15] The merchants who deal in these goods, who grew rich from business with the city, will keep their distance for fear of the punishment inflicted on her. Weeping and mourning, [16] they cry out:

> "Alas, alas, the great city,
>> dressed in fine linen
>> and purple and scarlet,
>> Adorned all in gold
>> and jewels and pearls!
> [17] In a single hour
>> this great wealth has been
>> destroyed!"

Every captain and navigator, all sailors and seafaring men, then stood at a distance [18] and cried out when they saw the smoke go up as the city burned to the ground: "What city could have compared with this great one!" [19] They poured dust on their heads and cried out, weeping and mourning:

> "Alas, alas, the great city,
>> in which all shipowners grew rich
>> from their profitable trade with her!
> In a single hour
>> her destruction has come about!"

14: Hos 10, 5.   16: 17, 4; Ez 27, 27-29.

18, 11: Ironically, the merchants weep not for Babylon-Rome, but for their lost markets; cf Ez 27, 36.

[20] Rejoice over her, you heavens, you saints, apostles and prophets! For God has exacted punishment from her on your account.

[21] A powerful angel picked up a stone like a huge millstone and hurled it into the sea and said:

> "Babylon the great city
>> shall be cast down like this, with violence,
>> and nevermore be found!
> [22] No tunes of harpists and minstrels,
>> of flutists and trumpeters,
>> shall ever again be heard in you!
> No craftsmen in any trade
>> shall ever again be found in you!
> No sound of the millstone
>> shall ever again be heard in you!
> [23] No light from a burning lamp
>> shall ever again shine out in you!
> No voices of bride and groom
>> shall ever again be heard in you!
> Because your merchants were the
>> world's nobility,
>> you led all nations astray by your sorcery.

[24] "In her was found the blood of prophets and saints and of all who were slain on the earth."

19

[1] After this I heard what sounded like the loud song of a great assembly in heaven. They were singing:

> "Alleluia!
> Salvation, glory and might belong to our God,
>> [2] for his judgments are true and just!
> He had condemned the great harlot
>> who corrupted the earth with her harlotry.
> He has avenged the blood of his servants
>> which was shed by her hand."

[3] Once more they sang "Alleluia!" And as the smoke began to rise from her forever and ever, [4] the four and twenty elders and the four living creatures fell down and worshiped God seated on the throne and sang, "Amen! Alleluia!"

20: Jer 51, 48.
21: Jer 51, 63f.
22: Is 24, 8; Ez 26, 13.

24: Mt 23, 35-37.
19, 2: Dn 3, 27.
4: Is 34, 10.

⁵ A voice coming from the throne cried out:

Song of Victory

"Praise our God, all you his servants,
the small and the great, who revere him!"

⁶ Then I heard what sounded like the shouts of a great crowd, or the roaring of the deep, or mighty peals of thunder, as they cried:

"Alleluia!
The Lord is king,
our God, the Almighty!
⁷ Let us rejoice and be glad,
and give him glory!
For this is the wedding day of the Lamb;
his bride has prepared herself for the wedding.
⁸ She has been given a dress to wear
made of finest linen, brilliant white."

(The linen dress is the virtuous deeds of God's saints.)

⁹ The angel then said to me: "Write this down: Happy are they who have been invited to the wedding feast of the Lamb." The angel continued, "These words are true; they come from God." ¹⁰ I fell at his feet to worship him, but he said to me, "No, get up! I am merely a fellow servant with you and your brothers who gives witness to Jesus. Worship God alone. The prophetic spirit proves itself by witnessing to Jesus."

V: DESTRUCTION OF PAGAN NATIONS

The King of Kings

¹¹ The heavens were opened, and as I looked on, a white horse appeared; its rider was called "The Faithful and True." Justice is his standard in passing judgment and in waging war.

7: Mt 22, 9; Eph 5, 27.   8: Is 61, 10.   9: Mt 22, 2; Lk 14, 16.

19, 7: *The wedding day of the Lamb:* symbol of God's reign about to begin (21, 1-22, 5); see note on 10, 7. *His bride:* the church (2 Cor 11, 2; Eph 5, 22-27). Marriage is one of the biblical metaphors used to describe the covenant relationship between God and his people (Hos 2, 16-22; Is 54, 5f; 62, 5; Ez 16, 6-14). Hence, idolatry and apostasy are viewed as adultery and prostitution (Hos 2, 4-15; Ez 16, 15-63); see note on 14, 4.
19, 8: See note on 14, 12f.
19, 9: *Happy:* See note on 1, 3.
19, 10: *The prophetic spirit . . . Jesus:* As the prophets were inspired to proclaim God's word, so the Christian is called to give witness to the Word of God (v 13) made flesh; cf 1, 2; 6, 9; 12, 17.
19, 11-16: Symbolic description of the exalted Christ (1, 13-16), who, together with the armies of heaven, overcomes the beast and its followers (17, 14).

[12] His eyes blazed like fire, and on his head were many diadems. Inscribed on his person was a name known to no one but himself. [13] He wore a cloak that had been dipped in blood, and his name was the Word of God. [14] The armies of heaven were behind him riding white horses and dressed in fine linen, pure and white. [15] Out of his mouth came a sharp sword for striking down the nations. He will shepherd them with an iron rod; it is he who will tread out in the winepress the blazing wrath of God the Almighty. [16] A name was written on the part of the cloak that covered his thigh: "King of kings and Lord of lords."

[17] Next I saw an angel standing on the sun. He cried out in a loud voice to all the birds flying in midheaven: "Come! Gather together for the great feast God has prepared for you! [18] You are to eat the flesh of kings, of commanders and warriors, of horses and their riders; the flesh of all men, the free and the slave, the small and the great." [19] Then I saw the beast and the kings of the earth, and the armies they had mustered to do battle with the One riding the horse, and with his army. [20] The beast was captured along with the false prophet who performed in its presence the prodigies that led men astray, making them accept the mark of the beast and worship its image. Both were hurled down alive into the fiery pool of burning sulphur. [21] The rest were slain by the sword which came out of the mouth of the One who rode the horse, and all the birds gorged themselves on the flesh of the slain.

20

Thousand-Year Reign

[1] Then I saw an angel come down from heaven, holding the

13: Is 63, 1.
14: Jn 1, 1.
15: Ps 2, 9.

16: 17, 14; Is 63, 3;
1 Tm 6, 15.
17: Ez 39, 17.

19, 12: *A name . . . no one but himself:* in Semitic thought, the name conveyed the reality of the person; cf Mt 11, 27; Lk 10, 22.
19, 13: *Had been dipped in:* other ancient MSS read "had been sprinkled with"; cf v 15. *The Word of God:* Christ is the revelation of the Father (Jn 1, 1.14; 1 Jn 2, 14).
19, 15: The treading of *the winepress* is a prophetic symbol used to describe the destruction of God's enemies (Is 63, 1-6; Jl 4, 13).
19, 17f. 21: Gruesome imagery borrowed from Ez 39, 4.17-20.
19, 20: *Beast . . . false prophet:* see notes on chapter 13. *The fiery pool . . . sulphur:* symbol of hell (14, 10; 20, 10.14f), different from the abyss; see note on 9, 1.
20, 1-6: Like the other numerical values in this book, *the thousand years* are not to be taken literally; they symbolize the long period of time between the chaining up of Satan (a symbol for Christ's resurrection-victory over death and the forces of evil) and the end of the world. During this time God's people share in the glorious reign of God which is present to them

key to the abyss and a huge chain in his hand. [2] He seized the dragon, the ancient serpent, who is the devil or Satan, and chained him up for a thousand years. [3] The angel hurled him into the abyss, which he closed and sealed over him. He did this so that the dragon might not lead the nations astray until the thousand years are over. After this, the dragon is to be released for a short time.

[4] Then I saw some thrones. Those who were sitting on them were empowered to pass judgment. I also saw the spirits of those who had been beheaded for their witness to Jesus and the word of God, those who had never worshiped the beast or its image nor accepted its mark on their foreheads or their hands. They came to life again and reigned with Christ for a thousand years. [5] The others who were dead did not come to life till the thousand years were over. This is the first resurrection; [6] happy and holy are they who share in the first resurrection! The second death will have no claim on them; they shall serve God and Christ as priests, and shall reign with him for a thousand years.

[7] When the thousand years are over, Satan will be released from his prison. [8] He will go out to seduce the nations in all four corners of the earth, and muster for war the troops of Gog and Magog, numerous as the sands of the sea. [9] They invaded the whole country and surrounded the beloved city where God's people were encamped; but fire came down from heaven and devoured them. [10] The devil who led them astray was hurled into the pool of burning sulphur, where the beast and the false prophet had also been thrown. There they will be tortured day and night, forever and ever.

The Last Judgment

[11] Next I saw a large white throne and the One who sat on

20, 2: Gn 3, 1.
4: Mt 19, 28.
8: Ez 38, 2.9; 39, 2.

9: Ez 38, 22.
11: Rom 2, 6.

---

in virtue of their baptism-victory over death and sin (Rom 6, 1-8; Jn 5, 24f; 16, 33; 1 Jn 3, 14; Eph 2, 1).
20, 1: *Abyss:* see note on 9, 1.
20, 2: *Dragon . . . serpent . . . Satan:* see notes on 12, 3.9f.15.
20, 4: *Beast . . . mark:* see chapter 13 and its notes.
20, 6: *Happy:* see note on 1, 3. *Second death:* see note on 2, 11. *Priests:* as in 1, 6; 5, 10; 22, 3; cf 1 Pt 2, 9.
20, 7-10: A description of the symbolic battle to take place when Satan is released at the end of time, *when the thousand years are over;* see note on vv 1-6.
20, 8: *Gog and Magog:* symbols of all pagan nations; the names are taken from Ez 38, 1—39, 20.
20, 9: *The whole country:* Palestine. *The beloved city:* Jerusalem; see note on 14, 1.

it. The earth and the sky fled from his presence until they could no longer be seen. [12] I saw the dead, the great and the lowly, standing before the throne. Lastly, among the scrolls, the book of the living was opened. The dead were judged according to their conduct as recorded on the scrolls. [13] The sea gave up its dead; then death and the nether world gave up their dead. Each person was judged according to his conduct. [14] Then death and the nether world were hurled into the pool of fire, which is the second death; [15] anyone whose name was not found inscribed in the book of the living was hurled into this pool of fire.

VI: NEW CREATION

21

New Heavens and New Earth

[1] Then I saw new heavens and a new earth. The former heavens and the former earth had passed away, and the sea was no longer. [2] I also saw a new Jerusalem, the holy city, coming down out of heaven from God, beautiful as a bride prepared to meet her husband. [3] I heard a loud voice from the throne cry out: "This is God's dwelling among men. He shall dwell with them and they shall be his people and he shall be their God who is always with them. [4] He shall wipe every tear from their eyes, and there shall be no more death or mourning, crying out or pain, for the former world has passed away."

[5] The One who sat on the throne said to me, "See, I make all things new!" Then he said, "Write these matters down, for the words are trustworthy and true!" [6] He went on to say: "These words are already fulfilled! I am the Alpha and the Omega, the Beginning and the End. To anyone who thirsts I will give to drink without cost from the spring of life-giving

---

21, 1: Is 65, 17; 66, 22;
2 Pt 3, 13.
3: Ez 37, 27.

4: 7, 17; Is 25, 8; 35, 10.
5: Is 43, 19; 2 Cor 5, 17.
6: 22, 17; Is 55, 1.

20, 12: *The book of the living:* see note on 3, 4f. *Judged . . . scrolls:* see note on 14, 12f.
20, 13: *The nether world:* see note on 1, 18.
20, 14: *Second death:* see note on 2, 11.
21, 1—22, 5: A description of God's eternal kingdom in heaven under the symbols of new heavens and a new earth (Is 65, 17-25; 66, 22).
21, 2: *New Jerusalem . . . bride:* symbol of the church (Gal 4, 26); see note on 19, 7.
21, 3f: Language taken from Ez 37, 27; Is 8, 8; 25, 8; 35, 10; cf 7, 17.
21, 5: *The one . . . on the throne:* God himself; cf 4, 1-11.
21, 6: *These words . . . fulfilled:* God's reign has already begun; see note on 20, 1-6. *Alpha and . . . Omega:* see note on 1, 8. *Lifegiving water:* see note on 7, 17.

water. [7] He who wins the victory shall inherit these gifts; I will be his God and he shall be my son. [8] As for the cowards and traitors to the faith, the depraved and murderers, the fornicators and sorcerers, the idol-worshipers and deceivers of every sort —their lot is the fiery pool of burning sulphur, the second death!"

The New Jerusalem

[9] One of the seven angels who held the seven bowls filled with the seven last plagues came and said to me, "Come, I will show you the woman who is the bride of the Lamb." [10] He carried me away in spirit to the top of a very high mountain and showed me the holy city Jerusalem coming down out of heaven from God. [11] It gleamed with the splendor of God. The city had the radiance of a precious jewel that sparkled like a diamond. [12] Its wall, massive and high, had twelve gates at which twelve angels were stationed. Twelve names were written on the gates, the names of the twelve tribes of Israel. [13] There were three gates facing east, three north, three south, and three west. [14] The wall of the city had twelve courses of stones as its foundation, on which were written the names of the twelve apostles of the Lamb.

[15] The one who spoke to me held a rod of gold for measuring the city, its gates, and its wall. [16] The city is perfectly square, its length and its width being the same. He measured the city with the rod and found it twelve thousand furlongs in length, in width, and in height. [17] Its wall measured a hundred and forty-four cubits in height by the unit of measurement the angel used. [18] The wall was constructed of jasper; the

---

7: 2 Sm 7, 14.
10: Heb 11, 10.
11: Is 60, 1f.

13: Ez 48, 31-35.
14: Eph 2, 20.
18: Is 54, 11f.

21, 7: *The victory:* over the forces of evil; see the conclusions of the seven letters (2, 7.11.17.26; 3, 5.12.21). *He shall be my son:* the victorious Christian enjoys divine sonship by adoption (Gal 4, 4-7; Rom 8, 14-17); see note on 2, 26ff.
21, 8: *Cowards:* their conviction is so weak that they deny Christ in time of trial and become *traitors. Second death:* see note on 2, 11.
21, 9—22, 5: Symbolic description of the new Jerusalem, the church. Most of the images are borrowed from Ez 40—48.
21, 9: *The woman . . . bride of the Lamb:* the church (v 2), the new Jerusalem (v 10).
21, 14: *Courses of stones . . . apostles:* cf Eph 2, 19f.
21, 15ff: The city is shaped like a gigantic cube, a symbol of perfection (cf 1 Kgs 6, 19f). The measurements of the city and its wall are multiples of the symbolic number twelve; see note on 7, 4-8. *Twelve thousand furlongs:* literally, 12,000 stadia, about 1500 miles; see note on 14, 20. The *cubit* was about 18 inches.
21, 18-21: The gold and precious gems symbolize the beauty and excellence of the church; cf Ex 28, 15-21; Is 54, 11f! Tb 13, 16f.

city was of pure gold, crystal-clear. [19] The foundation of the city wall was ornate with precious stones of every sort: the first course of stones was jasper, the second sapphire, the third chalcedony, the fourth emerald, [20] the fifth sardonyx, the sixth carnelian, the seventh chrysolite, the eighth beryl, the ninth topaz, the tenth chrysoprase, the eleventh hyacinth, and the twelfth amethyst. [21] The twelve gates were twelve pearls, each made of a single pearl; and the streets of the city were of pure gold, transparent as glass.

[22] I saw no temple in the city. The Lord, God the Almighty, is its temple—he and the Lamb. [23] The city had no need of sun or moon, for the glory of God gave it light, and its lamp was the Lamb. [24] The nations shall walk by its light; to it the kings of the earth shall bring their treasures. [25] During the day its gates shall never be shut, and there shall be no night. [26] The treasures and wealth of the nations shall be brought here, [27] but nothing profane shall enter it, nor anyone who is a liar or has done a detestable act. Only those shall enter whose names are inscribed in the book of the living kept by the Lamb.

22

[1] The angel then showed me the river of life-giving water, clear as crystal, which issued from the throne of God and of the Lamb [2] and flowed down the middle of the streets. On either side of the river grew the trees of life which produce fruit twelve times a year, once each month; their leaves serve as medicine for the nations. [3] Nothing deserving a curse shall be found there. The throne of God and of the Lamb shall be there, and his servants shall serve him faithfully. [4] They shall see him face to face and bear his name on their foreheads. [5] The night shall be no more. They will need no light from lamps or the sun, for the Lord God shall give them light, and they shall reign forever.

23: Is 60, 19f; Jn 2, 19-21;
   2 Cor 3, 18.
24: Is 60, 3.
25: Is 60, 11.
27: Is 35, 8; 52, 1;

2 Pt 3, 13.
22, 1: Ez 47, 1-12.
   4: 1 Cor 13, 12; 1 Jn 3, 2.
   5: Is 60, 20.

21, 22: *Christ is present throughout the church; hence, no temple is needed* as an earthly dwelling for God; cf Mt 18, 20; 28, 20; Jn 4, 21.
21, 23: *Lamp . . . Lamb:* cf Jn 8, 12.
21, 24-27: *All men of good will are welcome in the church;* cf Is 60, 1.3.5.11. *The book of the living:* see note on 3, 4f.
22, 1.17: *Life-giving water:* see note on 7, 17.
22, 2: *The tree of life:* cf v 14; see note on 2, 7. *Fruit . . . medicine:* cf Ez 47, 12.
22, 4: *See him face to face:* cf Mt 5, 8; 1 Cor 13, 12; 1 Jn 3, 2.

VII: EPILOGUE

⁶ The angel said to me: "These words are trustworthy and true; the Lord, the God of prophetic spirits, has sent his angel so show his servants what must happen very soon."

⁷ "Remember, I am coming soon! Happy the man who heeds the prophetic message of this book!"

⁸ It is I, John, who heard and saw all these things, and when I heard and saw them I fell down to worship at the feet of the angel who showed them to me. ⁹ But he said to me: "No, get up! I am merely a fellow servant with you and your brothers the prophets and those who heed the message of this book. Worship God alone!"

¹⁰ Then someone said to me: "Do not seal up the prophetic words of this book, for the appointed time is near! ¹¹ Let the wicked continue in their wicked ways, the depraved in their depravity! The virtuous must live on in their virtue and the holy ones in their holiness!

¹² "Remember, I am coming soon! I bring with me the reward that will be given to each man as his conduct deserves. ¹³ I am the Alpha and the Omega, the First and the Last, the Beginning and the End! ¹⁴ Happy are they who wash their robes so as to have free access to the tree of life and enter the city through its gates! ¹⁵ Outside are the dogs and sorcerers, the fornicators and murderers, the idol-worshipers and all who love falsehood.

¹⁶ "It is I, Jesus, who have sent my angel to give you this testimony about the churches. I am the Root and Offspring of David, the Morning Star shining bright."

¹⁷ The Spirit and the Bride say, "Come!" Let him who hears answer, "Come!" Let him who is thirsty come ˙forward; let all who desire it accept the gift of life-giving water.

¹⁸ I myself give witness to all who hear the prophetic words of this book. If anyone adds to these words, God will visit him with all the plagues described herein! ¹⁹ If anyone takes

---

10: 10, 4.
12: Is 40, 10; 62, 13.
13: 1, 8; Is 41, 4; 44, 6.

17: Is 55, 1.
18: Dt 4, 2.

22, 7.12.20: *I am coming soon:* Christ is the speaker; see note on 1, 3.
22, 7.14: *Happy:* see note on 1, 3.
22, 10: *The appointed time:* see note on 1, 3.
22, 13: Christ applies to himself the words used by God in 1, 8.
22, 14: *The city:* heavenly Jerusalem; see note on 21, 2.
22, 16: *The Root . . . of David:* see note on 5, 5. *Morning Star:* see note on 2, 26ff.
22, 17: *Bride:* the church; see note on 21, 2.

from the words of this prophetic book, God will take away his share in the tree of life and the holy city described here!

²⁰ The One who gives this testimony says, "Yes, I am coming soon!" Amen! Come, Lord Jesus!

²¹ The grace of the Lord Jesus be with you all. Amen!

22, 20: *Come, Lord Jesus:* a liturgical refrain, similar to the Aramaic expression *Marana tha,* "Our Lord, come!" in 1 Cor 16, 22. It was a prayer for the coming of Christ in glory at the parousia; see note on 1, 3.